If you're wondering why you should buy this new edition of *Essentials of American Government,* here are 10 good reasons!

1. The **2008 presidential campaigns and election** is explored throughout the book, including a look at the 2008 primary season, the party conventions, the role of the media, the historic nomination and election of Barack Obama, and voter turnout. Figures and tables are completely up to date with information on the 2008 election.

2. New **Roots of** and **Toward Reform** sections at the beginning and end of each chapter highlight the importance of the history of American government, and draw attention to the dynamic cycle of reassessment and reform that allows the United States to continually evolve and change.

3. **Illustrated Historical Timelines** provide you with a simple, effective, and inviting way to view the development of key American government topics and issues, like the right to privacy, political parties, civil rights legislation, campaign tactics, the development of the news media, and the war on terrorism.

4. New **"Ideas Into Action"** boxes show how political participation affects government while providing you with doable, practical, and useful suggestions for active involvement in the political process.

5. New the comm United St stronger comparative perspective to the text on a wide range of issues, including global environmentalism, indigenous legal systems, and parliamentary systems and their impact on parties and the executive branch.

6. Expanded and updated coverage of **civil rights issues affecting Hispanic Americans,** including a new timeline of important moments in Latino/a and Hispanic American rights. Chapter 5 also includes a new section on civil rights issues affecting Asian Americans, along with discussions of same-sex marriage, pay equity legislation, and living wage campaigns on campus.

7. Complete coverage of **the outcome of the 2008 congressional elections** and the makeup of the 111th Congress is included, as well as a discussion of increased congressional oversight of the Bush administration during the 110th Congress (see Chapter 6).

8. The Bush administration's economic policies and **efforts in 2008 to combat economic woes** are explored in Chapter 13.

9. Information on controversies related to the **war on terrorism and the wars in Iraq and Afghanistan** has been updated (see Chapter 14).

10. **MyPoliSciLab,** our Website that offers a wide array of multimedia activities—videos, simulations, exercises, and online newsfeeds—has been completely integrated with this edition to make learning more effective.

ELECTORAL COLLEGE VOTES IN THE 2008 ELECTION

THE UNITED STATES
A political map showing the number of electoral votes per state

A political map with states drawn in proportion to the number of electoral votes

Nebraska splits its electoral votes; four went to McCain and one to Obama.

● Obama victory
● McCain victory

Essentials of
American
GOVERNMENT

Essentials of American GOVERNMENT

ROOTS AND REFORM

2009 Edition

Karen O'Connor

Jonathan N. Helfat Distinguished Professor of Political Science
American University

Larry J. Sabato

University Professor and Robert Kent Gooch Professor of Politics
University of Virginia

Alixandra B. Yanus

University of North Carolina–Chapel Hill

Longman
New York San Francisco Boston
London Toronto Sydney Tokyo Singapore Madrid
Mexico City Munich Paris Cape Town Hong Kong Montreal

Editor-in-Chief: Eric Stano
Assistant Development Manager: David B. Kear
Development Editor: Melissa Mashburn
Associate Development Editor: Donna Garnier
Marketing Manager: Lindsey Prudhomme
Production Manager: Eric Jorgensen
Project Coordination, Text Design, and Electronic Page Makeup: Electronic Publishing Services Inc., NYC
Senior Cover Design Manager: Nancy Danahy
Cover Designer: Bernadette Skok
Cover Photo: Eric L. Wheater/Lonely Planet Images
Photo Researcher: Jody Potter
Image Permission Coordination: Frances Toepfer
Senior Manufacturing Buyer: Alfred C. Dorsey
Printer and Binder: RR Donnelley & Sons Company
Cover Printer: Lehigh/Phoenix Color Corporation

For permission to use copyrighted material, grateful acknowledgment is made to the copyright holders acknowledged throughout the book, which are hereby made part of this copyright page.

p. 2, The Granger Collection; p. 3, Eric L. Wheater/Lonely Planet Images; p. 24, Joseph Sohm/Visions of America/Corbis; p. 25, Michael Ventura/Alamy; p. 82, Bettmann/Corbis; p. 83, Susan Walsh/AP/Wide World Photos; p. 108, The Advertising Archives; p. 109, Kevin Clark/The Washington Post; p. 140, Flip Schulke/Corbis; p. 141, Chip Somodevilla/Getty Images; p. 170, The Granger Collection; p. 171, Doug Mills/The New York Times/Redux Pictures; p. 196, George Eastman House/Getty Images; p. 197, Dennis Brack; p. 220, Hulton Archive/Getty Images; p. 221, Ron Edmonds/AP/Wide World Photos; p. 244, Photograph by Abdon Daoud Ackad, Collection of the Supreme Court of the United States; p. 245, Doug Mills/The New York Times/Redux Pictures; p. 276, W. Eugene Smith/Time Life Pictures/Getty Images; p. 277, Jeff Haynes/Reuters/Landov; p. 312, Bettmann/Corbis; p. 313, Jae C. Hong/AP/Wide World Photos; p. 344, The Granger Collection; p. 345, Win McNamee/Getty Images; p. 382, Bettmann/Corbis; p. 383, Purdy/Sipa Press; p. 412, K.J. Historical/Corbis; p. 413, Chip Somodevilla/Getty Images

Library of Congress Cataloging-in-Publication Data
American government / Karen O'Connor ... [et al.].
   p. cm.
Includes bibliographical references and index.
ISBN 978-0-205-66283-8   1. United States—Politics and government. I. O'Connor, Karen, 1952-
JK276.A5475 2009
320.473—dc22

              2008046830

2345678910—DJC—11 10 09

Longman
is an imprint of

www.pearsonhighered.com

ISBN-13: 978-0-205-66284-5 (Essentials Texas)
ISBN-10: 0-205-66284-6
ISBN-13: 978-0-205-66283-8 (Essentials)
ISBN-10: 0-205-66283-8

To Meghan,
who grew up with this book

Karen O'Connor

To my Government 101 students
over the years, who all know that
"politics is a good thing"

Larry J. Sabato

For my family: You've never loved government,
but have always loved me

Alixandra B. Yanus

Contents

Preface   xvii

PART 1

FOUNDATIONS OF GOVERNMENT

CHAPTER 1   The Political Landscape   2

Roots of American Government: What Are They and Why Are They Important?   5

Functions of Government   5
Ideas Into Action   The American's Creed   6
Establishing Justice   6
Ensuring Domestic Tranquility   6
Providing for the Common Defense   7
Promoting the General Welfare   7
Securing the Blessings of Liberty   7
Types of Government   7

The Philosophical Origins of American Government   8

The Reformation and the Enlightenment: Questioning the Divine Right of Kings   8
Hobbes, Locke, and the Social Contract Theory of Government   9
Devising a National Government in the American Colonies   10

American Political Culture and the Basic Tenets of American Democracy   10

Personal Liberty   10
Equality   10
Popular Consent, Majority Rule, and Popular Sovereignty   11
Civil Society   11

Individualism   11
Religious Faith and Religious Freedom   11

Political Ideology: Its Role in the World and in American Politics   12

Prevailing American Political Ideologies   12
Conservatism   12
Liberalism   13
Problems with Political Labels   13

Changing Characteristics of the American People   13

Changing Size and Population   14
Changing Demographics of the U.S. Population   15
Changes in Racial and Ethnic Composition   15
Changes in Age Cohort Composition   15
Changes in Family and Family Size   15
Join the Debate   The Huntington Theory of Hispanization   16

Toward Reform: Population Changes and Americans' Attitudes Toward Government   18

Attitudinal Change and Reform   19
High Expectations   20
Redefining Our Expectations Concerning Reform   20
Analyzing Visuals   Faith in Institutions   21

CHAPTER 2   The Constitution   24

Roots of the New American Nation   26

Trade and Taxation   27
Timeline   Key Events Leading to American Independence   28
First Steps Toward Independence   28
The First Continental Congresses   29
The Declaration of Independence   30

The First Attempt at Government: The Articles of Confederation   31

Problems Under the Articles of Confederation   32

The Miracle at Philadelphia: Writing the U.S. Constitution 32

Analyzing Visuals Framers or Troublemakers? 33
The Characteristics and Motives of the Framers 33
The Virginia and New Jersey Plans 34
Constitutional Compromises 35
Unfinished Business Affecting the Executive Branch 36

The U.S. Constitution 36

The Basic Principles of the Constitution 36
Federalism 37
Separation of Powers 37
Checks and Balances 38
The Articles of the Constitution 38
Article I: The Legislative Branch 38
Article II: The Executive Branch 39
Join the Debate The Equal Opportunity to Govern Amendment 40
Article III: The Judicial Branch 40
Articles IV Through VII 42

The Drive for Ratification of the U.S. Constitution 42

Federalists versus Anti-Federalists 42
The Federalist Papers 43
Ratifying the Constitution 44
Ideas Into Action Celebrating the Constitution 45
Amending the Constitution: The Bill of Rights 45

Toward Reform: Methods of Amending the U.S. Constitution 45

Formal Methods of Amending the Constitution 46
The Living Constitution Article V 47
Informal Methods of Amending the Constitution 48
Judicial Interpretation 48
Social and Cultural Change 48
Politics Now Politics and the Flag 49

ANNOTATED CONSTITUTION 52

CHAPTER 3 Federalism 82

Roots of the Federal System and the Constitutional Allocation of Governmental Powers 85

National Powers Under the Constitution 86
State Powers Under the Constitution 87
Concurrent Powers Under the Constitution 87
Powers Denied Under the Constitution 87
Relations Among the States 88
The Living Constitution Article IV, Section 1 89
Relations within the States: Local Government 90

Federalism and the Marshall Court 90

McCulloch v. Maryland (1819) 90
Gibbons v. Ogden (1824) 91

Dual Federalism: The Taney Court, Slavery, and the Civil War 91

Dred Scott and the Advent of the Civil War 92
The Civil War, Its Aftermath, and the Continuation of Dual Federalism 92
Setting the Stage for a Stronger National Government 93

Cooperative Federalism: The New Deal and the Growth of National Government 93

The New Deal 94
The Changing Nature of Federalism: From Layer Cake to Marble Cake 95
Federal Grants and National Efforts to Influence the States 95
Join the Debate Federalism and the Environment 96

New Federalism: Returning Power to the States 98

The Reagan Revolution 98
The Devolution Revolution 99
Politics Now No Child Left Behind 100
Federalism Under the Bush Administration 100

Toward Reform: A New Judicial Federalism? 101

> Ideas Into Action   Violence on Campus 102
>
> Analyzing Visuals   State-by-State Report Card on Access to Abortion 103

CHAPTER 4   Civil Liberties   108

Roots of Civil Liberties: The Bill of Rights   111

The Incorporation Doctrine: The Bill of Rights Made Applicable to the States 111
Selective Incorporation and Fundamental Freedoms 112

First Amendment Guarantees: Freedom of Religion   113

The Establishment Clause 113

> Politics Now   Religious Accommodation on College Campuses 115

The Free Exercise Clause 115

First Amendment Guarantees: Freedoms of Speech, Press, Assembly, and Petition   116

Freedom of Speech and the Press 116
The Alien and Sedition Acts 116
Slavery, the Civil War, and Rights Curtailments 117
World War I and Anti-Governmental Speech 117
Protected Speech and Publications 118
Prior Restraint 118
Symbolic Speech 118
Hate Speech, Unpopular Speech, and Speech Zones 118

> Ideas Into Action   Political Speech and Mandatory Student Fees 119

Unprotected Speech and Publications 119
Libel and Slander 120
Fighting Words 120
Obscenity 120
Freedoms of Assembly and Petition 121

The Second Amendment: The Right to Keep and Bear Arms   121

The Rights of Criminal Defendants   122

The Fourth Amendment and Searches and Seizures 122
The Fifth Amendment: Self-Incrimination and Double Jeopardy 123
The Fourth and Fifth Amendments and the Exclusionary Rule 125
The Sixth Amendment and the Right to Counsel 125
The Sixth Amendment and Jury Trials 126
The Eighth Amendment and Cruel and Unusual Punishment 126

The Right to Privacy   127

> Join the Debate   The Death Penalty 128

Birth Control 129

> The Living Constitution   Ninth Amendment 130

Abortion 130

> Timeline   The Supreme Court and the Right to Privacy 132

Homosexuality 132
The Right to Die 133

Toward Reform: Civil Liberties and Combating Terrorism   134

The First Amendment 134
The Fourth Amendment 134
Due Process Rights 134

> Analyzing Visuals   Water-Boarding 135

CHAPTER 5   Civil Rights   140

Roots of Suffrage 1800–1890   142

Slavery and Congress 143
The First Civil Rights Movements: Abolition and Women's Rights 143
The 1850s: The Calm Before the Storm 143
The Civil War and Its Aftermath: Civil Rights Laws and Constitutional Amendments 144

> The Living Constitution   Thirteenth Amendment, Section 1 145

Civil Rights, Congress, and the Supreme Court 145

The Push for Equality, 1890–1954   146

The Founding of Key Groups 147
Litigating for Equality 148

The Civil Rights Movement   149

School Desegregation After *Brown* 150
A New Move for African American Rights 150
Formation of New Groups 150
The Civil Rights Act of 1964 151

> Analyzing Visuals   Police Confront Civil Rights Demonstrators in Birmingham 152

The Women's Rights Movement   153

Litigation for Equal Rights 153
The Equal Protection Clause and Constitutional Standards of Review 154
Statutory Remedies for Sex Discrimination 156

Other Groups Mobilize for Rights   157

Hispanic Americans 157

Timeline   Important Moments in Hispanic American Rights   158

American Indians   159
Asian and Pacific Americans   160
Gays and Lesbians   161
Politics Now   Gay and Lesbian Rights   162
Ideas Into Action   Accommodating College Students with Disabilities   163
Americans with Disabilities   163
Join the Debate   Determining A Living Wage   164

Toward Reform: Civil Rights, Affirmative Action, and Pay Equity   165

Affirmative Action   166
Pay Equity and Other Issues of Workplace Discrimination   166

PART 2
INSTITUTIONS OF GOVERNMENT

CHAPTER 6   Congress   170

Roots of the Legislative Branch of Government   172

How Congress Is Organized   174

The Role of Political Parties in Organizing Congress   174
The House of Representatives   175
The Speaker of the House   176
The Living Constitution   Article 1, Section 8, Clause 4   177
Other House Leaders   177
Politics Now   Leadership Styles of the Speaker of the House   178
The Senate   178
The Committee System   179
Types of Committees   179
Committee Membership   181
Committee Chairs   181

The Members of Congress   182

Running for and Staying in Office   182
Congressional Demographics   183
Theories of Representation   183

How Members Make Decisions   184

Party   184
Constituents   184

Analyzing Visuals   Approval Ratings of Congress and Individual Representatives   185
Colleagues and Caucuses   185
Interest Groups, Lobbyists, and Political Action Committees   186
Staff and Support Agencies   186
Ideas Into Action   Be a Congressional Intern   187

The Law-Making Function of Congress   187

How A Bill Becomes A Law: The Textbook Version   187
Join the Debate   Minority Party Rights in Congress   190

Toward Reform: Congressional Checks on the Executive and Judicial Branches   190

The Shifting Balance of Power   191
Foreign Policy and National Security   192
Confirmation of Presidential Appointments   193
The Impeachment Process   193
Congress and the Judiciary   193

CHAPTER 7   The Presidency   196

Roots of the Office of President of the United States   199

Presidential Qualifications and Terms of Office   199
Rules of Succession   200
The Living Constitution   Twenty-Fifth Amendment, Section 2   201

The Constitutional Powers of the President   201

The Appointment Power   202
The Power to Convene Congress   202
The Power to Make Treaties   202
Veto Power   203
The Power to Preside over the Military as Commander in Chief   203
The Pardoning Power   205

The Development and Expansion of Presidential Power   205

Join the Debate   The War Powers Act   206

The Presidential Establishment   209

The Vice President   209
The Cabinet   209
The First Lady   210
The Executive Office of the President (EOP)   211
The White House Staff   211

Presidential Leadership and the Importance of Public Opinion 211

  Presidential Leadership 212
  Going Public: Mobilizing Public Opinion 212
  The Public's Perception of Presidential Performance 212
    Ideas Into Action Exploring Presidential Visits 213
    Analyzing Visuals Presidential Approval Ratings Since 1981 214

Toward Reform: The President as Policy Maker 214

  The President's Role in Proposing and Facilitating Legislation 215
  The Budgetary Process and Legislative Implementation 215
    Politics Now Are Signing Statements Constitutional? 216
  Policy Making Through Executive Order 217

CHAPTER 8 The Executive Branch and the Federal Bureaucracy 220

Roots of the Federal Bureaucracy 223

  The Civil War and the Growth of Government 223
  From the Spoils System to the Merit System 223
  Regulating the Economy 224
  The Growth of Government in the Twentieth Century 224
    Analyzing Visuals Federal Employees in the Executive Branch, 1789–2005 225

The Modern Bureaucracy 226

  Who Are Bureaucrats? 226
  Formal Organization 229
  Cabinet Departments 229
  Government Corporations 230
  Independent Executive Agencies 230
    The Living Constitution Article II, Section 2, Clause 1 231
  Independent Regulatory Commissions 231
  Government Workers and Political Involvement 232

How the Bureaucracy Works 233

  Making Policy 235
  Rule Making 235
  Administrative Adjudication 235
    Ideas Into Action Enforcing Gender Equity in College Athletics 236

Toward Reform: Making Agencies Accountable 236

    Politics Now The Bush Administration and Bureaucratic Control 237
  Executive Control 237
    Join the Debate Funding the War in Iraq 238
  Congressional Control 240
  Judicial Control 240

CHAPTER 9 The Judiciary 244

Roots of the Federal Judiciary 247

    The Living Constitution Article III, Section 1 248
  The Judiciary Act of 1789 and the Creation of the Federal Judicial System 249
    Join the Debate Senate Advice and Consent on Judicial Nominations 250
  The Marshall Court: *Marbury* v. *Madison* (1803) and Judicial Review 252

The American Legal System 254

  Jurisdiction 254
  Criminal and Civil Law 254

The Federal Court System 256

  District Courts 256
  The Courts of Appeals 257
  The Supreme Court 257

How Federal Court Judges Are Selected 258

  Who are Federal Judges? 259
  Appointments to the U.S. Supreme Court 259
  Nomination Criteria 259
    Analyzing Visuals Race, Ethnicity, and Gender of Federal Court Appointees 260
  Competence 260
  Ideology or Policy Preferences 260
  Rewards 261
  Pursuit of Political Support From Various Groups 261
  Religion 261
  Race, Ethnicity, and Gender 261
  The Supreme Court Confirmation Process 261
  Investigation 261
  Lobbying by Interest Groups 262
  The Senate Committee Hearings and Senate Vote 262

The Supreme Court Today 262

  Deciding to Hear a Case 262
    Politics Now Should Supreme Court Proceedings Be Televised? 263

Writs of *Certiorari* and the Rule of Four   264
The Role of Clerks   264
How Does a Case Survive the Process?   266
The Federal Government   267
Conflict Among the Courts of Appeals   267
Interest Group Participation   267
Ideas Into Action   Be a Friend of the Court   268
Hearing and Deciding the Case   268
Oral Arguments   268
The Conference and the Vote   268
Writing Opinions   269

Judicial Philosophy and Decision Making   269

Judicial Philosophy, Original Intent, and Ideology   269
Models of Judicial Decision Making   270
Behavioral Characteristics   270
The Attitudinal Model   270
The Strategic Model   270
Public Opinion   271

Toward Reform: Power, Policy Making, and the Court   271

Policy Making   272
Implementing Court Decisions   272

PART 3

POLITICAL BEHAVIOR

CHAPTER 10   Public Opinion and The News Media   276

Roots of Political Values: Political Socialization   278

The Family   278
School and Peers   279
Join the Debate   Teaching Civics in American High Schools   280
The Mass Media   280
Religious Beliefs   282
Race and Ethnicity   283
Gender   283
Age   284
Region   284
The Impact of Events   285

Public Opinion and Polling   285

The History of Public Opinion Research   286

Traditional Public Opinion Polls   287
Determining the Content and Phrasing the Questions   287
Politics Now   Cell Phones Challenge Pollsters   288
Selecting the Sample   288
Contacting Respondents   289
Political Polls   289
Push Polls   289
Tracking Polls   289
Exit Polls   290
Shortcomings of Polling   290
Margin of Error   290
Sampling Error   291
Limited Respondent Options   291
Lack of Information   291
Difficulty Measuring Intensity   291

Why We Form and Express Political Opinions   291

Personal Benefits   292
Political Knowledge   292
Cues from Leaders or Opinion Makers   292
Political Ideology   293

The Evolution of News Media in the United States   293

Print Media   293
Timeline   The Development of American News Media   294
The Living Constitution   First Amendment   296
Radio News   297
Television News   297
The New Media   298
Ideas Into Action   Where Do Young People Get Their Campaign News?   299
Current Media Trends   300
The Influence of Media Giants   300
Media Consolidation   301
Increasing Use of Experts   301
Narrowcasting   302
Technological Innovation   302

Rules Governing the Media   302

Journalistic Standards   302
Government Regulation of the Electronic Media   303
Content Regulation   303
Efforts to Control the News Media   304

How the Media Cover Politics   305

How the Press and Public Figures Interact   305
Covering the Presidency   306
Covering Congress   306
Covering the Supreme Court   307

Toward Reform: Media Influence, Media Bias, and Public Confidence 307

   Media Influence 307
   Media Bias 308
   The Public's Perception of the Media 309

CHAPTER 11   Political Parties and Interest Groups   312

Roots of the American Party System   314

   The Birth of American Political Parties   315
   The Living Constitution   317
   The Early Parties Fade   318
   Democrats and Republicans: The Golden Age   318
   The Modern Era   319
   Realignment   320
   Secular Realignment   320
   Dealignment and the Strength of Political Parties   321

The Functions and Organization of the American Party System   322

   What Do Parties Do?   322
   Mobilizing Support and Gathering Power   322
   A Force for Stability and Moderation   322
   Unity, Linkage, and Accountability   322
   The Electioneering Function   322
   Party As a Voting and Issue Cue   324
   Policy Formulation and Promotion   324
   Legislative Organization   324
   Crashing the Party: Minor Parties in the American Two-Party System   325

The Party Organization   326

   National Committees   326
   Politics Now The Impact of a National Committee Chair 327
   Leadership   327
   National Conventions   328
   States and Localities   328
   Sources of Party Identification   328
   Group Affiliations   329

Interest Group Structure and Functions 330

   Interest Group Formation   331
   Interest Group Maintenance   332
   The Development of American Interest Groups   332
   The Rise of the Interest Group State   334
   What Do Interest Groups Do?   335
   Lobbying   335
   Ideas Into Action   Guns on Campus   336
   Election Activities   337

Join the Debate   Should There Be Limits on Interest Group Participation?   338
Analyzing Visuals   Interest Group Ratings of Selected Members of Congress   340

Toward Reform: Regulating Interest Groups and Lobbyists 341

CHAPTER 12   Voting, Elections, and Campaigns   344

Roots of Voting Behavior   347

   Patterns in Voter Turnout   347
   Education and Income   347
   Politics Now   Can Turnout Aid One Candidate? 348
   Age   348
   Ideas Into Action   Motivating Young Voters   349
   Gender   349
   Race and Ethnicity   349
   Timeline   The Expansion of Voting Rights   350
   Interest in Politics   351
   Why Is Voter Turnout So Low?   352
   Too Busy   352
   Difficulty of Registration   352
   Difficulty of Absentee Voting   352
   Number of Elections   353
   Patterns in Vote Choice   353
   Party Identification   353
   Issues   353
   Join the Debate   Should Felons Be Allowed to Vote?   354
   Types of Elections   355

Presidential Elections   356

   The Nomination Campaign   356
   The Living Constitution   357
   Primaries Versus Caucuses   358
   The Party Conventions   358
   Delegate Selection   359
   The General Election Campaign   359
   The Key Players: The Candidate and the Campaign Staff   360
   The Candidate   360
   The Campaign Staff   360
   The Candidate's Professional Staff   361
   The Electoral College: How Presidents Are Elected   361
   The Electoral College in the Nineteenth Century   362
   The Electoral College in the Twentieth and Twenty-First Centuries   362

Congressional Elections 364
- **The Incumbency Advantage 364**
  - Redistricting 364
  - The Impact of Scandals 365
  - Presidential Coattails 365
- **Midterm Elections 365**
- **The 2008 Congressional Elections 365**

The Media's Role in the Campaign Process 367
- **Paid Media 367**
- **Free Media 368**
- **The New Media 368**

The Main Event: The 2008 Presidential Campaign 369
- **The Party Nomination Battles 370**
- **The Democratic and Republican Conventions 371**
- **The Debates and the General Election Campaign 372**
- **Election Results and Analysis 374**

Toward Reform: Campaign Finance 375
- **Current Rules 376**
  - Individual Contributions 376
  - Political Action Committee (PAC) Contributions 377
  - Political Party Contributions 378
  - Member-to-Candidate Contributions 378
  - Candidates' Personal Contributions 378
  - Public Funds 378
  - **Analyzing Visuals** The Ten Most Active 527 Groups in 2008 379
- **Soft Money and the 527 Loophole 379**

PART 4

PUBLIC POLICY

CHAPTER 13 Social and Economic Policy 382

Roots of Public Policy: The Policy-Making Process 385
- **Problem Recognition and Definition 386**
- **Agenda Setting 387**
- **Policy Formulation 387**
- **Policy Adoption 387**
- **Budgeting 388**
- **Policy Implementation 388**
  - **Politics Now** Supreme Court Action on Clean Air 389
- **Policy Evaluation 391**

Social Welfare Policy 391
- **The Origins of Social Welfare 392**
  - Income Security 392
  - Health Care 393
- **Social Welfare 393**
  - Non-Means-Based Programs 394
  - **Analyzing Visuals** Unemployment Rates by State 396
  - Means-Tested Programs 397
  - The Effectiveness of Income Security Programs 398
- **Health Care 399**
  - Medicare 400
  - Medicaid 400

Toward Reform: Economic Policy 401
- **The Nineteenth Century 401**
  - **The Living Constitution** Sixteenth Amendment 402
- **The Progressive Era 402**
  - Financial Reforms 403
  - Agriculture and Labor 404
  - Industry Regulations 404
- **Economic and Social Regulations 404**
- **Deregulation 404**
- **Stabilizing the Economy 406**
  - Monetary Policy: Controlling the Money Supply 406
  - **Ideas Into Action** Discovering Your Tax Burden 407
  - **Join the Debate** Economic Stimulus Payments 408
  - Fiscal Policy: Taxing and Spending 408

CHAPTER 14 Foreign and Defense Policy 412

Roots of U.S. Foreign and Defense Policy 415
- **The Living Constitution** Article I, Section 8 416
- **Détente and Human Rights: 1969–1981 417**
- **Containment Revisited and Renewed: 1981–1989 418**
- **Searching for a New International Order: 1989–2001 418**
  - **Timeline** Major Acts of Terrorism Affecting the United States, 1990–Present 420
- **The War on Terrorism: 2001 to the Present 420**
  - **Join the Debate** Should the United States Pull Out of the United Nations? 422
  - **Ideas Into Action** The Impact of the War on Terrorism on American Campuses 425

Foreign and Defense Policy Decision Making 425
- **The Executive Branch 425**
  - The President 426

The Departments of State and Defense 426
The Department of Homeland Security 427
Congress 427
  Politics Now Private Security Firms in Iraq 428
The Military-Industrial Complex 430
The News Media 430
  Analyzing Visuals Abu Ghraib Prisoner Abuse 431
The Public 431

Twenty-First-Century Challenges 432
Promoting Democracy in the Middle East 433
Transnational Threats to Peace 433

Appendices
  I   The Declaration of Independence 436
  II   Fedreralist No. 10 438
  III Federalist No. 51 441
  IV   Presidents, Congresses, and Chief Justices:
       1789–2009 443

Selected Supreme Court Cases 446

Glossary 454

Notes 465

Index 475

Preface

We believe that one cannot fully understand the actions, issues, and policy decisions facing the U.S. government, its constituent states, or "the people" unless these issues are examined from the perspective of how they have evolved over time. Consequently, the title of this book is *Essentials of American Government: Roots and Reform*. In its pages, we try to examine how the United States is governed today by looking not just at present structures and behavior but also at the *Framers' intentions and how they have been implemented and adapted over the years*. For example, we believe that it is critical to an understanding of the role of political parties in the United States to understand the Framers' fears of factionalism, how parties evolved, and when and why realignments in party identification occurred.

To understand all levels of American government, students must appreciate its constitutional underpinnings. Our text includes a full, *annotated* Constitution of the United States and a boxed feature, "The Living Constitution," to ensure that students understand and appreciate the role of the Constitution in American government and their everyday lives.

In addition to the constitutional and historical origins of American government, we explore issues that the Framers could never have envisioned, and how the basic institutions of government have changed in responding to these new demands. For instance, no one more than two centuries ago could have foreseen election campaigns in an age when nearly all American homes contain television sets and the Internet allows instant access to information from across the nation and around the globe. Moreover, citizen demands and expectations routinely force government reforms, making an understanding of the dynamics of change essential for introductory students.

Our overriding concern is that students understand their government as it exists today, so that they may become better citizens and make better choices. Careful updating in every edition to reflect the significant events that affect government and citizens alike is crucial to insuring a book that accurately communicates where the United States is as a nation. We believe that by providing students with information about government, and by explaining why it is important and why their participation counts, students will come to see that politics can be a good thing.

What's Changed in This Edition?

This edition has been substantially revised throughout to capture the historic events of the last two years and reflect the latest scholarship. **Chapter 1** provides updated demographic data, an expanded section on religious faith and religious freedom, an expanded discussion of the immigration policy debate, and expanded coverage of symbolic expressions of American political culture. **Chapter 2** includes a new "Key Events Leading to American Independence" timeline and a new table comparing the Articles of Confederation to the Constitution. **Chapter 3** includes an expanded discussion of federalism and the Roberts Court. A new "Living Constitution" box on the Full Faith and Credit Clause references the legalization of same-sex marriage in California and Massachusetts. **Chapter 4**'s new opening vignette discusses the Supreme Court's ruling in the Supreme Court case *D. C. v. Heller*. This chapter also features expanded coverage of the debate over the death penalty, including a new "Join the Debate" box devoted to this topic. **Chapter 5** features expanded and updated coverage of civil rights issues affecting Hispanic Americans, including a new timeline of important moments in Latino/a and Hispanic American rights. The chapter also includes a new section on civil rights issues affecting Asian Americans. Updated discussions of same-sex marriage, pay equity legislation, and living wage campaigns on campus are also included. **Chapter 6** includes complete coverage of the outcome of the 2008 congressional elections and the makeup of the 111th Congress, and features a discussion of increased congressional oversight of the Bush administration during the 110th Congress. **Chapter 7** considers the impact of President George W. Bush's two terms in office and discusses the 2008 presidential election in the context of the Bush legacy. The "Politics Now" feature examines the debate over the constitutionality of presidential signing statements. **Chapter 8** includes an expanded and updated discussion of the use of private contractors to perform jobs formerly done by government employees. **Chapter 9** features a new opening vignette on the Roberts Court and offers updates on the Supreme Court's 2007–2008 term and models of judicial decision making. **Chapter 10** features a new vignette regarding the 2008 Iowa Caucus entrance polls and a "Timeline" feature discussing the development of the news media. **Chapter 11** has been updated to reflect the impact of technology and campaign finance reform on party activities. It includes a new "Ideas Into Action" feature about interest group efforts to legalize guns on college campuses and a new "Toward Reform" section related to regulating interest groups and lobbyists. **Chapter**

12 features new data and updated figures on election results, voter turnout, and demographics in the 2008 presidential and congressional elections. **Chapter 13** features a new opening vignette on health care reform and the 2008 presidential election and includes new sections on the Bush Administration's economic policies and efforts in 2008 to combat economic woes. **Chapter 14** includes updated information on controversies related to the War on Terrorism and the wars in Iraq and Afghanistan.

Historical Perspective

Every chapter uses history to serve three purposes: First, to show how institutions and processes have evolved to their present states; second, to provide some of the color that makes information memorable; and third, to provide students with a more thorough appreciation that our government was born amid burning issues of representation and power, issues that continue to smolder today. A richer historical texture helps to explain the present.

NEW! **Roots of** and **Toward Reform**

sections highlight the text's emphasis on the importance of the history of American government, as well as the dynamic cycle of reassessment and reform that allows the United States to continue to evolve. Every chapter begins with a "Roots of" section that gives a historical overview of the topic at hand and ends with a "Toward Reform" section devoted to a particularly contentious aspect of the topic being discussed.

Toward Reform: Civil Liberties and Combating Terrorism

After September 11, 2001, the Bush administration, Congress, and th courts all operated in what Secretary of State Condoleezza Rice dubbe "an alternate reality," where Bill of Rights guarantees were suspended in a time of war.[127] The USA Patriot Act, the Military Commissions Act, and a series of secre Department of Justice memos all altered the state of civil liberties in the Unite States. affected

Roots of Civil Liberties: The Bill of Rights

In 1787, most state constitutions explicitly protected a va personal liberties such as speech, religion, freedom from unrea searches and seizures, and trial by jury. It was clear that the new federal system lished by the Constitution would redistribute power between the national gove and the states. Without an explicit guarantee of specific civil liberties, co national government be trusted to uphold the freedoms already granted to citi their states?

As discussed in chapter 2, recognition of the increased power that would by the new national government led Anti-Federalists to stress the need for

NEW! **Illustrated Timelines** provide students with a clear and visual understanding of the development of key topics in American Government.

Timelines include key events leading to American Independence, the Supreme Court and the right to privacy, the development of American political parties, and the War on Terrorism.

Timeline: The Supreme Court and the Right to Privacy

1965 *Griswold v. Connecticut*—The right to privacy is explained by the Court and used to justify striking down a Connecticut statute prohibiting married couples' access to birth control.

1973 *Roe v. Wade*—The Court finds that a woman has a right to have an abortion based on her right to privacy.

1980 *Harris v. McRae*—The Court upholds the Hyde Amendment, ruling that federal funds cannot be used to pay for poor women's abortions.

1986 *Bowers v. Hardwick*—The Court upholds Georgia's sodomy law, finding that gay men and lesbians have no privacy rights.

1989 *Webster v. Reproductive Health Services*-The Court comes close to overruling *Roe*; invites states to fashion abortion restrictions.

1992 *Planned Parenthood of Southeastern Pennsylvania v. Casey*—By the narrowest of margins, the Court limits *Roe* by abolishing its trimester approach.

2003 *Lawrence v. Texas*—In overruling *Bowers*, the Court, for the first time, concludes that the right to privacy applies to homosexuals.

2007 *Gonzales Carhart*—Supreme upholds the federal Birth Abortion Ban

The Living Constitution reflects the authors' emphasis on the origins of America's democratic system. To further support the text's emphasis on the constitutional underpinnings of government and politics, this boxed feature appears in every chapter. Each feature examines the chapter's topic in light of what the Constitution says or does not say about it.

The Living Constitution

The enumeration in the Constitution, of certain rights, shall not be construed to deny or disparage others retained by the people.

—NINH AMENDMENT

...dment simply reiterates the belief that ...t specifically enumerated in the Bill of ...ist and are retained by the people. It ...o assuage the concerns of Federalists, ...s Madison, who feared that the enu- ...so many rights and liberties in the first ...ments to the Constitution would result ...l of rights that were not enumerated ... ...65, the Ninth Amendment...

...of Rights implied as retained. Since 1965, the Court has ruled in favor of a host of fundamental liberties guaranteed by the Ninth Amendment, often in combination with other specific guarantees, including the right to have an abortion.

CRITICAL THINKING QUESTIONS

The Constitution of the United States of America, carefully annotated to make it accessible to students, is placed between Chapters 2 and 3, providing students with a careful walkthrough of this seminal document.

AMENDMENT VIII

Excessive bail shall not be required, nor excessive fines imposed, nor cruel and unusual punishments inflicted.

For an amendment of so few words, the Eighth Amendment has generated an enormous volume of commentary and litigation since its ratification. This should not be surprising, as the three major provisions of the amendment deal with some of the most sensitive and emotionally charged issues involving the rights of criminal defendants.

POLITICS NOW

Source: THE NEW YORK TIMES   August 7, 2007

Religious Accommodation on College Campuses

Universities Install Footbaths to Benefit Muslims, and Not Everyone Is Pleased

TAMAR LEWIN

DEARBORN, Mich. — When pools of water began accumulating on the floor in some restrooms at the University of Michigan-Dearborn, and the sinks pulling away from the walls, the problem was easy to pinpoint. On this campus, more ...

in the new student union.

"My sister told me about it, and I didn't believe it," said Najla Malaibari, a graduate student at Eastern Michigan. "I was, 'No way,' and she said, 'Yeah, go crazy.' It really is convenient."

But after a Muslim student at Minneapolis Community and Technical College slipped and hurt herself last fall while washing her feet in a sink, word got out there that the college was considering installing a footbath, and a local columnist accused the college of double standard — stopping a campus coffee cart from playing Christmas music but taking a different attitude...

versity claims it's available for Western students as well, but, traditionally, Western students don't wash their feet five times day."

"They're building a structure for a particular religious tradition," Mr. Downs added, "and the Constitution says the government isn't supposed to endorse a particular religion."

The American Civil Liberties Union...

Discussion Questions

1. Does the Clark County ordinance violate any First Amendment guarantees? If it does, how can the statute be altered so that it is no longer unconstitutional?

Politics Now boxes provide in-depth examinations of contemporary issues, showcasing the book's currency and serving as a counterbalance to the text's thorough treatment of America's origins and history. Excerpts from news articles are followed by "Discussion Questions" that allow students to analyze current political issues for themselves.

Thinking Globally

Saudi Arabia and Free Exercise of Religion

In Saudi Arabia, public demonstration of religious affiliation or sentiment is forbidden except for Sunni Muslims who follow the austere Wahhabi interpretation of Islam. Public worship by non-Muslims is banned, and places of worship other than mosques are not permitted. The kingdom's Shi'a Muslim minority's religious practice is tightly controlled, and the construction of Shi'a mosques and religious community centers is restricted.

- Is it surprising that some countries officially support one religion at the expense of others? Why or why not?
- To what extent, should the United States pressure its allies, such as Saudi Arabia, to adhere more closely to American constitutional values of freedom of religion?
- What criteria would you use to evaluate the level of religious freedom in a country?

NEW! **Thinking Globally** features underscore the commonalities and differences between the United States and other nations to provide students with a comparative perspective on a range of issues, including global environmentalism, indigenous legal systems in nations like Australia, and parliamentary systems and their impact on parties and the executive branch. Thinking Globally features occur three or more times in each chapter and consist of a brief overview of a key comparative topic followed by critical thinking questions.

Putting It into Action

The new and revised pedagogical features help students actively engage the material, focus on key concepts, and become stronger political participants.

WHAT SHOULD I KNOW ABOUT . . .
- the roots of civil liberties and the Bill of Rights?
- First Amendment guarantees of freedom of religion?
- First Amendment guar[antees] of [freedom of] speech, press, assembl[y]
- the Second Amendmen[t] bear arms?
- the rights of criminal d[efendants]
- the right to privacy?
- civil liberties and comb[at]

★ Third, we will consider the meanings of other *First Amend[ment] freedoms of speech, press, assembly, and petition.*

★ Fourth, we will Review *the Second Amendment* and *the ri[ght to bear] arms.*

★ Fifth, we will analyze *the rights of criminal defendants* four[d] and how those rights have [been interpreted by the] Court.

★ Sixth, we will explore *the right [to privacy].*

★ Finally, we will examine ho[w] *[civil] liberties.*

First Amendment Guarantees: Freedom of Religion

Many of the Framers were religious men, but they knew wha[t the] new nation was not founded with religious freedom as one of i[ts] many colonists had fled Europe to escape religious persecution [and] persecuted those who d[isagreed]. theless, in 1774, the col[onies] passed a law establishing [...] the colonies. The First [...] announcing its "astonish[...] lish . . . a religion [Cath[olic] bigotry, persecution, mu[...]

WHAT SHOULD I HAVE LEARNED?
- **What are the roots of civil liberties and the Bill of Rights i[...]**

  Most of the Framers originally opposed the Bill of Rights. A[...] however, continued to stress the need for a bill of rights dur[ing the] ratification of the Constitution, and some states tried to ma[ke] contingent on the addition of a bill of rights. Thus, during i[ts first] Congress sent the first ten amendments to the Constitution [to] the states for their ratification. Later, the addition of the Fo[urteenth] allowed the Supreme Court to apply some of the amendmen[ts] through a process called selective incorporation.

- **What are the First Amendment guarantees of freedom of [religion?]**

  The First Amendment guarantees freedom of religion. The [...] which prohibits the national government from establishing [...] according to Supreme Court interpretation, create an absolu[...] church and state. While the national and state governments [...] give direct aid to religious groups, many forms of aid, especi[ally to] children, have been held to be constitutionally permissible. [...] has generally barred organized prayer in public schools. The [...] adopted an accommodationist approach when interpreting t[...]

NEW! ### What Should I Know?
and
What Should I Have Learned?

sections allow students to preview and review the key topics and concepts explored in each chapter. Every chapter begins with a set of "What Should I Know?" questions tied to the sections within the chapter. These questions, as well as a bulleted list of section descriptions that follows the opening vignette, preview the key content of the chapter and help to focus student attention on the overall chapter structure. A "What Should I Have Learned?" section at the end of every chapter revisits each "What Should I Know?" question and answers it with a succinct summary paragraph.

TO LEARN MORE— —TO DO MORE
To learn more about the Supreme Court's decision in *District of Columbia v. Heller* (2008), go to www.oyez.org and search on the name of the case.

NEW! ### To Learn More— To Do More features serve as a
capstone to every chapter's opening vignette and provide students with an online reference for participation in or further information about the vignette's topic.

Join the Debate

The Death Penalty

Overview: Challenges to the use of the death penalty are rising. In 2007, the U.S. Supreme Court agreed to take the case of *Baze v. Rees*, which questioned whether the method of lethal injection used by thirty-six states was potentially so painful as to violate the Eighth Amendment ban on cruel and unusual punishment. When the Court took the case, it in effect put a moratorium on executions until it ruled in the spring of 2008 that the method did not violate the Constitution. In 2007, forty-one people were put to death, the fewest since 1999, and New Jersey became the first state since 1965 to abolish the use of the death penalty. Although individuals and some government entities are having second thoughts about the death penalty, not everyone agrees that there is a problem. The federal government and thirty-eight states use the death penalty.

The debate over the use of capital punishment raises issues about the fundamental fairness of our system of justice. A major concern is that innocent people might be put to death, despite all the procedural safeguards in our court system to prevent mistakes. It is, of course, regrettable when someone is convicted of a crime he or she did not commit, even when they are only fined or imprisoned. Obviously there is no way of making amends when someone is executed.

Some of the current controversy related to the death penalty comes from advances in the use of DNA evidence. The Innocence Project, a nonprofit organization, has been working since 1992 to use DNA evidence to exonerate those wrongly convicted of crimes.* As of March 2008, the group's efforts have led to the release of 214 people, 16 of them on death row. In addition, between 1977 and 2007, another 108 people have been released from death rows because mistakes were made in eyewitness accounts, line-ups, police questioning,

and court proceedings. The obvious question is whether there were others who should have been released.

The major justification for the death penalty is captured in the slogan: "A life for a life." The consequence for taking someone else's life is the loss of the criminal's life. In turn, supporters of the death penalty believe that such a grave consequence will deter people from committing murder. There does not, however, appear to be a correlation between the death penalty and low homicide rates. Texas, for example, executes more people than all the rest of the states combined. Yet, Texas consistently has one of the highest murder rates in the country. And, as a whole, southern states use the death penalty more than any other region. The homicide rate in 2007 for the South was 42 per 100,000 people, in contrast to the rate of 17 per 100,000 people in the Northeast and Midwest.

Another concern with the death penalty is the racial and gender disparities in those who are executed. It is extremely

rare for a woman to be sent to the death chamber. And, a person is less likely to be executed if he or she is white. In 2007, for example, 53 percent of the 41 people executed were white, 37 percent were African American, and 10 percent were Hispanic—figures that do not match the racial composition of the general population. A crucial aspect of the debate regarding the death penalty is disagreement about whether the court system is biased and if convictions and executions reflect more general patterns of discrimination in society.

Arguments IN FAVOR of the Death Penalty

- The death penalty is just because it is used primarily to execute those who take the lives of others. Killing someone is the most egregious crime and act of violence, and societies must respond with the most severe punishment possible for murderers.

- The death penalty will deter at least some people from committing

capital offenses. Although some murders will occur in a fit of rage and passion, we need to make those who plot to kill another human being think about the possible consequences if they go ahead with their plan.

- It is costly to keep convicted murderers in prison for the rest of their lives. The cost to taxpayers to keep someone in prison is about $30,000 per year. It makes little economic sense for society to clothe, feed, and care for a murderer for the rest of his or her life.

Arguments AGAINST the Death Penalty

- Mistakes are inevitably going to be made, and innocent people are going to be put to death for crimes they did not commit. The consequence of executing an innocent person is beyond remedy. We simply cannot risk mistakes when life is at stake.

- The United States is alone among Western countries in continuing to have the death penalty. Canada, Australia, and all European nations are among the 91 countries that have completely abolished the death penalty. The United States is in the company of repressive nations such as China, Saudi Arabia, and Malaysia in its use of the death penalty.

- It actually costs more to execute someone than it does to imprison the person for life. The Urban Institute released a study on March 6, 2008, that showed the state of Maryland spent an average of $37.2

How do states vary in their application of the death penalty? This cartoon offers a social commentary on the administration of the death penalty in Texas, which leads the nation in the number of executions.

million for each of the five executions it conducted since it reinstated the death penalty in 1978. Although this figure is higher than those cited in other studies, the general finding is consistent with analyses that cite the high costs of appeals in capital cases and the high costs of running death rows.

Continuing the Debate

1. Should the states and the federal government abolish the death penalty? If not, for what crimes should the death penalty be allowed?
2. How, if at all, can mistakes in our criminal justice system be avoided? Do gender and racial disparities in executions suggest that the system is unfair?

To Follow the Debate Online, Go To:

www. prodeathpenalty.com, which advocates keeping and expanding the use of the death penalty and includes a list of print and media resources plus links to other supportive sites.

www. deathpenaltyinfo.org for a wide array of studies and statistics on the death penalty as well as coverage of current events related to the death penalty and arguments

pewforum.org/death-penalty/, which provides information, statistics, and arguments related to the death penalty.

www.innocenceproject.org.

Join the Debate boxes explore provocative, student-oriented topics and provide extensive, well-balanced coverage of both sides of a debate. Each box begins with a topic overview, provides accessible and detailed summaries of opposing arguments related to the issue, and ends with critical thinking questions that allow students to examine their own stance on the topic and suggested readings for further research. New topics in this edition include the death penalty, the living wage movement, budget allocations for the Iraq War, and voting rights for felons.

Ideas Into Action

Celebrating the Constitution

In late 2004, Senator Robert C. Byrd (D–WV) introduced legislation that called on all educational institutions receiving federal funds—from kindergarten through grade 12 to colleges, universities, and even law schools—to set aside September 17 of each year to conduct educational programs concerning the U.S. Constitution. When Public Law 108-447 passed, educational institutions around the United States began to question just what types of programs were required. The selection of September 17 was not random; the U.S. Constitution was sent to the states for ratification on that date.

Since 2005, educational institutions around the United States have chosen to celebrate what is now called Constitution Day in a variety of ways. The National Constitution Center has taken the lead in publicizing unique

and thoughtful ways for schools to observe Constitution Day. Among those highlighted are "celebrate your state" events, discussions on how the U.S. Supreme Court can change the law and make policy, grade school celebrations where students wear red, white, and blue and learn about the Preamble; and interactive Web-based activities for all ages.

- Visit the C-SPAN classroom Web site at www.c-spanclassroom.org. What activities might you and your classmates use to teach about the Constitution at a local elementary school?
- What kinds of activities [...] celebrate Constitution [...]
- What programs or pro[...] government class engage[...] Constitution Day to your[...]
- For more Constitution D[...] www.constitutionday.us.

NEW! **Ideas into Action** boxes emphasize political participation by highlighting current issues of interest to students and providing discussion questions, online resources for further research, and concrete suggestions for active involvement. Topics include celebrating Constitution Day, becoming a Congressional intern, and filing an *amicus curiae* brief.

Visual literacy—the ability to analyze, interpret, synthesize, and apply visual information—is essential in today's world. We receive much information from the written and spoken word, but much also comes in visual forms. We are used to thinking about reading written texts critically, but we do not always think about "reading" visuals in this way. We should, for images and informational graphics can tell us a lot if we read and consider them carefully. In order to emphasize these skills, the "Analyzing Visuals" feature in each chapter prompts students to think about the images and informational graphics they will encounter throughout this text, as well as those they see every day in the newspaper, in magazines, on the Web, on television, and in books. Critical thinking questions assist students in learning how to analyze visuals.

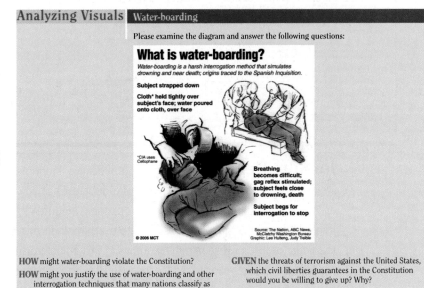

Analyzing Visuals | Water-boarding

Please examine the diagram and answer the following questions:

What is water-boarding?

HOW might water-boarding violate the Constitution?

HOW might you justify the use of water-boarding and other interrogation techniques that many nations classify as torture?

GIVEN the threats of terrorism against the United States, which civil liberties guarantees in the Constitution would you be willing to give up? Why?

Tables

Tables are the least "visual" of the visuals and consist of textual information and/or numerical data arranged in tabular form, in columns and rows. Tables are frequently used when exact information is required and when orderly arrangement is necessary to locate and, in many cases, to compare the information.

Here are a few questions to guide students' analysis of the tables in this book:

- What is the purpose of the table? What information does it show? There is usually a title that offers a sense of the table's purpose.
- What information is provided in the column headings (provided in the top row)? How are the rows labeled?
- Is there a time period indicated, such as January to June 2007? Or, are the data as of a specific date, such as June 30, 2007?
- If the table shows numerical data, what do these data represent? In what units? Dollars a special interest lobby provides to a political party? Estimated life expectancy in years?
- What is the source of the information presented in the table?

TABLE 4.3 Major Forms of Municipal Government

Form of Government	1984	2002
Council–Manager	3,387 (48.5%)	2,290 (34.7%)
Mayor–Council	3,011 (43.1%)	3,686 (55.8%)
Commission	143 (2.0%)	176 (2.7%)
Town Meeting	337 (4.8%)	370 (5.6%)
Representative Town Meeting	63 (.9%)	81 (1.2%)
Total[a]	6,981 (100%)	6,603 (100%)

[a] Totals for U.S. local governments represent only those municipalities with populations of 2,500 and greater. There are close to 30,000 local governments with populations under 2,500.
Source: Statistics from "Inside the Year Book: Cumulative Distributions of U.S. Municipalities," *The Municipal Year Books* 1984–2002, International City/County Management Association (ICMA), Washington, DC.

Charts and Graphs

Charts and graphs depict numerical data in visual forms. Examples that students will encounter throughout this text are line graphs, pie charts, and bar graphs. Line graphs show a progression, usually over time (as in Social Security Costs and Revenues, 1970–2008). Pie charts (such as the distribution of federal civilian employment) demonstrate how a whole (total federal civilian employment) is divided into its parts (employees in each branch). Bar graphs compare values across categories, showing how proportions are related to each other (as in the numbers of women and minorities in Congress). Bar graphs can present data either horizontally or vertically.

Here are a few questions to guide student analysis:

- What is the purpose of the chart or graph? What information does it provide? Or, what is being measured? There is usually a title that indicates the subject and purpose of the figure.
- Is there a time period shown, such as January to June 2008? Or, are the data as of a specific date, such as June 30, 2008? Are the data shown at multiple intervals over a fixed period, or at one particular point in time?
- What do the units represent? Dollars a candidate spends on a campaign? Number of voters versus number of nonvoters in Texas? If there are two or more sets of figures, what are the relationships among them?
- What is the source? Is it government information? Private polling information? A newspaper? A private organization? A corporation? An individual?
- Is the type of chart or graph appropriate for the information that is provided? For example, a line graph assumes a smooth progression from one data point to the next. Is that assumption valid for the data shown?
- Is there distortion in the visual representation of the information? Are the intervals equal? Does the area shown distort the actual amount or the proportion?

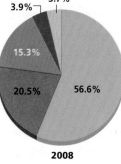

1967

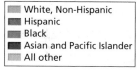

2008

- White, Non-Hispanic
- Hispanic
- Black
- Asian and Pacific Islander
- All other

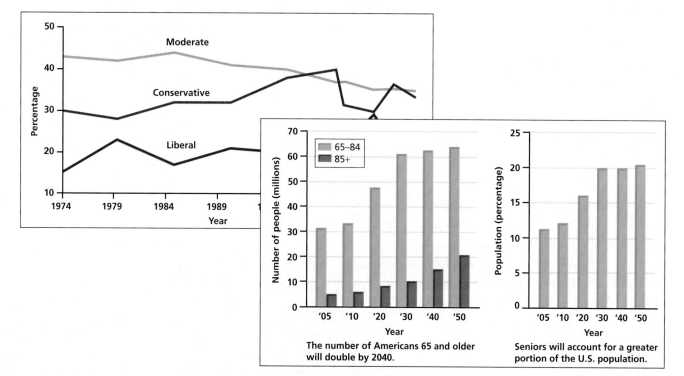

The number of Americans 65 and older will double by 2040.

Seniors will account for a greater portion of the U.S. population.

Maps

Maps—of the United States, of particular regions, or of the world—are frequently used in political analysis to illustrate demographic, social, economic, and political issues and trends.

Here are a few questions to guide student analysis:

- Is there a title that identifies the purpose or subject of the map?
- What does the map key/legend show? What are the factors that the map is analyzing?
- What is the region being shown?
- What source is given for the map?
- Maps usually depict a specific point in time. What is the point in time being shown on the map?

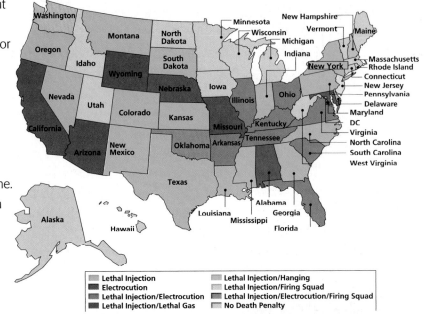

Lethal Injection	Lethal Injection/Hanging
Electrocution	Lethal Injection/Firing Squad
Lethal Injection/Electrocution	Lethal Injection/Electrocution/Firing Squad
Lethal Injection/Lethal Gas	No Death Penalty

News Photographs

Photos can have a dramatic—and often immediate—impact on politics and government. Visual images usually evoke a stronger emotional response from people than do written descriptions. For this reason, individuals and organizations have learned to use photographs as a means to document events, make arguments, offer evidence, and even in some cases to manipulate the viewer into having a particular response.

Here are a few questions to guide student analysis:

- When was the photograph taken?
- What is the subject of the photograph?

- Why was the photo taken? What appears to be the purpose of the photograph?
- Is it spontaneous or posed? Did the subject know he or she was being photographed?
- Who was responsible for the photo? (An individual, agency, or organization?) Can you discern the photographer's attitude toward the subject?
- Is there a caption? If so, what kind of information does it provide? Does it identify the subject of the photo? Does it provide an interpretation of the subject?

Political Cartoons

Some of the most interesting commentary on American politics takes place in the form of political cartoons. The cartoonist's goal is to comment on and/or criticize political figures, policies, or events. The cartoonist uses several techniques to accomplish this goal, including exaggeration, irony, and juxtaposition. For example, the cartoonist may point out how the results of governmental policies are the opposite of their intended effects (irony). In other cartoons, two people, ideas, or events that don't belong together may be joined to make a point (juxtaposition). Knowledge of current events is helpful in interpreting political cartoons.

Here are a few questions to guide student analysis:

- What labels appear on objects or people in the cartoon? Cartoonists will often label some of the elements. For example, a building with columns might be labeled "U.S. Supreme Court."
- What do the caption or title contribute to the meaning or impact of the cartoon?
- Can any of the people shown be identified? Presidents, well-known members of Congress, and world leaders are often shown with specific characteristics that help to identify them.
- Can the event being depicted be identified? Historical events, such as the American Revolution, or contemporary events, such as the 2008 presidential election, are often the subject matter for cartoons.

'Three-fourths of a penny for your thoughts...'

- What are the elements of the cartoon? Objects often represent ideas or events. For example, a donkey is often used to depict the Democratic Party.
- How are the characters interacting? What do the speech bubbles contribute to the cartoon?
- What is the overall message of the cartoon? Can you determine what the cartoonist's position is on the subject?

Resources in Print and Online

Name of Supplement	Available in Print	Available Online	Instructor or Student Supplement	Description
American Government Study Site 0205727409		✔	Both	Online set of practice tests, Web links, and flashcards organized by major topics and arranged according to this book's table of contents. www.pearsonamericangovernment.com.
Instructor's Manual 0205684408	✔	✔	Instructor	Offers chapter summaries, teaching ideas, discussion topics, and Web activities incorporating recent political news.
Test Bank 0205684416	✔	✔	Instructor	Contains over 200 questions per chapter in multiple-choice, true-false, short-answer, and essay format. Questions address all levels of Bloom's taxonomy and have been both reviewed and class-tested for accuracy and effectiveness.
MyTest 0205684386		✔	Instructor	This flexible, online test generating software includes all questions found in the printed Test Bank.
Study Guide 0205684394	✔		Student	Contains learning objectives, chapter summaries, and practice tests.
PowerPoint Presentation 0205684424		✔	Instructor	Slides include a lecture outline of the text along with graphics from the book. Available on the Instructor-Resource Center.*
Digital Transparency Masters 0205684092		✔	Instructor	These PDF slides contain all maps, figures, and tables found in the text. Available on the Instructor Resource Center.*
Longman Political Science Video Program		✔	Instructor	Qualified college adopters can peruse our list of videos for the American government classroom.
You Decide! Current Debates in American Politics, 2009 Edition 020568405X	✔		Student	This debate-style reader by John Rourke of the University of Connecticut examines provocative issues in American politics today by presenting various sides of key topics. Available at no additional charge when ordered packaged with this text.
Voices of Dissent: Critical Readings in American Politics, Eighth Edition 0205697976	✔		Student	This collection of critical essays assembled by William Grover of St. Michael's College and Joseph Peschek of Hamline University goes beyond the debate between mainstream liberalism and conservatism to fundamentally challenge the status quo.
Writing in Political Science, Third Edition 0321217357	✔		Student	This guide by Diane Schmidt of California State University–Chico takes students through all aspects of writing in political science step-by-step.
Choices: An American Government Database Reader		✔	Both	This customizable reader allows instructors to choose from a database of over 300 readings to create a reader that exactly matches their course needs. Go to www.pearsoncustom.com/database/choices.html for more information.
Ten Things That Every American Government Student Should Read 020528969X	✔		Student	Edited by Karen O'Connor of American University. We asked American government instructors across the country to vote for the 10 things beyond the text that they believe every student should read and put them in this brief and useful reader. Available at no additional charge when ordered packaged with the text.
American Government: Readings and Cases, Eighteenth Edition 0205697984	✔		Student	Edited by Peter Woll of Brandeis University, this longtime best-selling reader provides a strong, balanced blend of classic readings and cases that illustrate and amplify important concepts in American government, alongside extremely current selections drawn from today's issues and literature. Available at a discount when ordered packaged with this text.
Penguin-Longman Value Bundles	✔		Student	Longman offers 25 Penguin Putnam titles at more than a 60 percent discount when packaged with any Longman text. Go to www.pearsonhighered.com/penguin for more information.
Longman State Politics Series	✔		Student	These primers on state and local government and political issues are available at no extra cost when shrink-wrapped with the text. Available for Texas, California, and Georgia.

*The Instructor Resource Center can be found at www.pearsonhighered.com/educator

Improve Results With

Designed to amplify a traditional course in numerous ways or to administer a course online, **MyPoliSciLab** combines pedagogy and assessment with an array of multimedia activities—videos, simulations, exercises, and online newsfeeds—to make learning more effective for all types of students. Now featuring the combined resources, assets, and activities of both Prentice Hall and Longman Publishers, this new release of **MyPoliSciLab** is visually richer and even more interactive than previous iterations—a quantum leap forward in design with more points of assessment and interconnectivity between concepts.

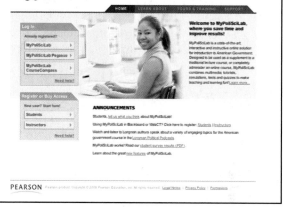

TEACHING AND LEARNING TOOLS

✓ **Assessment**: Comprehensive online diagnostic tools—learning objectives, study guides, flashcards, and pre- and post-tests—help students gauge and improve their understanding.

✓ **E-book:** Identical in content and design to the printed text, an e-book provides students access to their text wherever and whenever they need it.

✓ *UPDATED!* **PoliSci News Review:** A series of weekly articles and video clips—from traditional and non-traditional news sources—recaps the most important political news stories, followed by quizzes that test students' understanding.

✓ *NEW!* **ABC News RSS feed:** MyPoliSciLab provides an online feed from ABC News, updated hourly, to keep students current.

✓ **ABC News Video Clips**: Over 60 high-interest 2- to 4-minute clips provide historical snapshots in each chapter of key political issues and offer opportunities to launch discussions.

✓ *UPDATED!* **Roundtable and Debate Video Clips**: These video clips feature professors discussing key concepts from ideologically diverse perspectives and debating politically charged issues.

✓ **Student Polling:** Updated weekly with timely, provocative questions, the polling feature lets students voice their opinions in nationwide polls and view how their peers across the country see the same issue.

✓ **Political Podcasts:** Featuring some of Pearson's most respected authors, these video podcasts present short, instructive—and even entertaining—lectures on key topics that students can download and play at their convenience.

✓ *NEW!* **Student Podcasts:** The new MyPoliSciLab allows students to record and download their own videos for peer-to-peer learning.

INTERACTIVE ACTIVITIES

✓ **New and Updated Simulations:** Featuring an appealing new graphic interface, these role-playing simulations help students experience political decision-making in a way they never have before—including new "mini activities" that prepare students to make the right decisions.

✓ *NEW!* **Debate Exercises:** These provocative new exercises present classic and contemporary views on core controversies, ask students to take a position, and then show them the potential consequences of taking that stand.

✓ **More Focused Comparative Exercises:** These exercises have been revised in scope to concentrate on a more specific issue when comparing the US to other political systems, giving students a more concrete foundation on which to analyze key similarities and differences.

✓ **More Interactive Timelines:** With redesigned media and graphics, these timelines let students step through the evolution of some aspect of politics and now include more interactive questions throughout.

✓ **More Dynamic Visual Literacy Exercises:** These revised exercises offer attractive new graphs, charts, and tables and more opportunities to manipulate and interpret political data.

✓ **Expanded Participation Activities:** Reflecting our county's growing political interest, these expanded activities give students ideas and instructions for getting involved in all aspects of politics.

Icons in the margin of this book direct students to the activities on MyPoliSciLab related to the topics they are studying.

ONLINE ADMINISTRATION

No matter what course management system you use—or if you do not use one at all, but still wish to easily capture your students grades and track their performance—Pearson has a **MyPoliSciLab** option to suit your needs. Contact one of Pearson's Technology Specialists for more information or assistance.

A **MyPoliSciLab** access code is no additional cost when packaged with selected Pearson American Government texts. To get started, contact your local Pearson Publisher's Representative at **www.pearsonhighered.com/replocator.**

Acknowledgments

Karen O'Connor thanks the thousands of students in her American Government courses at Emory and American University who, over the years, have pushed her to learn more about American government and to have fun in the process. She especially thanks her American University colleagues who offered books and suggestions for this most recent revision—especially David Lublin. Her former professor and longtime friend and co-author, Nancy E. McGlen, has offered support for more than three decades. Her former students, too, have contributed in various ways to this project, especially John R. Hermann, Sue Davis, and Laura van Assendelft. For this edition of the book, Jon L. Weakley, an American politics student who first had the foresight (or the stupidity) to offer help during the 2006 election updates process, provided necessary reinforcement and enthusiasm. Jon's copyediting skills, love of the electoral process, and unlimited patience have significantly improved this text.

For the last four editions of the book, Alixandra B. Yanus of the University of North Carolina at Chapel Hill offered invaluable assistance and unflagging support. This edition marks Ali's formal participation as an author, where her fresh perspective on politics and ideas about things of interest to students, as well as her keen eye for the typo, her research abilities, and her unbelievably hard work, have resulted in numerous improvements.

Larry J. Sabato would like to acknowledge all of the students from his University of Virginia Introduction to American Politics classes and the many student interns at the UVA Center for Politics who have offered valuable suggestions and an abundance of thoughtful feedback. A massive textbook project like this one needs the very best assistance an author can find, and this author was lucky enough to find some marvelously talented people. Jeff Gulati, assistant professor of political science at Bentley University, worked endless hours researching the new edition and weaving together beautifully constructed sections on recent American politics. His original contributions to sections on new campaign technologies, technological innovations transforming the traditional news media, and the rise of the Internet and other forms of "new media" are particularly noteworthy. As always, the staff of the University of Virginia Center for Politics and a team of extraordinary interns contributed in many important ways toward the successful completion of this volume, especially my chief of staff Ken Stroupe, Mary Brown, Cordel Faulk, Rhodes Cook, Dan Keyserling, Paul Wiley, Isaac Wood and Brandon Gould. Their commitment to excellence is also obvious in their work for the Center's Crystal Ball website (www.centerforpolitics.org/crystalball)—a very useful resource in completing this volume. Finally, Larry extends his thanks to the faculty and staff of the Department of Politics at UVA, especially Debbie Best and Department Chairman Jeffrey Legro.

Alixandra B. Yanus thanks Karen O'Connor, who has been both mentor and "mom," for the opportunity to work on this textbook. She also acknowledges the support of her colleagues at the University of North Carolina at Chapel Hill, without whom the journey would be long and lonely. Most especially, she is grateful to her parents, Karen and Mark Yanus, for the assistance, encouragement, and guidance they have provided throughout her life. She also appreciates the patience and devotion of Daniel P. Tappen, who watches the Mets when she has to work, and takes her to Phillies games when she doesn't.

Particular thanks go to Dennis L. Dresang at the University of Wisconsin–Madison, who has once again brought a keen eye and insightful analysis to chapter 4 (State and Local Government) and has written new Join the Debate features in the book; Christopher Borick at Muhlenberg College, who thoroughly revised chapters 17 and 18 (Domestic Policy and Economic Policy); and Kiki Caruson of the University of South Florida, who tackled the rapidly shifting landscape of chapter 19 (Foreign and Defense Policy) for this edition and also drafted the Thinking Globally features. Our continued thanks go to Steven Koven at the University of Louisville and Daniel S. Papp of the University System of Georgia, whose earlier work on the policy chapters continues to serve as such a strong foundation. We also thank Brian Bearry of the University of Texas at Dallas for his past help with many of the Join the Debate features.

In the now many years we have been writing and rewriting this book, we have been blessed to have been helped by many people at Longman. Eric Stano has been a fantastic editor as well as fun to work with. Our development editor, Melissa Mashburn, has been a stern taskmaster with a political junkie's eye for extensive updating. Our marketing manager, Lindsey Prudhomme, has done a terrific job. We would also like to acknowledge the tireless efforts of the Pearson Education sales force. In the end, we hope that all of these talented people see how much their work and support have helped us to write a better book.

Many of our peers reviewed past editions of the book and earned our gratitude in the process. We list a number who reviewed recent editions here:

Danny Adkison, *Oklahoma State University*

Weston H. Agor, *University of Texas at El Paso*

Victor Aikhionbare, *Salt Lake Community College*

James Anderson, *Texas A&M University*

William Arp, *Southern University, Baton Rouge*

Judith Baer, *Texas A&M University*

Vanessa Baird, *University of Colorado, Boulder*

Ruth Bamberger, *Drury College*

Christine Barbour, *Indiana University*

Ken Baxter, *San Joaquin Delta College*

Brian Bearry, *University of Texas at Dallas*

Jon Bond, *Texas A&M University*

Stephen A. Borrelli, *University of Alabama*

Ann Bowman, *University of South Carolina*

Robert C. Bradley, *Illinois State University*

Holly Brasher, *University of Alabama, Birmingham*

Michelle Brophy-Baermann, *University of Wisconsin*

Gary Brown, *Montgomery College*

John Francis Burke, *University of Houston–Downtown*

Kevin Buterbaugh, *Northwest Missouri State University*

Mark Byrnes, *Middle Tennessee State University*

Greg Caldeira, *Ohio State University*

John H. Calhoun, *Palm Beach Atlantic University*

David E. Camacho, *Northern Arizona University*

Alan R. Carter, *Schenectady County Community College*

Carl D. Cavalli, *North Georgia College and State University*

Steve Chan, *University of Colorado*

Richard Christofferson, Sr., *University of Wisconsin–Stevens Point*

David Cingranelli, *SUNY Binghamton*

Clarke E. Cochran, *Texas Tech University*

Paul W. Cook, *Cy-Fair College*

Tracy Cook, *Central Texas College*

Kevin Corder, *Western Michigan University*

Anne N. Costain, *University of Colorado*

Cary Covington, *University of Iowa*

Lorrie Clemo, *SUNY Oswego*

Stephen C. Craig, *University of Florida*

Lane Crothers, *Illinois State University*

Abraham L. Davis, *Morehouse College*

Robert DiClerico, *West Virginia University*

John Dinan, *Wake Forest University*

John Domino, *Sam Houston State University*

Keith L. Dougherty, *University of Georgia*

David E. Dupree, *Victor Valley College*

Craig F. Emmert, *Texas Tech University*

Walle Engedayehu, *Prairie View A&M University*

Alan S. Engel, *Miami University*

Timothy Fackler, *University of Nevada, Las Vegas*

Frank B. Feigert, *University of North Texas*

Terri S. Fine, *University of Central Florida*

Evelyn Fink, *University of Nebraska*

Scott R. Furlong, *University of Wisconsin–Green Bay*

James D. Gleason, *Victoria College*

Dana K. Glencross, *Oklahoma City Community College*

Sheldon Goldman, *University of Massachusetts, Amherst*

Doris Graber, *University of Illinois at Chicago*

Jeffrey D. Green, *University of Montana*

Roger W. Green, *University of North Dakota*

James Michael Greig, *University of North Texas*

Charles Hadley, *University of New Orleans*

Mel Hailey, *Abilene Christian University*

William K. Hall, *Bradley University*

Robert L. Hardgrave, Jr., *University of Texas at Austin*

Chip Hauss, *George Mason University/University of Reading*

Stacia L. Haynie, *Louisiana State University*

John R. Hermann, *Trinity University*

Marjorie Hershey, *Indiana University*

Justin Holmes, *University of Minnesota*

Steven Alan Holmes, *Bakersfield College*

Jerry Hopkins, *East Texas Baptist University*

Tim Howard, *North Harris College*

John C. Hughes, *Oklahoma City Community College*

Jon Hurwitz, *SUNY Buffalo*

Thomas Hyde, *Pfeiffer University*

Joseph Ignagni, *University of Texas at Arlington*

Willoughby Jarrell, *Kennesaw State College*

Susan M. Johnson, *University of Wisconsin–Whitewater*

Dennis Judd, *University of Missouri–St. Louis*

Ngozi Kamalu, *Fayetteville State University*

Carol J. Kamper, *Rochester Community College*

David Kennedy, *Montgomery College*

Kenneth Kennedy, *College of San Mateo*

Donald F. Kettl, *University of Wisconsin*

Quentin Kidd, *Christopher Newport University*

John Kincaid, *Lafayette College*

Karen M. King, *Bowling Green State University*

Alec Kirby, *University of Wisconsin–Stout*

Aaron Knight, *Houston Community College*

John F. Kozlowicz, *University of Wisconsin–Whitewater*

Jonathan E. Kranz, *John Jay College of Criminal Justice*

John C. Kuzenski, *The Citadel*

Mark Landis, *Hofstra University*

Sue Lee, *North Lake College*

Ted Lewis, *Collin County Community College*

Matt Lindstrom, *St. John's University*

Brad Lockerbie, *University of Georgia*

Susan MacFarland, *Gainesville College*

Cecilia Manrique, *University of Wisconsin–La Crosse*

Larry Martinez, *California State University–Long Beach*

Lynn Mather, *SUNY Buffalo*

Laurel A. Mayer, *Sinclair Community College*

Steve Mazurana, *University of Northern Colorado*

Clifton McCleskey, *University of Virginia*

Percival Robert McDonagh, *Catholic University*
James L. McDowell, *Indiana State University*
Carl E. Meacham, *SUNY Oneonta*
Stephen S. Meinhold, *University of North Carolina–Wilmington*
John Mercurio, *San Diego State University*
Mark C. Miller, *Clark University*
Kenneth F. Mott, *Gettysburg College*
Joseph Nogee, *University of Houston*
John O'Callaghan, *Suffolk University*
Bruce Oppenheimer, *Vanderbilt University*
Richard Pacelle, *Georgia Southern University*
Marian Lief Palley, *University of Delaware*
David R. Penna, *Gallaudet University*
Ron Pettus, *St. Charles Community College*
Richard M. Pious, *Columbia University*
David H. Provost, *California State University–Fresno*
Lawrence J. Redlinger, *University of Texas at Dallas*
James A. Rhodes, *Luther College*
Leroy N. Rieselbach, *Indiana University*
David Robertson, *Public Policy Research Centers, University of Missouri–St. Louis*
David Robinson, *University of Houston–Downtown*
Norman Rodriguez, *John Wood Community College*
David W. Rohde, *Duke University*
Frank Rourke, *Johns Hopkins University*
Thomas Rowan, *Chicago State University*
Donald Roy, *Ferris State University*
Ronald Rubin, *City University of New York, Borough of Manhattan Community College*
Bruce L. Sanders, *MacComb Community College*
Denise Scheberle, *University of Wisconsin–Green Bay*
Gaye Lynn Scott, *Austin Community College*
Martin P. Sellers, *Campbell University*
Daniel M. Shea, *University of Akron*

John N. Short, *University of Arkansas–Monticello*
Michael Eric Siegel, *American University*
Mark Silverstein, *Boston University*
James R. Simmons, *University of Wisconsin–Oshkosh*
Andrea Simpson, *University of Richmond*
Philip M. Simpson, *Cameron University*
Elliott E. Slotnick, *Ohio State University*
Michael W. Sonnleitner, *Portland Community College*
Frank J. Sorauf, *University of Minnesota*
David Sprick, *University of Missouri, Kansas City*
Gerald Stanglin, *Cedar Valley College*
C. S. Tai, *University of Arkansas–Pine Bluff*
Leena Thacker-Kumer, *University of Houston–Downtown*
Richard J. Timpone, *SUNY Stony Brook*
Albert C. Waite, *Central Texas College*
Brian Walsh, *University of Maryland*
Shirley Anne Warshaw, *Gettysburg College*
Matt Wetstein, *San Joaquin Delta College*
Richard Whaley, *Marian College*
Rich Whisonant, *York Technical College*
Harold Wingfield, *Kennesaw State University*
Martin Wiseman, *Mississippi State University*
Kevan Yenerall, *Bridgewater College*
Finally, we'd also like to thank our peers who reviewed and aided in the development of the current edition:
Brian Dille, *Odessa College*
Robert Locander, *North Harris College*
Billy Monroe, *University of Texas at Dallas*
Dana Morales, *Montgomery College*
Katarina Moyon, *Winthrop University*
Kathleen Sedille, *College of DuPage*
Robert Sullivan, *Dallas Baptist University*
Ron Velten, *Grayson County College*

Essentials of
American
GOVERNMENT

1

The Political Landscape

We the People of the United States, in Order to form a more perfect Union, establish Justice, insure domestic Tranquility, provide for the common defence, promote the general Welfare, and secure the Blessings of Liberty to ourselves and our Posterity, do ordain and establish this Constitution for the United States of America.

These are the words that begin the Preamble to the United States Constitution. Written in 1787 by a group of men we today refer to as the Framers, this document, which expresses sentiments echoed in later written statements such as the Pledge of Allegiance and the American's Creed, has guided our nation, its government, its politics, its institutions, and its inhabitants for over 200 years.

When the Preamble to the U.S. Constitution was written, the phrases "We the People" and "ourselves" meant something very different from what they do today. After all, voting largely was limited to property-owning white males. Indians, slaves, and women could not vote. Today, through the expansion of the right to vote, the

phrase "the People" encompasses men and women of all races, ethnic origins, and social and economic statuses—a variety of peoples and interests. The Framers could not have imagined the range of people today who are eligible to vote. The Framers would be amazed, as well, at the array of services and programs the government— especially the national government—provides. They further would be surprised to see how the physical boundaries and the composition of the population have changed over the past 200 plus years. And, they might well wonder, "How did we get here?"

In the goals it outlines, the Preamble to the Constitution describes what the people of the United States can expect from their government. The Pledge of Allegiance, adopted in 1892 during a time of political turmoil and a great influx of immigrants, calls on all to profess their dedication to the American flag and for all it stands: *"I pledge allegiance to the Flag of the United States of America, and to the Republic for which it stands, one Nation, indivisible, with liberty and justice for all."* (The phrasing was changed to "one Nation under God" in 1954.)

Americans believe that each generation should hand down to the next not only a better America, but an improved economic, educational, and social status. In general, Americans long have been optimistic about their nation, its institutions, and its future. Thomas Jefferson saw the United States as the world's

WHAT SHOULD I KNOW ABOUT . . .

- the roots of American government?
- the philosophical origins of American government?
- American political culture and the characteristics of American democracy?
- political ideology, its role in the world, and its role in American politics?
- the changing characteristics of the American people?
- population changes and Americans' attitudes toward government?

"best hope"; Abraham Lincoln echoed these sentiments when he called it the "last, best hope on earth."[1]

But, in the wake of the September 11, 2001, terrorist attacks, the wars in Iraq and Afghanistan, and natural disasters and economic troubles at home, citizens today question how well the U.S. government can deliver on the goals set out in the Preamble and the Pledge of Allegiance. Few Americans classify the union as "perfect"; many feel excluded from "Justice" and the "Blessings of Liberty," and even our leaders do not believe that our domestic situation is particularly tranquil, as evidenced by the continuing debates about the best means to protect America. Still, in appraising how well government functions, it is imperative to look at not only the roots of the political system, but also how it has been reformed over time through amendment, legislation, common usage, and changing social mores.

Perhaps because reform is usually incremental and takes so much time, some Americans put little faith in government or do not care much at all about it. Many believe that they have no influence in its decision making, or they do not see any positive benefits from it in their lives. Yet, ironically, in times of emergency, be it a terrorist attack or a natural disaster, or in the face of rising food and gas prices, many people immediately look to their government for help. And when citizens are concerned about their lives and the state of the nation, they often call for reform. During the 2008 presidential nominating season, candidates made much of the need for "change." Yet how that change was to be accomplished remained quite vague.

TO LEARN MORE—
—TO DO MORE

Learn about the history of the Pledge of Allegiance at www.home-ofheroes.com. Search "Pledge of Allegiance" from the site's home page. Discuss if it is time, again, to refocus on American ideals as the government debates immigration and citizenship issues.

In this text, we present you with the tools that you need to understand how our political system has evolved and to prepare you to understand the changes that are yet to come. If you approach the study of American government and politics with an open mind, it should help you become a better citizen. We hope that you learn to ask questions, to understand how various issues have come to be important, and to see why a particular law was enacted, how it was implemented, and if it is in need of reform. We further hope that, with such understanding, you will learn not to accept at face value everything you see on the television news, hear on the radio, or read in the newspaper and on the Internet, especially in the blogosphere. Work to understand your government, and use your vote and other forms of participation to help ensure that your government works for you.

We recognize that the discourse of politics has changed dramatically even in the last few years: it is easier to become informed about the political process and to get involved in campaigns and elections than ever before. We also believe that a thorough understanding of the workings of government will allow you to question and think about the political system—the good parts and the bad—and decide for yourself the advantages and disadvantages of possible changes and reforms. Equipped with such an understanding, you likely will become a better informed and more active participant in the political process.

Every long journey begins with a single step. In this chapter, we will discuss the roots of American government and why they are important. We will then explore American political culture and the basic tenets of American democracy. We will also discuss political ideology and its role in the world and in American politics. We will then turn to the changing characteristics of the American people. Finally, we will discuss changes in population and Americans' attitudes and their implication for government reform.

Roots of American Government: What Are They and Why Are They Important?

Throughout history, all sorts of societies have organized themselves into a variety of governments, small and large, simple and complex, democratic and nondemocratic, elected and nonelected. A **government** is the formal vehicle through which policies are made and affairs of state are conducted. In fact, the term "government" is derived from the Greek for "to pilot a ship," which is appropriate, since we expect governments to guide "the ship of state." As we explore throughout this text, governments are often a result of trial and error, experiment, compromise, and sometimes bloodshed.

Unlike schools, banks, or corporations, the actions of government are binding on all citizens. A **citizen**, by law, is a member of the political community who, by nature of being born in a particular nation or having become a naturalized citizen, is entitled to all of the security and freedoms guaranteed by the government. In exchange, citizens must obey the government, its laws, and its constitution. Citzens also are expected to support their government through exercising their right to vote, paying taxes, and, if they are eligible, submitting themselves to military service.

As we explore American government in this text, we are referring to the web of formal administrative structures that exist on the national, state, and local levels. But, these governments do not exist in a vacuum. A variety of external forces such as the media, political parties, and interest groups influence the day-to-day workings of governments. Thus, we explore government in the context of **politics**, the study of what has been called "who gets what, when, and how," or more simply, the process of how policy decisions get made. While all governments share to greater or lesser degrees the need to provide certain key functions, to whom they provide these benefits, which benefits they provide, when they provide them, and how they are provided vary tremendously across as well as within nations.

government
The formal vehicle through which policies are made and affairs of state are conducted.

citizen
Member of the political community to whom certain rights and obligations are attached.

politics
The study of who gets what, when, and how—or how policy decisions are made.

Functions of Government

The Framers of the Constitution clearly recognized the need for a new government. As our opening vignette underscores, in attempting "to form a more perfect Union," the Framers, through the Constitution, set out several key functions of government, as well as governmental guarantees to the people that have continuing relevance today. As discussed below, several of the Framers' ideas centered on their belief that the major function of government was creating mechanisms to allow individuals to solve conflicts in an orderly and peaceful manner. Just how much authority one must give up to governments in exchange for this kind of security, however, has vexed political philosophers as well as politicians for ages. Still, several enduring

Comparing Political Landscapes

Ideas Into Action

The American's Creed

Times of war often lead to patriotic displays intended to bolster support for home and country. As dissension among Americans swirled around U.S. involvement in World War I, a national contest was held to codify an "American's Creed." The winning entry, written by William Tyler Page in 1917 and adopted by the U.S. House of Representatives in 1918, states:

> I believe in the United States of America as a Government of the people, by the people, for the people, whose just powers are derived from the consent of the government; a democracy in a Republic; a sovereign Nation of many sovereign States; a perfect Union, one and inseparable; established upon those principles of freedom, equality, justice and humanity for which American patriots sacrificed their lives and fortunes.
>
> I therefore believe it is my duty to my country to love it, to support its Constitution, to obey its laws, to respect its flag and to defend it against all enemies.

The similarities between the American's Creed and the Declaration of Independence are clear, but in times of political disagreement over American policies abroad, such statements of solidarity can lead to disagreements over what American citizens owe their nation and how best they can defend it against "all enemies." Are politicians who wear flag pins on their lapels more patriotic than those who do not? To what extent may citizens actively oppose their governments' policies while still remaining loyal citizens? Does citizenship require voiced disagreement as well as support? The spirited debate on these issues will continue.

- How would you change the American's Creed to make it more relevant to twenty-first-century America? Does the creed omit or underplay aspects of citizenship that you believe are important? Does it emphasize aspects of citizenship that should be downplayed or left out?
- Examine the language of the American's Creed and research the myriad allusions it makes to other historical documents. How are these documents important to modern American society?
- Draft a new version of the American's Creed, making it both specific to the United States and also relevant to twenty-first-century America.

---

principles are evident in the Declaration of Independence, the Constitution, the Pledge of Allegiance, and the American's Creed. (To learn more about the enduring principles of the United States, see Ideas into Action: The American's Creed.)

Thinking Globally

The European Union

The European Union (EU) was established in 1993. It is now composed of twenty-seven countries, including fifteen Western European nations, eight Eastern European nations, and the island nations of Malta and Cyprus. The European Union has achieved a great deal of cross-national integration with respect to economic, diplomatic, and technical matters. Political and military integration of the member nations has been more difficult to accomplish.

- If the United States were to enter into a union of nations similar to the European Union, which countries would be its natural partners?
- What functions of government might such a union of countries facilitate if the United States were a party to it?

ESTABLISHING JUSTICE One of the first things expected from governments is a system of laws that allows individuals to abide by a common set of principles. Societies adhering to the rule of law allow for the rational dispensing of justice by acknowledged legal authorities. Thus, today, the Bill of Rights entitles people to a trial by jury, to be informed of the charges against them, and to be tried in a courtroom presided over by an impartial judge. The Constitution created a federal judicial system to dispense justice, but the Bill of Rights specified a host of rights guaranteed to all citizens in an effort to establish justice.

INSURING DOMESTIC TRANQUILITY As we will discuss throughout this text, the role of government in insuring domestic tranquility is a subject of much debate. In times of crisis such as the terrorist attacks of September 11, 2001, the U.S. government, as well as state and local governments, took extraordinary measures to contain the threat of terrorism from abroad as well as within the United States. Local governments also have police forces, the states have national guards, and the federal government can always call up troops to quell any threats.

PROVIDING FOR THE COMMON DEFENSE The Constitution calls for the president to be the commander in chief of the armed forces, and Congress is given the authority to raise an army. The Framers recognized that one of the major purposes of government is to provide for the defense of its citizens. As highlighted in Figure 1.1, the defense budget is a considerable proportion of all federal outlays.

PROMOTING THE GENERAL WELFARE When the Framers added "promoting the general Welfare" to their list of key government functions, they never envisioned how the involvement of the government at all levels would expand so tremendously. In fact, promoting the general welfare was more of an ideal than a mandate for the new national government. Over time, however, our notions of what governments should do have expanded along with the number and size of governments. As we discuss throughout this text, however, there is no universal agreement on the scope of what governments should do.

SECURING THE BLESSINGS OF LIBERTY A well-functioning government that enjoys the support of its citizenry is one of the best ways to "secure the Blessings of Liberty" for its people. In a free society, citizens enjoy a wide range of liberties and freedoms and feel free to prosper. They are free to criticize the government and to petition it when they disagree with its policies or have a grievance.

   Taken together, these principal functions of government and the guarantees they provide to citizens permeate our lives. Whether it is your ability to obtain a low-interest student loan, buy a formerly prescription-only drug over the counter, or be licensed to drive a car at a particular age, government plays a major role. And, without government-sponsored research, we would not have cellular telephones or the Internet.

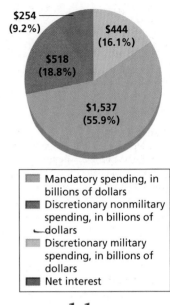

$254 (9.2%)
$444 (16.1%)
$518 (18.8%)
$1,537 (55.9%)

- Mandatory spending, in billions of dollars
- Discretionary nonmilitary spending, in billions of dollars
- Discretionary military spending, in billions of dollars
- Net interest

FIGURE 1.1 Allocation of the Federal Budget, 2008

Source: Fiscal Year 2008 Budget, www.whitehouse.gov/omb/budget/fy2008/pdf/spec.pdf, Table 25-1.

Types of Government

Early theorists such as Plato and Aristotle tried to categorize governments by who participates, who governs, and how much authority those who govern enjoy. As revealed in Table 1.1, a **monarchy**, the form of government explicitly rejected by the Framers, is defined by the rule of one in the interest of all of his or her subjects. The Framers also rejected adopting an aristocracy, which is defined as government by the few in the service of the many.

   The least appealing of Aristotle's classifications of government is **totalitarianism**, a form of government that he considered rule by "tyranny." Tyrants rule their countries to benefit themselves. This was the case in Iraq under Saddam Hussein. In tyrannical or totalitarian systems, the leader exercises unlimited power, and individuals have no personal rights or liberties. Generally, these systems tend to be ruled in the

monarchy
A form of government in which power is vested in hereditary kings and queens who govern in the interests of all.

totalitarianism
A form of government in which power resides in a leader who rules according to self-interest and without regard for individual rights and liberties.

TABLE 1.1 Aristotle's Classifications of Government

Rule by	In Whose Interest?	
	Public	Self
One	Monarchy	Tyranny
The Few	Aristocracy	Oligarchy
The Many	Polity	Democracy

Source: Aristotle, *Politics* 3, 7.

name of a particular religion or orthodoxy, an ideology, or a personality cult organized around a supreme leader.

oligarchy
A form of government in which the right to participate is conditioned on the possession of wealth, social status, military position, or achievement.

democracy
A system of government that gives power to the people, whether directly or through elected representatives.

Another unappealing form of government, an **oligarchy**, occurs when a few people rule in their own interest. In an oligarchy, participation in government is conditioned on the possession of wealth, social status, military position, or achievement.

Aristotle called rule of the many for the benefit of all citizens a "polity" and referred to rule of the many to benefit themselves as a "democracy." The term **democracy** is derived from the Greek words *demos* (the people) and *kratia* (power or authority) and may be used to refer to any system of government that gives power to the people, either directly, or indirectly through elected representatives. Ironically, Aristotle was quite troubled by the idea of democracy, although he believed it better than tyranny or oligarchy. He strongly believed that the collective judgment of the many was preferable to that of a few.

The majority of governments worldwide are democracies to one extent or another. In most democracies, contrary to Aristotle's fears, the "many"—or in the case of the United States and as noted in our chapter opening vignette, "the People"—are the ruling power, albeit through their elected leaders.

The Philosophical Origins of American Government

The current American political system did not spring into being overnight. It is the result of philosophy, trial and error, and even luck. To begin our examination of why we have the type of government we have today, we will look at the theories of government that influenced the Framers who drafted the Constitution and created the United States of America.

The Reformation and the Enlightenment: Questioning the Divine Right of Kings

In the third century, as the Roman Empire began to fall, kings throughout Europe began to rule their countries absolutely, claiming their right to govern came directly from God. Thus, since it was thought to be God's will that a particular monarch ruled a country, the people in that country had no right to question their monarch's authority or agitate for a voice in their government's operation.

Mayflower Compact
Document written by the Pilgrims while at sea enumerating the scope of their government and its expectations of citizens.

social contract
An agreement between the people and their government signifying their consent to be governed.

The intellectual and religious developments of the Reformation and Enlightenment periods of the sixteenth and seventeenth centuries encouraged people to seek alternatives to absolute monarchies and to ponder new methods of governance. In the late sixteenth century, radical Protestants split from the Church of England, which was created by King Henry VIII when the Roman Catholic Church forbade him to divorce and remarry. Known as Puritans, these new Protestants believed in their ability to speak directly to God, and they established self-governing congregations. But, they were persecuted for their religious beliefs by the English monarchy. The Pilgrims were the first group of these Protestants to flee religious persecution and settle in America. There they established self-governing congregations and were responsible for the first widespread appearance of self-government in the American colonies. The **Mayflower Compact**, the document setting up their new government, was deemed sufficiently important to be written while the Pilgrims were still at sea. It took the form of a **social contract**, or agreement between the people and their government signifying their consent to be governed.

Hobbes, Locke, and the Social Contract Theory of Government

Two English theorists of the seventeenth century, Thomas Hobbes (1588–1679) and John Locke (1632–1704), built on conventional notions about the role of government and the relationship of the government to the people in proposing a **social contract theory** of government. They argued that all individuals were free and equal by natural right. This freedom, in turn, required that all men and women give their consent to be governed.

In Hobbes's *Leviathan* (1651), he argued pessimistically that humanity's natural state was one of war. Government, Hobbes theorized, particularly a monarchy, was necessary to restrain humanity's bestial tendencies because life without government was but a "state of nature." Without written, enforceable rules, people would live like animals—foraging for food, stealing, and killing when necessary. To escape the horrors of the natural state and to protect their lives, Hobbes argued, people must give up certain rights to government. Without government, Hobbes warned, life would be "solitary, poor, nasty, brutish, and short"—a constant struggle to survive against the evil of others. For these reasons, governments had to intrude on people's rights and liberties to better control society and to provide the necessary safeguards for property.

Hobbes argued strongly for a single ruler, no matter how evil, to guarantee the rights of the weak against the strong. Leviathan, a biblical sea monster, was his characterization of an all-powerful government. Strict adherence to Leviathan's laws, however all-encompassing or intrusive on liberty, was a small price to pay for living in a civilized society.

In contrast to Hobbes, John Locke, like many other political philosophers of the era, took the basic survival of humanity for granted. Locke argued that a government's major responsibility was the preservation of private property, an idea that ultimately found its way into the U.S. Constitution. In two of his works—*Second Treatise on Civil Government* (1689) and *Essay Concerning Human Understanding* (1690)—Locke not only denied the divine right of kings to govern but argued that individuals were born equal and with natural rights that no king had the power to void. Under Locke's conception of social contract theory, the consent of the people is the only true basis of any sovereign's right to rule. According to Locke, people form governments largely to preserve life, liberty, and property, and to ensure justice. If governments act improperly, they break their contract with the people and therefore no longer enjoy the consent of the governed. Because he believed that true justice comes from the law, Locke argued that the branch of government that makes laws—as opposed to the one that enforces or interprets laws—should be the most powerful.

Locke believed that having a chief executive to administer laws was important, but that he should necessarily be limited by law or by the social contract with the governed. Locke's writings influenced many American colonists, especially Thomas Jefferson, whose original draft of the Declaration of Independence noted the rights to "life, liberty, and property" as key reasons to separate from England.[2] This document was "pure Locke" because it based the justification for the split with England on the English government's violation of the social contract with the American colonists.

social contract theory
The belief that people are free and equal by natural right, and that this in turn requires that all people give their consent to be governed; espoused by John Locke and influential in the writing of the Declaration of Independence.

Why did Hobbes support rule by a monarch? The title page from Thomas Hobbes's *Leviathan* (1651) depicts a giant ruler whose body consists of the bodies of his subjects. This is symbolic of the people coming together under one ruler.

Photo courtesy: Bettmann/CORBIS

Devising a National Government in the American Colonies

The American colonists rejected a system with a strong ruler, like the British monarchy, when they declared their independence. The colonists also were fearful of replicating the landed and titled system of the British aristocracy. They viewed the formation of a representative form of government as far more in keeping with the ideas of social contract theorists and their own traditions.

The earliest forms of government in the colonies, such as the New England town meeting, where all citizens gather to discuss and decide issues facing the town, were characterized by **direct democracy.** This tradition, however, soon proved unworkable as more and more settlers came to the New World. Therefore, many town meetings were replaced by mechanisms of **indirect democracy** (this is also called representative democracy), which call for the election of representatives to a governmental decision-making body. The Virginia House of Burgesses, created in 1619, exemplifies this tradition.

Still, many citizens were uncomfortable with the term democracy because it conjured up Hobbesian fears of the people and mob rule. Instead, they preferred the term **republic**, which implied a system of government in which the interests of the people were represented by more educated or wealthier citizens who were responsible to those who elected them. Today, representative democracies are more commonly called republics, and the words democracy and republic often are used interchangeably.

direct democracy
A system of government in which members of the polity meet to discuss all policy decisions and then agree to abide by majority rule.

indirect (representative) democracy
A system of government that gives citizens the opportunity to vote for representatives who will work on their behalf.

republic
A government rooted in the consent of the governed; a representative or indirect democracy.

American Political Culture and the Basic Tenets of American Democracy

As described previously, the Framers devised a representative democratic system to govern the United States. This system is based on a number of underlying concepts and distinguishing characteristics that sometimes conflict with one another. Taken together, these ideas lie at the core of American political culture. More specifically, **political culture** can be defined as commonly shared attitudes, beliefs, and core values about how government should operate. American political culture emphasizes the values of personal liberty, equality, popular consent and majority rule, popular sovereignty, civil society, individualism, and religious faith.

political culture
Commonly shared attitudes, beliefs, and core values about how government should operate.

Personal Liberty

Personal liberty is perhaps the single most important characteristic of American democracy. The Constitution itself was written to ensure life and liberty. Over the years, however, our concepts of liberty have changed and evolved from freedom *from* to freedom *to*. The Framers intended Americans to be free from governmental infringements on freedom of religion and speech, from unreasonable searches and seizure, and so on. The addition of the Fourteenth Amendment to the Constitution and its emphasis on due process and on equal protection of the laws as well as the subsequent passage of laws guaranteeing civil rights, however, expanded Americans' concept of liberty to include demands for freedom to work or go to school without discrimination.

personal liberty
A key characteristic of U.S. democracy. Initially meaning freedom *from* governmental interference, today it includes demands for freedom *to* engage in a variety of practices without governmental interference or discrimination.

Equality

Another key characteristic of our democracy is **political equality**. A belief in political equality reflects Americans' emphasis on the importance of the individual.

political equality
The principle that all citizens are equal in the political process, as implied by the phrase "one person, one vote."

Although some individuals clearly wield more political clout than others, the adage "one person, one vote" implies a sense of political equality for all.

Popular Consent, Majority Rule, and Popular Sovereignty

Popular consent, the idea that governments must draw their powers from the consent of the governed, is another distinguishing characteristic of American democracy. Derived from John Locke's social contract theory, the notion of popular consent was central to the Declaration of Independence. Today, a citizen's willingness to vote represents his or her consent to be governed and is thus an essential premise of democracy.

Majority rule, another core political value, means that the majority (normally 50 percent of the total votes cast plus one) of citizens in any political unit should elect officials and determine policies. This principle holds for both voters and their elected representatives. Yet, the American system also stresses the need to preserve minority rights, as evidenced by the myriad protections of individual rights and liberties found in the Bill of Rights.

Popular sovereignty, or the notion that the ultimate authority in society rests with the people, has its basis in **natural law**. Ultimately, political authority rests with the people, who can create, abolish, or alter their governments. The idea that all governments derive their power from the people is found in the Declaration of Independence and the U.S. Constitution, but the term popular sovereignty did not come into wide use until pre–Civil War debates over slavery. At that time, supporters of popular sovereignty argued that the citizens of new states seeking admission to the union should be able to decide whether or not their states would allow slavery within their borders.

popular consent
The principle that governments must draw their powers from the consent of the governed.

majority rule
The central premise of direct democracy in which only policies that collectively garner the support of a majority of voters will be made into law.

popular sovereignty
The notion that the ultimate authority in society rests with the people.

natural law
A doctrine that society should be governed by certain ethical principles that are part of nature and, as such, can be understood by reason.

Civil Society

Several of these hallmarks of our political culture also are fundamental to what many commentators now term **civil society**. This term is used to describe the society created when citizens are allowed to organize and express their views publicly as they engage in an open debate about public policy.[3] The U.S. government routinely makes grants to nongovernmental organizations, professional associations, civic education groups, and women's groups to encourage the kind of participation in the political system that Americans often take for granted.

civil society
Society created when citizens are allowed to organize and express their views publicly as they engage in an open debate about public policy.

Individualism

Although many core political tenets concern protecting the rights of others, tremendous value is placed on the individual in American democracy. All individuals are deemed rational and fair and endowed, as Thomas Jefferson proclaimed in the Declaration of Independence, "with certain unalienable rights." Even today, many view individualism, which holds that the primary function of government is to enable the individual to achieve his or her highest level of development, as a mixed blessing.

What Are American Civic Values?

Religious Faith and Religious Freedom

Most Americans profess to have strong religious beliefs, and the United States is the most churchgoing nation in the world. It is overwhelmingly Christian, with a growing number of Christian evangelicals who, since 1980, have played an exceptionally important role in American politics, defining the political positions of the Republican Party, in particular. People of religious faith often have very firm beliefs on social issues such as contraception and abortion, same-sex marriage, the right of

Thinking Globally

Christianity and Islam

Christianity is the largest and most widely spread religion in the world. Christianity is most prevalent in Europe, Latin America, and North America. Muslims represent the second largest group and the most rapidly growing religion. The Muslim religion is concentrated in the Middle East, Asia, and Africa.

- In what ways has religious faith united countries and in what ways has it divided them?
- Identify some of the different ways religion plays a role in public policy making—either in the United States or in other countries.

homosexual people to adopt children, and the use of stem cells for medical research. The concerns of people of strong religious faith continue to play a major role in shaping the political agenda of the nation.

Political Ideology: Its Role in the World and in American Politics

Political ideologies are sets or systems of beliefs that shape the thinking of individuals and how they view the world, especially in regard to issues of "race, nationality, the role and function of government, the relations between men and women, human responsibility for the natural environment, and many other matters."[4] Isaiah Berlin, a noted historian and philosopher, believed that two factors shaped the twentieth century. One was science and technology. The other was "the great ideological storms that have altered the lives of virtually all mankind: the Russian Revolution and its aftermath—totalitarian tyrannies of both right and left and the explosions of nationalism, racism, and in places, of religious bigotry, which interestingly enough, not one among the most perceptive social thinkers of the nineteenth century had ever predicted."[5]

Political scientists note that ideologies perform four key functions:

1. *Explanation.* Ideologies can provide us with reasons for why social and political conditions are the way they are, especially in time of crisis.
2. *Evaluation.* Ideologies can provide the standards for evaluating social conditions and political institutions and events.
3. *Orientation.* Ideologies can provide a sense of identity. Much like a compass, ideologies provide individuals with an orientation toward issues and a position within the world.
4. *Political Program.* Ideologies help people to make political choices and guide their political actions.

Prevailing American Political Ideologies

In America today, one most often hears about conservative, moderate, or liberal political ideologies. (To learn more about the distribution of ideologies in the United States, see Figure 1.2.) These ideologies often translate into political party support, which in turn affects how one votes at the polls. A small proportion of Americans also refer to themselves as **libertarians**, which means they oppose government interference in personal liberties, but pollsters rarely offer respondents the opportunity to label themselves as such. In the American context, political ideologies are often tied into which political party an individual supports, which in turn affects how one votes at the polls and the outcome of elections.

CONSERVATISM A conservative generally believes that government is best when it governs least. They want less government, especially in terms of regulation of the economy. Conservatives favor local and state action over federal intervention, and they emphasize fiscal responsibility.

political ideology
The coherent set of values and beliefs about the purpose and scope of government held by groups and individuals.

libertarians
One who favors a free market economy and no governmental interference in personal liberties.

conservative
One who believes that government is best that governs least and that big government can only infringe on individual, personal, and economic rights.

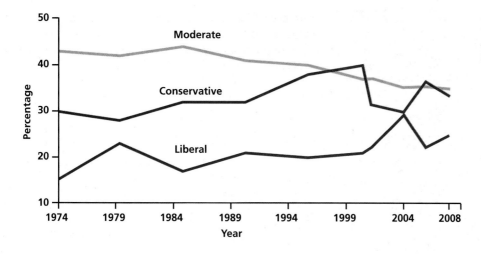

FIGURE **1.2**
Adult Ideological
Self-Identification,
1974–2008
Source: Roper Center at the University of Connecticut, *Public Opinion Online*, Roper iPoll.

Conservatives are likely to support smaller, less activist governments and believe that domestic problems such as homelessness, poverty, and discrimination are better dealt with by the private sector than by the government. Since the 1970s, a growing number of **social conservative** voters (sometimes referred to as the Religious Right) increasingly have affected politics and policies in the United States. Social conservatives believe that moral decay must be stemmed and that traditional moral teachings should be supported and furthered by the government. While a majority of social conservatives are evangelical Protestants and Roman Catholics, some Jews and many Muslims are also social conservatives.

social conservative
One who believes that traditional moral teachings should be supported and furthered by the government.

LIBERALISM A **liberal** is one who seeks to change the political, economic, and social status quo to foster the development of equality and the well-being of individuals.[6] The meanings of the words liberal and liberalism have changed over time, but in the modern United States, liberals generally value equality over other aspects of shared political culture. They are supportive of well-funded government social welfare programs that seek to protect individuals from economic disadvantages or to correct past injustices, and they generally oppose government efforts to regulate private behavior or infringe on civil rights and liberties.

liberal
One who favors governmental involvement in the economy and in the provision of social services and who takes an activist role in protecting the rights of women, the elderly, minorities, and the environment.

Problems with Political Labels

In a perfect world, liberals would be liberal and conservatives would be conservative. Studies reveal, however, that many people who call themselves conservative actually take fairly liberal positions on many policy issues. Thus, most people prefer to be categorized as moderates.

Changing Characteristics of the American People

Americans have many things in common beyond their political culture. Most Americans share a common language—English—and have similar aspirations for themselves and their families. Most agree that they would rather live in the United States than anywhere else, and that an indirect democracy, with all of its warts, is still the best system of government. Most Americans highly value education and want to send their children to the best schools possible, viewing a good education as the key to success. Despite these similarities, politicians, media commentators, and citizens themselves tend to focus on differences among Americans, in large part because these differences contribute to political conflicts among the electorate. Although it is true that the United States and its population are undergoing rapid change, this is not necessarily a new phenomenon.

Changing Size and Population

One year after the U.S. Constitution was ratified, fewer than 4 million Americans lived in the thirteen states. Most were united by a single language and a shared Protestant-Christian heritage, and those who voted were white male property owners. The Constitution mandated that each of the sixty-five members of the original House of Representatives should represent 30,000 people.

As the nation grew larger with the addition of new states, as revealed in Figure 1.3, the population also grew. Although the geographic size of the United States has remained stable since the addition of Alaska and Hawaii in 1959, in 2008 there were more than 304 million Americans, and a single member of the House of Representatives from Montana represented more than 944,000 people.

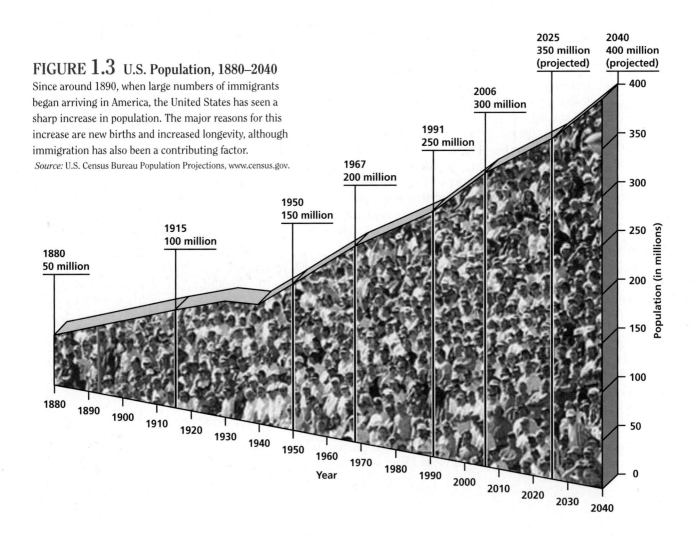

FIGURE 1.3 U.S. Population, 1880–2040

Since around 1890, when large numbers of immigrants began arriving in America, the United States has seen a sharp increase in population. The major reasons for this increase are new births and increased longevity, although immigration has also been a contributing factor.

Source: U.S. Census Bureau Population Projections, www.census.gov.

1880
50 million

1915
100 million

1950
150 million

1967
200 million

1991
250 million

2006
300 million

2025
350 million
(projected)

2040
400 million
(projected)

Population (in millions)

Changing Demographics of the U.S. Population

As the physical size and population of the United States have changed, so have many of the assumptions on which it was founded. Much of this dynamism actually stems from changes in demographics, or the characteristics of the American population, which have occurred throughout our history. Below, we look at some of these demographic characteristics and then discuss some of the implications of these changes for how our nation is governed.

CHANGES IN RACIAL AND ETHNIC COMPOSITION From the start, the American population has been altered constantly by the arrival of immigrants from various regions—Western Europeans fleeing religious persecution in the 1600s to early 1700s, Chinese laborers arriving to work on the railroads following the Gold Rush in 1848, Irish Catholics escaping the potato famine in the 1850s, Northern and Eastern Europeans from the 1880s to 1910s, and most recently, South and Southeast Asians, Cubans, and Mexicans, among others.

Immigration to the United States peaked in the first decade of the 1900s, when nearly 9 million people, many of them from Eastern Europe, entered the country. The United States did not see another major wave of immigration until the late 1980s, when nearly 2 million immigrants were admitted in one year.

While immigration has been a continual source of changing demographics in America, race and ethnicity have also played major roles in the development and course of politics in the United States. As revealed in Figure 1.4, the racial and ethnic balance in America has changed dramatically, with the proportion of Hispanics growing at the quickest rate. What the figure does not show is that 40 percent of Americans under age twenty-five are members of a minority group, a fact that will have a significant impact not only on the demographics of the American polity. (To learn more about immigration debates today, see Join the Debate: The Huntington Theory of Hispanization.)

CHANGES IN AGE COHORT COMPOSITION Just as the racial and ethnic composition of the American population is changing, so too is the average age. "For decades, the U.S. was described as a nation of the young because the number of persons under the age of twenty greatly outnumber[ed] those sixty-five and older," but this is no longer the case.[7] Because of changes in patterns of fertility, life expectancy, and immigration, the nation's age profile has changed drastically. When the United States was founded, the average life expectancy was thirty-five years; by 2008, it was eighty years for women and seventy-five years for men.

An aging population increases a host of costly demands on the government. In 2008, the first of the Baby Boomers (the 76.8 million people who were born between 1946 and 1964) reached age sixty-two and qualified for Social Security; in 2011, they will reach sixty-five and qualify for Medicare.[8] As Table 1.2 reveals, an aging America poses a great financial burden on working Americans, whose proportion of the population is rapidly declining.

These dramatic changes could potentially pit younger people against older people and result in dramatic cuts in benefits to the elderly and increased taxes for younger workers. Moreover, the elderly often vote against programs favored by younger voters, such as money for new schools and other items that they no longer view as important. At the same time, younger voters are less likely to support some things important to seniors, such as Medicare and prescription drug reform.

CHANGES IN FAMILY AND FAMILY SIZE In the past, familial gender roles were clearly defined. Women did housework and men worked in the fields. Large families were imperative; children were a source of cheap farm labor.

Using the Census to Understand Who Americans Are

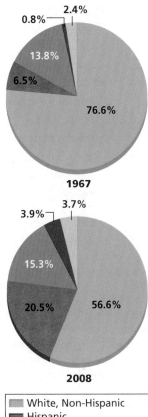

1967

2008

- White, Non-Hispanic
- Hispanic
- Black
- Asian and Pacific Islander
- All other

FIGURE 1.4 Race and Ethnicity in America, 1967 and 2008

Source: U.S. Census Bureau, 2008 Statistical Abstract of the United States.

You Are the Mayor and Need to Get a Town Budget Passed

Join the Debate

The Huntington Theory of Hispanization

OVERVIEW: Many observers of American culture and politics argue that one of the United States' greatest strengths is its ability to absorb and assimilate into the social body the diverse customs and values of different peoples. These commentators highlight the contributions to politics, the arts and sciences, national defense, and the common good made by American Indians and by various waves of immigrants— including those brought against their will during the years of slavery. Traditionalists such as Harvard professor Samuel Huntington contend that the American melting pot has been successful in part because, historically, new Americans have absorbed the fundamental political principles of the United States as their own. Though there are numerous cultures within the country, Huntington insists that there is one shared American culture based on the values espoused in the Declaration of Independence—that is, American political culture is based on the fundamental principles of equality, individual rights, and government by consent. In order for the love of freedom and self-government to be nurtured and maintained, he argues, American core principles must be accepted and protected by all citizens.

Huntington theorizes that during the latter part of the twentieth and into the twenty-first century, there has been a new wave of immigration into the United States unlike any other; he considers immigration from Mexico and Latin America to be potentially destructive of original American political principles. According to Huntington's highly controversial thesis, this immigration wave is unique in that there is a political agenda within part of the Hispanic community to "reclaim" the lands ceded to the United States after both the Texas war for independence and the Mexican-American War.

Furthermore, Huntington argues, no other nation has had to contend with a long, contiguous border that immigrants can cross rather freely to maintain familial, economic, and cultural ties, thereby fostering a type of dual national or cultural allegiance (or, at worst, immigrant loyalty to the home country) that can weaken ties to American core values. Finally, he contends, Hispanic immigrants have created linguistic and cultural enclaves within the United States (areas of Los Angeles and Miami, for example) in which there is no need to learn the language, history, and political values of their adopted nation, thus further eroding social and political bonds between citizens.

Huntington's thesis raises serious questions. Are American core ideals so exceptional that only people who share those values should be allowed citizenship? Do new immigrants from Latin America have political and social beliefs different from or opposed to America's core values? Has American history shown that, ultimately, most immigrants and their descendents embrace the principles that underlie the U.S. Constitution and American political culture? If Huntington is right, how might we reconcile the apparent demand by U.S. employers for Latino/a workers with the threat that Huntington describes?

Arguments IN FAVOR of Huntington's Thesis

- The core political values found in the Declaration of Independence and the Constitution are essential to maintain freedom and protect rights. It may be that original American principles run the risk of being replaced by ideals that advocate forms of government or politics opposed to liberty, self-government, and individual rights, thus changing the character of the American regime.

- American institutions and political culture pursue "justice as the end of government . . . as the end of civil society." American ideals can be a guide for all to live together effectively in peace and harmony, rather than an end in themselves. These principles allow most individuals to pursue their unique conception of the American dream, relatively free from interference by the government and others.

- A shared language and civic education bind citizens together. Teaching multiple languages and cultural viewpoints denies common civic education and creates competing sources of identity that will weaken citizens' attachments to one another and to their government.

Arguments AGAINST Huntington's Thesis

- Historically, certain waves of immigrants were incorrectly thought to be opposed to American values. Benjamin Franklin expressed concerns that German immigrants could not be assimilated into colonial American life because of their culture and history, and Irish Catholic immigrants were accused of both giving allegiance to the pope and being anti-republican in political outlook—fears that proved to be unfounded.

- Bilingualism in the Hispanic community does not indicate the creation of competing sources of social and political identity. Bilingual people who use English and Spanish—or any other language—are not differing from or opposing American core political values. These values, in fact, have roots in French, Greek, and German philosophies, not just British ones.

- American political culture is more than its Anglo-Protestant core. A strength of the American experience is its ability to absorb different cultures and values and transform them into one unique political society. It took both the successive waves of immigration

Photo courtesy: The New York Public Library/Art Resource, NY

THE HIGH TIDE OF IMMIGRATION—A NATIONAL MENACE.

Immigration statistics for the past year show that the influx of foreigners was the greatest in our history, and that the hard-working peasants are now being supplanted by the criminals and outlaws of all Europe.

Is immigration a problem? Concern over immigration is not a new phenomenon, as this cartoon from the early 1900s depicts.

and the freeing of the slaves to move the United States toward the realization of the ideals espoused in the Declaration of Independence.

Continuing the Debate

1. Does the issue of Hispanic immigration threaten American sovereignty and values? Do demonstrations by pro- and anti-immigrant groups signal a significant shift in U.S. history? Explain your thinking.

2. Is American political culture more than its core principles and institutions? What other values and institutions add to the United States' claim that it is a true "melting pot" or multicultural society?

To Follow the Debate Online, Go To:

www.whitehouse.gov to research the current administration's immigration policies.

www.aila.net, the Web site of the American Immigration Lawyer's Association, which provides information on the status of the immigration issue in court.

www.fairus.org for the views of the Federation for American Immigration Reform, which generally has advocated against allowing undocumented immigrants living in the United States to stay.

www.immigrationadvocates.org, the Web site of the Immigration Advocates Network, a partnership of religious, legal, and policy groups that works to strengthen the rights of immigrants by providing an online resource and communication site.

TABLE 1.2 Government, Health Care, and Costs

Examine the costs associated with the medical interventions listed in the table. Does the government have a role in providing the latest health care options to its citizens, regardless of cost? Should access to expensive new technologies and treatments like these be limited to those who can afford them or those who have health insurance policies willing to pay for such interventions?

Costs per New Medical Intervention

Treatment	What It Does or Would Do	Cost to Medicare per Additional Year of Life
Anti-aging compound for healthy people	$1-a-day compound adds 10 years to life	$11,245
Treatment for acute stroke	New drug reduces cell death after stroke	$28,024
Anti-aging compound for unhealthy people	$1-a-day compound adds 10 years to life	$38,105
Alzheimer's prevention	New drug delays onset of disease	$102,774
Implantable cardioverter defibrillator	Controls heart rhythm	$131,892
Diabetes prevention	Insulin-sensitizing drug reduces disease	$188,316
Pacemakers for atrial fibrillation	New generation of pacemakers	$1,795,850

Source: Rand and *USA Today* (October 25, 2005): 2B.

Industrialization and knowledge of birth control methods began to put a dent in the size of American families by the early 1900s. No longer needing children to work for the survival of the household unit on the farm, couples began to limit the sizes of their families.

The look of Ameican households also changed dramatically. In 1940, nine out of ten households were traditional family households. By 2006, just 67.4 percent of children under eighteen lived with both parents. In fact, almost 25 percent of children under eighteen lived with just one of their parents; the majority of those children (more than 21 percent) lived with their mother. Moreover, by 2006, almost 27 percent of all households consisted of a single person, a trend that is in part illustrative of the aging American population and declining marriage rate.

Toward Reform: Population Changes and Americans' Attitudes Toward Government

Today, 86 percent of Americans believe that illegal immigration is a serious problem, and several states have attempted to deny drivers' licenses or access to other public services to undocumented immigrants.[9] Many believe that the numbers of immigrants, legal and illegal, arriving at our shores will lead to disastrous consequences.

Such anti-immigration sentiments are hardly new. In fact, American history is replete with examples of Americans set against any new immigration. In the 1840s, for example, the Know Nothing Party arose in part to oppose immigration from Roman Catholic nations, charging that the pope was going to organize the slaughter of all Protestants in the United States. In the 1920s, the Ku Klux Klan, which had over 5 million members, called for barring immigration to stem the tide of Roman Catholic and Jewish immigrants into the nation.

Demographics affect politics and government because an individual's perspective influences how he or she hears debates on various issues. Thus, African Americans, for example, viewed the government's initial slow response to the plight of the poor and displaced after Hurricane Katrina more unfavorably than did whites.[10]

These cleavages and the emphasis many politicians put on our demographic differences play out in many ways in American politics. Baby Boomers and the elderly object to changes in Social Security or Medicare that adversely affect them, while young Americans are more likely to vote for politicians who support change, if they vote at all. Many policies are targeted at one group or the other, further exacerbating differences—real or imagined—and lawmakers often find themselves the target of many different factions. This diversity can make it difficult to devise coherent policies to "promote the general Welfare," as promised in the Constitution.

Attitudinal Change and Reform

Americans' views about, and expectations of, government and democracy affect the political system at all levels. It has now become part of our political culture to expect negative campaigns, dishonest politicians, and political pundits who make their living bashing politicians and the political process. How Americans view politics, the economy, and their ability to achieve the **American dream**—an American ideal of a happy and successful life, which often includes wealth, a house, a better life for one's children, and for some, the ability to grow up to be president—is influenced by their political ideology as well as by their social, economic, educational, and personal circumstances.

Since the early 1990s, the major sources of most individuals' on-the-air news—the four major networks (ABC, CBS, FOX, and NBC) along with CNN and C-SPAN—have been supplemented dramatically as the number of news and quasi-news outlets has grown exponentially. First there were weekly programs such as *Dateline* on the regular networks. Next came FOX News, MSNBC, and CNBC—all competing for similar audiences. During the 2008 election, more people turned to a cable news program than to the regular networks for their political coverage.

The Internet has also developed as an instantaneous source of news, as well as rumor, about politics. The growth of blogs has allowed consumers to report the news themselves, commenting on events as they occur, sometimes in an unflattering manner.

The competition for news stories, as well as the instantaneous nature of these communications, often highlights the negative, the sensational, the sound bite, and the extreme. It's hard to remain upbeat about America or politics amid the media's focus on personality and scandal. It's hard to remain positive about the fate of Americans and their families if you watch news shows that feature guests trying to outshout each other or campaign ads that highlight only the negative.

American dream
An American ideal of a happy, successful life, which often includes wealth, a house, a better life for one's children, and for some, the ability to grow up to be president.

TIMELINE

Major Technological Innovations That Have Changed the Political Landscape

Photo courtesy: Chris Hondros / Getty Images

How has the face of the United States changed? Barack Obama was the first African American to be elected to the U.S. presidency.

We also cannot ignore how Americans are now viewed abroad. For centuries, immigrants have come to our shores to be part of the American dream—but now, to some people in Europe, the Middle East, and elsewhere, America is no longer the beacon it once was. The spread of American culture as embodied by fast-food chains and American television along with the United States' unpopular involvement in Iraq, has intensified the stereotype of the "ugly American." Negative perceptions of the United States increasingly affect America's relations around the world.

High Expectations

In roughly the first 150 years of our nation's history, the federal government had few responsibilities, and its citizens had few expectations of it beyond national defense, printing money, and collecting tariffs and taxes. The state governments were generally far more powerful than the federal government in matters affecting the everyday lives of Americans (see chapter 3).

As the nation and its economy grew in size and complexity, the federal government took on more responsibilities, such as regulating some businesses, providing poverty relief, and inspecting food. Then, in response to the Great Depression of the 1930s, President Franklin D. Roosevelt's New Deal government programs proliferated in almost every area of American life, including job creation, income security, and aid to the poor. Since then, many Americans have looked to the government for solutions to all kinds of problems.

Redefining Our Expectations Concerning Reform

Today, many Americans lack faith in the country's institutions. (To learn more about Americans' confidence in institutions, see Analyzing Visuals: Faith in Institutions.) And, a 2008 poll revealed that eight in ten Americans think the country is headed in the wrong direction.[11] These concerns make it even easier for citizens to blame the government for all kinds of woes—personal as well as societal—or to fail to credit governments for the things they do well. Many Americans, for example, enjoy a remarkably high standard of living, and much of it is due to governmental programs and protections.

Although all governments have problems, it is important to stress the good they can do. In the aftermath of the Great Depression in the United States, for example, the federal government created the Social Security program, which dramatically decreased poverty among the elderly. Our contract laws and judicial system provide an efficient framework for business, while assuring consumers some recourse in the courts should someone fail to deliver as promised. Government-guaranteed student loan programs make it possible for many students to attend college. Government-sponsored research has contributed to the development of new medicines to improve life expectancy. Thus, Americans live longer today than ever before, far more are high school graduates, and the Internet and the development of cable television have dramatically changed how Americans live and work. And, as more women have equal opportunities with men in the labor force, more families also own their own homes although the economic downturn has made this more difficult.

Just as it is important to recognize that governments serve many important purposes, it is also important to recognize that government and politics are not static.

Analyzing Visuals　Faith in Institutions

This line graph shows the percentages of Americans declaring they had a "great deal" of confidence in American institutions. Examine the graph and answer the following questions:

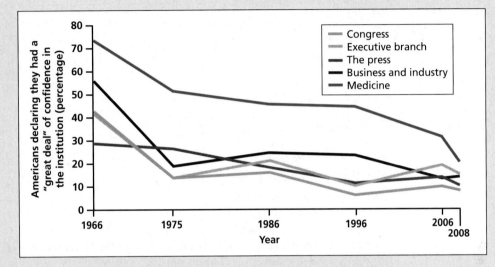

WHAT institution receives the highest rating? The lowest rating?

WHAT institution has shown the steepest decline in ratings since 1966? What institution has shown the least decline in ratings since 1966?

WHAT factors might explain the overall decline in faith in American institutions?

Sources: Newsweek (January 8, 1996): 32; *Public Perspective* 8 (February/March 1994): 4; Lexis-Nexis RPOLL; *Washington Post* (June 13, 2006): A2; Roper Center iPoll, 2008.

Politics, moreover, involves conflicts over different and sometimes opposing ideologies, and these ideologies are very much influenced by one's racial, economic, and historical experiences. These divisions are real and affect the political process at all levels. It is clear to most Americans today that politics and government no longer can be counted on to cure all of America's ills. Government, however, will always play a major role. True political leaders will need to help Americans come to terms with America as it is today—not as it was in the past.

WHAT SHOULD I HAVE LEARNED?

In this chapter, we have answered the followed questions:

■ **What are the roots of American government?**

Governments, which are made up of individuals and institutions, are the vehicles through which policies are made and affairs of state are conducted. We need governments to maintain order because governments alone can use force legitimately. Governments have many functions. In the U.S. context, most of these are included in the Preamble to the Constitution. Governments take many forms depending on the number who rule as well as whose interests are represented.

■ **What are the philosophical origins of American government?**

The American political system is based on several principles that have their roots in classical Greek ideas about democracy. The ideas of social contract theorists John Locke and Thomas Hobbes, who held the belief that people are free and equal by natural right, have continuing implications for our ideas of the proper role of government in our indirect democracy.

■ **What defines American political culture and what are the tenets of American democracy?**

Key tenets of Americans' shared political culture are personal liberty, equality, popular consent and majority rule, popular sovereignty, civil society, individualism, and religious faith.

■ **What is the role of political ideology in the United States and the world?**

Ideologies, the belief systems that shape the thinking of individuals and how they view the world, play a powerful role in politics here and abroad. Most Americans identify themselves as conservatives, liberals, or moderates.

■ **What are the changing characteristics of the American people?**

Several characteristics of the American electorate can help us understand how the system continues to evolve and change. Chief among these are changes in size, population, and demographics.

■ **How do population changes and Americans' attitudes toward government affect policies and efforts toward reform?**

Shifts in population have created controversy in the American electorate throughout America's history. Membership in a demographic group is likely to affect one's outlook on government policies. Moreover, Americans have high and often unrealistic expectations of government yet often fail to appreciate how much their government actually does for them. Americans' failing trust in institutions also explains some of the apathy evidenced in the electorate.

Key Terms

American dream, p. 19
citizen, p. 5
civil society, p. 11
conservative, p. 12
democracy, p. 8
direct democracy, p. 10
government, p. 5
indirect (representative)
    democracy, p. 10
liberal, p. 13

libertarian, p. 12
majority rule, p. 11
Mayflower Compact, p. 8
monarchy, p. 7
natural law, p. 11
oligarchy, p. 8
personal liberty, p. 10
political culture, p. 10
political equality, p. 10
political ideology, p. 12

politics, p. 5
popular consent, p. 11
popular sovereignty, p. 11
republic, p. 10
social conservative, p. 13
social contract, p. 8
social contract theory, p. 9
totalitarianism, p. 7

Researching the Political Landscape

In the Library

Almond, Gabriel A., and Sidney Verba. *Civic Culture: Political Attitudes and Democracy in Five Nations*, new ed. New York: Sage, 1989.

Ball, Terence, and Richard Dagger. *Political Ideologies and the Democratic Ideal*, 7th ed. New York: Longman, 2008.

Dahl, Robert A. *Polyarchy: Participation and Opposition*. New Haven, CT: Yale University Press, 1972.

Elshtain, Jean Bethke. *Democracy on Trial*. New York: Basic Books, 1995.

Fiorina, Morris P., Samuel J. Abrams, and Jeremy C. Pope. *Culture War? The Myth of a Polarized America*, 2nd ed. New York: Longman, 2006.

Fournier, Ron, Douglas B. Sosnick, and Matthew J. Dowd. *Applebee's America: How Successful Political, Business, and Religious Leaders Connect with the New American Community*. New York: Simon and Schuster, 2006.

Jamieson, Kathleen Hall. *Everything You Think You Know About Politics...and Why You're Wrong*. New York: Basic Books, 2000.

Hobbes, Thomas. *Leviathan* ed. Richard Tuck. New York: Cambridge University Press, 1996.

Hochschild, Jennifer L. *Facing Up to the American Dream: Race, Class, and the Soul of the Nation*. Princeton, NJ: Princeton University Press, 1996.

Locke, John. *Two Treatises of Government* ed. Peter Lasleti. New York: Cambridge University Press, 1988.

Nye, Joseph S., Jr. *The Paradox of American Power: Why the World's Superpower Can't Go It Alone*. New York: Oxford University Press, 2002.

Putnam, Robert D. *Bowling Alone: Collapse and Revival of the American Community*. New York: Simon and Schuster, 2001.

Skocpol, Theda, and Morris P. Fiorina, eds. *Civic Engagement in American Democracy*. Washington, DC: Brookings Institution Press, 1999.

Verba, Sidney, Kay Schlozman, and Henry Brady. *Voice and Equality: Civic Volunteerism in American Politics*, 2nd ed. Cambridge, MA: Harvard University Press, 2002.

Zakaria, Fareed. *The Future of Freedom: Illiberal Democracy at Home and Abroad*. New York: Norton, 2004.

On the Web

To learn more about Thomas Hobbes and John Locke, do key word searches on their names or see **www.iep.utm.edu/h/hobmoral.htm** and **www.utm.edu/research/iep/l/locke.htm**.

To learn more about your political ideology, go to the Political Compass at **www.politicalcompass.org**.

To learn about the policy positions and attitudes of American conservatives, go to the American Conservative Union home page at **www.conservative.org**

To learn more about the policy positions and attitudes of American liberals, go to the Liberal Oasis home page at **www.liberaloasis.com**.

To learn more about the policy positions and attitudes of American libertarians, go to the *Rational Review* home page at **www.rationalreview.com/**.

To learn more about shifts in the American population, go to the U.S. Census Bureau's home page at **www.census.gov**. Notice the population clocks in the upper-right corner of the home page that show the current population of the United States as well as the world population. Detailed information about population projections and on families and household composition may be accessed here.

sure domestic Tranquility, provide for the common and our Posterity, do ordain and establish this Consti

Article I

Section 1. All Legislative Powers herein granted shall be vested in a Congress of the United States, which shall consist of a Senate and House of Representatives.

Section 2. The House of Representatives shall be composed of Members chosen every second Year by the People of the several States...

THE
THIRTEEN COLON
AT THE END OF THE COLONIA
English Mile

The Constitution

At age eighteen, all American citizens are eligible to vote in state and national elections. This has not always been the case. It took an amendment to the U.S. Constitution—one of only seventeen that have been added since the Bill of Rights was ratified in 1791—to guarantee the vote to those under twenty-one years of age.

In 1942, during World War II, Representative Jennings Randolph (D–WV) proposed that the voting age be lowered to eighteen, believing that since young men were old enough to be drafted to fight and die for their country, they also should be allowed to vote. He continued to reintroduce his proposal during every session of Congress, and in 1954, President Dwight D. Eisenhower endorsed the idea in his State of the Union message. Presidents Lyndon B. Johnson and Richard M. Nixon—men who had also called upon the nation's young men to fight on foreign shores—echoed his appeal.[1]

During the 1960s, the campaign to lower the voting age took on a new sense of urgency as hundreds of thousands of young men were drafted to fight in Vietnam, and thousands of men and women were killed in action. "Old Enough to Fight, Old Enough to Vote," was one popular slogan of the day. By 1970, four states—the U.S. Constitution allows states to set the eligibility requirements for their voters—had

■ The U.S. Constitution, written in 1787, has proved to be an enduring and flexible document.

lowered their voting ages to eighteen. Later that year, Congress passed legislation lowering the voting age in national, state, and local elections to eighteen.

The state of Oregon, however, challenged the constitutionality of the law in court, arguing that Congress had not been given the authority to establish a uniform voting age in state and local government elections by the Constitution. The U.S. Supreme Court agreed.[2] The decision from the sharply divided Court meant that those under age twenty-one could vote in national elections but that the states were free to prohibit them from voting in state and local elections. The decision presented the states with a logistical nightmare. States setting the voting age at twenty-one would be forced to keep two sets of registration books: one for voters twenty-one and over, and one for voters under twenty-one.

Jennings Randolph, by then a senator from West Virginia, reintroduced his proposed amendment to lower the national voting age to eighteen.[3] Within three months of the Supreme Court's decision, Congress sent the proposed Twenty-Sixth Amendment to the states for their ratification. The required three-fourths of the states approved the amendment within three months—making its adoption on June 30, 1971, the quickest in the history of the constitutional amending process.

However, until the 2008 election cycle, young people never voted in large numbers. Issues of concern to those under the age of twenty-

WHAT SHOULD I KNOW ABOUT . . .

■ the roots of the new American nation?
■ the Articles of Confederation?
■ the writing of the U.S. Constitution?
■ the basic principles of the U.S. Constitution?
■ the drive for ratification of the U.S. Constitution?
■ methods of amending the U.S. Constitution?

25

five, including a possible draft, Internet privacy, reproductive rights, credit card and cell phone rules and regulations, rising college tuition, and the continuance of student loan programs, seemed to do little to energize young voters. While voter registration drives and voter awareness campaigns by groups such as Rock the Vote helped some, it was the Democratic primary race where young voters for the first time began to make a difference in electoral outcomes. Barack Obama's campaign for the Democratic presidential nod energized young people in a way never before seen. Those aged eighteen to twenty-nine affiliated Democratic 2 to 1. In Iowa, for example, young people accounted for 22 percent of caucus goers—the same percentage as those over age sixty-five!

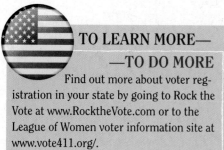

TO LEARN MORE—
—TO DO MORE

Find out more about voter registration in your state by going to Rock the Vote at www.RocktheVote.com or to the League of Women voter information site at www.vote411.org/.

A t its roots, the U.S. Constitution was never intended to be easy to change. The process by which it could be changed or amended was made time consuming and difficult. Over the years, thousands of amendments—including those to prohibit child labor, provide equal rights for women, grant statehood to the District of Columbia, balance the federal budget, and ban flag burning—have been debated or sent to the states for their approval, only to die slow deaths. Only twenty-seven amendments have successfully made their way into the Constitution. What the Framers wrote in Philadelphia has continued to work, in spite of increasing demands on and dissatisfaction with our national government. Although Americans often clamor for reform, perhaps they are happier with the system of government created by the Framers than they realize.

The ideas that went into the making of the Constitution and the ways that it has evolved to address the problems of a growing and changing nation are at the core of our discussion in this chapter. First, we will examine the roots of the new nation and the circumstances surrounding the Declaration of Independence and the break with Great Britain. After discussing the first attempts at American government created by the Articles of Confederation, we will examine the circumstances surrounding writing a constitution and will review the results of the Framers' efforts—the U.S. Constitution. Finally, we will present the drive for ratification and address methods of amending the Constitution.

oots of the New American Nation

Starting in the early seventeenth century, colonists came to the New World for a variety of reasons. Often, as detailed in chapter 1, it was to escape religious persecution. Others came seeking a new start on a continent where land was plentiful. The independence and diversity of the settlers in the New World made the question of how best to rule the new colonies a tricky one. More than merely an ocean separated England from the colonies; the colonists were independent people, and it soon became clear that the crown could not govern its subjects in the colonies with the same close rein used at home. King James I thus allowed some local participation in decision making through arrangements such as the first elected colonial assembly, the Virginia House of Burgesses formed in 1619, and the elected General Court that governed the Massachusetts Bay colony after 1629. Almost all of the colonists agreed that the king ruled by divine right, but English monarchs allowed the colonists significant liberties in terms of self-government, religious practices, and economic organization. For 140 years, this system worked fairly well.[4]

By the early 1760s, however, a century and a half of physical separation, development of colonial industry, and the relative self-governance of the colonies led to weakening ties with—and loyalties to—the crown. By this time, each of the thirteen colonies had drafted its own written constitution, which provided the fundamental rules or laws for each colony. Moreover, many of the most oppressive British traditions—feudalism, a rigid class system, and the absolute authority of the king—were absent in the New World. Land was abundant. The guild and craft systems that severely limited entry into many skilled professions in England did not exist in the colonies. Although religion was central to the lives of most colonists, there was no single state church.

Trade and Taxation

Mercantilism, an economic theory designed to increase a nation's wealth through the development of commercial industry and a favorable balance of trade, justified Britain's maintenance of strict import/export controls on the colonies. After 1650, for example, Parliament passed a series of navigation acts to prevent its chief rival, Holland, from trading with the English colonies. From 1650 until well into the 1700s, England tried to regulate colonial imports and exports, believing that it was critical to export more goods than it imported as a way of increasing the gold and silver in its treasury. These policies, however, were difficult to enforce and were widely ignored by the colonists, who saw little self-benefit in them. Thus, for years, an unwritten agreement existed. The colonists relinquished to the crown and the British Parliament the authority to regulate trade and conduct international affairs, but they retained the right to levy their own taxes.

This fragile agreement was soon put to the test. The French and Indian War, fought from 1756 to 1763 on the western frontier of the colonies and in Canada, was part of a global war initiated by the British. This American phase of what was called the Seven Years' War was fought between England and France with its Indian allies. In North America, its immediate cause was the rival claims of those two European nations for the lands between the Allegheny Mountains and the Mississippi River. What ultimately became the first Treaty of Paris, signed in 1763, not only signaled the end of the war but also greatly increased the size of land claimed by Great Britain in North America. The colonists expected that with the Indian problem on the western frontier now under control, westward migration and settlement could begin in earnest. In 1763, they were shocked when the crown decreed that there was to be no further westward movement by British subjects. Parliament believed that expansion into Indian territory would lead to new expenditures for the defense of the settlers, draining the British treasury.

To raise money to pay for the war as well as the expenses of administering the colonies, Parliament enacted the Sugar Act in 1764. This act placed taxes on sugar, wine, coffee, and other products commonly exported to the colonies. A postwar colonial depression heightened resentment of the tax. Major protest, however, failed to materialize until imposition of the Stamp Act by the British Parliament in 1765. This law required that all paper items bought and sold in the colonies carry a stamp mandated by the crown. The tax itself was not offensive to the colonists. However, they feared this act would establish a precedent for the British Parliament not only to regulate commerce in the colonies, but also to raise revenues from the colonists without the approval of the colonial governments. Around the colonies, the political cry "no taxation without representation" became prominent.

Colonists were outraged. Men throughout the colonies organized the Sons of Liberty under the leadership of Samuel Adams and Patrick Henry. Women formed the Daughters of Liberty. Protests against the Stamp Act were violent and loud. Riots, often led by the Sons of Liberty, broke out. They were especially violent in Boston, where the colonial governor's home was burned by an angry mob, and British stamp agents charged with collecting the tax were threatened. A boycott of goods needing the stamps as well as British imports also was organized.

mercantilism
An economic theory designed to increase a nation's wealth through the development of commercial industry and a favorable balance of trade.

Timeline: Key Events Leading to American Independence

1763 The Treaty of Paris—Ends the French and Indian War. France cedes its claims to any lands east of the Mississippi River, greatly expanding the size of the land claimed by Great Britain in North America.

1767 The Townshend Acts are passed by British Parliament—These acts impose duties on a host of colonial imports, including the colonists' favorite drink, tea.

1765 At the urging of Samuel Adams, the Stamp Act Congress convenes in New York—Adams later begins the Committees of Correspondence.

1770 The Boston Massacre—British troops open fire on a mob, killing five colonists.

First Steps Toward Independence

Stamp Act Congress
Meeting of representatives of nine of the thirteen colonies held in New York City in 1765, during which representatives drafted a document to send to the king listing how their rights had been violated.

In 1765, at the urgings of Samuel Adams, nine of the thirteen colonies sent representatives to a meeting in New York City, where a detailed list of crown violations of the colonists' fundamental rights was drafted. Known as the **Stamp Act Congress**, this gathering was the first official meeting of the colonies and the first step toward creating a unified nation. Attendees defined what they thought to be the proper relationship between colonial governments and the British Parliament; they ardently believed Parliament had no authority to tax them without colonial representation in that body. In contrast, the British believed that direct representation of the colonists was impractical and that members of Parliament represented the best interests of all the English, including the colonists.

The Stamp Act Congress and its petitions to the crown did little to stop the onslaught of taxing measures. Parliament did, however, repeal the Stamp Act and revise the Sugar Act in 1766, largely because of the uproar made by British merchants who were losing large sums of money as a result of the boycotts. Rather than appeasing the colonists, however, these actions emboldened them to increase their resistance. In 1767, Parliament enacted the Townshend Acts, which imposed duties on all kinds of colonial imports, including tea. Responses from the Sons and Daughters of Liberty were immediate. Another boycott was announced, and almost all colonists gave up their favorite drink in a united show of resistance to the tax and British authority.[5] Tensions continued to run high, especially after the British sent 4,000 troops to Boston. On March 5, 1770, English troops opened fire on a mob that included disgruntled dock workers, whose jobs had

Who was Samuel Adams? Today, Samuel Adams (1722–1803) is well known for the beer that bears his name. His original claim to fame was as a leader against the British and loyalist oppressors (although he did bankrupt his family's brewery business).

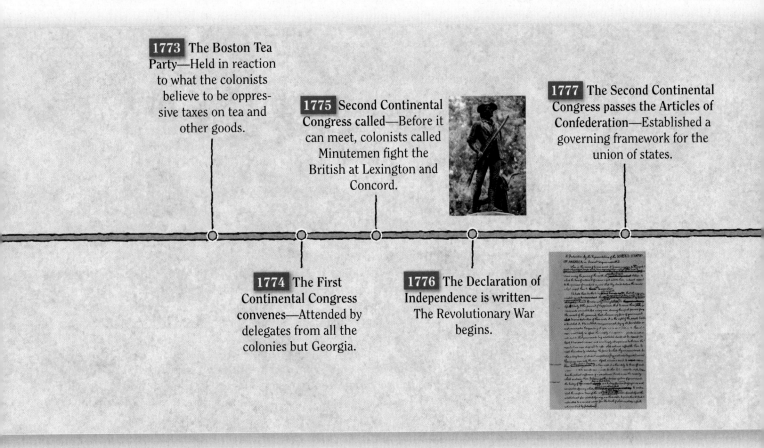

1773 The Boston Tea Party—Held in reaction to what the colonists believe to be oppressive taxes on tea and other goods.

1775 Second Continental Congress called—Before it can meet, colonists called Minutemen fight the British at Lexington and Concord.

1777 The Second Continental Congress passes the Articles of Confederation—Established a governing framework for the union of states.

1774 The First Continental Congress convenes—Attended by delegates from all the colonies but Georgia.

1776 The Declaration of Independence is written—The Revolutionary War begins.

been taken by British soldiers, and members of the Sons of Liberty, who were taunting the soldiers in front of the Boston Customs House. Five colonists were killed in what became known as the Boston Massacre. Following this confrontation, all duties except those on tea were lifted. The tea tax, however, continued to be a symbolic irritant.

In 1773, despite dissent in England over the treatment of the colonies, Parliament passed the Tea Act, granting a monopoly to the financially strapped East India Company to sell the tea imported from Britain. The company was allowed to funnel business to American merchants loyal to the crown, thereby undercutting colonial merchants, who could sell only tea imported from other nations. The effect was to drive down the price of tea and to hurt colonial merchants.

When the next shipment of tea arrived in Boston from Great Britain, the colonists responded by throwing the Boston Tea Party. Similar tea parties were held in other colonies. When the news of these actions reached King George III, he flew into a rage against the actions of his disloyal subjects. "The die is now cast," the king told his prime minister. "The colonies must either submit or triumph."

King George's first act of retaliation was to persuade Parliament to pass the Coercive Acts of 1774. Known in the colonies as the Intolerable Acts, they contained a key provision calling for a total blockade of Boston Harbor until restitution was made for the tea. Another provision reinforced the Quartering Act. It gave royal governors the authority to house British soldiers in the homes of private citizens, allowing Britain to send an additional 4,000 soldiers to patrol Boston.

The Continental Congresses

The British could never have guessed how the cumulative impact of these actions would unite the colonists. **Committees of Correspondence**—organizations in each of the American colonies to keep colonists informed—spread the word, and food and money were sent to the people of Boston from all over the thirteen colonies. The tax itself was no longer the key issue; now the extent of British authority over the colonies was the far more important question. At the request of the colonial assemblies of

Committees of Correspondence Organizations in each of the American colonies created to keep colonists abreast of developments with the British; served as powerful molders of public opinion against the British.

Massachusetts and Virginia, all but Georgia's colonial assembly agreed to select a group of delegates to attend a continental congress authorized to communicate with the king on behalf of the now-united colonies.

The **First Continental Congress** met in Philadelphia from September 5 to October 26, 1774. It was made up of fifty-six delegates. The colonists had yet to think of breaking with Great Britain; at this point, they simply wanted to iron out their differences with the king. By October, they had agreed on a series of resolutions to oppose the Coercive Acts and to establish a formal organization to boycott British goods. The Congress also drafted a Declaration of Rights and Resolves, which called for colonial rights of petition and assembly, trial by peers, freedom from a standing army, and the selection of representative councils to levy taxes.

King George refused to yield, tensions continued to rise, and a **Second Continental Congress** was deemed necessary. Before it could meet, fighting broke out early in the morning of April 19, 1775, at Lexington and Concord, Massachusetts, with what Ralph Waldo Emerson called "the shot heard round the world." Eight colonial soldiers, called Minutemen, were killed, and 16,000 British troops besieged Boston.

When the Second Continental Congress convened in Philadelphia on May 10, 1775, delegates were united by their increased hostility to Great Britain. In a final attempt to avert conflict, the Second Continental Congress adopted the Olive Branch Petition on July 5, 1775, asking the king to end hostilities. King George rejected the petition and sent an additional 20,000 troops to quell the rebellion.

The Declaration of Independence

In January 1776, Thomas Paine, with the support and encouragement of Benjamin Franklin, issued (at first anonymously) *Common Sense*, a pamphlet forcefully arguing for independence from Great Britain. *Common Sense* galvanized the American public against reconciliation with England. On May 15, 1776, Virginia became the first colony to call for independence, instructing one of its delegates to the Second Continental Congress to introduce a resolution to that effect. On June 7, 1776, Richard Henry Lee of Virginia rose to move "that these United Colonies are, and of right ought to be, free and independent States, and that all connection between them and the State of Great Britain is, and ought to be, dissolved." His three-part resolution—which called for independence, the formation of foreign alliances, and preparation of a plan of confederation—triggered hot debate among the delegates. A proclamation of independence from Great Britain was treason, a crime punishable by death. Although six of the thirteen colonies had already instructed their delegates to vote for independence, the Second Continental Congress was suspended to allow its delegates to return home to their respective colonial legislatures for final instructions. Independence was not a move to be taken lightly.

Committees were set up to consider each point of Richard Henry Lee's proposal. A committee of five was selected to begin work on the **Declaration of Independence**. The Congress selected Benjamin Franklin of Pennsylvania, John Adams of Massachusetts, Robert Livingston of New York, and Roger Sherman of Connecticut as members of the committee. Adams lobbied hard for a Southerner to add balance. Thus, owing to his southern origin as well as his "peculiar felicity of expression," Thomas Jefferson of Virginia was selected as chair.

On July 2, 1776, twelve of the thirteen colonies (with New York abstaining) voted for independence. Two days later, the Second Continental Congress voted to adopt the Declaration of Independence largely penned by Thomas Jefferson. On July 9, 1776, the Declaration, now with the approval of New York, was read aloud in Philadelphia.[6]

First Continental Congress
Meeting held in Philadelphia from September 5 to October 26, 1774, in which fifty-six delegates (from every colony except Georgia) adopted a resolution in opposition to the Coercive Acts.

Second Continental Congress
Meeting that convened in Philadelphia on May 10, 1775, at which it was decided that an army should be raised and George Washington of Virginia was named commander in chief.

Declaration of Independence
Document drafted by Thomas Jefferson in 1776 that proclaimed the right of the American colonies to separate from Great Britain.

Photo Courtesy: Kevin Fleming/Corbis

Who were colonial soldiers? Colonial soldiers, also known as Minutemen, were farmers, lawyers, and tradesmen from across the colonies. Their efforts were essential to the war for independence.

In simple but eloquent language, Jefferson set out the reasons for the colonies' separation from Great Britain. Most of his stirring rhetoric drew heavily on the works of seventeenth- and eighteenth-century political philosophers, particularly the English philosopher John Locke, who argued that individuals who give their consent to be governed have the right to resist or remove rulers who deviate from those purposes.

It is easy to see the colonists' debt to John Locke. In ringing language, the Declaration of Independence proclaims:

> We hold these truths to be self-evident, that all men are created equal, that they are endowed by their Creator with certain unalienable Rights, that among these are Life, Liberty and the pursuit of Happiness.

The Declaration also justified the colonists' break with the crown, clarified their notions of the proper form of government, and enumerated the wrongs that the colonists had suffered under British rule. After the Declaration was signed and transmitted to the king, the Revolutionary War waged on, and the Continental Congress attempted to fashion a new united government.

Thinking Globally

India's Independence

In 1947, following 150 years of British colonial rule, India became an independent nation. Unlike the United States, India achieved independence without a military revolution. Instead, India's people won their independence through mass nonviolent resistance to British rule, which led to political compromise and British withdrawal.

- The colonists' desire for independence led to war; India's did not. What factors facilitate a country's path to independence and what factors complicate it?
- Was the Revolutionary War inevitable? Was a political solution between the American colonies and Great Britain possible? Why or why not?

The First Attempt at Government: The Articles of Confederation

The British had no written constitution. The delegates to the Second Continental Congress were attempting to codify arrangements that had never before been put into legal terminology. To make things more complicated, the delegates had to arrive at these decisions in a wartime atmosphere. Nevertheless, in late 1777, the **Articles of Confederation**, creating a loose "league of friendship" between the thirteen sovereign or independent colonies, were passed by the Congress and presented to the states for their ratification. The Articles were finally ratified by all thirteen states in March 1781.

Unlike Great Britain's unitary system of government, wherein all of the powers of the government reside in the national government, the national government in a confederation derives all of its powers directly from the states. Thus, the national government in a confederacy is weaker than the sum of its parts, and the states often consider themselves independent nation-states linked together only for limited purposes such as national defense. So, the Articles of Confederation proposed the following:

- A national government with a Congress empowered to make peace, coin money, appoint officers for an army, control the post office, and negotiate with Indian tribes.
- Each state's retention of its independence and sovereignty, or ultimate authority, to govern within its territories.
- One vote in the Continental Congress for each state, regardless of size.
- The vote of nine states to pass any measure (a unanimous vote for any amendment).
- The selection and payment of delegates to the Congress by their respective state legislatures.

Articles of Confederation
The compact among the thirteen original colonies that created a loose league of friendship, with the national government drawing its powers from the states.

What happened during Shays's Rebellion? With Daniel Shays in the lead, a group of farmers and Continental Army veterans marched on the courthouse in Springfield, Massachusetts, to stop the state court from foreclosing on their farms. Unrest such as this prompted quick action to remedy the weakness of the Articles of Confederation.

Problems Under the Articles of Confederation

By 1784, just one year after the Revolutionary Army was disbanded, governing the new nation under the Articles of Confederation proved unworkable.[7] Congress rarely could assemble the required quorum of nine states to conduct business. Even when it did meet, there was little agreement among the states on any policies. To raise revenue to pay off war debts and run the government, various land, poll, and liquor taxes were proposed. But, since Congress had no specific power to tax, all these proposals were rejected. At one point, Congress was even driven out of Philadelphia (then the capital of the new national government) by its own unpaid army.

Although the national government could coin money, it had no resources to back up the value of its currency. Continental dollars were worth little, and trade between states became chaotic as some states began to coin their own money. Another weakness was that the Articles of Confederation did not allow Congress to regulate commerce among the states or with foreign nations. As a result, individual states attempted to enter into agreements with other countries, and foreign nations were suspicious of trade agreements made with the Congress of the Confederation.

The Articles of Confederation, moreover, had no provision for a judicial system to handle the growing number of economic conflicts and boundary disputes among the individual states. Several states claimed the same lands to the west, and Pennsylvania and Virginia went to war with each other.

The Articles' greatest weakness was the lack of a strong central government. Although states had operated independently before the war, during the war they acceded to the national government's authority to wage armed conflict. Once the war was over, however, each state resumed its sovereign status and was unwilling to give up rights, such as the power to tax, to an untested national government. Consequently, the government was unable to force the states to abide by the provisions of the Treaty of Paris, signed in 1783.

The crumbling economy was made worse by a series of bad harvests that failed to produce cash crops, thus making it difficult for farmers to get out of debt quickly. George Washington and Alexander Hamilton, both interested in the questions of trade and frontier expansion, soon saw the need for a stronger national government with the authority to act to solve some of these problems.

The Miracle at Philadelphia: Writing the U.S. Constitution

On February 21, 1787, in the throes of economic turmoil and with domestic tranquility gone haywire, the Congress passed an official resolution. It called for a Constitutional Convention in Philadelphia for "the sole and express purpose of revising the Articles of Confederation."

However, many delegates that gathered in sweltering Philadelphia on May 25, 1787, were prepared to take potentially treasonous steps to preserve the union. For

Analyzing Visuals | Framers or Troublemakers?

This political cartoon was published during the controversy surrounding revelations that President George W. Bush had authorized domestic surveillance activities as part of his proclaimed "War on Terror." Examine the cartoon and then answer the following questions:

Photo Courtesy: Nick Anderson/Cartoonist Group

WHAT meeting is the cartoonist depicting in this illustration?

WHAT activity are the "troublemakers" engaged in?

WHAT point is the cartoonist trying to communicate in this cartoon?

example, on the first day the convention was in session, Edmund Randolph and James Madison of Virginia proposed fifteen resolutions creating an entirely new government (later known as the Virginia Plan). Their enthusiasm, however, was not universal. Many delegates, including William Paterson of New Jersey, considered these resolutions to be in violation of the convention's charter, and proposed the New Jersey Plan, which took greater steps to preserve the Articles. These proposals met heated debate on the convention's floor.

The Characteristics and Motives of the Framers

The fifty-five delegates who attended the Constitutional Convention labored long and hard that hot summer. Owing to the high stakes of their action, all of the convention's work was conducted behind closed doors. George Washington of Virginia, who was unanimously elected the convention's presiding officer, cautioned delegates not to reveal details of the convention even to their family members. (To learn more about the secretive aspects of the convention, see Analyzing Visuals.)

All of the delegates to the Constitutional Convention were men; hence, they often are referred to as the "Founding Fathers." In this text, we generally refer to them as the Framers, because their work provided the framework for the new United States government. Most of them were quite young; many were in their twenties and thirties, and only one—Franklin at eighty-one—was quite old. Several owned slaves. The

constitution
A document establishing the structure, functions, and limitations of a government.

Framers brought with them a vast amount of political, educational, legal, and business experience. It is clear that they were an exceptional lot who ultimately produced a brilliant **constitution**, or document establishing the structure, functions, and limitations of a government.

However, debate about the Framers' motives filled the air during the ratification struggle and has provided grist for the mill of historians and political scientists over the years. In his *Economic Interpretation of the Constitution of the United States* (1913), Charles A. Beard argued that the 1780s were a critical period not for the nation as a whole, but rather for businessmen who feared that a weak, decentralized government could harm their economic interests.[8] Beard argued that the merchants wanted a strong national government to promote industry and trade, to protect private property, and most importantly, to ensure payment of the public debt—much of which was owed to them.

By the 1950s, this view had fallen into disfavor when other historians were unable to find direct links between wealth and the Framers' motives for establishing the Constitution and others faulted Beard's failure to consider the impact of religion and individual views about government.[9] In the 1960s, however, another group of historians began to argue that social and economic factors were, in fact, important motives for supporting the Constitution. In *The Anti-Federalists* (1961), Jackson Turner Main posited that while the Constitution's supporters might not have been the united group of creditors suggested by Beard, they were wealthier, came from higher social strata, and had greater concern for maintaining the prevailing social order than the general public.[10] In 1969, Gordon S. Wood's *The Creation of the American Republic* resurrected this debate. Wood deemphasized economics to argue that major social divisions explained different groups' support for (or opposition to) the new Constitution. He concluded that the Framers were representatives of a class that favored order and stability over some of the more radical ideas that had inspired the American Revolutionary War and the break with Britain.[11]

The Virginia and New Jersey Plans

Virginia Plan
The first general plan for the Constitution offered in Philadelphia. Its key points were a bicameral legislature, and an executive and a judiciary chosen by the national legislature.

The **Virginia Plan**, proposed by James Madison and Edmund Randolph, called for a national system based heavily on the European nation-state model, wherein the national government derives its powers from the people and not from the member states.

Its key features included:

- Creation of a powerful central government with three branches—the legislative, executive, and judicial.
- A two-house legislature with one house elected directly by the people, the other chosen from among persons nominated by the state legislatures.
- A legislature with the power to select the executive and the judiciary.

In general, smaller states such as New Jersey and Connecticut felt comfortable with the arrangements under the Articles of Confederation. These states offered another model of government, the **New Jersey Plan**. Its key features included:

New Jersey Plan
A framework for the Constitution proposed by a group of small states. Its key points were a one-house legislature with one vote for each state, a Congress with the ability to raise revenue, and a Supreme Court with members appointed for life.

- Strengthening the Articles, not replacing them.
- Creating a one-house legislature with one vote for each state and with representatives chosen by state legislatures.
- Giving Congress the power to raise revenue from duties on imports and from postal service fees.
- Creating a Supreme Court with members appointed for life by the executive officers.

Constitutional Compromises

The most serious disagreement between the Virginia and New Jersey plans concerned state representation in Congress. When a deadlock loomed, Connecticut offered its own compromise. Representation in the House of Representatives would be determined by population and each state would have an equal vote in the Senate. Again, there was a stalemate.

A committee to work out an agreement soon reported back what became known as the **Great Compromise**. Taking ideas from both the Virginia and New Jersey plans, it recommended:

- A two-house, or bicameral, legislature.
- In one house of the legislature (later called the House of Representatives), there would be fifty-six representatives—one representative for every 30,000 inhabitants. Representatives would be elected directly by the people.
- That house should have the power to originate all bills for raising and spending money.
- In the second house of the legislature (later called the Senate), each state should have an equal vote, and representatives would be selected by the state legislatures.
- In dividing power between the national and state governments, national power would be supreme.[12]

Great Compromise
The final decision of the Constitutional Convention to create a two-house legislature with the lower house elected by the people and with powers divided between the two houses. It also made national law supreme.

The Great Compromise ultimately met with the approval of all states in attendance. The smaller states were pleased because they got equal representation in the Senate; the larger states were satisfied with the proportional representation in the House of Representatives. The small states then would dominate the Senate while the large states, such as Virginia and Pennsylvania, would control the House. But, because both houses had to pass any legislation, neither body could dominate the other.

The Great Compromise dealt with one major concern of the Framers—how best to treat the differences in large and small states—but other problems stemming largely from regional differences remained. Slavery, which formed the basis of much of the southern states' cotton economy, was one of the thorniest issues to address. To reach an agreement on the Constitution, the Framers had to craft a compromise that balanced southern commercial interests with comparable northern concerns. Eventually the Framers agreed that Northerners would support continuing the slave trade for twenty more years, as well as a twenty-year ban on taxing exports to protect the cotton trade, while Southerners consented to a provision requiring only a majority vote on navigation laws, and the national government was given the authority to regulate foreign commerce. It was also agreed that the Senate would have the power to ratify treaties by a two-thirds majority, which assuaged the fears of southern states, who made up more than one-third of the nation.

Another sticking point concerning slavery remained: how to determine state population for purposes of representation in the House of Representatives. Slaves could not vote, but the southern states wanted them included for purposes of determining population. After considerable dissension, it was decided that population for purposes of representation and the apportionment of direct taxes would be calculated by adding the "whole Number of Free Persons" to "three-fifths of all other Persons." "All other Persons" was the delegates' euphemistic way of referring to slaves. Known as the **Three-Fifths Compromise**, this highly political deal assured that the South would hold 47 percent of the House—enough to prevent attacks on slavery but not so much as to foster the spread of slavery northward.

Three-Fifths Compromise
Agreement reached at the Constitutional Convention stipulating that each slave was to be counted as three-fifths of a person for purposes of determining population for representation in the U.S. House of Representatives.

Unfinished Business Affecting the Executive Branch

The Framers next turned to fashioning an executive branch. While they agreed on the idea of a one-person executive, they could not settle on the length of the term of office, nor on how the chief executive should be selected. With Shays's Rebellion still fresh in their minds, the delegates feared putting too much power, including selection of a president, into the hands of the lower classes. At the same time, representatives from the smaller states feared that the selection of the chief executive by the legislature would put additional power into the hands of the large states.

Amid these fears, the Committee on Unfinished Portions, whose sole responsibility was to iron out problems and disagreements concerning the office of chief executive, conducted its work. The committee recommended that the presidential term of office be fixed at four years instead of seven, as had earlier been proposed. By choosing not to mention a period of time within which the chief executive would be eligible for reelection, they made it possible for a president to serve more than one term.

The Framers also created the Electoral College. The Electoral College system gave individual states a key role, because each state would select electors equal to the number of representatives it had in the House and Senate. It was a vague compromise that removed election of the president and vice president from both the Congress and the people and put it in the hands of electors whose method of selection would be left to the states.

In drafting the new Constitution, the Framers also were careful to include a provision for removal of the chief executive. The House of Representatives was given the sole responsibility of investigating and charging a president or vice president with "Treason, Bribery, or other high Crimes and Misdemeanors." A majority vote then would result in issuing articles of impeachment against the president or vice president. In turn, the Senate was given sole responsibility to try the president or vice president on the charges issued by the House. A two-thirds vote of the Senate was required to convict and remove the president or the vice president from office.

The U.S. Constitution

Comparing Constitutions

After the compromise on the presidency, work proceeded quickly on the remaining sections of the Constitution. The Preamble to the Constitution, the last section to be drafted, contains exceptionally powerful language that forms the bedrock of American political tradition. Its opening line, "We the People of the United States," boldly proclaimed that a loose confederation of states no longer existed. Instead, there was but one American people and nation. And, the opening explained the source of the government's power: it came directly from the people.

The Constitution then explained the need for the new outline of government: "in Order to form a more perfect Union" indirectly acknowledged the weaknesses of the Articles of Confederation in governing a growing nation. Next, the optimistic goals of the Framers for the new nation were set out: to "establish Justice, insure domestic Tranquility, provide for the common defence, promote the general Welfare, and secure the Blessings of Liberty to ourselves and our Posterity;" followed by the formal creation of a new government: "do ordain and establish this Constitution for the United States of America." The Constitution was approved by the delegates from all twelve states in attendance on September 17, 1787.

The Basic Principles of the Constitution

separation of powers
A way of dividing the power of government among the legislative, executive, and judicial branches, each staffed separately, with equality and independence of each branch ensured by the Constitution.

checks and balances
A constitutionally mandated structure that gives each of the three branches of government some degree of oversight and control over the actions of the others.

The proposed structure of the new national government owed much to the writings of the French philosopher Montesquieu (1689–1755), who advocated distinct functions for each branch of government, called **separation of powers**, with a system of **checks and balances** between each branch. The Constitution's concern with the distribution of power between states and the national government also reveals the heavy influence of political philosophers, as well as the colonists' experience under the Articles of Confederation.[13]

FEDERALISM The question before and during the convention was how much power states would give up to the national government. Given the nation's experiences under the Articles of Confederation, the Framers believed that a strong national government was necessary for the new nation's survival. However, they were reluctant to create a powerful government after the model of Britain, the country from which they had just won their independence. Its unitary system was not even considered by the colonists. Instead, they employed a system (now known as the **federal system**) that divides the power of government between a strong national government and the individual states, with national power being supreme.

SEPARATION OF POWERS Separation of powers is simply a way of parceling out power among the three branches of government. Its three key features are:

1. Three distinct branches of government: the legislative, the executive, and the judicial.
2. Three separately staffed branches of government to exercise these functions.
3. Constitutional equality and independence of each branch.

As illustrated in Figure 2.1, the Framers were careful to create a system in which law-making, law-enforcing, and law-interpreting functions were assigned to independent

federal system
Plan of government in which power is divided between the national government and the state governments and in which independent states are bound together under one national government, whose power is supreme.

FIGURE 2.1 Separation of Powers and Checks and Balances under the U.S. Constitution

LEGISLATIVE BRANCH POWERS
Pass all federal laws
Pass the federal budget
Declare war
Approve treaties and
  presidential appointments
Establish lower federal courts
  and the number of judges

Legislative Checks on the Executive
Impeach the president
Reject legislation or funding the president wants
Refuse to confirm nominees or approve treaties
Override the president's veto by a two-thirds vote

Executive Checks on the Legislative
Veto legislation
Call Congress into special session
Implement (or fail to implement) laws
passed by Congress

EXECUTIVE BRANCH POWERS
Enforce federal laws and court orders
Propose legislation to Congress
Make foreign treaties
Nominate officers of the United
  States government and federal
  judges
Serve as commander in chief of the
  armed forces
Pardon people convicted in federal
  courts or grant reprieves

Judicial Checks on the Legislative
Rule federal and state laws
unconstitutional

Judicial Checks on the Executive
Declare executive branch
actions unconstitutional
Chief justice presides over
impeachment trial

JUDICIAL BRANCH POWERS
Interpret federal laws and U.S.
Constitution
Review the decisions of lower state
and federal courts

Legislative Checks on the Judicial
Change the number and
jurisdiction of federal courts
Impeach federal judges
Propose constitutional amendments to
override judicial decisions

Executive Checks on the Judicial
Appoint federal judges
Refuse to implement decisions

branches of government. On the national level (and in most states), only the legislature has the authority to make laws; the chief executive enforces laws; and the judiciary interprets them. Moreover, initially, members of the House of Representatives, members of the Senate, the president, and members of the federal courts were selected by and were therefore responsible to different constituencies.

The Framers could not have foreseen the intermingling of governmental functions that has since evolved. Locke, in fact, cautioned against giving a legislature the ability to delegate its powers. In Article I of the Constitution, the legislative power is vested in the Congress. But, the president is also given legislative power via his ability to veto legislation, although his veto can be overridden by a two-thirds vote in Congress. Judicial interpretation, including judicial review, a process cemented by the 1803 decision in *Marbury* v. *Madison*, then helps to clarify the implementation of legislation enacted through this process. So, instead of a pure system of separation of powers, a symbiotic, or interdependent, relationship among the three branches of government has existed from the beginning. Or, as one scholar has explained, there are "separated institutions sharing powers."[14]

CHECKS AND BALANCES The separation of powers among the three branches of the national government is not complete. According to Montesquieu and the Framers, the powers of each branch (as well as the two houses of the national legislature and between the states and the national government) could be used to check the powers of the other two branches of government. The power of each branch of government is checked, or limited, and balanced because the legislative, executive, and judicial branches share some authority and no branch has exclusive domain over any single activity. The creation of this system allowed the Framers to minimize the threat of tyranny from any one branch. Thus, for almost every power granted to one branch, an equal control was established in the other two branches.

The Articles of the Constitution

The document finally signed by the Framers condensed numerous resolutions into a Preamble and seven separate articles remedying many of the deficiencies within the Articles of Confederation. (To learn more about the differences between the Articles of Confederation, the Constitution see Table 2.1.) The first three articles established the three branches of government, defined their internal operations, and clarified their relationships with one another. The four remaining articles define the relationships among the states, declare national law to be supreme, and set out methods of amending the Constitution.

ARTICLE I: THE LEGISLATIVE BRANCH Article I vests all legislative powers in the Congress and establishes a bicameral legislature, consisting of the Senate and the House of Representatives. It also sets out the qualifications for holding office in each house, the terms of office, the methods of selection of representatives and senators, and the system of apportionment among the states to determine membership in the House of Representatives.

One of the most important sections of Article I is section 8. It carefully lists the powers the Framers wished the new Congress to possess. These specified or **enumerated powers** contain many key provisions that had been denied to the Continental Congress under the Articles of Confederation.

After careful enumeration of seventeen powers of Congress in Article I, section 8, a final, general clause authorizing Congress to "make all Laws which shall be necessary and proper for carrying into Execution the foregoing Powers" was added to Article I. Often referred to as the elastic clause, the **necessary and proper clause** has been a source of tremendous congressional activity never anticipated by the Framers, including the passage of laws that regulate the environment, welfare programs, education,

The American System of Checks
and Balances

enumerated powers
Seventeen specific powers granted to Congress under Article I, section 8, of the Constitution.

necessary and proper clause
The final paragraph of Article I, section 8, of the Constitution, which gives Congress the authority to pass all laws "necessary and proper" to carry out the enumerated powers specified in the Constitution; also called the elastic clause.

TABLE 2.1 Comparing the Articles of Confederation and the U.S. Constitution

The United States has operated under two constitutions. The first, the Articles of Confederation, was in effect from March 1, 1781, when it was ratified by Maryland. The second, the Constitution, replaced the Articles when it was ratified by New Hampshire on June 21, 1788. The two documents have much in common—they were established by the same people (sometimes literally the same exact people, though mostly just in terms of contemporaries). But, they differ more than they resemble each other, when one looks at the details.

	Articles of Confederation	Constitution
Formal name of the nation	The United States of America	Not specified, but referred to in the Preamble as "the United States of America"
Legislature	Unicameral, called Congress	Bicameral, called Congress, divided into the House of Representatives and the Senate
Members of Congress	Between two and seven members per state	Two senators per state, representatives apportioned according to population of each state
Voting in Congress	One vote per state	One vote per representative or senator
Appointment of members	All appointed by state legislatures, in the manner each legislature directed	Representatives elected by popular vote; senators appointed by state legislatures
Term of legislative office	One year	Two years for representatives, six for senators
Term limit for legislative office	No more than three out of every six years	None
Congressional pay	Paid by states	Paid by the federal government
When Congress is not in session	A committee of states had the full powers of Congress	The President of the United States can call for Congress to assemble
Chair of legislature	President of Congress	Speaker of the House of Representatives; U.S. vice president is president of the Senate
Executive	None	President
National judiciary	Maritime judiciary established—other courts left to states	Supreme Court established, as well as other courts Congress deems necessary
Adjudicator of disputes between states	Congress	U.S. Supreme Court
New states	Admitted upon agreement of nine states (special exemption provided for Canada)	Admitted upon agreement of majority of Congress
Amendment	When agreed upon by all states	When agreed upon by three-fourths of the states
Navy	Congress authorized to build a navy; states authorized to equip warships to counter piracy	Congress authorized to build a navy; states not allowed to keep ships of war
Army	Congress to decide on size of force and to requisition troops from each state according to population	Congress authorized to raise and support armies
Power to coin money	United States and the states	United States only
Ex post facto *laws*	Not forbidden	Forbidden of both the states and the Congress
Bills of attainder	Not forbidden	Forbidden of both the states and the Congress
Taxes	Apportioned by Congress, collected by the states	Laid and collected by Congress
Ratification	Unanimous consent required	Consent of nine states required

and communication. The necessary and proper clause, also called the elastic clause, is the basis for the **implied powers** that Congress uses to execute its other powers.

implied powers
Powers derived from the enumerated powers and the necessary and proper clause. These powers are not stated specifically but are considered to be reasonably implied through the exercise of delegated powers.

ARTICLE II: THE EXECUTIVE BRANCH Article II vests the executive power, that is, the authority to execute the laws of the nation, in a president of the United States. Section 1 sets the president's term of office at four years and explains the Electoral College. It also states the qualifications for office and describes a mechanism to replace the president in case of death, disability, or removal.

The powers and duties of the president are set out in section 3. Among the most important of these are the president's role as commander in chief of the armed forces, the authority to make treaties with the consent of the Senate, and the authority to "appoint Ambassadors, other public Ministers and Consuls, the Judges of the supreme Court, and all other Officers of the United States." Other sections of Article II instruct the president to report directly to Congress "from time to time," in what has come to be known as the State of the Union Address, and to "take Care that the Laws be faithfully executed." Section 4 provides the mechanism for removal of the president, vice president, and other officers of the United States.

Join the Debate

The Equal Opportunity to Govern Amendment

OVERVIEW: Article II, section 1, clause 5, of the U.S. Constitution declares: "No person except a natural-born citizen, or a citizen of the United States at the time of the Adoption of this Constitution, shall be eligible to the Office of President." Why would the Framers put such a restriction on the qualifications for president of the United States? In a letter to George Washington, John Jay, who later became Chief Justice of the Supreme Court, argued that the duty of commander in chief was too important to be given to a foreign-born person—the potential for conflict of interest, danger, and appearance of impropriety in matters of war and foreign policy should not be left to chance. Charles Pinckney, a South Carolina delegate to the Constitutional Convention, expressed concern that foreign governments would use whatever means necessary to influence international events, and he cited the example of Russia, Prussia, and Austria manipulating the election of Stanislaus II to the Polish throne—only to divide Polish lands among themselves. Furthermore, Pinckney contended that the clause would ensure the "experience" of American politics and principles and guarantee "attachment to the country" so as to further eliminate the potential for mischief and foreign intrigue.

As soon as it became clear that Senator John McCain (R-AZ) was going to be the 2008 presidential candidate of the Republican Party, legal scholars and political figures began to debate whether he was eligible under Article II, section 1, of the U.S. Constitution. John McCain was born in the Panama Canal Zone, where his parents—U.S. citizens—were stationed. McCain's father was a U.S. Navy officer. There is no clear legislative or judicial definition of "natural-born." Other presidential candidates, such as Barry Goldwater, George Romney, and Lowell Weicker Jr. were also born outside the United States to parents who were citizens, but they were not elected president. The common assumption, however, is that "natural-born" includes the circumstances of McCain's birth.

More controversial is whether naturalized citizens (those who were citizens of a foreign country but became U.S. citizens and pledged allegiance to this country) should be allowed to serve as president. The election of Austrian-born Arnold Schwarzenegger and of Canadian-born Jennifer Granholm to the governorships of California and Michigan, respectively, reopened this debate. Why shouldn't naturalized citizens be eligible for president? Many naturalized citizens have performed great service to their adopted country; both Henry Kissinger (born in Germany) and Madeleine Albright (born in Czechoslovakia) performed admirably as secretary of state, and over 700 foreign-born Congressional Medal of Honor recipients have demonstrated patriotism and the willingness to die for the country they embraced. With these

viewpoints in mind, in July 2003, Senator Orrin Hatch (R–UT) introduced the Equal Opportunity to Govern Amendment to strike the natural-born citizen clause from the Constitution. The proposed amendment takes into account the Framers' fear of foreign intervention and of divided loyalty by placing a lengthy citizenship requirement—twenty years— before naturalized citizens become eligible to run for presidential office.

Arguments IN FAVOR of the Equal Opportunity to Govern Amendment

- The United States is in part composed of its immigrant population, and they should have the opportunity to run for all political offices. America is a nation of immigrants and many of the

---

Article II also limits the presidency to natural-born citizens. A more new amendment would be needed to change that qualification. (To learn about the natural-born citizen clause, see Join the Debate: The Equal Opportunity to Govern Amendment.)

ARTICLE III: THE JUDICIAL BRANCH Article III establishes a Supreme Court and defines its jurisdiction. During the Philadelphia meeting, the small and large states differed significantly as to the desirability of an independent judiciary and on the role of state courts in the national court system. The smaller states feared that a strong

Framers were foreign born, notably Alexander Hamilton, who helped shape Washington's administration and the executive branch. The Constitution allows for naturalized citizens to attain other high political office, such as Speaker of the House, senator, or Supreme Court justice; why should naturalized citizens be denied the presidency?

- **The natural-born citizen clause has outlived its usefulness.** The problems that existed in 1787 either have changed or do not exist in the twenty-first century. The amendment process was created to allow for historical and political change, and ratification of the Equal Opportunity to Govern Amendment will increase the talent pool of presidential nominees, thus increasing the quality and choice of presidential aspirants for the American people.

- **The natural-born citizen clause is discriminatory.** The clause is un-American in that it denies equality of opportunity for all American citizens. Naturalized citizens serve in the military, pay taxes, run for local, state, and federal office, endure the same national hardships and crises, and add to the overall quality of American life; thus, naturalized citizens should have the same rights and privileges as the native born.

Arguments AGAINST the Equal Opportunity to Govern Amendment

- **Foreign governments still attempt to have undue influence in American politics.** The Framers were correct in assuming foreign governments attempt to manipulate American politics. For example, in 1999, the Democratic National Committee returned over $600,000 in campaign contributions to Chinese nationals attempting to gain influence with the Clinton administration. The clause was meant to be another institutional safeguard against presidential corruption.

- **Running for president is not a right.** The office of the president is an institution designed for republican purposes. The Framers strongly believed that foreign influence within the U.S. government must be restricted (the language was unanimously adopted by the Constitutional Convention) and thus they restricted the right to run for presidential office.

- **There is no public movement or outcry to remove this clause from the Constitution.** Many constitutional scholars argue the Constitution should be amended only for pressing reasons, and amendments should be construed with a view to the well-being of future generations. Foreign policy and events are too fluid and too volatile to risk undermining the president's foreign policy and commander-in-chief authority. Until the American people determine otherwise, the clause should remain.

Continuing the Debate

1. Is the natural-born citizen clause of the U.S. Constitution discriminatory? Should the Constitution be amended to realize the principle of political equality? Explain your answer.
2. Did the Framers create a true institutional barrier to help prevent corruption by foreign governments? Explain your answer.

To Follow the Debate Online, Go To:

writ.news.findlaw.com/dean/20041008.html and read John W. Dean's essay "The Pernicious 'Natural Born' Clause of the Constitution: Why Immigrants like Governors Schwarzenegger and Granholm Ought to Be Able to Become Presidents," which provides legal analyses of this issue, discusses the history of the natural-born citizen clause, and argues for change.

lawreview.kentlaw.edu/ articles/81-1/ Herlihy.pdf and read a law review article by Sarah P. Herlihy, "Amending the Natural Born Citizen Requirement: Globalization as the Impetus and the Obstacle," which reviews the history and weighs the arguments for and against changing this clause in the Constitution.

www.nytimes.com/2008/02/ 28/us/ politics/28mccain.html for a *New York Times* article that discusses the application of the natural-born citizen clause to John McCain.

unelected judiciary would trample on their liberties. In compromise, Congress was permitted, but not required, to establish lower national courts. Thus, state courts and the national court system would exist side by side with distinct areas of authority. Federal courts were given authority to decide cases arising under federal law. The U.S. Supreme Court was also given the power to settle disputes between states, or between a state and the national government.

Although some delegates to the convention urged that the president be allowed to remove federal judges, ultimately judges were given appointments for life, presuming "good behavior." And, like the president's, their salaries cannot be lowered while they hold office. This provision was adopted to ensure that the legislature did not attempt to punish the Supreme Court or any other judges for unpopular decisions.

ARTICLES IV THROUGH VII The remainder of the articles in the Constitution attempted to anticipate problems that might occur in the operation of the new national government as well as its relations to the states. Article IV begins with what is called the **full faith and credit clause**, which mandates that states honor the laws and judicial proceedings of the other states. Article IV also includes the mechanisms for admitting new states to the union.

Article V (discussed in greater detail on p. 46) specifies how amendments can be added to the Constitution. The Bill of Rights, which added ten amendments to the Constitution in 1791, was one of the first items of business when the First Congress met in 1789.

Article VI contains the supremacy clause, which asserts the basic primacy of the Constitution and national law over state laws and constitutions. The **supremacy clause** provides that the "Constitution, and the laws of the United States" as well as all treaties are to be the supreme law of the land. All national and state officers and judges are bound by national law and take oaths to support the federal Constitution above any state law or constitution. Because of the supremacy clause, any legitimate exercise of national power supersedes any state laws or action, in a process that is called preemption, further discussed in chapter 3. Without the supremacy clause and the federal court's ability to invoke it, the national government would have little actual enforceable power; thus, many commentators call the supremacy clause the linchpin of the entire federal system.

Article VI also specifies that no religious test shall be required for holding any office. This mandate is strengthed by the separation of church and state guarantee that was quickly added to the Constitution when the First Amendment was ratified.

The seventh and final article of the Constitution concerns the procedures for ratification of the new Constitution: nine of the thirteen states would have to agree to, or ratify, its new provisions before it would become the supreme law of the land.

The Drive for Ratification of the U.S. Constitution

The Second Continental Congress immediately accepted the work of the convention and forwarded the proposed Constitution to the states for their vote. It was by no means certain, however, that the new Constitution would be adopted. From the fall of 1787 to the summer of 1788, the proposed Constitution was debated hotly around the nation.

Federalists versus Anti-Federalists

Almost as soon as the ink was dry on the last signature to the Constitution, those who favored the new strong national government chose to call themselves **Federalists**. They were well aware that many people still generally opposed the notion of a strong national government. Thus, they did not want to risk being labeled nationalists, so they tried to get the upper hand in the debate by nicknaming their opponents **Anti-Federalists**. Those put in the latter category insisted that they were instead Federal Republicans, who believed in a federal system. As noted in Table 2.2, Anti-Federalists argued that they simply wanted to protect state governments from the tyranny of a too powerful national government.[15]

full faith and credit clause
Provision of the Constitution that mandates states to honor the laws and judicial proceedings of other states.

supremacy clause
Portion of Article VI of the U.S. Constitution mandating that national law is supreme to (that is, supersedes) all other laws passed by the states or by any other subdivision of government.

Federalists
Those who favored a stronger national government and supported the proposed U.S. Constitution; later became the first U.S. political party.

Anti-Federalists
Those who favored strong state governments and a weak national government; opposed the ratification of the U.S. Constitution.

TABLE 2.2 Federalists and Anti-Federalists Compared

	Federalists	Anti-Federalists
Who were they?	Property owners, landed rich, merchants of Northeast and Middle Atlantic states	Small farmers, shopkeepers, laborers
Political philosophy	Elitist: saw themselves and those of their class as most fit to govern (others were to be governed)	Believed in the decency of "the common man" and in participatory democracy; viewed elites as corrupt; sought greater protection of individual rights
Type of government favored	Powerful central government; two-house legislature; upper house (six-year term) further removed from the people, whom they distrusted	Wanted stronger state governments (closer to the people) at the expense of the powers of the national government; sought smaller electoral districts, frequent elections, referendum and recall, and a large unicameral legislature to provide for greater class and occupational representation
Alliances	Pro-British, anti-French	Anti-British, pro-French

Federalists and Anti-Federalists participated in the mass meetings that were held in state legislatures to discuss the pros and cons of the new plan. Tempers ran high at public meetings, where differences between the opposing groups were highlighted. Fervent debates were published in newspapers, which played a powerful role in the adoption process.

Comparing Political Landscapes

The Federalist Papers

One name stood out from all the rest: "Publius" (Latin for "the people"). Between October 1787 and May 1788, eighty-five articles written under that pen name routinely appeared in newspapers in New York, a state where ratification was in doubt. Most were written by Alexander Hamilton and James Madison. Hamilton, a young, fiery New Yorker born in the British West Indies, wrote fifty-one; Madison, a Virginian who later served as the fourth president, wrote twenty-six; jointly they penned another three. John Jay, also of New York, and later the first chief justice of the United States, wrote five of the pieces. These eighty-five essays became known as *The Federalist Papers*.

Forced on the defensive, the Anti-Federalists responded to *The Federalist Papers* with their own series of letters written under the pen names "Brutus" and "Cato," two ancient Romans famous for their intolerance of tyranny. These letters (actually essays) undertook a line-by-line critique of the Constitution.

Anti-Federalists argued that a strong central government would render the states powerless.[16] They stressed the strengths the government had been granted under the Articles of Confederation, and argued that the Articles, not the proposed Constitution, created a true federal system. Moreover, they argued that the strong national government would tax heavily, that the Supreme Court would overwhelm the states by invalidating state laws, and that the president eventually would have too much power, as commander in chief of a large and powerful army.[17]

In particular, the Anti-Federalists feared the power of the national government to run roughshod over the liberties of the people. They proposed that the taxing power of Congress be limited, that the executive be curbed by a council, that the military consist of state militias rather than a national force, and that the jurisdiction of the Supreme Court be limited to prevent it from reviewing and potentially overturning the decisions of state courts. But, their most effective argument concerned the absence of a bill of rights in the Constitution. James Madison answered these criticisms in *Federalist Nos. 10 and*

The Federalist Papers
A series of eighty-five political papers written by Alexander Hamilton, and James Madison and John Jay in support of ratification of the U.S. Constitution.

Why were *The Federalist Papers* written?
The Federalist Papers highlighted the reasons for the structure of the new government and its benefits.

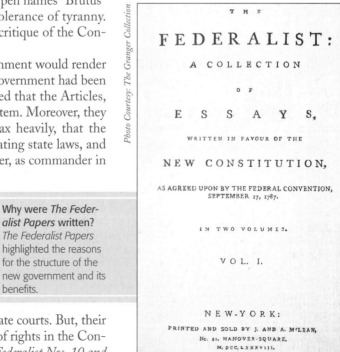

Photo Courtesy: The Granger Collection

THE

FEDERALIST:

A COLLECTION

OF

ESSAYS,

WRITTEN IN FAVOUR OF THE

NEW CONSTITUTION,

AS AGREED UPON BY THE FEDERAL CONVENTION, SEPTEMBER 17, 1787.

IN TWO VOLUMES.

VOL. I.

NEW-YORK:

PRINTED AND SOLD BY J. AND A. M'LEAN,
No. 41, HANOVER-SQUARE.
M,DCC,LXXXVIII.

51. (The texts of these two essays are printed in Appendices III and IV.) In *Federalist No. 10*, Madison pointed out that the voters would not always succeed in electing "enlightened statesmen" as their representatives. The greatest threat to individual liberties would therefore come from factions within the government, who might place narrow interests above broader national interests and the rights of citizens. While recognizing that no form of government could protect the country from unscrupulous politicians, Madison argued that the organization of the new government would minimize the effects of political factions. The great advantage of a federal system, Madison maintained, was that it created the "happy combination" of a national government too large to be controlled by any single faction, and several state governments that would be smaller and more responsive to local needs. Moreover, he argued in *Federalist No. 51* that the proposed federal government's separation of powers would prohibit any one branch from either dominating the national government or violating the rights of citizens.

Thinking Globally

The British System

Unlike the United States, Great Britain does not have a written constitution, nor is there a document comparable to the Bill of Rights that guarantees certain individual liberties to the British people. In the United States, the ultimate arbiter of what is constitutional is the U.S. Supreme Court. In Britain, the ultimate authority is Parliament, and the country's unwritten constitution can easily be changed by a majority vote of that legislative body.

- If the U.S. Constitution could be altered by a majority vote in Congress, what kinds of changes might you predict?
- Does the Supreme Court in the United States have too much power to decide what the government may or may not do? Explain your answers.

Ratifying the Constitution

Debate continued in the thirteen states as votes were taken from December 1787 to June 1788, in accordance with the ratifying process laid out in Article VII of the proposed Constitution. Three states acted quickly to ratify the new Constitution. Two small states, Delaware and New Jersey, voted to ratify before the large states could rethink the notion of equal representation of the states in the Senate. Pennsylvania, where Federalists were well organized, was also one of the first three states to ratify. Massachusetts assented to the new government but tempered its support by calling for an immediate addition of amendments, including one protecting personal rights. New Hampshire became the crucial ninth state to ratify on June 21, 1788. This action completed the ratification process outlined in Article VII of the Constitution and marked the beginning of a new nation. But, New York and Virginia, which at that time accounted for more than 40 percent of the new nation's population, had not yet ratified the Constitution. Thus, the practical future of the new nation remained in doubt.

Hamilton in New York and Madison in Virginia worked feverishly to convince delegates to their state conventions to vote for the new government. In New York, sentiment against the Constitution ran high. In Albany, fighting resulting in injuries and death broke out over ratification. When news of Virginia's acceptance of the Constitution reached the New York convention, Hamilton finally was able to convince a majority of those present to follow suit by a narrow margin of three votes. Both states also recommended the addition of a series of structural amend-

SIMULATION

You Are Proposing a Constitutional Amendment

TABLE 2.3 The Bill of Rights

First Amendment	Freedom of religion, speech, press, and assembly
Second Amendment	The right to bear arms
Third Amendment	Prohibition against quartering of troops in private homes
Fourth Amendment	Prohibition against unreasonable searches and seizures
Ffith Amendment	Rights guaranteed to the accused: requirement for grand jury indictment; protections against doube jeopardy, self-incrimination; due process
Sixth Amendment	Right to a speedy and public trial before an impartial jury, to cross-examine witness, and to have counsel
Seventh Amendment	Right to a trial by jury in civil suits
Eight Amendment	Prohibition against bail fines, and cruel and unusual punishment
Ninth Amendment	Rights not listed in the Constitution retained by the people
Tenth Amendment	States or people reserve those powers not denied to them by the Constitution or delegated to the national government

Celebrating the Constitution

In late 2004, Senator Robert C. Byrd (D–WV) introduced legislation that called on all educational institutions receiving federal funds—from kindergarten through grade 12 to colleges, universities, and even law schools—to set aside September 17 of each year to conduct educational programs concerning the U.S. Constitution. When Public Law 108-447 passed, educational institutions around the United States began to question just what types of programs were required. The selection of September 17 was not random; the U.S. Constitution was sent to the states for ratification on that date.

Since 2005, educational institutions around the United States have chosen to celebrate what is now called Constitution Day in a variety of ways. The National Constitution Center has taken the lead in publicizing unique and thoughtful ways for schools to observe Constitution Day. Among those highlighted are "celebrate your state" events, discussions on how the U.S. Supreme Court can change the law and make policy, grade school celebrations where students wear red, white, and blue and learn about the Preamble; and interactive Web-based activities for all ages.

- Visit the C-SPAN classroom Web site at **www.c-spanclassroom.org**. What activities might you and your classmates use to teach about the Constitution at a local elementary school?
- What kinds of activities are planned on your campus to celebrate Constitution Day?
- What programs or projects could your American government class engage in to bring recognition of Constitution Day to your campus?
- For more Constitution Day suggestions, go to www.constitutionday.us.

ments and a bill of rights. (To learn more about the Constitution, see Ideas Into Action: Studying the Constitution.)

Amending the Constitution: The Bill of Rights

Once the Constitution was ratified, elections were held. When Congress convened, it immediately sent a set of amendments to the states for their ratification. An amendment authorizing the enlargement of the House of Representatives and another to prevent members of the House from raising their own salaries failed to garner favorable votes in the necessary three-fourths of the states. The remaining ten amendments, known as the **Bill of Rights**, were ratified by 1791 in accordance with the procedures set out in the Constitution. Sought by Anti-Federalists as a protection for individual liberties, they offered numerous specific limitations on the national government's ability to interfere with a wide variety of personal liberties, some of which were already guaranteed by many state constitutions. (To learn more about the Bill of Rights, see Table 2.3.)

Bill of Rights
The first ten amendments to the U.S. Constitution, which largely guarantee specific rights and liberties.

Toward Reform: Methods of Amending the U.S. Constitution

The Framers did not want to fashion a government that could be too influenced by the whims of the people. Therefore, they made the formal amendment process a slow one to ensure that the Constitution was not impulsively amended. In keeping with this intent, only seventeen amendments have been added since the addition of the Bill of Rights. However, informal amendments,

Photo Courtesy: U.S. Department of Interior. National Park Service. Edison National Historical Site.

Why are constitutional amendments repealed? For all its moral support from groups such as the Women's Christian Temperance Union (WCTU), whose members invaded bars to protest the sale of alcoholic beverages, the Eighteenth (Prohibition) Amendment was a disaster. Among its side effects was the rise of powerful crime organizations responsible for illegal sales of alcoholic beverages. Once proposed, it took only ten months to ratify the Twenty-First Amendment, which repealed the Prohibition Amendment.

prompted by judicial interpretation and cultural and social change, have had a tremendous impact on the Constitution.

Formal Methods of Amending the Constitution

Article V of the Constitution creates a two-stage amendment process: proposal and ratification.[18] The Constitution specifies two ways to accomplish each stage. As illustrated in Figure 2.2, amendments to the Constitution can be proposed by: (1) a vote of two-thirds of the members in both houses of Congress; or, (2) a vote of two-thirds of the state legislatures specifically requesting Congress to call a national convention to propose amendments. (To learn more about the amendment process, see The Living Constitution.)

The second method has never been used. Historically, it has served as a fairly effective threat, forcing Congress to consider amendments that might otherwise never have been debated.

The ratification process is fairly straightforward. When Congress votes to propose an amendment, the Constitution specifies that the ratification process must occur in one of two ways: (1) a favorable vote in three-fourths of the state legislatures; or, (2) a favorable vote in specially called ratifying conventions in three-fourths of the states.

The Constitution itself was ratified by the favorable vote of nine states in specially called ratifying conventions. The Framers feared that the power of special interests in state legislatures would prevent a positive vote on the new Constitution. Since ratification of the Constitution, however, only one ratifying convention has been called. The Eighteenth Amendment, which outlawed the sale of alcoholic beverages nationwide, was ratified by the first method—a vote in state legislatures. Millions of people broke the law, others died from drinking homemade liquor, and still others made their fortunes selling bootleg or illegal liquor. After a decade of these problems, Congress decided to act. An additional amendment—the Twenty-First—was proposed to repeal the Eighteenth Amendment. It was sent to the states for ratification, but with a call for ratifying conventions, not a vote in the state legislatures.[19] Members of Congress correctly predicted that the move to repeal the

FIGURE 2.2 Methods of Amending the Constitution

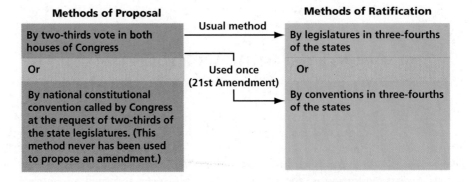

The Living Constitution

The Congress, whenever two thirds of both houses shall deem it necessary, shall propose amendments to this Constitution, or, on the application of the legislatures of two thirds of the several states, shall call a convention for proposing amendments, which, in either case, shall be valid to all intents and purposes, as part of this Constitution, when ratified by the legislatures of three fourths of the several states, or by conventions in three fourths thereof, as the one or the other mode of ratification may be proposed by the Congress.

—ARTICLE V

With this article, the Framers acknowledged the potential need to change or amend the Constitution. This article provides for two methods to propose amendments: by a two-thirds vote of both houses of Congress or by a two-thirds vote of the state legislatures. It also specifies two alternative methods of ratification of proposed amendments: by a three-quarters vote of the state legislatures, or by a similar vote in specially called state ratifying conventions.

During the Constitutional Convention in Philadelphia, the Framers were divided as to how frequently or how easily the Constitution was to be amended. The original suggestion was to allow the document to be amended "when soever it shall seem necessary." Some delegates wanted to entrust this authority to the state legislatures; however, others feared that it would give states too much power. James Madison alleviated these fears by suggesting that both Congress and the states have a role in the process.

In the late 1960s and early 1970s, leaders of the new women's rights movement sought passage of the Equal Rights Amendment (ERA). Their efforts were rewarded when the ERA was approved in the House and Senate by overwhelming majorities in 1972 and then sent out to the states for their approval. In spite of tremendous lobbying, a strong anti-ERA movement emerged and the amendment failed to gain approval in three-quarters of the state legislatures.

The failed battles for the ERA as well as other amendments, including one to prohibit child labor and another to grant statehood to the District of Columbia, underscore how difficult it is to amend the Constitution. Thus, unlike the constitutions of individual states or many other nations, the U.S. Constitution rarely has been amended.

Still, the ERA has been proposed in every session of Congress since 1923. In 2007, it was renamed the Women's Equality Amendment by its sponsors.

CRITICAL THINKING QUESTIONS

1. Should women's rights advocates press for a women's equality amendment? Why or why not?
2. Does your state already have an equal rights amendment? What does it guarantee?

Eighteenth Amendment would encounter opposition in the statehouses, which were largely controlled by elected conservative rural legislators.

The intensity of efforts to amend the Constitution has varied considerably, depending on the nature of the change proposed. Whereas the Twenty-First Amendment took only ten months to ratify, an equal rights amendment (ERA) was introduced in every session of Congress from 1923 until 1972, when Congress finally voted favorably for it. Even then, years of lobbying by women's groups were insufficient to garner necessary state support. By 1982, the congressionally mandated date

TIMELINE

The History of Constitutional Amendments

for ratification, only thirty-five states—three short of the number required—had voted favorably on the amendment.[20] One of the most recent, concerted efforts would amend the Constitution to prohibit flag burning. (To learn more about these efforts, see Politics Now: Politics and the Flag.)

Informal Methods of Amending the Constitution

The formal amendment process is not the only way that the Constitution has been changed over time. Judicial interpretation and cultural and social change also have had a major impact on the way the Constitution has evolved.

JUDICIAL INTERPRETATION As early as 1803, the Supreme Court declared in *Marbury* v. *Madison* that the federal courts had the power to nullify acts of the nation's government when they were found to be in conflict with the Constitution.[21] Over the years, this check on the other branches of government and on the states has increased the authority of the Court and significantly altered the meaning of various provisions of the Constitution, a fact that prompted President Woodrow Wilson to call the Supreme Court "a constitutional convention in continuous session." (More detail on the Supreme Court's role in interpreting the Constitution is found in chapters 4, 5, and 9 especially, as well as in other chapters in this book.)

Today, some analysts argue that the original intent of the Framers, as evidenced in *The Federalist Papers*, as well as in private notes taken by James Madison at the Constitutional Convention, should govern judicial interpretation of the Constitution.[22] Others argue that the Framers knew that a changing society needed an elastic, flexible document that could adapt to the ages.[23] In all likelihood, the vagueness of the document was purposeful. Those in attendance in Philadelphia recognized that they could not agree on everything and that it was wiser to leave interpretation to future generations.

SOCIAL AND CULTURAL CHANGE Even the most far-sighted of those in attendance at the Constitutional Convention could not have anticipated the vast changes that have occurred in the United States. For example, although many people were uncomfortable with the Three-Fifths Compromise and others hoped for the abolition of slavery, none could have imagined that an African American would one day become president of the United States. Likewise, few of the Framers could have anticipated the diverse roles that women would play in American society. The Constitution has evolved to accommodate such social and cultural changes. Thus, although there is no specific amendment guaranteeing women equal protection of the law, the federal courts have interpreted the Constitution to prohibit many forms of gender discrimination, thereby recognizing cultural and societal change.

Social change has also caused changes in the way institutions of government act. As problems such as the Great Depression appeared national in scope, Congress took on more and more power at the expense of the states to solve economic and social crises. In fact, Yale law professor Bruce Ackerman argues that on certain occasions, extraordinary times call for extraordinary measures such as the New Deal that, in effect, amend the Constitution. Thus, congressional passage (and the Supreme

POLITICS NOW

Source: WASHINGTON POST   June 28, 2006   Page A1

Politics and the Flag

Senate Rejects Flag Desecration Amendment

CHARLES BABINGTON

The Senate rejected by a single vote yesterday an effort to amend the Constitution to allow Congress to ban desecration of the American flag, after a two-day debate freighted with political calculations and sharp disputes over the limits of free speech.

The 66 to 34 vote fell just short of the two-thirds majority required to approve a constitutional amendment and submit it to the states for ratification. It marked the latest setback for congressional attempts to supersede Supreme Court decisions in

1989 and 1990. Justices narrowly ruled that burning and other desecrations of the flag are protected as free speech under the First Amendment. . . .

GOP [Republican] congressional leaders have offered up several measures in recent weeks that are important to their conservative political base—including an amendment banning same-sex marriage and further cuts in the estate tax—culminating with yesterday's vote on flag burning.

Polls show that most Americans want flag desecration outlawed, and the amendment's proponents said they were trying to stop justices from thwarting the public's will. They said that burning a U.S. flag in public—while rare these days—is a reprehensible insult to the nation's founders and a dishonor to the Americans who died fighting tyranny.

The amendment's opponents agreed that flag burning is repugnant, but argued that U.S. troops died to preserve freedoms that include controversial political statements.

Discussion Questions

1. *If the only approved way to dispose of an American flag is through burning, how can the government differentiate between appropriate and illegal flag burning?*
2. *Since a majority of the American public is opposed to flag desecration, how might lawmakers prohibit the practice in light of the Supreme Court's ruling that burning the flag is constitutionally protected speech?*

Court's eventual acceptance) of sweeping New Deal legislation that altered the balance of power between the national government and the states truly changed the Constitution without benefit of amendment.[24] Still, in spite of massive changes such as these, the Constitution survives, changed and ever changing after more than 200 years.

WHAT SHOULD I HAVE LEARNED?

The U.S. Constitution has proven to be a remarkably enduring document. In explaining how and why the Constitution came into being, this chapter has answered the following questions:

■ **What are the roots of the new American nation?**

While settlers came to the New World for a variety of reasons, most remained loyal to Great Britain and considered themselves subjects of the king. Over the years, as new generations of Americans were born on colonial soil, those ties weakened. A series of taxes levied by the crown ultimately led the colonists to convene a Continental Congress and to declare their independence.

■ **What is the significance of the Articles of Confederation?**

The Articles of Confederation (1781) created a loose league of friendship between the new national government and the states. Numerous weaknesses in the new government became apparent by 1784. Among the major flaws were Congress's inability to tax or regulate commerce, the absence of an executive to administer the government, the lack of a strong central government, and no judiciary.

■ **What occurred at the Constitutional Convention and how was the U.S. Constitution's structure agreed upon?**

When the weaknesses under the Articles of Confederation became apparent, the states called for a meeting to reform them. The Constitutional Convention (1787) quickly threw out the Articles of Confederation and fashioned a new, more workable form of government. The Constitution was the result of a series of compromises, including those over representation, over issues involving large and small states, and over how to determine population. Compromises were also made about how members of each branch of government were to be selected. The Electoral College was created to give states a key role in the selection of the president.

■ **What ideas and principles are embodied in the U.S. Constitution?**

The proposed U.S. Constitution created a federal system that drew heavily on Montesquieu's ideas about separation of powers. These ideas concerned a way of parceling out power among the three branches of government, and checks and balances to prevent any one branch from having too much power.

■ **How was the U.S. Constitution ratified?**

The drive for ratification became a fierce fight between Federalists and Anti-Federalists. Federalists lobbied for the strong national government created by the Constitution; Anti-Federalists favored greater state power.

■ **How can the Constitution be amended?**

The Framers did not want to fashion a government that could respond to the whims of the people. Therefore, they designed a deliberate two-stage formal amendment process that required approval on the federal and state levels; this process has rarely been used. However, informal amendments, prompted by judicial interpretation and by cultural and social change, have had a tremendous impact on the Constitution.

Key Terms

Anti-Federalists, p. 42
Articles of Confederation, p. 31
Bill of Rights, p. 45
checks and balances, p. 36
Committees of Correspondence, p. 29
confederation, p. 30
constitution, p. 34
Declaration of Independence, p. 30
enumerated powers, p. 38

federal system, p. 37
The Federalist Papers, p. 43
Federalists, p. 42
First Continental Congress, p. 30
full faith and credit clause, p. 42
Great Compromise, p. 35
implied powers, p. 39
mercantilism, p. 27
necessary and proper clause, p. 38

New Jersey Plan, p. 34
Second Continental Congress, p. 30
separation of powers, p. 36
Stamp Act Congress, p. 28
supremacy clause, p. 42
Three-Fifths Compromise, p. 35
Virginia Plan, p. 34

Researching the Constitution

In the Library

Ackerman, Bruce. *The Failure of the Founding Fathers: Jefferson, Marshall, and the Rise of Presidential Democracy,* new ed. Cambridge, MA: Belknap Press, 2007.

Ackerman, Bruce. *We the People: Transformations,* new ed. Cambridge, MA: Belknap Press, 2000.

Beard, Charles A. *An Economic Interpretation of the Constitution of the United States,* reissue ed. Mineola, NY: Dover, 2004.

Bowen, Catherine Drinker. *Miracle at Philadelphia.* Boston: Little, Brown, 1986.

Breyer, Stephen. *Active Liberty: Interpreting Our Democratic Constitution.* New York: Vintage, 2007.

Brinkley, Alan, Nelson W. Polsby, and Kathleen M. Sullivan. *New Federalist Papers: Essays in Defense of the Constitution.* New York: Norton, 1997.

Dahl, Robert A. *How Democratic is the American Constitution?* 2nd ed. New Haven, CT: Yale University Press, 2004.

Hamilton, Alexander, James Madison, and John Jay. *The Federalist Papers.* New York: Bantam Books, 1989 (first published in 1788).

Lynch, Joseph M. *Negotiating the Constitution: The Earliest Debates over Original Intent.* Ithaca, NY: Cornell University Press, 2005.

Main, Jackson Turner. *The Anti-Federalists: Critics of the Constitution, 1781–1788.* Chapel Hill: University of North Carolina Press, 2004.

———. *The Social Structure of Revolutionary America.* Princeton, NJ: Princeton University Press, 1965.

Rossiter, Clinton. *1787: Grand Convention,* reissue ed. New York: Norton, 1987.

Sabato, Larry J. *A More Perfect Constitution.* New York: Walker 2008.

Stewart, David O. *The Summer of 1787: The Men Who Invented the Constitution.* New York: Simon and Schuster, 2007.

Simon, James F. *What Kind of Nation: Thomas Jefferson, John Marshall, and the Epic Struggle to Create a United States.* New York: Simon and Schuster, 2003.

Storing, Herbert J. *What the Anti-Federalists Were For.* Chicago: University of Chicago Press, 1981.

Sunstein, Cass R. *Designing Democracy: What Constitutions Do.* New York: Oxford University Press, 2001.

Tushnet, Mark, ed. *Taking the Constitution Away from the Courts.* Princeton, NJ: Princeton University Press, 2002.

———. *The Constitution in Wartime: Beyond Alarmism and Complacency.* Durham, NC: Duke University Press, 2005.

Wood, Gordon S. *The Creation of the American Republic, 1776–1787,* reissue ed. New York: Norton, 1993.

On the Web

Learn more about the founding of the United States, the Articles of Confederation, and the writing and ratification of the Constitution at the educational resources page of the House of Representatives Web site at **www.house.gov/house/Educate.shtml**.

Learn more about the Declaration of Independence, the Constitution, the Bill of Rights, and the Framers at the National Archives site, which includes biographical sketches and demographic information at **www.archives.gov/exhibits/charters/charters.html**.

The Avalon Project at Yale Law School includes the text of eighteenth-century documents related to the national founding and the Revolutionary War, many of which are discussed in this chapter. Go to **www.yale.edu/lawweb/avalon/18th.htm**.

The Constitution of the United States of America

We the People of the United States, in Order to form a more perfect Union, establish Justice, insure domestic Tranquility, provide for the common defence, promote the general Welfare, and secure the Blessings of Liberty to ourselves and our Posterity, do ordain and establish this Constitution for the United States of America.

ARTICLE I

1.

All legislative Powers herein granted shall be vested in a Congress of the United States, which shall consist of a Senate and House of Representatives.

Article I is the longest and most detailed of any of the articles, sections, or amendments that make up the United States Constitution. By *enumerating* the powers of Congress, the Framers attached limits to the enormous authority they had vested in the legislative branch. At the same time, the allocation of certain powers to Congress ensured that the legislative branch would maintain control over certain vital areas of public policy and that it would be protected from incursions by the executive and judicial branches. Moreover, by clearly vesting Congress with certain powers (for example, the power to regulate interstate commerce), Article I established a water's edge for the exercise of state power in what were now national affairs.

Originally, Article I also contained restrictions limiting the amendment of several of its provisions, a feature found nowhere else in the Constitution. Section 4 prohibited Congress from making any law banning the importation of slaves until 1808, and section 9 prohibited Congress from levying an income tax on the general population. Neither section is operative any longer. Section 4 expired on its own, and section 9 was modified by passage of the Sixteenth Amendment, which established the income tax (see page 88).

Despite the great care the Framers took to limit the exercise of congressional authority to those powers enumerated in Article I, the power of Congress has grown tremendously since the nation's founding. Under Chief Justice John Marshall (1801–1835), the U.S. Supreme Court interpreted the Constitution to favor the power of the national government over the states and to permit Congress to exercise both its *enumerated* (the power to regulate interstate commerce) and *implied* (the necessary and proper clause) powers in broad fashion. With only the occasional exception, the Court has never really challenged the legislative power vested in Congress to engage in numerous areas of public policy that some constitutional scholars (and politicians and voters) believe are the province of the states. Perhaps the only area in which legislative power has diminished over the years has been the war-making power granted to Congress, something that lawmakers, for all their occasional criticism of presidential conduct of foreign policy, have ceded to the executive branch rather willingly.

Section 2.

The House of Representatives shall be composed of Members chosen every second Year by the People of the several States, and the Electors in each State shall have the Qualifications requisite for Electors of the most numerous Branch of the State Legislature.

No person shall be a Representative who shall not have attained to the Age of twenty five Years, and been seven Years a Citizen of the United States, and who shall not, when elected, be an Inhabitant of that State in which he shall be chosen.

The qualifications clause, which sets out the age and residency requirements for individuals who wish to run for the House of Representatives, became the centerpiece of a national debate that emerged during the late 1980s and early 1990s over term limits for members of Congress. In *U.S. Term Limits* v. *Thornton* (1995), the Supreme Court ruled that section 2, clause 2, did not specify any other qualification to serve in the House other than age and residency (as did section 3, clause 3, to run for the Senate). Thus, no state could restrict an individual's right to run for Congress. The Court ruled that any modification to

the qualifications clause would have to come through a constitutional amendment.

Representatives and direct Taxes shall be apportioned among the several States which may be included within this Union, according to their respective Numbers which shall be determined by adding to the whole Number of free Persons, including those bound to Service for a Term of Years, and excluding Indians not taxed, three fifths of all other Persons. The actual Enumeration shall be made within three Years after the first Meeting of the Congress of the United States, and within every subsequent Term ten Years, in such Manner as they shall by Law direct. The Number of Representatives shall not exceed one for every thirty Thousand, but each State shall have at Least one Representative; and until such enumerations shall be made, the State of New Hampshire shall be entitled to chuse three, Massachusetts eight, Rhode-Island and Providence Plantations one, Connecticut five, New-York six, New Jersey four, Pennsylvania eight, Delaware one, Maryland six, Virginia ten, North Carolina five, South Carolina five, and Georgia three.

Under the Articles of Confederation, "direct" taxes (such as taxes on property) were apportioned based on land value, not population. This encouraged states to diminish the value of their land in order to reduce their tax burden. Prior to the Constitutional Convention of 1787, several prominent delegates met to discuss—and ultimately propose—changing the method for direct taxation from land value to the population of each state. A major sticking point among the delegates on this issue was how to count slaves for taxation purposes. Southern states wanted to diminish the value of slaves for tax purposes, while northern states wanted to count slaves as closer to a full person. On the other hand, southern states wanted to count slaves as "whole persons" for purposes of representation to increase their power in the House of Representatives, but northern states rejected this proposal. Ultimately, the delegates settled on the "Three-Fifths Compromise," which treated each slave as three-fifths of a person for tax and representation purposes.

At the beginning, the Three-Fifths Compromise enhanced southern power in the House. In 1790, when the 1st Congress convened, the South held 45 percent of the seats, despite a significantly smaller free population than the North. Over time, however, the South saw its power in the House diminish. By the 1830s, the South held just over 30 percent of House seats, which gave it just enough power to thwart northern initiatives on slavery questions and territorial issues, but not enough power to defeat the growing power of the North to control commercial and economic policy. This standoff between the North and South led to such events as South Carolina Senator John C. Calhoun's doctrine of nullification and secession, which argued that a state could nullify any federal law not consistent with regional or state interests. By the 1850s, the Three-Fifths Compromise had made the South dependent on expanding the number of slaveholding territories eligible for admission to the union and a judicial system sympathetic to slaveholding interests. The Three-Fifths Compromise was repealed by section 2 of the Fourteenth Amendment (see pages 86–87).

When vacancies happen in the Representation from any State, the Executive Authority thereof shall issue Writs of Election to fill such Vacancies.

This clause permits the governor of a state to call an election to replace any member of the House of Representatives who is unable to complete a term of office due to death, resignation, or removal from the House. In some cases, a governor will appoint a successor to fill out a term; in other cases, the governor will call a special election. A governor's decision is shaped less by constitutional guidelines and more by partisan interests. For example, a Democratic governor might choose to appoint a Democratic successor if he or she believes that a Republican candidate might have an advantage in a special election.

The House of Representatives shall chuse their speaker and other Officers; and shall have the sole Power of Impeachment.

Clause 5 establishes the only officer of the House of Representatives—the Speaker. The remaining offices (party leaders, whips, and so on) are created by the House.

The House also has the sole power of impeachment against members of the executive and judicial branches. The House, like the Senate, is responsible for disciplining its own members. In *Nixon* v. *U.S.* (1993), the Supreme Court ruled that government officials who are the subject of impeachment proceedings may not challenge them in court. The Court ruled that the sole power given to the House over impeachment precludes judicial intervention.

Section 3.

The Senate of the United States shall be composed of two Senators from each State chosen by the Legislature thereof, for six Years; and each Senator shall have one Vote.

The provision of this clause establishing the election of senators by state legislatures was repealed by the Seventeenth Amendment (see page 88).

Immediately after they shall be assembled in Consequence of the first Election, they shall be divided as equally as may be into three Classes. The Seats of the Senators of the first Class shall be vacated at the Expiration of the second year, of the second Class at the Expiration of the fourth Year, and of the third Class at the Expiration of the sixth Year, so that one third may be chosen every second Year and if Vacancies happen by Resignation, or otherwise, during the Recess of the Legislature of any State, the Executive thereof may make temporary Appointments until the next Meeting of the Legislature, which shall then fill such Vacancies.

Vacancies for senators are handled the same way as vacancies for representatives—through appointment or special election. The Seventeenth Amendment modified the language authorizing the state legislature to choose a replacement for a vacant Senate position.

No Person shall be a Senator who shall not have attained to the Age of thirty Years, and been nine Years a Citizen of the United States, and who shall not, when elected, be an Inhabitant of that State for which he shall be chosen.

The Vice President of the United States shall be President of the Senate, but shall have no Vote, unless they be equally divided.

Clause 4 gives the vice president the authority to vote to break a tie in the Senate. This is the only constitutional duty the Constitution specifies for the vice president. As president of the Senate, the vice president also presides over procedural matters of that body, although this is not a responsibility that vice presidents really have ever shouldered.

The Senate shall chuse their other Officers, and also a President pro tempore, in the Absence of the Vice President, or when he shall exercise the Office of President of the United States.

Clause 5 creates the position of *president pro tempore* (the president of the time), the only Senate office established by the Constitution to handle the duties of the vice president set out in section 3, clause 4.

The Senate shall have the sole Power to try all Impeachments. When sitting for that Purpose, they shall be on Oath or Affirmation. When the President of the United States is tried, the Chief Justice shall preside: And no Person shall be convicted without the Concurrence of two thirds of the Members present.

Judgment in Cases of Impeachment shall not extend further than to removal from Office, and disqualification to hold and enjoy any Office of honor, Trust or Profit under the United States; but the Party convicted shall nevertheless be liable and subject to Indictment, Trial, Judgment and Punishment, according to law.

Just as the House of Representatives has the sole power to bring impeachment against executive and judicial branch officials, the Senate has the sole power to try all impeachments. Unless the president is facing trial in the Senate, the vice president serves as the presiding officer. In 1998, President Bill Clinton was tried on two articles of impeachment (four were brought against him in the House) and found not guilty on each count. The presiding officer in President Clinton's impeachment trial was Chief Justice William H. Rehnquist.

A conviction results in the removal of an official from office. It does not prohibit subsequent civil or criminal action against that individual. Nor does it prohibit an impeached and convicted official from returning to federal office. In 1989, Alcee Hastings, a trial judge with ten years experience on the U.S. District Court for the Southern District of Florida, was convicted on impeachment charges and removed from office. In 1992, he ran successfully for the 23rd District seat of the U.S. House of Representatives, where he continues to serve as of this writing.

Section 4.

The Times, Places and Manner of holding Elections for Senators and Representatives, shall be prescribed in each State by the Legislature thereof; but the Congress may at any time by Law make or alter such Regulations, except as to the Places of chusing Senators.

The Congress shall assemble at least once in every Year, and such Meeting shall be on the first Monday in December, unless they shall by Law appoint a different Day.

Section 4 authorizes the states to establish the rules governing elections for members of Congress, but Congress has never hesitated to exercise its law-making power in this area when it has believed that improvements were necessary to improve the electoral process. The first such action did not come until 1842, when Congress passed legislation making elections to the House based on single-member districts, not from the general population. By the turn of the twentieth

century, Congress had passed legislation establishing additional criteria such as the rough equality of population among districts and territorial compactness and contiguity. Article I, section 4, is one of the three main areas from which Congress derives the power to regulate the electoral process. The other two are the necessary and proper clause of Article I, section 8, clause 3, and section 2 of the Fifteenth Amendment.

Section 5.

Each House shall be the Judge of the Elections, Returns and Qualifications of its own Members, and a Majority of each shall constitute a Quorum to do business; but a smaller Number may adjourn from day to day, and may be authorized to compel the Attendance of absent Members, in such Manner, and under such Penalties as each House may provide.

Each House may determine the Rules of its Proceedings, punish its Members for disorderly Behaviour, and with the Concurrence of two thirds, expel a Member.

Clause 2 gives power to the House and Senate to establish the rules and decorum for each chamber. Expulsion from either the House or the Senate does not preclude a member from running for congressional office again or serving in any other official capacity. In *Powell* v. *McCormack* (1969), the Supreme Court ruled that the House's decision to exclude an individual from the chamber despite having been elected was different from the expulsion of a sitting representative.

Each House shall keep a Journal of its Proceedings, and from time to time publish the same, excepting such Parts as may in their judgment require Secrecy; and the Yeas and Nays of the Members of either House on any question shall, at the Desire of one fifth of those present, be entered on the Journal.

The *Congressional Record* is the official journal of Congress. Justice Joseph Story, in his much praised scholarly treatment of the U.S. Constitution, *Commentaries on the Constitution* (1833), said the purpose of this clause was "to insure publicity to the proceedings of the legislature, and a correspondent responsibility of the members to their respective constituents." Recorded votes (and yea-or-nay voice votes, if agreed to by one-fifth of the House or Senate), speeches, and other public business are contained in the *Congressional Record*.

Neither House, during the Session of Congress, shall, without the Consent of the other, adjourn for more than three days, nor to any other Place than that in which the two Houses shall be sitting.

Section 6.

The Senators and Representatives shall receive a Compensation for their Services, to be ascertained by Law, and paid out of the Treasury of the United States. They shall in all Cases, except Treason, Felony and Breach of the Peace, be privileged from Arrest during their Attendance at the Session of their respective Houses, and in going to and returning from the same; and for any Speech or Debate in either House, they shall not be questioned in any other Place.

The Twenty-Seventh Amendment, ratified in 1992, now governs the procedures for compensation of members of Congress. From the nation's founding until 1967, Congress had determined the salaries of its members. Then, Congress passed legislation giving the president the responsibility to recommend salary levels for members of Congress, since the president already had the responsibility to recommend pay levels for other federal officials. In 1989, as part of the Ethics Reform Act, Congress established a new system of pay raises and cost-of-living adjustments based on a particular vote.

Clause 1 also protects the right of senators and representatives from criminal prosecution for any "Speech or Debate" made in Congress. This protection stemmed from lessons drawn from the persistent conflicts between the House of Commons and the Tudor and Stuart monarchies in Great Britain, who used their power to bring civil and criminal actions against legislators whose opinions were deemed seditious or dangerous. The 1689 English Bill of Rights contained protection for legislators to conduct their business in Parliament free from such fears, and the Framers believed that such protection was essential for Congress under the Constitution. The Supreme Court has held, however, in *Gravel* v. *U.S.* (1972), that the speech or debate clause does not immunize senators or representatives from criminal inquiry if their activities in the Senate or House are the result of alleged or proven illegal action.

The privilege from arrest clause has little application in contemporary America. The clause applies only to arrests in civil suits, which were fairly common when the Constitution was ratified. The Court has interpreted the phrase "except Treason, Felony or Breach of the Peace" to make members eligible for arrest for crimes that would fall into that category. For example, a member of Congress is eligible if he or she commits a serious traffic offense, such as drunk or reckless driving, on the way to or from legislative business.

No Senator or Representative shall, during the Time for which he was elected, be appointed to any civil Office under the Authority of the United States, which shall have been created, or the Emoluments whereof shall have been encreased during such time; and no Person holding any Office under the United States, shall be a Member of either House during his Continuance in Office.

Clause 2 prohibits any senator or representative from holding a simultaneous office in the legislative or executive branches. This is one of the least controversial provisions of the Constitution. Indeed, there is no judicial interpretation of its meaning.

The general purpose of this clause is to prevent one branch of government from having an undue influence on another by creating dual incentives. It is also another safeguard in the separation of powers.

Section 7.

All Bills for raising Revenue shall originate in the House of Representatives; but the Senate may propose or concur with Amendments as on other Bills.

The power to raise revenue found in clause 1 is unique to the House of Representatives. In _Federalist No. 58_, James Madison argued that vesting such authority in the House was a key feature of the separation of powers. No bill either raising or lowering taxes may originate in the Senate. Legislation that creates incidental revenue may begin in the Senate, as long as the legislation does not involve taxation.

Every Bill which shall have passed the House of Representatives and the Senate, shall, before it become a Law, be presented to the President of the United States; If he approve he shall sign it, but if not he shall return it, with his Objections to that House in which it shall have originated, who shall enter the Objections at large on their Journal, and proceed to reconsider it. If after such Reconsideration two thirds of that House shall agree to pass the Bill, it shall be sent, together with the Objections, to the other House, by which it shall likewise be reconsidered, and if approved by two thirds of that House, it shall become a Law. But in all such Cases the Votes of both Houses shall be determined by Yeas and Nays, and the Names of the Persons voting for and against the Bill shall be entered on the Journal of each House respectively. If any Bill shall not be returned by the President within ten Days (Sundays excepted) after it shall have been presented to him, the Same shall be a Law, in like Manner as if he had signed it, unless the Congress by their

Adjournment prevent its Return, in which Case it shall not be a Law.

This clause establishes several key features of presidential-congressional relations in the flow of the legislative process. For a bill to become law, it must be passed by the House and Senate, and it must be signed by the president. The Supreme Court has ruled that the veto regulations outlined in this clause serve two purposes. First, by giving the president ten days to consider a bill for approval, clause 2 provides the president with ample time to consider legislation and protects him from having to approve legislation in the wake of congressional adjournment. But clause 2 also provides Congress with a countervailing power to override a presidential veto, a procedure that requires a two-thirds vote in each chamber.

Every Order, Resolution, or Vote to which the Concurrence of the Senate and House of Representatives may be necessary (except on a question of Adjournment) shall be presented to the President of the United States; and before the Same shall take Effect, shall be approved by him, or being disapproved by him, shall be repassed by two thirds of the Senate and House of Representatives, according to the Rules and Limitations prescribed in the Case of a Bill.

Clause 3 covers the presentation of resolutions, not actual legislation. For any resolution to have the force of law, it must be presented to the president for approval. Should the president veto the resolution, Congress may override this veto in the same manner expressed in section 7, clause 2. Resolutions that do not have the force of law do not require presidential approval. Preliminary votes taken on constitutional amendments and other legislative matters covered by clause 3 do not require presentation to the president.

This clause has been the subject of two major Supreme Court decisions dealing with the separation of powers. In _I.N.S._ v. _Chadha_ (1983), the Court ruled that the House-only legislative veto, a practice begun during the 1930s to give Congress power to control power delegated to a rapidly expanding executive branch, violated both the bicameralism principles of Article I, section 1, and the presentment clause of section 7, clause 3. At the time, the ruling struck down about 200 legislative vetoes that had been included in various pieces of congressional legislation. In _Clinton_ v. _New York_ (1998), the Court ruled that the line-item veto passed by Congress to give the president the power to veto specific provisions of legislation rather than an entire bill violated the presentment clause of Article I, section 7, clause 3. The Court claimed that the line-item

veto permitted the president to "repeal certain laws," a power that belonged to Congress and not the president.

Section 8.

The Congress shall have Power To lay and collect Taxes, Duties, Imposts and Excises, to pay the Debts and provide for the common Defence and general Welfare of the United States; but all Duties, Imposts and Excises shall be uniform throughout the United States;

To borrow Money on the credit of the United States;

To regulate Commerce with foreign Nations, and among the several States, and with the Indian Tribes;

To establish a uniform Rule of Naturalization, and uniform Laws on the subject of Bankruptcies throughout the United States;

To coin Money, regulate the Value thereof, and of foreign Coin, and fix the Standard of Weights and Measures;

To provide for the Punishment of counterfeiting the Securities and current Coin of the United States;

To establish Post Offices and post Roads;

To promote the Progress of Science and useful Arts, by securing for limited Times to Authors and Inventors exclusive Right to their respective Writings and Discoveries;

To constitute Tribunals inferior to the supreme Court;

To define and punish Piracies and Felonies committed on the high Seas, and Offences against the Law of Nations;

To declare War, grant Letters of Marque and Reprisal, and make rules concerning Captures on Land and Water;

To raise and support Armies, but no Appropriation of Money to that Use shall be for a longer Term than two Years;

To provide and maintain a Navy;

To make Rules for the Government and Regulation of the land and naval Forces;

To provide for calling forth the Militia to execute the Laws of the Union, suppress Insurrections and repel Invasions;

To provide for organizing, arming, and disciplining, the Militia, and for governing such Part of them as may be employed in the Service of the United States, reserving to the States respectively, the Appointment of the Officers, and the Authority of training the Militia according to the discipline prescribed by Congress;

To exercise exclusive Legislation in all Cases whatsoever, over such District (not exceeding ten Miles square) as may, by Cession of particular States, and the Acceptance of Congress, become the Seat of the Government of the United States, and to exercise like Authority over all Places purchased by the Consent of the Legislature of the State in which the Same shall be for the Erection of Forts, Magazines, Arsenals, dock-Yards, and other needful Buildings;—And

Article I, section 8, clause 1, is, in many ways, the engine of congressional power. First, clause 1 gives Congress the power to tax and spend, a power the Supreme Court has interpreted as "exhaustive" and "reaching every subject." Second, in giving Congress the power to provide for the common defense and general welfare, it offers no specific constraint on what Congress may spend public funds for and how much it may spend. Third, section 8 gives Congress complete authority in numerous areas of policy that affect Americans at home and abroad on a massive scale. These powers include the power to regulate interstate commerce (which Congress has relied on to establish federal civil rights law), to make war (a power that Congress, since the end of World War II in 1945, has increasingly deferred to the president), and to establish the federal judicial system.

Clause 1 is often cited by constitutional scholars as an example of how the Constitution constrains legislative power by limiting the powers that Congress may exercise. To a certain extent, this is true. But, it is also true that the Court has granted Congress extensive power to legislate in certain areas that bear only a tangential relationship to the specific language of some of the provisions of clause 1. For example, in *Katzenbach* v. *McClung* (1964), the Court turned back a challenge to the constitutionality of the Civil Rights Act of 1964, which Congress had passed under its authority to regulate interstate commerce. The Court ruled that racial discrimination had an adverse effect on the free flow of commerce.

Clause 2 establishes the seat of the federal government—first New York City, now Washington, D.C. The clause also makes Congress the legislative body of the nation's capital, a power that extends to other federal bodies, such as forts, military bases, and other places where federal buildings are located.

To make all Laws which shall be necessary and proper for carrying into Execution the foregoing Powers, and all other Powers vested by this

Constitution in the Government of the United States, or in any Department or Officer thereof.

Better known as the necessary and proper clause, this provision of Article I was one of the most contested points between Federalists and Anti-Federalists during the ratification debates over the Constitution. Anti-Federalists feared that the language was too broad and all-encompassing, and, if interpreted by a Supreme Court sympathetic to the nationalist ambitions of the Federalist Party, would give Congress limitless power to exercise legislative authority over state and local matters. In *McCulloch* v. *Maryland* (1819), Chief Justice John Marshall offered what constitutional scholars believe remains the definitive interpretation of the necessary and proper clause. While *McCulloch* certainly did cement the power of Congress in the federal system, the expansive definition given the necessary and proper clause by the Court is also testament to the flexible nature of the Constitution, and why so few amendments have been added to the original document.

Section 9.

The Migration or Importation of such Persons as any of the States now existing shall think proper to admit, shall not be prohibited by the Congress prior to the Year one thousand eight hundred and eight, but a Tax or duty may be imposed on such Importation, not exceeding ten dollars for each Person.

Like the other provisions of the Constitution that refer to slavery, such as the Three-Fifths Compromise, section 9 creates policy governing the institution without ever mentioning the word. The importation clause was a compromise between slave traders, who wanted to continue the practice, and opponents of slavery, who needed southern support to ratify the Constitution. In 1808, Congress passed legislation banning the importation of slaves; until then, Congress used its power to tax slaves brought to the United States.

The Privilege of the Writ of Habeas Corpus shall not be suspended, unless when in Cases of Rebellion or Invasion the public Safety may require it.

Clause 2 is the only place where the writ of habeas corpus—the "Great Writ," as it was known to the Framers—is mentioned in the Constitution. Only the federal government is bound by clause 2. The writ may only be suspended in times of crisis and rebellion, and then it is Congress that has the power, not the president. In *Boumediene v. Bush* (2008), the Supreme Court ruled that the provision of the Military Commissions Act of 2006 stripping the federal courts of their jurisdiction to hear habeas corpus petitions from detainees, regardless of their status as American citizens or foreign nationals, being held at a military prison at Guantanamo Bay, Cuba, was unconstitutional.

No Bill of Attainder or ex post facto Law shall be passed.

A bill of attainder is a legislative act punishing a person with "pains and penalties" without the benefit of a hearing or trial. The fundamental purpose of the ban on bills of attainder is to prevent trial by legislature and other arbitrary punishments for persons vulnerable to extra-judicial proceedings. An *ex post facto law* is one passed making a previously committed civil or criminal action subject to penalty. In *Calder* v. *Bull* (1798), the Court ruled that the ban on *ex post facto* laws applied only to penal and criminal actions. A similar restriction on the states is found in Article I, section 10, clause 1.

No Capitation, or other direct, Tax shall be laid, unless in Proportion to the Census or Enumeration herein before directed to be taken.

This clause, which originally prohibited Congress from levying an income tax, was modified by the Sixteenth Amendment, passed in 1913 (see page 88).

No Tax or Duty shall be laid on Articles exported from any State.

Clause 5 prohibits Congress from levying a tax on any good or article exported from a state to a foreign country or to another state. Many southern states feared that northern members of Congress would attempt to weaken the South's slave-based economy by taxing exports. This clause prohibited such action. Congress may prohibit the shipment of certain items from one state to another and to other countries.

No Preference shall be given by any Regulation of Commerce or Revenue to the Ports of one State over those of another: nor shall Vessels bound to, or from, one State, be obliged to enter, clear, or pay Duties in another.

Congress is prohibited from making laws regulating trade that favor one state over another. Clause 6 also prohibits Congress from establishing preferences for certain ports or trade centers over others, although it may, under its power to regulate interstate commerce, pass laws that incidentally benefit certain states or maritime outlets. The Supreme Court has ruled that states are not bound by the limitations on Congress expressed in this clause.

No money shall be drawn from the Treasury, but in Consequence of Appropriations made by Law; and a regular Statement and Account of the Receipts and Expenditures of all public Money shall be published from time to time.

Clause 7 serves two fundamental purposes. First, the clause prohibits any governmental body receiving federal funds from spending those funds without the approval of Congress. Once Congress has determined that federal funds are to be spent in a certain way, the executive branch may not exercise any discretion over that decision. Second, by restricting executive control of spending power, the clause firmly reinforces congressional authority over revenue and spending, a key feature of the separation of powers.

No Title of Nobility shall be granted by the United States: And no Person holding any Office of Profit or Trust under them, shall, without the Consent of the Congress, accept of any present, Emolument, Office, or Title, of any kind whatever, from any King, Prince, or foreign State.

This provision is among the first school-taught lessons about the Constitution. To reinforce the commitment to representative democracy, the Framers prohibited a title of nobility from being conferred on any public official. This clause also prohibits any government official from accepting compensation, gifts, or similar benefits from any foreign government for services rendered without the consent of Congress.

Section 10.

No state shall enter into any Treaty, Alliance, or Confederation; grant Letters of Marque and Reprisal; coin Money; emit Bills of Credit; make any Thing but gold and silver Coin a Tender in Payment of Debts; pass any Bill of Attainder, ex post facto Law, or Law impairing the Obligation of Contracts, or grant any Title of Nobility.

This clause denies several powers to the states that were once permissible under the Articles of Confederation, and it emphasizes the Framers' commitment under the Constitution to a strong national government with Congress as the centrifugal force. During the Civil War, the Union relied on this clause in support of its view that the Confederate states had no legal existence but instead were merely "states in rebellion" against the United States.

The restrictions on states passing either bills of attainder or ex post facto laws have come into play at various points in American history. During Reconstruction, several states enacted legislation prohibiting any individual who aided the Confederacy from entering certain professions or enjoying other benefits available to citizens who remained loyal to the Union. The Supreme Court struck down these laws on the grounds that they violated this clause.

The provision prohibiting states from passing any law "impairing the Obligation of Contracts," better known as the contract clause, has been the subject of considerable litigation before the Supreme Court. The contract clause was intended to bar the states from interfering in private contracts between consensual parties and was considered an important limit on the power of states to restrict the fledgling national economic order of the early republic. Early on, the Court considered many laws that restricted the terms set out in private contracts as unconstitutional. But as the United States became a more industrial society, and as citizen demands grew for government regulation of the economy, the environment, and social welfare benefits, the Court softened its position on the contract clause to permit states to make laws that served a reasonable public interest. A key case involving the contract clause is *Home Building and Loan Association* v. *Blaisdell* (1934). In *Blaisdell*, the Court ruled that a Depression-era law passed by the Minnesota legislature forgiving mortgage payments by homeowners to banks did not violate the contract clause.

No State shall, without the Consent of the Congress, lay any Imposts or Duties on Imports or Exports, except what may be absolutely necessary for executing its inspection Laws: and the net Produce of all Duties and Imposts, laid by any State on Imports or Exports, shall be for the Use of the Treasury of the United States, and all such Laws shall be subject to the Revision and Controul of the Congress.

No state may tax goods leaving or entering a state, although it may charge reasonable fees for inspections considered necessary to the public interest. The restriction on import and export taxes applies only to those goods entering from or leaving for a foreign country.

No State shall, without the Consent of Congress, lay any Duty of Tonnage, keep Troops, or Ships of War in time of Peace, enter into any Agreement or Compact with another State, or with a foreign Power, or engage in War, unless actually invaded, or in such imminent Danger as will not admit of delay.

Clause 3 cements the power of Congress to control acts of war and make treaties with foreign countries. The Framers wanted to correct any perception to the contrary gained from the Articles of Confederation that states were free to act independently of the national government on negotiated matters with foreign countries. They also wanted to ensure that any state that entered into a compact with another state—something this clause does not prohibit—must receive permission from Congress.

ARTICLE II

Section 1.

The executive Power shall be vested in a President of the United States of America. He shall hold his Office during the Term of four Years, and, together with the Vice President, chosen for the same Term, be elected as follows.

In *Federalist No. 70*, Alexander Hamilton argued for an "energetic executive" branch headed by a single, elected president not necessarily beholden to the majority party in Congress. Hamilton believed that a nationally elected president would not be bound by the narrow, parochial interests that drove legislative law-making. The president would possess both the veto power over Congress and a platform from which to articulate a national vision in both domestic and foreign affairs.

Hamilton believed that the constitutional boundaries placed on executive power through the separation of powers and the fact that the president was accountable to a national electorate constrained any possibility that the office would come to resemble the monarchies of Europe. However, most presidential scholars agree that the modern presidency has grown in power precisely because of the general nature of the enabling powers of Article II.

Each State shall appoint, in such Manner as the Legislature thereof may direct, a Number of Electors, equal to the whole Number of Senators and Representatives to which the State may be entitled in the Congress; but no Senator or Representative, or Person holding an Office of Trust of Profit under the United States, shall be appointed an Elector.

Clause 2 established the Electoral College and set the number of electors from each state at the total of senators and representatives serving in Congress.

The Electors shall meet in their respective States, and vote by Ballot for two Persons, of whom one at least shall not be an Inhabitant of the same State with themselves. And they shall make a List of all the Persons voted for, and, of the Number of Votes for each; which List they shall sign and certify, and transmit sealed to the Seat of the Government of the United States, directed to the President of the Senate. The President of the Senate shall, in the Presence of the Senate and House of Representatives, open all the Certificates, and the Votes shall then be counted. The Person having the greatest Number of Votes shall be the President, if such Number be a Majority of the whole Number of Electors appointed; and if there be more than one who have such Majority, and have an equal Number of Votes, then the House of Representatives shall immediately chuse by Ballot one of them for President; and if no Person have a Majority, then from the five highest on the List the said House shall in like Manner chuse the President. But in chusing the President, the Votes shall be taken by States, the Representation from each State having one Vote; A quorum for this Purpose shall consist of a Member or Members from two thirds of the States, and a Majority of all the States shall be necessary to a Choice. In every Case, after the Choice of the President, the Person having the greatest Number of Votes of the Electors shall be the Vice President. But if there should remain two or more who have equal Votes, the Senate shall chuse from them by Ballot the Vice President.

This provision of section 1 described the rules for calling the Electoral College to vote for president and vice president. Originally, the electors did not vote separately for president and vice president. After the 1800 election, which saw Thomas Jefferson and Aaron Burr receive the identical number of electoral votes even though it was clear that Jefferson was the presidential candidate and Burr the vice presidential candidate, the nation ratified the Twelfth Amendment (see page 85).

The Twelfth Amendment did not resolve what many constitutional scholars today believe are the inadequacies of the Electoral College system. In 1824, the presidential election ended in a four-way tie, and the House of Representatives elected second-place finisher John Quincy Adams president. In 1876, Benjamin Harrison lost the popular vote but won the presidency after recounts awarded him an Electoral College majority. But perhaps the most controversial election of all came in 2000, when George W. Bush, who lost the popular contest to Al Gore by approximately 500,000 votes, was named the presidential victor after a six-week court battle over the vote count in Florida. After the Supreme Court ruled against the position of Al Gore that a recount of the Florida popular vote should continue until all votes had been counted, an outcome that would have left the nation without a president-elect for several more weeks, Bush was awarded Florida's electoral votes, which gave him 271, just one more than he needed to win the office. Outraged Democrats pledged to mount a case for Electoral College reform, but, as was so often the case before, nothing happened.

The Congress may determine the Time of chusing the Electors, and the Day on which they shall give their Votes; which Day shall be the same throughout the United States.

No Person except a natural born Citizen, or a Citizen of the United States, at the time of the Adoption of this Constitution, shall be eligible to the Office of President; neither shall any Person be eligible to that Office who shall not have attained to the Age of thirty five Years, and been fourteen Years a Resident within the United States.

This provision of Article II is referred to as the presidential eligibility clause. In addition to setting out the age and resident requirements of presidential aspirants, this clause defines who may *not* run for president—any foreign-born individual who has nonetheless obtained United States citizenship. For example, Michigan Governor Jennifer Granholm, who has lived in the United States since she was four years old, may not run for president because she was born in Canada. The same is true for California Governor Arnold Schwarzenegger, who was born in Austria but has lived in the United States his entire adult life. Judicial interpretation of the presidential eligibility clause has not resolved the question of whether children born to U.S. citizens are eligible to run for president if they meet the residency requirements.

In Case of the Removal of the President from Office, or of his Death, Resignation, or Inability to discharge the Powers and Duties of the said Office, the Same shall devolve on the Vice President, and the Congress may by Law provide for the Case of Removal, Death, Resignation or Inability, both of the President and Vice President, declaring what Officer shall then act as President, and such Officer shall act accordingly, until the Disability be removed, or a President shall be elected.

This presidential succession clause has been modified by the Twenty-Fifth Amendment (see page 92).

The President shall, at stated Times, receive for his Services, a Compensation, which shall neither be encreased nor diminished during the Period for which he shall have been elected, and he shall not receive within that Period any other Emolument from the United States, or any of them.

Presidential compensation, like compensation for members of Congress, may not be increased for the current occupant of the office. The president is not eligible for any other public compensation during time in office. However, the president may continue to receive income such as interest on investments or book royalties.

Before he enter on the Execution of his Office, he shall take the following Oath or Affirmation:—"I do solemnly swear (or affirm) that I will faithfully execute the Office of President of the United States, and will to the best of my Ability, preserve, protect and defend the Constitution of the United States."

Since George Washington's inaugural in 1789, each president has added the phrase "so help me God" to the end of the presidential oath. Although Abraham Lincoln cited the oath to justify his suspension of the writ of *habeas corpus* during the Civil War, no other president has relied on the oath to justify action that stretched the boundaries of executive power. Presidents taking extraordinary action either at home or abroad have relied on either the commander in chief clause of section 2, clause 1, or the provision of section 3 authorizing the president to "faithfully execut[e]" the laws of the United States.

Section 2.

The President shall be Commander in Chief of the Army and Navy of the United States, and of the Militia of the several States, when called into the actual Service of the United States; he may require the Opinion, in writing, of the principal Officer in each of the executive Departments, upon any Subject relating to the Duties of their respective Offices, and he shall have Power to grant Reprieves and Pardons for Offences against the United States, except in Cases of Impeachment.

Section 2, clause 1, establishes the president as commander in chief of the Army and Navy of the United States. In modern times, that authority has extended to the Air Force, the Marines, and all other branches of the armed forces operating under the command of the United States, including state militias, reserve units, and national guards. Article I provides that Congress, and not the president, has the power to declare war. But, since World War II, no American president has received or requested a declaration of war to commit the armed forces to military conflicts, including those clearly acknowledged as large-scale war (Korea, Vietnam, the 1991 Persian Gulf War, Afghanistan, and the Iraq War). For these conflicts, the president received congressional *authorization* to use force, but not an Article I declaration.

Although the Supreme Court has ruled that the president has *inherent* power—that is, power to carry out the essential functions of his office in times of crisis, war or emergencies that are not *expressly* spelled out under Article II—it has not concluded that such power is unlimited. In *Youngstown Sheet & Tube* v. *Sawyer* (1952), the Court ruled that President Harry S Truman did not have the power to seize control of the nation's steel mills to continue the production of munitions and

other war supplies without congressional authorization. More recently, the Court ruled in *Hamdan* v. *Rumsfeld* (2006) that President George W. Bush exceeded his authority when he established military commissions that had not been approved by Congress to try detainees and other "enemy combatants" captured in the War on Terror. The Court ruled that since Congress had not approved of President Bush's system of military tribunals, prisoners were entitled to the protections of the Geneva Convention and the procedural rights of the Uniform Code of Military Justice. Congress passed the Military Commissions Act to address the Court's concerns.

Clause 1 also implicitly creates the Cabinet by authorizing the president to request the opinion "in writing" of the principal officers of the executive branch. The power to create Cabinet-level offices resides with Congress, not the president.

Presidential power to pardon is broad and limited only in cases of impeachment. Perhaps the most controversial pardon in American political history was President Gerald R. Ford's decision to pardon former President Richard M. Nixon, who resigned his office on August 8, 1974, after news reports and congressional inquiries strongly implicated him in the Watergate scandal. A real possibility existed that President Nixon could be tried on criminal charges as the result of his alleged activities during the Watergate scandal.

He shall have Power, by and with the Advice and Consent of the Senate, to make Treaties, provided two thirds of the Senators present concur; and he shall nominate, and by and with the Advice and Consent of the Senate, shall appoint Ambassadors, other public Ministers and Consuls, Judges of the supreme Court, and all other Officers of the United States, whose Appointments are not herein otherwise provided for, and which shall be established by Law: but the Congress may by Law vest the Appointment of such inferior Officers, as they think proper, in the President alone, in the Courts of Law, or in the Heads of Departments.

The President shall have Power to fill up all Vacancies that may happen during the Recess of the Senate, by granting Commissions which shall expire at the End of their next Session.

Clause 2 describes several powers the president may exercise in conjunction with the advice and consent of the Senate. These powers include the power, upon the approval of two-thirds of the Senate, to make treaties with foreign countries. But, the Constitution is silent on the question of whether a president (or Congress) may terminate a treaty by refusing to honor it or simply repealing it outright. When President Jimmy Carter terminated a treaty with China over the objection of Congress, several members sought a judicial resolution of the action; the Court, however, did not decide the case on the merits and offered no resolution on the matter. The president does not require a two-thirds majority for approval of appointments to the federal judiciary, foreign ambassadorships, Cabinet-level positions, high-ranking positions in non-Cabinet agencies, and high-level military offices. But, the fact that the Senate must approve presidential appointments in these areas provides Congress (senators often listen to the constituents of House members on controversial choices) with an important check on presidential power to shape the contours of the executive branch.

Section 3.

He shall from time to time give to the Congress Information of the State of the Union, and recommend to their Consideration such Measures as he shall judge necessary and expedient; he may, on extraordinary Occasions, convene both Houses, or either of them, and in Case of Disagreement between them, with Respect to the Time of Adjournment, he may adjourn them to such Time as he shall think proper; he shall receive Ambassadors and other public Ministers; he shall take Care that the Laws be faithfully executed, and shall Commission all the Officers of the United States.

The president is required to deliver a State of the Union message to Congress each year. The nation's first two presidents, George Washington and John Adams, delivered their addresses in person. But the nation's third president, Thomas Jefferson, believed that the practice too closely resembled the Speech from the Throne delivered by British royalty. Instead, Jefferson prepared remarks for recitation before Congress by an assistant or clerk of Congress. Every American president after Jefferson followed suit until Woodrow Wilson renewed the original practice after his first year in office. Now, the State of the Union Address is a major media event, although it is less an assessment of the nation's health and happiness and more a presidential wish-list for policy initiatives and the touting of partisan accomplishments.

The final provision of section 3 authorizing the president to faithfully execute the laws of the United States has proven controversial over the years. Presidents have cited this broad language to justify such far-reaching action as the suspension of the writ of *habeas corpus,* as President Abraham Lincoln did during the Civil War before being rebuffed by the Supreme Court in *Ex parte McCardle* (1867), and the doctrine of executive privilege, which, as asserted by various presidents, permits the executive branch to withhold sensitive information from the public or the other branches of government for national security reasons. The Court has been of two minds about the doctrine of executive privilege. On the one hand, the Court has said in such cases as *New York Times* v. *U.S.* (1971) and *U.S.* v. *Nixon* (1974) that the president has the power to withhold information to protect vital secrets and the nation's security. On the other hand, the Court has said, in ruling against the assertion of executive privilege in these two cases, that only an exceptional and demonstrated case can justify allowing the president to withhold information.

Section 4.

The President, Vice President and all civil Officers of the United States, shall be removed from Office on Impeachment for, and Conviction of, Treason, Bribery, or other High Crimes and Misdemeanors.

Presidential impeachment, like impeachment of the other described offices in section 4, is the responsibility of the House of Representatives. There is no judicial definition to what constitutes a high crime or misdemeanor. Complicating the matter further is that only the House and Senate are given responsibility over the impeachment process. No federal official subject to impeachment may challenge the action in federal court, as the Supreme Court has ruled that the rules governing impeachment are not actionable in court. Only two presidents, Andrew Johnson in 1868 and Bill Clinton in 1998, have ever been impeached. Neither president was convicted by the Senate of the charges brought against them.

ARTICLE III

Section 1.

The judicial Power of the United States, shall be vested in one supreme Court, and in such inferior Courts as the Congress may from time to time ordain and establish. The Judges, both of the supreme and inferior Courts, shall hold their Offices during good Behaviour, and shall, at stated Times, receive for their Services, a Compensation, which shall not be diminished during their Continuance in Office.

Like the power of Congress and the executive branch under Articles I and II, respectively, of the Constitution, the power of the federal judiciary has developed as the result of constitutional silences and ambiguities. Article III establishes only one federal court, the Supreme Court, and leaves to Congress the power to establish "inferior" courts as it deems necessary. Many students are surprised to learn that the power of judicial review was established by Congress, not the Supreme Court. Although the Court did articulate the power of judicial review in *Marbury* v. *Madison* (1803), that decision only applied to the power of the federal courts to review federal laws. The power of the federal courts to review state laws that allegedly trespassed upon the Constitution was established by the Judiciary Act of 1789. But, on the fundamental question of what constitutes the foundation and scope of judicial power, there is little doubt that the Court, not Congress, has been the foremost exponent of its own authority. Often, the Court has justified its authority to limit the power of the other branches to regulate its affairs by pointing to other provisions of the Constitution, most notably the supremacy clause of Article VI and section 5 of the Fourteenth Amendment, as well as Article III.

Section 2.

The judicial Power shall extend to all Cases, in Law and Equity, arising under this Constitution, the Laws of the United States, and Treaties made, or which shall be made, under their Authority;—to all Cases affecting Ambassadors, other public Ministers and Consuls;—to all Cases of admiralty and maritime Jurisdiction;—to Controversies to which the United States shall be a Party;—to Controversies between two or more States;—between a State and Citizens of another State;—between Citizens of different States;— between Citizens of the same State claiming Lands under Grants of different States,—and between a State, or the Citizens thereof, and foreign States, Citizens or Subjects.

In all Cases affecting Ambassadors, other public Ministers and Consuls, and those in which a State shall be Party, the supreme Court shall have original Jurisdiction. In all the other Cases before mentioned, the supreme Court shall have appellate Jurisdiction, both as to Law and Fact, with such Exceptions, and under such Regulations as the Congress shall make.

The Trial of all Crimes, except in Cases of Impeachment, shall be by Jury; and such Trial shall be held in the State where the said Crimes shall have been committed; but when not committed within any State, the Trial shall be at such Place or Places as the Congress may by Law have directed.

Section 1 invests the judicial power in "one Supreme Court," but it is in section 2 that we find the source of much of the controversy of the exercise of this power since *Marbury* was decided. By extending the judicial power to all "Cases, in Law and Equity, arising under the Constitution, [and] the laws of the United States," section 2 authorizes the Court to both decide matters of law and, if necessary, mandate a remedy commensurate with the degree of a constitutional violation. For example, in *Swann* v. *Charlotte-Mecklenburg Board of Education* (1971), the Court ruled that a lower court, having found that a school system had failed to meet desegregation requirements, had the power to order busing and other remedies to the constitutional violations it found in *Brown* v. *Board of Education* (1954).

Federal judicial power no longer extends to cases involving lawsuits between a state and citizens of another state. This provision was superceded by the Eleventh Amendment.

Section 2 also includes the exceptions and regulations clause. This clause has been used by congressional opponents of some of the Court's more controversial and generally liberal decisions. Although most scholars believe the clause limits the power of Congress to create broad jurisdiction for the courts it creates, others have argued that it permits Congress to strip the federal courts of jurisdiction to hear particular cases. Some opponents of the Court's decisions legalizing abortion, authorizing school busing, and upholding affirmative action have attempted to curb the power of federal courts to rule in such areas by stripping them of jurisdiction in such cases. To date, no president has ever signed such legislation.

Section 3.

Treason against the United States, shall consist only in levying War against them, or in adhering to their Enemies, giving them Aid and Comfort. No Person shall be convicted of Treason unless on the Testimony of two Witnesses to the same overt Act, or on Confession in open Court.

The Congress shall have Power to declare the Punishment of Treason, but no Attainder of Treason shall work Corruption of Blood, or Forfeiture except during the Life of the Person attainted.

Article III defines the only crime mentioned by the Constitution: treason.

ARTICLE IV

Section 1.

Full Faith and Credit shall be given in each State to the public Acts, Records, and judicial Proceedings of every other State. And the Congress may by general Laws prescribe the Manner in which such Acts, Records and Proceedings shall be proved, and the Effect thereof.

The full faith and credit clause rests on principles borrowed from international law that require one country to recognize contracts made in another country absent a compelling public policy reason to the contrary. Here, this principle, referred to in the law as comity, applied to the relationship between the states. For example, a driver's license issued in Ohio is good in Montana. The full and faith credit clause also requires a state to recognize public acts and court proceedings of another state. For the most part, interpretation of the full faith and credit clause has not been controversial. That may well change, as advocates of same-sex marriage have suggested that such a marriage performed in one state must be recognized in another state, as is the case with heterosexual marriage. A constitutional challenge to the clause may well center on the public policy exception recognized in other areas of law.

Section 2.

The Citizens of each State shall be entitled to all Privileges and Immunities of Citizens in the several States.

A Person charged in any State with Treason, Felony, or other Crime, who shall flee from Justice, and be found in another State, shall on Demand of the executive Authority of the State from which he fled, be delivered up, to be removed to the State having Jurisdiction of the Crime.

The extradition clause requires that the governor of one state deliver a fugitive from justice to the state from which that fugitive fled. Congress passed the Fugitive Act of 1793 to give definition to this provision, but the federal government has no authority to compel state authorities to extradite a fugitive from one state to another. A state may, however, sue another state in federal court to force the return of a fugitive.

No Person held to Service or Labour in one State under the Laws thereof, escaping into another, shall, in Consequence of any Law or Regulation therein, be discharged from such Service or Labour, but shall be delivered up on Claim of the Party to whom such Service or Labour may be due.

The fugitive slave clause, which required any state, including those outside the slave-holding states of the South, to return escaped slaves to their owners, was repealed in 1865 by the Thirteenth Amendment. Prior to 1865, Congress passed laws in 1793 and 1850 to enforce the clause, leaving states without power to make concurrent laws on the subject, ensuring that the southern states would always have the Constitution on their side to protect slavery.

Section 3.

New States may be admitted by the Congress into this Union; but no new State shall be formed or erected within the Jurisdiction of any other State; nor any State be formed by the Junction of two or more States, or Parts of States, without the Consent of the Legislatures of the States concerned as well as of the Congress.

The Congress shall have Power to dispose of and make all needful Rules and Regulations respecting the Territory or other Property belonging to the United States; and nothing in this Constitution shall be so construed as to Prejudice any Claims of the United States, or of any particular State.

Section 4.

The United States shall guarantee to every State in this Union a Republican Form of Government, and shall protect each of them against Invasion; and on Application of the Legislature, or of the Executive (when the Legislature cannot be convened) against domestic Violence.

ARTICLE V

The Congress, whenever two thirds of both Houses shall deem it necessary, shall propose Amendments to this Constitution, or, on the Application of the Legislatures of two thirds of the several States, shall call a Convention for proposing Amendments, which, in either Case, shall be valid to all Intents and Purposes, as Part of this Constitution, when ratified by the Legislatures of three fourths of the several States, or by Conventions in three fourths thereof, as the one or the other Mode of Ratification may be proposed by the Congress; Provided that no Amendment which may be made prior to the Year One thousand eight hundred and eight shall in any Manner affect the first and fourth Clauses in the Ninth Section of the first Article; and that no State, without its Consent, shall be deprived of its equal Suffrage in the Senate.

Changes to the Articles of Confederation had required the unanimous approval of the states. But, Article V of the U.S. Constitution offers multiple options—none of which require unanimity—for constitutional change. Article V was quite crucial to the ratification of the Constitution. Federalists who supported the Constitu-

tion wanted to ensure that any additions or modifications to the nation's charter would require the approval of more than a simple majority of citizens. This is why any amendment coming out of Congress requires two-thirds of the House and Senate for approval. The same is true for the rule requiring three-fourths of the states to ratify an amendment (either through conventions or state legislative action). Anti-Federalists who either opposed the Constitution or had reservations about key sections of it were soothed by the prospect of an amending process that did not require the unanimous approval of the states.

Only twenty-seven amendments since 1789 have been added to the Constitution, the first fifteen of which were added by 1870. Since 1933, when the nation repealed Prohibition by passing the Twenty-First Amendment, the Constitution has been amended only six times. In the modern constitutional era, efforts to amend the Constitution generally have centered on unhappiness with Supreme Court decisions (on school prayer, flag burning, school busing, abortion rights) or state court rulings with national implications (such as same-sex marriage) rather than any structural defect in the original Constitution (unlike woman suffrage or presidential succession) or a seismic political event (the Civil War). To date, none of these efforts have been successful.

ARTICLE VI

All Debts contracted and Engagements entered into, before the Adoption of this Constitution, shall be as valid against the United States under this Constitution, as under the Confederation.

This Constitution, and the Laws of the United States which shall be made in Pursuance thereof; and all Treaties made, or which shall be made, under the Authority of the United States, shall be the supreme Law of the Land; and the Judges in every State shall be bound thereby, any Thing in the Constitution or Laws of any State to the Contrary notwithstanding.

The Senators and Representatives before mentioned, and the Members of the several State Legislatures, and all executive and judicial Officers, both of the United States and of the several States, shall be bound by Oath or Affirmation, to support this Constitution; but no religious Test shall ever be required as a Qualification to any Office or public Trust under the United States.

Article VI made the national government responsible for all debts incurred by the Revolutionary War. This ensured that manufacturing and banking interests

would be repaid for the losses they sustained during the conflict. But the most important provisions of Article VI by far are contained in its second and third clauses.

Clause 2 took another major step forward for national power and away from the confederate approach to government structure of the Articles of Confederation. By making "this Constitution" and all laws made under its authority the "supreme Law of the Land," Article VI created what constitutional scholars call the supremacy clause. The Supreme Court has invoked the supremacy clause on several occasions to rebut challenges mounted by states to its decisions or acts of Congress. Among the more notable decisions by the Supreme Court that have cited the supremacy clause to mandate compliance with a previous ruling is *Cooper* v. *Aaron* (1958). In *Cooper*, the Court cited the supremacy clause in rejecting the argument of Governor Orval Faubus of Arkansas claiming that local schools were not obligated to follow the *Brown* v. *Board of Education* (1954) ruling. The Court said that *Brown* was the law of the land and, as such, all school boards were required to comply with its requirement to desegregate their schools.

Although most Americans rightly point to the First Amendment as the baseline for the guarantee for religious freedom, clause 3 of Article VI contains an important contribution to this principle—the ban on religious tests or qualifications to hold public office. Holders of public office, no matter how great or small, were required to affirm their allegiance to the Constitution and the laws of the United States, but they could not be required to profess a belief in God or meet any other religious qualification. Numerous states nonetheless ignored this requirement until 1961, when the Supreme Court ruled in *Torcaso* v. *Watkins* that states could not administer religious oaths to holders of public office.

ARTICLE VII

The Ratification of the Conventions of nine States, shall be sufficient for the Establishment of this Constitution between the States so ratifying the Same.

Done in Convention by the Unanimous Consent of the States present the Seventeenth Day of September in the Year of our Lord one thousand seven hundred and Eighty seven and of the Independence of the United States of America the Twelfth. IN WITNESS whereof We have hereunto subscribed our Names,

G. WASHINGTON,
Presid't. and deputy from Virginia

Attest
WILLIAM JACKSON,
Secretary

DELAWARE
George Read
Gunning Bedford, Jr.
John Dickinson
Richard Basset
Jacob Broom

MASSACHUSETTS
BAY
Nathaniel Gorham
Rufus King

CONNECTICUT
William Samuel
 Johnson
Roger Sherman

NEW YORK
Alexander Hamilton

NEW JERSEY
William Livingston
David Brearley
William Paterson
Jonathan Dayton

PENNSYLVANIA
Benjamin Franklin
Thomas Mifflin
Robert Morris
George Clymer
Thomas FitzSimons
Jared Ingersoll
James Wilson
Gouverneur Morris

NEW HAMPSHIRE
John Langdon
Nicholas Gilman

MARYLAND
James McHenry
Daniel of St. Thomas
 Jenifer
Daniel Carroll

VIRGINIA
John Blair
James Madison, Jr.

NORTH CAROLINA
William Blount
Richard Dobbs
 Spaight
Hugh Williamson

SOUTH CAROLINA
John Rutledge
Charles Cotesworth
 Pinckney
Charles Pinckney
Pierce Butler

GEORGIA
William Few
Abraham Baldwin

Articles in addition to, and amendment of the Constitution of the United States of America, proposed by Congress and ratified by the Legislatures of the several states, pursuant to the Fifth Article of the original Constitution.

(The first ten amendments were passed by Congress on September 25, 1789, and were ratified on December 15, 1791.)

AMENDMENT I

Congress shall make no law respecting an establishment of religion, or prohibiting the free exercise thereof; or abridging the freedom of speech, or of the press; or the right of the people peaceably to assemble, and to petition the Government for a redress of grievances.

For many Americans, the First Amendment represents the core of what the Bill of Rights stands for: limits on government power to limit or compel religious beliefs, the right to hold political opinions and express them, protection for a free press, the right to assemble peaceably, and the right to petition, through protest or the ballot, the government for a redress of political grievances. But it is also important to remember that the First Amendment, like most of the Bill of Rights, did not apply to state governments until the Supreme Court began to apply their substantive guarantees through the Fourteenth Amendment, a process that did not begin until 1925 in *Gitlow* v. *New York*.

Until then, state and local governments often failed to honor the rights and liberties that Congress, and by extension the national government, was expressly forbidden by the Constitution from withholding. For example, southern states, prior to the Civil War, outlawed pro-abolition literature; numerous states continued to collect taxes on behalf of state-sponsored churches and religious education; newspapers often were forbidden from publishing exposes on industry or political leaders because such speech was considered seditious and thus subject to prior restraint; and public protests on behalf of unpopular causes were often banned by state breach of peace laws.

The Supreme Court has recognized other important rights implied by the enumerated guarantees of the First Amendment. These include the right to association, even when such association might come in the form of clubs or organizations that discriminate on the basis of race, sex, or religion, and the right to personal privacy, which the Supreme Court held in *Griswold* v. *Connecticut* (1965) was based in part on the right of married couples to make decisions about contraception, a decision protected by one's personal religious and political beliefs.

AMENDMENT II

A well regulated Militia, being necessary to the security of a free State, the right of the people to keep and bear Arms, shall not be infringed.

Few issues in American politics generate as much emotional heat as the extent to which Americans have a right to keep and bear arms. Supporters of broad gun ownership rights, such as the National Rifle Association, argue that the Second Amendment protects an almost absolute individual right to own just about any small arm that can be manufactured, whether for reasons of sport or self-defense. Proponents of gun control, such as the Brady Campaign to Prevent Gun Violence, argue that the amendment creates no such individual right, but refers instead to the Framers' belief—now outdated—that citizen militias had the right to form to protect themselves against other states and, if need be, the national government. Under this view, Congress and the states are free to regulate gun ownership and use as they see fit, provided that the national and state governments are within their constitutional orbit of power to do so.

In 1939, the Supreme Court, for the first time, offered an interpretation of the Second Amendment. There, a unanimous Court upheld a federal law requiring the registration of sawed-off shotguns purchased for personal use. The justices also rejected the argument the Second Amendment established an individual right to keep and bear arms; the Court did, however, leave open the question by holding that not all weapons were intended for militia use only. Almost seventy years later, the Court revisited the question in *D.C.* v. *Heller* (2008), holding this time that a local law banning the possession of handguns in the home was unconstitutional. The justices also ruled that another provision of the same law requiring that all "long guns" be kept unloaded and non-functional was unconstitutional.

AMENDMENT III

No Soldier shall, in time of peace be quartered in any house, without the consent of the Owner, nor in time of war, but in a manner to be prescribed by law.

Among the complaints directed at King George III in the Declaration of Independence was the colonial-era practice of quartering large numbers of troops in private homes. The practice of quartering soldiers, along with the forced maintenance of British standing armies in times of peace without the consent of the colonial legislatures, formed a major component of the political grievances directed at the British crown. The Third Amendment was intended to protect individuals and their property from the abuse common to the practice of quartering soldiers.

AMENDMENT IV

The right of the people to be secure in their persons, houses, papers, and effects, against unreasonable searches and seizures, shall not be violated, and no warrants shall issue, but upon probable cause, supported by Oath or affirmation, and particularly describing the place to be searched, and the persons or things to be seized.

Although the Fourth Amendment is often discussed in tandem with the Fifth, Sixth, and Eighth Amendments—the other major provisions of the Bill of Rights outlining the criminal due process guarantees of citizens—it shares a similar undercurrent that motivated the adoption of the Third Amendment: to eliminate the practice of British officers from using the general writ of assistance to enter private homes, conduct searches, and seize personal property. British officers had not been required to offer a specific reason for a search or justify the taking of particular items. In most cases, the writ of assistance was used to confiscate items considered to have violated the strict British customs laws of the colonial era.

The twin pillars of the Fourth Amendment, the probable cause and warrant requirements, are a direct reflection of the disdain the Framers had for the Revolutionary-era practices of the British. But, like the First Amendment, the guarantees of the Fourth Amendment did not apply to state and local law enforcement practices until well after the ratification of the Fourteenth Amendment. Until *Wolf* v. *Colorado* (1949), when the Court ruled that the Fourteenth Amendment made the Fourth Amendment binding on the states, evidence seized in violation of the probable cause or warrant requirements could be used against a criminal suspect. The Court's best-known decision on the Fourth Amendment, *Mapp* v. *Ohio* (1961), which established the exclusionary rule, also marked the high-water point in the rights afforded to criminal suspects challenging an unlawful search. Since the late 1970s, the Court has steadily added exceptions to the Fourth Amendment to permit law enforcement officers to engage in warrantless searches and seizures, provided that such practices meet a threshold of reasonableness in the context of the circumstances under which they are undertaken.

AMENDMENT V

No person shall be held to answer for a capital, or otherwise infamous crime, unless on a presentment or indictment of a Grand Jury, except in cases arising in the land or naval forces, or in the Militia, when in actual service in time of War or public danger; nor shall any person be subject for the same offence to be twice put in jeopardy of life or limb; nor shall be compelled in any criminal case to be a witness against himself, nor be deprived of life, liberty, or property, without due process of law; nor shall private property be taken for public use, without just compensation.

The Fifth Amendment, along with the Sixth Amendment, is the legacy of the ruthless and secretive tactics that figured prominently in the colonial-era system of British justice. By requiring that no person could be held for a "capital, or otherwise infamous" crime except upon indictment by a grand jury, the Fifth Amendment took an important step toward making the criminal indictment process a public function. Along with the public trial and trial by jury guarantees of the Sixth Amendment, the grand jury provision of the Fifth Amendment established that the government would have to make its case against the accused in public. Also, by guaranteeing that no person could be compelled to testify against himself or herself in a criminal proceeding, the Fifth Amendment highlighted the adversarial nature of the American criminal justice system, a feature that is distinct from its British counterpart. "Pleading the Fifth" is permissible in any criminal, civil, administrative, judicial, or investigatory context. *Miranda* v. *Arizona* (1966), one of the most famous rulings of the Supreme Court, established a right to silence that combined the ban against self-incrimination of the Fifth Amendment with the Sixth Amendment's guarantee of the assistance of counsel. The right to silence, unlike the ban against self-incrimination, extends to any aspect of an interrogation.

The Fifth Amendment also forbids double jeopardy, which prohibits the prosecution of a crime against the same person in the same jurisdiction twice, and prevents the government from taking life, liberty, or property without due process of law. This phrase was reproduced in the Fourteenth Amendment, placing an identical set of constraints on the states. The Court has applied all the guarantees of the Fifth Amendment, with the exception of the grand jury provision, to the states through the due process clause of the Fourteenth Amendment. Some constitutional scholars also consider the due process clause of the Fifth Amendment to embrace an equal protection provision when applied to federal cases.

The final provision of the Fifth Amendment prohibits the government from taking private property for public use without just compensation. Litigation on the takings clause, as some scholars refer to this provision, has generally centered on two major questions. The first is what constitutes a taking, either by the government's decision to seize private property or by regulating it to the point where its value is greatly diminished. The second question centers on what the appropriate level of compensation is for owners who have successfully established a taking.

The Supreme Court has taken an expansive definition of what it means to "take" private land for "public use." In *Kelo* v. *New London* (2004), the Court ruled that government could take private property and then sell it to private developers so long as that property was slated for economic development that would benefit the surrounding community. This marked the first time the Court had authorized a taking for something other than public use by governmental authorities.

AMENDMENT VI

In all criminal prosecutions, the accused shall enjoy the right to a speedy and public trial, by an impartial jury of the State and district wherein the crime shall have been committed, which district shall have been previously ascertained by law, and to be informed of the nature and cause of the accusation; to be confronted with the witnesses against him; to have compulsory process for obtaining witnesses in his favor, and to have the assistance of counsel for his defence.

The centerpiece of the constitutional guarantees afforded to individuals facing criminal prosecution, the Sixth Amendment sets out eight specific rights, more than any other provision of the Bill of Rights. As with the Fifth Amendment, the core features of the Sixth Amendment build upon the unfortunate legacy of the repressive practices of colonial-era Britain. The very first provision of the Sixth Amendment mandates that individuals subject to criminal prosecution receive "a speedy and public trial"; it then requires that all such trials take place in public, with the defendant informed of the cause and nature of the accusation against him or her. The common theme underlying these sections of the Sixth Amendment, as well as those requiring witnesses for the prosecution to testify in public, allowing the defendant to produce witnesses on his or her own behalf, and securing the assistance of counsel, is that any citizen threatened with the deprivation of liberty is entitled to have the case made against him or her in public. The Fifth Amendment also required the government to produce evidence that did not rely on confessions and self-incrimination. And, it required that any such evidence must be acquired lawfully and

with the knowledge of a public magistrate. The Sixth Amendment establishes, in principle, the American criminal justice system as one that is open and public.

Since the vast majority of criminal prosecutions in the United States are undertaken by state and local authorities, the parchment promises of the Sixth Amendment did not extend to most Americans until the Supreme Court began incorporating the guarantees of the Bill of Rights to the states through the Fourteenth Amendment. Perhaps the best-known case involving the Sixth Amendment is *Gideon* v. *Wainwright* (1963), which held that all persons accused of a serious crime are entitled to an attorney, even if they cannot afford one, a rule that was soon extended to cover misdemeanors as well. Three years later, the Supreme Court fused the right to counsel rule established in *Gideon* with the Fifth Amendment ban against self-incrimination to create the principles animating *Miranda* v. *Arizona*. For a long time, the Court had never interpreted the Fifth and Sixth Amendments to mean that individuals had rights to criminal due process guarantees if they did not know about them or could not afford them. Decisions such as *Gideon* and *Miranda* offered a clear departure from this position.

The speedy and public trial clauses only require that criminal trials take place in public within a reasonable amount of time after the period of indictment, and that juries in such cases are unbiased. Americans also often cite the Sixth Amendment as entitling them to a trial by a "jury of one's peers." This is true to the extent individuals are entitled to a trial in the jurisdiction where the crime is alleged to have been committed. It does not mean, however, that they are entitled to a trial by persons of a similar age or background, for example.

AMENDMENT VII

In Suits at common law, where the value in controversy shall exceed twenty dollars, the right of trial by jury shall be preserved, and no fact tried by a jury, shall be otherwise re-examined in any Court of the United States, than according to the rules of the common law.

One feature of the British courts that the Framers sought to preserve in the American civil law system was the distinction between courts of common law and courts of equity. Common law courts heard cases involving strict legal rules, while equity courts based their decisions on principles of fairness and totality of circumstances. Common law courts featured juries that were authorized to return verdicts entitling plaintiffs to financial compensation for losses incurred, whereas equity courts relied upon judges to make determinations about appropriate relief for successful parties. Relief in equity courts did not consist of monetary awards, but injunctions, cease-and-desist orders, and so on. The Seventh Amendment carried over this British feature into the Constitution.

In 1938, Congress amended the Federal Rules of Civil Procedure to combine the function of civil common law and equity courts. In cases involving both legal and equitable claims, a federal judge must first decide the issue of law before moving to the equitable relief, or remedy, component of the trial. Judges are permitted to instruct juries on matters of law and fact, and may emphasize certain facts or legal issues to the jury in their instructions to the jury. But, the jury alone decides guilt or innocence. In some extraordinary cases, a judge may overturn the verdict of a jury. This happens only when a judge believes the jury has disregarded completely the facts and evidence before it in reaching a verdict.

Congress has also changed the $20 threshold for the right to a trial by jury. The amount is now $75,000. Finally, the Seventh Amendment has never been incorporated to the states through the Fourteenth Amendment.

AMENDMENT VIII

Excessive bail shall not be required, nor excessive fines imposed, nor cruel and unusual punishments inflicted.

For an amendment of so few words, the Eighth Amendment has generated an enormous volume of commentary and litigation since its ratification. This should not be surprising, as the three major provisions of the amendment deal with some of the most sensitive and emotionally charged issues involving the rights of criminal defendants.

The origin of the excessive bail clause stems from the reforms to the British system instituted by the 1689 English Bill of Rights. Having had limited success in preventing law enforcement officials from detaining suspects by imposing outrageous bail requirements, Britain amended previous laws to say that "excessive bail ought not to be required." Much like the British model, the Eighth Amendment does not state what an "excessive bail" is or the particular criminal offense that warrants a high bail amount. The Supreme Court has offered two fundamental rules on the excessive bail clause. First, a judge has the discretion to decide if a criminal offense is sufficiently serious to justify high bail. Second, a judge has the power, under *U.S.* v. *Salerno* (1987), to deny a criminal defendant bail as a "preventative measure." In both such cases, a judge's action must be considered proportionate to the nature of the criminal offense for which an individual stands accused.

Like the excessive bail clause, the excessive fines clause is rooted in the English Bill of Rights. The clause applies only to criminal proceedings, not civil litigation. For example, a tobacco company cannot appeal what it believes is an excessive jury award under this clause. An indigent criminal defendant, however, can challenge a fine levied in connection with a criminal conviction.

The most controversial section of the Eighth Amendment is the clause forbidding cruel and unusual punishments. The absence of such a guarantee from the Constitution was a major impetus for the adoption of the Bill of Rights. While most historians agree that the Framers wanted to prohibit barbaric forms of punishment, including torture, as well as arbitrary and disproportionate penalties, there is little consensus on what specific punishments met this definition. By the late 1800s, the Supreme Court had ruled that such punishments as public burning, disembowelment, and drawing and quartering crossed the Eighth Amendment barrier. In *Weems* v. *U.S.* (1910), the Court went the additional of step of concluding that any punishment considered "excessive" would violate the cruel and unusual punishment clause. And, in *Solem* v. *Helm* (1983), the Court developed a "proportionality" standard that required punishments, even simple incarceration, to bear a rational relationship to the offense.

The Court has never ruled, however, that the death penalty per se violates the Eighth Amendment. It has developed certain rules and exceptions governing the application of the death penalty, such as requiring a criminal defendant actually to have killed, or attempted to have killed, a victim. It has also ruled that the mentally retarded, as a class, are exempt from the death penalty. But it has also issued highly controversial decisions concluding, for example, that neither racial disparities in the application of capital punishment nor juvenile status at the time the offense was committed violate the Eighth Amendment. Except for a four-year ban on the practice between 1972 and 1976, the death penalty has always been an available punishment in the American criminal justice system.

AMENDMENT IX

The enumeration in the Constitution, of certain rights, shall not be construed to deny or disparage others retained by the people.

A major point of contention between the Federalists and Anti-Federalists was the need for a bill of rights. In *Federalist No. 84*, Alexander Hamilton argued that a bill of rights was unnecessary, as there was no need to place limits on the power of government to do things that it was not authorized by the Constitution to do. Hamilton also argued that it would be impossible to list all the rights "retained by the people." Protecting some rights but not others would suggest that Americans had surrendered certain rights to their government when, in Hamilton's view, the Constitution did nothing of the sort.

Given his well-deserved reputation for unbridled national power, Hamilton's views have often been dismissed as a cynical ploy to sidestep any meaningful discussion of the Bill of Rights and speed along the ratification process. But, James Madison, along with Thomas Jefferson, held a much deeper belief in the need for a bill of rights. Madison also believed that the enumeration of certain rights and liberties in the Constitution should not be understood to deny others that exist as a condition of citizenship in a free society. Madison, the primary author of the Bill of Rights, included the Ninth Amendment to underscore this belief.

The Supreme Court has never offered a clear and definitive interpretation of the Ninth Amendment, primarily because it has been wary of giving such general language any substantive definition. The amendment has been cited in such decisions as *Griswold* v. *Connecticut* (1965) and *Richmond Newspapers* v. *Virginia* (1980) along with other constitutional amendments to bolster the case on behalf of an asserted constitutional right. The difficulty in constructing a specific meaning for the Ninth Amendment can be illustrated by the fact that both supporters and opponents of legal abortion have cited it to defend the feasibility of their respective positions.

AMENDMENT X

The powers not delegated to the United States by the Constitution, nor prohibited by it to the States, are reserved to the States respectively, or to the people.

The Tenth Amendment generated little controversy during the ratification process over the Bill of Rights. As the Supreme Court later ruled in *U.S.* v. *Darby Lumber Co.* (1941), the Tenth Amendment states a truism about the relationship between the boundaries of national and state power—that the states retain those powers not specifically set out in the Constitution as belonging to the national government. There is little in the history in the debate over the Tenth Amendment to suggest that its language is anything other than declaratory. Indeed, the refusal of the 1st Congress to insert the word "expressly" before "delegated" strongly suggests that James Madison, who offered the most thorough explanation of the amendment during the floor debates, intended to leave room for this relationship to evolve as future events made necessary.

The earliest political and constitutional developments involving the Tenth Amendment tilted the balance of power firmly in favor of national power. Alexander Hamilton's vision for a national bank to consolidate the nation's currency and trading position was realized in *McCullough* v. *Maryland* (1819), in which the Court held that Article I granted Congress broad power to make all laws "necessary and proper" to the exercise of its legislative power. By no means, however, did *McCullough* settle the argument over the power reserved to the states. Led by Chief Justice Roger B. Taney, the Court handed down several decisions in the three decades leading up to the Civil War that offered substantial protection to the southern states on the matters closest to their hearts: slavery and economic sovereignty. From the period after the Civil War until the New Deal, the Court continued to shield states from congressional legislation designed to regulate the economy and promote social and political reform. After the constitutional revolution of 1937, when the Court threw its support behind the New Deal, Congress received a blank constitutional check to engage in the regulatory action that featured an unprecedented level of federal intervention in economic and social matters once the purview of the states, one that would last almost sixty years.

Beginning in *New York* v. *U.S.* (1992), however, the Court, in striking down a key provision of a federal environmental law, began to revisit the New Deal assumptions that underlay its modern interpretation of the Tenth Amendment. A few years later, in *U.S.* v. *Lopez* (1995), it invalidated a federal gun control law on the ground that Congress lacked authority under the commerce clause to regulate gun possession. And, in *U.S.* v. *Printz* (1997), the Tenth Amendment explicitly was cited to strike down an important section of the Brady Bill, a congressional law that required states to conduct background checks on prospective gun buyers. Although the Court has not returned to the dual federalism posture on the Tenth Amendment that it built from the years between the Taney Court and the triumph of the New Deal, these decisions make clear that the constitutional status of the states as actors in the federal system has been dramatically strengthened.

AMENDMENT XI
(Ratified on February 7, 1795)

The Judicial power of the United States shall not be construed to extend to any suit in law or equity, commenced or prosecuted against one of the United States by Citizens of another State, or by Citizens or Subjects of any Foreign State.

The Eleventh Amendment was prompted by one of the earliest notable decisions of the Supreme Court, *Chisolm* v. *Georgia* (1793). In *Chisolm*, the Court held that Article III and the enforcement provision of the Judiciary Act of 1789 permitted a citizen of one state to bring suit against another state in federal court. Almost immediately after *Chisolm*, the Eleventh Amendment was introduced and promptly ratified, as the states saw this decision as a threat to their sovereignty under the new Constitution. The amendment was passed in less than a year, which, by the standards of the era, was remarkably fast.

The Eleventh Amendment nullified the result in *Chisolm* but did not completely bar a citizen from bringing suit against a state in federal court. Citizens may bring lawsuits against state officials in federal court if they can satisfy the requirement that their rights under federal constitutional or statutory law have been violated. The Eleventh Amendment has not been extensively litigated in modern times, but the extent to which states are immune under federal law from citizen lawsuits has reemerged as an important constitutional question in recent years. For example, the Court has said in several cases that the doctrine of sovereign immunity prevents citizens from suing state agencies under the Americans with Disabilities Act of 1990. But, as recently as 2003, the Court, in *Nevada* v. *Hibbs*, ruled that the Family and Medical Leave Act of 1993 did not immunize state government agencies against lawsuits brought by former state employees. States are also free to waive their immunity and consent to a lawsuit.

AMENDMENT XII
(Ratified on June 15, 1804)

The Electors shall meet in their respective states, and vote by ballot for President and Vice-President, one of whom, at least, shall not be an inhabitant of the same state with themselves; they shall name in their ballots the person voted for as President, and in distinct ballots the person voted for as Vice-President, and they shall make distinct lists of all persons voted for as President, and of all persons voted for as Vice-President, and of the number of votes for each, which lists they shall sign and certify, and transmit sealed to the seat of the government of the United States, directed to the President of the Senate;—The President of the Senate shall, in the presence of the Senate and House of Representatives, open all the certificates and the votes shall then be counted;—The person having the greatest number of votes for President, shall be the President, if such number be a majority of the whole number of Electors appointed;

and if no person have such majority; then from the persons having the highest numbers not exceeding three on the list of those voted for as President, the House of Representatives shall choose immediately, by ballot, the President. But in choosing the President, the votes shall be taken by states, the representation from each state having one vote; a quorum for this purpose shall consist of a member or members from two-thirds of the states, and a majority of all the states shall be necessary to a choice. And if the House of Representatives shall not choose a President whenever the right of choice shall devolve upon them, before the fourth day of March next following, then the Vice-President shall act as President, as in the case of the death or other constitutional disability of the President.—The person having the greatest number of votes as Vice-President, shall be the Vice-President, if such number be a majority of the whole number of Electors appointed, and if no person have a majority, then from the two highest numbers on the list, the Senate shall choose the Vice-President; a quorum for the purpose shall consist of two-thirds of the whole number of Senators, and a majority of the whole number shall be necessary to a choice. But no person constitutionally ineligible to the office of President shall be eligible to that of Vice-President of the United States.

The Twelfth Amendment was added to the Constitution after the 1800 presidential election was thrown into the House of Representatives. Thomas Jefferson and Aaron Burr, running on the Democratic-Republican Party ticket, each received seventy-three electoral votes for president, even though everyone knew that Jefferson was the presidential candidate and Burr the vice presidential candidate. This was possible because Article II, section 1, did not require electors to vote for president and vice president separately. The Twelfth Amendment remedied this deficiency by requiring electors to cast their votes for president and vice president separately.

Whether it intended to or not, the Twelfth Amendment took a major step toward institutionalizing the party system in the United States. The 1796 election yielded a president and vice president from different parties, a clear indication that partisan differences were emerging in a distinct form. The 1800 election simply highlighted the problem further. By requiring electors to make their presidential and vice presidential choices separately, the Twelfth Amendment conceded that a party system in American politics had indeed evolved, an inevitable but nonetheless disappointing development to the architects of the original constitutional vision.

AMENDMENT XIII
(Ratified on December 6, 1865)

Section 1.

Neither slavery nor involuntary servitude, except as a punishment for crime whereof the party shall have been duly convicted, shall exist within the United States, or any place subject to their jurisdiction.

Section 2.

Congress shall have power to enforce this article by appropriate legislation.

The Thirteenth, Fourteenth, and Fifteenth Amendments are known collectively as the Civil War Amendments.

In anticipation of a Union victory, the Thirteenth Amendment was passed by Congress and sent to the states for ratification before the end of the Civil War. The amendment not only formally abolished slavery and involuntary servitude; it also served as the constitutional foundation for the nation's first major civil rights legislation, the Civil Rights Act of 1866. This law extended numerous rights to African Americans previously held in servitude as well as those having "free" status during the Civil War, including the right to purchase, rent, and sell personal property, to bring suit in federal court, to enter into contracts, and to receive the full and equal benefit of all laws "enjoyed by white citizens." The Thirteenth Amendment overturned the pre–Civil War decision of the Supreme Court, *Dred Scott* v. *Sandford* (1857), which held that slaves were not people entitled to constitutional rights, but property subject to the civil law binding them to their masters.

In modern times, the Court has ruled that the Thirteenth Amendment prohibits any action that recognizes a "badge" or "condition" of slavery, such as housing discrimination and certain forms of employment discrimination. The Department of Justice also has used the Thirteenth Amendment to file lawsuits against manufacturing sweatshops and other criminal enterprises in which persons are forced to work without compensation.

AMENDMENT XIV
(Ratified on July 9, 1868)

Section 1.

All persons born or naturalized in the United States, and subject to the jurisdiction thereof, are citizens of the United States and of the State wherein they reside. No State shall make or enforce any law which shall abridge the privileges or immunities of citizens of the United States; nor shall any State deprive any person of life, liberty, or property, without due process of law; nor deny to any person within its jurisdiction the equal protection of the laws.

Many constitutional scholars believe the Fourteenth Amendment is the most important addition to the Constitution since the Bill of Rights was ratified in 1791. In addition to serving as a cornerstone of Reconstruction policy, section 1 eliminated the distinction between the rights and liberties of Americans as citizens of their respective states and those to which they were entitled under the Bill of Rights as citizens of the United States. The Republican leadership that drafted and steered the Fourteenth Amendment to passage left no doubt that the three major provisions of section 1, which placed express limits on state power to abridge rights and liberties protected as a condition of national citizenship, were intended to make the Bill of Rights binding upon the states, thus overruling *Barron* v. *Baltimore* (1833). Although the Supreme Court has never endorsed this view, the selective incorporation of the Bill of Rights to the states during the twentieth century through the Fourteenth Amendment ultimately made the Reconstruction-era vision of the Republicans a reality. The former Confederate states were required to ratify the Fourteenth Amendment to qualify for readmission into the Union.

Section 2.

Representatives shall be apportioned among the several States according to their respective numbers, counting the whole number of persons in each State, excluding Indians not taxed. But when the right to vote at any election for the choice of electors for President and Vice President of the United States, Representatives in Congress, the Executive and Judicial officers of a State, or the members of the Legislature thereof, is denied to any of the male inhabitants of such State, being twenty-one years of age, and citizens of the United States, or in any way abridged, except for participation in rebellion, or other crime, the basis of representation therein shall be reduced in the proportion which the number of such male citizens shall bear to the whole number of male citizens twenty-one years of age in such State.

Section 2 established two major changes to the Constitution. First, by stating that representatives from each state would be apportioned based on the number of "whole" persons in each state, section 2 modified the Three-Fifths Compromise of Article 1, section 2, clause 3, of the original Constitution. Note, however, that section 2 still called for the exclusion of Indians "not taxed" from the apportionment criteria. Second, section 2, for

the first time anywhere in the Constitution, mentions that only "male" inhabitants of the states age twenty-one or older would be counted toward representation in the House of Representatives and eligible to vote.

The Military Reconstruction Act of 1867 had strengthened Republican power in the southern states by stripping former Confederates of the right to vote, a law that, in conjunction with the gradual addition of blacks to the voting rolls, made enactment of the Fourteenth Amendment possible. Section 2 temporarily solidified the Republican presence in the South by eliminating from apportionment counts any person that participated in the rebellion against the Union.

Section 3.

No person shall be a Senator or Representative in Congress, or elector of President and Vice President, or hold any office, civil or military, under the United States, or under any State, who, having previously taken an oath, as a member of Congress, or as an officer of the United States, or as a member of any State legislature, or as an executive or judicial officer of any State, to support the Constitution of the United States, shall have engaged in insurrection or rebellion against the same, or given aid or comfort to the enemies thereof. But Congress may by a vote of two-thirds of each House, remove such disability.

Section 3 also reflected the power of the Reconstruction-era Republicans over the South. By eliminating the eligibility of former Confederates for public office or to serve as an elector for president or vice president, the Republicans strengthened their presence in Congress and throughout national politics. This measure also allowed African Americans to run for and hold office in the South, which they were doing by 1870, the same year the Fifteenth Amendment was ratified.

In December 1868, five months after the ratification of the Fourteenth Amendment, President Andrew Johnson declared universal amnesty for all former Confederates. This measure had the effect of returning white politicians and by extension the Democratic Party to power in the South. Republican concern over this development was a major force behind the adoption of the Fifteenth Amendment, which was viewed as an instrument to protect Republican political power by securing black enfranchisement. However, Republican president Ulysses S. Grant, who defeated Johnson in 1868, pardoned all but a few hundred remaining Confederate sympathizers by signing the Amnesty Act of 1872. Decisions such as these began the gradual undoing of Republican commitment to black civil rights in the South.

Section 4.

The validity of the public debt of the United States, authorized by law, including debts incurred for payment of pensions and bounties for services in suppressing insurrection or rebellion, shall not be questioned. But neither the United States nor any State shall assume or pay any debt or obligation incurred in aid of insurrection or rebellion against the United States, or any claim for the loss or emancipation of any slave, but all such debts, obligations and claims shall be held illegal and void.

Section 4 repudiated the South's desire to have Congress forgive the Confederacy's war debts. It also rejected any claim that former slaveholders had to be compensated for the loss of their slaves.

Section 5.

The Congress shall have power to enforce, by appropriate legislation, the provisions of this article.

By giving Congress the power to enforce the provisions of the Fourteenth Amendment, section 5 reiterated the post–Civil War emphasis on national citizenship and the limit on state power to deny individuals their constitutional rights. Section 5 also extended congressional law-making power beyond those areas outlined in Article I. But, the Court has taken a mixed view of the scope of congressional power to enforce the Fourteenth Amendment. In *Katzenbach* v. *Morgan* (1966), for example, the Supreme Court offered a broad ruling on the section 5 power of Congress. It held that Congress could enact laws establishing rights beyond what the Court said the Constitution required, as long as such laws were designed to establish a remedial constitutional right or protect citizens from a potential constitutional violation. In other cases, such as *City of Boerne* v. *Flores* (1997) and *U.S.* v. *Morrison* (2000), the Court ruled that Congress may not intrude upon the authority of the judicial branch to define the meaning of the Constitution or intrude on the power of the states to make laws within their own domain.

AMENDMENT XV
(Ratified on February 3, 1870)

Section 1.

The right of citizens of the United States to vote shall not be denied or abridged by the United States or by any State on account of race, color, or previous condition of servitude.

Section 2.

The Congress shall have power to enforce this article by appropriate legislation.

The Fifteenth Amendment was the most controversial of the Civil War Amendments, both for what it did and did not do. Although the adoption of the Thirteenth and Fourteenth Amendments made clear that blacks could not be returned to their pre–Civil War slavery, enthusiasm for a constitutional right of black suffrage, even among the northern states, was another matter. On the one hand, the extension of voting rights to blacks was the most dramatic outcome of the Civil War. The former Confederate states had to ratify the Fifteenth Amendment as a condition for readmission into the Union. On the other hand, the rejection of proposed language forbidding discrimination on the basis of property ownership, education, or religious belief gave states the power to regulate the vote as they wished. And, with the collapse of Reconstruction after the 1876 election, southern states implemented laws created by this opening with full force, successfully crippling black voter registration for generations to come in the region where most African Americans lived. Full enfranchisement for African Americans would not arrive until the passage of the Voting Rights Act of 1965, almost one hundred years after the ratification of the Fifteenth Amendment.

The Fifteenth Amendment also divided woman's rights organizations that had campaigned on behalf of abolition and black enfranchisement. Feminists such as Elizabeth Cady Stanton and Susan B. Anthony were furious over the exclusion of women from the Fifteenth Amendment and opposed its ratification, while others, such as Lucy Stone, were willing to support black voting rights at the expense of woman suffrage, leaving that battle for another day. The Supreme Court sided with those who opposed female enfranchisement, ruling in *Minor* v. *Happersett* (1875) that the Fourteenth Amendment did not recognize among the privileges and immunities of American citizenship a constitutional right to vote.

AMENDMENT XVI
(Ratified on February 3, 1913)

The Congress shall have power to lay and collect taxes on incomes, from whatever source derived, without apportionment among the several States, and without regard to any census or enumeration.

The Sixteenth Amendment was a response to the Supreme Court's sharply divided ruling in *Pollock* v. *Farmers' Loan & Trust Co.* (1895), which struck down the Income Tax Act of 1894 as unconstitutional. The

Court, by a 5–4 margin, held that the law violated Article I, section 9, which prevented Congress from enacting a direct tax (on individuals) unless in proportion to the U.S. Census. In some ways, this was a curious holding, since the Court had permitted Congress to enact a direct tax on individuals during the Civil War. Between the *Pollock* decision and the enactment of the Sixteenth Amendment, the Court approved of taxes levied on corporations, as such taxes were not really taxes but "excises" levied on "incidents of ownership."

Anti-tax groups have claimed the Sixteenth Amendment was never properly ratified and is thus unconstitutional. The federal courts have rejected that view and have sanctioned and fined individuals who have brought such frivolous challenges to court.

AMENDMENT XVII
(Ratified on April 8, 1913)

The Senate of the United States shall be composed of two Senators from each State, elected by the people thereof, for six years; and each Senator shall have one vote. The electors in each State shall have the qualifications requisite for electors of the most numerous branch of the State legislatures.

When vacancies happen in the representation of any State in the Senate, the executive authority of such State shall issue writs of election to fill such vacancies: Provided, That the legislature of any State may empower the executive thereof to make temporary appointments until the people fill the vacancies by election as the legislature may direct.

This amendment shall not be so construed as to affect the election or term of any Senator chosen before it becomes valid as part of the Constitution.

The Seventeenth Amendment repealed the language in Article I, section 3, of the original Constitution, which called for the election of U.S. senators by state legislatures. This method had its roots in the selection of delegates to the Constitutional Convention, who were chosen by the state legislatures. It was also the preferred method of the Framers, who believed that having state legislatures elect senators would strengthen the relationship between the states and the national government, and also contribute to the stability of Congress by removing popular electoral pressure from the upper chamber.

Dissatisfaction set in with this method during the period leading up to the Civil War, especially by the 1850s. Indiana, for example, deeply divided between Union supporters in the northern part of the state and

Confederate sympathizers in the southern part, could not agree on the selection of senators and was without representation for two years. After the Civil War, numerous Senate elections were tainted by corruption, and many more resulted in ties that prevented seating senators in a timely fashion. In 1899, Delaware's election was so mired in controversy that it did not have representation in the Senate for four years.

The ratification of the Seventeenth Amendment was the result of almost two decades of persistent efforts at reform. By 1912, twenty-nine states had changed their election laws to require the popular election of senators. In the years before that, constitutional amendments were introduced on a regular basis calling for the popular election of senators. Although many powerful legislators entrenched in the Senate resisted such change, the tide of reform, now aided by journalists and scholars sympathetic to the cause, proved too powerful to withstand. One year after the Seventeenth Amendment was sent to the states for ratification, all members of the Senate were elected by the popular vote.

AMENDMENT XVIII
(Ratified on January 16, 1919)

Section 1.

After one year from the ratification of this article the manufacture, sale, or transportation of intoxicating liquors within, the importation thereof into, or the exportation thereof from the United States and all territory subject to the jurisdiction thereof for beverage purposes is hereby prohibited.

Section 2.

The Congress and the several States shall have concurrent power to enforce this article by appropriate legislation.

Section 3.

This article shall be inoperative unless it shall have been ratified as an amendment to the Constitution by the legislatures of the several States, as provided in the Constitution, within seven years from the date of the submission hereof to the States by the Congress.

The Eighteenth Amendment was the end result of a crusade against the consumption of alcoholic beverages than began during the early nineteenth century. A combination of Christian organizations emboldened by the second Great Awakening and women's groups, who believed alcohol contributed greatly to domestic violence and poverty, campaigned to abolish the manufacture, sale, and use of alcoholic beverages in the United States. Their campaign was moderately successful in the pre–Civil War era. By 1855, thirteen states had banned the sale of "intoxicating" beverages. By the end of the Civil War, however, ten states had repealed their prohibition laws.

Another wave of anti-alcohol campaigning soon emerged, however, as the Women's Christian Temperance Union, founded in 1874 and 250,000 strong by 1911, and the Anti-Saloon League, founded in 1913, pressed the case for Prohibition. Among the arguments offered by supporters of Prohibition were that the cereal grains used in the manufacture of beer and liquor diverted valuable resources from food supplies and that the malaise of drunkenness sapped the strength of manufacturing production at home and the conduct of America's soldiers in World War I. Underneath the formal case for Prohibition was a considerable anti-immigrant sentiment, as many Prohibitionists considered the waves of Italian, Irish, Poles, and German immigrants unduly dependent on alcohol.

In 1919, Congress passed the Eighteenth Amendment over President Woodrow Wilson's veto. That same year, Congress passed the Volstead Act, which implemented Prohibition and authorized law enforcement to target illegal shipments of alcohol into the United States (mostly from Canada, which, ironically, also mandated Prohibition in most of its provinces during this time) as well as alcoholic beverages illegally manufactured in the United States. Evidence remains inconclusive over just how successful the Eighteenth Amendment was in reducing alcohol consumption in the United States. More certain was the billion-dollar windfall that Prohibition created for organized crime, as well as small-time smugglers and bootleggers.

AMENDMENT XIX
(Ratified on August 18, 1920)

The right of citizens of the United States to vote shall not be denied or abridged by the United States or by any State on account of sex.

Congress shall have power to enforce this article by appropriate legislation.

The two major woman's rights organizations of the nineteenth century most active in the battle for female enfranchisement were the National Woman Suffrage Association (NWSA) and the American Woman Suffrage Association (AWSA). NWSA campaigned for a constitutional amendment modeled on the Fifteenth Amendment, which had secured African American voting rights, while AWSA preferred to pursue women's voting rights through state-level legislative initiatives. In 1890, the two organizations combined to form the National American Woman Suffrage Association. By 1919, the NAWSA, the newer, more radical National Woman's Party, and other activists had secured congressional passage of the Nineteenth Amendment by a broad margin. It was ratified by the states just over a year later.

The Nineteenth Amendment, however, did not free black women from the voting restrictions that southern states placed in the way of African Americans. They and other minorities were not protected from such restrictions until the passage of the Voting Rights Act of 1965.

AMENDMENT XX
(Ratified on February 6, 1933)

Section 1.

The terms of the President and Vice President shall end at noon on the 20th day of January, and the terms of Senators and Representatives at noon on the 3d day of January, of the years in which such terms would have ended if this article had not been ratified; and the terms of their successors shall then begin.

Section 2.

The Congress shall assemble at least once in every year, and such meeting shall begin at noon on the 3d day of January, unless they shall by law appoint a different day.

Section 3.

If, at the time fixed for the beginning of the term of the President, the President elect shall have died, the Vice President elect shall become President. If a President shall not have been chosen before the time fixed for the beginning of his term, or if the President elect shall have failed to qualify, then the Vice President elect shall act as President until a President shall have qualified; and the Congress may by law provide for the case wherein neither a President elect nor a Vice President elect shall have qualified, declaring who shall then act as President, or the manner in which one who is to act shall be selected, and such person shall act accordingly until a President or Vice President shall have qualified.

Section 4.

The Congress may by law provide for the case of the death of any of the persons from whom the House of Representatives may choose a President whenever the rights of choice shall have devolved upon them, and for the case of the death of any of the persons from whom the Senate may choose a Vice President whenever the right of choice shall have devolved upon them.

Section 5.

Sections 1 and 2 shall take effect on the 15th day of October following the ratification of this article.

Section 6.

This article shall be inoperative unless it shall have been ratified as an amendment to the Constitution by the legislatures of three-fourths of the several States within seven years from the date of its submission.

The Twentieth Amendment is often called the lame duck amendment because its fundamental purpose was to shorten the time between the November elections, particularly in a presidential election year, and the starting date of the new presidential term and the commencement of the new congressional session. The amendment modified section 1 of the Twelfth Amendment by moving the beginning of the annual legislative session from March 4 to January 3. This change meant that the newly elected Congress would decide any presidential election thrown into the House of Representatives. It also eliminated the possibility that the nation would have to endure two additional months without a chief executive.

The Twentieth Amendment also modified Article I of the Constitution by placing a fixed time—noon—to begin the congressional session.

AMENDMENT XXI
(Ratified on December 5, 1933)

Section 1.

The eighteenth article of amendment to the Constitution of the United States is hereby repealed.

Section 2.

The transportation or importation into any State, Territory, or possession of the United States for delivery or use therein of intoxicating liquors, in violation of the laws thereof, is hereby prohibited.

Section 3.

This article shall be inoperative unless it shall have been ratified as an amendment to the Constitution by conventions in the several States, as provided in the Constitution, within seven years from the date of the submission hereof to the States by the Congress.

The Twenty-First Amendment repealed the Eighteenth Amendment, which was the first and last time that a constitutional amendment has been repealed. The Twenty-First Amendment is also the only amendment to the Constitution approved by state ratifying conventions rather than a popular vote.

By the late 1920s, Americans had tired of Prohibition, and the arrival of the Great Depression in 1929 did nothing to lift their spirits. Few public officials, well aware of the extensive criminal enterprises that had grown up around Prohibition and had made a mockery of the practice, attempted to defend Prohibition as a success. Indeed, Franklin D. Roosevelt, in his initial bid for the presidency in 1932, made the repeal of Prohibition a campaign promise. In January 1933, Congress amended the Volstead Act to permit the sale of alcoholic beverages with an alcohol content of 3.2 percent. The ratification of the Twenty-First Amendment in December returned absolute control of the regulation of alcohol to the states. States are now free to regulate alcohol as they see fit. They may, for example, limit the quantity and type of alcohol sold to consumers, or ban alcohol sales completely. The Supreme Court, in *South Carolina* v. *Dole* (1984), ruled that Congress may require the states to set a certain age for the consumption of alcohol in return for participation in a federal program without violating the Twenty-First Amendment.

AMENDMENT XXII
(Ratified on February 27, 1951)

Section 1.

No person shall be elected to the office of the President more than twice, and no person who has held the office of President, or acted as President, for more than two years of a term to which some other person was elected President shall be elected to the office of the President more than once. But this Article shall not apply to any person holding the office of President when this Article was proposed by the Congress, and shall not prevent any person who may be holding the office of President, or acting as President, during the term within which this Article becomes operative from holding the office of President or acting as President during the remainder of such term.

Section 2.

This article shall be inoperative unless it shall have been ratified as an amendment to the Constitution by the legislatures of three-fourths of the several States within seven years from the date of its submission to the States by the Congress.

Thomas Jefferson, who served as the third president of the United States, was the first person of public stature to suggest a constitutional provision limiting presidential terms. "If some termination to the services of the chief Magistrate be not fixed by the Constitution," said Jefferson, "or supplied by practice, his office, nominally four years, will in fact become for life." Until Ulysses S. Grant's unsuccessful attempt to secure his party's nomination to a third term, no other president attempted to extend the two-term limit that had operated in principle. Theodore Roosevelt, having ascended to the presidency after the assassination of William McKinley in 1901, was elected to his second term in 1904. He then sat out a term, and then ran against Woodrow Wilson in the 1912 election and lost.

The first president to serve more than two terms was Franklin D. Roosevelt, and it was his success that inspired the enactment of the Twenty-Second Amendment. In 1946, Republicans took control of Congress for the first time in sixteen years and were determined to guard against such future Democratic dynasties. A year later, Congress, in one of the most party-line votes in the history of the amending process, approved the Twenty-Second Amendment. Every Republican member of the House and Senate who voted on the amendment voted for it. The remaining votes came almost exclusively from southern Democrats, whose relationship with Roosevelt was never more than a marriage of convenience. Ironically, some Republicans began to call for the repeal of the Twenty-Second Amendment toward the end of popular Republican Dwight D. Eisenhower's second term in 1956. A similar movement emerged in the late 1980s toward the end of Republican Ronald Reagan's second term. The American public at large, however, has shown little enthusiasm for repealing the Twenty-Second Amendment.

AMENDMENT XXIII
(Ratified on March 29, 1961)

Section 1.

The District constituting the seat of Government of the United States shall appoint in such manner as the Congress may direct:

A number of electors of President and Vice President equal to the whole number of Senators and Representatives in Congress to which the District would be entitled if it were a State, but in no event more than the least populous State; they shall be in addition to those appointed by the States, but they shall be considered, for the purposes of the election of President and Vice President, to be electors appointed by a State; and they shall meet in the District and perform such duties as provided by the twelfth article of amendment.

Section 2.

The Congress shall have power to enforce this article by appropriate legislation.

Article II, section 2, of the Constitution limits participation in presidential elections to citizens who reside in the states. The Twenty-Third Amendment amended this provision to include residents of the District of Columbia. Since the District was envisioned as the seat of the national government with a transient population, the Constitution afforded no right of representation to its residents in Congress. By the time the Twenty-Third Amendment was ratified, the District had a greater population than twelve states.

In 1978, Congress introduced a constitutional amendment to give the District of Columbia representation in the House and the Senate. By 1985, the ratification period for the amendment expired without the necessary three-fourths approval from the states.

AMENDMENT XXIV
(Ratified on January 23, 1964)

Section 1.

The right of citizens of the United States to vote in any primary or other election for President or Vice President, for electors for President or Vice President, or for Senator or Representative in Congress, shall not be denied or abridged by the United States or any State by reason of failure to pay any poll tax or other tax.

Section 2.

The Congress shall have power to enforce this article by appropriate legislation.

The Twenty-Fourth Amendment continued the work of the Fifteenth Amendment. By abolishing the poll tax, the amendment eliminated one of the most popular tools used by voting registrars to prevent most African Americans and other minorities from taking part in the electoral process. Property ownership and literacy tests as conditions of the franchise extended back to the colonial era and were not particular to any region of the United States. But, the poll tax was a southern invention, coming after the enactment of the Fifteenth Amendment. By the fall of Reconstruction in 1877, eleven southern states had enacted poll tax laws. The poll tax was disproportionately enforced against poor African American voters and, in some cases, poor whites.

Congress had begun to debate a constitutional amendment to abolish the poll tax as far back as 1939, but it took the momentum of the civil rights movement to move this process forward. Shortly after the ratification of the Twenty-Fourth Amendment, Congress enacted the Civil Rights Act of 1964, the most sweeping and effective federal civil rights law to date. By the time of ratification of the Twenty-Fourth Amendment, only five states had poll taxes on their books. Spurred on by the spirit of the times, Congress enacted the Voting Rights Act of 1965, which enforced the poll tax ban of the Twenty-Fourth Amendment and also abolished literacy tests, property qualifications, and other obstacles to voter registration. In 1966, in *Harper* v. *Board of Elections*, the Supreme Court rejected a constitutional challenge to the historic voting rights law.

AMENDMENT XXV
(Ratified on February 10, 1967)

Section 1.

In case of the removal of the President from office or of his death or resignation, the Vice President shall become President.

Section 2.

Whenever there is a vacancy in the office of the Vice President, the President shall nominate a Vice President who shall take office upon confirmation by a majority vote of both Houses of Congress.

Section 3.

Whenever the President transmits to the President pro tempore of the Senate and the Speaker of the House of Representatives his written declaration that he is unable to discharge the powers and duties of his office, and until he transmits to them a written declaration to the contrary, such powers and duties shall be discharged by the Vice President as Acting President.

Section 4.

Whenever the Vice President and a majority of either the principal officers of the executive departments or of such other body as Congress may by law provide, transmit to the President pro tempore of the Senate and the Speaker of the House of Representatives their written declaration that the President is unable to discharge the powers and duties of his office, the Vice President shall immediately assume the powers and duties of the office as Acting President.

Thereafter, when the President transmits to the President pro tempore of the Senate and the Speaker of the House of Representatives his written declaration that no inability exists, he shall resume the powers and duties of his office unless the Vice President and a majority of either the principal officers of the executive department or of such other body as Congress may by law provide, transmit within four days to the President pro tempore of the Senate and the Speaker of the House of Representatives their written declaration that the President is unable to discharge the powers and duties of his office. Thereupon Congress shall decide the issue, assembling within forty-eight hours for that purpose if not in session. If the Congress, within twenty-one days after receipt of the latter written declaration, or, if Congress is not in session, within twenty-one days after Congress is required to assemble, determines by two-thirds vote of both Houses that the President is unable to discharge the powers and duties of his office, the Vice President shall continue to discharge the same as Acting President; otherwise, the President shall resume the powers and duties of his office.

Several tragedies to the men who occupied the offices of president and vice president and the lack of constitutional clarity about the path of succession in event of presidential and vice presidential disability spurred the enactment of the Twenty-Fifth Amendment.

Whether the vice president was merely an acting president or assumed the permanent powers of the office for the remainder of the term upon the death of a president was answered in 1841 when John Tyler became president upon the death of William Henry Harrison, who died only a month after his inauguration. Seven more presidents died in office before the enactment of the Twenty-Fifth Amendment,

and in each case the vice president assumed the presidency without controversy. What this amendment answered that the original Constitution did not was the method of vice presidential succession. The vice presidency often went unfilled for months at a time as the result of constitutional ambiguity. Since the enactment of the amendment, there have been two occasions when the president appointed a vice president. Both took place during the second term of President Richard M. Nixon. For the first time in United States history, the nation witnessed a presidential term served out by two men, President Gerald R. Ford and Vice President Nelson A. Rockefeller, neither of whom had been elected to the position.

The Twenty-Fifth Amendment also settled the path of succession in the event of presidential disability. This provision of the amendment was prompted by the memories of James Garfield lying in a coma for eighty days after being struck by an assassin's bullet and Woodrow Wilson's bedridden state for the last eighteen months of his term after a stroke. The first president to invoke the disability provision of the Twenty-Fifth Amendment was Ronald Reagan, who made Vice President George Bush acting president for eight hours while he underwent surgery. The only other time a president invoked this provision came in 2002, when George W. Bush underwent minor surgery and transferred the powers of his office to Vice President Dick Cheney.

The provision authorizing the vice president, in consultation with Congress and members of the Cabinet, to declare the president disabled has never been invoked.

AMENDMENT XXVI
(Ratified on July 1, 1971)

Section 1.

The right of citizens of the United States, who are eighteen years of age or older, to vote shall not be denied or abridged by the United States or by any State on account of age.

Section 2.

The Congress shall have power to enforce this article by appropriate legislation.

The Twenty-Sixth Amendment was a direct response to the unpopularity of the Vietnam War and was spurred by calls to lower the voting age to eighteen so that draft-eligible men could voice their opinion on the war through the ballot box. In 1970, Congress had amended

the Voting Rights Act of 1965 to lower the voting age to eighteen in all national, state, and local elections. Many states resisted compliance, claiming that Congress, while having the power to establish the voting age in national elections, had no such authority in state and local elections. In *Oregon* v. *Mitchell* (1970), the Supreme Court agreed with that view. Congress responded by drafting the Twenty-Sixth Amendment, and the states ratified it quickly and without controversy.

AMENDMENT XXVII
(Ratified on May 7, 1992)

No law, varying the compensation for the services of the Senators and Representatives shall take effect until an election of Representatives shall have intervened.

The Twenty-Seventh Amendment originally was introduced in 1789 during the 1st Congress as one of the original twelve amendments to the Constitution. Only six of the necessary eleven (of thirteen) states had ratified the amendment by 1791. As more states came into the union, the prospect of the amendment's passage only dwindled. No additional state ratified the amendment until 1873, when Ohio approved its addition to the Constitution.

Sometime in the early 1980s, a University of Texas student discovered the amendment and launched an intensive effort to bring it to the public's attention for ratification. The amendment's core purpose, preventing members of Congress from raising their salaries during the terms in which they served, meshed well with another grassroots movement that began during this time, the campaign to impose term limits on members of the House and Senate. Nothing in the nation's constitutional or statutory law prohibited the resurrection of the Twenty-Seventh Amendment for voter approval. In 1939, the Supreme Court had ruled in *Coleman* v. *Miller* that amendments could remain indefinitely before the public unless Congress had set a specific time limit on the ratification process. By 1992, the amendment had received the necessary three-fourths approval of the states, making it the last successful effort to amend the Constitution. The Twenty-Seventh Amendment has not, however, barred Congress from increasing its compensation through annual cost-of-living-adjustments.

Federalism

O n August 26, 2005, New Orleans, Louisiana, and other low-lying Gulf Coast areas in Mississippi and Alabama braced for a Category 5 hurricane named Katrina. In preparation for the coming storm, Louisiana Governor Kathleen Blanco and Mississippi Governor Haley Barbour declared states of emergency in their jurisdictions and asked President George W. Bush to follow suit at the federal level. The White House responded by authorizing the Federal Emergency Management Agency (FEMA) "to identify, mobilize, and provide at its discretion, equipment and resources necessary to alleviate the impacts of the emergency."[1]

On Sunday, August 28, Mayor Ray Nagin issued the first-ever mandatory evacuation of New Orleans amid warnings that the levees, built by the U.S. Army Corps of Engineers, might not hold, thereby flooding the city. As massive evacuations of the coast occurred, Marty Bahamonde, a Boston-based FEMA official, was sent to New Orleans to be the eyes and ears of FEMA Director Michael Brown. The Louisiana National Guard asked FEMA for 700 buses to help evacuate the poor who had no other method of transportation; FEMA sent 100.

When the storm hit land on August 29 as a Category 3 storm, it looked as if damages might not be as bad as predicted. Still, thousands of largely poor and elderly New Orleans citizens were forced to take refuge in the Superdome and the Convention Center. As feared, the levees gave way, flooding entire sections of New Orleans and basically destroying one of the poorest areas of the city. Many residents were stranded in their homes, some on their rooftops.

The situation quickly deteriorated when a large proportion of New Orleans police failed to show up for work and Mayor Nagin and Governor Blanco seemed unable to agree on strategies to deal with the colossal disaster. Both, however, pleaded for more federal assistance, but their pleas fell on deaf ears. Various levels of government appeared either paralyzed or unaware of the disaster in Louisiana and other coastal areas. One government official who was not able to ignore the situation was FEMA agent Bahamonde, who sent increasingly desperate e-mails back to the FEMA director. Using his Blackberry, Bahamonde, who was in the Superdome with thousands of evacuees, told Brown: "Sir, I know that you know the situation is past critical .... Hotels are kicking people out, thousands gathering in the streets with no food or water .... Estimates are that many will die within hours. We are out of food and running out of water." Still, assistance did not come quickly.

■ **Residents of the Gulf Coast are no strangers to natural disaster.** At left, a scene in Louisiana after the Great Mississippi Flood of 1927. At right, Governor Kathleen Blanco, President George W. Bush, and Mayor Ray Nagin survey damage in New Orleans in the wake of Hurricane Katrina.

WHAT SHOULD I KNOW ABOUT . . .

- the roots of the federal system and the constitutional allocation of governmental powers?
- federalism and the Marshall Court?
- dual federalism before and after the Civil War?
- cooperative federalism during the New Deal and the growth of national government?
- New Federalism and returning power to the states?
- Supreme Court rulings related to a new judicial federalism?

By Thursday, September 1, New Orleans Homeland Security Director Terry Ebbert said, "This is a national disgrace. FEMA has been here three days yet there is not command and control." Mayor Nagin sent out an SOS to FEMA and was told by FEMA Director Brown that Brown had heard "no reports of unrest."

With many local and state employees without homes or ways to get to work, and with nearly all forms of communication failing, hundreds died in New Orleans. The official response made clear that there was no effective coordination between the local, state, and national governments, nor any real agreement as to which level of government was responsible for what in this tragedy. [2]

This breakdown in intergovernmental communications, as well as other difficulties in coordinating post-Katrina recovery efforts, led local, state, and national governments to reevaluate their emergency response and disaster relief plans. Citizens, too, voiced their dissatisfaction with the way the various governments responded to Hurricane Katrina. Governor Blanco, for example, chose not to run for a second term out of fear that she would not win.

Almost exactly three years after Katrina hit the Gulf Coast, the reformed emergency response plans throughout the Gulf Region, as well as the new levees around the city of New Orleans constructed by the Army Corps of Engineers were tested by a Category 2 hurricane named Gustav. Much to the pleasant surprise of citizens and observers alike, the lessons offered by Katrina appeared to have been learned.

Local, state, and national governments had prepared for a worst-case scenario, establishing a clear chain of command and cooperating with one another to assure the safety of the citizens. Evacuations throughout Texas, Louisiana, Alabama, and Mississippi went smoothly.

President Bush, who had faced heavy criticism for his administration's handling of Hurricane Katrina, summarized the various governments' response to Hurricane Gustav by saying, "The coordination on this storm [was] a lot better than during Katrina. It was clearly a spirit of sharing assets, of listening to somebody's problems and saying, "How can we best address them?" "[3]

TO LEARN MORE— —TO DO MORE
Find out how you can get involved with hurricane rebuilding efforts by visiting the Hands on Network at www.handsonnetwork.org/hurricane-relief.

From its very beginning, the challenge for the United States of America was to preserve the traditional independence and rights of the states while establishing an effective national government. The Framers, fearing tyranny, divided powers between the state and the national governments. At each level, moreover, powers were divided among executive, legislative, and judicial branches. The people are the ultimate power from which both the national government and the state governments derive their power.

Although most of the delegates to the Constitutional Convention favored a strong federal government, they knew that some compromise about the distribution of powers would be necessary. Some of the Framers wanted to continue with the confederate form of government defined in the Articles of Confederation; others wanted a more centralized system, similar to that of Great Britain. Their solution was to create the world's first federal system (although the word "federal" never appears in the U.S.

Constitution). The thirteen sovereign or independent states were bound together under one national government.

Today, the Constitution ultimately binds more than 89,000 different governments at the national, state, and local levels (To learn more about governments in the United States, see Figure 3.1). The Constitution lays out the duties, obligations, and powers of each of these units. Throughout history, however, this relationship has been reshaped continually by crises, historical evolution, public expectations, and judicial interpretation. All these forces have had tremendous influence on who makes policy decisions and how these decisions get made, as is underscored in our opening vignette.

To understand the current relationship between the states and the federal government and to better grasp some of the issues that arise from this constantly changing relationship, in this chapter, we will look at the roots of the federal system and the governmental powers under the Constitution created by the Framers. After we explore federalism and how it was molded by the Marshall Court, we will examine the development of dual federalism before and after the Civil War. Following a discussion of cooperative federalism and the growth of national government, we will consider New Federalism, especially the movement toward returning power to the states. Finally, we will examine the Supreme Court's efforts toward reform and a new judicial federalism.

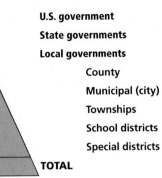

1	U.S. government
50	State governments
89,476	Local governments
3,033	County
19,492	Municipal (city)
16,519	Townships
13,051	School districts
37,387	Special districts
89,527	TOTAL

FIGURE 3.1 Number of Governments in the United States

Source: U.S. Census Bureau, www.census.gov/govs/cog/GovOrgTab033ss.html

Roots of the Federal System and the Constitutional Allocation of Governmental Powers

The United States was the first country to adopt a **federal system** of government. This system of government, where the national government and state governments derive all authority from the people, was designed to remedy many of the problems experienced under the Articles of Confederation.

The new system of government also had to be different from the **unitary system** found in Great Britain, where the local and regional governments derived all their power from a strong national government. (To learn more about these forms of government, see Figure 3.2.) Having been under the rule of English kings, whom they considered tyrants, the Framers feared centralizing power in one government or institution. Therefore, they made both the state and the federal government accountable to the people at large. While the governments shared some powers, such as the ability to tax, each government was supreme in some spheres, as described in the following section.

The federal system as conceived by the Framers has proven tremendously effective. Since the creation of the U.S. system, many other nations, including Canada (1867), Mexico (1917), and Russia (1993), have adopted federal systems in their constitutions.

Comparing Federal and Unitary Systems

federal system
System of government where the national government and state governments share power, derive all authority from the people, and the powers of the government are specified in a Constitution.

unitary system
System of government where the local and regional governments derive all authority from a strong national government.

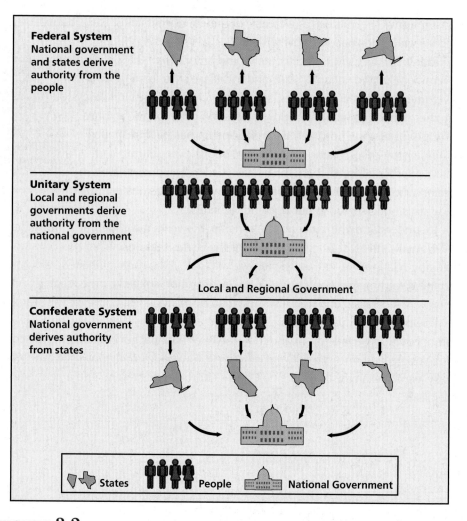

FIGURE 3.2 The Federal, Unitary, and Confederate Systems of Government
The source of governmental authority and power differs dramatically in various systems of government.

enumerated powers
Specific powers granted to Congress under Article I, section 8, of the Constitution; these powers include taxation, coinage of money, regulation of commerce, and the authority to provide for a national defense.

necessary and proper clause
The final paragraph of Article I, section 8, of the Constitution, which gives Congress the authority to pass all laws "necessary and proper" to carry out the enumerated powers specified in the Constitution; also called the elastic clause.

implied powers
Powers derived from enumerated powers and the necessary and proper clause. These powers are not stated specifically but are considered to be reasonably implied through the exercise of delegated powers.

National Powers Under the Constitution

Chief among the exclusive powers of the national government are the authorities to coin money, conduct foreign relations, provide for an army and navy, declare war, and establish a national court system. All of these powers set out in Article I, section 8, of the Constitution are called **enumerated powers.** Article I, section 8, also contains the **necessary and proper clause** (also called the elastic clause), which gives Congress the authority to enact any laws "necessary and proper" for carrying out any of its enumerated powers. These powers derived from enumerated powers and the necessary and proper clause are known as **implied powers.**

The federal government's right to tax was also clearly set out in the Constitution. The Framers wanted to avoid the financial problems that the national government experienced under the Articles of Confederation. If the national government was to be strong, its power to raise revenue had to be unquestionable. Although the new national government had no power under the Constitution to levy a national income tax, that was changed by the passage of the Sixteenth Amendment in 1913. Eventually, as discussed later in this chapter, this new taxing power became a powerful catalyst for further expansion of the national government.

Article VI of the federal Constitution underscores the notion that the national government is to be supreme in situations of conflict between state and national law. It declares that the U.S. Constitution, the laws of the United States, and its treaties, are to be "the supreme Law of the Land; and the Judges in every State shall be bound thereby." In spite of this explicit language, the meaning of what is called the **supremacy clause** has been subject to continuous judicial interpretation.

State Powers Under the Constitution

Because states had all the power at the time the Constitution was written, the Framers felt no need, as they did for the new national government, to list and restate the powers of the states. Article I, however, allows states to set the "Times, Places, and Manner, for holding elections for senators and representatives." Article II requires that each state appoint electors to vote for president. And, Article IV provides each state a "Republican Form of Government," meaning one that represents the citizens of the state.

It was not until the **Tenth Amendment,** the final part of the Bill of Rights, that the states' powers were described in greater detail: "The powers not delegated to the United States by the Constitution, nor prohibited by it to the States, are reserved to the States respectively, or to the people." These powers, often called the states' **reserve** or **police powers,** include the ability to legislate for the public health, safety, and morals of their citizens. Today, the states' rights to legislate under their police powers are used as the rationale for many states' restrictions on abortion. Similarly, some states now fund stem-cell research, in sharp contrast to the federal government. Police powers are also the basis for state criminal laws, including varied laws concerning the death penalty.

Concurrent Powers Under the Constitution

As revealed in Figure 3.3, national and state powers overlap. The area where the systems overlap represents **concurrent powers**—powers shared by the national and state governments. States already had the power to tax; the Constitution extended this power to the national government as well. Other important concurrent powers include the right to borrow money, establish courts, and make and enforce laws necessary to carry out these powers.

Powers Denied Under the Constitution

Some powers are explicitly denied to the national government or the states under Article I of the Constitution. In keeping with the Framers' desire to forge a national economy, for example, states are prohibited from entering treaties, coining money, or impairing obligation of contracts. States also are prohibited from entering into compacts with other states without express congressional approval. In a similar vein, Congress is barred from favoring one state over another in regulating commerce, and it cannot lay duties on items exported from any state.

State governments (as well as the national government) are denied the authority to take arbitrary actions affecting constitutional rights and liberties. Neither national nor state governments may pass a **bill of attainder,** a law declaring an act illegal without a judicial trial. The Constitution also bars the national and state govern-

Thinking Globally
Federal and Unitary Systems

The United States, Germany, Russia, Nigeria, and Brazil are just some of the countries that have a federal system of government. Most of the world's nations, including Great Britain, France, China, Japan, and Iran, have unitary systems of power with authority concentrated in the central government. Although federal states are relatively few in number, they tend to be large and politically important.

- What factors encourage the adoption of a federal system rather than a unitary one?
- What features do the federal countries listed have in common? How are they different?

supremacy clause
Portion of Article VI of the Constitution mandating that national law is supreme to (that is, supersedes) all other laws passed by the states or by any other subdivision of government.

Tenth Amendment
The final part of the Bill of Rights that defines the basic principle of American federalism in stating: "The powers not delegated to the United States by the Constitution, nor prohibited by it to the States, are reserved to the States respectively, or to the people."

reserve (or police) powers
Powers reserved to the states by the Tenth Amendment that lie at the foundation of a state's right to legislate for the public health and welfare of its citizens.

concurrent powers
Authority possessed by both the state and national governments that may be exercised concurrently as long as that power is not exclusively within the scope of national power or in conflict with national law.

Comparing Federal and Unitary Systems

bill of attainder
A law declaring an act illegal without a judicial trial.

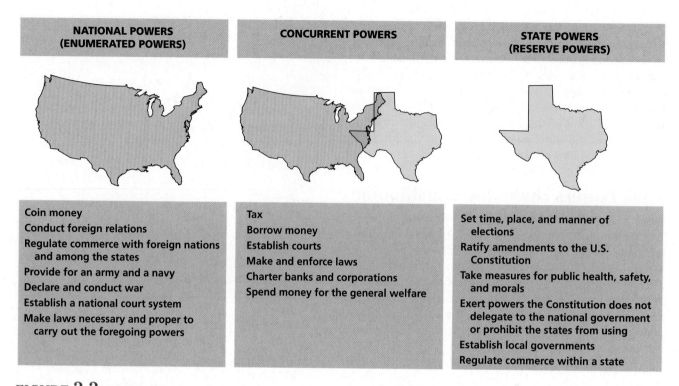

NATIONAL POWERS (ENUMERATED POWERS)	CONCURRENT POWERS	STATE POWERS (RESERVE POWERS)
Coin money	Tax	Set time, place, and manner of elections
Conduct foreign relations	Borrow money	Ratify amendments to the U.S. Constitution
Regulate commerce with foreign nations and among the states	Establish courts	Take measures for public health, safety, and morals
Provide for an army and a navy	Make and enforce laws	Exert powers the Constitution does not delegate to the national government or prohibit the states from using
Declare and conduct war	Charter banks and corporations	Establish local governments
Establish a national court system	Spend money for the general welfare	Regulate commerce within a state
Make laws necessary and proper to carry out the foregoing powers		

FIGURE 3.3 The Distribution of Governmental Power in the Federal System

ex post facto law
Law that makes an act punishable as a crime even if the action was legal at the time it was committed.

ments from passing *ex post facto* **laws,** laws that make an act punishable as a crime even if the action was legal at the time it was committed. (To learn more about civil rights and liberties, see chapters 4 and 5.)

Relations Among the States

In addition to delineating the relationship of the states with the national government, the Constitution provides a mechanism for resolving interstate disputes and facilitating relations among states. To avoid any sense of favoritism, it provides that disputes between states be settled directly by the U.S. Supreme Court under its original jurisdiction as mandated by Article III of the Constitution (see chapter 9). Moreover, Article IV requires that each state give "Full Faith and Credit . . . to the public Acts, Records and judicial Proceedings of every other State." The **full faith and credit clause** ensures that judicial decrees and contracts made in one state will be binding and enforceable in another, thereby facilitating trade and other commercial relationships. Full faith and credit cases continue to make their way through the judicial system. For example, a state's refusal to honor same-sex marriage contracts poses interesting constitutional questions. States can vary considerably on social issues. (To learn more about the full faith and credit clause, see The Living Constitution: Article IV, Section 1.)

full faith and credit clause
Section of Article IV of the Constitution that ensures judicial decrees and contracts made in one state will be binding and enforceable in any other state.

privileges and immunities clause
Part of Article IV of the Constitution guaranteeing that the citizens of each state are afforded the same rights as citizens of all other states.

Article IV also contains the **privileges and immunities clause**, guaranteeing that the citizens of each state are afforded the same rights as citizens of all other states. In addition, Article IV contains the **extradition clause**, which requires states to extradite, or return, criminals to states where they have been convicted or are to stand trial.

extradition clause
Part of Article IV of the Constitution that requires states to extradite, or return, criminals to states where they have been convicted or are to stand trial.

To facilitate relations among states, Article 1, section 10, clause 3, of the U.S. Constitution sets the legal foundation for interstate cooperation in the form of

The Living Constitution

Full Faith and Credit shall be given in each State to the public Acts, Records, and judicial Proceedings of every other State. And the Congress may by general Laws prescribe the Manner in which such Acts, Records, and Proceedings shall be proved, and the Effect thereof.

—ARTICLE IV, SECTION 1

The full faith and credit clause in Article IV of the Constitution rests on principles borrowed from international law that require one country to recognize contracts made in another country absent a compelling public policy reason to the contrary. In the United States, this principle applies to the relationship between the states.

The full faith and credit clause requires a state to recognize public acts and court proceedings of another state. In 1997, the Supreme Court ruled that the full faith and credit clause mandates that state courts always honor the judgments of other state courts, even if to do so is against state public policy or existing state laws. Failure to do so would allow a single state to "rule the world," said Supreme Court Justice Ruth Bader Ginsburg during oral argument.[a]

For the most part, interpretation of the full faith and credit clause has not been controversial. That is likely to change, however, as advocates of same-sex marriage have suggested that marriages of same-sex couples performed and legally sanctioned in one state must be recognized in another state, as is the case with heterosexual marriages.

In the mid 1990s, the possible legalization of marriage between same-sex couples threw numerous state legislatures and the U.S. Congress into a virtual frenzy. Twenty-five states passed laws in 1996 or 1997 to bar legal recognition of same-sex marriages. The U.S. Congress also got into the act by passing what is called the Defense of Marriage Act (DOMA), which President Bill Clinton signed into law in 1996. It was designed to undercut possible state recognition of same-sex marriages. This federal law permits states to disregard same-sex marriages even if they are legal in other states. The U.S. Constitution, however, doesn't give Congress the authority to create exceptions to the full faith and credit clause of the Constitution. With the legalization of same-sex marriages in Massachusetts in 2004 and in Connecticut in 2008, years of litigation are likely to ensue in states that refuse to recognize same-sex unions.

CRITICAL THINKING QUESTIONS

1. How should the Supreme Court rule on a challenge to a state's refusal to recognize a legally valid marriage from Connecticut or Massachusetts? Explain your reasoning.
2. Is a federal law such as DOMA consistent with the wishes of the Framers, who left regulation of marriage largely to the states?

[a]Oral argument by Thomas in *Baker* v. *General Motors Corporation*, 522 U.S. 222 (1998), noted in Linda Greenhouse, "Court Weighs Whether One State Must Obey Another's Courts," *New York Times* (October 16, 1997): A25.

---

interstate compacts, contracts between states that carry the force of law. It reads, "No State shall, without the consent of Congress . . . enter into any Agreement or Compact with another state." Before 1920, interstate compacts were largely bistate compacts that addressed boundary disputes or acted to help two states accomplish some objective.

More than 200 interstate compacts exist today. While some deal with rudimentary items such as state boundaries, others help states carry out their policy objectives, and they play an important role in helping states carry out their functions. Although

interstate compacts
Contracts between states that carry the force of law; generally now used as a tool to address multistate policy concerns.

TABLE 3.1 Compacts by the Numbers

Interstate compacts with 25 or more members	13
Least compact memberships by a state (HI & WI)	14
Most compact memberships by a state (NH & VA)	42
Average compact memberships by a state	27
Compacts developed prior to 1920	36
Compacts developed since 1920	150+
Interstate compacts currently in operation	200+

Source: Council of State Governments, www.csg.org.

several bistate compacts still exist, other compacts have as many as fifty signatories.[4] The Drivers License Compact, for example, was signed by all fifty states to facilitate nationwide recognition of licenses issued in the respective states. (To learn more about interstate compacts, see Table 3.1.)

Relations within the States: Local Governments

The Constitution gives local governments, including counties, municipalities, townships, and school districts, no independent standing. Thus, their authority is not granted directly by the people but through state governments, which establish or charter administrative subdivisions to execute the duties of the state government on a smaller scale.

Thinking Globally

Mexico's Federal System

Mexico has a federal structure of government, but in practice, the central government is much more powerful than its thirty-one state and numerous municipal governments, in part because it controls a significant proportion of the nation's total revenue. Over the past twenty years, Mexico has taken some steps to decentralize power. Movement toward a U.S.-style system of government, however, has been met with opposition from federal officials and state governors who remain resistant to the idea of sharing power with local governments.

- What steps could Mexico's central government take to empower local governments and foster local control?
- How might Mexico's central government encourage those in state government to view local governments and municipalities as partners and not as competitors?

TIMELINE

Federalism and the Supreme Court

McCulloch v. *Maryland* (1819)
The Supreme Court upheld the power of the national government and denied the right of a state to tax the federal bank using the Constitution's supremacy clause. The Court's broad interpretation of the necessary and proper clause paved the way for later rulings upholding expansive federal powers.

Federalism and the Marshall Court

The nature of federalism, including its allocation of power between the national government and the states, has changed dramatically over the past two hundred years. Much of this change is due to the rulings of the U.S. Supreme Court, which has played a major role in defining the federal system because the distribution of power between the national and state governments is not clearly delineated in the Constitution. Few Supreme Courts have had a greater impact on the federal–state relationship than the one headed by Chief Justice John Marshall (1801–1835). In a series of decisions, he and his associates carved out an important role for the Court in defining the balance of power between the national government and the states. Two rulings in the early 1800s, *McCulloch* v. *Maryland* (1819) and *Gibbons* v. *Ogden* (1824), were particularly important.

McCulloch v. *Maryland* (1819)

McCulloch v. *Maryland* **(1819)** was the first major Supreme Court decision of the Marshall Court to define the relationship between the national and state governments. In 1816, Congress chartered the Second Bank of the United States. (The charter of the First Bank had been allowed to expire.) In 1818, the Maryland state legislature levied a tax requiring all banks not chartered by Maryland (that is, the Second Bank of the United States) to: (1) buy stamped paper from the state on which the Second Bank's notes were to be issued; (2) pay the state $15,000 a year, or, (3) go out of business. James McCulloch, the head cashier of the Baltimore branch of the Bank of the United States, refused to pay the tax, and Maryland brought suit against him. After losing in a Maryland state court, McCulloch appealed the decision to the U.S. Supreme Court by order of the U.S. secretary of the treasury. In a unanimous opinion, the Court answered the two central questions that had been presented to it: Did Congress have the authority to charter a bank? If it did, could a state tax it?

Chief Justice John Marshall's answer to the first question—whether Congress had the right to establish a bank or another type of corporation—continues to stand as the classic exposition of the doctrine of implied powers and as a reaffirmation of the authority of a strong national government. Although the word "bank" cannot be found in the Constitution, the Constitution enumerates powers that give Congress the authority to levy and collect taxes, issue a currency, and borrow funds. From these enumerated powers, Marshall found, it was reasonable to imply that Congress had the power to charter a bank, which could be considered "necessary and proper" to the exercise of its aforementioned enumerated powers.

Marshall next addressed the question of whether a federal bank could be taxed by any state government. To Marshall, this was not a difficult question. The national government was dependent on the people, not the states, for its powers. In addition, Marshall noted, the Constitution specifically calls for the national law to be supreme. "The power to tax involves the power to destroy," wrote Marshall.[5] Thus, the state tax violated the supremacy clause, because individual states cannot interfere with the operations of the national government, whose laws are supreme.

The Court's decision in *McCulloch* has far-reaching consequences even today. The necessary and proper clause is used to justify federal action in many areas, including social welfare problems. Furthermore, had Marshall allowed the state of Maryland to tax the federal bank, it is possible that states could have attempted to tax all federal agencies located within their boundaries, a costly proposition that could have driven the federal government into insurmountable debt.

Gibbons v. *Ogden* (1824)

Shortly after *McCulloch*, the Marshall Court had another opportunity to rule in favor of a broad interpretation of the scope of national power. ***Gibbons* v. *Ogden* (1824)** involved a dispute that arose after the New York State legislature granted to Robert Fulton the exclusive right to operate steamboats on the Hudson River. Simultaneously, Congress licensed a ship to sail on the same waters. By the time the case reached the Supreme Court, it was complicated both factually and procedurally. Suffice it to say that both New York and New Jersey wanted to control shipping on the lower Hudson River. But, *Gibbons* actually addressed one simple, very important question: what was the scope of Congress's authority under the commerce clause? The states argued that "commerce," as mentioned in Article I, should be interpreted narrowly to include only direct dealings in products. In *Gibbons*, however, the Supreme Court ruled that Congress's power to regulate interstate commerce included the power to regulate commercial activity as well, and that the commerce power had no limits except those specifically found in the Constitution. Thus, New York had no constitutional authority to grant a monopoly to a single steamboat operator, an act that interfered with interstate commerce.[6] Like the necessary and proper clause, today the commerce clause has been used by Congress—with varying degrees of success—to justify federal legislation concerning regulation of highways, the stock market, and violence against women.

Gibbons v. *Ogden* (1824)
The Supreme Court upheld broad congressional power to regulate interstate commerce. The Court's broad interpretation of the Constitution's commerce clause paved the way for later rulings upholding expansive federal powers.

Dual Federalism: The Taney Court, Slavery, and the Civil War

In spite of nationalist Marshall Court decisions such as *McCulloch* and *Gibbons*, strong debate continued in the United States over national versus state power. It was under the leadership of Chief Justice Marshall's successor, Roger B. Taney (1835–1863), that the Supreme Court articulated the notions of concurrent power

dual federalism
The belief that having separate and equally powerful levels of government is the best arrangement.

and **dual federalism.** Dual federalism posits that having separate and equally powerful state and national governments is the best arrangement. Adherents of this theory typically believe that the national government should not exceed its constitutionally enumerated powers, and as stated in the Tenth Amendment, all other powers are, and should be, reserved to the states or to the people.

Dred Scott and the Advent of the Civil War

During the Taney Court era, the role of the Supreme Court as the arbiter of competing national and state interests became troublesome when the justices were called upon to deal with the controversial issue of slavery. In cases such as *Dred Scott* v. *Sandford* (1857), the Court tried to manage the slavery issue by resolving questions of ownership, the status of fugitive slaves, and slavery in the new territories.[6] These cases generally were settled in favor of slavery and states' rights within the framework of dual federalism. In *Dred Scott*, for example, the Taney Court, in declaring the Missouri Compromise unconstitutional, ruled that Congress lacked the authority to ban slavery in the territories. This decision seemed to rule out any nationally legislated solution to the slavery question, leaving the problem in the hands of the state legislatures and the people, who did not have the power to impose their will on other states.

The Civil War, Its Aftermath, and the Continuation of Dual Federalism

The Civil War (1861–1865) forever changed the nature of federalism. In the aftermath of the war, the national government grew in size and power. It also attempted to impose its will on the state governments through the Thirteenth, Fourteenth, and Fifteenth Amendments. These three amendments, known collectively as the Civil War Amendments, prohibited slavery and granted civil and political rights, including voting rights, to African Americans.

The U.S. Supreme Court, however, continued to adhere to its belief in the concept of dual federalism. Therefore, in spite of the growth of the national government's powers, the importance of the state governments' powers was not diminished until 1933, when the next major change in the federal system occurred. Generally, the Court upheld any laws passed under the states' police powers, which allow states to pass laws to protect the general welfare of their citizens. These laws affected commerce, labor relations, and manufacturing. After the Court's decision in *Plessy* v. *Ferguson* (1896), in which the Court ruled that state maintenance of "separate but equal" facilities for blacks and whites was constitutional, most civil rights and voting cases also became state matters, in spite of the Civil War Amendments.[7]

Photo courtesy: The Granger Collection

Who was Dred Scott? Born into slavery around 1795, Dred Scott became the named plaintiff in a case with major ramifications for the federal system. In 1833, Scott was sold by his original owners, the Blow family, to Dr. Emerson in St. Louis, Missouri. When Emerson died in 1843, Scott tried to buy his freedom. Before he could, however, he was transferred to Emerson's widow, who moved to New York, leaving Scott in the custody of his first owners, the Blows. Some of the Blows (Henry Blow later founded the anti-slavery Free Soil Party) and other abolitionists gave money to support a test case seeking Scott's freedom. They believed that Scott's residence with the Emerson family in Illinois and later in the Wisconsin Territory, which both prohibited slavery, made Scott a free man. After many delays, the U.S. Supreme Court ruled 7–2 in 1857 that Scott was not a citizen of the United States. "Slaves," said the Court, "were never thought of or spoken of except as property." Despite this ruling, Dred Scott was given his freedom when the Emerson family permanently returned him to the anti-slavery Blows. He died of tuberculosis less than one year later.

The Court also developed legal doctrine in a series of cases that reinforced the national government's ability to regulate commerce. By the 1930s, these two somewhat contradictory approaches led to confusion: states, for example, could not tax gasoline used by federal vehicles,[8] and the national government could not tax the sale of motorcycles to city police departments.[9] In this period, the Court, however, did recognize the need for national control over new technological developments, such as the telegraph.[10] And, beginning in the 1880s, the Court allowed Congress to regulate many aspects of economic relationships, such as monopolies, an area of regulation formerly thought to be in the exclusive realm of the states. Passage of laws such as the Interstate Commerce Act in 1887 and the Sherman Anti-Trust Act in 1890 allowed Congress to establish itself as an important player in the growing national economy.

Setting the Stage for a Stronger National Government

In 1895, the U.S. Supreme Court found a congressional effort to tax personal incomes unconstitutional, although an earlier Court had found a similar tax levied during the Civil War constitutional.[11] Thus, Congress and the state legislatures were moved to ratify the **Sixteenth Amendment.** The Sixteenth Amendment gave Congress the power to levy and collect taxes on incomes without apportioning them among the states. The revenues taken in by the federal government through taxation of personal income "removed a major constraint on the federal government by giving it access to almost unlimited revenues."[12] If money is power, the income tax and the revenues it generated greatly enhanced the power of the federal government and its ability to enter policy areas where it formerly had few funds to spend.

Sixteenth Amendment
Authorized Congress to enact a national income tax.

The **Seventeenth Amendment,** ratified in 1913, similarly enhanced the power of the national government at the expense of the states. This amendment terminated the state legislatures' election of senators and put their election in the hands of the people. With senators no longer directly accountable to the state legislators who elected them, states lost their principal protectors in Congress. Coupled with the Sixteenth Amendment, this amendment paved the way for more drastic changes in the relationship between national and state governments in the United States.

Seventeenth Amendment
Made senators directly elected by the people; removed their selection from state legislatures.

Cooperative Federalism: The New Deal and the Growth of National Government

The era of dual federalism came to an abrupt end in the 1930s. While the ratification of the Sixteenth and Seventeenth Amendments set the stage for expanded national government, the catalyst for dual federalism's demise was a series of economic events that ended in the cataclysm of the Great Depression:

- Throughout the 1920s, bank failures were common.
- In 1921, the nation experienced a severe slump in agricultural prices.
- In 1926, the construction industry went into decline.
- In the summer of 1929, inventories of consumer goods and automobiles were at an all-time high.
- On October 29, 1929, stock prices, which had risen steadily since 1926, crashed, taking with them the entire national economy.

Despite the severity of these indicators, Presidents Calvin Coolidge and Herbert Hoover took little action, believing that the national depression was an amalgamation of state economic crises that should be dealt with by state and local governments. However, by 1933, the situation could no longer be ignored.

The New Deal

Rampant unemployment (historians estimate it was as high as 40 to 50 percent) was the hallmark of the Great Depression. In 1933, to combat severe problems facing the nation, newly elected President Franklin D. Roosevelt (FDR) proposed a variety of innovative programs, collectively called the "New Deal," and ushered in a new era in American politics. FDR used the full power of the office of the president as well as his highly effective communication skills to sell the American public and Congress on a new level of government intervention intended to stabilize the economy and reduce suffering. Most politicians during the New Deal period (1933–1939) agreed that to find national solutions to the Depression, which was affecting the citizens of every state in the union, the national government would have to exercise tremendous authority.

In the first few weeks of the legislative session after FDR's inauguration, Congress passed a series of acts creating new federal agencies and programs proposed by the president. These new agencies, often known by their initials, created what many termed an alphabetocracy. Among the more significant programs were the Federal Housing Administration (FHA), which provided federal financing for new home construction; the Civilian Conservation Corps (CCC), a work relief program for farmers and homeowners; the Agricultural Adjustment Administration (AAA) and the National Recovery Administration (NRA), which imposed restrictions on production in agriculture and many industries while also providing subsidies to farmers.

New Deal programs forced all levels of government to work cooperatively with one another. Indeed, local governments—mainly in big cities—became a third partner in the federal system as FDR relied on big-city Democratic political machines to turn out voters to support his programs. Cities were embraced as equal partners in an intergovernmental system for the first time and became players in the national political arena because many members of Congress wanted to bypass state legislatures, where urban interests usually were underrepresented significantly.

New Deal programs also enlarged the scope of the national government. Those who feared this unprecedented use of national power quickly challenged the constitutionality of the programs in court.

Through the mid-1930s, the Supreme Court continued to rule that certain aspects of New Deal programs went beyond the authority of Congress to regulate commerce. The Court's *laissez-faire*, or hands-off, attitude toward the economy was reflected in a series of decisions ruling various aspects of New Deal programs unconstitutional.

FDR and the Congress were livid. FDR's frustration with the Court prompted him to suggest what ultimately was nicknamed his "Court-packing plan." Knowing that he could do little to change the minds of those already on the Court, FDR suggested enlarging its size from nine to thirteen justices. This would have given him the opportunity to pack the Court with a majority of justices predisposed toward the constitutional validity of the New Deal.

Even though Roosevelt was popular, the Court-packing plan was not. Congress and the public were outraged that he even suggested tampering with an institution of government. Nevertheless, the Court appeared to respond to this threat. In 1937, it reversed its series of anti–New Deal decisions, concluding that Congress (and therefore the national government) had the authority to legislate in any area so long as what was regulated affected commerce in any way. The Court also upheld the consti-

Thinking Globally

Sweden's Social Welfare System

Sweden has an extensive social welfare system that provides a wide range of benefits and services to its citizens, from child care to retirement funds. Sweden has long maintained one of the world's lowest poverty levels and one of the highest rates of egalitarianism in terms of income distribution. Many claim that Sweden is a successful example of what is referred to as "social democracy."

- To what degree should government policy emphasize egalitarianism over individualism?
- Is a more comprehensive government-sponsored system of social benefits a possibility in the United States? If so, what would such a system look like? If not, why not?

tutionality of the bulk of the massive New Deal relief programs, including the National Labor Relations Act of 1935, which authorized collective bargaining between unions and employees;[13] the Fair Labor Standards Act of 1938, which prohibited the interstate shipment of goods made by employees earning less than the federally mandated minimum wage;[14] and the Agricultural Adjustment Act of 1938, which provided crop subsidies to farmers.[15] Congress then used this newly recognized power to legislate in a wide array of areas, including maximum hour and minimum wage laws and regulation of child labor.

The Changing Nature of Federalism: From Layer Cake to Marble Cake

Before the Depression and the New Deal, most political scientists likened the federal system to a layer cake: each level or layer of government—national, state, and local— had clearly defined powers and responsibilities. After the New Deal, however, the nature of the federal system changed. Government now looked something like a marble cake:

> Wherever you slice through it you reveal an inseparable mixture of differently colored ingredients. . . . Vertical and diagonal lines almost obliterate the horizontal ones, and in some places there are unexpected whirls and an imperceptible merging of colors, so that it is difficult to tell where one ends and the other begins.[16]

The metaphor of marble cake federalism refers to what political scientists call **cooperative federalism,** a term that describes the intertwined relationship among the national, state, and local governments that began with the New Deal. (To learn more about cooperative federalism in practice, see Join the Debate: Federalism and the Environment.) States began to take a secondary, albeit important, cooperative role in the scheme of governance, as did many cities. Nowhere is this shift in power from the states to the national government clearer than in the growth of federal grant programs that began in earnest during the New Deal. Between the New Deal and the 1990s, the tremendous growth in these programs, and in federal government spending in general, changed the nature and discussion of federalism from "How much power should the national government have?" to "How much say in the policies of the states can the national government buy?" During the 1970s energy crisis, for example, the national government initially imposed a national 55 mph speed limit on the states.

cooperative federalism
The interwined relationship between the national, state and local governments that began with the New Deal.

Federal Grants and National Efforts to Influence the States

As early as 1790, Congress appropriated funds for the states to pay debts incurred during the Revolutionary War. But, it wasn't until the Civil War that Congress enacted its first true federal grant program, which allocated federal funds to the states for a specific purpose. Most commentators believe the start of this redistribution of funds began with the Morrill Land Grant Act of 1862, which gave each state 30,000 acres of public land for each representative in Congress. Income from the sale of these lands was to be earmarked for the establishment and support of agricultural and mechanical arts colleges. Sixty-nine land-grant colleges—including Texas A&M University, the University of Georgia, and Michigan State University—were founded or significantly assisted by the federal funds.

As we have seen, Franklin D. Roosevelt's New Deal program increased the flow of federal dollars to the states with the infusion of massive federal dollars for a variety of public works programs, including building and road construction. In the boom times of World War II, even more new federal programs were introduced. By the 1950s and

Join the Debate

Federalism and the Environment

Overview: The Environmental Protection Act, passed during Richard M. Nixon's presidency, provided the federal government with responsibility for protecting the environment. Because pollution is inherently interstate, there is good reason to defer to the federal government for environmental protection. The Interstate Commerce Clause of the Constitution provides the legal foundation for the federal government to play the dominant role in this arena. But, should this prevent states from regarding federal standards as minimum requirements and going further if they are so inclined? And, what if state officials are convinced that the federal government is not fulfilling its responsibilities? Should federal standards act as a floor or a ceiling for state laws?

States, particularly on the West Coast and in the Northeast, have repeatedly sued the federal government over powers and responsibilities to protect the In 2006, when the George W. Bush administration relaxed restrictions on the amount of pollution allowed after industries repaired or modernized their plants, twelve states in the Northeast filed suit. Some of these same states plus California, Arizona, Minnesota, and Illinois filed a suit in 2007 when the federal Environmental Protection Agency (EPA) weakened regulations requiring businesses and industries to report the toxic chemicals they use, store, and release. In late 2007 and early 2008, states and the federal government went head-to-head on two other environmental issues. First, California led nine states in requiring cars and trucks to get more miles per gallon than the federal government mandated. President Bush objected and the EPA asserted that the federal rules prevailed. Second, fifteen states established higher standards than the federal government in curbing greenhouse-gas emissions from the tailpipes of cars, thereby defying a federal edict that only Washington can impose such rules.

The concerns raised by environmental issues apply more broadly to public policy and the governance of our society. The federal government funds Medicare, the major health care program for the elderly. States and the federal government jointly provide health care for the poor, with the federal government establishing minimum standards and guidelines for how much states can provide above the minimum. Education is the primary responsibility of states, but—as pointed out in the Politics Now feature in this chapter—the federal government is seeking to set standards through the No Child Left Behind Act.

The question of the power of the federal government in contrast to the power of state governments is central to the concept and the realities of federalism. Should the federal government set limits on how much a state wants to do for its citizens? Can policy makers in Washington, D.C., be responsive to the different opportunities and needs throughout the country?

Arguments IN FAVOR of Federal Dominance in Environmental Protection

- The intergovernmental nature of pollution requires a national approach to environmental issues. A state can have lax pollution standards in order to minimize costs to the industries within its boundaries and suffer minimal consequences while causing more serious hazards for its neighbors. Federal regulations protect everyone.

- Industries cannot be expected to produce vehicles, appliances, and other goods that meet a wide variety of standards set by different states. Car manufacturers, as an example, might have to design and build several different vehicles to comply with a mosaic of requirements. This would necessarily result in inefficiencies likely to hurt the competitiveness of U.S. companies and increase costs to consumers.

- Environmental issues require a level of scientific expertise that is most likely to reside in the federal government. The identification of toxic substances and the design of strategies to reduce or eliminate these substances is a matter of scientific inquiry and discovery. Federal, not state, resources should support the

1960s, federal grant-in-aid programs were well entrenched. They often defined federal/state relationships and made the national government a major player in domestic policy. Until the 1960s, however, most federal grant programs were constructed in cooperation with the states and were designed to assist the states in the furtherance of their traditional responsibilities to protect the health, welfare, and safety of their citizens.

Arguments AGAINST Federal Dominance in Environmental Protection

- Political dynamics make the federal government an unreliable advocate for environmental protection. Not all presidents put a premium on environmental protection. Congress is susceptible to pressures from lobbyists that are more concerned with short-term profits for corporations than with the long-term consequences of pollution.

- States should be able to exceed federal standards. State governments should have discretion to respond to the needs of different regions of the country by going above minimal requirements. It is appropriate for the federal government to establish basic national standards, but it should not place limits on states who, for whatever reason, wish to do better.

- The federal government should allow states to exert leadership in public policy. California led the way in establishing higher automobile standards for pollution control in the 1960s. California has a large share of the nation's automobile market and thus was able to exert this kind of influence. Smaller states, by themselves, are not likely to exert pressure to establish new national standards, so fears of change being driven by any one state are unwarranted. States are more likely to act in coalition with others, and the largest states, like California, are likely to exert the most influence.

What role should government play in protecting the environment? Environmental groups favor stronger actions by all levels of government to protect air and water quality and promote clean energy. Here, members of Greenpeace hang a banner at a coal-burning power plant to protest the Bush Administration's energy policies.

Photo Courtesy: Laura Lombardi/Greenpeace/Zuma Press

Continuing the Debate

1. What policy roles should states play on the one hand and the federal government play on the other?
2. Have technological developments and the development of a national and even global economy relegated states in our federal system to relatively meaningless positions?

To Follow the Debate Online, Go To:

www.epa.gov, the Web site of the Environmental Protection Agency, the major federal body responsible for developing and enforcing environmental policies.

www.sierraclub.org, the Web site of the Sierra Club, a national, grassroots organization that is one of the major advocates for environmental protection and has joined lawsuits against the federal government and state governments, depending on the specific issues.

www.uschamber.com, the Web site of the U.S. Chamber of Commerce, one of the major advocates for businesses. It posts policy positions on its site and lobbies the federal government on behalf of its member businesses.

Most of these programs were **categorical grants,** ones for which Congress appropriates funds for specific purposes. Categorical grants allocate federal dollars by a precise formula and are subject to detailed conditions imposed by the national government, often on a matching basis; that is, states must contribute money to match federal funds, although the national government may pay as much as 90 percent of the total.

categorical grant
Grants that allocated federal funds to states for a specific purpose.

By the early 1960s, as concern about the poor and minorities rose, and as states (especially in the South) were blamed for perpetuating discrimination, those in power in the national government saw grants as a way to force states to behave in ways desired by the national government.[17] If the states would not cooperate with the national government to further its goals, it would withhold funds.

In 1964, the Democratic administration of President Lyndon B. Johnson (LBJ) launched its "Great Society" program, which included what LBJ called a "War on Poverty." The Great Society program was a broad attempt to combat poverty and discrimination. In a frenzy of activity in Washington not seen since the New Deal, federal funds were channeled to states, to local governments, and even directly to citizen action groups in an effort to alleviate social ills that the states had been unable or unwilling to remedy. Money was allocated for urban renewal, education, and poverty programs, including Head Start and job training. The move to fund local groups directly was made by the most liberal members of Congress to bypass not only conservative state legislatures, but also conservative mayors and councils in cities such as Chicago, who were perceived as disinclined to help their poor, often African American, constituencies. Thus, these programs often pitted governors and mayors against community activists, who became key players in the distribution of federal dollars.

These new grants altered the fragile federal/state balance of power that had been at the core of many older federal grant programs. During the Johnson administration, the national government began to use federal grants as a way to further what federal (and not state) officials perceived to be national needs. Grants based on what states wanted or believed they needed began to decline, while grants based on what the national government wanted states to do to foster national goals increased dramatically. From pollution to economic development and law enforcement, creating a federal grant seemed like the perfect solution to every problem.[18]

Not all federal programs mandating state or local action came with federal money, however. And, while presidents during the 1970s voiced their opposition to big government, their efforts to rein it in were largely unsuccessful.

New Federalism: Returning Power to the States

New Federalism
Federal–state relationship proposed by Reagan administration during the 1980s; hallmark is returning administrative powers to the state governments.

In 1980, former California Governor Ronald Reagan was elected president, pledging to advance what he called **New Federalism** and a return of power to the states. This policy set the tone for the federal–state relationship that was maintained from the 1980s until 2001. Presidents and Congresses took steps to shrink the size of the federal government in favor of programs administered by state governments. President Bill Clinton, a Democrat, lauded the demise of big government. And, on the campaign trail in 2000, Republican candidate George W. Bush also seemed committed to this devolution. The September 11, 2001, terrorist attacks, however, led to substantial growth in the power and scope of the federal government.

The Reagan Revolution

The Republican Reagan Revolution had at its heart strong views about the role of states in the federal system. While many Democrats and liberal interest groups argued that federal grants were an effective way to raise the level of services provided to the poor; others, including Reagan, attacked them as imposing national priorities on the states. In part to curtail federal spending, Reagan almost immediately proposed massive cuts in federal domestic programs and drastic income tax cuts. Declining federal revenues dramatically altered the relationships among federal, state, and local governments. For the first time in thirty years, federal aid to state and local governments declined.[19] Reagan persuaded Congress to consolidate many categorical grants into far fewer, less restrictive **block grants**—broad grants to states for specific activities such as secondary education or health services, with few strings attached. He also ended general revenue sharing, which had provided significant restricted funds to the states.

By the end of the presidencies of Ronald Reagan and George Bush in 1993, most block grants fell into one of four categories: health, income security, education, or transportation. Yet, many politicians, including most state governors, urged the consolidation of even more programs into block grants. Calls to reform the welfare system, particularly to allow the states more latitude in an effort to get back to the Hamiltonian notion of states as laboratories of experiment, seemed popular with citizens and governments alike.

block grant
Broad grant with few strings attached; given to states by the federal government for general categories of activity, such as secondary education or health services.

The Devolution Revolution

In 1994, Republican candidates for the House of Representatives joined together in their support for the Contract with America, a campaign document proposed by then House Minority Whip Newt Gingrich (R–GA). In it, Republican candidates pledged to force a national debate on the role of the national government in regard to the states. A top priority was scaling back the federal government, an effort that some commentators called the devolution revolution.

Running under a clear set of priorities contained in the Contract, Republican candidates took back the House of Representatives for the first time in more than forty years. A majority of the legislative proposals based on the Contract passed the House of Representatives during the first one hundred days of the 104th Congress. However, very few of the Contract's proposals, including acts requiring a balanced budget, tax reforms, and term limits, passed the Senate and became law.

On some issues, however, the Republicans were able to achieve their goals. For example, before 1995, **unfunded mandates,** national laws that direct state or local governments to comply with federal rules or regulations (such as clean air or water standards) but contain no federal funding to defray the cost of meeting these requirements, absorbed nearly 30 percent of some local budgets. Republicans in Congress, loyal to the concerns of these governments, secured passage of the Unfunded Mandates Reform Act of 1995. This act prevented Congress from passing costly federal programs without debate on how to fund them and addressed a primary concern for state governments.

Another important act passed by the Republican-controlled Congress and signed into law by President Bill Clinton was the Personal Responsibility and Work Opportunity Reconciliation Act of 1996. This legislation replaced the existing welfare program, known as Aid to Families with Dependent Children (AFDC), with a program known as Temporary Assistance for Needy Families (TANF). TANF returned much of the administrative power for welfare programs to the states and became a hallmark of the devolution revolution.

In the short run, these and other programs, coupled with a growing economy, produced record federal and state budget surpluses. States were in the best fiscal shape they had been in since the 1970s. According to the National Conference of State Legislatures, total state budget surpluses in 1998 exceeded $30 billion. These tax surpluses allowed many states to increase spending, while other states offered their residents steep tax cuts. Mississippi, for example, increased its per capita spending by 42.4 percent, while Alaska opted to reduce taxes by 44.2 percent.[20]

unfunded mandates
National laws that direct state or local governments to comply with federal rules or regulations (such as clean air or water standards) but contain little or no federal funding to defray the cost of meeting these requirements.

VISUAL LITERACY

Federalism and Regulations

What was the devolution revolution?
Here, then House Minority Whip Newt Gingrich (R–GA) promotes the tenets of the Contract with America in 1994. A top priority of the program was to scale back the scope and size of the federal government. Though some of the Contract's proposals became law, most of its goals remained unfulfilled.

Photo Courtesy: John Duricka/AP/Wide World Photos

Source: AUGUSTA CHRONICLE   December 31, 2006   Page 006

No Child Left Behind

Test Scores Are Stagnant Despite No Child Left Behind

JULIA SELLERS

Aiken County pupils' scores have remained the same over the years—even with No Child Left Behind. Schools are being labeled as "failing" because administrators are having a hard time meeting requirements under the federal act, school officials said.

"When people see, 'Oh, it's a failing school,' they don't look to see that everybody's giving their best effort," said Sarah Emerling, a Busbee Elementary School special-education teacher.

David Mathis, the associate superintendent for administration, said the district's curriculum is correctly aligned and the test scores remain above state averages. The biggest frustration for the county is in the fine details of the federal act. "I don't see where No Child Left Behind has helped the system because the playing field from state to state is not level," Dr. Mathis said. "When we can play on a level playing field, I think it will have more substance to it. The concept of No Child Left Behind is a good one—no one has a desire to leave a child behind—but good policy should be supported by good practice."

The lack of federal funding hinders districts in improving low-scoring areas. "There are four-year-old programs that are organized out of federal funds, but it is never enough," Dr. Mathis said. "If the federal government fully funded programs they mandate, then we could close that gap."

Ms. Emerling, however, said the government will never change the policy if more people aren't vocal about the inconsistencies. "A parent has so much more power to make their concerns known; you always see teachers rallying against this, but not enough parents are," Ms. Emerling said. "Get in touch with legislators and local politicians."

Discussion Questions

1. What oversight role should the federal government play with regard to powers left to the states, such as education?
2. What should be the source of funding for schools? Less affluent school districts and states contend that more funds should come from the federal level, while more affluent districts and states tend to believe that funding decisions should be left to state and local governments. What compromise might ensure that every child in the United States has an equal opportunity to a quality education?

Federalism Under the Bush Administration

On the campaign trail in 2000, then Governor George W. Bush (R–TX) made it clear that he would follow in the tradition of former Republican President Ronald Reagan in moving to return power to the states.[21] Yet, no one could have foreseen the circumstances that would surround much of Bush's presidency. A struggling economy, terrorist attacks on the World Trade Center and the Pentagon, the invasion of Afghanistan, and the continuing costly war in Iraq, as well as the rising costs of education and welfare, produced state and federal budget deficits that would have been unimaginable only a few years before.

By 2003, many state governments faced budget shortfalls of more than $30 billion. Because state governments, unlike the federal government, are required to balance their budgets, governors and legislators struggled to make ends meet. Some states raised taxes, and others cut services, including school construction and infrastructure repairs. These dramatic changes helped nearly all of the states to project surpluses—albeit small—for fiscal year 2006.

The federal government was not so lucky; by November 2007, it struggled with a record $9.1 trillion debt, with the wars in Iraq and Afghanistan estimated to cost each American as much as $8,000.[22] This deficit had a number of sources, including President Bush's 2001 tax cuts, spending on the wars in Iraq and Afghanistan, costs associated with the dramatic expansion of the federal government after the September 11, 2001, terrorist attacks, and Hurricanes Katrina and Rita. In addition, the No Child Left Behind Act, which imposed a host of federal requirements on everything from class size to accountability testing, increased burdens on the federal coffers.[23]

The No Child Left Behind Act was viewed by many as an unprecedented usurpation of state and local powers. However, this trend of **preemption**, or allowing the

preemption
A concept derived from the Constitution's supremacy clause that allows the national government to override or preempt state or local actions in certain areas.

national government to override state or local actions in certain areas, is not new. The growth of preemption statutes, laws that allow the federal government to assume partial or full responsibility for state and local governmental functions, began in 1965 during the Johnson administration. Since then, Congress has used its authority under the Commerce Clause to preempt state laws. However, until recently, preemption statutes generally were supported by Democrats in Congress and the White House, not Republicans. The Bush administration's support of this law reflects a new era in preemption. (To learn more about preemption, see Politics Now: No Child Left Behind.)

Toward Reform: A New Judicial Federalism?

The role of the Supreme Court of the United States in determining the parameters of federalism cannot be underestimated. Neither can the role of the executive branch in advocating certain positions before the Court. Although in the 1930s Congress passed sweeping New Deal legislation, it was not until the Supreme Court finally reversed itself and found those programs constitutional that any real change occurred in the federal–state relationship. From the New Deal until the 1980s, the Supreme Court's impact on the federal system generally was to expand the national government's authority at the expense of the states.

Beginning in the late 1980s, however, the Court's willingness to allow Congress to regulate in a variety of areas waned. Once Ronald Reagan was elected president, he attempted to appoint new justices committed to the notion of states' rights and to rolling back federal intervention in matters that many Republicans believed were state responsibilities.

Mario M. Cuomo, a former Democratic New York governor, has referred to the decisions of what he called the Reagan-Bush Court as creating "a kind of new judicial federalism." According to Cuomo, this new federalism could be characterized by the Court's withdrawal of "rights and emphases previously thought to be national."[24] Illustrative of this trend are many of the Supreme Court's decisions in abortion cases. In *Webster* v. *Reproductive Health Services* (1989), for example, the Court first gave new latitude—and even encouragement—to the states to fashion more restrictive abortion laws.[25] Since *Webster*, most states have enacted new restrictions on abortion, with parental consent, informed consent or waiting periods, or bans on late-term or "partial birth" abortions being the most common. (To learn more, see Analyzing Visuals: State-by-State Report Card on Access to Abortion.) The Court consistently has upheld the authority of the individual states to limit a minor's access to abortion through imposition of parental consent or notification laws. Still, as discussed in chapter 5, in *Stenberg* v. *Carhart* (2000) the Supreme Court under Chief Justice William H. Rehnquist ruled that a state law limiting "partial birth" abortions without any provision to save a woman's health was unconstitutional.[26] And, in 2006, a unanimous Roberts Court ruled that states seeking to restrict minors' access to abortion must allow for some exceptions for medical emergencies.[27] But, in 2007, the Roberts Court upheld the

How does the Supreme Court affect the federal–state relationship? Since 1989, the Supreme Court has often deferred to state courts as well as judgments of the state legislatures.

Photo courtesy: Herblock/The Herb Block Foundation

"I GUESS I JUST HADN'T NOTICED IT BEFORE"

SUPREME COURT OF THE VARIOUS STATES

OVERRULING OF CONGRESS ON STATE EMPLOYEES RIGHTS

©2000 HERBLOCK

Violence on Campus

Violence is not a new trend on college campuses, but only recently has it been under the public eye. In 1990, Congress passed the Jeanne Clery Disclosure of Campus Security Policy and Campus Crime Statistics Act, which requires campuses to report all incidences of violence to students, to the community, and the U.S. Department of Education. According to the data, nearly 200,000 instances of crime were reported on campuses in 2005.[a] The prevalence of certain crimes on U.S. college and university campuses is surprising. For example, the American Association of University Women (AAUW) reports that nearly one-third of college women have been sexually harassed in a physical manner.[b]

One issue that hinders crime prevention is the coordination of federal, state, local, and campus officials. Following a mass shooting in 2007 at Virginia Tech, for example, it was revealed that the student gunman had been deemed mentally ill by state courts and that multiple complaints from fellow students had led to psychological counseling. Because much of this information was confidential and not shared among the various levels of administration, many students concluded that they were not warned about a potential danger and, furthermore, not enough was done to prevent the tragedy.[c]

In response to the wake-up call caused by the shooting, many universities reevaluated their crime prevention and emergency preparedness programs. Many universities across the country are turning to a technology that over 95 percentage of college students carry with them on a daily basis: cell phones.[d]

Hundreds of colleges and universities have begun to use text message alerts, sent to warn students of emergency situations. While proponents say the messages will help minimize disaster, others warn that not all students will receive the notifications because many professors prohibit cell phone use in class.

- Find out what program your college or university has put into place to prepare for emergency situations.
- Acquaint yourself with crisis protocol so that you and other students can be informed about what to do in emergency situations. Encourage your school to test its systems, and make suggestions on how to improve the process it has implemented.

---

[a]*Crime in the United States 2005,* Department of Justice, Federal Bureau of Investigation, September 2006.
[b]Catherine Hill and Elena Silva, *Drawing the Line: Sexual Harassment on Campus,* Washington, DC, AAUW Educational Foundation, 2006.
[c]"Killer's Manifesto: 'You Forced Me into a Corner,'" *Massacre at Virginia Tech,* CNN.com, April 18, 2007, www.cnn.com/2007/US/04/18/vtech.shooting/index.html.
[d]Thomas Frank, "Schools Weigh Text Alerts for Crises," USAtoday.com, April 23, 2007, www.usatoday.com/tech/news/techpolicy/2007-04-23-text-alerts-vt_n.htm.

---

constitutionality of the federal Partial Birth Abortion Act, the provisions of which were nearly identical to those struck down in *Stenberg* revealing the Court's continued preference to defer to the states when abortion is involved.[28]

Since 1989, the Supreme Court has also decided numerous cases in other issue areas related to federalism. From 1995–2005, especially, the Rehnquist Court made a number of closely divided decisions related to the balance of power between the federal and state governments. For example, in *U.S.* v. *Lopez* (1995), which involved the conviction of a student charged with carrying a concealed handgun onto school property, a five-person majority of the Court ruled that Congress lacked constitutional authority under the commerce clause to regulate guns within 1,000 feet of a school.[29] The majority concluded that local gun control laws, even those involving schools, were a state, not a federal, matter.

One year later, again a badly divided Rehnquist Court ruled that Congress lacked the authority to require states to negotiate with Indian tribes about gaming and casinos.[30] The U.S. Constitution specifically gives Congress the right to deal with Indian tribes, but the Court found that Florida's **sovereign immunity** protected the state from this kind of congressional directive about how to conduct its business. In 1997, the Court decided two more major cases dealing with the scope of Congress's authority to regulate in areas historically left to the province of the states: zoning and local law enforcement. In one, a majority of the Court ruled that sections of the Religious Freedom Restoration Act were unconstitutional because Congress lacked the authority to

sovereign immunity
The right of a state to be free from a lawsuit unless it gives permission to the suit. Under the Eleventh Amendment, all states are considered sovereign.

Examine the map created by NARAL Pro-Choice America, a liberal interest group, and answer the following questions:

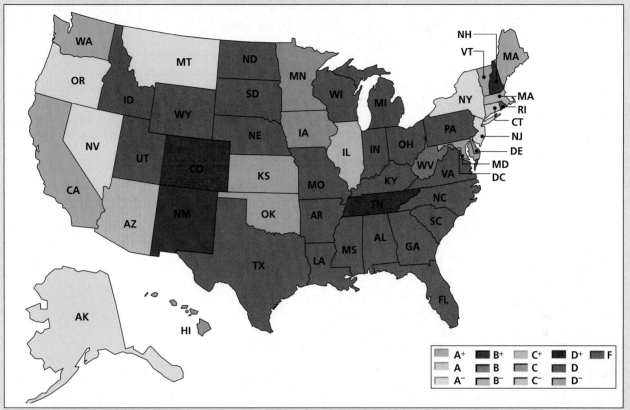

WHAT, if anything, do the states that receive A's have in common? What, if anything, do the states that receive D's and F's have in common?

HOW might factors such as political culture, geography, and characteristics of the population influence a state's laws concerning abortion?

WHAT criteria would a group opposing abortion, such as the National Right to Life Committee, use to grade the states? How would its criteria differ from those of NARAL Pro-Choice America?

Source: NARAL Pro-Choice America/NARAL Foundation, "Who Decides? A State-by-State Review of Abortion and Reproductive Rights, 2007," www.prochoiceamerica.org. Reprinted by permission.

meddle in local zoning regulations, even if a church was involved.[31] Another 5–4 majority ruled that Congress lacked the authority to require local law enforcement officials to conduct background checks on handgun purchasers until the federal government was able to implement a national system.[32] In 1999, in another case involving sovereign immunity, a slim majority of the Supreme Court ruled that Congress lacked the authority to change patent laws in a manner that would negatively affect a state's right to assert its immunity from lawsuits.[33] And, in 2000, the Court ruled that Congress had exceeded its powers in enacting some provisions of the Violence Against Women Act.[34] (To learn more, see Ideas into Action: Violence on Campus.)

As *New York Times* Supreme Court reporter Linda Greenhouse once noted, "a hallmark of the Rehnquist Court [was] a re-examination of the country's most basic constitutional arrangements, resulting in decisions that demanded a new respect for the sovereignty of the states and placed corresponding restrictions on the powers of Congress."[35] A careful analysis of Figure 3.4 demonstrates this point. During the 2002–2003 term, however, the Court took an unexpected turn in its federalism devolution revolution.[36] In a case opening states to lawsuits for alleged violations of the federal Family and Medical Leave Act (FMLA), Chief Justice William H. Rehnquist rejected Nevada's claim that it was immune from suit under FMLA.[37] But, as also is reflected in Figure 3.4, the Roberts Court's first decision involving federalism supported state power by limiting the federal government's right to block Oregon's physician assisted suicide law.[38]

Also in 2006, however, the Court's unanimous decision in *U.S.* v. *Georgia* supported federal authority by ruling that Congress had the power to interfere with state powers in situations where violations of the Eighth Amendment were alleged.[39] The extent to which the Roberts Court will ultimately throw its support to national or to state authority in our federal system remains to be seen, but the Court is clearly in a strong position to arbitrate the contentious balance of power in the American republic.

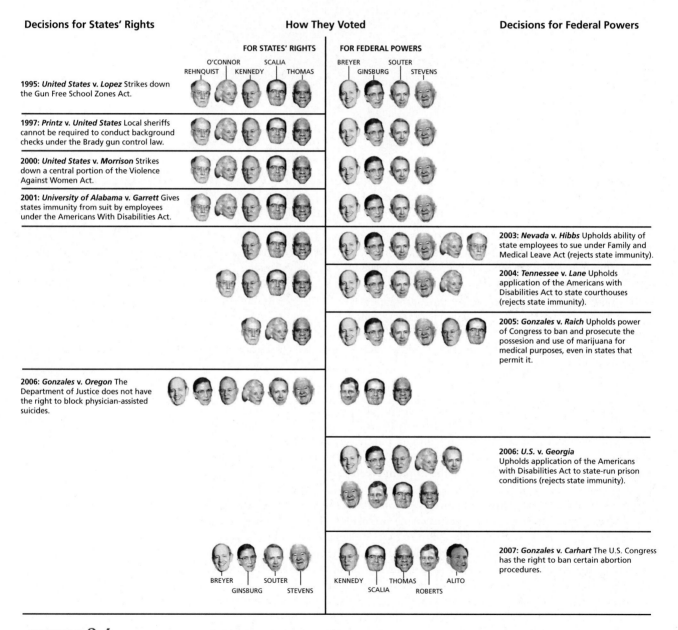

Decisions for States' Rights

How They Voted

Decisions for Federal Powers

FOR STATES' RIGHTS | FOR FEDERAL POWERS

O'CONNOR   SCALIA   BREYER   SOUTER
REHNQUIST   KENNEDY   THOMAS   GINSBURG   STEVENS

1995: *United States* **v.** *Lopez* Strikes down the Gun Free School Zones Act.

1997: *Printz* **v.** *United States* Local sheriffs cannot be required to conduct background checks under the Brady gun control law.

2000: *United States* **v.** *Morrison* Strikes down a central portion of the Violence Against Women Act.

2001: *University of Alabama* **v.** *Garrett* Gives states immunity from suit by employees under the Americans With Disabilities Act.

2003: *Nevada* **v.** *Hibbs* Upholds ability of state employees to sue under Family and Medical Leave Act (rejects state immunity).

2004: *Tennessee* **v.** *Lane* Upholds application of the Americans with Disabilities Act to state courthouses (rejects state immunity).

2005: *Gonzales* **v.** *Raich* Upholds power of Congress to ban and prosecute the possesion and use of marijuana for medical purposes, even in states that permit it.

2006: *Gonzales* **v.** *Oregon* The Department of Justice does not have the right to block physician-assisted suicides.

2006: *U.S.* **v.** *Georgia* Upholds application of the Americans with Disabilities Act to state-run prison conditions (rejects state immunity).

2007: *Gonzales* **v.** *Carhart* The U.S. Congress has the right to ban certain abortion procedures.

BREYER   SOUTER   KENNEDY   THOMAS   ALITO
GINSBURG   STEVENS   SCALIA   ROBERTS

FIGURE 3.4 The Rehnquist and Roberts Courts and Federalism

Source: New York Times (June 12, 2005): 3; *New York Times* (July 2, 2006): A18; Legal Information Institute at Cornell University Law School.

WHAT SHOULD I HAVE LEARNED?

The inadequacies of the confederate form of government created by the Articles of Confederation led the Framers to create a federal system of government that divided power between the national and state governments, with each ultimately responsible to the people. In describing the evolution of this system throughout American history, we have answered the following questions:

- **What are the roots of the federal system and how does the U.S. Constitution allocate governmental powers?**

    The national government has both enumerated and implied powers under the Constitution. An additional group of concurrent powers are shared by national and state governements. Other powers are reserved to the states or the people or expressly denied to both governments, although the national government is ultimately declared supreme. The Constitution also lays the groundwork for the Supreme Court to be the arbiter in disagreements between states.

- **What effect did the Marshall Court have on federalism?**

    Early on, the Supreme Court played a key role in defining the relationship and powers of the national government through its broad interpretations of the supremacy and commerce clauses.

- **What was the role of dual federalism before and after the Civil War?**

    For many years, dual federalism, as articulated by the Taney Court, tended to limit the national government's authority in areas such as slavery and civil rights, and was the norm in relations between the national and state governments. However, the beginnings of a departure from this view became evident with the ratification of the Sixteenth and Seventeenth Amendments in 1913.

- **What was the role of cooperative federalism during the New Deal and the growth of the national government?**

    The notion of a limited federal government ultimately fell by the wayside in the wake of the Great Depression and Franklin D. Roosevelt's New Deal. This growth in the size and role of the federal government escalated during the Lyndon B. Johnson administration and into the mid to late 1970s. Federal grants became popular solutions for a host of state and local problems.

- **How did New Federalism return power to the states?**

    After his election in 1980, Ronald Reagan tried to shrink the size and powers of the federal government through what he termed New Federalism. This trend continued through the 1990s, most notably through the contract with America. Initially, George W. Bush's administration seemed committed to this devolution, but the September 11, 2001, terrorist attacks led to substantial growth in the size of the federal government.

- **How have Supreme Court rulings created reform through a new judicial federalism?**

    The Rehnquist and Roberts Courts have redefined the parameters of federalism. While many of the decisions rendered in the 1990s supported state's rights, several recent decisions have expanded the powers of Congress. Thus, the Court has set an ambiguous course in determining the definition and role of federalism.

Key Terms

bill of attainder, p. 88
block grant, p. 99
categorical grant, p. 97
concurrent powers, p. 87
cooperative federalism, p. 95
dual federalism, p. 92
enumerated powers, p. 86
ex post facto law, p. 88
extradition clause, p. 88
federal system, p. 85

full faith and credit clause, p. 88
Gibbons v. *Ogden* (1824), p. 91
implied powers, p. 86
interstate compacts, p. 89
McCulloch v. *Maryland* (1819), p. 90
necessary and proper clause, p. 86
New Federalism, p. 98
preemption, p. 100
privileges and immunities clause, p. 88
reserve (or police) powers, p. 87

Seventeenth Amendment, p. 93
Sixteenth Amendment, p. 93
sovereign immunity, p. 102
supremacy clause, p. 87
Tenth Amendment, p. 87
unfunded mandates, p. 99
unitary system, p. 85

Researching Federalism

In the Library

Campbell, Tom. *Separation of Powers in Practice.* Stanford, CA: Stanford University Press, 2004.

Chemerinsky, Erwin. *Enhancing Government: Federalism for the 21st Century.* Stanford, CA: Stanford Law Books, 2008.

Derthick, Martha. *The Influence of Federal Grants.* Cambridge, MA: Harvard University Press, 1970.

Elazar, Daniel J., and John Kincaid, eds. *The Covenant Connection: From Federal Theology to Modern Federalism.* Lexington, MA: Lexington Books, 2000.

Finegold, Kenneth, and Theda Skocpol. *State and Party in America's New Deal.* Madison: University of Wisconsin Press, 1995.

Gerston, Larry N. *American Federalism: A Concise Introduction.* Armonk, NY: M.E. Sharpe, 2007.

Grodzins, Morton. *The American System: A View of Government in the United States.* Chicago: Rand McNally, 1966.

Kincaid, John, ed. *The Encyclopedia of American Federalism.* Washington, DC: CQ Press, 2005.

Manna, Paul. *School's In: Federalism and the National Education Agenda.* Washington, DC: Georgetown University Press, 2006.

McCabe, Neil Colman, ed. *Comparative Federalism in the Devolution Era.* Lanham, MD: Rowman and Littlefield, 2003.

Nagel, Robert F. *The Implosion of American Federalism.* New York: Oxford University Press, 2002.

O'Toole, Laurence, ed. *American Intergovernmental Relations: Foundations, Perspectives, and Issues.* Washington, DC: CQ Press, 2007.

Purcell, Edward, A. *Originalism, Federalism, and the American Constitutional Enterprises: A Historical Inquiry.* New Haven: Yale University Press, 2007.

Stephens, G. Ross, and Nelson Wikstrom. *American Intergovernmental Relations: A Fragmented Federal Polity.* New York: Oxford University Press, 2006.

Zimmerman, Joseph F. *Interstate Cooperation: Compacts and Administrative Agreements.* New York: Praeger, 2002.

On the Web

For a directory of federalism links, go to the American Council on Intergovernmental Relations at **govinfo.library.unt.edu/ amcouncil/index.html**

To learn more about your state and local governments, go to State and Local Government on the Net, **www.statelocalgov.net/,** which has links for thousands of state agencies and state and local governments.

The Landmark Supreme Courts cases site at **www. landmarkcases.org** provides the full text of *McCulloch* v. *Maryland* (1819) and *Gibbons* v. *Ogden* (1824).

The Oyez Project site at **www.oyez.org** provides a wealth of information on recent Supreme Court cases highlighted in the Toward Reform section of this chapter.

LIVE SAFELY...LIVE HAPPILY!

How to Clean a Gun and Keep Your Head...

Civil Liberties

The Supreme Court is frequently called upon to adjudicate disputes related to the scope of civil liberties protections in the United States. Issues such as free speech, trial by jury, and cruel and unusual punishment come before the Court at regular intervals. And, as a result, the judiciary has played a major role in defining the boundaries of these rights.

The right to bear arms has, however, received relatively little attention from the Supreme Court. In fact, before 2008, the Court had not directly considered the Second Amendment in nearly 70 years.

Despite the lack of Supreme Court intervention, gun control has remained a hot button issue in the federal and state legislatures. The federal government has placed waiting periods on the purchase of weapons, and prohibited the ownership of certain types of automatic and semi-automatic weapons. And, many states have enacted similar restrictions. Washington, D.C., for example, passed a total ban on handgun ownership in 1976.

For much of its 32-year history, this law went relatively unchallenged. But, in 2003, Robert A. Levy, a lawyer who worked as a constitutional fellow for the

libertarian Cato Institute, decided it was time to test the legality of the statute. Levy, who had never personally owned a gun, financed the litigation, recruited co-counsel, and hand-picked six plaintiffs who were willing to bring suit against the District. To illustrate the scope of the effects of the law, Levy assured that the plaintiffs were diverse in many ways. They included three men and three women, whose ages varied from 20 to 60. Four of the plaintiffs were white, while the other two were black. They lived in a variety of neighborhoods, and had a wide range of jobs, from lawyer to security guard.[1]

The case took five years to weave its way thorugh the federal judicial system, eventually reaching the Supreme Court in time for its 2007–08 term. The justices chose to hear oral arguments in the case, and in June of 2008, they handed down a 5-4 decision in the case of *D.C. v. Heller*. Writing for the majority, Justice Antonin Scalia acknowledged the problems that gun violence poses in American cities, but declared that the District of Columbia's ban on handgun ownership was unconstitutional.

The Court's majority opinion also included language declaring that the Second Amendment guaranteed "the right of law abiding, responsible citizens to use arms in defense of hearth and home." This statement clarified a longstanding dispute about whether the Amendment had been written to assure for the preservation of a

■ **The right to bear arms is an enduring civil liberty established by the Second Amendment.** At left, a gun safety pamphlet from the 1950s references the recreational aspects of hunting that were once taken for granted in the United States. At right, Dick Heller, the lead plaintiff in *D.C. v. Heller*, awaits the Supreme Court's ruling, with pro- and anti-gun protesters surrounding him.

⋆ WHAT SHOULD I KNOW ABOUT . . .

- the roots of civil liberties and the Bill of Rights?
- First Amendment guarantees of freedom of religion?
- First Amendment guarantees of freedom of speech, press, assembly, and petition?
- the Second Amendment right to keep and bear arms?
- the rights of criminal defendants?
- the right to privacy?
- civil liberties and combating terrorism?

well-trained militia, or whether the right to own a weapon also extended to ownership for private use. The majority's view was not well-received by the four dissenting justices, who charged that the opinion of the Court created a "dramatic upheavel in the law."[2]

Legal scholars expect that the D.C. case will lead to additional challenges out of other states and communities with restrictive legislation. The Supreme Court may also be asked to review these cases in the very near future. The question of whether the justices will decide to hear these cases, and if so, what decisions they will make, rests heavily on the composition and interests of the Court. In this way, Second Amendment rights are quite similar to many of the other rights and liberties we will consider in this chapter.

TO LEARN MORE—
—TO DO MORE
To learn more about the Supreme Court's decision in *D.C.* v. *Heller* (2008), go to www.oyez.org and search on the name of the case.

civil liberties
The personal guarantees and freedoms that the federal government cannot abridge by law, constitution, or judicial interpretation.

civil rights
The goverment-protected rights of individuals against arbitrary or discriminatory treatment.

When the Bill of Rights, which contains many of the most important protections of individual liberty, was written, its drafters were not thinking about issues such as abortion, gay rights, physician-assisted suicide, or many of the other personal liberties discussed in this chapter.

The Constitution is nonabsolute in the nature of most **civil liberties**. Civil liberties are the personal guarantees and freedoms that the federal government cannot abridge, either by law or judicial interpretation. As guarantees of "freedom to" action, they place limitations on the power of the government to restrain or dictate individuals' actions. **Civil rights**, in contrast, provide "freedom from" a host of discriminatory actions and place the burden of protecting individuals on the government. (Civil rights are discussed in chapter 5.)

Questions of civil liberties often present complex problems. We must decide how to determine the boundaries of speech and assembly. We must also consider how much infringement on our personal liberties we want to give the police or other government actors. Moreover, in an era of a war on terrorism, it is important to consider what liberties should be accorded to those suspected of terrorist activity.

Civil liberties issues often fall to the judiciary, who must balance the competing interests of the government and the people. Thus, in many of the cases discussed in this chapter, there is a conflict between an individual or group of individuals seeking to exercise what they believe to be a liberty, and the government, be it local, state, or national, seeking to control the exercise of that liberty in an attempt to keep order and preserve the rights (and safety) of others. In other cases, two liberties are in conflict, such as a physician's and her patients' rights to easy access to a medical clinic versus a pro-life advocate's liberty to picket that clinic. Many of the Supreme Court's recent decisions, as well as the actions of George W. Bush's administration in the aftermath of the September 11, 2001, terrorist attacks, are discussed in this chapter as we explore the various dimensions of civil liberties guarantees contained in the U.S. Constitution and the Bill of Rights.

In this chapter, we will first discuss the roots of civil liberties and the Bill of Rights. Afer surveying the meaning of one of the First Amendment's guarantees—freedom of religion—we will discuss the meanings of other First Amendment guarantees: freedom of speech, press, and assembly. Following a discussion of the Second

Amendment and the right to keep and bear arms, we will analyze the reasons for many of the rights of criminal defendants found in the Bill of Rights and how those rights have been expanded and contracted by the U.S. Supreme Court. We will then discuss the meaning of the right to privacy. Finally, we will examine how reforms to combat terrorism have affected civil liberties.

Roots of Civil Liberties: The Bill of Rights

The notion of adding a bill of rights to the Constitution was not a popular one at the Constitutional Convention. When George Mason of Virginia proposed that such a bill be added to the preface of the proposed Constitution, his resolution was defeated unanimously.[3] In the subsequent ratification debates, Federalists argued that a bill of rights was unnecessary. Not only did most state constitutions already contain those protections, but Federalists believed it was foolhardy to list things that the national government had no power to do.

The insistence of Anti-Federalists on a bill of rights, the fact that some states conditioned their ratification of the Constitution on the addition of these guarantees, and the disagreement among Federalists about writing specific liberty guarantees into the Constitution led to prompt congressional action to put an end to further controversy. This was a time when national stability and support for the new government particularly were needed. Thus, in 1789, Congress sent the proposed Bill of Rights to the states for ratification, which occurred in 1791.

The **Bill of Rights**, the first ten amendments to the Constitution, contains numerous specific guarantees, including those of free speech, press, and religion (for the full text, see the annotated Constitution that begins on page 52). The Ninth and Tenth Amendments, favored by the Federalists, note that the Bill of Rights is not exclusive. The **Ninth Amendment,** strongly favored by James Madison, makes it clear that this special listing of rights does not mean that others don't exist. The **Tenth Amendment** reiterates that powers not delegated to the national government are reserved to the states or to the people.

The Incorporation Doctrine: The Bill of Rights Made Applicable to the States

The Bill of Rights was intended to limit the powers of the national government to infringe on the rights and liberties of the citizenry. In *Barron v. Baltimore* (1833), the Supreme Court ruled that the national Bill of Rights limited only the actions of the U.S. government and not those of the states.[4] In 1868, however, the Fourteenth Amendment was added to the U.S. Constitution. Its language suggested the possibility that some or even all of the protections guaranteed in the Bill of Rights might be interpreted to prevent state infringement of those rights. Section 1 of the Fourteenth Amendment reads: "No State shall . . . deprive any person of life, liberty, or property, without due process of law." Questions about the scope of "liberty" as well as the meaning of "due process of law" continue even today to engage legal scholars and jurists.

Until nearly the turn of the century, the Supreme Court steadfastly rejected numerous arguments urging it to interpret the **due process clause** found in the Fourteenth Amendment as making various provisions contained in the Bill of Rights applicable to the states. In 1897, however, the Court began to increase its jurisdiction

Bill of Rights
The first ten amendments to the U.S. Constitution, which largely guarantee specific rights and liberties.

Ninth Amendment
Part of the Bill of Rights that reads "The enumeration in the Constitution, of certain rights, shall not be construed to deny or disparage others retained by the people."

Tenth Amendment
Part of the Bill of Rights that reiterates that powers not delegated to the national government are reserved to the states or to the people.

Balancing Liberty and Security in a Time of War

due process clause
Clause contained in the Fifth and Fourteenth Amendments. Over the years, it has been construed to guarantee to individuals a variety of rights ranging from economic liberty to criminal procedural rights to protection from arbitrary governmental action.

substantive due process
Judicial interpretation of the Fifth and Fourteenth Amendments' due process clauses that protects citizens from arbitrary or unjust laws.

over the states.[5] It began to hold states to a **substantive due process** standard whereby states had the legal burden to prove that their laws were a valid exercise of their power to regulate the health, welfare, or public morals of their citizens.

Interferences with state power, however, were rare. As a consequence, states continued to pass sedition laws (laws that made it illegal to speak or write any political criticism that threatened to diminish respect for the government, its laws, or public officials), anticipating that the Supreme Court would uphold their constitutionality. When Benjamin Gitlow, a member of the Socialist Party, printed 16,000 copies of a manifesto in which he urged workers to overthrow the U.S. government, he was convicted of violating a New York law that prohibited such advocacy. Although his conviction was upheld, in *Gitlow* v. *New York* (1925), the Supreme Court noted that the states were not completely free to limit forms of political expression. The court argued that certain "fundamental personal rights and liberties" were protected from state impairment by the Fourteenth Amendment's due process clause.[6]

incorporation doctrine
An interpretation of the Constitution that holds that the due process clause of the Fourteenth Amendment requires that state and local governments also guarantee the rights stated in the Bill of Rights.

Gitlow, with its finding that states could not abridge free speech protections, was the first step in the slow development of what is called the **incorporation doctrine**. After *Gitlow*, it took the Court six more years to incorporate another First Amendment freedom—that of the press. *Near* v. *Minnesota* (1931) was the first case in which the Supreme Court found that a state law violated freedom of the press as protected by the First Amendment.[7]

selective incorporation
A judicial doctrine whereby most but not all of the protections found in the Bill of Rights are made applicable to the states via the Fourteenth Amendment.

Selective Incorporation and Fundamental Freedoms

Not all the specific guarantees in the Bill of Rights have been made applicable to the states through the due process clause of the Fourteenth Amendment, as revealed in Table 5.1. Instead, the Court has used the process of **selective incorporation** to limit

TABLE 5.1 The Selective Incorporation of the Bill of Rights

Amendment	Right	Date	Case Incorporated
I	Speech	1925	*Gitlow* v. *New York*
	Press	1931	*Near* v. *Minnesota*
	Assembly	1937	*DeJonge* v. *Oregon*
	Religion	1940	*Cantwell* v. *Connecticut*
II	Bear arms	2008	*D.C.* v. *Heller*
III	No quartering of soldiers		Not incorporated (The quartering problem has not recurred since colonial times.)
IV	No unreasonable searches or seizures	1949	*Wolf* v. *Colorado*
	Exclusionary rule	1961	*Mapp* v. *Ohio*
V	Just compensation	1897	*Chicago, B&Q RR Co.* v. *Chicago*
	Self-incrimination	1964	*Malloy* v. *Hogan*
	Double jeopardy	1969	*Benton* v. *Maryland* (overruled *Palko* v. *Connecticut*)
	Grand jury indictment		Not incorporated (The trend in state criminal cases is away from grand juries.)
VI	Public trial	1948	*In re Oliver*
	Right to counsel	1963	*Gideon* v. *Wainwright*
	Confrontation of witnesses	1965	*Pointer* v. *Texas*
	Impartial trial	1966	*Parker* v. *Gladden*
	Speedy trial	1967	*Klopfer* v. *North Carolina*
	Compulsory trial	1967	*Washington* v. *Texas*
	Criminal jury trial	1968	*Duncan* v. *Louisiana*
VII	Civil jury trial		Not incorporated (Chief Justice Warren Burger wanted to abolish these trials.)
VIII	No cruel and unusual punishment	1962	*Robinson* v. *California*
	No excessive fines or bail		Not incorporated

the rights of states by protecting against abridgement of those liberties it considers most essential to order, liberty, and justice.

The rationale for selective incorporation was set out by the Court in *Palko* v. *Connecticut* (1937).[8] Frank Palko was charged with first-degree murder for killing two Connecticut police officers, found guilty of a lesser charge of second-degree murder, and sentenced to life imprisonment. Connecticut appealed. Palko was retried, found guilty of first-degree murder, and sentenced to death. Palko then appealed his second conviction, arguing that it violated the Fifth Amendment's prohibition against double jeopardy because the Fifth Amendment had been made applicable to the states by the due process clause of the Fourteenth Amendment.

The Supreme Court upheld Palko's second conviction and the death sentence. They also chose not to bind states to the Fifth Amendment's double jeopardy clause and concluded that protection from being tried twice (double jeopardy) was not a fundamental freedom. Palko died in Connecticut's gas chamber one year later. The Court's decision was overruled in 1969.

First Amendment Guarantees: Freedom of Religion

Many of the Framers were religious men, but they knew what evils could arise if the new nation was not founded with religious freedom as one of its core ideals. Although many colonists had fled Europe to escape religious persecution, most colonies actively persecuted those who did not belong to their predominant religious groups.

The Framers' distaste for a national church or religion was reflected in the Constitution. Article VI, for example, provides that "no religious Test shall ever be required as a Qualification to any Office or Public Trust under the United States." This simple statement, however, did not completely reassure those who feared the new Constitution would curtail individual liberty. Thus, the First Amendment to the Constitution soon was ratified to allay those fears.

The **First Amendment** to the Constitution begins, "Congress shall make no law respecting an establishment of religion, or prohibiting the free exercise thereof." This statement sets the boundaries of governmental action. The **establishment clause** ("Congress shall make no law respecting an establishment of religion") directs the national government not to involve itself in religion. The **free exercise clause** ("or prohibiting the free exercise thereof") guarantees citizens that the national government will not interfere with their practice of religion. These guarantees, however, are not absolute.

The Establishment Clause

Over the years, the Court has been divided over how to interpret the establishment clause. Does this clause erect a total wall between church and state, as favored by Thomas Jefferson, or is some governmental accommodation of religion allowed? While the Supreme Court has upheld the constitutionality of many kinds of church/state entanglements such as public funding to provide sign language interpreters for deaf students in religious schools,[9] the Court has held fast to the rule of strict separation between church and state when issues of prayer in school are involved. In *Engel* v. *Vitale* (1962), for example, the Court ruled that the recitation in public school classrooms of a brief nondenominational prayer drafted by the local school board was unconstitutional.[10]

The Court has gone back and forth in its effort to come up with a workable way to deal with church/state questions. In 1971, in *Lemon* v. *Kurtzman*, the Court tried to carve out a three-part test for laws dealing with religious establishment issues. According to the *Lemon* test, a practice or policy was constitutional if it: (1) had a secular pur-

First Amendment
Part of the Bill of Rights that imposes a number of restrictions on the federal government with respect to the civil liberties of the people, including freedom of religion, speech, press, assembly, and petition.

establishment clause
The first clause in the First Amendment; it prohibits the national government from establishing a national religion.

free exercise clause
The second clause of the First Amendment; it prohibits the U.S. government from interfering with a citizen's right to practice his or her religion.

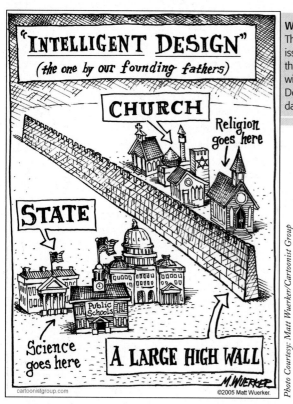

"INTELLIGENT DESIGN"
(the one by our founding fathers)

CHURCH

Religion goes here

STATE

Science goes here

A LARGE HIGH WALL

M. WUERKER

cartoonistgroup.com ©2005 Matt Wuerker

Public Schools

Photo Courtesy: Matt Wuerker/Cartoonist Group

pose; (2) neither advanced nor inhibited religion; and, (3) did not foster an excessive government entanglement with religion.[11] But, since the early 1980s, the Supreme Court often has sidestepped the *Lemon* test altogether and has appeared more willing to lower the wall between church and state so long as school prayer is not involved. In 1981, for example, the Court ruled unconstitutional a Missouri law prohibiting the use of state university buildings and grounds for "purposes of religious worship." The law had been used to ban religious groups from using school facilities.[12]

In 1995, the Court signaled that it was willing to lower the wall even further. In a case involving the University of Virginia, a 5–4 majority held that the university violated the free speech rights of a fundamentalist Christian group when it refused to fund the group's student magazine. The importance of this decision was highlighted by Justice David Souter, who noted in dissent: "The Court today, for the first time, approves direct funding of core religious activities by an arm of the state."[13]

For more than a quarter century, the Supreme Court basically allowed "books only" as an aid to religious schools, noting that the books go to children, not to the schools. But, in 2000, the Court voted 6–3 to uphold the constitutionality of a federal aid provision that allowed the government to lend books and computers to religious schools.[14] And, in 2002, by a bitterly divided 5–4 vote, the Supreme Court concluded that governments can give money to parents to allow them to send their children to private or religious schools.[15] Basically, the Court now appears willing to support programs so long as they provide aid to religious and nonreligious schools alike, and the money goes to persons who exercise free choice over how it is used.

Prayer in school also continues to be an issue. In 1992, the Court continued its unwillingness to allow organized prayer in public schools by finding unconstitutional the saying of prayer at a middle school graduation.[16] And, in 2000, the Court ruled that student-led, student-initiated prayer at high school football games violated the establishment clause.

Establishment issues, however, do not always focus on education. In 2005, for example, the Supreme Court in a 5–4 decision narrowly upheld the continued vitality of the *Lemon* test in holding that a privately donated courthouse display, which included the Ten Commandments and 300 other historical documents illustrating the evolution of American law, was a violation of the First Amendment's establishment clause. Court watchers now are waiting to see how the addition of two new justices to the Court will affect these closely divided opinions.[17]

Thinking Globally

Saudi Arabia and Free Exercise of Religion

In Saudi Arabia, public demonstration of religious affiliation or sentiment is forbidden except for Sunni Muslims who follow the austere Wahhabi interpretation of Islam. Public worship by non-Muslims is banned, and places of worship other than mosques are not permitted. The kingdom's Shi'a Muslim minority's religious practice is tightly controlled, and the construction of Shi'a mosques and religious community centers is restricted.

- Is it surprising that some countries officially support one religion at the expense of others? Why or why not?
- To what extent, should the United States pressure its allies, such as Saudi Arabia, to adhere more closely to American constitutional values of freedom of religion?
- What criteria would you use to evaluate the level of religious freedom in a country?

Source: THE NEW YORK TIMES   August 7, 2007

Religious Accommodation on College Campuses

Universities Install Footbaths to Benefit Muslims, and Not Everyone Is Pleased

TAMAR LEWIN

DEARBORN, Mich.—When pools of water began accumulating on the floor in some restrooms at the University of Michigan-Dearborn, and the sinks pulling away from the walls, the problem was easy to pinpoint. On this campus, more than 10 percent of the students are Muslims, and as part of ritual ablutions required before their five-times-a-day prayers, some were washing their feet in the sinks.

The solution seemed straightforward. After discussions with the Muslim Students' Association, the university announced that it would install $25,000 foot-washing stations in several restrooms.

But as a legal and political matter, that solution has not been quite so simple. When word of the plan got out this spring, it created instant controversy, with bloggers going on about the Islamification of the university, students divided on the use of their building-maintenance fees, and tricky legal questions about whether the plan is a legitimate accommodation of students' right to practice their religion—or unconstitutional government support for that religion.

Nationwide, more than a dozen universities have footbaths, many installed in new buildings. On some campuses, like George Mason University in Virginia, and Eastern Michigan University in Ypsilanti, Mich., there was no outcry. At Eastern Michigan, even some Muslim students were surprised by the appearance of the footbath—a single spigot delivering 45 seconds of water—in a partitioned corner of the restroom in the new student union.

"My sister told me about it, and I didn't believe it," said Najla Malaibari, a graduate student at Eastern Michigan. "I was, 'No way,' and she said, 'Yeah, go crazy.' It really is convenient."

But after a Muslim student at Minneapolis Community and Technical College slipped and hurt herself last fall while washing her feet in a sink, word got out there that the college was considering installing a footbath, and a local columnist accused the college of a double standard—stopping a campus coffee cart from playing Christmas music but taking a different attitude toward Islam.

"After the column, a Christian conservative group issued an action alert to its members, which prompted 3,000 e-mail and 600 voice messages to me and/or legislators," said Phil Davis, president of the college.

Mr. Davis said that after a legal briefing, the board concluded that installing footbaths was constitutional, and that the college hoped to have a plan in place by the next school year.

Here in Dearborn, the university called the footbaths a health and safety measure, not a religious decision. And it argued that while the footbaths may benefit Muslim students, they will be available to others, like lacrosse players who want to wash their feet.

Still, the plans are controversial.

On her Web site, Debbie Schlussel, a conservative lawyer and blogger in Southfield, Mich., posted, "Forget about the Constitutionally mandated separation of church and state … at least when it comes to mosque and state."

And in an editorial, the student newspaper, The Michigan Journal, worried that opponents would turn their hostility "on Muslim students at the university and Islam as a whole."

Hal Downs, president of the Michigan chapter of Americans United for Separation of Church and State, said, "The university claims it's available for Western students as well, but, traditionally, Western students don't wash their feet five times a day."

"They're building a structure for a particular religious tradition," Mr. Downs added, "and the Constitution says the government isn't supposed to endorse a particular religion."

The American Civil Liberties Union says the footbath issue is complex.

"Our policy is to object whenever public funds are spent on any brick and mortar component of religion," said Kary Moss, director of the Michigan Civil Liberties Union. "What makes this different, though, is that the footbaths themselves can be used by anyone, don't have any symbolic value and are not stylized in a religious way. They're in a regular restroom, and could be just as useful to a janitor filling up buckets, or someone coming off the basketball court, as to Muslim students."

Then, too, Ms. Moss said, the health and safety component is not normally part of religious accommodation cases.

"This came from the maintenance staff, which was worried about the wet floors," she said. "We were also aware that if the university said students could not wash their feet in the sink anymore, that could present a different civil liberties problem, interfering with Muslim students' ability to practice their religion."

Discussion Questions

1. *Do you agree with administrators at the University of Michigan that installation of footbaths are a health and safety issue and do not run afoul of First Amendment guarantees? Why or why not?*

2. *Do you believe that the same groups would object to the installation of footbaths if they were an accommodation for students practicing a religion other than Islam?*

The Free Exercise Clause

The free exercise clause of the First Amendment proclaims that "Congress shall make no law . . . prohibiting the free exercise [of religion]." Although the free exercise clause of the First Amendment guarantees individuals the right to be free from governmental interference in the exercise of their religion, this guarantee, like other First Amendment freedoms, is not absolute. When secular law comes into conflict with religious law, the right to exercise one's religious beliefs is often denied—especially if the religious beliefs in question are held by a minority or by an unpopular or "suspicious" group. (To learn about academic efforts to support free exercise, see Politics Now: Religious Accommodation on College Campuses.)

In 1990, for example, the Supreme Court ruled that the free exercise clause allowed Oregon to ban the use of sacramental peyote (an illegal hallucinogenic drug) in some Native American tribes' traditional religous services.[18] This decision prompted a dramatic outcry. Congressional response was passage of the Religous Freedom Restoration Act, which makes it harder for states to interfere with how citizens practice their religion. Although the Supreme Court ruled portions of the act unconstitutional in 1997, it continues to have some effect.[19] For example, in 2006, the U.S. Supreme court found that the use of Hoasca tea, which contains the controlled substance dimethyltryptamine (DMT), well-known for its hallucinogenic properties, was permissible free exercise of religion for memebers of the Brazilian-based O Centro Espirita Beneficente União do Vegetal church.[20]

First Amendment Guarantees: Freedoms of Speech, Press, Assembly, and Petition

Comparing Civil Liberties

Today, some members of Congress criticize the movie industry and reality television shows for pandering to the least common denominator of society. Other groups criticize popular musicians for lyrics that denigrate women. Such criticism often comes with calls for increased restrictions and greater regulation of media outlets. This leads many civil libertarians to believe that the rights to speak, print, and assemble freely are being seriously threatened.[21] (To learn more about content regulation, see chapter 10.)

Freedom of Speech and the Press

A democracy depends on a free exchange of ideas, and the First Amendment shows that the Framers were well aware of this fact. Historically, one of the most volatile areas of constitutional interpretation has been in the interpretation of the First Amendment's mandate that "Congress shall make no law . . . abridging the freedom of speech or of the press." Like the establishment and free exercise clauses of the First Amendment, the speech and press clauses have not been interpreted as absolute bans against government regulation. A lack of absolute meaning has led to thousands of cases seeking both broader and narrower judicial interpretations of the scope of the amendment. Over the years, the Court has employed a hierarchical approach in determining what the government can and cannot regulate, with some items getting greater protection than others. Generally, thoughts have received the greatest protection, and actions or deeds the least. Words have come somewhere in the middle, depending on their content and purpose.

THE ALIEN AND SEDITION ACTS When the First Amendment was ratified in 1791, it was considered to protect against **prior restraint** of speech or expression, or to guard against the prohibition of speech or publication before the fact. However, in 1798, the Federalist Congress with President John Adams's blessing enacted the Alien and Sedition Acts, which were designed to ban any criticism of the Federalist government by the growing numbers of Democratic-Republicans. These acts made the publication of "any false, scandalous writing against the government of the United States" a criminal offense. Although the law clearly ran in the face of the First Amendment's ban on prior restraint, the Adams administration and partisan Federalist judges successfully prosecuted and imposed fines and jail terms on at least ten Democratic-

prior restraint
Constitutional doctrine that prevents the government from prohibiting speech or publication before the fact; generally held to be in violation of the First Amendment.

Republican newspaper editors. The acts became a major issue in the 1800 presidential election campaign, which led to the election of Thomas Jefferson, a vocal opponent of the acts. He quickly pardoned all who had been convicted under their provisions and the Democratic-Republican Congress allowed the acts to expire.

Civil Liberties and National Security

SLAVERY, THE CIVIL WAR, AND RIGHTS CURTAILMENTS After the public outcry over the Alien and Sedition Acts, the national government largely refrained from regulating speech. But, in its place, the states, which were not yet bound by the Bill of Rights (through selective incorporation), began to prosecute those who published articles critical of governmental policies. In the 1830s, at the urgings of abolitionists (those who sought an end to slavery), the publication or dissemination of any positive information about slavery became a punishable offense in the North. In the opposite vein, in the South, supporters of slavery enacted laws to prohibit publication of any anti-slavery sentiments. Southern postmasters, for example, refused to deliver northern abolitionist papers, a step that amounted to censorship of the federal mail.

During the Civil War, President Abraham Lincoln took several steps that actually were unconstitutional. He made it unlawful to print any criticisms of the national government or of the Civil War, effectively suspending the free press protections of the First Amendment. Lincoln went so far as to order the arrest of several newspaper editors critical of his conduct of the war and ignored a Supreme Court decision saying that these practices were unconstitutional.

After the Civil War, states also began to prosecute individuals for seditious speech if they uttered or printed statements critical of the government. Between 1890 and 1900, for example, there were more than one hundred state prosecutions for sedition.[22] Moreover, by the dawn of the twentieth century, public opinion in the United States had grown increasingly hostile toward the commentary of Socialists and Communists who attempted to appeal to growing immigrant populations. Groups espousing socialism and communism became the targets of state laws curtailing speech and the written word. By the end of World War I, over thirty states had passed laws to punish seditious speech, and more than 1,900 individuals and over one hundred newspapers were prosecuted for violations.[23] In 1925, however, states' authority to regulate speech was severely restricted by the Court's decision in *Gitlow* v. *New York*.

WORLD WAR I AND ANTI-GOVERNMENTAL SPEECH The next major national efforts to restrict freedom of speech and the press did not occur until Congress, at the urging of President Woodrow Wilson during World War I, passed the Espionage Act in 1917. Nearly 2,000 Americans were convicted of violating its various provisions, especially those that made it illegal to urge resistance to the draft or to prohibit the distribution of anti-war leaflets. In *Schenck* v. *U.S.* (1919), the Supreme Court upheld this act, ruling that Congress had a right to restrict speech "of such a nature as to create a clear and present danger that will bring about the substantive evils that Congress has a right to prevent."[24] Under this **clear and present danger test,** the circumstances surrounding an incident are important. Under *Schenck*, anti-war leaflets, for example, may be permissible during peacetime, but during World War I they were considered to pose too much of a danger to be permissible.

For decades, the Supreme Court wrestled with what constituted a danger. Finally, in *Brandenburg* v. *Ohio* (1969), the Court fashioned a new test for deciding whether certain kinds of speech could be regulated by the government: the **direct incitement test.** Now, the government could punish the advocacy of illegal action only if "such advocacy is directed to inciting or producing imminent lawless action and is likely to incite or produce such action."[25] The requirement of "imminent lawless action" makes it more difficult for the government to punish speech and publication and is consistent with the Framers' notion of the special role played by these elements in a democratic society.

clear and present danger test
Test articulated by the Supreme Court in *Schenck* v. *U.S.* (1919) to draw the line between protected and unprotected speech; the Court looks to see "whether the words used" could "create a clear and present danger that they will bring about substantive evils" that Congress seeks "to prevent."

direct incitement test
Test articulated by the Supreme Court in *Brandenburg* v. *Ohio* (1969) that holds that advocacy of illegal action is protected by the First Amendment unless imminent lawless action is intended and likely to occur.

Why was the *Pentagon Papers* case important? A headline from the *New York Times* details legal proceedings in the *Pentagon Papers* case, formally called *New York Times Co. v. U.S.,* (1971) which was an important decision in establishing the boundaries of prior restraint.

What Speech is Protected by the Constitution?

Protected Speech and Publications

As discussed, the Supreme Court has refused to uphold the constitutionality of legislation that amounts to prior restraint of the press. Other types of speech and publication are also protected by the Court, including symbolic speech and hate speech.

PRIOR RESTRAINT With only a few exceptions, the Court has made it clear that it will not tolerate prior restraint of speech. For example, in *New York Times Co. v. U.S.* (1971) (also called the *Pentagon Papers* case), the Supreme Court ruled that the U.S. government could not block the publication of secret Department of Defense documents illegally furnished to the *Times* by anti-war activists.[26] In 1976, the Supreme Court went even further, noting in *Nebraska Press Association v. Stuart* (1976) that any attempt by the government to prevent expression carried "'a heavy presumption' against its constitutionality."[27]

symbolic speech
Symbols, signs, and other methods of expression generally also considered to be protected by the First Amendment.

SYMBOLIC SPEECH In addition to the general protection accorded to pure speech, the Supreme Court has extended the reach of the First Amendment to **symbolic speech**, a means of expression that includes symbols or signs. In the words of Justice John Marshall Harlan, these kinds of speech are part of the "free trade in ideas."[28] (To learn more about symbolic speech, see Ideas into Action: Political Speech and Mandatory Student Fees.)

The Supreme Court first acknowledged that symbolic speech was entitled to First Amendment protection in *Stromberg v. California* (1931).[29] There, the Court overturned a communist youth camp director's conviction under a state statute prohibiting the display of a red flag, a symbol of opposition to the U.S. government. In a similar vein, the right of high school students to wear black armbands to protest the Vietnam War was upheld in *Tinker v. Des Moines Independent Community School District* (1969).[30] Burning the American flag also has been held a form of protected symbolic speech, as discussed in chapter 2.

HATE SPEECH, UNPOPULAR SPEECH, AND SPEECH ZONES In the 1990s, a particularly thorny First Amendment issue emerged as cities and universities attempted to prohibit what they viewed as offensive hate speech. In *R.A.V. v. City of St. Paul* (1992), a St. Paul, Minnesota, ordinance that made it a crime to engage in speech or action likely to arouse "anger," "alarm," or "resentment" on the basis of race, color, creed, religion, or gender was at issue. The Court ruled 5–4 that a white teenager who burned a cross on a black family's front lawn, thereby committing a hate crime under the ordinance, could not be charged under that law because the First Amendment prevents governments from "silencing speech on the basis of its

Political Speech and Mandatory Student Fees

Universities across the United States often charge mandatory student fees that are used to pay for various activities and services across campus. These may include a range of health services (including sex education), student unions, technology, student publications, transportation, community service groups, and political organizations. Mandatory fees have increased in recent years at most universities, sometimes more sharply than tuition increases, especially at public universities. At the University of Wisconsin, Madison, for example, mandatory student fees increased nearly 20 percent in 2007, while tuition increased about 5 percent.[a]

The practice of charging mandatory fees can be controversial.[b] In March 2000, the U.S. Supreme Court ruled unanimously in *Board of Regents* v. *Southworth* that public universities could charge students a mandatory activity fee that could be used to facilitate extracurricular student political speech as long as the programs are neutral in their application.[c]

Scott Southworth, a law student at the University of Wisconsin, believed that the university's mandatory fee was a violation of his First Amendment right to free speech. He, along with several other law students, objected that their fees went to fund liberal groups. They particularly objected to the support of eighteen of the 125 various groups on campus that

benefited from the mandatory activity fee, including the Lesbian, Gay, Bisexual, and Transgender Center, the International Socialist Organization, and the campus women's law center.[d] The Court ruled against Southworth and for the university, underscoring the importance of universities being a forum for the free exchange of political and ideological ideas and objectives.

- Should universities be allowed to charge mandatory fees to all students, even those who do not use some of the services?
- Visit the Web site of your university or a university near you. What kind of mandatory fees are currently in place, and where do such fees go? How difficult is it to find information on the subject?
- Are you aware of any student organizations whose request for school funding has been rejected? If so, what reasons were given?.
- How is paying for student organizations a way universities can reinforce rights guaranteed by the First Amendment?

[a]Heather LaRoi, "Mandatory Student Fees Have Been Rising Faster than Tuition at UW Campuses," *Wisconsin State Journal* (November 4, 2007).
[b]Jordan Lorence, *FIRE's Guide to Student Fees and Legal Equality on Campus*. (Philadelphia: Foundation for Individual Rights in Education, 2003), 3–4.
[c]*Board of Regents* v. *Southworth*, 529 U.S. 217 (2000).
[d]"U.S. Court Upholds Student Fees Going to Controversial Groups," *Toronto Star* (March 23, 2000): NEXIS.

content."[31] In 2003, the Court narrowed this definition, ruling that state governments could constitutionally restrict cross burning when it occurred with the intent of racial intimidation.[32]

Two-thirds of colleges and universities have banned a variety of forms of speech or conduct that creates or fosters an intimidating, hostile, or offensive environment on campus. To prevent disruption of university activities, some universities have also created free speech zones that restrict the time, place, or manner of speech. Critics, including the ACLU, charge that free speech zones imply that speech can be limited on other parts of the campus, which they see as a violation of the First Amendment. They have filed a number of suits in district court, but to date none of these cases has been heard by the Supreme Court.

Unprotected Speech and Publications

Although the Supreme Court has allowed few governmental bans on most types of speech, some forms of expression are not protected. In 1942, the Supreme Court set out the rationale by which it would distinguish between protected and unprotected speech.

Thinking Globally
Free Speech or Hate Speech?

In 2007, as part of efforts to combat racism and hate crimes, the twenty-seven nations that comprise the European Union (EU) agreed to criminalize statements that deny or trivialize the Holocaust, the mass killing of Jews during World War II. The proposed rules call for the EU to impose up to three-year prison sentences for those convicted. A German court recently sentenced Ernst Zundel to five years in prison for inciting racial hatred and for his denial of the Holocaust.

- Is the European Union's ban on statements that deny the Holocaust too restrictive of free speech? Why or why not?
- Would such a ban be possible in the United States? Should such a ban be possible in the United States? Explain your answers.

According to the Court, libel, fighting words, obscenity, and lewdness are not protected by the First Amendment because "such expressions are no essential part of any exposition of ideals, and are of such slight social value as a step to truth that any benefit that may be derived from them is clearly outweighed by the social interest in order and morality."[33]

libel
False written statement or a written statement tending to call someone's reputation into disrepute.

slander
Untrue spoken statements that defame the character of a person.

New York Times Co. v. Sullivan (1964)
The Supreme Court concluded that "actual malice" must be proved to support a finding of libel against a public figure.

fighting words
Words that, "by their very utterance inflict injury or tend to incite an immediate breach of peace." Fighting words are not subject to the restrictions of the First Amendment.

LIBEL AND SLANDER   Libel is a written statement that defames the character of a person. If the statement is spoken, it is **slander**. In many nations—such as Great Britain, for example—it is relatively easy to sue someone for libel. In the United States, however, the standards of proof are much higher. A person who believes that he or she has been a victim of libel must show that the statements made were untrue. Truth is an absolute defense against the charge of libel, no matter how painful or embarrassing the revelations.

It is often more difficult for individuals the Supreme Court considers "public persons or public officials" to sue for libel or slander. ***New York Times Co. v. Sullivan* (1964)** was the first major libel case considered by the Supreme Court.[34] An Alabama state court found the *Times* guilty of libel for printing a full-page advertisement accusing Alabama officials of physically abusing African Americans during various civil rights protests. (The ad was paid for by civil rights activists, including former First Lady Eleanor Roosevelt.) The Supreme Court overturned the conviction and established that a finding of libel against a public official could stand only if there was a showing of "actual malice," or a knowing disregard for the truth. Proof that the statements were false or negligent was not sufficient to prove actual malice.

FIGHTING WORDS   In the 1942 case of *Chaplinsky* v. *New Hampshire*, the Court stated that **fighting words**, or words that, "by their very utterance inflict injury or tend or incite an immediate breach of peace" are not subject to the restrictions of the First Amendment.[35] Fighting words, which include "profanity, obscenity, and threats," are therefore able to be regulated by the federal and state governments. These words do not necessarily have to be spoken; fighting words can also come in the form of symbolic expression.

OBSCENITY   The current standard by which the court judges obscenity was laid out by Chief Justice Warren Burger, who wrote the opinion in *Miller* v. *California* (1973). The justices concluded that obscenity should be judged by "whether the work depicts or describes, in a patently offensive way, sexual conduct specifically defined by state law." The courts also were to determine "whether the work, taken as a whole, lacks serious literary, artistic, political, or scientific value." And, in place of the contemporary community standards gauge used in *Roth*, the Court defined community standards to refer to the locality in question, under the rationale that what is acceptable in New York City might not be acceptable in Maine or Mississippi.[36]

Time and contexts clearly have altered the Court's and, indeed, much of America's perceptions of what works are obscene. But, the Supreme Court has allowed communities great leeway in drafting statutes to deal with obscenity and, even more importantly, other forms of questionable expression. In 1991, for example, the Court voted 5–4 to allow Indiana to ban totally nude erotic dancing, concluding that the statute furthered a substantial governmental interest, and therefore was not in violation of the First Amendment.[37]

While lawmakers have been fairly effective in restricting the sale and distribution of obscene materials, monitoring the Internet has proven difficult for Congress. Since 1996, Congress has passed several laws designed to prohibit the transmission of obscene or "harmful" materials over the Internet to anyone under age eighteen. The U.S. Supreme Court has repeatedly found these laws unconstitutional.[38] Yet, in 2008, a seven-justice majority decided in *U.S.* v. *Williams* that the Protect Act, which outlawed the printing of material believed to be child pornography, was not overly broad and did not abridge the freedom of speech guaranteed by the First Amendment.[39]

Freedoms of Assembly and Petition

"Peaceful assembly for lawful discussion cannot be made a crime," Chief Justice Charles Evans Hughes wrote in the 1937 case of *DeJonge* v. *Oregon*, which incorporated the First Amendment's freedom of assembly clause to apply to the states.[40] Despite this clear declaration, and an even more ringing declaration in the First Amendment, the fundamental freedoms of assembly and petition have been among the most controversial, especially in times of war. As with other First Amendment freedoms, the Supreme Court often has become the arbiter between the freedom of the people to express dissent and government's authority to limit controversy in the name of national security.

Because the freedom to assemble is hinged on peaceful conduct, the freedoms of assembly and petition are related directly to the freedoms of speech and of the press. If the words or actions taken at any event cross the line of constitutionality, the event itself may no longer be protected by the Constitution. Absent that protection, leaders and attendees may be subject to governmental regulation and even criminal arrest, incarceration, or civil fines.

The Second Amendment: The Right to Keep and Bear Arms

Most colonies required all white men to keep and bear arms, and all white men in whole sections of the colonies were deputized to defend their settlements against Indians and European powers. These local militias were viewed as the best way to keep order and protect liberty. The Second Amendment was added to the Constitution to ensure that Congress could not pass laws to disarm state militias. This amendment appeased Anti-Federalists, who feared that the new Constitution would cause them to lose the right to "keep and bear arms" as well as an unstated right—the right to revolt against governmental tyranny.

Through the early 1920s, few state statutes were passed to regulate firearms (and generally these laws dealt with the possession of firearms by slaves). The Supreme Court's decision in *Barron* v. *Baltimore* (1833), which refused to incorporate the Bill of Rights to the state governments, prevented federal review of those state laws.[41] Moreover, in *Dred Scott* v. *Sandford* (1857) (see chapter 3), Chief Justice Roger B. Taney listed the right to own and carry arms as a basic right of citizenship.[42]

In 1934, Congress passed the National Firearms Act in response to the increase in organized crime that occurred in the 1920s and 1930s as a result of Prohibition. The act imposed taxes on automatic weapons and sawed-off shotguns. In *U.S.* v. *Miller* (1939), a unanimous Court upheld the constitutionality of the act, stating that the Second Amendment was intended to protect a citizen's right to own ordinary militia weapons and not sawed-off shotguns.[43] "For nearly seventy years following *Miller*, the court did not directly address the Second Amendment. Then, in the 2008 case of *D.C.* v. *Heller*, to the Court to ruled that the Second Amendment protects an individual's" right to own a firearm for personal use.[44] (To learn more about *D.C.* v. *Heller*, see the opening vignette.)

Congress and the executive branch, however, have been consistent players in the gun control debate. In the aftermath of the assassination attempt on President Ronald Reagan

Thinking Globally

Gun Control in Europe

Many European countries have very strict laws governing gun ownership. In Great Britain, it is illegal to own a handgun. In France, citizens may apply for a three-year permit only after demonstrating a clear need and completing an exhaustive background check. Laws in Switzerland and Germany are equally restrictive.

- Why is the issue of gun control so polarizing in the United States but not in Europe?
- Do you support any restrictions on the right to keep and bear arms? If so what? If not, why?

in 1981, many lawmakers called for passage of gun control legislation. At the forefront of that effort was Sarah Brady, the wife of James Brady, the presidential press secretary who was badly wounded and left partially disabled by John Hinckley Jr., President Reagan's assailant. In 1993, her efforts helped to win passage of the Brady Bill, which imposed a federal mandatory five-day waiting period on the purchase of handguns.

Perhaps more important than the Brady Bill was the ban on assault weapons signed by President Bill Clinton in 1994. This provision, which prohibited Americans from owning many of the most powerful types of guns, carried a ten-year time limit. It expired just before the 2004 presidential and congressional elections. Neither President George W. Bush nor the Republican-controlled Congress made any serious efforts to renew it.

The Rights of Criminal Defendants

Article I of the Constitution guarantees a number of rights for those accused of crimes. The Constitution guarantees **writs of *habeas corpus*,** court orders in which a judge requires authorities to prove that a prisoner is being held lawfully and that allows the prisoner to be freed if the judge is not persuaded by the government's case. Habeas corpus rights also imply that prisoners have a right to know what charges are being made against them.

Article I of the Constitution also prohibits ***ex post facto* laws,** or laws that apply to actions committed before the laws were passed. And, Article I prohibits **bills of attainder,** legislative acts that inflict punishment on individuals without judicial action.

The Fourth, Fifth, Sixth, and Eighth Amendments supplement these rights with a variety of procedural guarantees, often called due process rights. In this section, we examine how the courts have interpreted and applied these guarantees in an attempt to balance personal liberty and national safety and security.

The Fourth Amendment and Searches and Seizures

The **Fourth Amendment** to the Constitution protects people from unreasonable searches by the federal government. Moreover, in some detail, it sets out what may not be searched unless a warrant is issued, underscoring the Framers' concern with preventing government abuses.

The purpose of this amendment was to deny the national government the authority to make general searches. Over the years, in a number of decisions, the Supreme Court has interpreted the Fourth Amendment to allow the police to search: (1) the person arrested; (2) things in plain view of the accused person; and, (3) places or things that the arrested person could touch or reach or are otherwise in the arrestee's immediate control.

Warrantless searches often occur if police suspect that someone is committing or is about to commit a crime. In these situations, police may stop and frisk the individual under suspicion. In 1989, the Court ruled that there need be only a "reasonable suspicion" for stopping a suspect—a much lower standard than probable cause.[45]

Searches can also be made without a warrant if consent is obtained, and the Court has ruled that consent can be given by a variety of persons. It has ruled, for example, that police can search a bedroom occupied by two persons as long as they have the consent of one of them.[46] The same standard, however, does not apply to houses. In 2006, the Court ruled that the police could not conduct a warrantless search of a home if one of the occupants objected.[47]

---

writs of *habeas corpus*
Court orders in which a judge requires authorities to prove that a prisoner is being held lawfully and that allows the prisoner to be freed if the judge is not persuaded by the government's case. Habeas *corpus* rights imply that prisoners have a right to know what charges are being made against them.

***ex post facto* law**
From the Latin for "after the fact," a law that applies to actions committed before the law was passed. Prohibited by the Constitution.

bill of attainder
A legislative act that inflicts punishment on individuals without any kind of judicial action. Prohibited by the Constitution.

Fourth Amendment
Part of the Bill of Rights that reads: "The right of the people to be secure in their persons, houses, papers, and effects, against unreasonable searches and seizures, shall not be violated, and no Warrants shall issue, but upon probable cause, supported by Oath or affirmation, and particularly describing the place to be searched, and the persons or things to be seized."

SIMULATION
You are a Police Officer

In situations where no arrest occurs, police must obtain search warrants from a "neutral and detached magistrate" prior to conducting more extensive searches of houses, cars, offices, or any other place where an individual would reasonably have some expectation of privacy.[48] Police cannot get search warrants, for example, to require you to undergo surgery to remove a bullet that might be used to incriminate you, since your expectation of bodily privacy outweighs the need for evidence.[49] But, courts do not require search warrants in possible drunk driving situations. Thus, the police in some states can require you to take a Breathalyzer test to determine whether you have been drinking in excess of legal limits.[50]

Until passage of the USA Patriot Act, homes, too, were presumed to be private. Firefighters can enter your home to fight a fire without a warrant. But, if they decide to investigate the cause of the fire, they must obtain a warrant before their reentry.[51] In contrast, under the open fields doctrine first articulated by the Supreme Court in 1924, if you own a field, and even if you post "No Trespassing" signs, the police can search your field without a warrant to see if you are illegally growing marijuana, because you cannot reasonably expect privacy in an open field.[52]

Cars have proven problematic for police and the courts because of their mobile nature. As noted by Chief Justice William H. Taft as early as 1925, "the vehicle can quickly be moved out of the locality or jurisdiction in which the warrant must be sought."[53] Over the years, the Court has become increasingly lenient about the scope of automobile searches. In 2002, for example, an unusually unanimous Court ruled that when evaluating if a border patrol officer acted lawfully in stopping a suspicious minivan, the totality of the circumstances had to be considered. Wrote Chief Justice William H. Rehnquist, the "balance between the public interest and the individual's right to personal security," tilts in favor of a "standard less than probable cause in brief investigatory stops." This ruling gave law enforcement officers more leeway to pull over suspicious motorists.[54]

Testing for drugs is an especially thorny search and seizure issue. While many private employers and professional athletic organizations routinely require drug tests upon application or as a condition of employment, governmental requirements present constitutional questions about the scope of permissible searches and seizures. In 1989, the Supreme Court ruled that mandatory drug and alcohol testing of employees involved in accidents was constitutional.[55] In 1995, the Court upheld the constitutionally of random drug testing of public high school athletes.[56] And, in 2002, the Court upheld the constitutionality of a Tecumseh, Oklahoma, policy that required mandatory drug testing of high school students participating in any extracurricular activities. Thus, prospective band, choir, debate, or drama club members were subject to the same kind of random drug testing undergone by athletes.[57]

The Fifth Amendment: Self-Incrimination and Double Jeopardy

The **Fifth Amendment** provides that "No person shall be . . . compelled in any criminal case to be a witness against himself." "Taking the Fifth" is shorthand for exercising one's constitutional right not to self-incriminate. The Supreme Court has interpreted this guarantee to be "as broad as the mischief against which it seeks to guard," finding that criminal defendants do not have to take the stand at trial to answer questions, nor can a judge make mention of their failure to do so as evidence of guilt.[58] Moreover, lawyers cannot imply that a defendant who refuses to take the stand must be guilty or have something to hide.

This right not to incriminate oneself also means that prosecutors cannot use as evidence in a trial any of a defendant's statements or confessions that were not made voluntarily. As is the case in many areas of the law, however, judicial interpretation of the term voluntary has changed over time. In earlier times, it was not unusual for

Fifth Amendment
Part of the Bill of Rights that imposes a number of restrictions on the federal government with respect to the rights of persons suspected of committing a crime. It provides for indictment by a grand jury and protection against self-incrimination, and prevents the national government from denying a person life, liberty, or property without just due process of law. It also prevents the national government from taking property without fair compensation.

Who was Ernesto Miranda? Even though Ernesto Miranda's confession was not admitted as evidence at his retrial, the testimony of his ex-girlfriend and the victim were enough to convince the jury of his guilt. He served nine years in prison before he was paroled. After his release, he routinely sold autographed cards inscribed with what are called the *Miranda* rights now read to all suspects. In 1976, four years after his release, Miranda was stabbed to death in a Phoenix bar fight during a card game. Two *Miranda* cards were found on his body, and the person who killed him was read his *Miranda* rights upon his arrest.

***Miranda* v. *Arizona* (1966)**
A landmark Supreme Court ruling that held the Fifth Amendment requires that individuals arrested for a crime must be advised of their right to remain silent and to have counsel present.

***Miranda* rights**
Statements that must be made by the police informing a suspect of his or her constitutional rights protected by the Fifth Amendment, including the right to an attorney, provided by the court if the suspect cannot afford one.

double jeopardy clause
Part of the Fifth Amendment that protects individuals from being tried twice for the same offense.

police to beat defendants to obtain their confessions. In 1936, however, the Supreme Court ruled that convictions for murder based solely on confessions given after physical beatings were unconstitutional.[59] Police then began to resort to other measures to force confessions. Defendants, for example, were given the third degree—questioned for hours on end with no sleep or food, or threatened with physical violence until they were mentally beaten into giving confessions.

Miranda **v.** *Arizona* **(1966)** was the Supreme Court's response to these coercive efforts to obtain confessions that were not truly voluntary. On March 3, 1963, an eighteen-year-old girl was kidnapped and raped on the outskirts of Phoenix, Arizona. Ten days later, police arrested Ernesto Miranda, a poor, mentally disturbed man with a ninth-grade education. In a police-station lineup, the victim identified Miranda as her attacker. Police then took Miranda to a separate room and questioned him for two hours. At first he denied guilt. Eventually, however, he confessed to the crime and wrote and signed a brief statement describing the crime and admitting his guilt. At no time was he told that he did not have to answer any questions or that he could be represented by an attorney.

After Miranda's conviction, his case was appealed on the grounds that his Fifth Amendment right not to incriminate himself had been violated because his confession had been coerced. Writing for the Court, Chief Justice Earl Warren, himself a former district attorney and a former California state attorney general, noted that because police have a tremendous advantage in any interrogation situation, criminal suspects must be given greater protection. A confession obtained in the manner of Miranda's was not truly voluntary; thus, it was inadmissible at trial.

To provide guidelines for police to implement *Miranda*, the Court mandated that: "Prior to any questioning, the person must be warned that he has a right to remain silent, that any statements he does make may be used as evidence against him, and that he has a right to the presence of an attorney, either retained or appointed." In response to this mandate from the Court, police routinely began to read suspects what are now called their *Miranda* **rights**, a practice you undoubtedly have seen repeated over and over in movies and TV police dramas.

In 2003, the Court was faced with a new twist on *Miranda* rights. Samuel Patane was arrested in his home for violating a restraining order taken out by his girlfriend. As he was being arrested and was about to be read his rights, Patane interrupted the officers, saying that he knew them. The officers subsequently found guns in Patane's home, which as an ex-felon he was not allowed to possess. Patane later argued that the search was illegal because he was not Mirandized. A majority of the Court concluded that the guns could be used as evidence against Patane.[60]

The Fifth Amendment also mandates: "nor shall any person be subject for the same offense to be twice put in jeopardy of life or limb." This is called the **double jeopardy clause** and it protects individuals from being tried twice for the same offense. Thus, if a defendant is acquitted by a jury of a charge of murder, he or she cannot be retried for the offense even if new information is unearthed that could further point to guilt.

The Fourth and Fifth Amendments and the Exclusionary Rule

In *Weeks* v. *U.S.* (1914), the U.S. Supreme Court adopted the **exclusionary rule,** which bars the use of illegally seized evidence at trial. Thus, although the Fourth and Fifth Amendments do not prohibit the use of evidence obtained in violation of their provisions, the exclusionary rule is a judicially created remedy to deter constitutional violations. In *Weeks*, for example, the Court reasoned that allowing police and prosecutors to use the "fruits of a poisonous tree" (a tainted search) would only encourage that activity.[61]

In balancing the need to deter police misconduct against the possibility that guilty individuals could go free, the Warren Court decided that deterring police misconduct was most important. In *Mapp* v. *Ohio* (1961), the Warren Court ruled that "all evidence obtained by searches and seizures in violation of the Constitution, is inadmissible in a state court."[62] This historic and controversial case put law enforcement officers on notice that if they found evidence in violation of any constitutional rights, those efforts would be for naught because the tainted evidence could not be used in federal or state trials.

More recently, Congress and the federal courts have attempted to carve away at the exclusionary rule with a number of "good faith exceptions." These include allowing the use of tainted evidence in a variety of situations, especially when police have a search warrant and, in good faith, conduct the search on the assumption that the warrant is valid even though it is subsequently found invalid. Since the purpose of the exclusionary rule is to deter police misconduct, and in this situation there is no police misconduct, the courts have permitted the introduction at trial of the seized evidence. Another exception to the exclusionary rule is "inevitable discovery." Evidence illegally seized may be introduced if it would have been discovered anyway in the course of continuing investigation.

exclusionary rule
Judicially created rule that prohibits police from using illegally seized evidence at trial.

The Sixth Amendment and the Right to Counsel

The **Sixth Amendment** guarantees to an accused person "the Assistance of Counsel in his defense." In the past, this provision meant only that an individual could hire an attorney to represent him or her in court. Since most criminal defendants are too poor to hire private lawyers, this provision was of little assistance to many who found themselves on trial. Recognizing this, Congress required federal courts to provide an attorney for defendants who could not afford one. This was first required in capital cases (where the death penalty is a possibility); eventually, attorneys were provided to the poor in all federal criminal cases.[63]

Until the Court's decision in *Gideon* v. *Wainwright* (1963), criminal defendants were not entitled to lawyers in state courts.[64] Writing for the Court, Justice Hugo Black explained that "lawyers in criminal courts are necessities, not luxuries." Therefore, the Court concluded, the state must provide an attorney to indigent defendants in felony cases. Underscoring the Court's point, Gideon was acquitted when he was retried with a lawyer to argue his case.

The Burger and Rehnquist Courts gradually expanded the *Gideon* rule. The justices first applied this standard to cases that were not felonies[65] and, later, to many cases where probation and future penalties were possibilities. In 2008, the Court also ruled that the right to counsel began at the accused's first appearance before a judge.[66]

The issue of legal representation also extends to questions of competence. Various courts have held that lawyers who fell asleep during trial, failed to put on a defense, or were drunk during the proceedings were "adequate." In 2005, however, the Supreme Court ruled that the Sixth Amendment's guarantees required lawyers to take reasonable steps to prepare for their clients' trial and sentencing, including examining their prior criminal history.[67]

Sixth Amendment
Part of the Bill of Rights that sets out the basic requirements of procedural due process for federal courts to follow in criminal trials. These include speedy and public trials, impartial juries, trials in the state where crime was committed, notice of the charges, the right to confront and obtain favorable witnesses, and the right to counsel.

The Sixth Amendment and Jury Trials

The Sixth Amendment (and, to a lesser extent, Article III of the Constitution) provides that a person accused of a crime shall enjoy the right to a speedy and public trial by an impartial jury—that is, a trial in which a group of the accused's peers act as a fact-finding, deliberative body to determine guilt or innocence. It also provides defendants the right to confront witnesses against them.

Impartiality is a requirement of jury trials that has undergone significant change, with the method of selecting jurors being the most frequently challenged part of the process. Although potential individual jurors who have prejudged a case are not eligible to serve, no groups can be systematically excluded from serving. In 1880, for example, the Supreme Court ruled that African Americans could not be excluded from state jury pools (lists of those eligible to serve).[68] And, it was not until 1975 that the Court ruled that barring women from jury service violated the mandate that juries be made up of a "fair cross section" of the community.[69]

In 1986, the Court expanded the requirement that juries reflect a fair cross section of the community. Historically, lawyers had used peremptory challenges (those for which no cause needs to be given) to exclude African Americans from juries, especially when African Americans were criminal defendants. In *Batson* v. *Kentucky* (1986), the Court ruled that the use of peremptory challenges specifically to exclude African American jurors violated the equal protection clause of the Fourteenth Amendment.[70]

In 1994, the Supreme Court answered the major remaining unanswered question about jury selection: can lawyers exclude women from juries through their use of peremptory challenges? This question came up frequently because in rape trials and sex discrimination cases, one side or another often considers it advantageous to select jurors on the basis of their sex. The Supreme Court ruled that the equal protection clause prohibits discrimination in jury selection on the basis of gender. Thus, lawyers cannot strike all potential male jurors based on the belief that males might be more sympathetic to the arguments of a man charged in a paternity suit, a rape trial, or a domestic violence suit, for example.[71]

The right to confront witnesses at trial also is protected by the Sixth Amendment. In 1990, however, the Supreme Court ruled that this right was not absolute. In *Maryland* v. *Craig* (1990), the Court ruled that, constitutionally, the testimony of a six-year-old alleged child abuse victim via one-way closed circuit television was permissible. The clause's central purpose, said the Court, was to ensure the reliability of testimony by subjecting it to rigorous examination in an adversarial proceeding.[72] In this case, the child was questioned out of the presence of the defendant, who was in communication with his defense and prosecuting attorneys. The defendant, along with the judge and jury, watched the testimony.

The Eighth Amendment and Cruel and Unusual Punishment

Eighth Amendment
Part of the Bill of Rights that states: "Excessive bail shall not be required, nor excessive fines imposed, nor cruel and unusual punishments inflicted."

The **Eighth Amendment** prohibits "cruel and unusual punishments," a concept rooted in the English common-law tradition. Prior to the 1960s, however, little judicial attention was paid to the meaning of that phrase, especially in the context of the death penalty.

In the 1960s, the NAACP Legal Defense Fund (LDF), believing that the death penalty was applied more frequently to African Americans than to members of other groups, orchestrated a carefully designed legal attack on its constitutionality.[73] Public opinion polls revealed that in 1971, on the eve of the LDF's first major death sentence case to reach the Supreme Court, public support for the death penalty had fallen to below 50 percent. With the timing just right, in *Furman* v. *Georgia* (1972), the Supreme Court effectively put an end to capital punishment, at least in the short run.[74] The Court ruled that because the death penalty often was imposed in an arbitrary manner, it constituted cruel and unusual punishment in violation of the Eighth and Fourteenth Amendments.

Following *Furman*, several state legislatures enacted new laws designed to meet the Court's objections to the arbitrary nature of the sentence. In 1976, in *Gregg* v. *Georgia*, Georgia's rewritten death penalty statute was ruled constitutional by the Supreme Court in a 7–2 decision.[75] (To learn more about the controversy over the death penalty, See Join the Debate: The Death Penalty.) Unless the perpetrator of a crime was a minor at the time of the crime or mentally retarded, the Supreme Court currently is unwilling to intervene to overrule state courts' impositions of the death penalty, even when it appears to discriminate against African Americans.

At the state level, a move to at least stay executions took on momentum in March 2000 when Governor George Ryan (R–IL) ordered a moratorium on all executions. Ryan, a death penalty proponent, became disturbed by new evidence collected as a class project by Northwestern University students. The students unearthed information that led to the release of thirteen men on the state's death row. Soon thereafter, the Democratic governor of Maryland followed suit after receiving evidence that blacks were much more likely to be sentenced to death than whites; however, the Republican governor who succeeded him lifted the stay. Before leaving office in January 2003, Illinois Governor Ryan continued his anti-death-penalty crusade by commuting the sentences of 167 death-row inmates, giving them life in prison instead. This action constituted the single largest anti-death-penalty action since the Court's decision in *Gregg*, and it spurred national conversation on the death penalty, which, in recent polls, has seen its lowest levels of support since 1978.

Race and the Death Penalty

In another effort to verify that those on death row are not there wrongly, several states offer free DNA testing to death-row inmates. The U.S. Supreme Court recognized the potential exculpatory power of DNA evidence in *House* v. *Bell* (2006), in which the Court ruled a Tennessee death-row inmate who had exhausted other federal appeals was entitled to an exception to more stringent federal appeals rules due to DNA and related evidence suggesting his innocence.[76] The Court also revisited what can be considered cruel and unusual punishment in 2006 when it unanimously ruled that death-row inmates could challenge the drugs and procedures involved in lethal injections.[77] This "invitation" was followed by the Court's acceptance of a case challenging the cocktail of drugs used in lethal injections in Kentucky (and a number of other states). Many states issued a moratorium on the death penalty until the Court decided the case. In April 2008, the Court ruled that the combination of drugs used in these lethal injections did not constitute cruel and unusual punishment.[78]

Thinking Globally
The Death Penalty and Extradition

Mexico, which has no death penalty, will not extradite anyone facing possible execution to the United States. To guarantee extradition of criminals, U.S. prosecutors must agree to seek no more than life in prison. Other countries, including France and Canada, also demand such assurances from the U.S. government.

■ Were you surprised to learn that international agreements between nations can limit the types of sentences handed down to fugitives from the law? Why would justice officials agree to forgo the death penalty in such cases?

■ Canada, Australia, the European Union, and most of Central and South America have abolished the death penalty. What makes the United States so different in this regard?

The Right to Privacy

Privacy and Government Surveillance Powers

To this point, we have discussed rights and freedoms that have been derived fairly directly from specific guarantees contained in the Bill of Rights. However, the

Join the Debate

The Death Penalty

Overview: Challenges to the use of the death penalty are rising. In 2007, the United States Supreme Court agreed to take the case of *Baze* v. *Rees*, which questioned whether the method of lethal injection used by thirty-six states was potentially so painful as to violate the Eighth Amendment ban on cruel and unusual punishment. When the Court took the case, it in effect put a moratorium on executions until it ruled in the spring of 2008 that the method did not violate the Constitution. In 2007, forty-one people were put to death, the fewest since 1999, and New Jersey became the first state since 1965 to abolish the use of the death penalty. Although individuals and some government entities are having second thoughts about the death penalty, not everyone agrees that lthere is a problem. The federal government and thirty-eight states continue use the death penalty.

The debate over the use of capital punishment raises issues about the fundamental fairness of our system of justice. A major concern is that innocent people might be put to death, despite all the procedural safeguards in our court system to prevent mistakes. It is, of course, regrettable when someone is convicted of a crime he or she did not commit, even when they are only fined or imprisoned. Obviously there is no way of making amends when someone is executed.

Some of the current controversy related to the death penalty comes from advances in the use of DNA evidence. The Innocence Project, a nonprofit organization, has been working since 1992 to use DNA evidence to exonerate those wrongly convicted of crimes.[a] As of March 2008, the group's efforts have led to the release of 214 people, 16 of them on death row. In addition, between 1977 and 2007, another 108 people have been released from death rows because mistakes were made in eyewitness accounts, line-ups, police questioning,

and court proceedings. The obvious question is whether there were others who should have been released.

The major justification for the death penalty is captured in the slogan: "A life for a life." The consequence for taking someone else's life is the loss of the criminal's life. In turn, supporters of the death penalty believe that such a grave consequence will deter people from committing murder. There does not, however, appear to be a correlation between the death penalty and low homicide rates. Texas, for example, executes more people than all the rest of the states combined. Yet, Texas consistently has one of the highest murder rates in the country. And, as a whole, southern states use the death penalty more than any other region, but the homicide rate in 2007 for the South was 42 per 100,000 people, in contrast to the rate of 17 per 100,000 people in the Northeast and Midwest.

Another concern with the death penalty is the racial and gender disparities in those who are executed. It is extremely

rare for a woman to be sent to the death chamber. And, a person is less likely to be executed if he or she is white. In 2007, for example, 53 percent of the 41 people executed were white, 37 percent were African American, and 10 percent were Latino/a—figures that do not match the Racial composition of the general population. A crucial aspect of the debate regarding the death penalty is disagreement about whether the court system is biased and if convictions and executions reflect more general patterns of discrimination in society.

Arguments IN FAVOR of the Death Penalty

- The death penalty is just because it is used primarily to execute those who take the lives of others. Killing someone is the most egregious crime and act of violence, and societies must respond with the most severe punishment possible for murderers.

- The death penalty will deter at least some people from committing

---

right to privacy
The right to be left alone; a judicially created principle encompassing a variety of individual actions protected by the penumbras or shadows cast by several constitutional amendments, including the First, Third, Fourth, Ninth, and Fourteenth Amendments.

Supreme Court also has given protection to rights not enumerated specifically in the Constitution or Bill of Rights.

Although the Constitution is silent about the **right to privacy,** the Bill of Rights contains many indications that the Framers expected that some areas of life were off limits to governmental regulation. As early as 1928, Justice Louis Brandeis hailed privacy as "the right to be left alone—the most comprehensive of rights and the right most valued by civilized men."[79] It was not until 1965, however, that the Court

capital offenses. Although some murders will occur in a fit of rage and passion, we need to make those who plot to kill another human being think about the possible consequences if they go ahead with their plan.

- It is costly to keep convicted murderers in prison for the rest of their lives. The cost to taxpayers to keep someone in prison is about $30,000 per year. It makes little economic sense for society to clothe, feed, and care for a murderer for the rest of his or her life.

Arguments AGAINST the Death Penalty

- Mistakes are inevitably going to be made, and innocent people are going to be put to death for crimes they did not commit. The consequence of executing an innocent person is beyond remedy. We simply cannot risk mistakes when life is at stake.

- The United States is alone among Western countries in continuing to have the death penalty. Canada, Australia, and all European nations are among the 91 countries that have completely abolished the death penalty. The United States is in the company of repressive nations such as China, Saudi Arabia, and Malaysia in its use of the death penalty.

- It actually costs more to execute someone than it does to imprison the person for life. The Urban Institute released a study on March 6, 2008, that showed the state of Maryland spent an average of $37.2

How do states vary in their application of the death penalty? This cartoon offers a social commentary on the administration of the death penalty in Texas, which leads the nation in the number of executions.

Photo Courtesy: Nick Anderson/Cartoonist Group

million for each of the five executions it conducted since it reinstated the death penalty in 1978. Although this figure is higher than those cited in other studies, the general finding is consistent with analyses that cite the high costs of appeals in capital cases and the high costs of running death rows.

Continuing the Debate

1. Should the states and the federal government abolish the death penalty? If not, for what crimes should the death penalty be allowed?
2. How, if at all, can mistakes in our criminal justice system be avoided? Do gender and racial disparities in executions suggest that the system is unfair?

To Follow the Debate Online, Go To:

- www. prodeathpenalty.com, which advocates keeping and expanding the use of the death penalty and includes a list of print and media resources plus links to other supportive sites.

- www. deathpenaltyinfo.org for a wide array of studies and statistics on the death penalty as well as coverage of current events related to the death penalty and arguments

- pewforum.org/death-penalty/, which provides information, statistics, and arguments related to the death penalty.

ªwww.innocenceproject.org.

attempted to explain the origins of this right. (To learn more about the Ninth Amendment, see The Living Constitution.)

Birth Control

Today, most Americans take access to birth control as a matter of course. This wasn't always the case. *Griswold* v. *Connecticut* (1965) involved a challenge to the

The Living Constitution

The enumeration in the Constitution, of certain rights, shall not be construed to deny or disparage others retained by the people.

—NINTH AMENDMENT

This amendment simply reiterates the belief that rights not specifically enumerated in the Bill of Rights exist and are retained by the people. It was added to assuage the concerns of Federalists, such as James Madison, who feared that the enumeration of so many rights and liberties in the first eight amendments to the Constitution would result in the denial of rights that were not enumerated.

Until 1965, the Ninth Amendment was rarely mentioned by the Court. In that year, however, it was used for the first time by the Court as a positive affirmation of a particular liberty—marital privacy. Although privacy is not mentioned in the Constitution, it was—according to the Court—one of those fundamental freedoms that the drafters of the Bill of Rights implied as retained. Since 1965, the Court has ruled in favor of a host of fundamental liberties guaranteed by the Ninth Amendment, often in combination with other specific guarantees, including the right to have an abortion.

CRITICAL THINKING QUESTIONS

1. How can the U.S. justice system dictate the definition of a fundamental right if the Constitution does not specifically enumerate such rights?
2. How might public opinion affect judicial interpretations of the Ninth Amendment?
3. What others implied rights should be protected by the Ninth Amendment?

constitutionality of an 1879 Connecticut law prohibiting the dissemination of information about and/or the sale of contraceptives.[80] In *Griswold*, seven justices decided that various portions of the Bill of Rights, including the First, Third, Fourth, Ninth, and Fourteenth Amendments, cast what the Court called "penumbras" (unstated liberties on the fringes or in the shadow of more explicitly stated rights), thereby creating zones of privacy, including a married couple's right to plan a family. Thus, the Connecticut statute was ruled unconstitutional because it violated marital privacy, a right the Court concluded could be read into the U.S. Constitution through interpreting several amendments.

Later, the Court expanded the right of privacy to include the right of unmarried individuals to have access to contraceptives. "If the right of privacy means anything," wrote Justice William J. Brennan Jr., "it is the right of the individual, married or single, to be free from unwarranted governmental intrusion into matters so fundamentally affecting a person as the decision to bear or beget a child."[81] This right to privacy was to be the basis for later decisions from the Court, including the right to secure an abortion.

Roe v. Wade (1973)
The Supreme Court found that a woman's right to an abortion was protected by the right to privacy that could be implied from specific guarantees found in the Bill of Rights applied to the states through the Fourteenth Amendment.

Abortion

In 1973, the Supreme Court handed down one of its most controverial decisions, *Roe v. Wade*. Norma McCorvey, already a mother and an itinerant circus worker, was pregnant but unable to care for another child. Texas law allowed abortions only when they were necessary to save the life of the mother. Unable to secure a legal abortion and frightened by the conditions she found when she sought an illegal, back-alley abor-

What was the outcome of *Griswold* v. *Connecticut* (1965)? In this photo, Estelle Griswold (left), executive director of the Planned Parenthood League of Connecticut, and Cornelia Jahncke, its president, celebrate the Supreme Court's ruling *Griswold* v. *Connecticut* (1965). *Griswold* invalidated a Connecticut law that made selling contraceptives or disseminating information about contraception illegal.

tion, McCorvey turned to two young Texas lawyers who were looking for a plaintiff to bring a lawsuit to challenge Texas's restrictive statute. Before a final legal decision could be reached, McCorvey gave birth and put the baby up for adoption. Nevertheless, she allowed her lawyers to proceed with the case using her as their plaintiff, under the pseudonym Jane Roe.

When the case finally came before the Supreme Court, Justice Harry A. Blackmun, a former lawyer at the Mayo Clinic, relied heavily on medical evidence to rule that the Texas law violated a woman's constitutionally guaranteed right to privacy, which he argued included her decision to terminate a pregnancy. Writing for the majority in *Roe* v. *Wade* (1973), Blackmun divided pregnancy into three stages. In the first trimester, a woman's right to privacy gave her an absolute right (in consultation with her physician), free from state interference, to terminate her pregnancy. In the second trimester, the state's interest in the health of the mother gave it the right to regulate abortions—but only to protect the woman's health. Only in the third trimester—when the fetus becomes potentially viable—did the Court find that the state's interest in potential life outweighed a woman's privacy interests. Even in the third trimester, however, abortions to save the life or health of the mother were to be legal.[82]

Roe v. *Wade* unleashed a torrent of political controversy. From the 1970s through the present, the right to an abortion and its constitutional underpinnings in the right to privacy have been under attack by well-organized pro-life groups. The administrations of Ronald Reagan and George Bush were strong abortion opponents, and their Justice Departments regularly urged the Court to overrule *Roe*. They came close to victory in *Webster* v. *Reproductive Health Services* (1989).[83] In *Webster*, the Court upheld state-required fetal viability tests in the second trimester, even though these tests increased the cost of an abortion considerably. The Court also upheld Missouri's refusal to allow abortions to be performed in state-supported hospitals or by state-funded doctors or nurses. Perhaps most noteworthy, however, was that four justices seemed willing to overrule *Roe* v. *Wade* and that Justice Antonin Scalia publicly rebuked his colleague, Justice Sandra Day O'Connor, then the only woman on the Court, for failing to provide the critical fifth vote to overrule *Roe*.

After *Webster*, states began to enact more restrictive legislation. In *Planned Parenthood of Southeastern Pennsylvania* v. *Casey* (1992), Justices O'Connor, Anthony Kennedy, and David Souter, in a jointly authored opinion, wrote that Pennsylvania could limit abortions so long as its regulations did not pose "an undue burden" on pregnant women.[84] The narrowly supported standard, by which the Court upheld a twenty-four-hour waiting period and parental consent requirements, did not overrule *Roe*, but clearly limited its scope by abolishing its trimester approach and substituting the undue burden standard for the judicial standard used by the Court in *Roe*.

1965 *Griswold* v. *Connecticut*—The right to privacy is explained by the Court and used to justify striking down a Connecticut statute prohibiting married couples' access to birth control.

1980 *Harris* v. *McRae*—The Court upholds the Hyde Amendment, ruling that federal funds cannot be used to pay for poor women's abortions.

1973 *Roe* v. *Wade*—The Court finds that a woman has a right to have an abortion based on her right to privacy.

1986 *Bowers* v. *Hardwick*—The Court upholds Georgia's sodomy law, finding that gay men and lesbians have no privacy rights.

Homosexuality

It was not until 2003 that the U.S. Supreme Court ruled that an individual's constitutional right to privacy, which provided the basis for the *Griswold* (contraceptives) and *Roe* (abortion) decisions, prevented the state of Texas from criminalizing private sexual behavior. This monumental decision invalidated the laws of fourteen states.

In *Lawrence* v. *Texas* (2003), six members of the Court overruled its decision in *Bowers* v. *Hardwick* (1986) which had upheld anti-sodomy laws—and found that the Texas law was unconstitutional; five justices found it violated fundamental privacy rights.[85] Justice Sandra Day O'Connor agreed that the law was unconstitutional, but concluded that it was an equal protection violation. (To learn more about the equal protection clause of the Fourteenth Amendment, see chapter 5). Although Justice Antonin Scalia issued a stinging dissent, charging that "the Court has largely signed on to the so-called homosexual agenda," the majority of the Court was unswayed.[86]

Do all Americans deserve the same freedoms and liberties? Tyron Garner (left) and John Geddes Lawrence (center), the plaintiffs in *Lawrence v. Texas* (2003), are shown here with their attorney.

1989 *Webster v. Repro-ductive Health Services*—The Court comes close to overruling *Roe*; invites states to fashion abortion restrictions.

2003 *Lawrence v. Texas*—In overruling *Bowers*, the Court, for the first time, concludes that the right to privacy applies to homosexuals.

1992 *Planned Parenthood of Southeastern Pennsylvania v. Casey*—By the narrowest of margins, the Court limits *Roe* by abolishing its trimester approach.

2007 *Gonzales v. Carhart*—Supreme Court upholds the federal Partial Birth Abortion Ban Act.

The Right to Die

In 1990, the Supreme Court ruled 5–4 that parents could not withdraw a feeding tube from their comatose daughter after her doctors testified that she could live for many more years if the tube remained in place. Writing for the majority, Chief Justice William H. Rehnquist rejected any attempts to expand the right of privacy into this thorny area of social policy. The Court did note, however, that individuals could terminate medical treatment if they were able to express, or had done so in writing via a living will, their desire to have medical treatment terminated in the event they became incompetent.[87]

In 1997, the U.S. Supreme Court ruled unanimously that terminally ill persons do not have a constitutional right to physician assisted suicide. The Court's action upheld the laws of New York and Washington State that make it a crime for doctors to give life-ending drugs to mentally competent but terminally ill patients who wish to die.[88] But, Oregon enacted a right-to-die or assisted suicide law that allows physicians to prescribe drugs to terminally ill patients.

In November 2001, however, U.S. Attorney General John Ashcroft issued a legal opinion determining that assisted suicide is not "a legitimate medical purpose."[89] His memo also called for the revocation of physicians' prescription drug licenses, putting the state and the national government in conflict in an area that Republicans historically have argued is the province of state authority. Oregon officials immediately (and successfully) sought a court order blocking Ashcroft's attempt to interfere with implementation of Oregon law. Later, the Supreme Court ruled that the attorney general had overstepped his authority on every point.[90] Following this decision, in 2008, Washington voters approved an initiative that again allowed assisted suicide in that state.

oward Reform: Civil Liberties and Combating Terrorism

After September 11, 2001, the Bush administration, Congress, and the courts all operated in what Secretary of State Condoleezza Rice dubbed "an alternate reality," where Bill of Rights guarantees were suspended in a time of war.[91] The USA Patriot Act, the Military Commissions Act, and a series of secret Department of Justice memos all altered the state of civil liberties in the United States. Here, we detail the provisions of these actions and explain how they have affected the civil liberties discussed in this chapter.

The First Amendment

The USA Patriot Act, violates the First Amendment's free speech guarantees by barring those who have been subject to search orders from telling anyone about those orders, even in situations where no need for secrecy can be proven. It also authorizes the FBI to investigate citizens who choose to exercise their freedom of speech with no need to prove that any parts of their speech might be labeled illegal.

In addition, respect for religious practices has fallen by the wayside in the wake of the war on terrorism. For example, many Muslim detainees captured in Iraq and Afghanistan were fed pork, a violation of basic Muslim religious rules. Some were stripped naked in front of members of the opposite sex, another religious violation.

The Fourth Amendment

The USA Patriot Act enhances the ability of the government to curtail specific search and seizure restrictions in four areas. First, it allows the government to examine an individual's private records held by third parties. This includes allowing the FBI to force anyone, including physicians, libraries, bookshops, colleges and universities, and Internet service providers, to turn over all records they have on a particular individual. Second, it expands the government's right to search private property without notice to the owner. Third, according to the American Civil Liberties Union, the Act "expands a narrow exception to the Fourth Amendment that had been created for the collection of foreign intelligence information."[92] Finally, the Act expands an exception for spying that collects "addressing information" about where and to whom communications are going, as opposed to what is contained in the documents.

Judicial oversight of these new governmental powers is virtually nonexistent. Proper governmental authorities need only certify to a judge, without any evidence, that the requested search meets the statute's broad criteria. Moreover, the legislation deprives judges of the authority to reject such applications.

Due Process Rights

Illegal incarceration and torture are federal crimes, and the Supreme Court ruled in 2004 that detainees have a right to *habeas corpus*.[93] However, the Bush administration argued that under the Military Commissions Act of 2006, alien victims of torture had significantly reduced rights of *habeas corpus*. The Military Commissions Act also eliminated the right to bring any challenge to "detention, transfer, treatment, trial, or conditions of confinement" of detainees. It allowed the government to declare permanent resident aliens to be enemy combatants and enabled the government to jail these

Analyzing Visuals   Water-boarding

Please examine the diagram and answer the following questions:

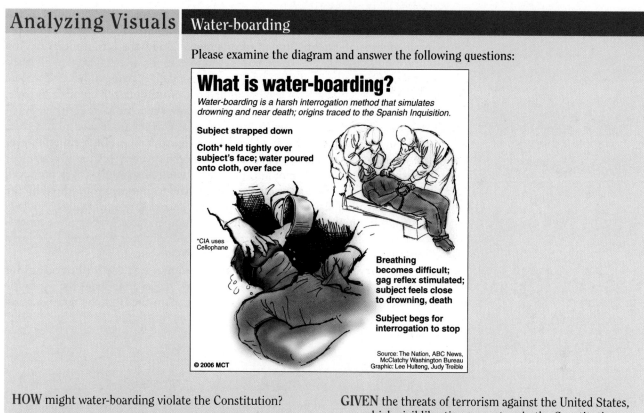

What is water-boarding?

Water-boarding is a harsh interrogation method that simulates drowning and near death; origins traced to the Spanish Inquisition.

Subject strapped down

Cloth* held tightly over subject's face; water poured onto cloth, over face

*CIA uses Cellophane

Breathing becomes difficult; gag reflex stimulated; subject feels close to drowning, death

Subject begs for interrogation to stop

Source: The Nation, ABC News, McClatchy Washington Bureau
Graphic: Lee Hulteng, Judy Treible

© 2006 MCT

HOW might water-boarding violate the Constitution?

HOW might you justify the use of water-boarding and other interrogation techniques that many nations classify as torture?

GIVEN the threats of terrorism against the United States, which civil liberties guarantees in the Constitution would you be willing to give up? Why?

people indefinitely without any opportunity to file a writ of *habeas corpus*. In 2008, in a surprising setback for the Bush administration, the Roberts Court ruled parts of the act unconstitutional, finding that any detainees could challenge their extended incarceration in federal court.[94]

Many suspected terrorists have also been held against their will in secret offshore prisons, known as black sites. In September 2006, President Bush acknowledged the existence of these facilities, moving fourteen such detainees to the detention facility at Guantanamo Bay, Cuba.

The Sixth Amendment right to trial by jury has also been curtailed by recent federal activity. Although those declared enemy combatants can no longer be held indefinitely for trial by military tribunals, they still do not have access to the evidence against them, and the evidence can be obtained through coercion or torture. These trials are closed, and people tried in these courts do not have a right to an attorney of their choosing. The federal government's activity in these tribunals was limited by the Supreme Court,[95] but the Military Commissions Act returned these powers to the executive branch.

Finally, the Eighth Amendment's prohibition on cruel and unusual punishment has been the subject of great controversy. Since shortly after the terrorist attacks of

September 11, 2001, there were rumors that many of the prisoners detained by the U.S. government were treated in ways that violated the Geneva Convention. In 2004, for example, photos of cruel treatment of prisoners held by the U.S. military in Abu Ghraib prison in Iraq surfaced. These photos led to calls for investigations at all levels of government. On the heels of this incident, the Justice Department declared torture "abhorrent" in a December 2004 legal memo. That position lasted but a short time. After Alberto Gonzales was sworn in as attorney general in February 2005, the department issued a secret memo. Provisions of this memo leaked to the press constituted "an expansive endorsement of the harshest interrogation techniques ever used by the Central Intelligence Agency."[96] According to one Justice Department memo, interrogation practices were not to be considered illegal unless they produced pain equivalent to organ failure or death. Among the techniques authorized by the government were combinations of "painful physical and psychological tactics, including head-slapping, simulated drowning, and frigid temperatures."[97] The most controversial of these techniques is water-boarding, which simulates drowning. (To learn more about this technique, see Analyzing Visuals: Water-boarding.)

The controversy over these interrogation techniques was one of the reasons for the resignation of Attorney General Gonzales in 2007. Questions about the appropriateness of such interrogation techniques were the main focus of the confirmation hearings of his successor, Michael Mukasey.

★ WHAT SHOULD I HAVE LEARNED?

■ **What are the roots of civil liberties and the Bill of Rights in the United States?**

Most of the Framers originally opposed the Bill of Rights. Anti-Federalists, however, continued to stress the need for a bill of rights during the drive for ratification of the Constitution, and some states tried to make their ratification contingent on the addition of a bill of rights. Thus, during its first session, Congress sent the first ten amendments to the Constitution, the Bill of Rights, to the states for their ratification. Later, the addition of the Fourteenth Amendment allowed the Supreme Court to apply some of the amendments to the states through a process called selective incorporation.

■ **What are the First Amendment guarantees of freedom of religion?**

The First Amendment guarantees freedom of religion. The establishment clause, which prohibits the national government from establishing a religion, does not, according to Supreme Court interpretation, create an absolute wall between church and state. While the national and state governments may generally not give direct aid to religious groups, many forms of aid, especially many that benefit children, have been held to be constitutionally permissible. In contrast, the Court has generally barred organized prayer in public schools. The Court largely has adopted an accommodationist approach when interpreting the free exercise clause by allowing some governmental regulation of religious practices.

■ **What are the First Amendment guarantees of freedom of speech, press, assembly, and petition?**

Historically, one of the most volatile areas of constitutional interpretation has been in the interpretation of the First Amendment's mandate that "Congress shall make no law . . . abridging the freedom of speech or of the press." Like the establishment and free exercise clauses of the First Amendment, the speech and press clauses have not been interpreted as absolute bans against government regulation.

Some areas of speech and publication are unconditionally protected by the First Amendment. Among these are prior restraint, symbolic speech, and hate speech. Other areas of speech and publication, however, are unprotected by the First Amendment. These include libel, fighting words, and obscenity and pornography.

The freedoms of peaceable assembly and petition are directly related to the freedoms of speech and of the press. As with other First Amendment rights, the Supreme Court has often become the arbiter between the right of the people to express dissent and government's right to limit controversy in the name of security.

■ **What is the Second Amendment right to keep and bear arms?**

Initially, the right to bear arms was envisioned as one dealing with state militias. Over the years, states and Congress have enacted various gun ownership restrictions with little Supreme Court interpretation as a guide to their ultimate constitutionality. In 2008, the Court ruled that gun ownership is a constitutionally protected individual right.

■ **What rights are guaranteed to criminal defendants in the United States?**

The Fourth, Fifth, Sixth, and Eighth Amendments provide a variety of procedural guarantees to individuals accused of crimes. In particular, the Fourth Amendment prohibits unreasonable searches and seizures, and the Court has generally refused to allow evidence seized in violation of this safeguard to be used at trial.

Among other rights, the Fifth Amendment guarantees that "no person shall be compelled to be a witness against himself." The Supreme Court has interpreted this provision to require that the government inform the accused of his or her right to remain silent. This provision has also been interpreted to require that illegally obtained confessions must be excluded at trial.

The Sixth Amendment's guarantee of "assistance of counsel" has been interpreted by the Supreme Court to require that the government provide counsel to defendants unable to pay for it in cases where prison sentences may be imposed. The Sixth Amendment also requires an impartial jury, although the meaning of impartial continues to evolve through judicial interpretation.

The Eighth Amendment's ban against "cruel and unusual punishments" has been held not to bar imposition of the death penalty or the use of lethal injection.

■ **What does the right to privacy encompass and what is the U.S. Supreme Court's rationale for this right?**

The right to privacy is a judicially created right carved from the penumbras (unstated liberties implied by more explicitly stated rights) of several amendments, including the First, Third, Fourth, Ninth, and Fourteenth Amendments. Statutes limiting access to birth control or abortion or banning homosexual acts have been ruled unconstitutional violations of the right to privacy. The Court, however, appears poised to allow some states to opt to allow their citizens the right to die under a physician's supervision.

■ **How have reforms to combat terrorism affected civil liberties?**

After the terrorist attacks of September 11, 2001, reform enacted by the Bush administration and Congress have dramatically altered civil liberties in the United States. Critics charge that a host of constitutional guarantees have been significantly compromised, while supporters say that these reforms are necessary to protect national security in a time of war.

Key Terms

Bill of Rights, p. 111
bill of attainder, p. 122
civil liberties, p. 110
civil rights, p. 110
clear and present danger test, p. 117
direct incitement test, p. 117
double jeopardy clause, p. 124
due process clause, p. 111
Eighth Amendment, p. 126
establishment clause, p. 113
ex post facto law, p. 122
exclusionary rule, p. 125

Fifth Amendment, p. 123
fighting words, p. 120
First Amendment, p. 113
Fourth Amendment, p. 122
free exercise clause, p. 113
incorporation doctrine, p. 112
libel, p. 120
Miranda rights, p. 124
Miranda v. *Arizona* (1966), p. 124
New York Times Co. v. *Sullivan*
    (1964), p. 120
Ninth Amendment, p. 111

prior restraint, p. 116
right to privacy, p. 128
Roe v. *Wade* (1973), p. 130
selective incorporation, p. 112
Sixth Amendment, p. 125
slander, p. 120
substantive due process, p. 112
symbolic speech, p. 118
Tenth Amendment, p. 111
writ of *habeas corpus*, p. 122

Researching Civil Liberties

In the Library

Abrams, Floyd. *Trials of the First Amendment*. New York: Viking, 2006.

Ackerman, Bruce. *Before the Next Attack: Preserving Civil Liberties in an Age of Terrorism*. New Haven, CT: Yale University Press, 2007.

Cole, David, and James X. Dempsey. *Terrorism and the Constitution: Sacrificing Civil Liberties in the Name of National Security*, 3rd ed. Washington, DC: First Amendment Foundation, 2006.

Darmer, M. Katherine B., Robert M. Baird, Stuart E. Rosenbaum, eds. *Civil Liberties vs. National Security in a Post 9/11 World*. New York: Prometheus, 2004.

Etzoni, Amitai, and Jason H. Marsh, eds. *Rights vs. Public Safety after 9/11: America in the Age of Terrorism*. Lanham, MD: Rowman and Littlefield, 2003.

Fiss, Owen M. *The Irony of Free Speech*, reprint ed. Cambridge, MA: Harvard University Press, 1998.

Gates, Henry Louis, Jr., ed. *Speaking of Race, Speaking of Sex: Hate Speech, Civil Rights, and Civil Liberties*. New York: New York University Press, 1995.

Ivers, Gregg, and Kevin T. McGuire, eds. *Creating Constitutional Change*. Charlottesville: University Press of Virginia, 2004.

Leone, Richard C., and Greg Anrig Jr., eds. *The War on Our Freedoms: Civil Liberties in an Age of Terrorism*. Public Affairs, 2003.

Lewis, Anthony. *Gideon's Trumpet*, reissue ed. New York: Vintage Books, 1989.

———. *Make No Law: The Sullivan Case and the First Amendment*, reprint ed. New York: Random House, 1992.

Lichtblau, Eric. *Bush's Law: The Remaking of American Justice*. New York:/Pantheon, 2008.

O'Brien, David M. *Animal Sacrifice and Religions Freedom: Church of the Lukumi Babalu Aye v. City of Hialeah*. Lawrence: University Press of Kansas, 2004.

———. *Constitutional Law and Politics, vol. 2: Civil Rights and Civil Liberties*, 6th ed. New York: Norton, 2005.

O'Connor, Karen. *No Neutral Ground: Abortion Politics in an Age of Absolutes*. Boulder, CO: Westview, 1996.

Romero, Anthony D., and Dina Temple-Raston. *In Defense of Our America: The Fight for Civil Liberites in the Age of Terror*. New York:/William Morron, 2007.

Sands, Philippe. *Torture Teams: Rumsfeld's Memo and the Betrayal of American Values*. New York: Palgrave Macmillan, 2008.

Weddington, Sarah. *A Question of Choice*, reprint ed. New York: Grosset Putnam, 1993.

On the Web

To compare differing views on civil liberties, including debates related to the war on terrorism, go to the home pages for the following groups:
The American Civil Liberties Union, **www.aclu.org**
People for the American Way, **www.pfaw.org**
The American Center for Law and Justice, **www.aclj.org**
The Federalist Society, **www.fed-soc.org/**

To learn more about the Supreme Court cases discussed in this chapter, go to Oyez: U.S. Supreme Court Media at **www.oyez.org**, and search on the case name. Or, go to the Legal Information Institute of Cornell University's Law School, **www.law.cornell.edu/supet/cases/topic. htm,** where you can search cases by topic.

To compare the different sides of the abortion debate, go to FLITE (Federal Legal Information Through Electronics) at **www.fedworld.gov/supcourt/.**

For more on civil liberties protections for homosexuals, go to Human Rights Campaign at **www.hrc.org**, and Lambda Legal at **www.lambdalegal.org.**

5

Civil Rights

For many years, the U.S. government has played an important role in enforcing civil rights in the nation. The passage of the Thirteenth, Fourteenth, and Fifteenth Amendments, for example, abolished slavery, guaranteed citizens equal protection of the laws, and granted the right to vote to newly freed male slaves. Much later, after a prolonged civil rights movement sparked by years of discrimination against African Americans, particularly in the South, the U.S. Congress passed sweeping anti-discrimination legislation in the Civil Rights Act of 1964 and the Voting Rights Act of 1965. The Civil Rights Act, in particular, banned discrimination in employment, public accommodations, and education based on race, creed, color, religion, national origin, or sex. Over the years, Congress has added prohibitions based on pregnancy and disability to the act.

The Civil Rights Act and all federal statutes prohibiting discrimination are enforced by the Civil Rights Division of the Department of Justice. The division is headed by an assistant attorney general, a political appointee, who reports to the chief law enforcement official of the United States, the attorney general.

In 2006, the Civil Rights Division was in turmoil. Almost 20 percent of its lawyers, a record number, left in 2005 when many took advantage of a buyout program that allowed them to retire early; other career lawyers took positions elsewhere because they were upset by what they perceived as the politicization of the division. Many of the lawyers, all career civil servants, believed they were being pressured to leave because they "did not share the administration's conservative view on civil rights laws."[1] Veteran lawyers charged that the political appointees in the division made hiring and policy decisions without consulting staff members with more expertise. Their allegations were supported when it was revealed in 2007 that Attorney General Alberto Gonzales, along with the White House, had interfered in the work of regional U.S. attorneys. Eight of these attorneys appeared to have been fired without just cause spurring congressional hearings and the indictment of a Gonzales aide.[2]

In addition to these personnel changes, since President George W. Bush took office and appointed those who shared his beliefs to key division spots, prosecutions of race and sex discrimination have decreased by 40 percent. Many division lawyers found their workloads shifted to immigration and deportation cases.[3]

Voting Rights Act enforcement, too, was politicized, according to many nonpolitical career lawyers in the division's voting rights section. According to them, those "who remain are barred from offering recommendations in major voting rights cases."[4] And, when the

■ **Who protects the civil rights of American citizens?** At left, non-violent protestors demanding voting rights for African Americans march across the Edmund Pettus Bridge on their way from Selma to Montgomery, Alabama, in March of 1965. At right, some of the U.S. attorneys who were fired by the Justice Department in 2006. The firings raised questions about the extent to which partisan politics rather than the rule of law was the guiding force during Alberto Gonzales's tenure as attorney general.

WHAT SHOULD I KNOW ABOUT . . .

- the roots of suffrage: 1800–1890?
- the push for equality: 1890–1954?
- the civil rights movement?
- the women's rights movement?
- how other groups have mobilized for civil rights?
- reforms affecting civil rights, affirmative action, and pay equity?

section involved itself in cases in Georgia, Mississippi, and Texas, it supported actions favoring the election of Republicans. With regard to the controversial Texas redistricting plan discussed in chapter 13, for example, the Attorney General acknowledged in December 2005 that Department of Justice officials had overruled a unanimous finding that aspects of the Texas plan would violate the Civil Rights Act of 1965.[5] In 2006, the U.S. Supreme Court ruled that states did not have to wait for a new U.S. Census to redraw district lines. The Court also found that one of the districts diluted the voting power of Hispanics and thus violated the Voting Rights Act.[6] The Obama administration is likely to refocus the agency's energies on civil rights enforcement.

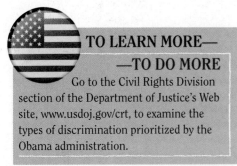

**TO LEARN MORE—
—TO DO MORE**
Go to the Civil Rights Division section of the Department of Justice's Web site, www.usdoj.gov/crt, to examine the types of discrimination prioritized by the Obama administration.

The Declaration of Independence, written in 1776, boldly proclaims: "We hold these truths to be self-evident, that all men are created equal, that they are endowed by their Creator with certain unalienable rights." And, although the Framers considered some equality issues, one entire class of citizens—slaves—were treated in the new Constitution more as property than as people. Delegates to the Constitutional Convention put political expediency before the immorality of slavery. Moreover, the Constitution considered white women full citizens for purposes of determining state population, but voting qualifications were left to the states, and none allowed women to vote at the time the Constitution was ratified.

civil rights
The government-protected rights of individuals against arbitrary or discriminatory treatment by governments or individuals.

Since the Constitution was written, concepts of **civil rights**, the government-protected rights of individuals against arbitrary or discriminatory treatment by governments or individuals based on categories such as race, sex, national origin, age, religion, or sexual orientation, have changed dramatically. The addition of the Fourteenth Amendment, one of three Civil War Amendments ratified from 1865 to 1870, introduced the notion of equality into the Constitution by specifying that a state could not deny "any person within its jurisdiction equal protection of the laws." Throughout history, the Fourteenth Amendment's equal protection guarantees have been the linchpin of efforts to expand upon the original intent of the amendment to allow its provisions to protect a variety of other groups from discrimination.

Since passage of the Civil War Amendments, there has been a fairly consistent pattern of expansion of civil rights to more and more groups. In this chapter, we will first discuss the roots of suffrage, 1800–1890. We will then examine African Americans' and women's next push for equality, 1890–1954. These topics lead to an analysis of the civil rights movement and the Civil Rights Act of 1964. After discussing the development of a new women's rights movement, we will present the efforts of other groups to mobilize for rights. Finally, we will explore reform efforts in civil rights.

Roots of Suffrage: 1800–1890

The period from 1800 to 1890 was one of tremendous change and upheaval in America. Despite the Civil War and the freeing of the slaves, the promise of equality guaranteed to African Americans by the Civil War Amendments failed to become a reality. Women's rights activists also

TIMELINE

The Struggle for Equal Protection

began to make claims for equality, often using the arguments enunciated for the abolition of slavery, but they too fell far short of their goals.

Slavery and Congress

As the nation grew westward in the early 1800s, conflicts between northern and southern states intensified over the admission of new states to the union with free or slave status. The first major crisis occurred in 1820, when Missouri applied for admission to the union as a slave state—that is, one in which slavery would be legal. Missouri's admission would have weighted the Senate in favor of slavery and therefore was opposed by northern senators. To resolve this conflict, Congress passed the Missouri Compromise of 1820. The Compromise prohibited slavery north of the geographical boundary at 36 degrees latitude. This act allowed Missouri to be admitted to the union as a slave state, and to maintain the balance of slave and free states, Maine was carved out of a portion of Massachusetts.

The First Civil Rights Movements: Abolition and Women's Rights

The Missouri Compromise solidified the South in its determination to keep slavery legal, but it also fueled the fervor of those who opposed slavery. William Lloyd Garrison, a white New Englander, galvanized the abolitionist movement in the early 1830s. Garrison, a newspaper editor, founded the American Anti-Slavery Society in 1833; by 1838, it had more than 250,000 members.

Slavery was not the only practice that people began to question in the decades following the Missouri Compromise. In 1840, for example, Elizabeth Cady Stanton and Lucretia Mott, who were to found the first women's rights movement, attended the 1840 meeting of the World Anti-Slavery Society in London with their husbands. After their long journey, they were not allowed to participate in the convention because they were women. As they sat in the balcony, apart from the male delegates, they paused to compare their status to that of the slaves they sought to free. They concluded that women were not much better off than slaves, and they resolved to meet to address these issues.

The first meeting for women's rights was held in Seneca Falls, New York, in 1848. The 300 people who attended passed resolutions calling for the abolition of legal, economic, and social discrimination against women. All of the resolutions reflected the attendees' dissatisfaction with contemporary moral codes, divorce and criminal laws, and the limited opportunities for women in education, the church, medicine, law, and politics. Ironically, only the call for "woman suffrage" (a call to give women the right to vote) failed to win unanimous approval.

The 1850s: The Calm Before The Storm

By 1850, much had changed in America. The Gold Rush had spurred westward migration, cities grew as people were lured from their farms, railroads and the telegraph increased mobility and communication, and immigrants flooded into the United States. The woman's movement gained momentum, and slavery continued to tear the nation apart. Harriet Beecher Stowe's *Uncle Tom's Cabin*, a novel that depicted the evils of slavery, further inflamed the country. *Uncle Tom's Cabin* sold more than 300,000 copies in 1852.

The tremendous national reaction to Stowe's work, which later prompted President Abraham Lincoln to call Stowe "the little woman who started the big war," had not yet faded when a new controversy over the Missouri Compromise of 1820 became the lightning rod for the first major civil rights case to be addressed by the U.S. Supreme Court. As discussed in chapter 3, in *Dred Scott* v. *Sandford* (1857), the Court ruled that the Missouri Compromise, which prohibited slavery north of a set geographical boundary, was unconstitutional. Furthermore, the Court went on to add that slaves were not

Thinking Globally

European Policies on Slavery

Slavery was outlawed in many nations long before ratification of the Thirteenth Amendment to the U.S. Constitution. In 1794, during the French Revolution, the French National Convention emancipated all slaves in French colonies. Napoleon reintroduced the practice of slavery in 1802, but by 1818 slavery was once again illegal. In Great Britain, the Great Emancipation Act of 1833 freed all slaves on British soil.

- In the United States, the issue of slavery helped to ignite a civil war. What factors contributed to this outcome?
- Why were Great Britain, France, and other European nations able to abolish slavery without igniting a civil war?

U.S. citizens, and as a consequence, slaves could not bring suits in federal court.

The Civil War and Its Aftermath: Civil Rights Laws and Constitutional Amendments

The Civil War had many causes, but slavery was clearly a key issue. During the war (1861–1865), abolitionists continued to press for an end to slavery. They were partially rewarded when President Abraham Lincoln issued the Emancipation Proclamation, which provided that all slaves in states still in active rebellion against the United States would be freed automatically on January 1, 1863. Designed as a measure to gain favor for the war in the North, the Emancipation Proclamation did not free all slaves—it freed only those who lived in the Confederacy. Complete abolition of slavery did not occur until congressional passage and ultimate ratification of the Thirteenth Amendment in 1865.

The **Thirteenth Amendment** was the first of the three Civil War Amendments. It banned all forms of "slavery [and] involuntary servitude." (To learn more about the Thirteenth Amendment, see The Living Constitution: Thirteenth Amendment, Section 1.) Although southern states were required to ratify the Thirteenth Amendment as a condition of their readmission to the Union after the war, most of the former Confederate states quickly passed laws that were designed to restrict opportunities for newly freed slaves. These **Black Codes** prohibited African Americans from voting, sitting on juries, or even appearing in public places. Although Black Codes differed from state to state, all empowered local law-enforcement officials to arrest unemployed blacks, fine them for vagrancy, and hire them out to employers to satisfy their fines. Some state codes went so far as to require African Americans to work on plantations or to be domestics. The Black Codes laid the groundwork for Jim Crow laws, which later would institute segregation in all walks of life in the South.

An outraged Congress enacted the Civil Rights Act of 1866 to invalidate some state Black Codes. President Andrew Johnson vetoed the legislation, but—for the first time in history—Congress overrode a presidential veto. The Civil Rights Act formally made African Americans citizens of the United States and gave the Congress and the federal courts the power to intervene when states attempted to restrict the citizenship rights of male African Americans in matters such as voting. Congress reasoned that African Americans were unlikely to fare well if they had to file discrimination complaints in state courts, where most judges were elected. Passage of a federal law allowed African Americans to challenge discriminatory state practices in the federal courts, where judges were appointed for life by the president.

Because controversy remained over the constitutionality of the act (since the Constitution gives states the right to determine qualifications of voters), the **Fourteenth Amendment** was proposed simultaneously with the Civil Rights Act to guarantee, among other things, citizenship to all freed slaves. Other key provisions of the Fourteenth Amendment barred states from abridging "the privileges or immunities of citizenship" or depriving "any person of life, liberty, or property without due process of law," or denying "any person within its jurisdiction the equal protection of the laws." Unlike the Thirteenth Amendment, which had near-unanimous support in the North, the Fourteenth Amendment was opposed by many women because it failed to guarantee suffrage for women. The **Fifteenth Amendment** was also passed by Congress in the aftermath of the Civil War. It guaranteed the "right of citizens" to vote regardless of their "race, color or previous condition of servitude." Sex was not mentioned.

Thirteenth Amendment
One of the three Civil War Amendments; specifically bans slavery in the United States.

Black Codes
Laws denying most legal rights to newly freed slaves; passed by southern states following the Civil War.

Fourteenth Amendment
One of the three Civil War Amendments; guarantees equal protection and due process of the law to all U.S. citizens.

Fifteenth Amendment
One of the three Civil War Amendments; specifically enfranchised newly freed male slaves.

The Living Constitution

Neither slavery nor involuntary servitude, except as a punishment for crime whereof the party shall have been duly convicted, shall exist within the United States, or any place subject to their jurisdiction.

—THIRTEENTH AMENDMENT, SECTION 1

This amendment, the first of three Civil War Amendments, abolished slavery throughout the United States and its territories. It also prohibited involuntary servitude.

Based on his wartime authority, in 1863 President Abraham Lincoln issued the Emancipation Proclamation abolishing slavery in the states that were in rebellion against the United States. Because Congress was considered to lack the constitutional authority to abolish slavery, after one unsuccessful attempt to garner the two-thirds vote necessary, the proposed Thirteenth Amendment was forwarded to the states on February 1, 1865. With its adoption, said one of its sponsors, it relieved Congress "of sectional strifes." Initially, some doubted if any groups other than newly freed African slaves were protected by the provisions of the amendment. Soon, however, the Supreme Court went on to clarify this question by noting: "If Mexican peonage or the Chinese coolie labor system shall develop slavery of the Mexican or Chinese race within our territory, this amendment may safely be trusted to make it void."

In the early 1990s, the Supreme Court was called on several times to construe section 1 of the amendment, especially in regard to involuntary servitude. Thus, provisions of an Alabama law that called for criminal sanctions and jail time for defaulting sharecroppers were considered unconstitutional, and Congress enacted a law banning this kind of involuntary servitude. More recently, the Court has found that compulsory high school community service programs do not violate the ban on involuntary servitude.

The Supreme Court and a host of lower federal and state courts have upheld criminal convictions of those who psychologically coerced mentally retarded farm laborers into service or who lured foreign workers to the United States with promises of jobs and then forced them to work long hours at little or no pay. Human trafficking, in fact, was targeted by the Bush administration as an especially onerous form of involuntary servitude. The U.S. Department of Justice began hundreds of investigations in an attempt to end this system.

CRITICAL THINKING QUESTIONS

1. Why would the Supreme Court rule that compulsory high school community service programs do not violate the Thirteenth Amendment?
2. Is forcing prison inmates to work as part of a "chain gang" a form of involuntary servitude? Why or why not?

Woman's rights activists were shocked. Abolitionists' continued support of the Fifteenth Amendment, which was ratified by the states in 1870, prompted many woman's rights supporters to leave the abolition movement and to work solely for the cause of women's rights. Twice burned, Susan B. Anthony and Elizabeth Cady Stanton decided to form their own group, the National Woman Suffrage Association (NWSA), to achieve that goal. (Another, more conservative group, the American Woman Suffrage Association, also was formed.) In spite of the NWSA's opposition, however, the Fifteenth Amendment was ratified by the states in 1870.

Civil Rights, Congress, and the Supreme Court

Continued southern resistance to African American equality led Congress to pass the Civil Rights Act of 1875, designed to grant equal access to public accommodations such

Jim Crow laws
Laws enacted by southern states that discriminated against blacks by creating "whites only" schools, theaters, hotels, and other public accommodations.

Civil Rights Cases (1883)
Name attached to five cases brought under the Civil Rights Act of 1875. In 1883, the Supreme Court decided that discrimination in a variety of public accommodations, including theaters, hotels, and railroads, could not be prohibited by the act because such discrimination was private discrimination and not state discrimination.

poll tax
A tax levied in many southern states and localities that had to be paid before an eligible voter could cast a ballot.

grandfather clause
Voting qualification provision in many southern states that allowed only those whose grandfathers had voted before Reconstruction to vote unless they passed a wealth or literacy test.

Plessy v. *Ferguson* (1896)
Supreme Court case that challenged a Louisiana statute requiring that railroads provide separate accommodations for blacks and whites. The Court found that separate but equal accommodations did not violate the equal protection clause of the Fourteenth Amendment.

as theaters, restaurants, and transportation. The act also prohibited the exclusion of African Americans from jury service. But after the end of federal occupation of the South in 1877, southern states quickly moved to limit African Americans' access to the ballot. Other forms of discrimination also were allowed by judicial decisions upholding **Jim Crow laws,** which required segregation in public schools and facilities, including railroads, restaurants, and theaters.

All these laws, at first glance, appeared to conflict with the Civil Rights Act of 1875. In 1883, however, a series of cases decided by the Supreme Court severely damaged the vitality of the 1875 act. The *Civil Rights Cases* **(1883)** were five separate cases involving the convictions of private individuals found to have violated the Civil Rights Act by refusing to extend accommodations to African Americans in theaters, a hotel, and a railroad.[7] In deciding these cases, the Supreme Court ruled that Congress could prohibit only state or governmental action and not private acts of discrimination. The Court thus seriously limited the scope of the Civil Rights Act by concluding that Congress had no authority to prohibit private discrimination in public accommodations. The Court's opinion in the *Civil Rights Cases* provided a moral reinforcement for the Jim Crow system. Southern states viewed the Court's ruling as an invitation to gut the reach and intent of the Thirteenth, Fourteenth, and Fifteenth Amendments.

In devising ways to make certain that African Americans did not vote, southern states had to avoid the intent of the Fifteenth Amendment. This amendment did not guarantee suffrage; it simply said that states could not deny anyone the right to vote on account of race or color. To exclude African Americans in a seemingly racially neutral way, southern states used three devices before the 1890s: (1) **poll taxes** (small taxes on the right to vote that often came due when poor African American sharecroppers had the least amount of money on hand); (2) some form of property-owning qualifications; and, (3) "literacy" or "understanding" tests, which allowed local voter registration officials to administer difficult reading-comprehension tests to potential voters whom they did not know.

To make certain that these laws did not further reduce the numbers of poor or uneducated white voters, many southern states added a **grandfather clause** to their voting qualification provisions, granting voting privileges to those who failed to pass a wealth or literacy test only if their grandfathers had voted before Reconstruction. Grandfather clauses effectively denied the descendents of slaves the right to vote.

While African Americans continued to face wide-ranging racism on all fronts, women also confronted discrimination. During this period, married women, by law, could not be recognized as legal entities. Women often were treated in the same category as juveniles and imbeciles, and in many states they were not entitled to wages, inheritances, or custody of their children.

The Push for Equality, 1890–1954

The Progressive era (1890–1920) was characterized by a concerted effort to reform political, economic, and social affairs. Prejudice against African Americans was just one target of progressive reform efforts. Distress over the inferior legal status of African Americans was aggravated by the U.S. Supreme Court's decision in *Plessy* v. *Ferguson* **(1896)**, a case that some commentators point to as the Court's darkest hour.[8]

In *Plessy*, the Court upheld the constitutionality of a Louisiana law mandating racial segregation on all public trains. The justices based their decision on their belief that separate facilities for blacks and whites provided equal protection of the laws. After all, they reasoned, African Americans were not prevented from riding the train; the Louisiana statute required only that the races travel separately. Justice John Marshall Harlan was the lone dissenter. He argued that "the Constitution is colorblind" and that it was senseless to hold constitutional a law "which, practically, puts the badge of servitude and degradation upon a large class of our fellow citizens."

The separate-but-equal doctrine enunciated in *Plessy* v. *Ferguson* soon came to mean only separate, as new legal avenues to discriminate against African Americans were enacted into law throughout the South. By 1900, equality for African Americans was far from the promise first offered by the Civil War Amendments. Again and again, the Supreme Court nullified the intent of the amendments and sanctioned racial segregation while the states avidly followed its lead.[9]

The Founding of Key Groups

By 1909, major race riots had occurred in several American cities, and progressive reformers were concerned about these outbreaks of violence and the possibility of others. Oswald Garrison Villard, the influential publisher of the *New York Evening Post*—and the grandson of William Lloyd Garrison—called a conference to discuss the problem. This group soon evolved into the National Association for the Advancement of Colored People (NAACP).

The NAACP was not the only new group. The struggle for women's rights was revitalized in 1890 when the National and American Woman Suffrage Associations merged into the National American Woman Suffrage Association (NAWSA). The suffrage movement was greatly facilitated by the proliferation of women's groups that emerged during the Progressive era. In addition to the rapidly growing temperance movement—the move to ban the sale of alcohol, which many women blamed for a variety of social ills—women's groups were created to seek protective legislation in the form of maximum hour or minimum wage laws for women and to work for improved sanitation, public morals, and education.

NAWSA based its claim to the right to vote largely on the fact that women, as mothers, should be enfranchised. Furthermore, although many members of the suffrage movement were NAACP members, the new women's movement—called the **suffrage movement** because of its focus on the vote alone and not on broader issues of women's rights—took on racist overtones. Suffragists argued that if undereducated African Americans could vote, why couldn't women?

Having roots in the Progressive movement gave the suffrage movement an exceptionally broad base that transformed NAWSA from a small organization of just over 10,000 members in the early 1890s to a true social movement of more than 2 million members in 1917. By 1920, a coalition of women's groups, led by NAWSA and the newer, more radical National Woman's Party, was able to secure ratification of the **Nineteenth Amendment** to the Constitution. It guaranteed all women the right to vote—fifty years after African American males were enfranchised by the Fifteenth Amendment.

After passage of the suffrage amendment in 1920, the fragile alliance of diverse women's groups that had come together to fight for the vote quickly disintegrated. Widespread organized activity on behalf of women's rights did not reemerge until the 1960s. In the meantime, the NAACP continued to fight racism and racial segregation. Its activities and those of others in the civil rights movement would later give impetus to a new women's movement.

Photo courtesy: The New York Public Library/Art Resource, NY

Why was the Niagara Movement founded? W. E. B. Du Bois (second from right in the second row, facing left) is pictured with the other original leaders of the Niagara Movement. This 1905 photo was taken on the Canadian side of Niagara Falls because no hotel on the U.S. side would accommodate the group's African American members. At the meeting, a list of injustices suffered by African Americans was detailed.

suffrage movement
The drive for voting rights for women that took place in the United States from 1890 to 1920.

Nineteenth Amendment
Amendment to the Constitution that guaranteed women the right to vote.

147

Litigating for Equality

During the 1930s, leaders of the NAACP began to sense that the time was right to launch a full-scale challenge in the federal courts to the constitutionality of *Plessy*'s separate-but-equal doctrine. The NAACP mapped out a long-range plan that would first target segregation in professional and graduate education. In 1935, all southern states maintained fully segregated elementary and secondary schools. Colleges and universities also were segregated, and most states did not provide for postgraduate education for African Americans. NAACP lawyers chose to target law schools because they were institutions that judges could well understand, and integration there would prove less threatening to most whites.

Lloyd Gaines, a graduate of Missouri's all-black Lincoln University, sought admission to the all-white University of Missouri Law School in 1936. He was immediately rejected. In the separate-but-equal spirit, the state offered to build a law school at Lincoln (although no funds were allocated for the project) or, if he didn't want to wait, to pay his tuition at an out-of-state law school. Gaines rejected the offer, sued, lost in the lower courts, and appealed to the U.S. Supreme Court.

Gaines's case was filed at an auspicious time. As discussed in chapter 3, a constitutional revolution of sorts occurred in Supreme Court decision making in 1937. Before this time, the Court was most receptive to and interested in the protection of economic liberties. In 1937, however, the Court reversed itself in a series of cases and began to place individual freedoms and personal liberties on a more protected footing. Thus, in 1938, Gaines's lawyers pleaded his appeal to a far more sympathetic Supreme Court. NAACP attorneys argued that the creation of a separate law school of a lesser caliber than that of the University of Missouri would not and could not afford Gaines an equal education. The justices agreed and ruled that Missouri had failed to meet the separate-but-equal requirements of *Plessy*. The Court ordered Missouri either to admit Gaines to the school or to set up a law school for him.[10]

Recognizing the importance of the Court's ruling, in 1939 the NAACP created a separate, tax-exempt legal defense fund to devise a strategy that would build on the Missouri case and bring about equal educational opportunities for all African American children. The first head of the NAACP Legal Defense and Educational Fund, commonly referred to as the LDF, was Thurgood Marshall, who later became the first African American to serve on the U.S. Supreme Court. Sensing that the Court would be more amenable to the NAACP's broader goals if it were first forced to address a variety of less threatening claims to educational opportunity, Marshall and the LDF brought a series of carefully crafted test cases to the Court.

The first case involved H. M. Sweatt, a forty-six-year-old African American mail carrier, who applied for admission to the all-white University of Texas Law School in 1946. Rejected on racial grounds, Sweatt sued. The judge gave the state six months to establish a law school or to admit Sweatt to the university. The state legislature saw the handwriting on the wall and authorized $3 million for the creation of the Texas State University for Negroes. One hundred thousand dollars of that money was to be for a new law school in Austin across the street from the state capitol building. It consisted of three small basement rooms, a library of 10,000 books, access to the state law library, and three part-time first-year instructors as the faculty. Sweatt declined the opportunity to obtain an education there and instead chose to continue his legal challenge.

Who were the leaders of the suffrage movement? Alice Paul and other members of the National Woman's Party picketed outside the White House to support woman suffrage. Although they were arrested, jailed, and force-fed, their efforts ultimately were successful; they are shown here celebrating.

Photo courtesy: Picture History

Eventually the Supreme Court handled this case together with another LDF case involving graduate education.[11] The eleven southern states filed an *amicus curiae* (friend of the court) brief, in which they argued that *Plessy* should govern both cases. The LDF received assistance, however, from an unexpected source—the U.S. government. In a dramatic departure from the past, the administration of President Harry S Truman filed a friend of the court brief, urging the Court to overrule *Plessy*. Although the Court did not overrule *Plessy*, the justices found that the measures taken by the states in each case failed to live up to the strictures of the separate-but-equal doctrine. The Court unanimously ruled that the remedies to each situation were inadequate to afford a sound education.

In 1950, after these decisions were handed down, the LDF concluded that the time had come to launch a full-scale attack on the separate-but-equal doctrine. The decisions of the Court were encouraging, and the position of the U.S. government and the population in general appeared to be more receptive to an outright overruling of *Plessy*.

The Challenge came in the form of **Brown v. Board of Education (1954),** four cases brought from different areas of the South and border states involving public elementary or high school systems that mandated separate schools for blacks and whites.[12] In *Brown*, LDF lawyers, again led by Thurgood Marshall, argued that *Plessy*'s separate-but-equal doctrine was unconstitutional under the **equal protection clause** of the Fourteenth Amendment, and that if the Court was still reluctant to overrule *Plessy*, the only way to equalize the schools was to integrate them. A major component of the LDF's strategy was to prove that the intellectual, psychological, and financial damage that befell African Americans as a result of segregation precluded any court from finding that equality was served by the separate-but-equal policy.

On May 17, 1954, Chief Justice Earl Warren delivered the fourth opinion of the day, *Brown v. Board of Education*. Writing for the Court, Warren stated:

> To separate [some school children] from others . . . solely because of their race generates a feeling of inferiority as to their status in the community that may affect their hearts and minds in a way very unlikely ever to be undone. We conclude, unanimously, that in the field of public education the doctrine of "separate but equal" has no place.

Brown was the most important civil rights case decided in the twentieth century.[13] It immediately evoked an uproar that shook the nation. Some segregationists called the day the decision was handed down Black Monday. The governor of South Carolina denounced the decision, saying, "Ending segregation would mark the beginning of the end of civilization in the South as we know it."[14]

Photo courtesy: Bettmann/Corbis

What did "separate but equal" look like? Here, George McLaurin, the plaintiff in one of the LDF's challenges to the "separate but equal doctrine," is shown outside his classroom. This was the university's shameful accommodation when a federal district court ordered his admission into the University of Oklahoma's doctoral program.

Brown v. Board of Education (1954)
U.S. Supreme Court decision holding that school segregation is inherently unconstitutional because it violates the Fourteenth Amendment's guarantee of equal protection

equal protection clause
Section of the Fourteenth Amendment that guarantees that all citizens receive "equal protection of the laws."

The Civil Rights Movement

Brown served as a catalyst for change, sparking the development of the modern civil rights movement. Women's work in that movement and the student protest movement that arose in reaction to the U.S. government's involvement in Vietnam gave women the experience needed to form their own organizations to press for full equality. As

TIMELINE

The Civil Rights Movement

African Americans and women became more and more successful, they served as models for other groups who sought equality—Hispanic Americans, American Indians, Asian and Pacific Americans, homosexuals, the disabled, and others.

School Desegregation After *Brown*

One year after *Brown*, in a case referred to as *Brown v. Board of Education II* (1955), the Court ruled that racially segregated systems must be dismantled "with all deliberate speed."[15] Many politicians in the South entered into a near conspiracy to avoid the mandates of *Brown II*. In Arkansas, for example, Governor Orval Faubus, who was facing a reelection bid, announced that he would not "be a party to any attempt to force acceptance of change to which people are overwhelmingly opposed."[16] The day before school was to begin, he announced that National Guardsmen would surround Little Rock's Central High School to prevent African American students from entering. While the federal courts in Arkansas continued to order the admission of African American children, the governor remained adamant. Finally, President Dwight D. Eisenhower sent federal troops to Little Rock to protect the rights of the nine students attending Central High.

In reaction to the governor's outrageous conduct, the Court broke with tradition and issued a unanimous decision in *Cooper v. Aaron* (1958), which was filed by the Little Rock School Board asking the federal district court for a two-and-one-half-year delay in implementation of its desegregation plans. Each justice signed the opinion individually, underscoring his individual support for the notion that "no state legislator or executive or judicial officer can war against the Constitution without violating his undertaking to support it."[17] The state's actions thus were ruled unconstitutional and its "evasive schemes" illegal.

A New Move for African American Rights

In 1955, soon after *Brown II*, the civil rights movement took another step forward—this time in Montgomery, Alabama. Rosa Parks, the local NAACP's Youth Council adviser, decided to challenge the constitutionality of the segregated bus system. First, Parks and other NAACP officials began to raise money for litigation and made speeches around town to garner public support. Then, on December 1, 1955, Rosa Parks made history when she refused to leave her seat on a bus to move to the back to make room for a white male passenger. She was arrested for violating an Alabama law banning integration of public facilities, including buses. After she was freed on bond, Parks and the NAACP decided to enlist city clergy to help her cause. At the same time, they distributed 35,000 handbills calling for African Americans to boycott the Montgomery bus system.

The boycott was led by a new, twenty-six-year-old minister, the Reverend Martin Luther King Jr. As it dragged on, Montgomery officials and local business owners began to harass the city's African American citizens. The residents held out, despite suffering personal hardship for their actions, ranging from harassment to job loss to bankruptcy. In 1956, a federal court ruled that the segregated bus system violated the equal protection clause of the Fourteenth Amendment. After a year of walking, black Montgomery residents ended their protest when city buses were ordered to integrate. The first effort at nonviolent protest had been successful. Organized boycotts and other forms of nonviolent protest, including sit-ins at segregated restaurants and bus stations, were to follow.

Formation of New Groups

The recognition and respect that the Reverend Martin Luther King Jr. earned within the African American community helped him to launch the Southern Christian Leadership Conference (SCLC) in 1957, soon after the end of the Montgomery bus boycott. Unlike the NAACP, which had northern origins and had come to rely largely on litigation as a means of achieving expanded equality, the SCLC had a southern base and was rooted more closely in black religious culture. The SCLC's philosophy reflected King's growing belief in the importance of nonviolent protest and civil disobedience.

Eventually, the SCLC and the Student Non-violent Coordinating Committee (SNCC), largely made up of activist college students, dominated the new civil rights movement. While the SCLC generally worked with church leaders in a community, SNCC was much more of a grass-roots organization. Always perceived as more radical than the SCLC, SNCC tended to focus its organizing activities on the young, both black and white.

In addition to joining the sit-in bandwagon, SNCC also came to lead what were called freedom rides, designed to focus attention on segregated public accommodations. Bands of college students and other civil rights activists traveled by bus throughout the South in an effort to force bus stations to desegregate.

While SNCC continued to sponsor sit-ins and freedom rides, in 1963 the Reverend Martin Luther King Jr. launched a series of massive nonviolent demonstrations in Birmingham, Alabama, long considered a major stronghold of segregation. Thousands of blacks and whites marched to Birmingham in a show of solidarity. Peaceful marchers were met there by the Birmingham police commissioner, who ordered his officers to use dogs, clubs, and fire hoses on the marchers. Americans across the nation were horrified as they witnessed the brutality and abuse heaped on the protesters on television. As the marchers hoped, the shocking scenes helped convince President John F. Kennedy to propose important civil rights legislation. (To learn more about the Civil Rights Movement, see Analyzing Visuals: Police Confront Civil Rights Demonstrators in Birmingham.)

The Civil Rights Act of 1964

Both the SCLC and SNCC sought full implementation of Supreme Court decisions dealing with race and an end to racial segregation and discrimination. The cumulative effect of collective actions including sit-ins, boycotts, marches, and freedom rides—as well as the tragic bombings and deaths inflicted in retaliation—led Congress to pass the first major piece of civil rights legislation since the post–Civil War era, the Civil Rights Act of 1964, followed the next year by the Voting Rights Act of 1965. Several events led to the consideration of the two pieces of legislation.

In 1963, President John F. Kennedy requested that Congress pass a law banning discrimination in public accommodations. Seizing the moment, the Reverend Martin Luther King Jr. called for a monumental march on Washington, D.C. to demonstrate widespread support for far-ranging anti-discrimination legislation. It was clear that national legislation outlawing discrimination were the only answer: southern legislators would never vote to repeal Jim Crow laws. The March on Washington for Jobs and Freedom was held in August 1963, only a few months after the Birmingham demonstrations. More than 250,000 people heard King deliver his famous "I Have a Dream" speech from the Lincoln Memorial. Before Congress had the opportunity to vote on any legislation, however, John F. Kennedy was assassinated on November 22, 1963, in Dallas, Texas.

When Vice President Lyndon B. Johnson, a southern-born, former Senate majority leader, succeeded Kennedy as president, he put civil rights reform at the top of his

Photo courtesy: Chicago Defender

How did Emmett Till's murder awaken a nation to racial injustice? The brutal 1955 murder of Emmett Till, a fourteen-year-old boy from Chicago, Illinois, heightened awareness of the injustices of the Jim Crow system in the South and helped to coalesce the nascent Civil Rights Movement. Till, who was visiting relatives in Mississippi, was accused of whistling at a white woman. He was kidnapped, beaten, mutilated, shot, and thrown in a river. His mother insisted on an open casket funeral, so that news media and mourners would understand the violence visited upon her child. Two suspects were acquitted of the killings, but later confessed their crime to a reporter.

Analyzing Visuals   Police Confront Civil Rights Demonstrators in Birmingham

Examine the May 1963 photograph by Charles Moore reprinted here. It was taken during a civil rights demonstration in Birmingham, Alabama, and was frequently reprinted and also discussed on the floor Congress during debate over the Civil Rights Act of 1964. After examining the photograph, answer the following questions:

Photo courtesy: Charles Moore/Black Star/Stock Photo

WHAT do you observe about the scene and the various people shown in the photograph?

WHAT do you notice about the man who is being attacked by the dogs? The other demonstrators? The police?

WHAT emotions does the picture evoke? Why do you think this image was an effective tool in the struggle for African Americans' civil rights?

legislative priority list, and civil rights activists gained a critical ally. Thus, through the 1960s, the movement subtly changed in focus from peaceful protest and litigation to legislative lobbying. Its focus broadened from integration of school and public facilities and voting rights to preventing housing and job discrimination and alleviating poverty.

In spite of strong presidential support and the sway of public opinion, the Civil Rights Act of 1964 did not sail through Congress. Southern senators, led by South Carolina's Strom Thurmond, a Democrat who later switched to the Republican Party, conducted the longest filibuster in the history of the Senate. For eight weeks, Thurmond led the effort to hold up voting on the civil rights bill until cloture was invoked and the filibuster ended. Once passed, the **Civil Rights Act of 1964**:

Civil Rights Act of 1964
Wide-ranging legislation passed by Congress to outlaw segregation in public facilities and discrimination in employment, education, and voting; created the Equal Employment Opportunity Commission.

- Outlawed arbitrary discrimination in voter registration and expedited voting rights lawsuits.
- Barred discrimination in public accommodations engaged in interstate commerce.
- Authorized the Department of Justice to initiate lawsuits to desegregate public facilities and schools.

- Provided for the witholding of federal funds from discriminatory state and local programs.
- Prohibited discrimination in employment on grounds of race, creed, color, religion, national origin, or sex.
- Created the Equal Employment Opportunity Commission (EEOC) to monitor and enforce the bans on employment discrimination.

As challenges were made to the Civil Rights Act of 1964, other changes continued to sweep the United States. African Americans in the North, who believed that their brothers and sisters in the South were making progress against discrimination, found themselves frustrated. Northern blacks were experiencing high unemployment, poverty, discrimination, and little political clout. Some, including Black Muslim leader Malcolm X, even argued that, to survive, African Americans must separate themselves from white culture in every way. These increased tensions resulted in riots in many major cities from 1964 to 1968, when many African Americans in the North took to the streets, burning and looting to vent their rage. The assassination of the Reverend Martin Luther King Jr. in 1968 triggered a new epidemic of race riots.

The Women's Rights Movement

Just as in the abolition movement in the 1800s, women from all walks of life participated in the civil rights movement. Women were important members of new groups such as SNCC and the SCLC as well as more traditional groups such as the NAACP, yet they often found themselves treated as second-class citizens. At one point during a SNCC national meeting, its chair proclaimed: "The only position for women in SNCC is prone."[18] Statements and attitudes such as these led some women to found early women's liberation groups that generally were quite radical but small in membership. Others founded more traditional groups such as the National Organization for Women (NOW). Some groups sought improved rights for women through lobbying for specific laws or a constitutional amendment to guarantee women equal rights; other groups, following the model of the NAACP LDF, turned to the courts.

TIMELINE

Women's Struggle for Equality

Litigation for Equal Rights

The paternalistic attitudes of the Supreme Court, and perhaps society as well, continued well into the 1970s. Said one U.S. Supreme Court justice, "Despite the enlightened emancipation of women from the restrictions and protections of bygone years, and their entry into many parts of community life formerly considered to be reserved to men, a woman is still regarded as the center of home and family life."[19]

These kinds of attitudes and decisions were insufficient to forge a new movement for women's rights. However, three events occurred to move women to action. In 1961, soon after his election, President John F. Kennedy created the President's Commission on the Status of Women, which was headed by former first lady Eleanor Roosevelt. The commission's report, *American Women*, released in 1963, documented pervasive discrimination against women in all walks of life. In addition, the civil rights movement and the publication of Betty Friedan's *The Feminine Mystique* (1963), led some women to question their lives and status in society. The passage of the Equal Pay Act in 1963 (which guaranteed women

Thinking Globally
Saudi Arabia and Women's Rights

In Saudi Arabia, women are prohibited from voting and driving and may only travel abroad or work with the permission of a male relative. In schools and universities, women are segregated from their male colleagues.

- Saudi Arabia is considered a strong U.S. ally. Should Saudi Arabia's lack of support for women's civil rights affect U.S. foreign policy toward Saudi Arabia? Explain your answer.

- What should be considered "women's rights"? Are they the same rights afforded to men or not?

equal pay for equal work) and the Civil Rights Act of 1964, which barred discrimination in employment based on sex as well as race (and other factors), motivated women to demand workplace equity.

In 1966, after the **Equal Employment Opportunity Commission** failed to enforce the law as it applied to sex discrimination, female activists formed the National Organization for Women. NOW was modeled closely on the NAACP. Its founders sought to work within the system to prevent discrimination. Initially, most of this activity was geared toward two goals: achievement of equality either by passage of an equal rights amendment to the Constitution, or by judicial decision.

Equal Employment Opportunity Commission
Federal agency created to enforce the Civil Rights Act of 1964, which forbids discrimination on the basis of race, creed, national origin, religion, or sex in hiring, promotion, or firing.

Not all women agreed with the notion of full equality for women. Nevertheless, from 1923 to 1972, a proposal for an equal rights amendment was made in every session of every Congress. Every president between Harry S Truman and Richard M. Nixon backed it, and by 1972 public opinion favored its ratification. In response to pressure from NOW, the National Women's Political Caucus, and a wide variety of other feminist groups, Congress voted in favor of the Equal Rights Amendment (ERA) by overwhelming majorities (84–8 in the Senate; 354–24 in the House). The amendment provided that:

> Equality of rights under the law shall not be denied or abridged by the United States or by any state on account of sex.
>
> The Congress shall have the power to enforce, by appropriate legislation, the provisions of this article.

Within a year, twenty-two states ratified the amendment, most by overwhelming margins, but the tide soon turned. In 1974 and 1975, the amendment only squeaked through the Montana and North Dakota legislatures, and two states—Nebraska and Tennessee—voted to rescind their earlier ratifications.

By 1978, one year before the deadline for ratification was to expire, thirty-five states had voted for the amendment—three short of the three-fourths necessary for ratification. Efforts in key states such as Illinois and Florida failed as opposition to the ERA intensified. Faced with the prospect of defeat, ERA supporters heavily lobbied Congress to extend the deadline for ratification. Congress extended the ratification period by three years, but to no avail. No additional states ratified the amendment, and three more rescinded their votes.

Women's Equality Amendment
Proposed amendment to the Constitution that states "Equality of rights under the law shall not be denied or abridged by the United States or any state on account of sex."

What began as a simple correction to the Constitution turned into a highly controversial proposed change. Even though large percentages of the public favored the ERA, opponents needed to stall ratification in only thirteen states while supporters had to convince legislators in thirty-eight. The success that women's rights activists were having in the courts was hurting the effort. When women first sought the ERA in the late 1960s, the Supreme Court had yet to rule that women were protected by the Fourteenth Amendment's equal protection clause from any kind of discrimination, thus highlighting the need for an amendment. But, as the Court widened its interpretation of the Constitution to protect women from some sorts of discrimination, many felt the need for a new amendment was less urgent. The proposed amendment died without being ratified on June 30, 1982. The recently renamed **Women's Equality Amendment** continues to be reintroduced in each session of Congress.

The Equal Protection Clause and Constitutional Standards of Review

The Fourteenth Amendment protects all U.S. citizens from state action that violates equal protection of the laws. Most laws, however, are subject to what is called the rational basis or minimum rationality test. This lowest level of scrutiny means that governments must allege a rational foundation for any distinctions they make. Early on, however, the Supreme Court decided that certain freedoms were entitled to a heightened standard of review. As early as 1937, the Supreme Court recognized that certain freedoms were so fundamental that a very heavy burden would be placed on any government that sought to restrict those rights. As discussed in chapter 4, when fundamental freedoms such as those guaranteed by the First Amendment or **suspect classifications** such as race are involved, the Court uses a heightened standard of review called **strict scrutiny** to determine the constitutional validity of the challenged practices, as detailed in Table 5.1.

In legal terms, this means that if a statute or governmental practice makes a classification based on race, the statute is presumed to be unconstitutional unless the state can provide "compelling affirmative justifications": that is, unless the state can prove the law in question is necessary to accomplish a permissible goal and that it is the least restrictive means through which that goal can be accomplished.

During the 1960s and into the 1970s, the Court routinely struck down as unconstitutional practices and statutes that discriminated on the basis of race. "Whites-only" public parks and recreational facilities, tax-exempt status for private schools that discriminated, and statutes prohibiting interracial marriage were declared unconstitutional. In contrast, the Court refused to consider whether the equal protection clause might apply to discrimination against women. Finally, in *Reed* v. *Reed* (1971), the Supreme Court ruled that an Idaho law granting a male parent automatic preference over a female parent as the administrator of their deceased child's estate violated the equal protection clause of the Fourteenth Amendment. Although the Court did not rule that sex was a suspect classification, it concluded that the equal protection clause of the Fourteenth Amendment prohibited unreasonable classifications based on sex.[20]

In *Craig* v. *Boren* (1976), the Court carved out a new test to be used in examining claims of sex discrimination: "to withstand constitutional challenge, ... classifications by gender must serve important governmental objectives and must be substantially related to achievement of those objectives.[21]"

Since 1976, the Court has applied the intermediate standard of constitutional review to most claims that it has heard involving gender. Thus, the following kinds of practices have been found to violate the Fourteenth Amendment:

- Single-sex public nursing schools.[22]
- Laws that consider males adults at twenty-one years but females at eighteen years.[23]

suspect classification
Category or class, such as race, that triggers the highest standard of scrutiny from the Supreme Court.

strict scrutiny
A heightened standard of review used by the Supreme Court to determine the constitutional validity of a challenged practice.

TABLE 5.1   The Equal Protection Clause and Standards of Review

Type of Classification: What kind of statutory classification is at issue?	Standard of Review: What standard of review will be used?	Test: What does the Court ask?	Example: How does the Court apply the test?
Fundamental freedoms (including religion, speech, assembly, press, privacy); Suspect classifications (including race, alienage, and national origin)	Strict scrutiny or heightened standard	Is classification necessary to the accomplishment of a permissible state goal? Is it the least restrictive way to reach that goal?	*Brown* v. *Board of Education* (1954): Racial segregation not necessary to accomplish the state's goal of educating its students.
Gender	Intermediate standard	Does the classification serve an important governmental objective, and is it substantially related to those ends?	*Craig* v. *Boren* (1976): Keeping drunk drivers off the roads may be an important governmental objective, but allowing eighteen- to twenty-one-year-old women to drink alcoholic beverages while prohibiting men of the same age from drinking is not substantially related to that goal.
Others (including age, wealth, mental retardation, and sexual orientation)	Minimum rationality standard	Is there any rational foundation for the discrimination?	*Romer* v. *Evans* (1996): Colorado state constitutional amendment denying equal rights to homosexuals is unconstitutional.

- Laws that allow women but not men to receive alimony.[24]
- State prosecutors' use of peremptory challenges to reject men or women to create more sympathetic juries.[25]
- Virginia's maintenance of an all-male military college, the Virginia Military Institute.[26]
- Different requirements for a child's acquisition of citizenship based on whether the citizen parent is a mother or a father.[27]

In contrast, the Court has upheld the following governmental practices and laws:

- Draft registration provisions for males only.[28]
- State statutory rape laws that apply only to female victims.[29]

The level of review used by the Court is crucial. Clearly, a statute excluding African Americans from draft registration would be unconstitutional. But, because gender is not subject to the same higher standard of review that is used in racial discrimination cases, the exclusion of women from the requirements of the Military Selective Service Act was ruled permissible because the government policy was considered to serve "important governmental objectives."[30]

This history has perhaps clarified why women's rights activists continue to argue that until the passage of the Women's Equality Amendment, women will never enjoy the same rights as men. An amendment would raise the level of scrutiny that the Court applies to gender-based claims, although there are clear indications that the Supreme Court favors requiring states to show "exceedingly persuasive justifications" for their actions.[31]

Statutory Remedies for Sex Discrimination

In part because of the limits of the intermediate standard of review and the fact that the equal protection clause applies only to governmental discrimination, women's rights activists began to bombard the courts with sex-discrimination cases.

A number of cases have been filed under the Equal Pay Act of 1963 and Title VII of the Civil Rights Act, which prohibits discrimination by private (and, after 1972, public) employers. Key victories under Title VII include:

- Consideration of sexual harassment as sex discrimination.[32]
- Inclusion of law firms, which many argued were private partnerships, in the coverage of the act.[33]
- A broad definition of what can be considered sexual harassment, which includes same-sex harassment.[34]
- Allowance of voluntary affirmative action programs to redress historical discrimination against women.[35]

Title IX
Provision of the Educational Amendments of 1972 that bars educational institutions receiving federal funds from discriminating against female students.

Other victories have come under **Title IX** of the Education Amendments of 1972, which bars educational institutions receiving federal funds from discriminating against female students. Title IX, which parallels Title VII, greatly expanded the opportunities for women in elementary, secondary, and postsecondary institutions. It bars educational institutions receiving federal funds from discriminating against female students. Since women's groups saw eradication of educational discrimination as key to improving other facets of women's lives, they lobbied for it heavily. They also litigate to make sure its provisions are enforced. (To learn more about Title IX, see Chapter 8.)

Other Groups Mobilize for Rights

African Americans and women are not the only groups that have suffered unequal treatment under the law. Denial of civil rights has also led many other disadvantaged groups to mobilize.

Hispanic Americans

As noted in Chapter 1, Hispanic Americans are the largest and fastest growing minority group in the United States. But, Latino/a immigration to the United States is not a new phenomenon. In 1910, the Mexican Revolution forced Mexicans seeking safety and employment into the United States. And, in 1916, New Mexico entered the union as an officially bilingual state—the only one in the United States.

These early groups, many of whom were from families who had owned land when parts of the Southwest were still in Mexico's control, formed the League of United Latin American Citizens (LULAC) in 1929. LULAC continues to be the largest Latino/a group in the United States, with local councils in every state and Puerto Rico.

A later influx of Puerto Rican immigrants mainly moved to New York City. Like Mexican immigrants before them, they tended to live in poverty in their own neighborhoods, where life was centered around the Roman Catholic Church and the customs of their homeland.

Despite the relative isolation of these groups, the first major victory for Latino/a rights came in 1954, the same year as *Brown*. In *Hernandez* v. *Texas*, the Supreme Court struck down discrimination based on ethnicity and class, ruling unanimously that Mexican Americans were entitled to a jury that included other Mexican Americans.[36]

A more extensive push for greater Hispanic rights began in the mid-1960s, just as a wave of Cuban immigrants began to establish homes in Florida, dramatically altering the political and social climate of Miami and other neighboring towns and cities. This new movement, marked by the establishment of the National Council of La Raza in 1968, included many tactics drawn from the African American civil rights movement, including sit-ins, boycotts, marches, and other activities designed to attract publicity to their cause. In one earlier example, in 1965, Cesar Chavez and Dolores Huerta organized migrant workers into the United Farm Workers Union, which would become the largest farm workers' union in the nation, and led them in a strike against growers in California. This strike was eventually coupled with a national boycott of several farm products.

Latino/as also have relied heavily on litigation to secure legal change. Key groups are the Mexican American Legal Defense and Educational Fund (MALDEF) and the Puerto Rican Legal Defense and Educational Fund. MALDEF was founded in 1968 after members of LULAC met with NAACP LDF leaders and, with their assistance, secured a $2.2-million start-up grant from the Ford Foundation. MALDEF was originally created to bring test cases before the Supreme Court to force school districts to allocate more funds to schools with predominantly low-income minority populations, to implement bilingual education programs, to force employers to hire Latino/as, and to challenge election rules and apportionment plans that undercount or dilute Latino/a voting power.

MALDEF has been successful in its efforts to expand voting rights and opportunities to Hispanic Americans under the Voting Rights Act of 1965 (renewed in 2006

Photo Courtesy: Library of Congress

What was the significance of the Supreme Court's decision in *Hernandez v. Texas*? *Hernandez* v. *Texas* (1954) was a landmark decision for Latino/a rights groups. Here, a San Antonio newspaper celebrates the Court's decision.

TIMELINE

The Mexican-American Civil Rights Movement

Timeline: Important Moments in Hispanic American Rights

1910 Mexican Revolution—Political turmoil during the Mexican Revolution forces Mexicans to seek safety and employment in the United States.

1929 League of United Latin American Citizens Formed—Several service organizations unite, creating LULAC, the largest Latino/a service organization in the country.

1954 *Hernandez* v. *Texas*—Supreme Court rules that the Fourteenth Amendment's equal protection rights apply to other racial groups, including Latino/as.

1916 New Mexico Becomes a State—New Mexico is granted statehood as an officially bilingual member of the union.

1939 *Grapes of Wrath* Published—John Steinbeck's novel draws attention to the plight of migrant farm workers.

1965 United Farm Workers Union Founded—The United Farm Workers Union, the largest farm workers union in the United States, has been important in coordinating strikes in California.

for ten years) and the U.S. Constitution's equal protection clause. In 1973, for example, it won a major victory when the Supreme Court ruled that multimember electoral districts (in which more than one person represents a single district) in Texas discriminated against African Americans and Latinos/as.[37]

MALDEF's success in educational equity cases came more slowly. In 1973, for example, in *San Antonio Independent School District* v. *Rodriguez*, the Supreme Court refused to find that a Texas law under which the state appropriated a set dollar amount to each school district per pupil, while allowing wealthier districts to enrich educational programs from other funds, violated the equal protection clause of the Fourteenth Amendment.[38] In 1989, however, MALDEF won a case in which a state district judge declared the state's entire method of financing public schools to be unconstitutional under the state constitution.[39] And, in 2004, it entered into a settlement with the state of California in a case brought four years earlier to address, in MALDEF's words, "the shocking inequities facing public school children across the state."[40]

MALDEF continues to litigate in a wide range of areas of concern to Latino/as. High on its agenda today are affirmative action, the admission of Latino/a students to state colleges and universities, health care for undocumented immigrants, and challenging redistricting practices that make it more difficult to elect Latino/a legislators. It also litigates to challenge many state redistricting plans to ensure that Hispanics are adequately represented.

MALDEF is also at the fore of legislative lobbying for expanded rights. Since 2002, it has worked to oppose restrictions concerning driver's license requirements for undocumented immigrants, to gain greater rights for Latino/a workers, and to ensure that redistricting plans do not silence Latino/a voters. MALDEF also focuses on the rights of Latino/a workers.

1965 Voting Rights Act of 1965—The Voting Rights Act of 1965, among other innovations, requires bilingual ballots in Spanish speaking communities.

1973 *San Antonio Independent School District* v. *Rodriguez*—MALDEF fails to convince the Supreme Court that educational funds should be distributed equally among school districts.

2006 *LULAC* v. *Perry*—The Supreme Court decides in Texas that a redistricting plan does not intentionally limit Latino/a representation.

1968 Legal Lobbying Groups Created—MALDEF and the Puerto Rican Legal Defense and Education Fund are founded in the image of the NAACP LDF.

2006 Day Without Immigrants—More than 1 million immigrants leave their jobs to march in cities across the United States to illustrate the importance of Latino/as and other immigrants to the American economy.

In 2006, MALDEF, LULAC, and hundreds of ad hoc groups of Latino/as, rallied to show their concern about various governmental proposals being offered concerning immigrants. On May 1, 2006, legal and illegal immigrants, supported by many American citizens, took the day off in what originally was to be an economic boycott called "Day Without Immigrants." Ultimately, more than 1 million marchers took to the streets in at least forty states to draw attention to the plight of immigrants, the vast majority of them of Hispanic origin.

American Indians

American Indians are the first true Americans, and their status under U.S. law is unique. Under the U.S. Constitution, Indian tribes are considered distinct governments, a situation that has affected American Indians' treatment by the Supreme Court in contrast to other groups of ethnic minorities.

It is estimated that there were as many as 10 million Indians in the New World at the time Europeans arrived in the 1400s. The actual number of Indians is hotly contested, with estimates varying from a high of 150–200 million to a low of 20–50 million throughout North and South America. By 1900, the number of Indians in the continental United States had plummeted to less than 2 million. Today, there are approximately 2.8 million.

It was not until the 1960s that Indians began to mobilize. During this time, Indian activists, many trained by the American

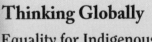

Thinking Globally

Equality for Indigenous People in Mexico

Chiapas is one of the poorest states in Mexico; it also boasts one of the largest concentrations of indigenous peoples. In 1994, a rebel movement known as the Zapatistas took control of several Chiapas cities. Its leaders demanded better treatment by the federal government for the Chiapas people. The rebels' actions focused the world's attention on the plight of many indigenous groups in Central and South America.

- What is the level of a country's responsibility to its indigenous people?
- Should indigenous peoples enjoy distinct or special rights because of their position as descendants of the original settlers of a particular region? Explain your reasoning.

159

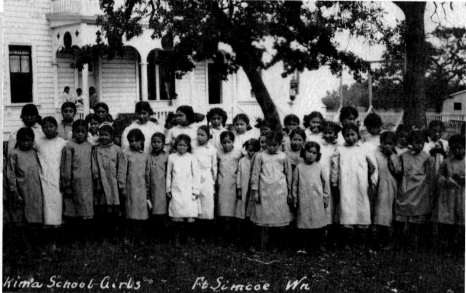

How were American Indians treated by the U.S. government? Indian children were forcibly removed from their homes beginning in the late 1800s and sent to boarding schools where they were pressured to give up their cultural traditions and tribal languages. Here, girls from the Yakima Reservation in Washington State are pictured in front of such a school in 1913.

Indian Law Center at the University of New Mexico, began to file hundreds of test cases in the federal courts involving tribal fishing rights, tribal land claims, and the taxation of tribal profits. The Native American Rights Fund (NARF), founded in 1970, became the NAACP LDF of the Indian rights movement.

American Indians have won some very important victories concerning hunting, fishing, and land rights. American Indian tribes all over America have sued to reclaim lands they say were stolen from them by the United States, often more than 200 years ago. Today, these land rights allow American Indians to play host to a number of casinos across the country, a phenomenon that has resulted in billions of dollars for Indian tribes. These improvements in Indians' economic affairs have helped to increase their political clout.

As a result, Indians are attempting to have their voices heard by electing more American Indians to office. In 2005, the Indigenous Democratic Network (INDN) was founded. Its campaign finance arm, INDN's List, is modeled after other political action committees and its purpose is to elect Indians and Democrats at the state and national level. INDN also trains candidates in "Campaign Camp" and encourages Indians to run for office.[41]

Asian and Pacific Americans

One of the most significant difficulties for Asian and Pacific Americans has been finding a Pan-Asian identity. Originally, Asian and Pacific Americans were far more likely to identify as Japanese, Chinese, Korean, or Filipino.[42] It was not until 1977 that the U.S. government decided to use the nomenclature "Asian and Pacific Islanders." Even this identity has been challenged by some subgroups; in the 1990s, native Hawaiians unsuccessfully requested to be categorized with American Indians, with whom they felt greater affinity.

Discrimination against Asian and Pacific immigrants developed over time in the United States. In 1868, Congress passed a law allowing free migration from China, but in 1882, Congress passed the Chinese Exclusion Act, which was the first to restrict the immigration of any identifiable nationality. This legislation implicitly invited more discriminatory laws against the Chinese, which closely paralleled the Jim Crow laws affecting African Americans.

Several Supreme Court cases also slowed the progress of Asian and Pacific Americans. But, in 1886, the Court ruled in *Yick Wo* v. *Hopkins* that a California law limiting immigrants' ability to open laundries violated the Fourteenth Amendment in its application.[43]

In 1922, the Court took a step backwards, ruling that Asian and Pacific Americans were not white and therefore not entitled to full citizenship rights.[44] Conditions became even worse, especially for those of Japanese descent, after the Japanese invasion of Pearl Harbor in 1941. In response to this action, President Franklin D. Roosevelt issued Executive Order 9066, which led to the internment of 120,000 Japanese Americans. Over two-thirds of those confined to internment camps were U.S. citizens.[45] The Supreme Court upheld the constitutionality of these camps in *Korematsu* v. *U.S.* (1944).[46]

During the 1960s and 1970s, Asian and Pacific Americans, like many other groups discussed in this chapter, began to organize for equal rights. Filipino farm workers, for example, joined with Mexicans to form the United Farm Workers Union. In 1973, the Movement for a Free Philippines emerged to oppose the government of Ferdinand Marcos, the President of the Philippines. Soon, it joined forces with the Friends of Filipino People, which ultimately established the Congress Education Project, a Washington, DC-based lobbying group. It and other Asian and Pacific Americans constituent groups largely were opposed to the Vietnam War. These groups, however, chose not to coordinate their actions.

In the 1970s and 1980s, Japanese Americans mobilized, lobbying the courts and Congress for reparations for their treatment during World War II. In 1988, Congress passed the Civil Liberties Act, which apologized to the interned and their descendants and offered reparations to them and their families. Today, myriad Asian and Pacific American groups target diverse political venues. In California, in particular, they have been successful in seeing more men and women elected at the local and state level.

Photo Courtesy: Russell Lee/Corbis

How were Japanese Americans treated during World War II? The internment of Japanese Americans during World War II was a low point in American history. In *Korematsu* v. *U.S.* (1944), the U.S. Supreme Court upheld the constitutionality of this action.

Gays and Lesbians

Until very recently, gays and lesbians have had an even harder time than other groups in achieving anything approximating equal rights.[47] However, gays and lesbians have, on average, far higher household incomes and educational levels than other minority groups, and they are beginning to convert these advantages into political clout at the ballot box and recently have benefited from changes in public opinion. As discussed in chapter 4, like African Americans and women, gays and lesbians initially did not fare well in the Supreme Court. In the late 1970s, the Lambda Legal Defense and Education Fund, the Lesbian Rights Project, and Gay and Lesbian Advocates and Defenders were founded by gay and lesbian activists dedicated to ending legal restrictions on the civil rights of homosexuals.[48] Although these groups have won important legal victories concerning HIV/AIDS discrimination, insurance policy survivor benefits, and even some employment issues, they generally were not as successful as other historically disadvantaged groups.[49]

In 1993, for example, President Bill Clinton tried to ban discrimination against homosexuals in the armed services. Congressional and military leaders led the effort against Clinton's proposal. Eventually, Clinton and Senate leaders compromised on what was called the "Don't Ask, Don't Tell" policy. It stipulated that gays and lesbians would no longer be asked if they were homosexual, but they were barred from revealing their sexual orientation (under threat of discharge from the service).[50] Although

POLITICS NOW

Source: OMAHA WORLD-HERALD   May 23, 2007   Page 1A

Gay and Lesbian Rights

Gay Discrimination Ban Again Fails to Become Nebraska Law

MARTHA STODDARD

State lawmakers Tuesday decided that Nebraska should not join Iowa and other states in prohibiting job discrimination against gays and lesbians. A 24–15 vote killed Legislative Bill 475, which had been introduced by State Sen. Ernie Chambers of Omaha. He sponsored the measure because of what he said is a need for its proposed protections. LB 475 would give homosexuals "what all of us take for granted: the right to earn an honest living," Chambers said. "We're not talking about anything other than the right to get a job."

Sen. Bill Avery of Lincoln said the bill had limited scope. It would have applied only to hiring, firing and promotions in the workplace, and it only covered people based on sexual orientation. Opposing the measure were Sen. Tony Fulton of Lincoln and others, who argued against giving special protections to gay and lesbian people in state law.

Fulton questioned whether the bill's protections would extend to pedophiles or transvestites wanting to be teachers. He said studies that show gay households have higher average incomes demonstrate that job discrimination is not a problem.

Sen. Tom Carlson of Holdrege said the bill is not needed as long as people keep private what goes on in their bedrooms. "I don't think we should unleash such things on the unsuspecting public," he said. "We're talking here about values. We're talking here about behavior. We're talking here about ethics."

LB 475 would have exempted small businesses and religious organizations from its provisions.

Nebraska law offers specific legal protection to gays and lesbians in two instances. The state's hate crimes law enhances penalties for crimes committed against people based on their sexual orientation. Language added to the state budget in 2005 bars recipients of biomedical research money from discriminating against gays and lesbians.

A state constitutional amendment bars same-sex couples from marrying.

Chambers said his bill would pass easily if senators were not afraid of political repercussions. When asked directly by Chambers, even some opponents of the bill said they did not believe an employer should be able to discriminate against a gay or lesbian person.

Discussion Questions

1. *Is a person's sexual orientation relevant to employment? Why or why not?*
2. *Are anti-discrimination laws "special protection," and if so, do they violate the Fourteenth Amendment?*
3. *To what extent should policy makers be able to impose their personal values in formulating civil rights laws and regulations?*

Civil Rights and Gay Adoption

this policy was initially viewed as a successful compromise, it has been called into question in recent years, as the wars in Iraq and Afghanistan have increased America's need for active-duty military personnel. Since the policy was adopted in 1994, at least 11,000 soldiers have been discharged for their sexual orientation.[51]

The public's views toward homosexuality have also changed, as signaled by the Court's 1996 decision in *Romer* v. *Evans*.[52] In this case, the Court ruled that an amendment to the Colorado constitution that denied homosexuals the right to seek protection from discrimination was unconstitutional under the equal protection clause of the Fourteenth Amendment.

In 2000, Vermont became the first state to recognize civil unions, marking another landmark in the struggle for equal rights for homosexuals. And, the Supreme Court's decision in *Lawrence* v. *Texas* (2003) reversed an earlier ruling by finding a Texas statute that banned sodomy to be unconstitutional.[53]

In November 2003, the Massachusetts Supreme Court ruled that denying homosexuals the right to civil marriage was unconstitutional under the state's constitution. The U.S. Supreme Court later refused to hear an appeal of this case, paving the way for the legality of marriage. In the 2004 and 2006 elections many conservative groups and Republican politicians made same-sex marriage a key issue. Referenda or amendments prohibiting same-sex marriage were placed on a number of state ballots, and most were passed overwhelmingly by voters.

In 2008, California and Connecticut joined Massachusetts in legalizing same-sex marriages. Same-sex couples traveled to California, especially, to legally marry. But, in November 2008, California voters passed a ballot proposition amending the state constitution in a manner that makes same-sex marriages illegal again; several organized interests have announced their intention to litigate on the legality of this proposition.

Accommodating College Students with Disabilities

Since the Americans with Disabilities Act (ADA) of 1990, universities across the United States have been trying to make facilities and services on campus more accessible to students with disabilities. According to the ADA, a disabled student is one who "has a physical or mental impairment that substantially limits major life activities." Not only are there testing and instructional modifications for students with learning disabilities, but wheelchair ramps, lifts, handlebars, and other accommodations have been put into place to assist those with physical disabilities.

The number of disabled students at colleges or universities has increased rapidly in recent years. Nearly 10 percent of the students in the State University of New York's system are considered disabled.[a] However, few universities have been fully effective in adapting facilities and services to meet the individual needs of these students. Many educational institutions lack formal structures and methods to help accommodate students with disabilities.[b] Failure to provide adequately maintained sidewalks, lack of benches and elevators, and the absence of listening systems in classrooms and auditoriums are among the many lapses. Fixing these problems has proven to be an expensive venture for educational systems, and some students have to pay for the services themselves.[c]

- How should schools pay for the staffing and equipment required to accommodate students with disabilities?
- Look for physical accommodations across your campus. Also, what programs or service are available for students with disabilities? Are the accommodations meeting the needs of the individuals who require them?

[a]National Council on Disability, *People with Disabilities and Postsecondary Education.*
[b]Robert A. Stodden, L. M. Galloway, and Norma Jean Stodden, "Secondary School Curricula Issues: Impact on Postsecondary Students with Disabilities," *Exceptional Children* 70 (2003): 9–25.
[c]Sara D. Knapp, "Disability Access at SUNY Campuses: 10 Years After the ADA," United University Professions' Disability Rights and Concerns Committee, April 2004, 19.

Americans with Disabilities

In the aftermath of World War II, many veterans returned to a nation unequipped to handle their disabilities. The Korean and Vietnam Wars made the problems of disabled veterans all the more clear. These veterans saw the successes of African Americans, women, and other minorities, and they too began to lobby for greater protection against discrimination.[54] In 1990, in coalition with other disabled people, veterans finally were able to convince Congress to pass the Americans with Disabilities Act (ADA). The statute defines a disabled person as someone with a physical or mental impairment that limits one or more "life activities," or who has a record of such impairment. It thus extends the protections of the Civil Rights Act of 1964 to all of those with physical or mental disabilities. It guarantees access to public facilities, employment, and communication services. It also requires employers to acquire or modify work equipment, adjust work schedules, and make existing facilities accessible to those with disabilities.

In 1999, the U.S. Supreme Court issued a series of four decisions redefining and limiting the scope of the ADA. The cumulative impact of these decisions was to limit dramatically the number of people who can claim coverage under the act. Moreover, these cases "could profoundly affect individuals with a range of impairments—from diabetes and hypertension to severe nearsightedness and hearing loss—who are able to function in society with the help of medicines or aids but whose impairments may still make employers consider them ineligible for certain jobs."[55] Thus, pilots who need glasses to correct their vision cannot claim discrimination when employers fail to hire them even though their vision is correctable.[56] In the 2004 case of *Tennessee* v. *Lane*, however, the Court ruled 5–4 that disabled persons could sue states that failed to make reasonable accommodations to assure that courthouses are handicapped accessible.[57] (To learn more about the ADA's impact on college campuses, see Ideas into Action: Accommodating College Students with Disabilities.)

You are the Mayor and Need to Make Civil Rights Decisions

Join the Debate

Determining a Living Wage

OVERVIEW: When the Reverend Martin Luther King Jr. was assassinated, he was visiting Memphis, Tennessee, to support African Americans in their struggle to raise poverty-level wages and to secure collective bargaining rights. As this chapter points out, there are various dimensions to civil rights. Economic justice is one of them. An example of such an economic justice issue is how best to determine the level of pay that workers should receive.

Most people are familiar with the concept of a minimum wage, which is the lowest hourly rate that employers can legally pay their workers. The federal government and all state governments except for Tennessee, Alabama, Mississippi, Louisiana, and South Carolina have passed laws setting a minimum wage. The federal minimum wage as of July 24, 2008, is $6.55 an hour. Thirty-four states mandate a higher rate than the federal minimum. A limitation of the minimum wage is that it is arbitrary and, because of political stalemates in Congress, may not change from year to year. The federal minimum wage was $5.15 per hour from 1997 to 2007—and because of inflation, the 2007 rate was worth only $4.04 when compared to a decade earlier.

In contrast to the minimum wage, a living wage refers to how much a person needs to earn in order to pay for a satisfactory level of housing, food, utilities, transportation, and health care. Since costs vary over time and vary depending on where you live, the living wage differs from place to place and changes over time.

College students around the country have been visible in the campaign for the adoption of living wage policies. United Students Against Sweatshops (USAS) has organized chapters on over sixty campuses and helped organize protests and other activities to get universities to commit to paying their employees at least a living wage. USAS has won victories at Georgetown, Stanford, Harvard, Washington University, and the University of Wisconsin–Madison.

The Association of Community Organizations for Reform Now (ACORN) is the nation's oldest and largest grassroots organization of low- and moderate-income people. ACORN'S over 200,000 members have pressed in almost ninety cities to get living wage ordinances adopted. These efforts have been successful in places like San Francisco, California; Madison, Wisconson, and Baltimore, Maryland. In 2007, Maryland enacted a living wage law covering the entire state.

Chambers of Commerce and other representatives of businesses warn that the victories achieved by living wage advocates are temporary and costly. The general philosophical argument is that market forces, not politics and government, should set wages.

Living wage opponents also argue that there are alternatives to living wage mandates if one is concerned about low-income people. There are public programs providing food stamps, energy and housing assistance, and other welfare programs for needy families and individuals. Those concerned about the adoption of living wage laws object in part because they do not see why a change is necessary.

Another concern with the concept of a living wage is the complexity of incorporating geographic variation. In response to this concern, Amy Glasmeier, director of the Pennsylvania State University Center for Policy Research on Energy, Environment, and Community Well-Being, has developed an online calculator that determines a living wage for specific communities throughout the United States. She uses federal government data from the Census Bureau, the Department of Agriculture, and the Department of Housing and Urban Development and includes a sample list of jobs and wages for each community.

The largest national nonprofit organization lobbying for expanded civil rights for the disabled is the American Association of People with Disabilities (AAPD). Acting on behalf of the over 56 million Americans who suffer from some form of disability, it works in coalition with other disability organizations to assure that the ADA is implemented fully. Civil rights groups such as the AAPD often find themselves working in concert with more radical disability rights groups such as Not Dead Yet. Not Dead Yet is one of many other disability groups actively opposing assisted suicide and euthanasia laws, believing that they infringe on the civil rights of people with disabilities, especially those who cannot advocate for themselves.

Arguments IN FAVOR of a Living Wage

- If people are working full-time, they should at least be able to afford basic housing, food, and other necessities for life. This is an issue of fairness and common sense, as has long been recognized. In 1891, for example, Pope Leo XIII issued an encyclical on economic justice. A fundamental right of individuals is to be able to survive if they work full-time for someone else.

- The living wage is sensitive to geographic variations in costs and changes in cost over time. The living wage concept is superior to the minimum wage because it is not static or arbitrary. Public policy supporting a living wage is essentially reminding employers to be realistic in setting wages, and to be responsive to local conditions rather than a national or statewide standard.

- Living wages will eliminate the need for many government welfare programs. The current system is unfair not only toward workers but also toward taxpayers. In the absence of a living wage requirement, employers are able to pay extremely low wages while their workers turn to the government for food stamps, housing assistance, and the like. This system essentially provides government subsidies so that companies may have low labor costs and higher profits.

Arguments AGAINST a Living Wage

- Governments should not be setting wages; that is the role of the market. The lowest wages go to the most unskilled and plentiful labor. Individuals who want to increase their earnings should select a job or career path where their labor is more valued in the economy, instead of putting political pressure on the government. The government sets artificial wages and is bound to disrupt natural market forces.

- Adoption of a living wage policy will result in loss of business and unemployment. By increasing labor costs through a living wage policy, government will force businesses to reduce the number of workers or to move to a community that doesn't have such a requirement. A business has to make a profit in order to survive and grow. Governments and communities benefit much more by encouraging business growth and development than by forcing businesses to reduce their workforce or close altogether.

- A living wage policy is going to hurt consumers. If government arbitrarily and artificially increases labor costs for businesses, some of those businesses are going to close, and consumers will no longer have access to those services or products. When businesses close, that affects general competition, which is important in keeping prices down and quality up. Again, consumers lose. And, as businesses pass their increased labor costs along to consumers by raising prices, consumers will not get more, but they will pay more.

Continuing the Debate

1. Is it the role of government to ensure a living wage for all workers? Why are why not?
2. Is it likely that employers will close or move their businesses rather than comply with a living wage law? Explain your reasoning.

To Follow the Debate Online, Go To:

http://www.livingwagecampaign.org
Association of Community Organizations for Reform Now (ACORN), which includes information about their campaign for a living wage and instructions for organizing at a local level.

http://www.ncpa.org
National Center for Policy Analysis, a nonprofit, nonpartisan organization that advocates for policy alternatives to government regulation and involvement in American business. They oppose living wage policies.

http://www.livingwage.geog.psu.edu
An online calculator identifies the living wage for a specific community. The information for each community includes housing, food, and other costs that determine the living wage and a sample list of jobs and wages in the community.

Toward Reform: Civil Rights, Affirmative Action, and Pay Equity

Since passage of major civil rights legislation in the 1960s and the Supreme Court's continued interest in upholding the civil rights of many groups, African Americans, women, Latino/as, American Indians, Asian and Pacific Americans, gays and lesbians, and the disabled have come much closer to the attainment of equal rights. Yet, all of these groups remain far from enjoying full equality under the Constitution and continue to seek reform by pushing for rights from all three branches of government. Enforcement of anti-discrimination laws varies based on administration priorities as well as the resources of private individuals to fund challenges to perceived discriminatory practices.

Affirmative Action

The civil rights debate centers on the question of equality of opportunity versus equality of results. Most civil rights and women's rights organizations argue that the lingering and pervasive burdens of racism and sexism can be overcome only by taking race or gender into account in fashioning remedies for discrimination. They argue that the Constitution is not and should not be blind to color or sex.

affirmative action
Policies designed to give special attention or compensatory treatment to members of a previously disadvantaged group.

Other groups believe that if it was once wrong to use labels to discriminate against a group, it should be wrong to use those same labels to help a group. They argue that laws should be neutral, or color-blind. According to this view, quotas and other forms of **affirmative action**, policies designed to give special attention or compensatory treatment to members of a previously disadvantaged group, should be illegal.

The debate over affirmative action and equality of opportunity became particularly intense during the presidential administration of Ronald Reagan. Shortly before his election. In 1978, the Supreme Court for the first time fully addressed the issue of affirmative action. In *Regents of the University of California* v. *Bakke* (1978), a sharply divided Court concluded that Bakke's rejection had been illegal because the use of strict quotas was inappropriate.[58] The medical school, however, was free to "take race into account." Other courts upheld this view until the later 1980s. Then in a three-month period in 1989, the Supreme Court handed down five civil rights decisions limiting affirmative action programs and making it harder to prove employment discrimination. In response, Congress passed the Civil Rights Act of 1991, which overruled these decisions.

Then in *Grutter* v. *Bollinger* (2003), the Court voted to uphold the constitutionality of the University of Michigan's law school admissions policy, which gave preference to minority applicants.[59] However, in a companion case, the Court struck down Michigan's undergraduate point system, which gave minority applicants twenty automatic points simply because they were minorities.[60]

Taken together, these cases set the stage for a new era in affirmative action in the United States. Although the use of strict quotas and automatic points is not constitutional, the Court clearly believes that there is a place for some preferential treatment, at least until greater racial and ethnic parity is achieved.

Pay Equity and Other Issues of Workplace Discrimination

Comparing Civil Rights

Race is not the only issue that continues to breed civil rights controversies. In fact, one of the largest barriers faced by minority groups living in the United States is the issue of pay equity, which, as already discussed, has an especially significant impact on female workers. The issue of pay equity for women received national attention through a lawsuit filed against the nation's largest employer, Wal-Mart. Six California women filed a claim against the chain, charging that they were the victims of gender discrimination.[61] These women asserted that they were paid lower wages and offered fewer opportunities for advancement than their male colleagues. In June 2004, a federal judge broadened their class action suit to include 1.6 million women. The lawsuit is still pending before the 9th Circuit Court of Appeals. Meanwhile, similar suits have been filed by employees at other big box stores, including Costco. (To learn more about a controversy related to pay equity, see Join the Debate: Determining a Living Wage.)

In 2007, the Supreme Court took up the issue of pay equity. The justices heard the case of Lilly Ledbetter, the lone female supervisor at a Goodyear tire factory in Alabama. Ledbetter charged that sex discrimination throughout her career had led her to earn substantially less than her male counterparts. In a 5–4 decision, the Court ruled that Ledbetter and other women could not seek redress of grievances for discrimination that had occurred over a period of years. [62]

Pay equity has also been a concern for Latino/as and other immigrants. Nine illegal immigrants who worked as janitors at Wal-Marts in New Jersey are suing the company for discriminating against them by paying them lower wages and giving them fewer benefits based solely on their ethnic origin. Another group of Wal-Mart employees from twenty-one states is also suing the corporation, claiming that executives knowingly conspired to hire illegal immigrants and, in doing so, violated the workers' civil rights by refusing to pay Social Security and other wage compensation benefits.[63] These suits are representative of a growing trend in discrimination suits filed by immigrants who believe they have been persecuted or disadvantaged following changes in security and immigration law since the September 11, 2001 terrorist attacks.

★ WHAT SHOULD I HAVE LEARNED?

While the Framers and other Americans basked in the glory of the newly adopted Constitution and Bill of Rights, their protections did not extend to all Americans. In this chapter, we have shown how rights have been expanded to ever-increasing segments of the population. To that end, we have addressed the following questions:

■ **What should I know about the roots of suffrage from 1800 through 1890?**

When the Framers tried to compromise on the issue of slavery, they only postponed dealing with a volatile question that would eventually rip the nation apart. Ultimately, the Civil War was fought to end slavery. Among its results were the triumph of the abolitionist position and the adoption of the Thirteenth, Fourteenth, and Fifteenth Amendments. During this period, women also sought expanded rights, especially the right to vote, but to no avail.

■ **How did African Americans and women push for equality from 1890 through 1954?**

Although the Civil War Amendments were added to the Constitution, the Supreme Court limited their application. As Jim Crow laws were passed throughout the South, the NAACP was founded in the early 1900s to press for equal rights for African Americans. Women's groups also were active during this period, successfully lobbying for passage of the Nineteenth Amendment, which assured them the right to vote. Groups, such as the National Consumers' League (NCL) began to view litigation as a means to an end, and went court to to argue for the constitutionality of legislation protecting women workers.

■ **What should I know about the civil rights movement?**

In 1954, the U.S. Supreme Court ruled in *Brown* v. *Board of Education* that racially-segregated state school systems were unconstitutional. This victory empowered African Americans as they sought an end to other forms of pervasive discrimination. Bus boycotts, sit-ins, freedom rides, pressure for voting rights, and massive nonviolent demonstrations became common tactics. This activity culminated in the passage of the Civil Rights Act of 1964, which gave African Americans another weapon in their legal arsenal.

■ **What should I know about the women's rights movement?**

After passage of the Civil Rights Act, a new women's rights movement arose. Several women's rights groups were created, and while some sought a constitutional amendment, others attempted to litigate under the equal protection clause. Over the years, the Supreme Court developed different tests to determine the constitutionality of various forms of discrimination. In general, strict scrutiny, the most stringent standard, was applied to race-based claims. An intermediate standard of review was developed to assess the constitutionality of sex discrimination claims.

■ **How did other groups mobilize for their civil rights?**

Building on the successes of African Americans and women, other groups, including Lationo/as Americans, American Indians, Asian and Pacific Americans, gays and lesbians, and the disabled, organized to litigate for expanded civil rights as well as to lobby for anti-discrimination laws.

■ **What should I know about reforms related to affirmative action and pay equity?**

The groups discussed in this chapter have yet to reach full equality. One policy, affirmative action, which was designed to remedy education and employment discrimination, continues to be very controversial. Gays, women, and immigrants continue to use the courts to seek remedies for costly employment discrimination.

Key Terms

affirmative action, p. 166
Black Codes, p. 144
Brown v. *Board of Education*
    (1954), p. 149
civil rights, p. 142
Civil Rights Act of 1964, p. 152
Civil Rights Cases (1883), p. 146
Equal Employment Opportunity
    Commission, p. 154

equal protection clause, p. 149
Fifteenth Amendment, p. 144
Fourteenth Amendment, p. 144
grandfather clause, p. 146
Jim Crow laws, p. 146
Nineteenth Amendment, p. 147
Plessy v. *Ferguson* (1896), p. 146
poll tax, p. 146
strict scrutiny, p. 155

suffrage movement, p. 147
suspect classification, p. 155
Thirteenth Amendment, p. 144
Title IX, p. 156
Women's Equality
    Amendment, p. 154

Researching Civil Rights

In the Library

Anderson, Terry H. *The Pursuit of Fairness: A History of Affirmative Action*. New York: Oxford University Press, 2005.

Delgado, Richard. *Justice at War: Civil Liberties and Civil Rights During Times of Crisis*. New York: New York University Press, 2005.

Freeman, Jo. *The Politics of Women's Liberation*. New York: Backinprint.com, 2000.

Guinier, Lani, and Susan Sturm. *Who's Qualified?* Boston: Beacon, 2001.

Kluger, Richard. *Simple Justice*, reprint ed. New York: Vintage, 2004.

Longmore, Paul, and Lauri Umansky. *The New Disability History: American Perspectives*. New York: New York University Press, 2001.

Mansbridge, Jane J. *Why We Lost the ERA*. Chicago: University of Chicago Press, 1986.

McClain, Paula D., and Joseph Stewart Jr. *"Can We All Get Along?": Racial and Ethnic Minorities in American Politics*, 4th ed. Boulder, CO: Westview, 2005.

McGlen, Nancy E., et al. *Women, Politics, and American Society*, 4th ed. New York: Longman, 2004.

Ramakrishnan, S. Karthick. *Democracy in Immigrant America: Changing Demographics and Political Participation*. Stanford, CA: Stanford University Press, 2005.

Reed, Adolph, Jr., ed. *Without Justice for All: The New Liberalism and Our Retreat from Racial Equity*. Boulder, CO: Westview, 2001.

Rodriguez, Clara E. *Changing Race: Latinos, the Census, and the History of Ethnicity in the United States*. New York: New York University Press, 2000.

Rosales, F. Arturo. *Chicano! The History of the Mexican American Civil Rights Movement*. Houston, TX: Arte Publico, 1996.

Wilkins, David E. *American Indian Politics and the American Political System*. New York: Rowman and Littlefield, 2006.

Williams, Juan. *Eyes on the Prize: America's Civil Rights Years, 1954–1965.* New York: Penguin, 1987.

Wilson, William Julius. *The Bridge over the Racial Divide: Rising Inequality and Coalition Politics,* 2nd ed. Berkeley: University of California Press, 2001.

Zia, Hellen. *Asian American Dreams: The Emergence of an American People.* New York: Farrar, Straus and Giroux, 2000.

On the Web

To learn more about the Civil Rights Division of the Department of Justice and its priorities, go to **www.usdoj.gov/crt/.**

To learn more about civil rights issues in the United States, go to **www.civilrights.org,** where a coalition of 150 civil rights organizations provides coverage of a host of civil rights issues as well as links to breaking news related to civil rights.

To read the full text of *Brown* v. *Board of Education* (1954) and other civil rights Supreme Court opinions, go to **www.oyez.org** and search on the case name.

To learn more about the civil rights era, go to the African American Odyssey section of the Library of Congress, **memory.loc.gov/ammem/aaohtml/exhibit/aointro.html,** and click on the last section, Civil Rights.

To learn more about the ACLU Women's Rights Project, go to **www.aclu.org/womensrights/index.html.**

To learn more about MALDEF, go to **www.maldef.org.**

To learn more about Asian and Pacific Americans' civil rights, go to the Web site for the Asian American Justice Center, **www.napalc.org.**

To learn more about the Native American Rights Fund, go to **www.narf.org.**

To learn more about the controversy surrounding same-sex marriage go to the Pew Forum on Religion and Public Life site, **pewforum.org/gay-marriage/.**

To learn more about disability advocacy groups, go to the Web site for the American Association of People with Disabilities, **www.aapd.com.**

6 Congress

On February 6, 2002, Representative Nancy Pelosi (D–CA) broke through a glass ceiling when she was sworn in as the Democratic House whip, becoming the first woman in history to win an elected position in the formal leadership of the U.S. House of Representatives.[1] The whip position has long been viewed as a stepping stone to becoming the Speaker of the House. House Speakers Tip O'Neill (D–MA) and Newt Gingrich (R–GA) were both former whips. As whip, it was Pelosi's responsibility to convince Democratic members of the House to vote together on the full range of bills before the 107th Congress.

First elected to Congress from California in 1986, Pelosi quickly made her mark as an advocate for human rights in China and as an effective fundraiser. Her fund-raising skills and years of experience in the House, in fact, helped her win the hotly contested race for the whip position. As part of the House leadership, she became the first woman to attend critical White House meetings, where, said Pelosi, "Susan B. Anthony and others are with me."[2]

Although the president's party traditionally loses seats in midterm elections, in 2002 House Republicans actually increased their majority. Critics charged that the Democrats lacked a consistent message. Therefore, soon after the election results were in, House Minority Leader Richard Gephardt (D–MO) resigned from his position, leaving Pelosi in line to succeed him. Representative Harold Ford (D–TN), one of the youngest members of the House, threw his hat into the ring to oppose Pelosi's campaign for the leader's position. Ford, a moderate, charged that Pelosi, who already was being referred to by conservatives as a "San Francisco liberal," was simply too liberal to lead the Democrats back to political viability in the 2004 elections. A majority of the members of the House Democratic Caucus, however, did not appear fazed by these charges; Pelosi was elected minority leader by an overwhelming majority of the caucus members.

In 2006, when Democrats regained control of Congress, Pelosi was catapulted into the role of Speaker. In shattering what she termed "the marble ceiling" as Speaker of the House, Pelosi became the first woman to hold that position and is second in line of succession to the presidency. Thus, more than 150 years after women first sought the right to vote, a female member of Congress now leads the House of Representatives.

■ **The position of Speaker of the House has changed dramatically in the last 200 years.** At left is House Speaker Henry Clay of Kentucky, the first powerful Speaker of the House. At right is current House Speaker Nancy Pelosi, shown celebrating Democratic gains in the 2006 congressional elections.

WHAT SHOULD I KNOW ABOUT . . .

- the roots of the legislative branch of government?
- how Congress is organized?
- the members of Congress?
- how members of Congress make decisions?
- the law-making function of Congress?
- congressional checks on the executive and judicial branches of government?

171

The Framers' original conception of the representational function of Congress was much narrower than it is today. Instead of regarding members of Congress as representatives of the people, those in attendance at the Constitutional Convention were extremely concerned with creating a legislative body that would be able to make laws to govern the new nation. Over time, Congress has attempted to maintain the role of a law- and policy-making institution, but changes in the demands made on the national government have allowed the executive and judicial branches to gain powers at the expense of the legislative. Moreover, the power and the importance of individual members have grown. Thus, the public doesn't think much about Congress itself, but somewhat ironically, citizens hold their own elected representatives in high esteem.

The dual roles that Congress plays contribute to this divide in public opinion. Members of Congress must combine and balance the roles of lawmaker and policy maker with being a representative of their district, their state, their party, and sometimes their race, ethnicity, or gender. Not surprisingly, this balancing act often results in role conflict.

In this chapter, we will analyze the powers of Congress and the competing roles members of Congress play as they represent the interests of their constituents, make laws, and oversee the actions of the other two branches of government. We will also see that as these functions have changed throughout U.S. history, so has Congress itself. We will first examine the roots of Congress--the legislative branch of government. We will then compare the two chambers and consider how their differences affect the course of legislation. After looking at the members of Congress, including how members get elected, and how they spend their days, we will examine the various factors that influence how members of Congress make decisions. We will also examine the lawmaking function of Congress. Finally, we will discuss reform efforts and congressional checks on the executive and judicial branches of government.

Roots of the Legislative Branch of Government

Article I of the Constitution describes the structure of the legislative branch of government we know today. As discussed in chapter 2, the Great Compromise at the Constitutional Convention resulted in the creation of an upper house, the Senate, and a lower house, the House of Representatives. Any two-house legislature, such as the one created by the Framers, is called a **bicameral legislature.** Each state is represented in the Senate by two senators, regardless of the state's population. The number of representatives each state sends to the House of Representatives, in contrast, is determined by that state's population.

The U.S. Constitution sets out the formal, or legal, requirements for membership in the House and Senate. As agreed to at the Constitutional Convention, House members are to be at least twenty-five years of age; senators, thirty. Members of the House are required to have been citizens of the United States for at least seven years; those elected to the Senate, for at least nine years. Both representatives and senators must be legal residents of the states from which they are elected.

Senators are elected for six-year terms, and originally they were elected by state legislatures because the Framers intended for senators to represent their states' interests

bicameral legislature
A legislature divided into two houses; the U.S. Congress and the state legislatures are bicameral except Nebraska, which is unicameral.

[Handwritten annotations:]

H.O.R + Senate
(25)   (30)

• 2 senators per state
• Reps determined by state's population.
• 25, citizens 7 yrs for House, 2 yr term
Senate 30, citizen 9 yrs, 6 yr term
both legal residents of states
1/3 reelected 2 yrs.

in the Senate. State legislators lost this influence over the Senate with the ratification of the Seventeenth Amendment in 1913, which provides for the direct election of senators by voters. Then, as now, one-third of all senators are up for reelection every two years.

Members of the House of Representatives are elected to two-year terms by a vote of the eligible electorate in each congressional district. The Framers expected that House members would be more responsible to the people, both because they were elected directly by them and because they were up for reelection every two years.

The U.S. Constitution requires that a census, which entails the counting of all Americans, be conducted every ten years. Until the first census could be taken, the Constitution fixed the number of representatives in the House of Representatives at sixty-five. In 1790, one member represented about 30,000 people. But, as the population of the new nation grew and states were added to the union, the House became larger and larger. In 1910, it expanded to 435 members, and in 1929, its size was fixed at that number by statute.

Each state is allotted its share of these 435 representatives based on its population. After each U.S. Census, the number of seats allotted to each state is adjusted by a constitutionally mandated process called **apportionment.** After seats are apportioned, congressional districts must be redrawn by state legislatures to reflect population shifts to ensure that each member in Congress represents approximately the same number of residents. This process of redrawing congressional districts to reflect increases or decreases in the number of seats allotted to a state, as well as population shifts within a state, is called **redistricting.** The Supreme Court has ruled that states may redraw districts more frequently than after each U.S. Census. The legal controversies and effects of redistricting are discussed in chapter 12.

The Constitution specifically gives Congress its most important power: the authority to make laws. No **bill** (proposed law) can become law without the consent of both houses. Examples of other powers shared by both houses include the power to declare war, raise an army and navy, coin money, regulate commerce, establish the federal courts and their jurisdiction, establish rules of immigration and naturalization, and "make all Laws which shall be necessary and proper for carrying into Execution the foregoing Powers." As interpreted by the U.S. Supreme Court, the necessary and proper clause, found at the end of Article I, section 8, when coupled with one or more of the specific powers enumerated in Article I, section 8, has allowed Congress to increase the scope of its authority, often at the expense of the states.

Reflecting the different constituencies and size of each house of Congress (as well as the Framers' intentions), Article I gives special, exclusive powers to each house in addition to their shared role in law-making. For example, as noted in Table 6.1, the Constitution specifies that all revenue bills must originate in the House of Representatives. Over the years, however, this mandate has been blurred, and it is not unusual to see budget bills being considered simultaneously in both houses, especially since, ultimately, each must approve all bills, whether or not they involve revenues. The House also has the power to charge the president, vice president, or other "civil officers," including federal judges, with "Treason, Bribery, or other high Crimes and Misdemeanors." Only the Senate is authorized to conduct trials of **impeachment,** with a two-thirds yea vote being necessary before a federal official can be removed from office.

The Senate has the sole authority to approve major presidential appointments, including federal judges, ambassadors, and Cabinet- and sub-Cabinet-level positions. The Senate, too, must approve all presidential treaties by a two-thirds vote.

Thinking Globally
Bicameral and Unicameral Legislatures Worldwide

Among the nations of the world, the most common legislative model is the bicameral parliament, congress, or assembly, with a lower chamber and an upper chamber—as in the United Kingdom, Canada, Australia, and the United States. However, a unicameral system—a single legislative body—is used in several established democracies, including Denmark, Sweden, Israel, New Zealand, South Korea, and Singapore.

- How would replacing the U.S. House and Senate with a single body affect the legislative process?
- Are unicameral systems likely to be more or less powerful than their bicameral counterparts? What are the potential weaknesses of a unicameral system? What are the potential weaknesses of a bicameral system?

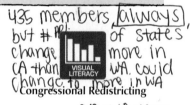

Congressional Redistricting

apportionment
The process of allotting congressional seats to each state following the decennial census according to their proportion of the population.

redistricting
The redrawing of congressional districts to reflect increases or decreases in seats allotted to the states, as well as population shifts within a state.

bill
A proposed law.

impeachment
The power delegated to the House of Representatives in the Constitution to charge the president, vice president, or other "civil officers," including federal judges, with "Treason, Bribery, or other high Crimes and Misdemeanors." This is the first step in the constitutional process of removing such government officials from office.

[Handwritten margin notes: 435 members always, but # ppl. of states change more in CA than WA. could change to more in WA — every 10 years — con: party (majority) can draw in favor — 650 ppl. per district — fixed # of seats (435) — $ bills in H.O.R. now blurred both houses b/c both pass it even w/ $ — Senate can impeach "civil officers" w/ 2/3 votes, approve major presidential appts, approve presidential treaties with 2/3 vote]

TABLE 6.1 Key Differences Between the House of Representatives and the Senate

Constitutional Differences	
House	Senate
435 voting members (apportioned by population)	100 voting members (two from each state)
Two-year terms	Six-year terms (one-third up for reelection every two years)
Initiates all revenue bills	Offers "advice and consent" on many major presidential appointments
Initiates impeachment procedures and passes articles of impeachment	Tries impeached officials Approves treaties

Differences in Operation	
House	Senate
More centralized, more formal; stronger leadership	Less centralized, less formal; weaker leadership
Committee on Rules fairly powerful in controlling time and rules of debate (in conjunction with the Speaker of the House)	No rules committee; limits on debate come through unanimous consent or cloture of filibuster
More impersonal	More personal
Power distributed less evenly	Power distributed more evenly
Members are highly specialized	Members are generalists
Emphasizes tax and revenue policy	Emphasizes foreign policy

Changes in the Institution	
House	Senate
Power centralized in the Speaker's inner circle of advisers	Senate workload increasing and institution becoming more formal; threat of filibusters more frequent than in the past
House procedures becoming more efficient	Becoming more difficult to pass legislation
Turnover is relatively high, although those seeking reelection almost always win	Turnover is moderate

How Congress Is Organized

Every two years, a new Congress is seated. After ascertaining the formal qualifications of new members, the Congress organizes itself as it prepares for the business of the coming session. Among the first items on its agenda are the election of new leaders and the adoption of rules for conducting its business. Each house has a hierarchical leadership structure that is closely tied to the key role of political parties in organizing Congress.

The Role of Political Parties in Organizing Congress

As demonstrated in Figure 6.1, the basic division in Congress is between majority and minority parties. The **majority party** is the party in each house with the most members. The **minority party** is the party in each house with the second most members. (To learn more about the 111th Congress, see Figure 6.2.) Parties play a key role in the committee system, an organizational feature of Congress that facilitates its law-making and oversight functions. The committees, controlled by the majority party in each house of Congress, often set the agendas.

At the beginning of each new Congress—the 111th Congress, for example, will sit in two sessions, one in 2009 and one in 2010—the members of each party gather in their party caucus or conference. Historically, these caucuses have enjoyed varied powers, but today the party caucuses—now called caucus by House Democrats and conference by House and Senate Republicans and Senate Democrats—have several roles, including nominating or electing party officers, reviewing committee assignments, discussing party policy, imposing party discipline, setting party themes, and coordinating

majority party
The political party in each house of Congress with the most members.

minority party
The political party in each house of Congress with the second most members.

TIMELINE

The Power of the Speaker of the House

HOUSE OF REPRESENTATIVES

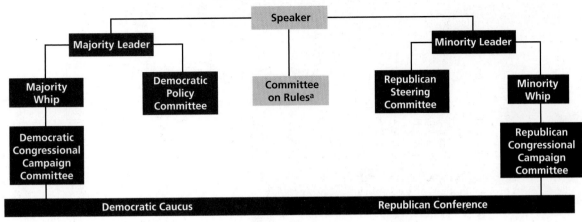

^aAlthough not strictly a party panel, the Committee on Rules in modern times functions largely as an arm of the majority leadership.

SENATE

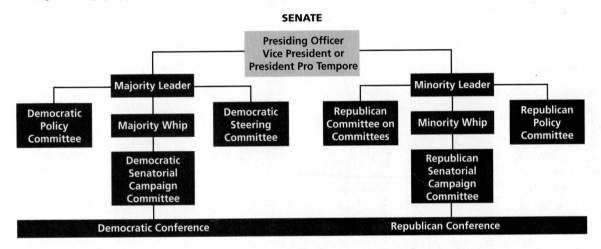

FIGURE 6.1 Organizational Structure of the House of Representatives and the Senate in the 111th Congress

Source: Adapted from Roger H. Davidson and Walter J. Oleszek, *Congress and its Members*, 10th ed. (Washington, DC: CQ Press, 2006.) Updated by the authors.

media, including talk radio. Conference and caucus chairs are recognized party leaders who work with other leaders in the House or Senate.[3]

Each caucus or conference has specialized committees that fulfill certain tasks. House Republicans, for example, have a Committee on Committees that makes committee assignments. The Democrats' Steering Committee performs this function. Each party also has congressional campaign committees to assist members in their reelection bids.

The House of Representatives

Even in the first Congress in 1789, the House of Representatives was almost three times larger than the Senate. It is not surprising, then, that from the beginning the House has been organized more tightly, structured more elaborately, and governed by stricter rules. Traditionally, loyalty to the party leadership and voting along party lines has been more common in the House than in the Senate. House leaders also play a key role in moving the business of the House along. Historically, the Speaker of the House, the majority and minority leaders, and the Republican and Democratic House whips have made up the party leadership that runs Congress. This group now has been expanded to include deputy whips of both parties, as well as those who head the Democratic Caucus and the Republican Conference.

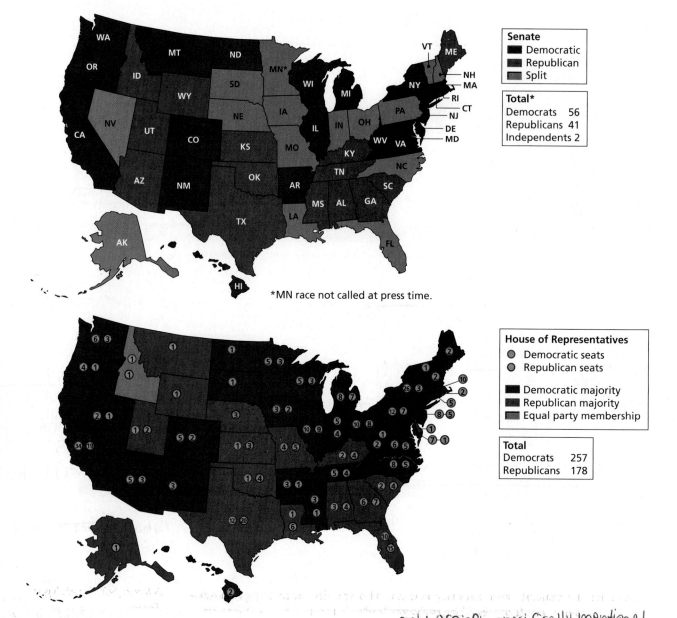

FIGURE 6.2 The 111th Congress

[handwritten: only officer specifically mentioned in constitution · elected by House only @ each new congress]

Speaker of the House
The only officer of the House of Representatives specifically mentioned in the Constitution; elected at the beginning of each new Congress by the entire House; traditionally a member of the majority party.

[handwritten: member of majority party in house long time · apprenticeship in other lead positions · oversees house business, official spokesperson, second in line of pres seccession · great political influence in chamber, smooth passage of party-backed legislation]

THE SPEAKER OF THE HOUSE The **Speaker of the House** is the only officer of the House of Representatives specifically mentioned in the Constitution. The entire House of Representatives elects the Speaker at the beginning of each new Congress. Traditionally, the Speaker is a member of the majority party, as are all committee chairs. Although typically not the member with the longest service, the Speaker generally has served in the House for a long time and in other House leadership positions as an apprenticeship.

The Speaker presides over the House of Representatives, oversees House business, and is the official spokesperson for the House, as well as being second in the line of presidential succession. Moreover, the Speaker is the House liaison with the president and generally has great political influence within the chamber. The Speaker is also expected to smooth the passage of party-backed legislation through the House. (To learn more about recent Speakers, see Politics Now: Leadership Styles of the Speakers of the House.)

The Living Constitution

The Congress shall have power . . . to establish a uniform Rule of Naturalization.

—ARTICLE 1, SECTION 8, CLAUSE 4

This article reiterates the sovereign power of the nation and places authority to draft laws concerning naturalization in the hands of Congress. Congress's power over naturalization is exclusive—meaning that no state can bestow U.S. citizenship on anyone. Citizenship is a privilege and Congress may make laws limiting or expanding the criteria.

The word *citizen* was not defined constitutionally until ratification in 1868 of the Fourteenth Amendment, which sets forth two kinds of citizenship: by birth and through naturalization. Throughout American history, Congress has imposed a variety of limits on naturalization, originally restricting it to "free, white persons." "Orientals" were excluded from eligibility in 1882. At one time those affiliated with the Communist Party and those who lacked "good moral character" (a phrase that was construed to bar homosexuals, drunkards, gamblers, and adulterers) were deemed unfit for citizenship. These restrictions no longer carry the force of law, but they do underscore the power of Congress in this matter.

Congress continues to retain the right to naturalize large classes of individuals, as it did in 2000 when it granted automatic citizenship rights to all minor children adopted abroad as long as both adoptive parents were American citizens. Naturalized citizens, however, do not necessarily enjoy the full rights of citizenship enjoyed by other Americans. Congress at any time, subject only to Supreme Court review, can limit the rights and liberties of naturalized citizens, especially in times of national crisis. In the wake of the September 11, 2001, terrorist attacks, when it was revealed that one-third of the forty-eight al-Qaeda-linked operatives who took part in some sort of terrorist activities against the United States were lawful permanent residents or naturalized citizens, Congress called for greater screening by the U.S. Citizenship and Immigration Service for potential terrorists.

CRITICAL THINKING QUESTIONS

1. Is Congress the appropriate institution to have the power over immigration and naturalization? Why or why not?
2. Is racial profiling by the U.S. Citizenship and Immigration Service and other government entities an appropriate action in the name of national security? Why or why not?

OTHER HOUSE LEADERS After the Speaker, the next most powerful people in the House are the majority and minority leaders, who are elected in their individual **party caucuses** or **conferences.** The **majority leader** is the second most important person in the House; his or her counterpart on the other side of the aisle (the House is organized so that if you are facing the front of the chamber, Democrats sit on the left side and Republicans on the right side of the center aisle) is the **minority leader.** The majority leader helps the Speaker schedule proposed legislation for debate on the House floor. In the past, both leaders worked closely with the Speaker. This relationship has changed in recent Congresses.

The Republican and Democratic **whips,** who are elected by party members in caucuses, assist the Speaker and majority and minority leaders in their leadership efforts. The position of whip originated in the British House of Commons, where it was named after the "whipper in," the rider who keeps the hounds together in a fox hunt. Party whips—who were first designated in the U.S. House of Representatives in 1899 and in the Senate in 1913—do, as their name suggests, try to whip fellow Democrats or Republicans into line on partisan issues. They try to maintain close contact with all members on important votes, prepare summaries of content and implications of bills, get "nose counts" during debates and votes, and in general get members to toe the party line. Whips and their deputy whips also serve as communications links, distributing word of the party line from leaders to rank-and-file members and alerting leaders to concerns in the ranks.

party caucus or conference
A formal gathering of all party members.

majority leader
The elected leader of the party controlling the most seats in the House of Representatives or the Senate; is second in authority to the Speaker of the House and in the Senate is regarded as its most powerful member.

minority leader
The elected leader of the party with the second highest number of elected representatives in the House of Representatives or the Senate.

whip
Key member who keeps close contact with all members of his or her party and takes nose counts on key votes, prepares summaries of bills, and in general acts as communications link within a party.

177

Source: POLITICO.COM   June 27, 2007

Leadership Styles of the Speaker of the House

Pelosi Forging Quieter Path than Gingrich

JOSEPHINE HEARN

Nancy Pelosi would never have made the mistake Newt Gingrich did in late 1995, when he complained to reporters over breakfast that President Clinton had not invited him to sit in the front of Air Force One. The *New York Daily News* had a field day, emblazoning on the next day's front page, "Cry Baby: Newt's Tantrum; He closed down the government because Clinton made him sit at the back of the plane." The remark kicked off the worst public relations episode of the Gingrich speakership.

Pelosi, six months into a speakership similar to Gingrich's in timing and national significance, is no fan of free-wheeling breakfasts with three dozen reporters. The California Democrat is more press-shy than the former Republican Speaker from Georgia, who reveled in his often unscripted role. Pelosi, though not immune to blunders, manages her image more carefully, limiting her media availabilities.

Though she and Gingrich came to power under similar circumstances—after widespread discontent with the ruling party swept the underdogs into power— Pelosi is developing a leadership style all her own. Either by natural temperament or political calculation, she has averted Gingrich's early missteps.

She polls ahead of Democratic leaders and Congress as a whole—and until recently enjoyed a roughly 15-point lead in approval ratings over Gingrich. Lately, she has about the same approval ratings as Gingrich did at this time, but her dis-approval ratings are lower.

To be sure, Pelosi has made her own mistakes. Her drop in the polls coin-cided with Democrats' failed show-down with the White House over with-drawing U.S. troops from Iraq. Her trip to Syria was widely panned. She famously miscalculated in backing Rep. John P. Murtha (D–PA) in the race for majority leader last fall. She has picked a nasty fight with House Energy and Commerce Chairman John Dingell (D–MI) over global warming legisla-tion. And congressional approval rat-ings are lower than ever.

But the Pelosi model has shown that a new majority need not hinge on a larger-than-life charismatic figure, as Gingrich was until his fall. Facing a hostile presi-dent of another party, much like Gingrich did, Pelosi is a quieter speaker. Among the public, twice as many people are unaware of Pelosi than were unaware of Gingrich.

Gingrich held 33 news conferences in his first three months, according to *Congressional Quarterly*. Many of them were solo events, televised nationally and loaded with colorful commentary. Pelosi conducted fewer than half that number during the same period, a rough count showed. And she has most often invited other lawmakers to join her.

To her critics, Pelosi's cloistered style is a weakness. "She's handled and protected like a prize fighter," said Rep. Jack Kingston (R–GA). "She has a good agent who only puts her in comfortable situa-tions. Newt would go behind enemy lines and not think twice about it."

But even Gingrich later regretted his penchant for the limelight. "I should have had much more media discipline," he said in 2003. "There's a side of me that's permanently analytical, that likes coming and giving the speech, and that side of me should not have been allowed out of the box for the entire time I was speaker."

Discussion Questions

1. *What are the effects of a Speaker's leadership style on the day-to-day operations of the House of Representatives?*
2. *What effect does a Speaker's leadership have on his or her party caucus?*
3. *Why is the Speaker's relationship with the press important?*

The Senate

The Constitution specifies that the presiding officer of the Senate is the vice presi-dent of the United States. Because he is not a member of the Senate, he votes only in the case of a tie. The official chair of the Senate is the **president pro tempore,** or pro tem, who is selected by the majority party and presides over the Senate in the absence of the vice president. The position of pro tem today is primarily an honorific office that generally goes to the most senior senator of the majority party. Once elected, the pro tem stays in that office until there is a change in the majority party in the Senate. Since presiding over the Senate can be a rather perfunctory duty, neither the vice pres-ident nor the president pro tempore actually perform the task very often. Instead, the duty of presiding over the Senate rotates among junior members of the chamber.

The true leader of the Senate is the majority leader, elected to the position by the majority party. Because the Senate is a smaller and more collegial body, the majority leader is not nearly as powerful as the Speaker of the House. The minority leader and the Republican and Democratic whips round out the leadership positions in the Senate and perform functions similar to those of their House counterparts. But, leading and whipping in the Senate can be quite a challenge. Senate rules always have given tremen-

president pro tempore
The official chair of the Senate; usu-ally the most senior member of the majority party.

dous power to individual senators; in most cases senators can offer any kind of amendments to legislation on the floor, and an individual senator can bring all work on the floor to a halt indefinitely through a filibuster unless three-fifths of the senators vote to cut him or her off.[4]

The Committee System

The saying "Congress in session is Congress on exhibition, whilst Congress in its committee rooms is Congress at work" may not be as true today as it was when Woodrow Wilson wrote it in 1885.[5] Still, "the work that takes place in the committee and subcommittee rooms of Capitol Hill is critical to the productivity and effectiveness of Congress."[6] Committees are especially important in the House of Representatives because of its size. The establishment of subcommittees allows for even greater specialization.

TYPES OF COMMITTEES There are four types of congressional committees: (1) standing; (2) joint; (3) conference; and, (4) select, or special.[7]

1. **Standing committees,** so called because they continue from one Congress to the next, are the committees to which bills are referred for consideration.
2. **Joint committees** are set up to expedite business between the houses and to help focus public attention on major matters, such as the economy, taxation, or scandals. They include members from both houses of Congress who conduct investigations or special studies.
3. **Conference committees** are special joint committees that reconcile differences in bills passed by the House and Senate. A conference committee is made up of those members from the House and Senate committees that originally considered the bill.
4. **Select (or special) committees** are temporary committees appointed for specific purposes. Generally such committees are established to conduct special investigations or studies and to report back to the chamber that established them.

In the 111th Congress, the House had nineteen standing committees, as shown in Table 6.2, each with an average of thirty-one members. Together, these standing committees had roughly ninety subcommittees that collectively act as the eyes, ears, and hands of the House. They consider issues roughly parallel to those of the departments represented in the president's Cabinet.

Although most committees in one house parallel those in the other, the House Committee on Rules, for which there is no counterpart in the Senate, plays a key role in the House's law-making process. Indicative of the importance of the Committee on Rules, majority party members are appointed directly by the Speaker. This committee

Thinking Globally
Proportional Representation

America's winner-take-all system for determining election outcomes effectively marginalizes minor parties. Independents serving in Congress generally caucus (assemble) with either the Democrats or the Republicans. In contrast, many countries with a parliamentary system of government rely on proportional representation. For example, Israel's unicameral parliament, the Knesset, awards seats to political parties in exact proportion to their share of the popular vote. The Knesset has operated successfully with numerous different parties represented and with no single party holding a majority.

- How would a proportional representation system affect the U.S. Congress?
- What are the advantages of a legislative system based on two or three major parties compared to one that incorporates many parties? What are the disadvantages?

standing committee
Committee to which proposed bills are referred: continue from one Congress to the next.

joint committee
Committees that includes members from both houses of Congress to conducts investigations or special studies.

conference committee
Special committee created to iron out differences between Senate and House versions of a specific piece of legislation.

select (or special) committee
Temporary committee appointed for specific purpose, such as conducting a special investigation or study.

Photo courtesy: Mark Wilson/Getty Images

How do congressional leaders handle a crisis? Senate Majority Leader Harry Reid (D–NV) and Senate Minority Leader Mitch McConnell (R–KY) hold a press conference announcing the Senate's successful passage of controversial financial bailout legislation on October 1, 2008. The House leadership passed the bill on Friday, October 3, after a failed initial attempt.

TABLE 6.2   Committees of the 111th Congress (with Subcommittee Examples in Italics)

Standing Committees	
House	**Senate**
Agriculture	Agriculture, Nutrition, & Forestry
Appropriations	Appropriations
Armed Services	Armed Services
Budget	Banking, Housing, & Urban Affairs
Education & Labor	Budget
Energy & Commerce	Commerce, Science, & Transportation
Financial Services	Energy & Natural Resources
Foreign Affairs	Environment & Public Works
Homeland Security	Finance
House Administration	Foreign Relations
Judiciary	Health, Education, Labor, & Pensions
Immigration, Citizenship, Refugees, Border Security, & International Law	Homeland Security & Governmental Affairs
Commercial & Administrative Law	Indian Affairs
Crime, Terrorism, & Homeland Security	Judiciary
Courts, the Internet, & Intellectual Property	*Administrative Oversight & the Courts*
The Constitution, Civil Rights, & Civil Liberties	*Antitrust, Competition Policy, & Consumer Rights*
Natural Resources	*Crime & Drugs*
Oversight & Government Reform	*Human Rights & the Law*
Rules	*Immigration, Refugees, & Border Security*
Science & Technology	*Terrorism, Technology, & Homeland Security*
Small Business	*The Constitution*
Standards of Official Conduct	Rules & Administration
Transportation & Infrastructure	Small Business & Entrepreneurship
Veterans Affairs	Veterans Affairs
Ways & Means	

Select, Special, and Other Committees		
House	**Senate**	**Joint Committees**
Permanent Select Intelligence	Select Ethics	Economics
Select Committee on Energy	Select Intelligence	Taxation
Independence & Global Warming	Special Aging	

reviews most bills after they come from a committee and before they go to the full chamber for consideration. Performing a traffic cop function, the Committee on Rules gives each bill what is called a rule, which contains the date the bill will come up for debate and the time that will be allotted for discussion, and often specifies what kinds of amendments can be offered. Bills considered under a closed rule cannot be amended.

Standing committees have considerable power. They can kill bills, amend them radically, or hurry them through the process. In the words of former President Woodrow Wilson, once a bill is referred to a committee, it "crosses a parliamentary bridge of sighs to dim dungeons of silence from whence it never will return."[8] Committees report out to the full House or Senate only a small fraction of the bills assigned to them. Bills can be forced out of a House committee by a **discharge petition** signed by a majority (218) of the House membership.

In the 111th Congress, the Senate had seventeen standing committees ranging in size from fifteen to twenty-nine members. It also had roughly seventy subcommittees, which allowed all majority party senators to chair at least one.

In contrast to the House, whose members hold few committee assignments (an average of 1.8 standing and three subcommittees), senators each serve on an average of three to four committees and seven subcommittees. Whereas the committee system allows House members to become policy or issue specialists, Senate members often are generalists. In the 111th Congress, Senator Kay Bailey Hutchison (R–TX), for

discharge petition
Petition that gives a majority of the House of Representatives the authority to bring an issue to the floor in the face of committee inaction.

example, served on several committees, including Appropriations; Commerce, Science, and Transportation; Veterans Affairs; and Rules and Administration. She also served on ten subcommittees, and was the chair of the Republican Policy Committee.

Senate committees enjoy the same power over framing legislation that House committees do, but the Senate, being an institution more open to individual input than the House, gives less deference to the work done in committees. In the Senate, legislation is more likely to be rewritten on the floor, where all senators can participate and add amendments at any time.

COMMITTEE MEMBERSHIP   Many newly elected members of Congress come into the body with their sights on certain committee assignments. Others are more flexible. Many legislators seeking committee assignments inform their party's selection committee of their preferences. They often request assignments based on their own interests or expertise or on a particular committee's ability to help their prospects for reelection. One political scientist has noted that committee assignments are to members what stocks are to investors—they seek to acquire those that will add to the value of their portfolios.[9]

Representatives often seek committee assignments that have access to what is known as **pork,** legislation that allows representatives to bring money and jobs to their districts in the form of public works programs, military bases, or other programs. Many of these programs are called **earmarks** because they are monies that an appropriations bill designates—"earmarks"—for specific projects within a member's district or state. Legislators who bring jobs and new public works programs back to their districts are hard to defeat when up for reelection. But, ironically, these are the programs that attract much of the public criticism directed at the federal government in general and Congress in particular. Thus, it is somewhat paradoxical that pork improves a member's chances for reelection.

Pork isn't the only motivator for those seeking strategic committee assignments.[10] Some committees, such as Energy and Commerce, facilitate reelection by giving House members influence over decisions that affect large campaign contributors. Other committees, such as Education and the Workforce or Judiciary, attract members eager to work on the policy responsibilities assigned to the committee even if the appointment does them little good at the ballot box. Another motivator for certain committee assignments is the desire to have power and influence within the chamber. The Appropriations and Budget Committees provide that kind of reward for some members.

In both the House and the Senate, committee membership generally reflects the party distribution within that chamber. For example, at the outset of the 111th Congress, Democrats held a majority of House seats and thus claimed about a fifty-eight percent share of the seats on several committees. On committees more critical to the operation of the House or to the setting of national policy, the majority often takes a disproportionate share of the slots. Since the Committee on Rules regulates access to the floor for legislation approved by other standing committees, control by the majority party is essential for it to manage the flow of legislation. For this reason, no matter how narrow the majority party's margin in the chamber, it makes up more than two-thirds of the Committee on Rules membership.

COMMITTEE CHAIRS   Committee chairs enjoy tremendous power and prestige. They are authorized to select all subcommittee chairs, call meetings, and recommend majority members to sit on conference committees. Committee chairs may even opt to kill a bill by refusing to schedule hearings on it. They also have a large committee staff at their disposal and are often recipients of favors from lobbyists, who recognize the chair's unique position of power. Personal skill, influence, and expertise are a chair's best allies.

pork
Legislation that allows representatives to bring home the bacon to their districts in the form of public works programs, military bases, or other programs designed to benefit their districts directly.

earmark
Funds in appropriations bill that provide dollars for particular purposes within a state or congressional district.

Committee chairs *(handwritten margin note)*

seniority
Time of continuous service on a committee.

interviewed by party leaders to show dem loyalty of party
term = 6 yrs. *(handwritten margin notes)*

Historically, committee chairs were the majority party members with the longest continuous service on the committee. Committee chairs in the House, unlike the Senate, are no longer selected by **seniority,** or time of continuous service on the committee. Instead, potential chairs interviewed by party leaders to ensure that candidates demonstrate loyalty to the party. The seniority system is also affected by term limits enacted by the House and Senate in 1995 and 1997, respectively. This term limit of six years for all committee chairs has forced many longtime committee chairs to step down or take over other committees.

The Members of Congress

Many members of Congress clearly relish their work, although there are indications that the high cost of living in Washington and maintaining two homes, political scandals, intense media scrutiny, the need to tackle hard issues, and a growth of party dissension are taking a toll on many members. It is also difficult to please two constituencies—party leaders, colleagues, and lobbyists in Washington, D.C., and constituents at home. Table 6.3 shows a representative day in the life of a member of Congress, both at home and in Washington.

Running for and Staying in Office

Despite the long hours and hard work required of senators and representatives, thousands aspire to these jobs every year. Yet, only 535 men and women (plus five nonvoting delegates) actually serve in the U.S. Congress. Membership in one of the two major political parties is almost always a prerequisite for election, because election laws in various states often discriminate against independents (those without party affiliation) and minor-party candidates.

535 ppl. in congress
being in office helps stay in office (name recognition, access to free media inside track to fund-raising. district drawn to favor *(handwritten margin notes)*

incumbency
The fact that being in office helps a person stay in office because of a variety of benefits that go with the position.

Unless serious scandal chance of defeat is minimal *(handwritten margin notes)*

Why is it So Hard to Defeat an Incumbent?

Incumbency helps members stay in office once they are elected.[11] It's often very difficult for outsiders to win because they don't have the advantages enjoyed by incumbents, including name recognition, access to free media, an inside track on fund-raising, and a district drawn to favor the incumbent. As illustrated in Analyzing Visuals: Approval Ratings of Congress and Individual Representatives, most Americans have higher regard for their own members of Congress than for Congress collectively. It is not surprising, then, that an average of 96 percent of the incumbents who seek reelection win their primary and general election races.[12] One study concluded that unless a member of Congress was involved in a serious scandal, his or her chances of defeat were minimal.[13]

TABLE 6.3 A Day in the Life of a Member of Congress

8:30 a.m.	Breakfast with a former member.
9:30 a.m.	Science Committee: Hearing.
10:00 a.m.	Private briefing by NASA officials for afternoon subcommittee hearing.
10:00 a.m.	Commerce Committee: Markup session of pending legistation
12:00 p.m.	Photo opportunity with Miss Universe.
12:00 p.m.	Lunch with visiting friend at Watergate Hotel.
1:30 p.m.	Science Committee: Subcommittee hearing.
1:30 p.m.	Commerce Committee: Subcommittee markup session of pending legislation.
2:00 p.m.	House convenes.
3:00 p.m.	Meeting with National Alliance for Animal Legislation official.
4:30 p.m.	Meeting with American Jewish Congress delegates.
5:00 p.m.	State University reception.
5:00 p.m.	Briefing by the commissioner of the Bureau of Labor Statistics on the uninsured.
5:30 p.m.	Reception/fundraiser for party whip.
6:00 p.m.	Reception/fundraiser for fellow member from the same state.
6:00 p.m.	Cajun foods reception sponsored by Louisiana member.
6:00 p.m.	Winetasting reception on behalf of New York wine industry sponsored by New York member.
10:45 p.m.	House adjourns.

[handwritten margin note:] congress is all over better than public · most senators + House members have college educations, 2/3 hold advanced degrees

Congressional Demographics

Congress is better educated, richer, more male, and more white than the general population. Most senators and members of the U.S. House of Representatives are college graduates. Over two-thirds of the members of each body also hold advanced degrees.[14] Many members of both houses have significant inherited wealth, but given their educational attainment, which is far higher than the average American's, it is not surprising to find so many wealthy members of Congress.

Almost 250 million members of Congress are millionaires. The Senate, in fact, is often called the Millionaires Club, and its members sport names including Rockefeller and Clinton. The median net worth of a senator in 2008 was $1.7 million, while the median net worth of a House member was $75,000.[15]

The average age of senators in the 111th Congress was sixty-two. Mark Pryor (D–AR) is the youngest senator. The average age of House members is fifty-six. Representative Aaron Schock (R–IL) was first elected to the House in 2008 and is the youngest member of Congress.

As revealed in Figure 6.3, the 1992 elections saw a record number of women, African Americans, and other minorities elected to Congress. By the 111th Congress, the total number of women members increased to at least seventy-four in the House and seventeen in the Senate. In 2009, the number of African Americans serving in the House held steady at thirty-nine. Until his election to the presidency, Barack Obama (D–IL) was the only African American in the Senate. In the 111th Congress, only twenty-four Hispanics served in the House. Three Hispanics served in the Senate. Also serving in the 111th Congress were two members of Asian or Pacific Islander heritage in the Senate and five in the House of Representatives. Only one American Indian, Tom Cole (R–OK), serves in the 111th Congress.

Interestingly, the 111th Congress included a historic number of Jewish members. Forty-five Jews served in Congress—thirteen in the Senate and thirty-two in the House of Representatives.

Occupationally, members of the Congress no longer are overwhelmingly lawyers, although lawyers continue to be the largest single occupational group. In the 111th Congress, 290 were former state legislators and 116 were former congressional staffers. The number of veterans in Congress, however, has continued to decline since the end of the Vietnam War.

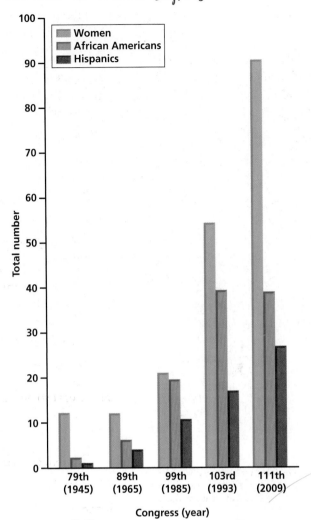

FIGURE **6.3** Female and Minority Members of Congress, Selected Years

Comparing Legislatures

Theories of Representation

Over the years, political theorists have offered various ideas about how constituents' interests are best represented in any legislative body. British political philosopher Edmund Burke (1729–1797), who also served in the British Parliament, believed that although he was elected from Bristol, it was his duty to represent the interests of the entire nation. He reasoned that elected officials were obliged to vote as they personally thought best. According to Burke, a representative should be a **trustee** who listens to the opinions of constituents and then can be trusted to use his or her own best judgment to make final decisions.

A second theory of representation holds that a representative should be a **delegate.** True delegates are representatives who vote the way their constituents would want them to, whether or not those opinions are the representative's. Delegates, therefore, must be

trustee
Role played by elected representatives who listen to constituents' opinions and then use their best judgment to make final decisions.

delegate
Role played by elected representatives who vote the way their constituents would want them to, regardless of their own opinions.

Photo courtesy: the Office of U.S. Senator Daniel Akaka

How diverse is Congress?
Senator Daniel Akaka (D–HI) is one of seven members of Congress whose ethnic background is Asian or Pacific American.

politico
Role played by elected representatives who act as trustees or as delegates, depending on the issue.

ready and willing to vote against their conscience or personal policy preferences if they know how their constituents feel about a particular issue.

Not surprisingly, members of Congress and other legislative bodies generally don't fall neatly into either category. It is often unclear how constituents feel about a particular issue, or there may be conflicting opinions within a single constituency. With these difficulties in mind, a third theory of representation holds that a **politico** alternately dons the hat of a trustee or delegate, depending on the issue. On an issue of great concern to their constituents, representatives most likely will vote as delegates; on other issues, perhaps those that are less visible, representatives will act as trustees and use their own best judgment.

How a representative views his or her role—as a trustee, delegate, or politico—may still not answer the question of whether it makes a difference if a representative or senator is male or female, African American, Latino/a, or Caucasian, young or old, gay or straight. Burke's ideas about representation don't even begin to address more practical issues of representation. Can a man, for example, represent the interests of women as well as a woman? Can a rich woman represent the interests of the poor? Are veterans more sensitive to veterans' issues?

How Members Make Decisions

As a bill makes its way through the labyrinth of the law-making process members are confronted with the question: "How should I vote?" Members adhere to their own personal beliefs on some matters, but their views often are moderated by other considerations. To avoid making any voting mistakes, members look to a variety of sources for cues.

Party

Members often look to party leaders for indicators of how to vote. Indeed, the whips in each chamber reinforce the need for party cohesion, particularly on issues of concern to the party. In fact, from 1970 to the mid-1990s, the incidence of party votes in which majorities of the two parties took opposing sides roughly doubled to more than 60 percent of all roll-call votes.[16] Under unified Republican control in the 107th Congress, for example, there was perfect party unity on all major votes taken in the House.[17] In the 108th Congress, Democratic senators demonstrated unanimity in filibustering several presidential judicial nominations to the U.S. Courts of Appeals. While some charged that this was not evidence of party unity, but instead elected officials taking their direction from major liberal special-interest groups, there can be no doubt that in both closely divided houses, party reigns supreme.[18] This has become increasingly evident during recent periods of **divided government**, the political condition in which different parties control the White House and Congress.

divided government
The political condition in which different political parties control the White House and Congress.

The Prepared Voter Kit

Constituents

Constituents—the people who live and vote in a representative's home district or state—are always in a member's mind when casting votes.[19] It is rare for a legislator to vote against the wishes of his or her constituents regularly, particularly on issues of welfare rights, domestic policy, or other highly salient issues.

Gauging how voters feel about any particular issue often is not easy. Because it is virtually impossible to know how the folks back home feel on all issues, representa-

Analyzing Visuals · Approval Ratings of Congress and Individual Representatives

Examine the line graph tracking approval ratings of Congress in general as well as of the respondents' individual representatives. Then, consider the following questions:

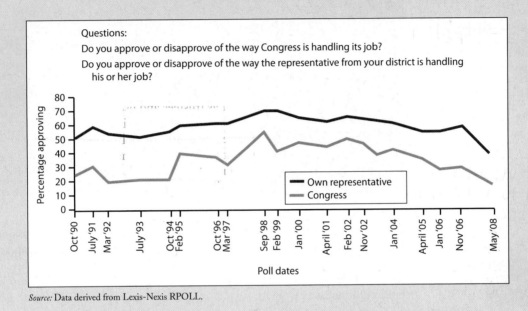

Questions:
Do you approve or disapprove of the way Congress is handling its job?
Do you approve or disapprove of the way the representative from your district is handling his or her job?

Source: Data derived from Lexis-Nexis RPOLL.

DO the data for approval of Congress and approval of one's own representative show similar trends over the period covered in the figure?

WHAT factors might account for the differences in the ratings of Congress and as a whole one's own representative in 2008?

IN general, why would the approval ratings for Congress be significantly lower than those for individual members?

---

tives' perceptions of their constituents' preferences is important. Even when voters have opinions, legislators may get little guidance if their district is narrowly divided. Abortion is an issue about which many voters feel passionately, but a legislator whose district has roughly equal numbers of pro-choice and pro-life advocates can satisfy only a portion of his or her constituents.

Colleagues and Caucuses

The range and complexity of issues confronting Congress mean that no one can be up to speed on more than a few topics. When members must vote on bills about which they know very little, they often turn for advice to colleagues who have served on the committee that handled the legislation. On issues that are of little interest to a legislator, **logrolling,** or vote trading, often occurs. Logrolling often takes place on specialized bills targeting money or projects to selected congressional districts. An unaffected member often will exchange a yea vote now for the promise of a future yea vote on a similar piece of specialized legislation.

Members may also look to other representatives who share common interests. Special-interest caucuses created around issues, home states, regions, congressional class, or other commonalities facilitate this communication. Prior to 1995, the power of these groups was even more evident, as several caucuses enjoyed formal status within the legislative body and were provided staff, office space, and budgets. Today, however, all caucuses are informal in nature, although some, such as the Black and

logrolling
Vote trading, voting yea to support a colleague's bill in return for a promise of future support.

Photo courtesy: the Office of U.S. Senator Barbara Mikulski

Can a man represent the interests of a woman as well as a woman? The sixteen women senators of the 110th Congress, pictured here, don't think so. The 2008 elections saw their numbers increase by one—Jeanne Shaheen (D–NH), while Elizabeth Dole (R–NC) was defeated by Kay Hagan (D–NC).

SIMULATION

You Are an Informed Voter Helping Your Classmates Decide How to Vote

How do staffers affect congressional decision making? Members of the Congressional Muslim Staffers Association like Sarah Bassal (left) and Amina Rubin (right) work to educate policy makers about Islam and Islamic beliefs.

Photo courtesy: Jamie Rose/The New York Times

Hispanic Caucuses, are far more organized than others. The Congressional Caucus for Women's Issues, for example, has formal elections of its Republican and Democratic co-chairs and vice chairs, its members provide staff to work on issues of common concern to caucus members, and staffers meet regularly to facilitate support for legislation of interest to women.

Interest Groups, Lobbyists, and Political Action Committees

A primary function of most lobbyists, whether they work for interest groups, trade associations, or large corporations, is to provide information to supportive or potentially supportive legislators, committees, and their staffs.[20] Interest groups also use grassroots appeals to pressure legislators by urging their members in a particular state or district to call, write, fax, or e-mail their senators or representatives. Lobbyists can't vote, but constituents back home can and do. The almost 5,000 political action committees (PACs) organized by interest groups are a major source of most members' campaign funding.

Staff and Support Agencies

Members of Congress rely heavily on members of their staffs for information on pending legislation.[21] House members have an average of seventeen staffers; senators have an average of forty. Staff are divided between D.C. and district offices. When a bill is nonideological or one on which the member has no real position, staff members can be very influential. In many offices, they are the greatest influence on their boss's votes. In many cases, lobbyists are just as likely to contact key staffers as they are members. And, in many of the recent major House lobbying scandals, it was staffers who ultimately faced criminal

Be a Congressional Intern

Senators and representatives cannot do their jobs by themselves. With so many demands on their time, both in Washington and their districts, these elected members rely on their staffs on a daily basis.

But, even professional staffers cannot do everything members of Congress require. Thus, advanced high school and college students are hired as interns to help with basic tasks. Interns answer phones, help with casework, respond to constituent letters and e-mails, and attend events on behalf of members. They work in both Washington, D.C., and district offices, and they are invaluable resources.

Internships provide students with an invaluable opportunity to learn about the day-to-day operations of Congress. In fact, a significant number of current members of Congress began their political careers as interns.

Explore the Web site of your senator or representative and learn what internship opportunities might be available to you. Then, consider the following questions:

- Do you know anyone who has worked for a member of Congress or a state legislator? What tasks did they perform?
- What skills might you learn as a congressional intern?
- How do your political views align with those of your representative or senator? How might this affect your experience as an intern in that person's office?

---

investigations or prosecutions for influence buying. (To learn about work opportunities in Congress, see Ideas into Action: Be a Congressional Intern.)

Congressional committees and subcommittees also have their own dedicated staff to assist committee members. Additional support for members comes from support personnel at the Congressional Research Service (CRS) at the Library of Congress, the Government Accountability Office (GAO), and the Congressional Budget Office (CBO).

The Law-Making Function of Congress

The organization of Congress allows it to fulfill its constitutional responsibilities, chief among which is its law-making function. It is through this power that Congress affects the day-to-day lives of all Americans and sets policy for the future. Proposals for legislation—be they about terrorism, Medicare, or tax policy—can come from the president, executive agencies, committee staffs, interest groups, or even private individuals. Only members of the House or Senate, however, can formally submit a bill for congressional consideration (although many are initially drafted by lobbyists). Once a bill is introduced by a member of Congress, it usually reaches a dead end. Of the approximately 10,000 bills introduced during the 110th session of Congress, fewer than 5 percent were made into law.

How A Bill Becomes A Law

A bill must survive several stages or roadblocks before it becomes a law. It must be approved by one or more standing committees and both chambers, and, if House and Senate versions differ, each house must accept a conference report resolving those differences. These multiple points of approval provide many opportunities for members to revise the content of legislation and may lead representatives to alter their views on a particular piece of legislation several times over. Thus, it is much easier to defeat a bill than it is to get one passed. As revealed in Figure 6.4, roadblocks (indicated by stop signs in the figure) exist at nearly every stage of the process.

The House and Senate have parallel processes, and often the same bill is introduced in each chamber at the same time. A bill must be introduced by a member of

How a Bill Becomes a Law

You Are a Member of Congress

Congress, but, in an attempt to show support for the aims of the bill, it is often sponsored by several other members (called co-sponsors).[22] Once introduced, the bill is sent to the clerk of the chamber, who gives it a number (for example, HR 1 or S 1—indicating House or Senate bill number one). The bill is then printed, distributed, and sent to the appropriate committee or committees for consideration.

The first action takes place within the committee, after a bill is referred there by the Speaker of the House or by the Senate majority leader. The committee usually refers the bill to one of its subcommittees, which researches the bill and decides whether to hold hearings on it. The subcommittee hearings provide the opportunity for those on both sides of the issue to voice their opinions. Since the passage of sunshine laws in the 1970s, most of these hearings are now open to the public. After the hearings, the bill is revised in subcommittee, and then the subcommittee votes to approve or defeat the bill. If the

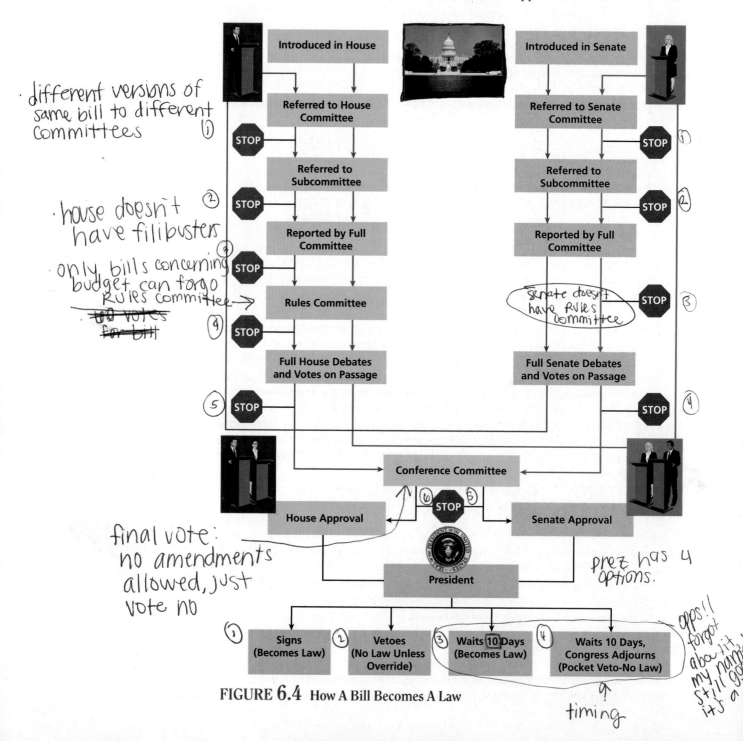

Handwritten annotations:
- different versions of same bill to different committees ①
- house doesn't have filibusters ②
- only bills concerning budget can forgo Rules committee → ~~no votes for bill~~
- Senate doesn't have Rules committee
- final vote: no amendments allowed, just vote no
- prez has 4 options.
- oops!! forgot about it, my name still good it's a B
- timing

FIGURE 6.4 How A Bill Becomes A Law

subcommittee votes in favor of the bill, it is returned to the full committee. There, during **markup,** committee members can add items to the bill and send it to the House or Senate floor with a favorable recommendation. It can also reject the bill (see Figure 6.4).

The second stage of action takes place on the House or Senate floor. As previously discussed, in the House, before a bill may be debated on the floor, it must be approved by the Committee on Rules and given a rule and a place on the calendar, or schedule. (House budget bills, however, don't go to the Committee on Rules.) In the House, the rule given to a bill determines the limits on the floor debate and specifies what types of amendments, if any, may be attached to the bill. Once the Committee on Rules considers the bill, it is put on the calendar.

When the day arrives for floor debate, the House may choose to form a Committee of the Whole. This procedure allows the House to deliberate with only one hundred members present, to expedite consideration of the bill. On the House floor, the bill is debated, amendments are offered, and a vote ultimately is taken by the full House. If the bill survives, it is sent to the Senate for consideration if it was not considered there simultaneously.

Unlike the House, where debate is necessarily limited given the size of the body, bills may be held up by a hold or a filibuster in the Senate. A **hold** is a tactic by which a senator asks to be informed before a particular bill is brought to the floor. This request signals the Senate leadership and the sponsors of the bill that a colleague may have objections to the bill and should be consulted before further action is taken.

Filibusters, which allow for unlimited debate on a bill (or on presidential appointments), grew out of the absence of rules to limit speech in the Senate. In contrast to a hold, a filibuster is a more formal and public way of halting action on a bill. There are no rules on the content of a filibuster as long as a senator keeps talking. A senator may read from a phone book, recite poetry, or read cookbooks to delay a vote. Often, a team of senators takes turns speaking to keep the filibuster going in the hope that a bill will be tabled or killed. In 1964, for example, a group of northern liberal senators continued a filibuster for eighty-two days in an effort to prevent amendments that would weaken a civil rights bill. Still, filibusters often are more of a threat than an actual event on the Senate floor, although members may use them in extreme circumstances. (To learn more about minority-majority relationships in Congress see Join the Debate: Minority Party Rights in Congress.)

There is only one way to end a filibuster. Sixty senators must sign a motion for **cloture.** After a cloture motion passes the Senate floor, members may spend no more than thirty additional hours debating the legislation at issue.

The third stage of action takes place when the two chambers of Congress approve different versions of the same bill. When this happens, they establish a conference committee to iron out the differences between the two versions. The conference committee, whose members often are from the original House and Senate committees, hammers out a compromise, which is returned to each chamber for a final vote. Sometimes the conference committee fails to agree and the bill dies there. No changes or amendments to the compromise version are allowed. If the bill is passed, it is sent to the president, who either signs it or **vetoes** it. If the bill is not passed in both houses, it dies.

The president has ten days to consider a bill. He has four options:

1. The president can sign the bill, at which point it becomes law.

2. The president can veto the bill, which is more likely to occur when the president is of a different party from the majority in Congress; Congress may override the president's veto with a two-thirds vote in each chamber, a very difficult task.

3. The president can wait the full ten days, at the end of which time the bill becomes law without his signature if Congress is still in session.

4. If the Congress adjourns before the ten days are up, the president can choose not to sign the bill, and it is considered pocket vetoed.

A **pocket veto** figuratively allows bills stashed in the president's pocket to die. The only way for a bill then to become law is for it to be reintroduced in the next ses-

markup
A process in which committee members offer changes to a bill before it goes to the floor in either house for a vote.

hold
A tactic by which a senator asks to be informed before a particular bill is brought to the floor. This allows the senator to stop the bill from coming to the floor until the hold is removed.

filibuster
A formal way of halting action on a bill by means of long speeches or unlimited debate in the Senate.

cloture
Mechanism requiring sixty senators to vote to cut off debate.

veto
Formal constitutional authority of the president to reject bills passed by both houses of the legislative body, thus preventing the bill from becoming law without further congressional activity.

pocket veto
If Congress adjourns during the ten days the president has to consider a bill passed by both houses of Congress, without the president's signature.

Join the Debate

Minority Party Rights in Congress

OVERVIEW: Some political commentators have concluded that the United States may be viewed as divided into two significant minorities representing the Republican and Democratic Party faithful. It follows, so the logic goes, that in the event of close elections, the governing process should strive to reflect the policy and political desires of the relatively nonpartisan "moderate middle" of the American electorate. Representatives typically are chosen by partisans in primary elections, however, and elected officials are compelled to at least try to enact party preferences. Should law-making rules be written to prevent legislative majorities from enforcing their agendas over the objections of the minority party? What rights should the minority party in a two-party system have to pursue its interests?

Article I, section 5, of the Constitution gives both chambers of Congress the authority to "determine the Rules of its Proceedings" and declares that a "Majority of each [chamber] shall constitute a Quorum to do business" (a quorum is the number of members required to transact affairs). Other than giving a legislative minority the right to "compel the Attendance of absent Members" (to ensure that a majority of representatives are available to conduct legislative business), the Constitution does not speak to minority party rights. And, the language of the Constitution plainly gives each chamber the power to determine its own manners of procedure, and hence the power to make rules governing the legislative process.

Nevertheless, the Framers did not foresee the rise of ideological political parties and their resulting political maneuvering. In fact, James Madison, in *Federalist No. 10*, argued that the Constitution would tend "to break and control the violence of faction." However, since parties have grown and developed, many observers believe that minority safeguards like the Senate's filibuster rule may be necessary to ensure that congressional governance reflects the policy desires of the broad majority of American voters. Other commentators see the filibuster as an opportunity for the minority party to obstruct the will of a majority. When in the minority in a closely divided Senate, both Republicans and Democrats have

blocked legislation on a wide variety of issues. In effect, as political scientists have observed, a supermajority of sixty votes is often needed to pass a bill, since it takes sixty votes to break a filibuster.

Arguments AGAINST Minority Party Rights in Congress

■ The Constitution is explicit where it requires supermajorities for political action. The Constitution plainly states when a supermajority is necessary for an act of government, and there are seven instances in the Constitution where this is necessary. For example, Article I requires that a two-thirds vote of each chamber is

sion and be put through the process all over again. Because Congress sets its own date of adjournment, technically the session could be continued the few extra days necessary to prevent a pocket veto. Extensions are unlikely, however, as sessions are scheduled to adjourn close to the November elections or the December holidays.

Toward Reform: Congressional Checks on the Executive and Judicial Branches

The Constitution envisioned that the Congress, the president, and the judiciary would have discrete powers, and that one branch would be able to hold the other in check. Over the years, and especially since the 1930s,

necessary to override a presidential veto, and Article II requires that a two-thirds vote of the Senate is necessary to ratify treaties. If the Framers wanted more than a simple majority vote to make law and policy, it would be embodied in the Constitution's text.

■ **Voters have the ability to unseat members of Congress.** If voters don't care for the legislative and political agenda of the majority party in Congress, they are competent enough to vote the party out of power. Voter disaffection with forty years of Democratic Party dominance of Congress, for example, led to the party being voted out of majority status in the 1994 midterm elections.

■ **Giving a legislative minority authority to stop legislation frustrates the will of the electorate.** Even in a closely divided electorate, the majority principle remains. Echoing the sentiment expressed in the Constitutional Convention, Thomas Jefferson argued that majority rule must necessarily be the rule for democratic government. The Framers believed that giving legislative minorities rights was essentially giving democratic government over to the rule of small elites.

Arguments IN FAVOR of Minority Party Rights in Congress

■ **Legislative majorities can be unjust.** Many people consider actions by legislative majorities to be harmful to the rights or lives of citizens. For example, some observers believe the Defense of Marriage Act, which gives states the authority to deny the legitimacy of same-sex marriages made in other states, is an infringement on the rights of individual citizens to marry. Allowing a minority party the right to impede legislation could provide a means for preventing unjust or unfair legislation.

■ **Giving the minority party legislative rights helps the deliberative process.** Allowing a minority party the right to slow down the legislative process will result in a better law. Giving the minority party assured rights would make certain there will be compromise and negotiation in the legislative process, and as a result, law and policy would be further filtered through deliberation and conciliation.

■ **Legislation should reflect the preferences of the electorate as a whole.** Representative democracy means representation for all, not just for a political majority. Giving the minority party the right to block legislation will ensure legislation and policy are crafted to reflect the diverse and broad policy preferences of the American electorate. Otherwise, legislation will reflect the ideological desires of only a portion of the American people.

Continuing the Debate

1. Should minority parties have the right to slow down or derail the passage of legislation sponsored by the majority party? Is this a violation of the Framers' majority principle? Why or why not?

2. Given that minority party representatives are duly elected by a majority of their constituents, what minority party protections seem appropriate?

To Follow the Debate Online, Go To:

www.fairvote.org

Advocates for majority rule and for limiting the rights of minority parties.

www.votesmart.org

Project Vote Smart, a nonprofit, nonpartisan organization, encourages participation in elections and provides information on topics like the role and strategies of minority and majority parties in Congress.

---

the president often has held the upper hand. In times of crisis or simply when it was unable to meet public demands for solutions, Congress willingly has handed over its authority to the chief executive. Even though the chief executive has been granted greater latitude, Congress does, of course, retain ultimate legislative authority to question executive actions and to halt administration activities by cutting off funds for programs a president wants. Congress also wields ultimate power over the president, since it can impeach and even remove him from office. Similar checks and balances affect relations between Congress and the courts.

The Shifting Balance of Power

From the the 1960s through the election of President George W. Bush, Congress increased its **oversight** of the executive branch. Oversight subcommittees became particularly prominent in the 1970s and 1980s as a means of promoting investigation and program review, to determine if an agency, department, or office is carrying out its responsibilities as intended by Congress.[23] Congressional oversight also includes checking on

oversight
Congressional review of the activities of an agency, department, or office.

Thinking Globally:

Legislative Power in Parliamentary Systems

The executive branch in most parliamentary systems is dependent upon the direct support of the legislative branch—the parliament. In the bulk of parliamentary systems, the head of government (typically called the prime minister) is chosen by the governing party or coalition of parties in the parliament.

- Do the principles of separation of powers and checks and balances that characterize American government help or hinder effective governance? In what ways?

- Under which system is the legislative branch more powerful? Why?

possible abuses of power by members of the military and governmental officials, including the president. The Republican-controlled Congress was especially mindful of its oversight duties during the Clinton administration. Not only did it regularly hold oversight hearings involving Cabinet secretaries, but it also launched several investigations of the Clintons themselves, such as Travelgate, the Clinton's investments in the failed Whitewater development in Arkansas, and, of course, President Bill Clinton's involvement with intern Monica Lewinsky which led to his impeachment in the House and trial in the Senate.

Historically, the key to Congress's performance of its oversight function is its ability to question members of the administration to see if they are enforcing and interpreting the laws as intended by Congress. These committee hearings, now routinely televised, are among Congress's most visible and dramatic actions. The hearings are not used simply to gather information. Hearings may focus on particular executive-branch actions and often signal that Congress believes changes in policy need to be made before an agency next comes before the committee to justify its budget. Hearings also are used to improve program administration. Since most members of House and Senate committees and subcommittees are interested in the issues under their jurisdiction, they often want to help and not hinder policy makers.

Although recent Congresses have abandoned some of their oversight function, members have additional means of oversight at their disposal. Legislators may augment their formal oversight of the executive branch by allowing citizens to appeal adverse bureaucratic decisions to agencies, Congress, and even the courts. The Congressional Review Act of 1996 allows Congress to nullify agency regulations by joint resolutions of legislative disapproval. This process, called **congressional review,** is another method of exercising congressional oversight.[24] The act provides Congress with sixty days to disapprove newly announced agency regulations, often passed to implement some congressional action. A regulation is disapproved if the resolution is passed by both chambers and signed by the president, or when Congress overrides a presidential veto of a disapproving resolution. Since its passage, only thirty-seven joint resolutions of disapproval relating to twenty-eight rules have been introduced.[25] To date, this act has been used only once—in 2001—when Congress and the president reversed Clinton administration ergonomics regulations, which were intended to prevent job-related repetitive stress injuries.

congressional review
A process whereby Congress can nullify agency regulations by a joint resolution of legislative disapproval.

FOREIGN POLICY AND NATIONAL SECURITY The Constitution divides foreign policy powers between the executive and the legislative branches. The president has the power to wage war and negotiate treaties, whereas the Congress has the power to declare war and the Senate has the power to ratify treaties. The executive branch, however, has become preeminent in foreign affairs despite the constitutional division of powers. This supremacy is partly due to a series of crises and the development of nuclear weapons in the twentieth century; both have necessitated quick decision making and secrecy, which are much easier to manage in the executive branch. Congress, with its 535 voting members, has a more difficult time reaching a consensus and keeping secrets.

After years of playing second fiddle to a series of presidents from Theodore Roosevelt to Richard M. Nixon, a "snoozing Congress" was "aroused" and seized for itself the authority and expertise necessary to go head to head with the chief executive.[26] In a delayed response to Lyndon B. Johnson's conduct of the Vietnam War, in 1973 Congress passed the **War Powers Act** over President Nixon's veto. This act requires presidents to obtain congressional approval before committing U.S. forces to a combat zone. It also requires them to notify Congress within forty-eight hours of committing troops to foreign soil. In addition, the president must withdraw troops within sixty days unless

War Powers Act
Passed by Congress in 1973; the president is limited in the deployment of troops overseas to a sixty-day period in peacetime (which can be extended for an extra thirty days to permit withdrawal) unless Congress explicitly gives its approval for a longer period.

Congress votes to declare war. The president also is required to consult with Congress, if at all possible, prior to committing troops.

The War Powers Act has been of limited effectiveness in claiming a larger congressional role in international crisis situations. Presidents Gerald R. Ford, Jimmy Carter, and Ronald Reagan never consulted Congress in advance of committing troops, citing the need for secrecy and swift movement, although each president did notify Congress shortly after the incidents. They contended that the War Powers Act was probably unconstitutional because it limits presidential prerogatives as commander in chief, as discussed in greater detail in chapter 7.

CONFIRMATION OF PRESIDENTIAL APPOINTMENTS   The Senate plays a special oversight function through its ability to confirm key members of the executive branch, as well as presidential appointments to the federal courts. As discussed in chapters 8 and 9, although the Senate generally confirms most presidential nominees, it does not always do so. A wise president considers senatorial reaction before nominating potentially controversial individuals to his administration or to the federal courts.

THE IMPEACHMENT PROCESS   As discussed earlier, the impeachment process is Congress's ultimate oversight of the U.S. president (as well as of federal court judges). The U.S. Constitution is quite vague about the impeachment process, and much of the debate about it concerns what is an impeachable offense. The Constitution specifies that a president can be impeached for treason, bribery, or other "high crimes and misdemeanors." Most commentators agree that this phrase was meant to mean significant abuses of power.

House and Senate rules control how the impeachment process operates. Yet, because the process is used so rarely, and under such disparate circumstances, there are few hard and fast rules. The U.S. House of Representatives has voted to impeach only seventeen federal officials. Of those, seven were convicted and removed from office and three resigned before the process described below was completed.

Only four resolutions against presidents have resulted in further action: (1) John Tyler, charged with corruption and misconduct in 1843; (2) Andrew Johnson, charged with serious misconduct in 1868; (3) Richard M. Nixon, charged with obstruction and the abuse of power in 1974; and, (4) Bill Clinton, charged with perjury and obstruction of justice in 1998.

Photo courtesy: Chip Somodevilla/Getty Images

How does congressional oversight function? Then Senate Armed Services Committee Chair John Warner (R–VA), ranking Democrat Carl Levin (D–MI), and committee members Robert Byrd (D–WV) and John McCain (R–AZ) caucus before holding a markup hearing about the Military Commissions Act of 2006. The act provides the president with unprecedented powers to detain and interrogate citizens and noncitizens accused of terrorism. While some observers believe that the compromise eventually worked out between the White House and members of Congress indicated appropriate congressional oversight, others believe that a number of the act's provisions are unconstitutional and compromise Congress's ability to review executive branch actions.

Congress and the Judiciary

Congress exercises its control over the judiciary in a variety of ways. As part of our system of checks and balances, the power of judicial review (discussed in chapters 2 and 9) gives the Supreme Court the power to review the constitutionality of acts of Congress. This is a potent power because Congress must ever be mindful to make sure that the laws that it passes are in accord with the U.S. Constitution. Congress also has the constitutional authority to establish the size of the Supreme Court, its appellate jurisdiction, the structure of the federal court system, and to allocate its budget. And, the Senate also has the authority to accept or reject presidential nominees to the federal courts (as well as top executive branch appointments).

In the case of federal district court appointments, senators often have considerable say in the nomination of judges from their states through **senatorial courtesy,** a process by which presidents generally defer to the senators who represent the state

senatorial courtesy
A process by which presidents, when selecting district court judges, defer to the senator in whose state the vacancy occurs.

where the vacancy occurs. The judicial nominees of both Presidents Bill Clinton and George W. Bush encountered a particularly hostile Senate. "Appointments have always been the battleground for policy disputes," says one political scientist. But now, "what's new is the rawness of it—all of the veneer is off."[27] (Nominations to the Supreme Court and lower federal courts are discussed in chapter 9.)

An equally potent form of congressional oversight of the judicial branch that involves both the House and the Senate is the setting of the jurisdiction of the federal courts. Originally, the jurisdiction, or ability of the federal courts to hear cases, was quite limited. Over time, however, as Congress legislated to regulate the economy and even crime, the caseload of the courts skyrocketed. But, no matter how busy federal judges are, it is ultimately up to the Congress to determine the number of judges on each court.

During the 109th Congress, several members, unhappy with Supreme Court decisions and the Senate's failure to pass a proposed constitutional amendment to ban same-sex marriage, began to push for a bill to prevent federal courts from hearing challenges to the federal Defense of Marriage Act. In the House, the Republican majority leader pledged to promote similar legislation to bar court challenges to the Pledge of Allegiance and other social issues, including abortion. When Congress rears the ugly head of jurisdiction, it is signaling to the federal courts that Congress believes federal judges have gone too far.

★ WHAT SHOULD I HAVE LEARNED?

The size and scope of Congress, and the demands put on it, have increased tremendously over the years. In presenting the important role that Congress plays in American politics, we have answered the following questions:

- **What are the roots of the legislative branch of government?** The Constitution created a bicameral legislature with members of each body to be elected differently, and thus to represent different constituencies. Article I of the Constitution sets forth qualifications for office, states age minimums, and specifies how legislators are to be distributed among the states. The Constitution also requires seats in the House of Representatives to be apportioned by population. Thus, after every U.S. Census, district lines must be redrawn to reflect population shifts. The Constitution also provides a vast array of enumerated and implied powers to Congress.

- **How is congress organized?** Political parties play a major role in the way Congress is organized. The Speaker of the House is traditionally a member of the majority party, and members of the majority party chair all committees. Because the House of Representatives is large, the Speaker enforces more rigid rules on the House than exist in the Senate. In addition to the party leaders, Congress has a labyrinth of committees and subcommittees that cover the entire range of government policies, often with a confusing tangle of shared responsibilities.

- **Who are the members of Congress?** Members of Congress live in two worlds—in their home districts and in the District of Columbia. They must attempt to appease two constituencies—party leaders, colleagues, and lobbyists in Washington, D.C., and constituents in their home districts.

- **How do the members of Congress make decisions?** A multitude of factors affect legislators as they decide policy issues. These include political party, constituents, colleagues and caucuses, staff and support agencies and interest groups, lobbyists, and political action committees.

- **How does Congress make laws?** The road to enacting a bill into law is long and strewn with obstacles, and only a small share of the proposals introduced become law. Legislation must be approved by committees in each house and on the floor of each chamber. In addition, most House legislation initially is considered by a subcommittee and must be approved by the House Committee on Rules before getting to the floor. Legislation that is passed in different forms by the two chambers must be resolved in a conference before going back to each chamber for a vote and then to the president, who can sign the proposal into law, veto it, or allow it to become law without his signature. If Congress adjourns within ten days of passing legislation, that bill will die if the president does not sign it.

■ **What are the major congressional checks on the executive and judicial branches?** Congress has attempted to oversee the actions of the president and the executive branch through committee hearing, the War Powers Act, and the power to confirm or reject presidential appointments. Its ultimate weapon is the power of impeachment and conviction. Congress also exercises its control over the judiciary in a variety of ways. It has the constitutional authority to establish the size of the Supreme Court, its appellate jurisdiction, and the structure of the federal court system.

Key Terms

apportionment, p. 173
bicameral legislature, p. 172
bill, p. 173
cloture, p. 189
conference committee, p. 179
congressional review, p. 192
delegate, p. 183
discharge petition, p. 180
divided government, p. 184
earmark, p. 181
filibuster, p. 189
hold, p. 189
impeachment, p. 173

incumbency, p. 182
joint committee, p. 179
logrolling, p. 185
majority leader, p. 177
majority party, p. 174
markup, p. 189
minority leader, p. 177
minority party, p. 174
oversight, p. 191
party caucus or conference, p. 177
pocket veto, p. 189
politico, p. 184
pork, p. 181

president pro tempore, p. 178
redistricting, p. 173
select (or special) committee, p. 179
senatorial courtesy, p. 193
seniority, p. 182
Speaker of the House, p. 176
standing committee, p. 179
trustee, p. 183
veto, p. 189
War Powers Act, p. 192
whip, p. 177

Researching Congress

In the Library

Adler, E. Scott, and John S. Lapinski. *The Macropolitics of Congress*. Princeton, NJ: Princeton University Press, 2006.

Bianco, William T., ed. *Congress on Display, Congress at Work*. Ann Arbor: University of Michigan Press, 2000.

Binder, Sarah A. *Stalemate: Causes and Consequences of Legislative Gridlock*. Washington, DC: Brookings Institute, 2003.

Cox, Gary W., and Mathew D. McCubbins. *Setting the Agenda: Responsible Party Government in the U.S. House of Representatives*. New York: Cambridge University Press, 2005.

Davidson, Roger H., Walter Oleszek, and Frances E. Lee. *Congress and Its Members*, 11th ed. Washington, DC: CQ Press, 2007.

Dodd, Lawrence C., and Bruce I. Oppenheimer, eds. *Congress Reconsidered*, 8th ed. Washington, DC: CQ Press, 2007.

Evans, Diana. *Greasing the Wheels: Using Pork Barrel Projects to Build Majority Coalitions in Congress*. New York: Cambridge University Press, 2004.

Fenno, Richard F., Jr. *Home Style: House Members in Their Districts*, reprint ed. New York: Longman, 2002.

Gertzog, Irwin N. *Women and Power on Capitol Hill: Reconstructing the Congressional Women's Caucus*. Boulder, CO: Lynne Rienner, 2004.

Mayhew, David R. *Congress: The Electoral Connection*, 2nd ed. New Haven, CT: Yale University Press, 2004.

O'Connor, Karen, ed. *Women in Congress: Running, Winning, and Ruling*. New York: Haworth, 2004.

Oleszek, Walter J. *Congressional Procedures and the Policy Process*, 7th ed. Washington, DC: CQ Press, 2007.

Price, David E. *The Congressional Experience: A View from the Hill*, 3rd ed. Boulder, CO: Westview, 2005.

Quirk, Paul J., and Sarah A. Binder, eds. *Institutions of American Democracy: The Legislative Branch*. New York: Oxford University Press, 2006.

Rosenthal, Cindy Simon, ed. *Women Transforming Congress*. Norman: University of Oklahoma Press, 2003.

Smith, Steven S. *Party Influence in Congress*. New York: Cambridge University Press, 2007.

Theriault, Sean M. *Party Polarization in Congress*. New York: Cambridge University Press, 2008.

On the Web

To learn more about the legislative branch, go to the official Web site of the Senate, **www.senate.gov**, and of the House of Representatives, **www.house.gov**.

The Library of Congress's home page for information related to the legislative branch is named Thomas, in honor of President Thomas Jefferson. From the home page at **thomas.loc.gov**, you can research roll call votes, committee reports, and the *Congressional Record*.

Project Vote Smart is a nonpartisan group dedicated to providing U.S. citizens with the factual information they need to be informed voters. The Web site **www.votesmart.org** provides biographical information about members of Congress and lists the grades given to elected representatives by a range of interest groups.

THE NATION MOURNS.

7

The Presidency

When Ronald Reagan died on June 5, 2004, many Americans, first in California and then in Washington, D.C., lined up for hours to pay their respects to the man who had been the fortieth president of the United States. Many people were able to see, for the first time in recent memory, the grandeur of a presidential state funeral. Reagan was the first president to lie in state in the Rotunda of the Capitol since Lyndon B. Johnson did in January 1973, and one of only nine American presidents to receive that honor.

Presidential funerals underscore the esteem with which most Americans accord the office of the president, regardless of its occupant. Just before the first president, George Washington, died, he made it known that he wanted his burial to be a quiet one, "without parade or funeral oration." He also asked that he not be buried for three days; at that time, it was not without precedent to make this kind of request out of fear of being buried alive. Despite these requests, Washington's funeral was a state occasion as hundreds of soldiers, with their rifles held backward, marched to Mount Vernon, Virginia, where he was interred. Across the nation, imitation funerals were held, and the military wore black armbands for six months.[1] It was during

Washington's memorial service that Henry Lee declared that the former president was "first in war, first in peace, and first in the hearts of his countrymen."[2]

When Abraham Lincoln died in 1865 after being wounded by an assassin's bullet, more than a dozen funerals were held for him. Hundreds of thousands of mourners lined the way as the train carrying his open casket traveled the 1,700 miles to Illinois, where he was buried next to the body of his young son, who had died three years earlier. Most presidents' bodies were transported to their final resting place by train, allowing ordinary Americans the opportunity to pay their respects as the train traveled long distances. When Franklin D. Roosevelt died in Warm Springs, Georgia, his body was transported to Washington, D.C., and then to Hyde Park, New York, where he, like Washington, was buried on his family's estate.

Today, one of the first things a president is asked to do upon taking office is to consider funeral plans. The military has a book 138 pages long devoted to the kind of ceremony and traditions that were so evident in the Reagan funeral: a horse-drawn caisson; a riderless horse with boots hung backward in the stirrups to indicate that the deceased will ride no more; a twenty-one-gun salute; a flyover by military aircraft. Each president's family, however, has personalized their private, yet also public opportunity to mourn. The Reagan family, for example, filed a 300-page plan for the

■ **Presidential funerals have been occasions for national mourning since the death of the United States' first president, George Washington.** At left, the nation mourns President Abraham Lincoln, the first American president to be assassinated. At right, current and former presidents and their wives attend a funeral service for President Ronald Reagan in the National Cathedral prior to his interment in California.

WHAT SHOULD I KNOW ABOUT ...

- the roots of the office of the president of the United States?
- the constitutional powers of the president?
- the development and expansion of presidential power?
- the presidential establishment?
- presidential leadership and the importance of public opinion?
- the president as policy maker?

197

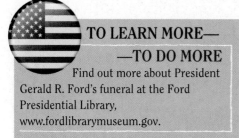

TO LEARN MORE—
—TO DO MORE
Find out more about President Gerald R. Ford's funeral at the Ford Presidential Library, www.fordlibrarymuseum.gov.

funeral in 1989 and updated it regularly. Former president Gerald R. Ford filed a plan that was enacted after his death 2006. Presidents Jimmy Carter and George Bush have also filed formal plans; Bill Clinton and George W. Bush have yet to do so.

The Reagan funeral also created a national time-out from the news of war, and even presidential campaigns were halted in respect for the deceased president. One historian commented that the event gave Americans the opportunity to "rediscover . . . what holds us together instead of what pulls us apart."[3] This is often the role of presidents—in life or in death.

Comparing Executive Branches

The authority granted to the president by the U.S. Constitution and through subsequent congressional legislation makes it a position with awesome power and responsibility. Not only did the Framers not envision such a powerful role for the president, but they could not have foreseen the skepticism with which many presidential actions are now greeted in the press, on talk radio, and on the Internet. Presidents have gone into policy arenas never dreamed of by the Framers. Imagine, for example, what the Framers might have thought about President George W. Bush's 2004 State of the Union message, in which he advocated colonizing Mars and addressed steroid use; or his 2006 address, in which he asked legislators to prohibit "the most egregious abuse of medical research—human cloning."

The modern media, used by successful presidents to help advance their agendas, have brought us closer to our presidents and made them seem more human, a mixed blessing for those trying to lead. Only two photographs exist of President Franklin D. Roosevelt in a wheelchair—his paralysis was a closely guarded secret. Five decades later, Bill Clinton was asked on national TV what kind of underwear he preferred (briefs). Later, revelations about his conduct with intern Monica Lewinsky made this disclosure seem tame. This demystification of the office of the president and increasing mistrust of government make governing a difficult job.

A president relies on more than the formal powers of office to lead the nation: public opinion and confidence are key components of his ability to get his programs adopted and his vision of the nation implemented. As political scientist Richard E. Neustadt has noted, the president's power often rests on his power to persuade.[4] To persuade, he not only must be able to forge links with members of Congress, but he also must have the support of the American people and the respect of foreign leaders.

The abilities to persuade and to marshal the informal powers of the presidency have become more important over time. In fact, the presidency of George W. Bush and the circumstances that surround it were dramatically different from the presidency of his father, George Bush (1989–1993). America is changing dramatically and so are the responsibilities of the president as well as people's expectations of the person who holds that office. Presidents in the last century battled the Great Depression, fascism, communism, and several wars involving American soldiers. The nation's forty-fourth president, Barack Obama, took office in 2009 with a number of pressing issues to tackle, including the wars in Iraq and Afghanistan and the global economic crisis.

The tension between public expectations about the presidency and the formal powers of the president permeate our discussion of how the office has evolved from its humble origins in Article II of the Constitution to its current stature. First, we will examine the roots of the office of the president of the United States and the constitutional powers of the president. We will then examine the development and expansion of presidential power and a more personalized presidency. After discussing the development of the presidential establishment, we will examine presidential leadership and the importance of public opinion. Finally, we will focus on reform efforts linked to the president's role as policy maker.

Roots of the Office of President of the United States

Under the Articles of Confederation, there was no executive branch of government; the eighteen different men who served as the president of the Continental Congress of the United States of America were president in name only—they held no actual authority or power in the new nation. When the delegates to the Constitutional Convention met in Philadelphia to fashion a new government, there was little dissention about the need for an executive branch to implement the laws made by Congress. Although some delegates suggested there should be multiple executives, eventually the Framers agreed that executive authority should be vested in one person. This agreement was relatively seamless because the Framers were sure that George Washington—whom they had trusted with their lives during the Revolutionary War—would become the first president of the new nation.

The manner of the president's election haunted the Framers for some time, and their solution to the dilemma—the creation of the Electoral College—is described in detail in chapter 12. We leave the resolution of that issue aside for now and turn instead to details of the issues the Framers resolved quickly.

Presidential Qualifications and Terms of Office

The Constitution requires that the president (and the vice president, whose major function is to succeed the president in the event of his death or disability) be a natural-born citizen of the United States, at least thirty-five years old, and a resident of the United States for at least fourteen years.

At one time the length of a president's term was controversial. Four-, seven-, and eleven-year terms with no eligibility for reelection were suggested by various delegates to the Constitutional Convention. The Framers ultimately reached agreement on a four-year term with eligibility for reelection. In the 1930s and 1940s, however, Franklin D. Roosevelt ran successfully in four elections as Americans fought first the Great Depression and then World War II. Despite Roosevelt's popularity, negative reaction to his long tenure in office ultimately led to passage (and ratification in 1951) of the **Twenty-Second Amendment.** It limits presidents to two four-year terms. A vice president who succeeds a president due to death, resignation, or impeachment is eligible for a total of ten years in office: two years of a president's remaining term and two elected terms, or more than two years of a president's term followed by one elected term.

During the Constitutional Convention, Benjamin Franklin was a staunch supporter of including a provision allowing for **impeachment**, the first step in a formal process to remove a specified official from office. He noted that "historically, the lack of power to impeach had necessitated recourse to assassination."[5] Not surprisingly, then, Franklin urged the rest of the delegates to formulate a legal mechanism to remove the president and vice president.

Comparing Chief Executives

Twenty-Second Amendment
Adopted in 1951, prevents a president from serving more than two terms, or more than ten years if he came to office via the death or impeachment of his predecessor.

impeachment
The power delegated to the House of Representatives in the Constitution to charge the president, vice president, or other "civil officers," including federal judges, with "Treason, Bribery, or other high Crimes and Misdemeanors." This is the first step in the constitutional process of removing such government officials from office.

Photo courtesy: Marcy Nighswander/AP/Wide World Photos

Who serves as president of the United States? Before Barack Obama, all of the people who served as president were white men. Here, five former presidents—Richard M. Nixon, Gerald R. Ford, Jimmy Carter, Ronald Reagan, and George Bush—gather to celebrate the opening of the Reagan Presidential Library in 1991.

The impeachment provision ultimately included in Article II was adopted as a check on the power of the president. As we discussed in detail in chapter 6, each house of Congress was given a role to play in the impeachment process to assure that the chief executive could be removed only for "Treason, Bribery, or other high Crimes and Misdemeanors." The House is empowered to vote to impeach the president by a simple majority vote. The Senate then acts as a court of law and tries the president for the charged offenses. A two-thirds majority vote in the Senate on any count contained in the articles of impeachment is necessary to remove the president from office.

In 1974, President Richard M. Nixon resigned from office rather than face the certainty of impeachment, trial, and removal from office for his role in covering up details about a break-in at the Democratic Party's national headquarters in the Watergate office complex. What came to be known simply as Watergate also produced a major decision from the Supreme Court on the scope of what is termed **executive privilege.** In **U.S. v. Nixon (1974),** the Supreme Court ruled unanimously that there was no overriding executive privilege that sanctioned the president's refusal to comply with a court order to produce information for use in the trial of the Watergate defendants.

Rules of Succession

Through 2009, eight presidents have died in office from illness or assassination. William H. Harrison was the first president to die in office—he caught a cold at his inauguration in 1841 and died one month later. (John Tyler thus became the first vice president to succeed to the presidency.) In 1865, Abraham Lincoln became the first president to be assassinated.

The Framers were aware that a system of orderly transfer of power was necessary; this was the primary reason they created the office of the vice president. To further clarify the order of presidential succession, in 1947, Congress passed the Presidential Succession Act, which lists—in order—those in line (after the vice president) to succeed the president

1. Speaker of the House of Representatives
2. President pro tempore of the Senate
3. Secretaries of state, treasury, and defense, and other Cabinet heads in order of the creation of their department.

The Succession Act has never been used because there has always been a vice president to take over when a president died in office. The **Twenty-Fifth Amendment,** in fact, was added to the Constitution in 1967 to assure that this will continue to be the case. Should a vacancy occur in the office of the vice president, the Twenty-Fifth Amendment directs the president to appoint a new vice president, subject to the approval (by a simple majority) of both houses of Congress. (To learn more, see The Living Constitution: Twenty-Fifth Amendment, Section 2.)

executive privilege
An implied presidential power that allows the president to refuse to disclose information regarding confidential conversations or national security to Congress or the judiciary.

U.S. v. Nixon (1974)
Key Supreme Court ruling on power of the president, finding that there is no absolute constitutional executive privilege to allow a president to refuse to comply with a court order to produce information needed in a criminal trial.

Twenty-Fifth Amendment
Adopted in 1967 to establish procedures for filling vacancies in the office of president and vice president as well as providing for procedures to deal with the disability of a president.

The Living Constitution

Whenever there is a vacancy in the office of the Vice President, the President shall nominate a Vice President who shall take office upon confirmation by a majority vote of both Houses of Congress.

—TWENTY-FIFTH AMENDMENT, SECTION 2

This clause of the Twenty-Fifth Amendment allows a president to fill a vacancy in the office of vice president with the consent of a simple majority of both Houses of Congress. The purpose of this amendment, which also deals with vacancies in the office of the president, was to remedy some structural flaws in Article II. When this amendment to the Constitution was proposed in 1965, (it was ratified in 1967), seven vice presidents had died in office and one had resigned. For over 20 percent of the nation's history there had been no vice president to assume the office of the president in case of his death or infirmity. When John F. Kennedy was assassinated, Vice President Lyndon B. Johnson became president and the office of vice president was vacant. Since Johnson had suffered a heart attack as vice president, members of Congress were anxious to remedy the problems that might occur should there be no vice president.

Richard M. Nixon followed Johnson as president, and during Nixon's presidency, the office of the vice president became empty twice! First, Nixon's vice president, Spiro T. Agnew, was forced to resign in the wake of charges of bribe taking, corruption, and income-tax evasion while an elected official in Maryland; he was replaced by popular House Minority Leader Gerald R. Ford (R–MI), who had no trouble getting a majority vote in both houses of Congress to confirm his nomination. When Nixon resigned rather than face sure impeachment, Ford became president and selected the former governor of New York, Nelson A. Rockefeller, to be his vice president. This chain of events set up for the first time in U.S. history a situation in which neither the president nor the vice president had been elected to those positions.

CRITICAL THINKING QUESTIONS

1. Why wasn't the Twenty-Fifth Amendment proposed until 1965? Why might a vice president be more necessary today than in the past?
2. Is it appropriate in a representative democracy to ever have a situation where both the president and the vice president have not been popularly elected?

The Constitutional Powers of the President

Though the Framers largely agreed about the need for a strong central government and a greatly empowered Congress, they did not agree about the proper role of the president or the sweep of his authority. In contrast to Article I's laundry list of enumerated powers for the Congress, Article II details few presidential powers. Perhaps the most important section of Article II is its first sentence: "The executive Power shall be vested in a President of the United States of America." Nonetheless, the sum total of the president's powers, enumerated below, allows him to become a major player in the policy process.

Thinking Globally

Impeachment in the Philippines

In the United States, use of the impeachment process by the Congress to remove the president is rare. In contrast, in the Philippines, opponents of President Gloria Macapagal Arroyo have filed an impeachment complaint alleging corruption against her every year since she won a disputed election in 2004.

- Is the impeachment process an effective tool for regulating presidential conduct? Why or why not?
- Should others in the executive branch be subject to impeachment? Should members of Congress be subject to impeachment? Explain your reasoning.

You Are the President and Need to Appoint a Supreme Court Justice

Cabinet
The formal body of presidential advisers who head the fifteen executive departments. Presidents often add others to this body of formal advisers.

The Appointment Power

To help the president enforce laws passed by Congress, the Constitution authorizes him to appoint, with the advice and consent of the Senate, "Ambassadors, other public Ministers and Consuls, judges of the supreme Court, and all other Officers of the United States, whose Appointments are not herein otherwise provided for, and which shall be established by Law." Although this section of the Constitution deals only with appointments, behind that language is a powerful policy-making tool. The president has the authority to make nearly 3,000 appointments to his administration (of which just over 1,000 require Senate confirmation). He also has the power to remove many of his appointees at will. In addition, he technically appoints more than 75,000 military personnel. Many of these appointees are in positions to wield substantial authority over the course and direction of public policy. Although Congress has the authority "to make all laws," through the president's enforcement power—and his chosen assistants—he often can set the policy agenda for the nation. And, especially in the context of his ability to make appointments to the federal courts, his influence can be felt far past his term of office.

It is not surprising, then, that selecting the right people is often one of a president's most important tasks. Presidents look for a blend of loyalty, competence, and integrity. Identifying these qualities in people is a major challenge that every new president faces. Recent presidents, especially Bill Clinton and George W. Bush, have made an effort to create a Cabinet and staff that, in President Clinton's terms, looks "more like America." (To learn more about the proportion of women appointees, see Table 7.1.)

In the past, when a president forwarded a nomination to the Senate for its approval, his selections traditionally were given great respect—especially those for the **Cabinet**, an advisory group selected by the president to help him make decisions and execute the laws. In fact, until the Clinton administration, the vast majority (97 percent) of all presidential nominations were confirmed.[6]

The Power to Convene Congress

The Constitution requires the president to inform the Congress periodically of "the State of the Union," and authorizes the president to convene either or both houses of Congress on "extraordinary Occasions." In *Federalist No. 77*, Hamilton justified the latter by noting that because the Senate and the chief executive enjoy concurrent powers to make treaties, "It might often be necessary to call it together with a view to this object, when it would be unnecessary and improper to convene the House of Representatives." The power to convene Congress was important when Congress did not sit in nearly year-round sessions.

The Power to Make Treaties

The president's power to make treaties with foreign nations is checked by the Constitution's stipulation that all treaties must be approved by at least two-thirds of the mem-

TABLE 7.1 Women on Presidential Teams: Carter to G. W. Bush

	Total Appointments	Total Women	Percentage Women
Jimmy Carter	1,087	191	17.6%
Ronald Reagan	2,349	277	11.8%
George Bush	1,079	215	19.9%
Bill Clinton	2,479	1,125	45.0%
George W. Bush[a]	2,786	1,017	36.0%

[a] Bush data include all political appointees through 2005 when his administration stopped making numbers public.
Sources: "Insiders Say White House Has Its Own Glass Ceiling," *Atlanta Journal and Constitution* (April 10, 1995): A/F; Judi Hasson, "Senate GOP Leader Lott Says He'll Work with Clinton," *USA Today* (December 4, 1996): 8A; and "The Growth of Political Appointees in the Bush Administration," U.S. House of Representatives, Committee on Government Reform—Minority Staff, May 2006.

bers of the Senate. The chief executive can also "receive ambassadors," wording that has been interpreted to allow the president to recognize the existence of other nations.

The Senate also may require substantial amendment of a treaty prior to its consent. When President Jimmy Carter proposed the controversial Panama Canal Treaty in 1977 to turn the canal over to Panama, for example, the Senate required several conditions to be ironed out before approving the canal's return.

Presidents may also "unsign" treaties, a practice often met with dismay from other signatories. For example, the Bush administration formally withdrew its support for the International Criminal Court (ICC). In a short, three-sentence letter to United Nations Secretary General Kofi Annan, the United States withdrew from efforts to create the first permanent court to prosecute war crimes, genocide, and other crimes against humanity. This treaty was formerly signed by President Bill Clinton and was scheduled to take effect July 1, 2002. Critics of the treaty argued that it could lead to politically motivated charges against U.S. troops in Afghanistan and Iraq.[7]

Presidents also often try to get around the constitutional "advice and consent" of the Senate requirement for ratification of treaties and the congressional approval requirement for trade agreements by entering into an **executive agreement,** which allows the president to form secret and highly sensitive arrangements with foreign nations without Senate approval. Presidents have used these agreements since the days of George Washington, and their use has been upheld by the courts. Although executive agreements are not binding on subsequent administrations, since 1900 they have been used far more frequently than treaties, further cementing the role of the president in foreign affairs, as revealed in Table 7.2.

Thinking Globally

The Executive Branch and Military Leadership

In the United States, the president serves as the commander in chief of the armed forces but is not a member of any branch of the military. Other countries, such as Pakistan, have a long history of presidents who simultaneously served as military leaders while in office. Former president of Pakistan Pervez Musharraf, for example, achieved power through a military coup in 1999 and relinquished his role as chief of the Pakistani Army with great reluctance after extensive pressure from Pakistani and foreign leaders.

- Is it necessary to draw a distinction between civilian leadership and military leadership as we do in the United States? Why or why not?
- Can you imagine a situation where a military overthrow of the government might occur in the United States? Explain your answer.

executive agreement
Formal government agreement entered into by the president that does not require the advice and consent of the U.S. Senate.

veto power
The formal, constitutional authority of the president to reject bills passed by both houses of Congress, thus preventing them from becoming law without further congressional action.

Veto Power

In keeping with the system of checks and balances, then, the president was given the veto power, but only as a "qualified negative." Although the president was given the authority to veto any act of Congress (with the exception of joint resolutions that propose constitutional amendments), Congress was given the authority to override an executive veto by a two-thirds vote in each house. The president's **veto power** is a powerful policy tool because Congress cannot usually muster enough votes to override a veto. Thus, in over 200 years, there have been approximately 2,500 presidential vetoes and only about a hundred have been overridden.

The Power to Preside Over the Military as Commander in Chief

One of the most important constitutional executive powers is the president's authority over the military. Article II states that the president is "Commander in Chief of the Army and Navy of the United States." While the Constitution specifically grants Congress the authority to declare war, presidents

TABLE 7.2 Treaties and Executive Agreements Concluded by the United States, 1789–2006

Years	Number of Treaties	Number of Executive Agreements
1789–1839	60	27
1839–1889	215	238
1889–1929	382	763
1930–1932	49	41
1933–1944 (F. Roosevelt)	131	369
1945–1952 (Truman)	132	1,324
1953–1960 (Eisenhower)	89	1,834
1961–1963 (Kennedy)	36	813
1964–1968 (L. Johnson)	67	1,083
1969–1974 (Nixon)	93	1,317
1975–1976 (Ford)	26	666
1977–1980 (Carter)	79	1,476
1981–1988 (Reagan)	125	2,840
1989–1992 (G. Bush)	67	1,350
1993–2000 (Clinton)	209	2,047
2001–2006 (G.W. Bush)	45	612

Note: Number of treaties includes those concluded during the indicated span of years. Some of these treaties did not receive the consent of the U.S. Senate. Varying definitions of what an executive agreement comprises and their entry-into-force date make the above numbers approximate.
Sources: 1789–1980: *Congressional Quarterly's Guide to Congress,* 291; 1981–2002: Office of the Assistant Legal Adviser for Treaty Affairs. U.S. Department of State; 2002–2006: www.saramitchell.org/MarshallPrins.pdf.

Photo courtesy: Bettmann/Corbis

Photo courtesy: Matt Reinstein/The Image Works

Chief law enforcer: Troops sent by President Dwight D. Eisenhower enforce a federal court decision ordering the integration of public schools in Little Rock, Arkansas.

Leader of the party: Ronald Reagan mobilized conservatives and changed the nature of the Republican Party.

Commander in Chief: President George. W. Bush speaks about the War in Iraq.

Photo courtesy: Hulton Archive/Getty Images

Photo courtesy: Ruth Fremson/AP/Wide World Photos

Shaper of public policy: President Richard M. Nixon cheers on the efforts of Apollo 11 astronauts.

Key player in the legislative process: President Bill Clinton at a bill signing ceremony.

Chief of state: President John F. Kennedy and his wife, Jacqueline, with the president of France and his wife during the Kennedys' widely publicized 1961 trip to that nation.

since Abraham Lincoln have used the commander in chief clause in conjunction with the chief executive's duty to "take Care that the Laws be faithfully executed" to wage war (and to broaden various powers).

Modern presidents continually clash with Congress over the ability to commence hostilities. Realizing that misinformation had led Congress largely to defer to the executive in the conduct of the Vietnam War, in 1973 Congress passed the **War Powers Act** to limit the president's authority to introduce American troops into hostile foreign lands without congressional approval. President Nixon vetoed the act, but it was overridden by a two-thirds majority in both houses of Congress.

Presidents since Nixon have continued to insist that the War Powers Act is an unconstitutional infringement of their executive power. Still, in 2001, President George W. Bush complied with the act when he sought, and both houses of Congress approved, a joint resolution authorizing the use of force against "those responsible for the recent [September 11] attacks launched against the United States." This resolution actually gave the president more open-ended authority to wage war than his father had received in 1991 to conduct the Persian Gulf War or President Johnson had received after the Gulf of Tonkin Resolution in 1964.[8] Later, in October 2002, after President Bush declared Iraq to be a "grave threat to peace," the House (296–133) and Senate (77–23) voted overwhelmingly to allow the president to use force in Iraq "as he determines to be necessary and appropriate," thereby conferring tremendous authority on the president to wage war. (To learn more about the controversies over this law, see Join the Debate: The War Powers Act.)

The Pardoning Power

Presidents can exercise a check on judicial power through their constitutional authority to grant reprieves or pardons. A **pardon** is an executive grant releasing an individual from the punishment or legal consequences of a crime before or after conviction, and restores all rights and privileges of citizenship. Presidents exercise complete pardoning power for federal offenses except in cases of impeachment, which cannot be pardoned. President Gerald R. Ford granted the most famous presidential pardon when he pardoned former President Richard M. Nixon—who had not been formally charged with any crime—"for any offenses against the United States, which he, Richard Nixon, has committed or may have committed while in office." This unilateral, absolute pardon prevented the former president from ever being tried for any crimes he may have committed. It also unleashed a torrent of public criticism against Ford and questions about whether Nixon had discussed the pardon with Ford before Nixon's resignation. Many analysts attribute Ford's defeat in his 1976 bid for the presidency to that pardon.

The Development and Expansion of Presidential Power

Every president brings to the position not only a vision of America, but also expectations about how to use presidential authority. But, most presidents find accomplishing their goals much more difficult than they envisioned. After President John F. Kennedy was in office two years, for example, he noted publicly that there were "greater limitations upon our ability to bring about a favorable result than I had imagined."[9] Similarly, as he was leaving office, President Harry S Truman mused about what surprises awaited his successor, Dwight D. Eisenhower, a former general: "He'll sit here and he'll say, 'Do this! Do that!' And nothing will happen. Poor Ike—it won't be a bit like the army. He'll find it very frustrating."[10]

SIMULATION

Presidential Leadership: Which Hat Do You Wear

War Powers Act
Passed by Congress in 1973; the president is limited in the deployment of troops overseas to a sixty-day period in peacetime (which can be extended for an extra thirty days to permit withdrawal) unless Congress explicitly gives its approval for a longer period.

pardon
An executive grant providing restoration of all rights and privileges of citizenship to a specific individual charged or convicted of a crime.

Join the Debate

The War Powers Act

OVERVIEW: While the Constitution divides the power to wage war between Congress and the president, scholars and politicians disagree on the specifics of the division. They also disagree on how this division should play out in specific circumstances. The Constitution gives Congress the authority to declare war, to make the rules that govern military forces, and to provide appropriations to the armed services. Yet, the president's constitutional jurisdiction over war powers has steadily increased since the nation's founding. Although President James Madison would not go to war with Great Britain in 1812 without a war declaration from Congress, the last six major American conflicts were conducted without formal declarations of war.

The War Powers Act of 1973, passed in the aftermath of the Vietnam War, was an attempt to rein in the war-making authority of the president by demanding, among other things, that the executive notify Congress when committing the U.S. military to hostile action. The War Powers Act requires the president to report to Congress "in every possible instance" within forty-eight hours after deploying the armed forces in combat. Implied in the law is the understanding that the information Congress receives will be timely and accurate. President Richard M. Nixon's veto of the act was overridden by both houses of Congress, but presidential administrations since Nixon's, Democratic and Republican alike, have agreed that the act infringes on the president's constitutional duty as commander in chief.

The intelligence the president and Congress receive is critically important when determining whether or not to engage in and support armed conflict but sometimes intelligence sources are flawed. For instance, in 1998, President Bill Clinton ordered the destruction of a pharmaceutical plant in Sudan based on faulty intelligence that the site produced nerve gas. In 2002–2003, President George W. Bush made the case for invading Iraq by asserting that the country harbored terrorists and possessed weapons of mass destruction (WMDs) that posed an imminent threat to the United States and the countries neighboring Iraq. These assertions, although not supported by evidence, loomed large in the national debate regarding whether to intervene in Iraq.

Complying with the War Powers Act, President Bush asked for and received authorization from Congress to use military force against Iraq if diplomatic efforts failed. Critics have charged that congressional authorization would not have been as forthcoming had the president and his administration not ignored or downplayed intelligence reports that contradicted their beliefs in the existence of WMDs and links between the Iraq government and terrorist organizations. The fact that WMDs were not found undermined the administration's credibility with many Americans, including members of Congress, as well as foreign nations. Some constitutional scholars have noted that intelligence failures, the rising death toll, and costs related to military action in Iraq suggest it is time for Congress to increase its oversight of the executive in foreign policy matters. Other scholars disagree, siding with executive branch officials who consider the War Powers Act an infringement on the president's constitutional authority.

Arguments IN FAVOR of the War Powers Act

- **The War Powers Act reflects the will of the American people.** The doctrine of civilian supremacy places ultimate war-making authority with the American people, and the War Powers Act reflects the will of the people as expressed through the representative institution of Congress.

- **The War Powers Act is an attempt by Congress to restore the balance of shared control of the military with the executive.** The act's stated purpose is to "fulfill the intent of the framers . . . and insure that the collective judgment of both the Congress and the president will apply to the introduction of United States Armed Forces into hostilities . . . and to the continued use of such forces." This is an attempt to return to the constitutional principle that waging war is to be shared by both branches of government.

A president's authority is limited by the formal powers enumerated in Article II of the Constitution and by the Supreme Court's interpretation of those constitutional provisions. How a president wields these powers is affected by the times in which the president serves, his confidantes and advisers, and the president's personality and leadership abilities. The 1950s postwar era of good feelings and eco-

- The War Powers Act is an additional check on the president's authority as commander in chief. The act is an attempt to prevent future presidents from engaging in hostilities of questionable importance to U.S. national security and to force deliberation within the government with regard to armed conflict. For example, had Congress known of President Lyndon B. Johnson's use of faulty or intentionally misleading information to increase U.S. military involvement in Vietnam, U.S. involvement in Southeast Asia may have taken a different, less costly, path in both lives and expenditures.

What authority do presidents have during wartime? President Lyndon B. Johnson's action during the Vietnam War led to the passage of the War Powers Act, which, at least in theory, restricts presidential power to deploy troops.

Source: Yoichi R. Okamoto/Picture History

Arguments AGAINST the War Powers Act

- International relations can be so volatile that the president must be able to act quickly and without hindrance to protect the nation and its people. The American executive was created in part to act quickly without relative interference during exceptional times of crisis. During extraordinary times, the president must take extraordinary means to defend the nation without undue interference from Congress. *Federalist No. 8* argues: "It is the nature of war to increase the executive at the expense of the legislative authority" as this is considered a natural shift in power.

- The Supreme Court has upheld an expanded interpretation of the president's authority. In *U.S. v. Curtiss-Wright* (1936), the Court argued that the president and "not

Congress has the better opportunity of knowing the conditions which prevail in foreign countries, and especially this is true during times of war. He has his confidential sources of information. . . . Secrecy in respect of information gathered by them may be highly necessary and the premature disclosure of it productive of harmful results." Thus, the Court concluded that the president is uniquely responsible in the area of foreign policy and war making.

- The Constitution has clearly defined the roles Congress should play in military action and there is no need to extend these powers. Congress has the authority to declare war, to establish military policies, and to fund military action. These are the appropriate checks on executive powers. Congress, for example, used the power of the purse to bring U.S. military activity to an end in Vietnam and in Somalia. The system of checks and balances is not broken, and thus does not need to be fixed.

Continuing the Debate

1. Is the War Powers Act constitutional? If Congress has the power to limit the war-making power of the executive, what implications does this have for U.S. national security?

2. Should Congress have access to the same information and intelligence regarding national security that is available to the president? Are there any circumstances where such information should be restricted to just the president and his or her closest advisers? Explain your answers.

To Follow the Debate Online, Go To:

www.fas.org/search.html, National security reports of the Congressional Research Service, an official agency of the U.S. Congress. The reports are listed when one enters "War Powers Act" into the search engine.

www.americansecurityproject.org/iraq_and_the_war_powers_act, Studies, resources, and position papers on foreign policy issues, including arguments about checks on the president, especially with regard to Iraq.

nomic prosperity presided over by the grandfatherly Eisenhower, for instance, called for a very different leader from the one needed by the Civil War–torn nation governed by Abraham Lincoln.

During that war, Lincoln argued that he needed to act quickly for the very survival of the nation. He suspended the writ of *habeas corpus*, which allows those in prison to petition to be released, citing the need to jail persons even suspected of disloyal practices. He ordered a blockade of southern ports, in effect initiating a war without the approval of Congress. He also closed the U.S. mails to treasonable correspondence.

Lincoln argued that the **inherent powers** of his office allowed him to circumvent the Constitution in a time of war or national crisis. Since the Constitution conferred on the president the duty to make sure that the laws of the United States are faithfully executed, reasoned Lincoln, the acts enumerated above were constitutional. He simply refused to allow the nation to crumble because of what he viewed as technical requirements of the Constitution. Because of his leadership during this crisis, Lincoln is generally ranked by historians as one of the best presidents. (To learn about another presidential ranking method, see Table 7.3.)

Presidential leadership has also become increasingly important with the development of new technology. Before the days of instantaneous communication, the nation could afford to allow Congress, with its relatively slow deliberative processes, to make most decisions. As times and technology have changed, however, so have the public's demands upon the president. The breakneck speed with which so many cable news networks and Internet sites report national and international events has intensified the public's expectation that, in a crisis, the president will be the individual to act quickly and decisively on behalf of the entire nation. Congress often is unable to respond to fast-changing events—especially in foreign affairs.

In the twentieth and twenty-first centuries, the general trend has been for presidential—as opposed to congressional—decision making to be more and more important. The start of this trend can be traced to the four-term presidency of Franklin D. Roosevelt (FDR), who led the nation through several crises.

FDR took office in 1933 in the midst of a major crisis—the Great Depression—during which a substantial portion of the U.S. workforce was unemployed. Noting the sorry state of the national economy in his Inaugural Address, FDR concluded: "This nation asks for action and action now." To jump-start the American economy, FDR asked Congress for and was given "broad executive powers to wage a war against the emergency, as great as the power that would be given to me if we were in fact invaded by a foreign foe."[11]

Just as Abraham Lincoln had taken bold steps upon his inauguration, Roosevelt also acted quickly. He immediately fashioned a plan for national recovery called the **New Deal,** a package of bold and controversial programs designed to invigorate the failing American economy (these are discussed in detail in chapter 3).

Roosevelt served an unprecedented twelve years in office; he was elected to four terms but died shortly after the beginning of this fourth term. During his years in office, the nation went from the economic war of the Great Depression to the real international conflict of World War II. The institution of the presidency changed profoundly and permanently as new federal agencies were created to implement New Deal.

Not only did FDR create a new bureaucracy to implement his pet programs, but he also personalized the presidency by establishing a new relationship between the president and the people. In his radio addresses, or fireside chats, as he liked to call them, he spoke directly to the public in a relaxed and informal manner about serious issues.

To his successors, FDR left the modern presidency, including a burgeoning federal bureaucracy (see chapter 8), an active and usually leading role in both domestic and foreign policy and legislation, and a nationalized executive office that used technology—first radio, then television, and now the Internet—to bring the president closer to the public than ever before.

inherent powers
Powers that belong to the national government simply because it is a sovereign body.

Rate the Presidents

New Deal
The name given to the program of "Relief, Recovery, Reform" begun by President Franklin D. Roosevelt in 1933 to bring the United States out of the Great Depression.

TABLE 7.3   Ranking U.S. Presidents

Who was the best president and who was the worst? Many surveys of scholars have been taken over the years to answer this question, and virtually all have ranked Abraham Lincoln among the best. A C-SPAN survey of fifty-eight historians from across the political spectrum came up with these results:

Five Best Presidents	Five Worst Presidents
1. Lincoln (best)	1. Buchanan (worst)
2. F. Roosevelt	2. A. Johnson
3. Washington	3. Pierce
4. T. Roosevelt	4. Harding
5. Truman	5. W. Harrison

Source: C-SPAN Survey of Presidential Leadership. www.cspan.com.

The Presidential Establishment

As the responsibilities and scope of presidential authority grew over the years, so did the executive branch, including the number of people working directly for the president in the White House. The vice president and his staff, the Cabinet, the first lady and her staff, the Executive Office of the President, and the White House staff all help the president fulfill his duties as chief executive.

The Vice President

Historically, presidents chose their vice presidents largely to balance—politically, geographically, or otherwise—the presidential ticket, with little thought given to the possibility that the vice president would become president. Franklin D. Roosevelt, for example, a liberal New Yorker, selected John Nance Garner, a conservative Texan, to be his running mate in 1932. After serving two terms, Garner—who openly disagreed with Roosevelt over many policies, including Roosevelt's decision to seek a third term—unsuccessfully sought the 1940 presidential nomination himself.

How much power a vice president has depends on how much the president is willing to give him. Jimmy Carter was the first president to give his vice president, Walter Mondale, more than ceremonial duties. In fact, Walter Mondale was the first vice president to have an office in the White House. No vice presidents, however, have ever enjoyed the access to, and ear of, the president to the extent of Vice President Dick Cheney. Some commentators argued that Cheney had a clearer agenda of where the United States should be moving, especially in terms of foreign affairs, than President George W. Bush.

The Cabinet

The Cabinet, which has no basis in the Constitution, is an informal institution based on practice and precedent whose membership is determined by tradition and presidential discretion. By custom, this advisory group selected by the president includes the heads of major executive departments. Presidents today also include their vice presidents in Cabinet meetings, as well as any other agency heads or officials to whom they would like to accord Cabinet-level status. As a body, the Cabinet's major function is to help the president execute the laws and assist him in making decisions.

As revealed in Table 7.4, over the years the Cabinet has grown along side the responsibilities of the national government. As interest groups, in particular, pressured Congress and the president to recognize their demands for services and governmental action, they often were rewarded by the creation of an executive

Why are vice presidents selected? Governor Sarah Palin of Alaska and Senator Joe Biden (D-DE) were chosen as vice presidential nominees for very different reasons. Both, however, helped to balance two historic presidential tickets.

Photo courtesy: Steve Kelley/Cartoonist Group

department. Since each was headed by a secretary who automatically became a member of the president's Cabinet, powerful clientele groups including farmers (Agriculture), business people (Commerce), workers (Labor), and teachers (Education) saw the creation of a department as increasing their access to the president.

While the size of the president's Cabinet has increased over the years, most presidents' reliance on their Cabinet secretaries has decreased. Some individual members of a president's Cabinet, however, may be very influential. To learn more about the Cabinet's role in executing U.S. policy, see chapter 8.

The First Lady

From the time of Martha Washington, first ladies (a term coined during the Civil War) have assisted presidents as informal advisers while making other, more public, and significant contributions to American society. Edith Bolling Galt Wilson, who became President Woodrow Wilson's surrogate after he was left partially paralyzed, and Eleanor Roosevelt, a tireless Democratic party activist were two of the most visible first ladies.

More recently, Laura Bush adopted a largely behind-the-scenes role with literacy the focus of her activities. The First Lady did, however, take to the campaign trail in 2002, 2004, and 2006, very effectively fund-raising on behalf of her husband and other Republican candidates, but returned to a behind-the-scenes role in 2008 as her husband's popularity plummeted.

TABLE 7.4   The U.S. Cabinet and Responsibilities of Each Executive Department

Department Head	Department	Date of Creation	Responsibilities
Secretary of State	Department of State	1789	Responsible for the making of foreign policy, including treaty negotiation
Secretary of the Treasury	Department of the Treasury	1789	Responsible for government funds and regulation of alcohol, firearms, and tobacco
Secretary of Defense	Department of Defense	1789	Responsible for national defense; current department created by consolidating the former Departments of War, the Army, the Navy, and the Air Force in 1947
Attorney General	Department of Justice	1870	Represents U.S. government in all federal courts, investigates and prosecutes violations of federal law
Secretary of the Interior	Department of the Interior	1849	Manages the nation's natural resources, including wildlife and public lands
Secretary of Agriculture	Department of Agriculture	1889	Assists farmers, oversees food-quality programs, administers food stamp and school lunch programs
Secretary of Commerce	Department of Commerce	1903	Aids businesses and conducts the U.S. Census (originally the Department of Commerce and Labor)
Secretary of Labor	Department of Labor	1913	Runs labor programs, keeps labor statistics, aids labor through enforcement of laws
Secretary of Health and Human Services	Department of Health and Human Services	1953	Runs health, welfare, and Social Security programs (originally the Department of Health, Education, and Welfare, lost its education function in 1979)
Secretary of Housing and Urban Development	Department of Housing and Urban Development	1965	Responsible for urban and housing programs
Secretary of Transportation	Department of Transportation	1966	Responsible for mass transportation and highway programs
Secretary of Energy	Department of Energy	1977	Responsible for energy policy and research, including atomic energy
Secretary of Education	Department of Education	1979	Responsible for the federal government's education programs
Secretary of Veterans Affairs	Department of Veterans Affairs	1989	Responsible for programs aiding veterans
Secretary of Homeland Security	Department of Homeland Security	2002	Responsible for all issues pertaining to homeland security

The Executive Office of the President (EOP)

The **Executive Office of the President (EOP)** was established by FDR in 1939 to oversee his New Deal programs. It was created to provide the president with a general staff to help him direct the diverse activities of the executive branch. In fact, it is a mini-bureaucracy of several advisers and offices located in the ornate Executive Office Building next to the White House on Pennsylvania Avenue, as well as in the White House itself, where the president's closest advisers often are located.

The EOP has expanded over time to include several advisory and policy-making agencies and task forces. Over time, the units of the EOP have become the prime policy makers in their fields of expertise as they play key roles in advancing the president's policy preferences. Among the EOP's most important members are the National Security Council, the Council of Economic Advisers, the Office of Management and Budget, the Office of the Vice President, and the Office of the U.S. Trade Representative.

The National Security Council (NSC) was established in 1947 to advise the president on American military affairs and foreign policy. The NSC is composed of the president, the vice president, and the secretaries of state and defense. The chair of the Joint Chiefs of Staff and the director of the Central Intelligence Agency also participate. Others such as the White House chief of staff and the general counsel may attend. The national security adviser runs the staff of the NSC, coordinates information and options, and advises the president.

Presidents can give clear indications of their policy preferences by the kinds of offices they include in the EOP. President George W. Bush, for example, not only moved or consolidated several offices when he became president in 2001, but he created a new Office of Faith-Based and Community Initiatives to help him achieve his goal of greater religious involvement in matters of domestic policy.

The White House Staff

Although presidents organize the White House staff in different ways, they typically have a chief of staff whose job is to facilitate the smooth running of the staff and the executive branch of government. Successful chiefs of staff also have protected the president from mistakes and helped implement policies to obtain the maximum political advantage for the president. Other key White House aides include the counselor to the president; domestic, foreign, and economic policy strategists; communications staff; White House counsel; and a lobbyist who acts as a liaison between the president and Congress.

White House staffers prefer to be located in the White House in spite of its small offices, but many staffers are relegated to the old Executive Office Building next door because White House office space is limited. In Washington, the size of the office is not the measure of power that it often is in corporations. Instead, power in the White House goes to those who have the president's ear and the offices closest to the Oval Office.

Presidential Leadership and the Importance of Public Opinion

A president's ability to get his programs adopted or implemented depends on many factors, including his leadership abilities, his personality and powers of persuasion, his ability to mobilize public opinion to support his actions, the public's perception of his performance, and Congress's perception of his public support.

Executive Office of the President (EOP)
Created in 1939 to help the president oversee the executive branch bureaucracy.

Presidential Leadership

Leadership is not an easy thing to exercise, and it remains an elusive concept for scholars to identify and measure, but it is important to all presidents seeking support for their programs and policies. Moreover, ideas about the importance of effective leaders have deep roots in our political culture. The leadership abilities of the great presidents—Washington, Jefferson, Lincoln, and FDR—have been extolled over and over again, leading us to fault modern presidents who fail to cloak themselves in the armor of leadership. Americans thus have come to believe that "if presidential leadership works some of the time, why not all of the time?"[12] This attitude, in turn, directly influences what we expect presidents to do and how we evaluate them. (To learn about presidential personalities, see Table 7.5.)

Research by political scientists shows that presidents can exercise leadership by increasing public attention to particular issues. Analyses of presidential State of the Union Addresses, for example, reveal that mentions of particular policies translate into more Americans mentioning those policies as the most important problems facing the nation.[13] Political scientist Richard E. Neustadt calls the president's ability to influence members of Congress and the public "the power to persuade." Neustadt believes this power is crucial to presidential leadership.[14]

Frequently, the difference between great and mediocre presidents centers on their ability to grasp the importance of leadership style. Truly great presidents, such as Lincoln and FDR, understood that the White House was a seat of power from which decisions could flow to shape the national destiny. They recognized that their day-to-day activities and how they went about them should be designed to bolster support for their policies and to secure congressional and popular backing that could translate their intuitive judgment into meaningful action. Mediocre presidents, on the other hand, have tended to regard the White House as "a stage for the presentation of performances to the public" or a fitting honor to cap a career.[15]

TABLE 7.5 Barber's Presidential Personalities

Political scientist James David Barber defines presidential character as the "way the president orients himself toward life." Barber believes that there are four presidential character types, based on energy level (whether the president is active or passive) and the degree of enjoyment a president finds in the job (whether the president has a positive or negative attitude). Barber believes that active and positive presidents are more successful than passive and negative presidents. Active-positive presidents, he argues, approach the presidency with a characteristic zest for life and have a drive to lead and succeed. In contrast, passive-negative presidents find themselves reacting to circumstances, are likely to take directions from others, and fail to make full use of the enormous resources of the executive office.

	Active	Passive
Positive	F. Roosevelt	Taft
	Truman	Harding
	Kennedy	Reagan
	Ford	
	Carter[a]	
	G. Bush	
Negative	Wilson	Coolidge
	Hoover	Eisenhower
	L. Johnson	
	Nixon	

[a] Some scholars think that Carter better fits the active-negative typology.

Source: James David Barber, *The Presidential Character: Predicting Performance in the White House*, 5th ed. (New York: Longman, 2008).

Going Public: Mobilizing Public Opinion

Even before radio, television, and the Internet, presidents tried to reach out to the public to gain support for their programs through what President Theodore Roosevelt called the bully pulpit. The development of commercial air travel and radio, newsreels, television, and computers have made direct communication to larger numbers of voters easier. Presidents, first ladies, and other presidential advisers travel all over the world to publicize their views and to build personal support as well as support for administration programs.

Direct, presidential appeals to the electorate like those often made by recent presidents are referred to as "going public."[16] Going public means that a president goes over the heads of members of Congress to gain support from the people, who can then place pressure on their elected officials in Washington. (To learn more about this tactic, see Ideas into Action: Exploring Presidential Visits.)

The Public's Perception of Presidential Performance

For presidents and other public figures, approval ratings are often used as tacit measures of their political capital:

Ideas Into Action

Exploring Presidential Visits

President Richard M. Nixon was the first president to visit all fifty states. Since Nixon's administration, chief executives have made a significant effort to visit each state during their term in office. President Bill Clinton, for example, took a one-day trip to Nebraska in November of 2000 in order to be able to say that he had visited each of the states. And, as of August 2008, President George W. Bush had visited every state but Vermont.

These visits may occur for any number of reasons—campaign events, policy speeches, or ceremonial visits. Presidents, for example, are often asked to give college commencement addresses. They may visit places of historical significance, commemorate historical events, or visit with foreign ambassadors.

State and local officials do not take presidential visits lightly. These visits often require significant preparation of security, although some events may not be accessible to the public.

Explore the history of your state or locality to learn more about presidential visits, both past and present.

- What presidents have visited your area? Did you attend any of these events? If so, what were they like?

- What local attractions or commemorations might be appropriate events for attracting the president? How might you go about bringing these events to the president's attention?

their ability to enact public policy simply because of their name and their office. Presidents who have high approval ratings, as President George W. Bush did in the immediate aftermath of the September 11, 2001 terrorist attacks, are assumed to be more powerful leaders with a mandate for action that comes largely by virtue of the high levels of public support they enjoy. They are often able to use their clout to push controversial legislation, such as the USA Patriot Act, through Congress. A public appearance from a popular president can even deliver a hotly contested congressional seat or gubernatorial contest to the president's party.

In sharp contrast, presidents with low approval ratings are often crippled in the policy arena. Their low ratings can actually prevent favored policies from being enacted on Capitol Hill, even when their party controls the legislature, as many of their partisans locked in close elections shy away from being seen or affiliated with an unpopular president. This was the case in 2008 when House Republicans did not want to be affiliated with the president's emergency financial bailout plan.

Presidential popularity, however, generally follows a cyclical pattern. These cycles have been recorded since 1938, when pollsters first began to track presidential popularity. Typically, presidents enjoy their highest level of public approval at the beginning of their terms and try to take advantage of this honeymoon period to get their programs passed by Congress as soon as possible. Each action a president takes, however, is divisive—some people will approve, and others will disapprove. Disapproval tends to have a negative cumulative effect on a president's approval rating. (To learn more about presidential approval, see Analyzing Visuals: Presidential Approval Ratings Since 1981.)

SIMULATION

You Are a President During a Nuclear Meltdown

How do presidents prepare to use their honeymoon period? Even before his election as the forty-fourth president of the United States, Barack Obama worked to fill key staff and cabinet positions. Obama named Congressman Rahm Emanuel (D–IL) as his chief of staff a mere two days after his election.

Photo courtesy: Mark Lyons/Getty Images

213

Analyzing Visuals | Presidential Approval Ratings Since 1981

Examine the line graph, which shows the percentage of the American public approving of presidents' performances from 1981 through 2008, and consider the following questions:

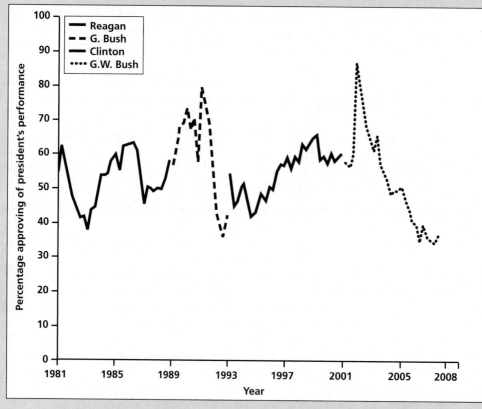

Source: Roper Center, University of Connecticut.

DO you notice a pattern in the approval ratings for two-term presidents Ronald Reagan, Bill Clinton, and George W. Bush?

WHICH president left office with the highest approval rating? The lowest approval rating?

BASED on your knowledge of President George W. Bush's terms in office, how would you explain the rise and fall of his approval ratings from 2001 to 2008?

Toward Reform: The President as Policy Maker

When FDR sent his first legislative package to Congress, he broke the traditional model of law-making.[17] As envisioned by the Framers, it was to be Congress that made the laws. Now FDR was claiming a leadership role for the president in the legislative process. Said the president of this new relationship: "It is the duty of the President to propose and it is the privilege of the Congress to dispose."[18] With those words and the actions that followed, FDR shifted the presidency into a law- and policy-maker role. Now the president and the executive branch not only executed the laws but generally suggested them, too.

The President's Role in Proposing and Facilitating Legislation

From FDR's presidency to the Republican-controlled 104th Congress, the public looked routinely to the president to formulate concrete legislative plans to propose to Congress, which subsequently adopted, modified, or rejected his plans for the nation. Then, in 1994, it appeared for a while that the electorate wanted Congress to reassert itself in the legislative process. In fact, the Contract with America was a Republican call for Congress to take the reins of the law-making process. But several Republican Congresses failed to pass many of the items of the Contract, and President Bill Clinton's continued forceful presence in the budgetary process made a resurgent role for Congress largely illusory. The same scenario held true for President George W. Bush, although by 2006, even some Republicans were concerned with Bush's continued deficit spending requests.

On the whole, presidents have a hard time getting Congress to pass their programs.[19] Passage is especially difficult if the president presides over a divided government, which occurs when the presidency and Congress are controlled by different political parties (see chapter 6). Recent research by political scientists, however, shows that presidents are much more likely to win on bills central to their announced agendas, such as President George W. Bush's victory on the Iraq war resolution, than to secure passage of legislation proposed by others.[20]

Because presidents generally experience declining support for policies they advocate throughout their terms, it is important that a president propose key plans early in his administration, during the honeymoon period, a time when the goodwill toward the president often allows a president to secure passage of legislation that he would not be able to gain at a later period. Even President Lyndon B. Johnson, who was able to get nearly 60 percent of his programs through Congress, noted: "You've got to give it all you can, that first year . . . before they start worrying about themselves. . . . You can't put anything through when half the Congress is thinking how to beat you."[21]

Another way a president can bolster support for his legislative package is to call on his political party. As the informal leader of his party, he should be able to use that position to his advantage in Congress, where party loyalty is very important. This strategy works best when the president has carried members of his party into office on his coattails, as was the case in the Johnson and Reagan landslides of 1964 and 1984, respectively. In fact, many scholars regard President Lyndon B. Johnson as the most effective legislative leader.[22] Not only had he served in the House and as Senate majority leader, but he also enjoyed a comfortable Democratic Party majority in Congress, and many Democrats owed their victories to his landslide win over his Republican challenger, Senator Barry Goldwater (R–AZ).[23]

The Budgetary Process and Legislative Implementation

Closely associated with a president's ability to pass legislation is his ability to secure funding for new and existing programs. A president sets national policy and priorities through his budget proposals and his continued insistence on their congressional passage. The budget proposal not only outlines the programs he wants but indicates the importance of each program by the amount of funding requested for each and for its associated agency or department.

Because the Framers gave Congress the power of the purse, Congress had primary responsibility for the budget process until 1930. The economic disaster set off by the stock market crash of 1929, however, gave FDR, once elected in 1932, the opportunity to assert himself in the congressional budgetary process, just as he inserted himself in the legislative process. In 1939, the Bureau of the Budget, which had been created in 1921 to help the president tell Congress how much money it would take to run the executive

POLITICS NOW

Source: THE BOSTON GLOBE   April 30, 2006

Are Signing Statements Constitutional?

George W. Bush Challenges Hundreds of Laws

CHARLIE SAVAGE

President Bush has quietly claimed the authority to disobey more than 750 laws enacted since he took office, asserting that he has the power to set aside any statute passed by Congress when it conflicts with his interpretation of the Constitution. Among the laws Bush said he can ignore are military rules and regulations, affirmative action provisions, requirements that Congress be told about immigration services problems, "whistle-blower" protections for nuclear regulatory officials, and safeguards against political interference in federally funded research.

Legal scholars say the scope and aggression of Bush's assertions that he can bypass laws represent a concerted effort to expand his power at the expense of Congress, upsetting the balance between the branches of government. The Constitution is clear in assigning to Congress the power to write the laws and to the president a duty "to take care that the laws be faithfully executed." Bush, however, has repeatedly declared that he does not need to "execute" a law he believes is unconstitutional. . . .

Far more than any predecessor, Bush has been aggressive about declaring his right to ignore vast swaths of laws—many of which he says infringe on power he believes the Constitution assigns to him

alone as the head of the executive branch or the commander in chief of the military. . . .

For the first five years of Bush's presidency, his legal claims attracted little attention in Congress or the media. Then, twice in recent months, Bush drew scrutiny after challenging new laws: a torture ban and a requirement that he give detailed reports to Congress about how he is using the Patriot Act. Bush administration spokesmen declined to make White House or Justice Department attorneys available to discuss any of Bush's challenges to the laws he has signed. Instead, they referred a *Globe* reporter to their response to questions about Bush's position that he could ignore provisions of the Patriot Act. They said at the time that Bush was following a practice that has "been used for several administrations" and that "the president will faithfully execute the law in a manner that is consistent with the Constitution." . . .

Bush . . . has signed every bill that reached his desk, often inviting the legislation's sponsors to signing ceremonies at which he lavishes praise upon their work.

Then, after the media and the lawmakers have left the White House, Bush quietly files "signing statements"—official documents in which a president lays out his legal interpretation of a bill for the federal bureaucracy to follow when implementing the new law. The statements are recorded in the *Federal Register*.

In his signing statements, Bush has repeatedly asserted that the Constitution gives him the right to ignore numerous sections of the bills—sometimes including provisions that were the subject of negotiations with Congress in order to get

lawmakers to pass the bill. He has appended such statements to more than one of every 10 bills he has signed. . . .

Though Bush has gone further than any previous president, his actions are not unprecedented. Since the early 19th century, American presidents have occasionally signed a large bill while declaring that they would not enforce a specific provision they believed was unconstitutional. On rare occasions, historians say, presidents also issued signing statements interpreting a law and explaining any concerns about it. But it was not until the mid-1980s, midway through the tenure of President Reagan, that it became common for the president to issue signing statements. . . .

Reagan's successors continued this practice. George H.W. Bush challenged 232 statutes over four years in office, and Bill Clinton objected to 140 laws over his eight years. . . .

Many of the challenges involved long-standing legal ambiguities and points of conflict between the president and Congress.

Discussion Questions

1. *Are signing statements a constitutional exercise of presidential power, or do they upset the system of checks and balances between the branches? Why or why not?*
2. *Why might presidents favor signing statements over the exercise of the veto power?*
3. *What other ways might presidents go about achieving the policy reforms they desire?*

Office of Management and Budget (OMB)
The office that prepares the president's annual budget proposal, reviews the budget and programs of the executive departments, supplies economic forecasts, and conducts detailed analyses of proposed bills and agency rules.

branch of government, was made part of the newly created Executive Office of the President. In 1970, President Nixon changed its name to the **Office of Management and Budget (OMB)** to clarify its function in the executive branch.

The OMB works exclusively for the president and employs hundreds of budget and policy experts. Key OMB responsibilities include preparing the president's annual budget proposal, designing the president's program, and reviewing the progress, budget, and program proposals of the executive department agencies. It also supplies economic forecasts to the president and conducts detailed analyses of proposed bills and agency rules. OMB reports allow the president to attach price tags to his legislative proposals and defend the presidential budget. The OMB budget is a huge document, and even those who prepare it have a hard time deciphering all of its provisions. Even so, the expertise of the OMB directors often gives them an advantage over members of Congress.

Policy Making Through Executive Order

Proposing legislation and using the budget to advance policy priorities are not the only ways that presidents can affect the policy process, especially in times of highly divided government. Major policy changes may be instituted when a president has issued an **executive order,** a rule or regulation issued by the president that has the effect of law. While many executive orders are issued to help clarify or implement legislation enacted by Congress, other executive orders have the effect of making new policy. President Truman also used an executive order to end segregation in the military, and affirmative action was institutionalized as national policy through Executive Order 11246, issued by Lyndon B. Johnson in 1966. More recently, President George W. Bush used executive orders to establish military tribunals and authorize wiretaps of suspected terrorists.

Executive orders have been used since the 1980s to set national policies toward abortion. President Ronald Reagan, for example, used an executive order to stop federal funding of fetal tissue research and to end federal funding of any groups providing abortion counseling. President Bill Clinton immediately rescinded those orders when he became president. One of President George W. Bush's first acts upon taking office was to issue an executive order reversing those Clinton orders.

George W. Bush also used executive orders to put his policy stamp on a wide array of important issues. After much soul searching, for example, he signed an executive order limiting federal funding of stem cell research to the sixty or so cell lines currently in the possession of scientific researchers.[24] An executive order also was used to allow military tribunals to try any foreigners captured by U.S. forces in Afghanistan or linked to the 9/11 terrorist acts.

In place of executive orders, presidents may also issue "signing statements" when signing legislation. Often these written statements merely comment on the bill signed, but they sometimes include controversial claims by the president that some part of the legislation is unconstitutional and that he intends to disregard it or to implement it in other ways. (To learn more about signing statements, see Politics Now: Are Signing Statements Constitutional?)

executive order
A rule or regulation issued by the president that has the effect of law. All executive orders must be published in the *Federal Register*.

Presidential Success in Polls and Congress

★ **WHAT SHOULD I HAVE LEARNED?**

Because the Framers feared a tyrannical monarch, they gave considerable thought to the office of the chief executive. Since ratification of the Constitution, the office has changed considerably—more through practice and need than from changes in the Constitution. In chronicling these changes, we have answered the following questions:

■ **What are the roots of the office of the president of the United States?**

Distrust of a too powerful leader led the Framers to create an executive office with limited powers. They mandated that a president be at least thirty-five years old, a natural-born citizen, and a resident of the United States for at least fourteen years, and they opted not to limit the president's term of office. To further guard against tyranny, they made provisions for the removal of the president.

■ **What are the constitutional powers of the president?**

The Framers gave the president a variety of specific constitutional powers in Article II, including the appointment power, the power to convene Congress, and the power to make treaties. The Constitution also gives the president the power to grant pardons and to veto acts of Congress. In addition, the president derives considerable power from being commander in chief of the military.

■ **How did presidential power develop and expand?**

The development of presidential power has depended on the personal force of those who have held the office. George Washington, in particular, took several actions to establish the primacy of the president in national affairs and as true chief executive of a strong national government. But, with only a few exceptions, subsequent presidents often let Congress dominate in national affairs. With the election of FDR, however, the power of the president increased, and presidential decision making became more important in national and foreign affairs.

■ **What offices make up the presidential establishment?**

As the responsibilities of the president have grown, so has the executive branch of government. Franklin D. Roosevelt established the Executive Office of the President to help him govern. Perhaps the most key policy advisers are those closest to the president: the vice president, the White House staff, some members of the Executive Office of the President, and sometimes, the first lady.

■ **How do public opinion and public perceptions of presidential leadership affect presidential success?**

To gain support for his programs or proposed budget, the president uses a variety of skills, including personal leadership and direct appeals to the public. How the president goes about winning support is determined by his leadership and personal style, affected by his character and his ability to persuade. Since the 1970s, however, the American public has been increasingly skeptical of presidential actions, and few presidents have enjoyed extended periods of the kind of popularity needed to help win support for programmatic change.

■ **How do presidents use their legislative proposals to affect and reform policy?**

Since FDR, the public has looked to the president to propose legislation to Congress. Through proposing legislation, advancing budgets, and involvement in the regulatory process, presidents make policy.

Key Terms

Cabinet, p. 202
executive agreement, p. 203
Executive Office of the President (EOP), p. 211
executive order, p. 217
executive privilege, p. 200

impeachment, p. 199
inherent powers, p. 208
New Deal, p. 208
Office of Management and Budget (OMB), p. 216
pardon, p. 205

Twenty-Fifth Amendment, p. 200
Twenty-Second Amendment, p. 199
U.S. v. *Nixon* (1974), p. 200
veto power, p. 203
War Powers Act, p. 205

Researching the Presidency

In the Library

Barber, James David. *The Presidential Character: Predicting Presidential Performance in the White House*, 5th ed. New York: Longman, 2008.

Cooper, Philip J. *By Order of the President: The Use and Abuse of Executive Direct Action*. Lawrence: University Press of Kansas, 2002.

Cronin, Thomas E., and Michael A. Genovese. *The Paradoxes of the American Presidency*, 2nd ed. New York: Oxford University Press, 2006.

Edwards, George C., III, and Desmond King. *The Polarized Presidency of George W. Bush*. New York: Oxford University Press, 2007.

Greenstein, Fred I. *The Presidential Difference: Leadership Style from FDR to George W. Bush*, 2nd ed. Princeton, NJ: Princeton University Press, 2004.

Martin, Janet M. *The American Presidency and Women: Promise, Performance, and Illusion*. College Station: Texas A&M University Press, 2003.

Milkis, Sidney M., and Michael T. Nelson. *The American Presidency: Origins and Development, 1776–2007*, 5th ed. Washington, DC: CQ Press, 2007.

Neustadt, Richard E. *Presidential Power and the Modern Presidents*. New York: Free Press, 1991.

Pfiffner, James P. *The Character Factor: How We Judge America's Presidents*. College Station: Texas A&M University Press, 2004.

———. *The Modern Presidency*, 5th ed. Belmont, CA: Wadsworth, 2007.

Pika, Joseph A., and John Anthony Maltese. *The Politics of the Presidency*, 7th ed. Washington, DC: CQ Press, 2008.

Rossiter, Clinton. *The American Presidency*, reprint ed. Baltimore, MD: Johns Hopkins University Press, 1987.

Skowronek, Stephen. *The Politics Presidents Make: Leadership from John Adams to Bill Clinton*. Cambridge, MA: Harvard University Press, 1997.

Warshaw, Shirley Anne. *The Keys to Power: Managing the Presidency*, 2nd ed. New York: Longman, 2005.

Wood, B. Dan. *The Politics of Economic Leadership: The Causes and Consequences of Presidential Rhetoric*. Princeton, NJ: Princeton University Press, 2007.

On the Web

To learn more about the office of the president, go to the official White House Web site, **www.whitehouse.gov**. There you can track current presidential initiatives and legislative priorities, read press briefings, and learn more about presidential nominations and executive orders.

To learn more about past presidents, go to the National Archives at **www.archives.gov/index.html**, where you can learn about the presidential libraries, view presidential documents, and hear audio of presidents speaking.

To learn more about the office of the vice president, go to **www.whitehouse.gov/vicepresident**.

To learn more about the initiatives favored by the first lady, go to **www.whitehouse.gov/firstlady**.

8

The Executive Branch and the Federal Bureaucracy

To maintain a secure homeland, planning is critical. And, at a time when federal resources are stretched to their limit given the high cost of military interventions in Iraq and Afghanistan, the U.S. government—especially its bureaucracy—is trying to prepare for what some are calling the next pandemic: avian flu.

Avian influenza, or H5N1—the designation scientists have given this particular strain of the influenza virus—has infected domesticated and migratory birds in more than fifty nations across Asia, Africa, and Europe. It has infected more than 250 people worldwide, with an astonishingly high death rate of more than 50 percent. Flu viruses mutate rapidly, and experts believe it is highly likely that this particular strain

of avian flu could become a global threat to humanity. The last major influenza pandemic occurred in 1918 and killed tens of millions of people worldwide.

Since it takes time to culture a reliable vaccine to protect people from getting easily transmitted viruses, a pandemic caused by a virus like H5N1, could outpace the abilities of governments to vaccinate their citizens or contain the outbreak. Even if the first widespread infections occurred in China, given the global travel patterns of U.S. citizens, a deadly virus likely would be on the ground in the United States within weeks. "If such an outbreak occurred, hospitals would become overwhelmed, riots would engulf vaccination clinics, and even power and food would be in short supply," concludes a draft of a plan the Bush administration developed as part of its initial planning to handle avian flu.[1]

On May 3, 2006, Frances Townsend, President George W. Bush's homeland security advisor, issued the administration's Pandemic Influenza Strategic Plan to get the nation ready for a 1918-style flu disaster, which left more than one-half million Americans dead. The new government plan outlined the responsibilities of every federal department and agency should the flu begin to spread quickly among humans. The secretary of health and human services was given major responsibility for health issues, and

■ Governments have been called upon to deal with public health crises for many years. At left, doctors tend to a patient during the 1918 Spanish flu epidemic. At right, Homeland Security Advisor Frances Townsend announces the Bush Administration's plan for a strategic response to the threat of avian flu.

★ WHAT SHOULD I KNOW ABOUT . . .
- the roots of the federal bureaucracy?
- the modern bureaucracy?
- how the bureaucracy works?
- making agencies accountable?

nonmedical emergency efforts and coordination were given to the secretary of homeland security. The secretary of state was given responsibility for international response issues.[2]

**TO LEARN MORE—
—TO DO MORE**
To learn more about U.S. preparedness in the event of a possible avian flu outbreak, go to the U.S. government avian and pandemic flu information site at www.pandemicflu.gov.

Critics were quick to point out that none of the secretaries were given emergency powers to spend additional monies, such as granting emergency medical coverage to the uninsured. Priorities as to how to allot any vaccines or interventional medicines were also left unanswered, as was any potential role for the military. "The real shortcoming of the plan is that it doesn't say who's in charge," said a top health official who fears the consequences of a disorganized response from the federal government.[3] Possibly further complicating a "national plan of action," the administration's plan places tremendous responsibility on state and local governments, who often are first responders in any emergency, and it has been criticized by the National Association of County and City Health Officials, who view the administration's plan as "the mother of all unfunded mandates."[4]

The plan, which suggests steps that state and local governments can take to prepare for a pandemic, calls for quarantine and travel restrictions, but the administration admits that such steps are largely stopgap measures. Its worst-case scenario foresees the deaths of nearly 2 million Americans and the need to hospitalize an additional 8.5 million people.

bureaucracy
A set of complex hierarchical departments, agencies, commissions, and their staffs that exist to help a chief executive officer carry out his or her duties. Bureaucracies may be private organizations or governmental units.

SIMULATION

You Are Deputy Director of the Census Bureau

In the American system, the **bureaucracy**, or the thousands of federal government agencies and institutions that implement and administer federal laws and programs, can be thought of as the part of the government that makes policy as it links together the three branches of the national government. Although Congress makes the laws, it must rely on bureaucrats in the executive branch to enforce and implement them. These agency determinations, in turn, are often challenged in the courts. Because most administrative agencies that make up part of the bureaucracy enjoy reputations for special expertise in clearly defined policy areas, the federal judiciary routinely defers to bureaucratic administrative decision makers.

The federal bureaucracy often is called the "fourth branch of government." Critics often charge that the bureaucracy is too large, too powerful, and too unaccountable to the people or even to elected officials. Many politicians, elected officials, and voters complain that the federal bureaucracy is too wasteful. However, few critics discuss the fact that laws and policies also are implemented by state and local bureaucracies and bureaucrats whose numbers are proportionately far larger, and often far less accountable, than those working for the federal government.

Many Americans are uncomfortable with the large role of the federal government in policy making. Nevertheless, recent studies show that most users of federal agencies rate quite favorably the agencies and the services they receive. Many of those polled by the Pew Research Center were frustrated by complicated rules and the slowness of a particular agency. Still, a majority gave most agencies overall high marks. Most of those polled drew sharp distinctions between particular agencies and the government as a whole. For example, 84 percent of physicians and pharmacists rated the Food and Drug Administration favorably, whereas only one-half of all those sampled were positive about the government in general.[5]

Harold D. Lasswell once defined political science as the "study of who gets what, when, and how."[6] It is by studying the bureaucracy that those questions can perhaps best be answered. To allow you to understand the role of the bureaucracy we will first examine the roots of the federal bureaucracy. Then, after examining the modern bureaucracy by discussing bureaucrats and the formal organization of the bureaucracy, we will consider how the bureaucracy works. Finally, we will discuss reform efforts intended to make agencies accountable.

Roots of the Federal Bureaucracy

In 1789, only three departments existed under the Articles of Confederation: Foreign Affairs, War, and Treasury. President George Washington inherited those departments, and soon, the head of each department was called its secretary and Foreign Affairs was renamed the Department of State. To provide the president with legal advice, Congress also created the office of attorney general. From the beginning, individuals appointed as Cabinet secretaries (as well as the attorney general) were subject to approval by the U.S. Senate, but they could be removed from office by the president alone. Even the first Congress realized how important it was that a president be surrounded by those in whom he had complete confidence and trust.

TIMELINE

The Evolution of the Federal Bureaucracy

Which U.S. president popularized the spoils system? Here, a political cartoonist depicts how President Andrew Jackson might have been immortalized for his use of the spoils system.

The Civil War and the Growth of Government

As discussed in chapter 3, the Civil War (1861–1865) permanently changed the nature of the federal bureaucracy. As the nation geared up for war, thousands of additional employees were added to existing departments. The Civil War also spawned the need for new government agencies. A series of poor harvests and distribution problems led President Abraham Lincoln (who understood that you need well-fed troops to conduct a war) to create the Department of Agriculture in 1862, although it was not given full Cabinet-level status until more than twenty years later.

The Pension Office was established in 1866 to pay benefits to the thousands of Union veterans who had fought in the war (more than 127,000 veterans initially were eligible for benefits). Justice, headed by the attorney general, was made a cabinet department in 1870, and other departments were added through 1900.

From the Spoils System to the Merit System

In 1831, describing President Andrew Jackson's populating the federal government with his political cronies, a New York senator commented, "To the victor belong the spoils." From his statement derives the term spoils system to describe the firing of public office holders of the defeated political party and their replacement with loyalists of a

Photo courtesy: Bettmann/Corbis

spoils system
The firing of public-office holders of a defeated political party and their replacement with loyalists of the newly elected party.

patronage
Jobs, grants, or other special favors that are given as rewards to friends and political allies for their support.

Pendleton Act
Reform measure that created the Civil Service Commission to administer a partial merit system. The act classified the federal service by grades, to which appointments were made based on the results of a competitive examination. It made it illegal for federal political appointees to be required to contribute to a particular political party.

civil service system
The legal system by which many federal bureaucrats are selected.

merit system
The system by which federal civil service jobs are classified into grades or levels, and appointments are made on the basis of performance on competitive examinations.

independent regulatory commission
An agency created by Congress that is generally concerned with a specific aspect of the economy.

new administration. The **spoils system** was a form of **patronage**, that is jobs, grants, or other special favors given as rewards to friends and political allies for their support. Political patronage often is defended as an essential element of the party system because it provides rewards and inducements for party workers. This system reached a high-water mark during Abraham Lincoln's presidency. By the time James A. Garfield, a former distinguished Civil War officer, was elected president in 1880, many reformers were calling for changes in the patronage system. On his election, thousands pressed Garfield for positions. Garfield resolved to reform the civil service, but his life was cut short by the bullets of an assassin who, ironically, was a frustrated job seeker.

Public reaction to Garfield's death and increasing criticism of the spoils system prompted Congress to pass the Civil Service Reform Act in 1883, more commonly known as the **Pendleton Act**, named in honor of its sponsor, Senator George H. Pendleton (D–OH). It established the principle of federal employment on the basis of open, competitive exams and created a bipartisan three-member Civil Service Commission, which operated until 1978. Initially, only about 10 percent of the positions in the federal **civil service system** were covered by the law, but later laws and executive orders extended coverage of the act to over 90 percent of all federal employees. This new system was called the **merit system**.

Regulating the Economy

As the nation grew, so did the bureaucracy. (To learn more, see Analyzing Visuals: Federal Employees in the Executive Branch, 1789–2005.) In the wake of the tremendous growth of big business (especially railroads), widespread price fixing, and other unfair business practices that occurred after the Civil War, Congress created the Interstate Commerce Commission (ICC) in 1887. In creating the ICC, Congress was reacting to public outcries over the exorbitant rates charged by railroad companies for hauling freight. It became the first **independent regulatory commission**, an agency outside a major executive department. Independent regulatory commissions such as the ICC, generally concerned with particular aspects of the economy, are created by Congress to be independent of direct presidential authority. Commission members are appointed by the president and hold their jobs for fixed terms, but they are not removable by the president unless they fail to uphold their oaths of office. The creation of the ICC also marked a shift in the focus of the bureaucracy from service to regulation. Its creation gave the government—in the shape of the bureaucracy—vast powers over individual and property rights.

As discussed in chapter 3, the ratification of the Sixteenth Amendment to the Constitution in 1913 affected the size and growth potential of government. It gave Congress the authority to implement a federal income tax to supplement the national treasury and provided a huge infusion of funds to support new federal agencies, services, and programs.

The Growth of Government in the Twentieth Century

The bureaucracy continued to grow after stock prices crashed in 1929 and the nation plunged into the Great Depression. To combat the resultant high unemployment and weak financial markets, President Franklin D. Roosevelt created hundreds of new government agencies to regulate business practices and various aspects of the national economy. Roosevelt believed that a national economic depression called for national intervention. Thus, the president proposed, and the Congress enacted, far-ranging economic legislation. The desperate mood of the nation supported these moves, as most Americans began to reconsider their ideas about the proper role of government and the provision of governmental services. Formerly, most Americans had believed in a hands-off approach; now they considered it the federal government's job to get the economy going and get Americans back to work.

Analyzing Visuals | Federal Employees in the Executive Branch, 1789–2005

Examine the line graph tracking the number of federal employees in the executive branch of the U.S. government from the eighteenth to the twenty-first century. After reviewing the data and balloons in the line graph and reading the material in this chapter on the origins and development of the executive branch and federal bureaucracy, answer the following questions:

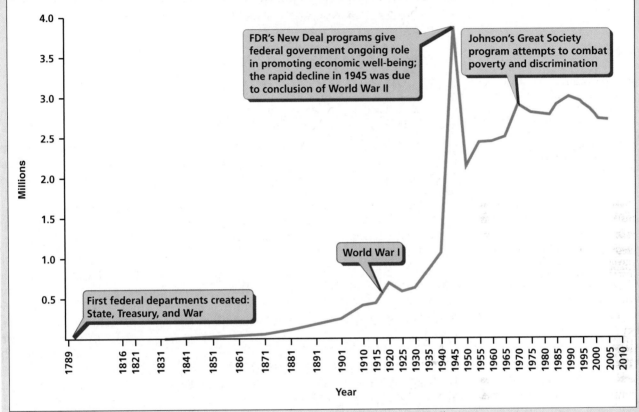

Source: Office of Personnel Management, *The Fact Book*, http://www.opm.gov/feddata/factbook/2005/factbook2005.pdf.

BEFORE the United States' involvement in World War II, what was the principal reason for the growth in the number of federal employees?

THE rapid decline in federal employees between 1945 and 1950 was a result of the end of World War II, but why

do you think the number of federal employees declined after 1970? Why might it have increased between 1975 and 1990?

WOULD you expect the Obama administration to hire more or fewer federal employees? Why?

World War II also prompted an expansion of the federal bureaucracy. Tax rates were increased to support the war, and they never again fell to prewar levels. After the war, this infusion of new monies and veterans' demands for services led to a variety of new programs and a much bigger government. The G.I. (Government Issue) Bill, for example, provided college loans for returning veterans and reduced mortgage rates to allow them to buy homes. The national government's involvement in these programs not only affected more people but also led to its greater involvement in more regulation. Homes bought with Veterans Housing Authority loans, for example, had to meet certain specifications. With these programs, Americans became increasingly accustomed to the national government's role in entirely new areas such as affordable middle-class housing and scholarships that allowed lower- and middle-class men their first opportunities for higher education.

Within two decades after World War II, the civil rights movement and President Lyndon B. Johnson's Great Society programs produced additional growth in the bureaucracy. The Equal Employment Opportunity Commission (EEOC) was created in 1965 by the Civil Rights Act of 1964. The Departments of Housing and Urban Development (HUD) and Transportation were created in 1965 and 1966, respectively. These expansions of the bureaucracy corresponded to increases in the president's power and his ability to persuade Congress that new agencies would be an effective way to solve pressing social problems.

The Modern Bureaucracy

The national government differs from private business in numerous ways. Governments exist for the public good, not to make money. Businesses are driven by a profit motive; government leaders, but not bureaucrats, are driven by reelection. Businesses get their money from customers; the national government gets its money from taxpayers. Another difference between a bureaucracy and a business is that it is difficult to determine to whom bureaucracies are responsible. Is it the president? Congress? The citizenry? Still, governments can learn much from business, and recent reform efforts have tried to apply business solutions to create a government that works better and costs less.

The different natures of government and business have a tremendous impact on the way the bureaucracy operates. Because all of the incentive in government "is in the direction of not making mistakes," public employees view risks and rewards very differently from their private-sector counterparts.[7] There is little reason for government employees to take risks or go beyond their assigned job tasks. In contrast, private employers are far more likely to reward ambition. The key to the modern bureaucracy is to understand who bureaucrats are, how the bureaucracy is organized, how organization and personnel affect each other, and how bureaucrats act within the political process. It also is key to understand that government cannot be run entirely like a business. An understanding of these facts and factors can help in the search for ways to motivate positive change in the bureaucracy.

Thinking Globally

Bureaucratic Independence in India and China

In India, the bureaucracy is considered the backbone of the country's government. It enjoys a high degree of autonomy and plays an important role in the public policy process. In contrast, China's civil servants have limited decision-making authority as the Communist Party functions as the principal policy-making organization.

- What level of independence should be extended to a government's bureaucracy? How might an independent bureaucracy facilitate the public policy process? How might it complicate it?
- Should civil service employees act as autonomous agents of government policy or as agents of the political party in power?

Who Are Bureaucrats?

Federal bureaucrats are career government employees who work in the executive branch in the Cabinet-level departments and independent agencies that comprise more than 2,000 bureaus, divisions, branches, offices, services, and other subunits of the federal government. There are more than 2.7 million federal workers in the executive branch. Nearly one-third of all civilian employees work in the U.S. Postal Service. The remaining federal civilian workers are spread out among the various executive departments and agencies throughout the United States. Most of these federal employees are paid according to what is called the "General Schedule" (GS). They advance within fifteen GS grades (as well as steps within those grades), moving into higher GS levels and salaries as their careers progress.

As a result of reforms during the Truman administration that built on the Pendleton Act, most civilian federal governmental employees today are selected by merit stan-

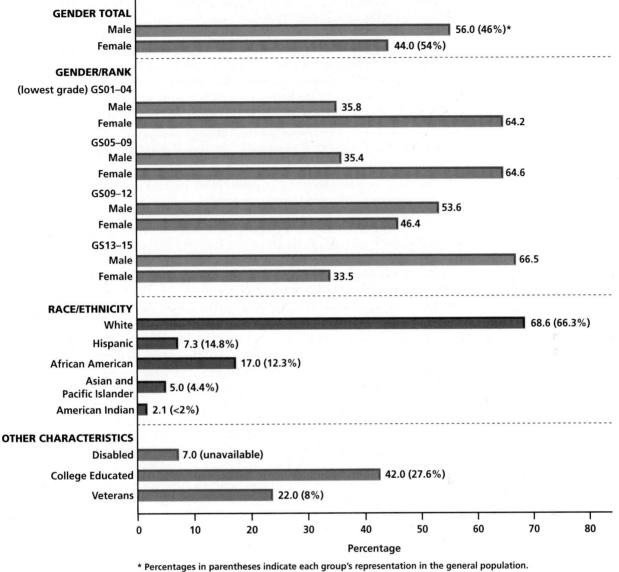

GENDER TOTAL
Male — 56.0 (46%)*
Female — 44.0 (54%)

GENDER/RANK
(lowest grade) GS01–04
Male — 35.8
Female — 64.2
GS05–09
Male — 35.4
Female — 64.6
GS09–12
Male — 53.6
Female — 46.4
GS13–15
Male — 66.5
Female — 33.5

RACE/ETHNICITY
White — 68.6 (66.3%)
Hispanic — 7.3 (14.8%)
African American — 17.0 (12.3%)
Asian and Pacific Islander — 5.0 (4.4%)
American Indian — 2.1 (<2%)

OTHER CHARACTERISTICS
Disabled — 7.0 (unavailable)
College Educated — 42.0 (27.6%)
Veterans — 22.0 (8%)

Percentage

* Percentages in parentheses indicate each group's representation in the general population.
Source: Office of Personnel Management, *2005 Fact Book*.

FIGURE 8.1 Characteristics and Rank Distribution of Federal Civilian Employees, 2004
This figure depicts the percentage of the federal civilian workforce in several categories. As you review the data displayed in the graph, consider the trends you observe across GS levels and overall.

dards, which include tests (such as civil service or foreign service exams) and educational criteria. Merit systems also protect federal employees from being fired for political reasons.

At the lower levels of the U.S. civil service, most positions are filled by competitive examinations. These usually involve a written test. Mid-level to upper ranges of federal positions do not normally require tests; instead, applicants submit resumes online. Personnel departments then evaluate potential candidates and rank candidates according to how well they fit a particular job opening. Only the names of those deemed "qualified" are then forwarded to the official filling the vacancy. This can be a time-consuming process; it often takes six to nine months before a position can be filled in this manner.

Comparing Bureaucracies

The remaining 10 percent of the federal workforce is made up of persons not covered by the civil service system. These positions generally fall into three categories:

1. *Appointive policy-making positions.* Nearly 3,000 people are presidential appointees. Some of these, including Cabinet secretaries and under- and assistant secretaries, are subject to Senate confirmation. These appointees, in turn, are responsible for appointing high-level policy-making assistants who form the top of the bureaucratic hierarchy. These are called "Schedule C" political appointees.

2. *Independent regulatory commissioners.* Although each president gets to appoint as many as one hundred commissioners, they become independent of his direct political influence once they take office.

3. *Low-level, nonpolicy patronage positions.* These types of positions generally concern secretarial assistants to policy makers.

**The Changing Face of the Federal
Bureaucracy**

More than 15,000 job skills are represented in the federal government. Government employees, whose average age is forty-seven, have an average length of service of seventeen years. They include forest rangers, FBI agents, foreign service officers, computer programmers, security guards, librarians, administrators, engineers, plumbers, lawyers, doctors, postal carriers, and zoologists, among others.

The diversity of government jobs mirrors the diversity of jobs in the private sector. The federal workforce is also diverse but under-represents African Americans and Hispanics, in particular, and the overall employment of women lags behind that of men. (To learn more about the distribution of the federal workforce, see Figure 8.1.) Women make up more than 60 percent of the lowest GS levels but have only raised their proportion of positions in the GS 13–15 ranks from 18 percent in 1990 to over 30 percent in 2004.[8]

There are about 332,500 federal workers in the nation's capital; the rest are located in regional, state, and local offices scattered throughout the country. To enhance efficiency, the United States is broken up into several regions, with most agencies having regional offices in one city in that region. (To learn more about agency regions, see Figure 8.2.) The decentralization of the bureaucracy facilitates accessibility to the public. The Social Security Administration, for example, has numerous offices so that its clients can have a place nearby to take their paperwork, questions, and problems. Decentralization also helps distribute jobs and incomes across the country.

FIGURE 8.2 Federal
**Agency Regions and City
Headquarters**

Source: Department of Health and Human
Services,
http://www.hhs.gov/images/regions.gif.

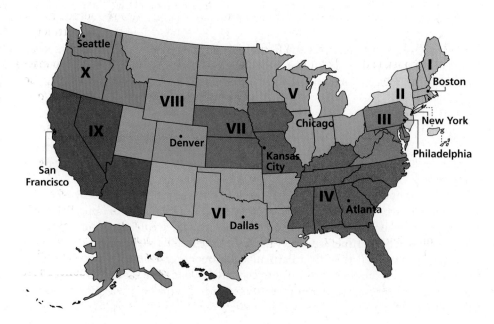

Many people complain that jobs in the federal government, especially highly skilled ones, are difficult to fill because they pay less than comparable positions in the private sector. Consequently, the military has enlisted private contractors at unprecedented rates to fill many bureaucratic positions in Iraq and other dangerous sites. Many of these private contractors are former government employees who can make much more money working for private companies. While the exact number of private contractors is unknown, it is estimated that the Bush administration added 2.4 million contractors to the existing 5.3 million contractors performing government work. This more than tripled the number of total military personnel and civil servants combined.[9]

Formal Organization

While even experts can't agree on the exact number of separate governmental agencies, commissions, and departments that make up the federal bureaucracy, there are at least 1,150 civilian agencies.[10] A distinctive feature of the executive bureaucracy is its traditional division into areas of specialization. For example, the Occupational Safety and Health Administration (OSHA) handles occupational safety, and the Department of State specializes in foreign affairs. It is not unusual, however, for more than one agency to be involved in a particular issue or for one agency to be involved in myriad issues. The vast authority and range of activities of the Department of Homeland Security are probably the best example of this phenomenon. In fact, numerous agencies often have authority in the same issue areas, making administration even more difficult. Agencies fall into four general types: (1) Cabinet departments; (2) government corporations; (3) independent executive agencies; and, (4) independent regulatory commissions.

CABINET DEPARTMENTS The fifteen Cabinet **departments** are major administrative units that have responsibility for conducting a broad area of government operations. (To learn more about the Cabinet, see The Living Constitution: Article II, Section 2, Clause 1.) Cabinet departments account for about 60 percent of the federal workforce. The vice president, the heads of all of the departments, as well as the heads of the Environmental Protection Agency (EPA), Office of Management and Budget (OMB), Office of National Drug Control Policy, the U.S. Trade Representative, and the president's chief of staff make up his formal Cabinet.

The executive branch departments depicted in Figure 8.3 are headed by Cabinet members called secretaries (except the Department of Justice, which is headed by the attorney general). The secretaries are responsible for establishing their department's general policy and overseeing its operations. As discussed in chapter 7, Cabinet secretaries are responsible directly to the president but are often viewed as having two masters—the president and those affected by their department. Cabinet secretaries also are tied to Congress, due to the appropriations process and given their discretion in implementing legislation and making rules and policy.

Although departments vary considerably in size, prestige, and power, they share certain features. Department status generally signifies a strong permanent national interest to promote a particular function. Each department covers a broad area of responsibility generally reflected by its name. Each secretary is assisted by one or more deputies or undersecretaries who take part of the administrative burden off the secretary's shoulders, as well as by several assistant secretaries who direct major programs within the department. In addition, each secretary has numerous assistants who help with planning, budgeting, personnel, legal services, public relations, and their key staff functions. Most departments are subdivided into bureaus, divisions, sections, or other smaller units, and it is at this level that the real work of each agency is done. Most departments are subdivided along functional lines, but the basis for division may be geography, work processes, or clientele. Clientele agencies are particularly subject to

departments
Major administrative unit with responsibility for a broad area of government operations. Departmental status usually indicates a permanent national interest in a particular governmental function, such as defense, commerce, or agriculture.

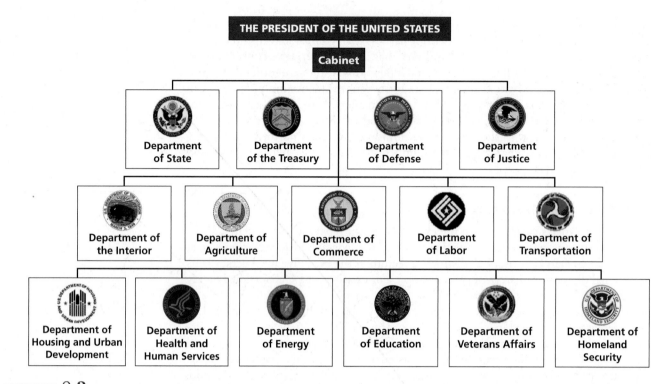

FIGURE 8.3 The Cabinet Departments

outside lobbying from organized interests in Washington. The clientele agencies and groups also are active at the regional level, where the agencies devote a substantial part of their resources to program implementation.

government corporation
Business established by Congress to perform functions that can be provided by private businesses.

GOVERNMENT CORPORATIONS **Government corporations** are the most recent addition to the bureaucracy. Dating from the early 1930s, they are businesses established by Congress to perform functions that could be provided by private businesses. The corporations are formed when the government chooses to engage in commercial activities that produce revenue, and require greater flexibility than Congress generally allows regular departments. Some of the better-known government corporations include Amtrak and the Federal Deposit Insurance Corporation (FDIC). Unlike other governmental agencies, government corporations charge for their services.

independent executive agency
Governmental unit that closely resembles a Cabinet department but has a narrower area of responsibility (such as the Central Intelligence Agency) and is not part of any Cabinet department.

INDEPENDENT EXECUTIVE AGENCIES **Independent executive agencies** closely resemble Cabinet departments but have narrower areas of responsibility. Generally speaking, independent agencies perform services rather than regulatory functions. The heads of these agencies are appointed by the president and serve, like Cabinet secretaries, at his pleasure.

Independent agencies exist apart from executive departments for practical or symbolic reasons. The National Aeronautics and Space Administration (NASA), for example, could have been placed within the Department of Defense. Such positioning, however, could have conjured up thoughts of a space program dedicated solely to military purposes, rather than to civilian satellite communication or scientific exploration. Similarly, the Environmental Protection Agency (EPA) could have been created within the Department of the Interior but instead was created as an independent agency in 1970 to administer federal programs aimed at controlling pollution and protecting the nation's environment. As an independent agency, the EPA is less indebted to the president on a day-to-day basis than it

The Living Constitution

The President . . . may require the Opinion, in writing, of the principal Officer in each of the executive Departments, upon any subject relating to the Duties of their respective Office.

—ARTICLE II, SECTION 2, CLAUSE 1

This clause, along with additional language designating that the president shall be the commander in chief, notes that the heads of departments are to serve as advisers to the president. There is no direct mention of the Cabinet in the Constitution.

This meager language is all that remains of the Framers' initial efforts to create a council to guide the president. Those in attendance at the Constitutional Convention largely favored the idea of a council but could not agree on who should be a part of that body. Some actually wanted to follow the British parliamentary model and create the Cabinet from members of the House and Senate, who would rotate into the bureaucracy; most, however, appeared to support the idea of the heads of departments along with the chief justice, who would preside when the president was unavailable. The resulting language above depicts a one-sided arrangement whereby the heads of executive departments must simply answer in writing questions put to them by the president.

The Cabinet of today differs totally from the structure envisioned by the Framers. George Washington was the first to convene a meeting of what he called his Cabinet. Some presidents have used their Cabinets as trusted advisers; others have used them to demonstrate that they are committed to political, racial, ethnic, or gender diversity, and have relied more on White House aides than particular Cabinet members. Who is included in the Cabinet, as well as how it is used, is solely up to the discretion of the sitting president with the approval of the U.S. Senate, although executive departments cannot be created or abolished without approval of both houses of Congress.

CRITICAL THINKING QUESTIONS

1. What are the advantages and disadvantages of having a Cabinet composed of heads of the departments?
2. What issues arise from requiring senatorial approval for Cabinet positions, and how does the Constitution remedy these issues?

would be if it were within a Cabinet department, although the president still has the ability to appoint its director and often intervenes on high-profile decisions.

INDEPENDENT REGULATORY COMMISSIONS Independent regulatory commissions are agencies created by Congress to exist outside the major departments to regulate a specific economic activity or interest. Because of the complexity of modern economic issues, Congress sought to create commissions that could develop expertise and provide continuity of policy with respect to economic issues because neither Congress nor the courts have the time or specific talents to do so. Examples include the National Labor Relations Board (NLRB), the Federal Reserve Board, the Federal Communications Commission (FCC), and the Securities and Exchange Commission (SEC).[11]

Older boards and commissions, such as the SEC and the Federal Reserve Board generally are charged with overseeing a certain industry. Most were created specifically to be free from partisan political pressure. Each is headed by a board composed of five to seven members (always an odd number, to avoid tie votes) who are selected by the

What do government corporations do? Workers install housing for turbines during the 1941 construction of the Tennessee Valley Authority's Cherokee Dam in Tennessee. Today, the TVA continues to provide electricity at reduced rates to millions of Americans living in Appalachia.

SIMULATION

You Are the President of MEDICORP

Photo courtesy: AP Wide World Photos

Thinking Globally

Nationalizing Venezuela's Oil Reserves

During the 1990s, Venezuela opened its economy to privatization, including the state-owned oil industry. Under President Hugo Chávez's leadership in 2007, Venezuela renationalized the nation's oil reserves, taking control of at least 60 percent of the shares in all oil operations in the country. Chávez maintains that this move ensures that the people of Venezuela profit from their nation's natural resources.

■ Are there sectors of the U.S. economy that should be controlled or managed by the government, especially in light of the recent financial crisis? Why or why not?

■ What is the proper balance between private ownership and government management of key sectors of the economy such as oil and gas production?

Hatch Act
The 1939 act to prohibit civil servants from taking activist roles in partisan campaigns. This act prohibited federal employees from making political contributions, working for a particular party, or campaigning for a particular candidate.

president and confirmed by the Senate for fixed, staggered terms to increase the chances of a bipartisan board. Unlike executive department heads, they cannot easily be removed by the president.

Newer regulatory boards are more concerned with how the business sector relates to public health and safety. The Occupational Safety and Health Administration (OSHA), for example, promotes job safety. These boards and commissions often lack autonomy and freedom from political pressures; they are generally headed by a single administrator who can be removed by the president. Thus, they are far more susceptible to the political wishes of the president who appoints them.

Government Workers and Political Involvement

As the number of federal employees and agencies grew during the 1930s, many Americans began to fear that the members of the civil service would play major roles not only in implementing public policy but also in electing members of Congress and even the president. Consequently, Congress enacted the Political Activities Act of 1939, commonly known as the **Hatch Act**, named in honor of its main sponsor, Senator Carl Hatch (D–NM). It was designed to prohibit federal employees from becoming directly involved in working for political candidates. Although this act allayed many critics' fears, other people argued that the Hatch Act was too extreme.

Today, government employees' political activities are regulated by the **Federal Employees Political Activities Act** of 1993. This liberalization of the Hatch Act allows employees to run for public office in nonpartisan elections, contribute money to political organizations, and campaign for or against candidates in partisan elections. Federal employees still, however, are prohibited from engaging in political activity while on duty, soliciting contributions from the general public, or running for office in partisan elections. (To learn more about the Federal Employees Political Activities Act, see Table 8.1.)

Photo courtesy: Karen Bleier/AFP/Getty Images

How the Bureaucracy Works

German sociologist Max Weber believed bureaucracies were a rational way for complex societies to organize themselves. Model bureaucracies, said Weber, are characterized by certain features, including:

1. A chain of command in which authority flows from top to bottom.
2. A division of labor whereby work is apportioned among specialized workers to increase productivity.

What government entity protects miners? The Mine Safety and Health Administration, part of the Department of Labor, has been responsible for protecting the safety and health of miners since 1978. A rash of mining disasters in West Virginia led to increased pressure for greater government oversight of mining companies. Here, Senator Robert Byrd (D–WV) meets with the family of Marty Bennet, one of twelve miners killed in a 2006 mine explosion.

Federal Employees Political Activities Act
The 1993 liberalization of the Hatch Act. Federal employees are now allowed to run for office in nonpartisan elections and to contribute money to campaigns in partisan elections.

TABLE 8.1 The Federal Employees Political Activities Act

Here are some examples of permissible and prohibited activities for federal employees under the Federal Employees Political Activities Act of 1993. Federal employees:

- **May** be candidates for public office in nonpartisan elections
- **May** assist in voter registration drives
- **May** express opinions about candidates and issues
- **May** contribute money to political organizations
- **May** attend political fund-raising functions
- **May** attend and be active at political rallies and meetings
- **May** join and be active members of a political party or club
- **May** sign nominating petitions
- **May** campaign for or against referendum questions, constitutional amendments, and municipal ordinances
- **May** campaign for or against candidates in partisan elections
- **May** make campaign speeches for candidates in partisan elections
- **May** distribute campaign literature in partisan elections
- **May** hold office in political clubs or parties
- **May not** use their official authority or influence to interfere with an election
- **May not** collect political contributions unless both individuals are members of the same federal labor organization or employee organization and the one solicited is not a subordinate employee
- **May not** knowingly solicit or discourage the political activity of any person who has business before the agency
- **May not** engage in political activity while on duty
- **May not** engage in political activity in any government office
- **May not** engage in political activity while wearing an official uniform
- **May not** engage in political activity while using a government vehicle
- **May not** solicit political contributions from the general public
- **May not** be candidates for public office in partisan elections

Source: U.S. Special Counsel's Office.

3. Clear lines of authority among workers and their superiors.

4. A goal orientation that determines structure, authority, and rules.

5. Impersonality, whereby all employees are treated fairly based on merit and all clients are served equally, without discrimination, according to established rules.

6. Productivity, whereby all work and actions are evaluated according to established rules.[12]

Clearly, this Weberian idea is somewhat idealistic, and even the best-run government agencies don't always work this way, but most are trying.

When Congress creates any kind of department, agency, or commission, it is actually delegating some of its powers listed in Article I, section 8, of the U.S. Constitution. Therefore, the laws creating departments, agencies, corporations, or commissions carefully describe their purpose and give them the authority to make numerous policy decisions, which have the effect of law. Congress recognizes that it does not have the time, expertise, or ability to involve itself in every detail of every program; therefore, it sets general guidelines for agency action and leaves it to the agency to work out the details. How agencies execute congressional wishes is called **implementation**, the process by which a law or policy is put into operation.

Historically, political scientists attempting to study how the bureaucracy made policy investigated what they termed **iron triangles**, a term refering to the relatively stable relationships and patterns of interaction that occurred among federal workers in agencies or departments, interest groups, and relevant congressional committees and subcommittees. (To learn more about iron triangles, see Figure 8.4.) Today, iron triangles no longer dominate most policy processes. Some do persist, however, such as the relationship between the Department of Veterans' Affairs, the House Committee on Veterans' Affairs, and the American Legion and the Veterans of Foreign Wars, the two largest veterans groups.

Many political scientists examining external influences on the modern bureaucracy prefer to examine **issue networks**. In general, issue networks, like iron triangles, include agency officials, members of Congress (and committee staffers), and interest group lobbyists. But, they also include lawyers, consultants, academics, public relations specialists, and sometimes even the courts. Unlike iron triangles, issue networks constantly are changing as members with technical expertise or newly interested parties become involved in issue areas.

As a result of the increasing complexity of many policy domains, many alliances have also been created within the bureaucracy. One such example is **interagency councils**, working groups that bring together representatives of several departments and agencies to facilitate the coordination of policy making and implementation. Depending on how well these councils are funded, they can be the prime movers of administration policy in any area where an interagency council exists. The U.S. Interagency Council on the Homeless, for example, was created in 1987 to coordinate the activities of the more than fifty governmental agencies and programs that work to alleviate homelessness.

In areas where there are extraordinarily complex policy problems, recent presidential administrations have created policy coordinating committees (PCCs) to facilitate interaction among agencies and departments at the subcabinet level. These PCCs gained increasing favor after the September 11, 2001 terrorist attacks. For example, the PCC on Terrorist Financing, which includes representatives from the Departments of Treasury, State, Defense, and Justice, along with the CIA and FBI, conducted a study that recommended to the president that he ask the Saudi government to take action against alleged terrorist financiers.[13]

implementation
The process by which a law or policy is put into operation by the bureaucracy.

iron triangle
The relatively stable relationships and patterns of interaction that occur among an agency, interest groups, and congressional committees or subcommittees.

issue network
The loose and informal relationships that exist among a large number of actors who work in broad policy areas.

interagency council
Working group created to facilitate coordination of policy making and implementation across a host of governmental agencies.

SIMULATION

You Are a Government Affairs Consultant in Texas

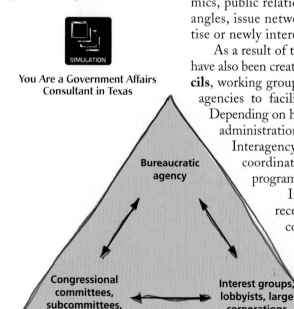

Bureaucratic agency

Congressional committees, subcommittees, and staff

Interest groups, lobbyists, large corporations

FIGURE 8.4 An Iron Triangle

Making Policy

The end product of all of these decision-making bodies is policy making. Policy making and implementation take place on both informal and formal levels. Practically, many decisions are left to individual government employees on a day-to-day basis. Department of Justice lawyers, for example, make daily decisions about whether or not to prosecute someone. Similarly, street-level Internal Revenue Service agents make many decisions during personal audits. These street-level bureaucrats make policy on two levels. First, they exercise wide discretion in decisions concerning citizens with whom they interact. Second, taken together, their individual actions add up to agency behavior.[14] Thus, how bureaucrats interpret and how they apply (or choose not to apply) various policies are equally important parts of the policy-making process.

Administrative discretion, the ability to make choices concerning the best way to implement congressional or executive intentions, also allows decision makers (whether they are in a Cabinet-level position or at the lowest GS levels) a tremendous amount of leeway. It is exercised through two formal administrative procedures: rule making and administrative adjudication.

RULE MAKING   **Rule making** is a quasi-legislative administrative process that results in regulations and has the characteristics of a legislative act. **Regulations** are the rules that govern the operation of all government programs and have the force of law. In essence, then, bureaucratic rule makers often act as lawmakers as well as law enforcers when they make rules or draft regulations to implement various congressional statutes. Some political scientists say that rule making "is the single most important function performed by agencies of government."[15]

Because regulations often involve political conflict, the 1946 Administrative Procedures Act established rule-making procedures to give everyone the chance to participate in the process. The act requires that: (1) public notice of the time, place, and nature of the rule-making proceedings be provided in the *Federal Register*; (2) interested parties be given the opportunity to submit written arguments and facts relevant to the rule; and, (3) the statutory purpose and basis of the rule be stated. Once rules are written, thirty days generally must elapse before they take effect.

Sometimes an agency is required by law to conduct a formal hearing before issuing rules. Evidence is gathered, and witnesses testify and are cross-examined by opposing interests. The process can take weeks, months, or even years, at the end of which agency administrators must review the entire record and then justify the new rules. Although cumbersome, the process has reduced criticism of some rules and bolstered the deference given by the courts to agency decisions. Many Americans are unaware of the opportunities available to them to influence government at this stage. As illustrated in Ideas into Action: Enforcing Gender Equity in College Athletics, women's groups and female athletes testified at hearings held around the country urging then Secretary of Education Roderick Paige not to revise existing Title IX regulations, although the Bush administration ultimately did.

ADMINISTRATIVE ADJUDICATION   **Administrative adjudication** is a quasi-judicial process in which a bureaucratic agency settles disputes between two parties in a manner similar to the way courts resolve disputes. Administrative adjudication is referred to as quasi judicial, because law-making by any body other than Congress or adjudication by any body other than the judiciary would be a violation of the constitutional principle of separation of powers.

Agencies regularly find that persons or businesses are not in compliance with the federal laws the agencies are charged with enforcing, or that they are in violation of an agency rule or regulation. To force compliance, some agencies resort to administrative adjudication, which generally is less formal than a trial. Several agencies and boards employ administrative law judges to conduct the hearings. Although these judges are employed by the agencies, they are strictly independent and cannot be removed except for gross misconduct.

administrative discretion
The ability of bureaucrats to make choices concerning the best way to implement congressional intentions.

rule making
A quasi-legislative administrative process that has the characteristics of a legislative act.

regulations
Rules that govern the operation of a particular government program that have the force of law.

You Are a Federal Administrator

administrative adjudication
A quasi-judicial process in which a bureaucratic agency settles disputes between two parties in a manner similar to the way courts resolve disputes.

Enforcing Gender Equity in College Athletics

During the late 1960s and early 1970s, women students at colleges and universities had few opportunities to participate in sports. To address the lack of athletic programs for women, the federal government passed Title IX of the Education Amendments Act of 1972. Title IX prohibits discrimination on the basis of sex in any education program receiving federal financial assistance. In order for a university to demonstrate compliance with the act, it must show that:

1. The university provides opportunities to women similar to the proportion of their enrollment in the student body; or
2. The university has developed programs for the underrepresented; or
3. The university has attempted to accommodate the interests of women who may want to become involved in affected programs.

By most measures, the law has achieved its goal and increased opportunities for women at educational institutions, especially in athletics. In the thirty years since the federal bureaucracy implemented Title IX, women have made significant gains in sports. By 2005, for example, there were 2.8 million girls playing high school sports, up from 294,000 in 1971. Similarly, there has been a five-fold increase in the number of women playing sports at the college level.[a]

Title IX has not gone without criticism. Some male alumni, for example, have protested when men's sports programs are cut to free up funds for athletic opportunities for women students. And, a number of federal regulations have loosened or reinterpreted Title IX. The Bush administration established a panel that held hearings on the implementation of Title IX. This panel clarified the standards for compliance with Title IX and decided that universities could demonstrate that they were meeting the needs of female students through e-mail surveys inquiring about their

Photo courtesy: Doug Mills/The New York Times

Who lobbies for Title IX enforcement? Soccer Olympian Julie Foudy joins members of the Congressional Women's Caucus to save Title IX.

interest in playing sports. Notably, the committee stated that if a student did not respond to the survey, the students would be counted as uninterested. Supporters of Title IX, however, argue that women who wish to play college sports don't simply decide to do so once they are enrolled in a university. The NCAA, too, has voiced its opposition to the survey, and through 2008, few universities have used surveys to demonstrate compliance.

- Is your college or university bound by the regulations of Title IX? Why or why not?
- How does your university demonstrate compliance with Title IX? Is this compliance consistent with what you observe on campus? In what ways?
- How might you increase awareness of women's sports programs on your campus? What assistance might you expect from the Obama administration?

[a]Katrina Vanden Heuvel, "Bush Targets Women's Sports," http://www. thenation. com/blogs/edcut/2310.

Toward Reform: Making Agencies Accountable

The question of to whom bureaucrats should be responsible is one that continually comes up in any debate about governmental accountability. Should the bureaucracy be answerable to itself? To organized interest groups? To its clientele? To the president? To Congress? Or to some combination of all of these? At times an agency becomes so removed from the public it serves that Congress must step in.

POLITICS NOW

Source: WASHINGTON POST   August 20, 2007   Page A1

The Bush Administration and Bureaucratic Control

As Democracy Push Falters, Bush Feels Like a 'Dissident'

PETER BAKER

By the time he arrived in Prague in June for a democracy conference, President Bush was frustrated. He had committed his presidency to working toward the goal of "ending tyranny in our world," yet the march of freedom seemed stalled. Just as aggravating was the sense that his own government was not committed to his vision.

As he sat down with opposition leaders from authoritarian societies around the world, he gave voice to his exasperation. "You're not the only dissident," Bush told Saad Eddin Ibrahim, a leader in the resistance to Egyptian President Hosni Mubarak. "I too am a dissident in Washington. Bureaucracy in the United States does not help change. It seems that Mubarak succeeded in brainwashing them."

If he needed more evidence, he would soon get it. In his speech that day, Bush vowed to order U.S. ambassadors in unfree nations to meet with dissidents and boasted that he had created a fund to help embattled human rights defenders. But the State Department did not send out the cable directing ambassadors to sit down with dissidents until two months later. And to this day, not a nickel has been transferred to the fund he touted.

Two and a half years after Bush pledged in his second inaugural address to spread democracy around the world, the grand project has bogged down in a bureaucratic and geopolitical morass, in the view of many activists, officials and even White House aides. Many in his administration never bought into the idea, and some undermined it, including his own vice president. The Iraq war has distracted Bush and, in some quarters, discredited his aspirations. And while he focuses his ire on bureaucracy, Bush at times has compromised the idealism of that speech in the muddy reality of guarding other U.S. interests.

Discussion Questions

1. *How does this excerpt underscore presidents' difficulties in controlling the bureaucracy?*
2. *How does the structure of the bureaucracy help or hinder policy making?*
3. *What remedies might be useful in solving the problems inherent in the U.S. bureaucracy? Consider whether particular remedies might lead to unintended consequences— would the solution create additional problems?*

Although many critics of the bureaucracy argue that federal employees should be responsive to the public interest, the public interest is difficult to define. As it turns out, several factors work to control the power of the bureaucracy, and to some degree, the same kinds of checks and balances that operate among the three branches of government serve to check the bureaucracy.

Executive Control

As the size and scope of the American national government, in general, and of the executive branch and the bureaucracy, in particular, have grown, presidents have delegated more and more power to bureaucrats. But, most presidents have continued to try to exercise some control over the bureaucracy, although they have often found that task more difficult than they first envisioned. (To learn more, see Politics Now: The Bush Administration and Bureaucratic Control.)

Recognizing these potential problems, presidents try to appoint the best possible people to carry out their wishes and policy preferences. Presidents make hundreds of appointments to the executive branch; in doing so, they have the opportunity to appoint individuals who share their views on a range of policies. Although presidential appointments make up a very small proportion of all federal jobs, presidents or the Cabinet secretaries usually fill most top policy-making positions.

Presidents, with the approval of Congress, can reorganize the bureaucracy. They also can make changes in an agency's annual budget requests and ignore legislative initiatives originating within the bureaucracy.

Join the Debate

Funding the War in Iraq

OVERVIEW: Funding and accountability are two of the issues raised by the military action and ensuing presence of the United States in Iraq. The operations of any government bureaucracy, civilian or military, depend on how much money there is to spend, the source of the money, and how the money is spent. In the federal government, the president typically proposes the amount and the source of funding, while Congress approves—perhaps with amendments and conditions—the request for funding. Then the relevant agency makes detailed spending decisions and proceeds with its operations, and Congress provides oversight to be sure the funds have been spent appropriately. The funding of the Iraq war has followed this general pattern with some important exceptions. President George W. Bush separated his requests for funding from the regular annual budgets, and the war in Iraq has been funded by borrowing money, rather than using current revenues. The Departments of Defense and State have relied very heavily on contracting with private companies for U.S. operations in Iraq, which has complicated oversight and accountability. Clearly, fundamental differences exist between the war in Iraq and the activities common to most other federal agencies. Do these differences necessitate the need for unusual funding arrangements?

When the United States began combat operations in Afghanistan in fiscal year 2002 and in Iraq in 2003, President George W. Bush made emergency requests for appropriating $18 billion and $78 billion respectively. Congress approved those requests. Although there had been planning prior to the commencement of military action, there were no requests for funding made in the regular budget process. To do so would have been highly unusual and might have compromised strategic and safety considerations about exactly when and how to begin the attacks.

As operations have continued, funding requests from the president have continued to be outside the regular budget process. Except for a slight decrease in 2004 to $74 billion, appropriations for continuing operations in Iraq and Afghanistan (funding requests since 2003 have combined the two operations) have increased steadily each year. As of March 2008, the total costs were $752 billion, with a pending request for another $101 billion. This is almost twelve times the total cost

predicted at the beginning of military action. Spending in Iraq in 2008 was at the rate of $2 billion per week. Despite these sums and the administration's intention of a long-term commitment, all funding requests were still for "emergency appropriations." Some senators and representatives in Congress sought, unsuccessfully, to amend the legislation funding operations in Iraq by requiring the administration to submit plans for withdrawing troops or by setting deadlines for cutting back on U.S. involvement.

An issue with both administrative and political implications is the source of funding. According to analyses by the Congressional Budget Office, only $16 billion (2 percent) of the money allocated for Iraq and Afghanistan comes from the regular budget of the Department of Defense. The rest is borrowed. On the one hand, this means that taxpayers currently are not sacrificing either by paying higher taxes or suffering cuts in other federal programs in order to pay for operations in Iraq and Afghanistan. However, this also means that taxpayers in the future

will have to pay the amounts borrowed, plus interest.

Congress relies on reports and evaluations prepared by members of the federal bureaucracy to oversee these expenditures. However, the extensive use of private contractors in Iraq makes oversight and accountability more challenging. Contractors have been used to provide logistical support for troops, to construct military bases and a new U.S. embassy in Iraq, to provide services to civilians, and to protect American diplomats and other officials. Using private vendors for many of the duties traditionally performed by military personnel frees soldiers for combat missions and avoids the creation of more government agencies and jobs. By 2008, the Government Accountability Office had completed over 130 studies of contracts used in operations in Iraq, frequently finding it difficult to trace where the money flowed and for what purpose it was spent. When instances of corruption or misbehavior were identified, contractors usually were not liable because they were not subject to either

U.S. domestic law or to Iraqi law. Congressional hearings and investigations began focusing on concerns about contracting in 2007, after Democrats gained control of both houses of Congress. Republicans questioned whether this was oversight or partisan posturing.

Arguments IN FAVOR of Special Arrangements for Funding the War in Iraq

- National security is essential. The need to protect the United States from acts of terrorism and aggression is so fundamental that it trumps business-as-usual procedures. The government should spend what it takes to provide for national security, and if that means borrowing money and making emergency appropriations, then that is what it must do.

- It is not possible to predict what must be spent to achieve peace and stability in various regions of the world. The planning and budgeting that federal agencies do to protect the environment, maintain transportation networks, and perform other activities are irrelevant for national security and military activities. The government must respond to threats as they emerge and to developments in countries like Iraq as they occur.

- Private companies can provide services more efficiently and less expensively than public bureaucracies, and in military situations they help soldiers focus on combat and security missions. A strength of the United States is the quality and competitiveness of its businesses. Contracts with private companies build on this strength and avoid some of the problems associated with public

bureaucracies. It is especially important to use private vendors to support military operations. The armed forces no longer rely on a draft, which means the military is leaner and must be more focused on its core mission.

Arguments AGAINST Special Arrangements for Funding the War in Iraq

- The security of the United States is not so dependent on what happens to Iraq that a blank check is justified. The justifications for attacking Iraq were based on faulty intelligence and flawed reasoning. The government must now proceed based on a plan that considers Iraq along with other national security and domestic needs. This means including funding for future operations in Iraq in the regular budget process and ending the policy of open-ended borrowing and spending.

- The future of Iraq should be determined by the people of Iraq, not the government of the United States. It is not appropriate to ask American taxpayers to fund operations that are constantly being undermined by violence among Iraqi groups and corruption among Iraqi officials. Funding should be limited and focused, and the U.S. government should let the Iraqis solve their own problems.

- Contractors operating in Iraq make huge profits and are not held accountable for their actions and expenditures. The argument that the government benefits from contracts with private companies fails to recognize that many of the most lucrative contracts were issued without a competitive bidding process. Reports by the inspectors

general of the Department of Defense and Department of State revealed performance problems and missing funds related to contracting in Iraq. Likewise, congressional investigations and reports by the Government Accountability Office cite waste and abuse.

Continuing the Debate

1. Should funding the war in Iraq be separate from the regular budget process? Should we continue to borrow money for operations in Iraq, or should we make cuts in other federal programs or raise taxes? Explain your reasoning.

2. Is it appropriate for Congress to tie funding for operations in Iraq to a requirement for preparing a withdrawal of some or all U.S. troops? Why or why not?

3. What changes do you expect the Obama administration will place on the use of private contractors in Iraq?

To Follow the Debate Online, Go To:

www.cbo.gov/ to find Congressional Budget Office analyses of funding the war in Iraq.

www. gao.gov/docsearch/ featured/oif.html, where the Governmental Accountability Office provides more than 130 reports on contracts for services and construction projects related to the war in Iraq.

www.iraqwarveterans.org, for information about support to military veterans of the Iraq War and their families and continuing U.S. efforts in Iraq.

www.mfso.org, the Web site of Military Families Speak Out, which advocates ending funding in order to halt U.S. involvement and casualties in Iraq.

executive order
Rule or regulation issued by the president that has the effect of law. All executive orders must be published in the *Federal Register*.

As discussed in chapter 7, presidents also can shape policy and provide direction to bureaucrats by issuing executive orders.[16] **Executive orders** are rules or regulations issued by the president that have the effect of law. For example, even before Congress acted to protect women from discrimination by the federal government, the National Organization for Women convinced President Lyndon B. Johnson to sign a 1967 executive order that amended an earlier one prohibiting the federal government from discriminating on the basis of race, color, religion, or national origin in the awarding of federal contracts, by adding to it the category of "gender." Although the president signed the order, the Office of Federal Contract Compliance, part of the Department of Labor's Employment Standards Administration, failed to draft appropriate guidelines for implementation of the order until several [17]

Congressional Control

Congress, too, historically has played an important role in checking the power of the bureaucracy. Constitutionally, it possesses the authority to create or abolish departments and agencies as well as to transfer agency functions, as was the case in the protracted debate over the creation of the Department of Homeland Security. In addition, it can expand or contract bureaucratic discretion and alter agency budgets. (To learn more about controversies related to funding the Iraq War, see Join the Debate: Funding the War in Iraq.) The Senate's authority to confirm (or reject) presidential appointments also gives Congress a check on the bureaucracy.

Congress uses many of its constitutional powers to exercise control over the bureaucracy. These include its investigatory powers. It is not at all unusual for a congressional committee or subcommittee to hold hearings on a particular problem and then direct the relevant agency to study the problem or find ways to remedy it. Representatives of the agencies also appear before these committees on a regular basis to inform members about agency activities and ongoing investigations.

Legislators also augment their formal oversight of the executive branch by allowing citizens to appeal adverse bureaucratic decisions to agencies, Congress, and even the courts. Congressional review, a procedure adopted by the 104th Congress, by which agency regulations can be nullified by joint resolutions of legislative disapproval, is another method of exercising congressional oversight. This form of oversight is discussed in greater detail in chapter 6.

Judicial Control

Whereas the president's and Congress's ongoing control over the actions of the bureaucracy is very direct, the judiciary's oversight function is less apparent. Still, federal judges, for example, can issue injunctions or orders to an executive agency even before a rule is promulgated formally, giving the federal judiciary a potent check on the bureaucracy.

The courts also have ruled that agencies must give all affected individuals their due process rights guaranteed by the U.S. Constitution. A Social Security recipient's checks cannot be stopped, for example, unless that individual is provided with reasonable notice and an opportunity for a hearing. On a more informal, indirect level, litigation, or even the threat of litigation, often exerts a strong influence on bureaucrats. Injured parties can bring suit against agencies for their failure to enforce a law, and can challenge agency interpretations of any law. In general, however, the courts give great weight to the opinions of bureaucrats and usually defer to their expertise.[18]

SIMULATION

You Are the Head of FEMA

The development of specialized courts, however, has altered the relationship of some agencies with the federal courts, apparently resulting in less judicial deference to agency rulings. Research by political scientists reveals that specialized courts such as the Court of International Trade, because of its jurists' expertise, defer less to agency decisions than do more generalized federal courts. Conversely, decisions from executive agencies are more likely to be reversed than those from more specialized independent regulatory commissions.[19]

WHAT SHOULD I HAVE LEARNED?

The bureaucracy plays a major role in America as a shaper of public policy, earning it the nickname the "fourth branch" of government. To explain the evolution and scope of bureaucratic power, in this chapter we have answered the following questions:

■ What are the roots of the federal bureaucracy?

The federal bureaucracy has changed dramatically since George Washington's time, when the executive branch had only three departments—State, War, and Treasury. As employment opportunities within the federal government increased, concurrent reforms in the civil service system assured that more and more jobs were filled according to merit and not by patronage. By the late 1800s, reform efforts led to further increases in the size of the bureaucracy, as independent regulatory commissions were created. In the wake of the Depression, many new agencies were created to get the national economy back on course as part of President Franklin D. Roosevelt's New Deal.

■ What are the key characteristics of the modern bureaucracy?

The modern bureaucracy is composed of more than 2.7 million civilian workers from all walks of life. In general, bureaucratic agencies fall into four categories: departments, government corporations, independent agencies, and independent regulatory commissions. The political activity of employees in the federal government is regulated by the Federal Employees Political Activities Act.

■ How does the bureaucracy work?

The bureaucracy gets much of its power from the Congress delegating its powers. A variety of formal and informal mechanisms have been created to help the bureaucracy work more efficiently. These mechanisms help the bureaucracy and bureaucrats make policy.

■ What controls are in place to make bureaucratic agencies accountable?

Agencies enjoy considerable discretion, but they are also subjected to many formal controls. The president, Congress, and the judiciary all exercise various degrees of control over the bureaucracy.

Key Terms

administrative adjudication, p. 235
administrative discretion, p. 235
bureaucracy, p. 222
civil service system, p. 224
department, p. 229
executive order, p. 240
Federal Employees Political Activities
    Act, p. 233

government corporation, p. 230
Hatch Act, p. 232
implementation, p. 234
independent executive agency, p. 230
independent regulatory commission,
    p. 224
interagency council, p. 234
iron triangle, p. 234

issue network, p. 234
merit system, p. 224
patronage, p. 224
Pendleton Act, p. 224
regulation, p. 235
rule making, p. 235
spoils system, p. 224

Researching the Executive Branch and the Federal Bureaucracy

In the Library

Aberbach, Joel D., and Bert A. Rockman. *In the Web of Politics: Three Decades of the U.S. Federal Executive*. Washington, DC: Brookings Institution, 2000.

Borrelli, MaryAnne. *The President's Cabinet: Gender, Power, and Representation*. Boulder, CO: Lynne Rienner, 2002.

Brehm, John, and Scott Gates. *Working, Shirking, and Sabotage: Bureaucratic Response to a Democratic Public*. Ann Arbor: University of Michigan Press, 1997.

Dolan, Julie A., and David H. Rosenbloom. *Representative Bureaucracy: Classic Readings and Continuing Controversies*. Armonk, NY: M. E. Sharpe, 2003.

Felbinger, Claire L., and Wendy A. Haynes, eds. *Outstanding Women in Public Administration: Leaders, Mentors, and Pioneers*. Armonk, NY: M. E. Sharpe, 2004.

Goodsell, Charles T. *The Case for Bureaucracy: A Public Administration Polemic*, 4th ed. Washington, DC: CQ Press, 2003.

Gormley, William T., and Steven J. Balla. *Bureaucracy and Democracy: Accountability and Perform*, 2nd ed. Washington, DC: CQ Press, 2007.

Ingraham, Patricia Wallace. *The Foundation of Merit: Public Service in American Democracy*. Baltimore, MD: Johns Hopkins University Press, 1995.

Ingraham, Patricia Wallace, and Laurence E. Lynn Jr. *The Art of Governance: Analyzing Management and Administration*. Washington, DC: Georgetown University Press, 2004.

Kerwin, Cornelius M. *Rulemaking: How Government Agencies Write Law and Make Policy*, 3rd ed. Washington, DC: CQ Press, 2003.

Meier, Kenneth J., and John Bohte. *Politics and the Bureaucracy*, 5th ed. Belmont, CA: Wadsworth, 2006.

Nigro, Lloyd G. et al. *The New Public Personnel Administration*, 6th ed. Belmont, CA: Wadsworth, 2006.

Peters, B. Guy. *The Politics of Bureaucracy*, 5th ed. New York: Routledge, 2001.

Richardson, William D. *Democracy, Bureaucracy and Character*. Lawrence: University Press of Kansas, 1997.

Stivers, Camilla. *Gender Images in Public Administration: Legitimacy and the Administrative State*, 2nd ed. Thousand Oaks, CA: Sage, 2002.

Twight, Charlotte. *Dependent on DC: The Rise of Federal Control over the Lives of Ordinary Americans*. New York: Palgrave Macmillan, 2002.

Wilson, James Q. *Bureaucracy: What Government Agencies Do and Why They Do It*, reprint ed. New York: Basic Books, 2000.

On the Web

To learn more about federal employees go to the Office of Personnel Management Web site at **www. opm.gov** or to the page listing demographic information, **www.opm.gov/feddata/factbook**. What percentage of federal employees share your gender? Your racial and ethnic background?

To learn more about rules, proposed rules, and notices of federal agencies and organizations, go to the home page for the *Federal Register* at **www.gpoaccess.gov/fr/index. html**.

To learn more about the Government Accountability Office, go to **www.gao.gov**. What resources are available to Congress? To the media? To the general public?

To learn more about the Congressional Budget Office, **www.cbo.gov**. How does the information on the CBO site differ from the information on the GAO site? After comparing information about the missions of both organizations, do you consider one or the other more important to the efficient, transparent functioning of the bureaucracy?

The Judiciary

The nine justices of the U.S. Supreme Court must work together to reach consensus on which cases to hear, how opinions are written, and ultimately, what precedents are established. Therefore, changing one or two justices on a nine-person court can have an important impact on the direction of the Court's decisions. In a body as closely divided as recent Courts, these changes can be particularly significant.

Thus, when Chief Justice John G. Roberts Jr. and Justice Samuel A. Alito Jr. were confirmed by the Senate to join the Court during its 2005–2006 term, many Court watchers began to speculate about how the Court's decisions would change. Most observers expected that with the addition of Roberts and Alito, the Court would become more conservative than the earlier Court led by Chief Justice William H. Rehnquist.

Roberts and Alito's first full term on the Court appeared to validate the speculation of Court watchers. The nation's highest court seemed increasingly conservative. Among other decisions, the Roberts Court upheld the first federal restriction on abortion procedures, limited employees' ability to sue for employment discrimination, and allowed school officials to limit speech that appeared to advocate

9

■ **The Supreme Court's power has increased markedly since the Founding of the United States.** At left, the Warren Court (1953-1969), pictured here in 1953, greatly expanded civil rights and liberties as well as the power of the federal government and the judiciary. At right, justices attend the funeral of Chief Justice William H. Rehnquist.

drug use. All of these decisions—and a full one-third of those handed down by the Court during its 2006–2007 term—were decided by a 5–4 margin.[1] Conservative Justices Antonin Scalia, Clarence Thomas, and Anthony Kennedy joined Roberts and Alito in opposing the liberal bloc of Justices John Paul Stevens, David Souter, Stephen Breyer, and Ruth Bader Ginsburg.

During the Roberts Court's second full term, however, the Court seemed to step back from the conservative rulings of the previous term. Although the Court handed down a significant victory for conservative gun rights advocates, the liberal bloc won major victories in a wide range of issue areas, including criminal rights, presidential power, and employment discrimination. More surprisingly, the deep divisions that marked the Roberts Court's first term were often absent. Many of the Court's major decisions were decided by 6–3 or even 7–2 margins.[2]

Thus, two full terms into the Roberts Court, observers were still struggling to define the difference that Chief Justice Roberts and Justice Alito have made on the decisions of the Supreme Court. Chief Justice Roberts's effect on the number and kinds of cases heard by the Court, on the other hand, is much clearer.

WHAT SHOULD I KNOW ABOUT . . .

- the roots of the federal judiciary?
- the American legal system?
- the federal court system?
- the selection of federal court judges?
- the Supreme Court today?
- judicial philosophy and decision making?
- the judiciary's power to affect policy?

245

During the 2006–2007 term, the Roberts Court decided only seventy-five cases. In 2007–2008, the Court decided seventy-four cases. These numbers are the lowest since 1953, when the Court was asked to hear about half as many cases as today.[3] They represent a significant reduction in the activity of the Court and suggest that the justices may be struggling to agree on which cases are most important. (As discussed later in this chapter, for the Court to hear a case, four justices must agree that it presents an important legal question.)

The issues addressed by these cases are also drastically different from those that were the focus of much of the work of the Rehnquist Court. While the Rehnquist Court favored cases on issues such as federalism and the Fourth Amendment, the Roberts Court seems to be focusing on topics such as discrimination, sentencing, and *habeas corpus*, going head to head with the Bush administration to come out against its use of war powers to justify the curtailment of the rights of prisoners at Guantanamo Bay.

It is clearly too early to completely understand the direction of the Court under Chief Justice Roberts. But, leaders from John Marshall to Earl Warren to Rehnquist have demonstrated the inherent power that comes with the office of chief justice of the United States. These officials and their associate justices have led the country through significant periods of political and legal change. In so doing, they have carved a significant role for the Supreme Court in the American policy-making process.

TO LEARN MORE—
—TO DO MORE

To learn more about the activities and justices of the Roberts Court, visit the Web site of the Supreme Court of the United States at www.supremecourtus.gov.

In 1787, when Alexander Hamilton wrote articles urging support for the U.S. Constitution, he firmly believed that the judiciary would prove to be the weakest of the three departments of government. In its formative years, the judiciary was, in Hamilton's words, "the least dangerous" branch. The judicial branch seemed so inconsequential that when the young national government made its move to the District of Columbia in 1800, Congress actually forgot to include any space to house the justices of the Supreme Court!

Today, the role of the courts, particularly the Supreme Court of the United States, is significantly different from that envisioned when the national government came into being. The "least dangerous branch" now is perceived by many as having too much power.

In this chapter, we will first look at the roots of the federal judiciary. After considering the American legal system and the concepts of civil and criminal law, we will discuss the federal court system composed of specialized courts, district courts, courts of appeals, and the Supreme Court, which is the ultimate authority on all federal law. Then, we will examine how federal court judges are selected. All appointments to the federal district courts, courts of appeals, and the Supreme Court are made by the president and are subject to Senate confirmation. Our study of the Supreme Court today will make clear that only a few of the millions of cases filed in courts around the United States every year eventually make their way to the Supreme Court through the lengthy appellate process. After an examination of judicial philosophy and decision making and how judicial decision making is based on a variety of legal and extra-legal factors, we will discuss reform efforts and judicial policy making and implementation.

A note on terminology: When we refer to the "Supreme Court," the "Court," or the "high Court" here, we always mean the U.S. Supreme Court, which sits at the pinnacle of the federal and state court systems. The Supreme Court is referred to by the name of the chief justice who presided over it during a particular period. For example, the Marshall Court is the Court presided over by John Marshall from 1801 to 1835, and the Roberts Court is the current Court that began in late 2005. When we use the term "courts," we refer to all federal or state courts unless otherwise noted.

Roots of the Federal Judiciary

Comparing Judicial Systems

The detailed notes James Madison took at the Constitutional Convention in Philadelphia make it clear that the Framers devoted little time to writing Article III, which created the judicial branch of government. The Framers believed that a federal judiciary posed little threat of tyranny. Anti-Federalists, however, objected to a judiciary whose members had life tenure and the ability to define "the supreme law of the land."

As discussed in chapter 2, the Framers also debated the need for any federal courts below the Supreme Court. Some argued in favor of deciding all cases in state courts, with only appeals going before the Supreme Court. Others argued for a system of federal courts. A compromise left the final choice to Congress, and Article III, section 1, begins simply by vesting "The judicial Power of the United States . . . in one supreme Court, and in such inferior Courts as the Congress may from time to time ordain and establish."

Article III, section 2 specifies the judicial power of the Supreme Court (To learn more about the Court's jurisdiction, see Table 9.1) and discusses the Court's original and appellate jurisdiction. This section also specifies that all federal crimes, except those involving impeachment, shall be tried by jury in the state in which the crime was committed. The third section of the article defines treason, and mandates that at least two witnesses appear in such cases.

Had the Supreme Court been viewed as the potential policy maker it is today, it is highly unlikely that the Framers would have provided for life tenure with "good behavior" for all federal judges in Article III. This feature was agreed on because the Framers did not want the justices (or any federal judges) subject to the whims of politics, the public, or politicians. Moreover, Alexander Hamilton argued in *Federalist No. 78* that the "independence of judges" was needed "to guard the Constitution and the rights of individuals." (To learn more about Article III and judicial compensation, see The Living Constitution: Article III, Section 1.)

TABLE 9.1 The Judicial Power of the United States Supreme Court

The following are the types of cases the Supreme Court was given the jurisdiction to hear as initially specified in Article III, section 2, of the Constitution:
- All cases arising under the Constitution and laws or treaties of the United States
- All cases of admiralty or maritime jurisdiction
- Cases in which the United States is a party
- Controversies between a state and citizens of another state (later modified by the Eleventh Amendment)
- Controversies between two or more states
- Controversies between citizens of different states
- Controversies between citizens of the same states claiming lands under grants in different states
- Controversies between a state, or the citizens thereof, and foreign states or citizens thereof
- All cases affecting ambassadors or other public ministers

The Living Constitution

The Judges both of the supreme and inferior Courts, shall . . . receive for their services, a compensation, which shall not be diminished during their continuance in office.

—ARTICLE III, SECTION 1

This section of Article III guarantees that the salaries of all federal judges will not be reduced during their service on the bench. During the Constitutional Convention, there was considerable debate over how to treat the payment of federal judges. Some believed that Congress should have an extra check on the judiciary by being able to reduce their salaries. This provision was a compromise after James Madison suggested that Congress have the authority to bar increases as well as decreases in the salaries of these unelected jurists. The delegates recognized that decreases, as well as no opportunity for raises, could negatively affect the perks associated with life tenure.

There has not been much controversy over this clause of the Constitution. When the federal income tax was first enacted, some judges unsuccessfully challenged it as a diminution of their salaries. Much more recently, Chief Justices William H. Rehnquist and John G. Roberts Jr. have repeatedly urged Congress to increase salaries for federal judges. As early as 1989, Rehnquist noted that "judicial salaries are the single greatest problem facing the federal judiciary today." Roberts, in his first state of the judiciary message, pointed out that the comparatively low salaries earned by federal judges drive away many well-qualified and diverse lawyers, compromising the independence of the American judiciary.

More and more federal judges are leaving the bench for more lucrative private practice. While a salary of $217,400 (for the chief justice) or $208,100 (for the other justices) may sound like a lot to most people, lawyers in large urban practices routinely earn more than double and triple that amount annually. Supreme Court clerks, moreover, now regularly receive $200,000 signing bonuses (in addition to large salaries) from law firms anxious to pay for their expertise.

CRITICAL THINKING QUESTIONS

1. What other checks on judicial power does Congress have?
2. Do you agree with Chief Justice Roberts's contention that judges are underpaid? Why or why not?

Some checks on the power of the judiciary were nonetheless included in the Constitution. The Constitution gives Congress the authority to alter the Court's jurisdiction (its ability to hear certain kinds of cases). Congress can also propose constitutional amendments that, if ratified, can effectively reverse judicial decisions, and it can impeach and remove federal judges. In one further check, it is the president who, with the "advice and consent" of the Senate, appoints all federal judges. (To learn more, see Join the Debate: Senate Advice and Consent on Judicial Nominations.)

The Court can, in turn, check the presidency by presiding over presidential impeachment. Article I, section 3, notes in discussing impeachment, "When the President of the United States is tried, the Chief Justice shall preside."

judicial review
Power of the courts to review acts of other branches of government and the states.

The Constitution, however, is silent on the Court's power of **judicial review**, which allows the judiciary to review acts of the other branches of government and the state. This question was not resolved until *Marbury* v. *Madison* (1803),[4] regarding acts of the national government, and *Martin* v. *Hunter's Lessee* (1816), regarding state law.[5]

The Judiciary Act of 1789 and the Creation of the Federal Judicial System

In spite of the Framers' intentions, the pervasive role of politics in the judicial branch quickly became evident with the passage of the Judiciary Act of 1789. Congress spent nearly the entire second half of its first session deliberating the various provisions of the act to give form and substance to the federal judiciary.

The **Judiciary Act of 1789** established the basic three-tiered structure of the federal court system. At the bottom are the federal district courts—at least one in each state. If the people participating in a lawsuit (called litigants) are unhappy with the district court's verdict, they can appeal their case to one of three circuit courts. Each circuit court, initially created to function as a trial court for important cases, was composed of one district court judge and two itinerant Supreme Court justices who met as a circuit court twice a year. It wasn't until 1891 that circuit courts (or, as we know them today, courts of appeals) took on their exclusively appellate function. The third tier of the federal judicial system created by the Judiciary Act of 1789 was the Supreme Court of the United States. Although the Constitution mentions "the supreme Court," it was silent on its size. In the Judiciary Act, Congress set the size of the Supreme Court at six—the chief justice plus five associate justices. After being reduced to five members in 1801, it later expanded and contracted, and finally the Court's size was fixed at nine in 1869.

The first session of the Court—presided over by John Jay, who was appointed chief justice of the United States by George Washington—initially had to be adjourned when less than half the justices attended. Later, once a sufficient number of justices assembled, the Court decided only one major case—*Chisholm* v. *Georgia* (1793). Moreover, as an indication of its lowly status, one associate justice left the Court to become chief justice of the South Carolina Supreme Court.

Thinking Globally
Judicial Review in Great Britain

The process of judicial review in Great Britain is less than fifty years old. It consists of a review by courts of the legality (not constitutionality) of a decision by an administrative authority. For example, an action by the Prime Minister may be negated if it is illegal, irrational, or involves a procedural impropriety.

- How important is judicial review to the governing process? Is it surprising that a country such as Great Britain only recently adopted the power of judicial review?
- Does the power of judicial review give the courts too much power? Why or why not?

Judiciary Act of 1789
Established the basic three-tiered structure of the federal court system.

Photo courtesy: Architect of the U.S. Capitol

Where did the Supreme Court hear cases in the eighteenth and nineteenth centuries? From 1819 to 1860, the Supreme Court met in this small room in the basement of the U.S. Capitol building. It is now known as the "Old Supreme Court Chamber." This was far from its only meeting place, however. The Supreme Court first met on February 1, 1790, in the Merchants Exchange Building in New York City. When the nation's capital moved to Philadelphia in 1790, the Court moved with it, establishing chambers first in the state house (Independence Hall) and later in City Hall. After the federal government established Washington, D.C., as the permanent capital in 1800, the Court changed its meeting place a half-dozen times before it moved into its own building in 1935.

Join the Debate

Senate Advice and Consent
On Judicial Nominations

OVERVIEW: Article II of the Constitution gives the president sole authority to make judicial and executive appointments, and it gives the Senate the power to confirm the chief executive's choices. Article I of the Constitution gives the Senate authority to determine its own rules including procedural devices such as the filibuster to slow or stop legislative and political action. Any senator can use the filibuster to delay a vote on a political nominee. A two-thirds majority vote is needed to invoke cloture, thereby ending the filibuster, while only a simple majority (50 percent plus one) is needed to confirm a nominee. Historically, the Senate generally has confirmed the president's nominees, and it was only in 1955 that the tradition of judicial appointees regularly appearing before the Senate Judiciary Committee began (the first potential justice to appear before the Senate did so in 1916). The Senate generally has played a narrow role in the confirmation process and usually has deferred to the president's wishes. Precedent for filibustering Supreme Court nominees, however, was set in 1968 when President Lyndon B. Johnson's choice for chief justice, Abe Fortas, was blocked by the Republican minority. But it was with the controversial Supreme Court nomination of Judge Robert H. Bork in 1987 that confirmation politics took a contentious turn. The Senate voted against Bork's nomination after unprecedented pressure from civil and women's rights groups who believed his conservative judicial views would roll back civil liberties protections.

Senate Democrats, while in the minority in 2005 and 2006, argued that the use of the filibuster is necessary to help moderate the ideological make-up of the federal bench, noting that Republicans made similar arguments when they were in the minority and opposed some of former President Bill Clinton's judicial nominees. During this time, the Senate's Republican majority threatened to use the somewhat arcane rules of the chamber to bar filibusters on judicial nominations. Those opposed to judicial filibusters argue that the minority party has no right to thwart the majority's constitutional advice and consent role. They argue that the Constitution

requires a simple majority to confirm nominees—the Constitution is explicit when it requires a two-thirds or three-quarters supermajority vote—and judicial filibusters have the effect of denying the Senate majority its right to exercise consent.

Arguments AGAINST Allowing Filibusters in the Senate's Confirmation Process

- Article II of the Constitution gives the president sole authority to make judicial nominations. Some scholars argue that the president has full power over the nomination process. The Senate's role is merely to provide

advice and consent on already chosen nominees with a vote approving or blocking a nominee

- There is nothing in the Constitution creating or giving protection to judicial filibusters. Article I, section 5, gives each chamber the authority to determine its own rules of procedure by a simple majority vote. If the Senate, in order to change with the times, wishes to abolish the filibuster, it has the full authority of the Constitution behind it.

- The Constitution's Framers intended only a simple majority vote for the advice and consent clause. Alexander Hamilton explains in *Federalist Nos. 76* and *77* that the advice and

In its first decade, the Court took several actions to mold the new nation. First, by declining to give George Washington advice on the legality of some of his actions, the justices attempted to establish the Supreme Court as an independent, nonpolitical branch of government. The early Court also tried to advance principles

consent function would be exercised "by the whole body, by [the] entire branch of the legislature." That is, the advice and consent would reflect the majority's will. A faction should not be allowed to thwart a legitimate majority's will.

Arguments IN FAVOR of Filibusters in the Senate's Confirmation Process

■ **Filibusters are necessary to maintain the ideological balance of the federal courts.** Filibusters on judicial nominees allow the minority party to check a president's attempt to stack the judiciary with members espousing one political philosophy. Maintaining ideological diversity will allow different constitutional interpretations and understandings, thus adding depth to our knowledge of constitutional jurisprudence.

■ **The Framers intended for the Senate to be a deliberative body.** The Constitution's writers intended for Senate debate to be slow, deliberate, and reasoned. The idea was to create a small legislative body in which all views would be aired in the marketplace of ideas. The filibuster keeps the debate open. Besides, if two-thirds of the Senate support cloture, the filibuster ends.

How far should the Senate go in blocking a president's judicial nominees? President George W. Bush meets with conservative judge Priscilla Owen at the White House. It took more than four years to confirm Owen to a position on the Fifth Circuit Court of Appeals.

■ **Senate rules benefit both political parties and their partisans.** No party remains in the majority forever. History shows that both parties spend significant time in both majority and minority status. Altering the rules to suit partisan politics practically ensures that minority party members will engage in the same tactics and politics once they regain majority standing and the cycle of bitter partisan politics will continue.

Continuing the Debate

1. Should a dedicated minority be able to delay the will of the majority? Why or why not?
2. Should a president strive to place nonpartisan judges on the federal bench? Why or why not?

To Follow the Debate Online, Go To:

www.senate.gov/reference/ reference_index_subjects/Filibuster_vrd. htm, where the Senate provides a link to several reports on the use and implications of the filibuster.

www.civilrights.org/issues/nominations, a Web site developed by coalition of over 180 civil rights groups to advocate for a number of issues, including the preservation of the filibuster rule in the Senate as a way of preventing a president from appointing judges opposed to civil rights.

www.committeeforjustice.org, which favors the appointment of conservative judges and argues for changing Senate rules so that the filibuster rule no longer would apply to the confirmation of judicial nominees.

Photo courtesy: J. Scott Applewhite/AP Wide World Photos

of nationalism and to maintain the national government's supremacy over the states. Finally, in a series of circuit and Supreme Court decisions, the justices paved the way for announcement of the doctrine of judicial review by the third chief justice, John Marshall.

Timeline: The Development of the Supreme Court

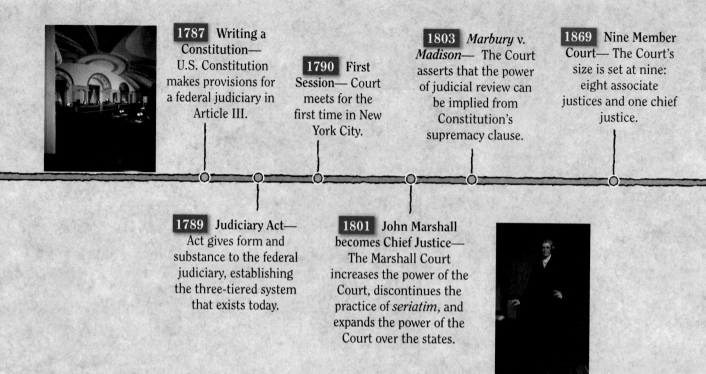

1787 Writing a Constitution— U.S. Constitution makes provisions for a federal judiciary in Article III.

1790 First Session— Court meets for the first time in New York City.

1803 *Marbury* v. *Madison*— The Court asserts that the power of judicial review can be implied from Constitution's supremacy clause.

1869 Nine Member Court— The Court's size is set at nine: eight associate justices and one chief justice.

1789 Judiciary Act— Act gives form and substance to the federal judiciary, establishing the three-tiered system that exists today.

1801 John Marshall becomes Chief Justice— The Marshall Court increases the power of the Court, discontinues the practice of *seriatim*, and expands the power of the Court over the states.

The Marshall Court: *Marbury* v. *Madison* (1803) and Judicial Review

Chief Justices of the Supreme Court

John Marshall was appointed chief justice by President John Adams in 1801, three years after he declined to accept a nomination as associate justice. An ardent Federalist, Marshall is considered the most important justice to serve on the high Court. Part of his reputation is the result of the duration of his service and the historical significance of this period in our nation's history.

As chief justice, Marshall helped to establish the Court as a co-equal branch of government. He began the practice of issuing opinions on behalf of the Court so that the justices would speak as a court and not as six individuals. example, discontinued the practice of *seriatim* (Latin for "in a series") opinions, which was the custom of the King's Bench in Great Britain. Prior to the Marshall Court, the justices delivered their individual opinions in order. For the Court to take its place as an equal branch of government, Marshall believed, the justices needed to speak as a Court and not as six individuals. In fact, during Marshall's first four years in office, the Court routinely spoke as one, and the chief justice wrote twenty-four of its twenty-six opinions.

The Marshall Court also established the authority of the Supreme Court over the judiciaries of the various states.[6] In addition, the Court established the supremacy of the federal government and Congress over state governments through a broad interpretation of the necessary and proper clause in *McCulloch* v. *Maryland* (1819), discussed in detail in chapter 3.[7]

Marshall also claimed the right of judicial review, from which the Supreme Court derives much of its day-to-day power and impact on the policy process. This established the Court as the final arbiter of constitutional questions, with the right to declare congressional acts void.[8]

Alexander Hamilton first publicly endorsed the idea of judicial review in *Federalist No. 78*, noting, "Whenever a particular statute contravenes the Constitution, it will be the duty of the judicial tribunals to adhere to the latter and disregard the former." Nonetheless, because judicial review is not mentioned in the U.S. Con-

Marbury v. Madison (1803)
Case in which the Supreme Court first asserted the power of judicial review by finding that the congressional statute extending the Court's original jurisdiction was unconstitutional.

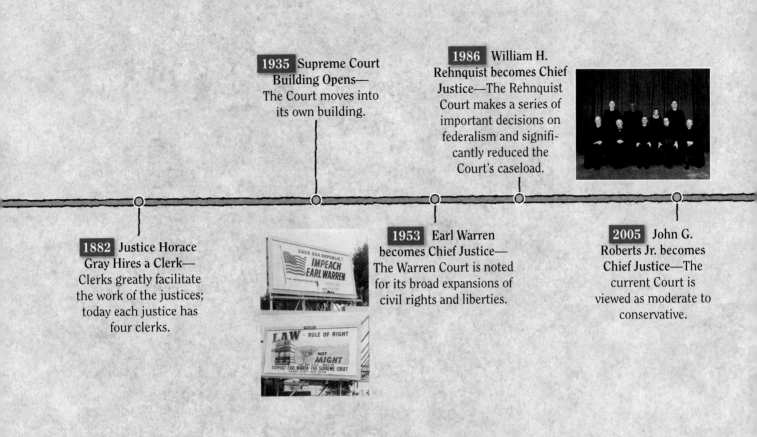

1935 Supreme Court Building Opens— The Court moves into its own building.

1986 William H. Rehnquist becomes Chief Justice—The Rehnquist Court makes a series of important decisions on federalism and significantly reduced the Court's caseload.

1882 Justice Horace Gray Hires a Clerk— Clerks greatly facilitate the work of the justices; today each justice has four clerks.

1953 Earl Warren becomes Chief Justice— The Warren Court is noted for its broad expansions of civil rights and liberties.

2005 John G. Roberts Jr. becomes Chief Justice—The current Court is viewed as moderate to conservative.

stitution, the actual authority of the Supreme Court to review the constitutionality of acts of Congress was an unsettled question. But, in *Marbury* v. *Madison* **(1803)**, Chief Justice John Marshall claimed this sweeping authority for the Court by asserting that the right of judicial review could be implied from the Constitution's supremacy clause.[9]

Marbury v. *Madison* arose amid a sea of political controversy. In the final hours of the Adams administration, William Marbury was appointed a justice of the peace for the District of Columbia. But, in the confusion of winding up matters, Adams's secretary of state failed to deliver Marbury's commission. Marbury then asked James Madison, Thomas Jefferson's secretary of state, for the commission. Under direct orders from Jefferson, who was irate over the Adams administration's last-minute appointment of several Federalist judges (quickly confirmed by the Federalist Senate), Madison refused to turn over the commission. Marbury and three other Adams appointees who were in the same situation then filed a writ of *mandamus* (a legal motion) asking the Supreme Court to order Madison to deliver their commissions.

Photo courtesy: Boston Athenaeum

Who was John Marshall? A single person can make a major difference in the development of an institution. Such was the case with John Marshall (1755–1835), who dominated the Supreme Court during his thirty-four years as chief justice. More of a politician than a lawyer, Marshall served as a delegate to the Virginia legislature and played an instrumental role in Virginia's ratification of the U.S. Constitution in 1787. He became secretary of state in 1800 under John Adams. When Oliver Ellsworth resigned as chief justice of the United States in 1800, Adams nominated Marshall. Marshall served on the Court until the day he died, participating in more than 1,000 decisions and authoring more than 500 opinions.

Political tensions ran high as the Court met to hear the case. Jefferson threatened to ignore any order of the Court. Marshall realized that he and the prestige of the Court could be devastated by any refusal of the executive branch to comply with the decision. Responding to this challenge, in a brilliant opinion that in many sections reads more like a lecture to Jefferson than a discussion of the merits of Marbury's claim, Marshall concluded that although Marbury and the others were entitled to their commissions, the Court lacked the power to issue the writ sought by Marbury. In *Marbury* v. *Madison*, Marshall further ruled that the parts of the Judiciary Act of 1789 that extended the original jurisdiction of the Court to allow it to issue writs were inconsistent with the Constitution and therefore unconstitutional.

Although the immediate effect of the decision was to deny power to the Court, its long-term effect was to establish the implied power of judicial review. Said Marshall, writing for the Court, "it is emphatically the province and duty of the judicial department to say what the law is." Since *Marbury*, the Court has routinely exercised the power of judicial review to determine the constitutionality of acts of Congress, the executive branch, and the states.

The American Legal System

The judicial system in the United States can best be described as a dual system consisting of the federal court system and the judicial systems of the fifty states, as illustrated in Figure 9.1. Cases may arise in either system. Both systems are basically three-tiered. At the bottom of the system are **trial courts**, where litigation begins. In the middle are appellate courts in the state systems and the courts of appeals in the federal system. At the top of each pyramid sits a court of last resort. The federal courts of appeals and Supreme Court as well as state courts of appeals and supreme courts are **appellate courts** that, with few exceptions, review on appeal only cases that already have been decided in lower courts. These courts generally hear matters of both civil and criminal law.

Jurisdiction

Before a state or federal court can hear a case, it must have **jurisdiction**, the authority to hear and decide the issues in that case. The jurisdiction of the federal courts is controlled by the U.S. Constitution and by statute. Jurisdiction is conferred based on issues, the amount of money involved in a dispute, or the type of offense. Procedurally, we speak of two types of jurisdiction: original and appellate. **Original jurisdiction** refers to a court's authority to hear disputes as a trial court and may occur on the federal or state level. For example, the child custody case between Britney Spears and Kevin Federline began in a California state trial court of original jurisdiction. In contrast, the legal battle over the constitutionality of the federal Partial Birth Abortion Ban Act began in several federal district courts. More than 90 percent of all cases, whether state or federal, end in a court of original jurisdiction. **Appellate jurisdiction** refers to a court's ability to review cases already decided by a trial court. Appellate courts ordinarily do not review the factual record. Instead, they review legal procedures to make certain that the law was applied properly to the issues presented in the case.

Criminal and Civil Law

Criminal law is the body of law that regulates individual conduct and is enforced by the state and national governments.[10] Crimes are graded as felonies, misdemeanors, or offenses, according to their severity. Some acts—for example, murder, rape, and robbery—are considered crimes in all states. Although all states outlaw murder, their

trial court
Court of original jurisdiction where cases begin.

appellate court
Court that generally reviews only findings of law made by lower courts.

jurisdiction
Authority vested in a particular court to hear and decide the issues in any particular case.

original jurisdiction
The jurisdiction of courts that hear a case first, usually in a trial. These courts determine the facts of a case.

appellate jurisdiction
The power vested in particular courts to review and/or revise the decision of a lower court.

criminal law
Codes of behavior related to the protection of property and individual safety.

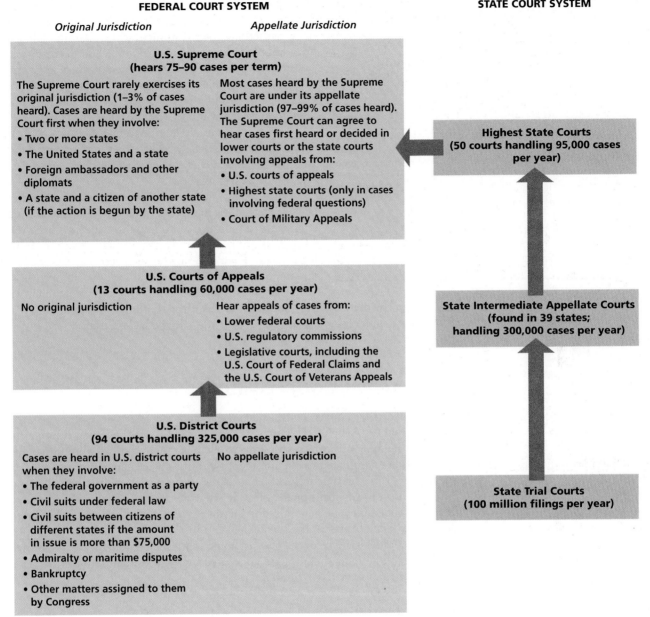

FEDERAL COURT SYSTEM

Original Jurisdiction   *Appellate Jurisdiction*

STATE COURT SYSTEM

U.S. Supreme Court
(hears 75–90 cases per term)

The Supreme Court rarely exercises its original jurisdiction (1–3% of cases heard). Cases are heard by the Supreme Court first when they involve:
• Two or more states
• The United States and a state
• Foreign ambassadors and other diplomats
• A state and a citizen of another state (if the action is begun by the state)

Most cases heard by the Supreme Court are under its appellate jurisdiction (97–99% of cases heard). The Supreme Court can agree to hear cases first heard or decided in lower courts or the state courts involving appeals from:
• U.S. courts of appeals
• Highest state courts (only in cases involving federal questions)
• Court of Military Appeals

Highest State Courts
(50 courts handling 95,000 cases per year)

U.S. Courts of Appeals
(13 courts handling 60,000 cases per year)

No original jurisdiction

Hear appeals of cases from:
• Lower federal courts
• U.S. regulatory commissions
• Legislative courts, including the U.S. Court of Federal Claims and the U.S. Court of Veterans Appeals

State Intermediate Appellate Courts
(found in 39 states; handling 300,000 cases per year)

U.S. District Courts
(94 courts handling 325,000 cases per year)

Cases are heard in U.S. district courts when they involve:
• The federal government as a party
• Civil suits under federal law
• Civil suits between citizens of different states if the amount in issue is more than $75,000
• Admiralty or maritime disputes
• Bankruptcy
• Other matters assigned to them by Congress

No appellate jurisdiction

State Trial Courts
(100 million filings per year)

FIGURE 9.1 The Dual Structure of the American Court System

penal, or criminal, codes treat the crime quite differently; some states, for example, allow the death penalty for murder, while others prohibit the use of capital punishment. Other practices—such as gambling—are illegal only in some states.

Criminal law assumes that society itself is the victim of the illegal act; therefore, the government prosecutes, or brings an action, on behalf of an injured party (acting as a plaintiff) in criminal but not civil cases. Criminal cases are traditionally in the purview of the states. But, a burgeoning set of federal criminal laws is contributing significantly to delays in the federal courts.

Civil law is the body of law that regulates the conduct and relationships between private individuals or companies. Because the actions at issue in civil law do not constitute a threat to society at large, people who believe they have been injured by another party must take action on their own to seek judicial relief. Civil cases, then, involve lawsuits filed to recover something of value, whether it is the right to vote, fair treatment, or monetary compensation for an item or service that cannot be recovered.

civil law
Codes of behavior related to business and contractual relationships between groups and individuals.

SIMULATION

You Are a Young Lawyer

constitutional courts
Federal courts specifically created by the U.S. Constitution or by Congress pursuant to its authority in Article III.

legislative courts
Courts established by Congress for specialized purposes, such as the Court of Military Appeals.

Each civil or criminal case has a plaintiff, or petitioner, who brings charges against a defendant, or respondent. Sometimes the government is the plaintiff. The government may bring civil charges on behalf of the citizens of the state or the national government against a person or corporation for violating the law, but it is always the government that brings a criminal case. When cases are initiated, they are known first by the name of the petitioner. In *Marbury* v. *Madison*, William Marbury was the plaintiff, suing the defendants, the U.S. government and James Madison as its secretary of state, for not delivering Marbury's judicial commission.

During trials, judges often must interpret the intent of laws enacted by Congress and state legislatures. To do so, they read reports, testimony, and debates on the relevant legislation and study the results of other similar legal cases. They also rely on the presentations made by lawyers in their briefs and at trial.

Another important component of most civil and criminal cases is the jury. This body acts as the ultimate finder of fact and plays an important role in determining the culpability of the individual on trial.

The Federal Court System

The federal district courts, courts of appeals, and the Supreme Court are called **constitutional** (or Article III) **courts** because Article III of the Constitution either established them or authorized Congress to establish them. Judges who preside over these courts are nominated by the president (with the advice and consent of the Senate), and they serve lifetime terms, as long as they engage in "good behavior."

In addition to constitutional courts, **legislative courts** are set up by Congress, under its implied powers, generally for special purposes. The U.S. territorial courts (which hear federal cases in the territories) and the U.S. Court of Veterans Appeals are examples of legislative courts, or what some call Article I courts. The judges who preside over these federal courts are appointed by the president (subject to Senate confirmation) and serve fixed, limited terms.

District Courts

As we have seen, Congress created U.S. district courts when it enacted the Judiciary Act of 1789. District courts are federal trial courts of original jurisdiction. There are currently ninety-four federal district courts. No district court cuts across state lines. Every state has at least one federal district court, and the most populous states—California, Texas, and New York—each have four.[11]

Federal district courts, where the bulk of the judicial work takes place in the federal system, have original jurisdiction over only specific types of cases. Although the rules governing district court jurisdiction can be complex, cases heard in federal district courts by a single judge (with or without a jury) generally fall into one of three categories:

1. They involve the federal government as a party.
2. They present a federal question based on a claim under the U.S. Constitution, a treaty with another nation, or a federal statute.
3. They involve civil suits in which citizens are from different states, and the amount of money at issue is more than $75,000.[12]

Each federal judicial district has a U.S. attorney, who is nominated by the president and confirmed by the Senate. The U.S. attorney in each district is that district's chief law enforcement officer. The number of assistant U.S. attorneys in each district depends on the amount of litigation. U.S. attorneys, like district attorneys within the states, have a considerable amount of discretion as to whether they pursue criminal or civil investigations or file charges against individuals or corporations.

The Courts of Appeals

The losing party in a case heard and decided in a federal district court can appeal the decision to the appropriate court of appeals. The United States courts of appeals (known as the circuit courts of appeals prior to 1948) are the intermediate appellate courts in the federal system and were established in 1789 to hear appeals from federal district courts. There are currently eleven numbered courts of appeals. A twelfth, the U.S. Court of Appeals for the D.C. Circuit, handles most appeals involving federal regulatory commissions and agencies, including, for example, the National Labor Relations Board and the Securities and Exchange Commission. The thirteenth federal appeals court is the U.S. Court of Appeals for the Federal Circuit, which deals with patents and contract and financial claims against the federal government.

The number of judges within each court of appeals varies—depending on the workload and the complexity of the cases—and ranges from six to nearly thirty. Each court is supervised by a chief judge, the most senior judge in terms of service below the age of sixty-five, who can serve no more than seven years. In deciding cases, judges are divided into rotating three-judge panels, made up of the active judges within the court of appeals, visiting judges (primarily district judges from the same court), and retired judges. In rare cases, all the judges in a court of appeals may choose to sit together (*en banc*) to decide a case by majority vote.

The courts of appeals have no original jurisdiction. Rather, Congress has granted these courts appellate jurisdiction over two general categories of cases: appeals from criminal and civil cases from the district courts, and appeals from administrative agencies. Once a decision is made by a federal court of appeals, a litigant no longer has an automatic right to an appeal. The losing party may submit a petition to the U.S. Supreme Court to hear the case, but the Court grants few of these requests.

In general, courts of appeals try to correct errors of law and procedure that have occurred in lower courts or administrative agencies. Courts of appeals hear no new testimony; instead, lawyers submit written arguments in what is called a **brief** (also submitted in trial courts), and they then appear to present and argue the case orally to the court.

Decisions of any court of appeals are binding on only the courts within its geographic confines, but decisions of the U.S. Supreme Court are binding throughout the nation and establish national **precedents**. This reliance on past decisions or precedents to formulate decisions in new cases is called *stare decisis* (a Latin phrase meaning "let the decision stand"). The principle of *stare decisis* allows for continuity and predictability in our judicial system. Although *stare decisis* can be helpful in predicting decisions, at times judges carve out new ground and ignore, decline to follow, or even overrule precedents to reach a different conclusion in a case involving similar circumstances. This is a major reason why so much litigation exsists in America today. Parties to a suit know that the outcome of a case is not always predictable; if such prediction were possible, there would be little reason to go to court.

The Supreme Court

The U.S. Supreme Court, as we saw in the opening vignette, is often at the center of the storm of highly controversial issues that have yet to be resolved successfully in the political process. It reviews cases from the U.S. courts of appeals and state supreme

brief
A document containing the legal written arguments in a case filed with a court by a party prior to a hearing or trial.

precedent
A prior judicial decision that serves as a rule for settling subsequent cases of a similar nature.

stare decisis
In court rulings, a reliance on past decisions or precedents to formulate decisions in new cases.

courts (as well as other courts of last resort) and acts as the final interpreter of the U.S. Constitution. The Court not only decides major cases with tremendous policy significance each year, but it also ensures uniformity in the interpretation of national laws and the Constitution, resolves conflicts among the states, and maintains the supremacy of national law in the federal system.

Since 1869, the U.S. Supreme Court has consisted of eight associate justices and one chief justice, who is nominated by the president specifically for that position. There is no special significance about the number nine, and the Constitution is silent about the size of the Court. Between 1789 and 1869, Congress periodically altered the size of the Court. The lowest number of justices on the Court was six; the most, ten. Through December 2008, only 110 justices had served on the Court, and there had been seventeen chief justices (To learn more about chief justices of the Supreme Court, see Appendix IV).

How Federal Court Judges Are Selected

The selection of federal judges is often a very political process with important political ramifications because judges are nominated by the president and must be confirmed by the U.S. Senate. Presidents, in general, try to select well-qualified men and women for the bench. But, these appointments also provide a president with the opportunity to put his philosophical stamp on the federal courts. (To learn more about how presidents affect the judiciary, see Table 9.2.) Nominees, however, while generally members of the nominating president's party, usually are vetted through the senator's offices of the states where the district court or court of appeals vacancy occurs. In the Clinton White House, candidates for district court generally came from recommendations by Democratic senators, "or in the absence of a Democratic senator, from the Democratic members of the House of Representatives or other high ranking Democratic Party politicians."[13] This process by which presidents generally defer selection of district court judges to the choice of senators of their own party who represent the state where the vacancy occurs is known as **senatorial courtesy**.

senatorial courtesy
Process by which presidents generally defer selection of district court judges to the choice of senators of their own party who represent the state where the vacancy occurs.

TABLE 9.2 How A President Affects the Federal Judiciary

The table depicts the number of judges appointed by each president and shows how quickly a president can make an impact on the make-up of the courts.

President	Appointed to Supreme Court	Appointed to Courts of Appeals[a]	Appointed to District Courts[b]	Total Appointed	Total Number of Judgeships[c]	Percentage of Judgeships Filled by President
Johnson (1963–1969)	2	40	122	164	449	37
Nixon (1969–1974)	4	45	179	228	504	45
Ford (1974–1977)	1	12	52	65	504	13
Carter (1977–1981)	0	56	202	258	657	39
Reagan (1981–1989)	3	78	290	368	740	50
Bush (1989–1993)	2	37	148	185	825	22
Clinton (1993–2001)	2	66	305	373	841	44
G. W. Bush (2001–2009)[d]	2	57	287	344	866	40

[a]Does not include the U. S. Court of Appeals for the Federal Circuit
[b]Includes district courts in the territories
[c]Total judgeships authorized in president's last year in office
[d]George W. Bush data through September 1, 2008

Source: "Imprints on the Bench," *CQ Weekly Report* (January 19, 2001): 173. Reprinted by permission of Copyright Clearance Center on behalf of Congressional Quarterly, Inc. Updated by authors.

Who are Federal Judges?

Typically, federal district court judges have held other political offices, such as those of state court judge or prosecutor. Most have been involved in politics, which is what usually brings them into consideration for a position on the federal bench.

Increasingly, most judicial nominees have had prior judicial experience. White males continue to dominate the federal courts, but since the 1970s, most presidents have pledged (with varying degrees of success) to do their best to appoint more African Americans, Hispanics, women, and other underrepresented groups to the federal bench. (To learn more, see Analyzing Visuals: Race, Ethnicity, and Gender of District Court Appointees.)

Appointments to the U.S. Supreme Court

Like other federal court judges, the justices of the Supreme Court are nominated by the president and must be confirmed by the Senate. Historically, because of the special place the Supreme Court enjoys in our constitutional system, its nominees have encountered more opposition than have district court or court of appeals nominees. As the role of the Court has increased over time, so too has the amount of attention given to nominees. With this increased attention has come greater opposition, especially to nominees with controversial views. (To learn more about the current Court, see Table 9.3.)

Nomination Criteria

Justice Sandra Day O'Connor once remarked that "You have to be lucky" to be appointed to the Court.[14] Although luck is certainly important, over the years nominations to the

TABLE 9.3 The Supreme Court, 2008

	Year of Birth	Year of Appointment	Political Party	Law School	Appointing President	Religion	Prior Judicial Experience	Prior Government Experience
John G. Roberts Jr.	1955	2005	R	Harvard	G. W. Bush	Roman Catholic	U.S. Court of Appeals	Dept. of Justice, White House counsel
John Paul Stevens	1920	1975	R	Chicago	Ford	Nondenominational Protestant	U.S. Court of Appeals	Associate Counsel, House Judiciary Committee
Antonin Scalia	1936	1986	R	Harvard	Reagan	Roman Catholic	U.S. Court of Appeals	Assistant attorney general, Office of Legal Counsel
Anthony Kennedy	1936	1988	R	Harvard	Reagan	Roman Catholic	U.S. Court of Appeals	
David Souter	1939	1990	R	Harvard	Bush	Episcopalian	U.S. Court of Appeals	New Hampshire assistant attorney general
Clarence Thomas	1948	1991	R	Yale	Bush	Roman Catholic	U.S. Court of Appeals	Chair, Equal Employment Opportunity Commission
Ruth Bader Ginsburg	1933	1993	D	Columbia/ Harvard	Clinton	Jewish	U.S. Court of Appeals	
Stephen Breyer	1938	1994	D	Harvard	Clinton	Jewish	U.S. Court of Appeals	Chief counsel, Senate Judiciary Committee
Samuel A. Alito Jr.	1950	2006	R	Yale	G. W. Bush	Roman Catholic	U.S. Court of Appeals	Dept. of Justice, U.S. Attorney.

Analyzing Visuals | Race, Ethnicity, and Gender of Federal Court Appointees

Examine the bar graphs, which show some of the characteristics of federal court appointees from President Jimmy Carter to President George W. Bush, and consider the following questions:

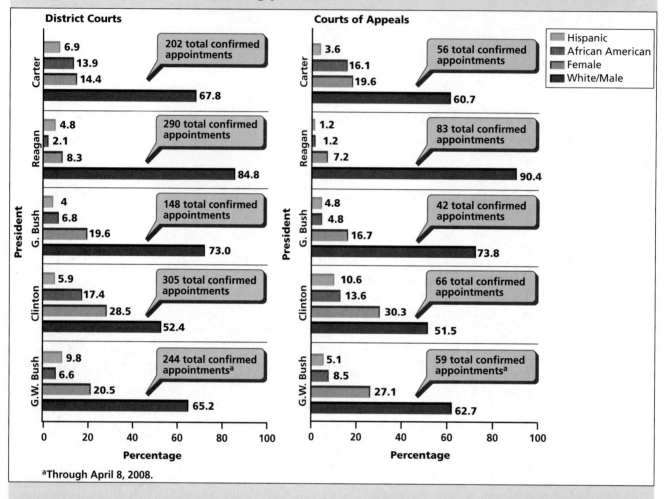

^aThrough April 8, 2008.

Source: Federal Judges Biographical database, www.fjc.gov/public/home.nsf/hisj.

ARE there differences between appointments made by Democratic presidents (Carter and Clinton) and Republican presidents? Can you identify any trends in appointees over time?

WHICH groups are most underrepresented?

SHOULD race, ethnicity, and gender matter in presidential appointments? Why or why not?

bench have been made for a variety of reasons. At least six criteria are especially important: competence, ideology or policy preferences, rewards, pursuit of political support, religion, and race and gender.

COMPETENCE Most prospective nominees are expected to have had at least some judicial or governmental experience. For example, John Jay, the first chief justice, was one of the authors of *The Federalist Papers* and was active in New York politics. In 2008, all nine sitting Supreme Court justices had prior judicial experience.

IDEOLOGY OR POLICY PREFERENCES Most presidents seek to appoint individuals who share their policy preferences, and almost all have political goals in mind when they appoint a justice. Presidents Franklin D. Roosevelt, Richard M. Nixon, and Ronald Reagan were very successful in molding the Court to their own political beliefs.

REWARDS Historically, many of those appointed to the Supreme Court have been personal friends of presidents. Abraham Lincoln, for example, appointed one of his key political advisers to the Court. Lyndon B. Johnson appointed his longtime friend Abe Fortas to the bench. Most presidents also select justices of their own party affiliation. Chief Justice John G. Roberts Jr. and Justice Samuel A. Alito Jr., for example, both Republicans, worked in the Department of Justice during the Reagan and George Bush administrations. Roberts also served as associate White House counsel under Reagan.

PURSUIT OF POLITICAL SUPPORT FROM VARIOUS GROUPS During Ronald Reagan's successful campaign for the presidency in 1980, some of his advisers feared that the gender gap would hurt him. Polls repeatedly showed that he was far less popular with female voters than with men. To gain support from women, Reagan announced during his campaign that should he win, he would appoint a woman to fill the first vacancy on the Court. When Justice Potter Stewart, a moderate, announced his retirement from the bench, under pressure from women's rights groups, President Reagan nominated Sandra Day O'Connor of the Arizona Court of Appeals to fill the vacancy.

RELIGION Through early 2009, of the 110 justices who served on the Court, almost all have been members of traditional Protestant faiths.[15] Only eleven have been Catholic and only seven have been Jewish.[16] Today, more Catholics—Roberts, Scalia, Kennedy, Thomas, and Alito—serve on the court than at any other point in history.

RACE, ETHNICITY, AND GENDER Through 2008, only two African Americans and two women have served on the Court. Race was undoubtedly a critical issue in the appointment of Clarence Thomas to replace Thurgood Marshall, the first African American justice. But, President George Bush refused to acknowledge his wish to retain a black seat on the Court. Instead, he announced that he was "picking the best man for the job on the merits," a claim that was met with considerable skepticism by many observers.

The Supreme Court Confirmation Process

The Constitution gives the Senate the authority to approve all nominees to the federal bench. As detailed below, the Senate Judiciary Committee investigates the nominees, holds hearings, and votes on its recommendation for Senate action. At this stage, the committee may reject a nominee or send the nomination to the full Senate for a vote. The full Senate then deliberates on the nominee before voting. A simple majority vote is required for confirmation.

INVESTIGATION As a president begins to narrow the list of possible nominees to the Supreme Court, those names are sent to the Federal Bureau of Investigation for a background check. After a formal nomination is made and

What does the confirmation process entail? When Samuel A. Alito Jr. was nominated for a seat on the Supreme Court, the result was a high-stakes confirmation battle that involved a number of interest groups. Here, Alito signs autographs for supporters on the way to his confirmation hearing.

Photo courtesy: Joshua Roberts/Reuters/Landov

sent to the Senate, the Senate Judiciary Committee begins its own investigation. (The same process is used for nominees to the lower federal courts, although such investigations rarely are as extensive as for Supreme Court nominees.)

LOBBYING BY INTEREST GROUPS   Many groups are keenly interested in the nomination process. In 1987, for example, the nomination of Judge Robert H. Bork to the Supreme Court led liberal groups to launch an extensive radio, television, and print media campaign against the nominee. These interest groups decried Bork's actions as solicitor general, especially his firing of the Watergate special prosecutor at the request of President Richard M. Nixon, as well as his political beliefs.

More and more, interest groups are also getting involved in district court and court of appeals nominations. They recognize that these appointments often pave the way for future nominees to the Supreme Court.

THE SENATE COMMITTEE HEARINGS AND SENATE VOTE   After hearings are concluded, the Senate Judiciary Committee usually makes a recommendation to the full Senate. Any rejections of presidential nominees to the Supreme Court generally occur only after the Senate Judiciary Committee has recommended against a nominee's appointment. Few recent confirmations have been close; Clarence Thomas's 52–48 vote in 1991 and Samuel A. Alito Jr.'s 58–42 vote in 2006 were the closest in recent history.

The Supreme Court Today

Given the judicial system's vast size and substantial, although often indirect, power over so many aspects of our lives, it is surprising that so many Americans know next to nothing about the judicial system, in general, and the U.S. Supreme Court, in particular.

Even after the attention the Court received during the nominations of John G. Roberts Jr. and Samuel A. Alito Jr., more than half of those Americans surveyed in early 2006 could not name one member of the Court; virtually no one could name all nine members of the Court. As revealed in Table 9.4, Sandra Day O'Connor, the first woman appointed to the Court, was the most well-known justice. Still, only about a quarter of those polled could name her.

While much of this ignorance can be blamed on the American public's lack of interest, the Court has also taken great pains to ensure its privacy and sense of decorum. Its rites and rituals contribute to the Court's mystique and encourage a "cult of the robe."[17] Consider, for example, the way Supreme Court proceedings are conducted. Oral arguments are not televised, and deliberations concerning the outcome of cases are conducted in utmost secrecy. In contrast, C-SPAN brings us daily coverage of various congressional hearings and floor debate on bills and important national issues, and CNN (and sometimes other networks) provides extensive coverage of many important state court trials. The Supreme Court, however, remains adamant in its refusal to televise its proceedings—including public oral arguments, although it now allows the release of same-day audio tapes of oral arguments. (To learn about efforts to open Supreme Court proceedings to the media, see Politics Now: Should Supreme Court Proceedings Be Televised?)

Case Overload

Deciding to Hear a Case

Just over 9,600 cases were filed at the Supreme Court in its 2007–2008 term; 75 were heard, and 74 decisions were issued. In contrast, from 1790 to 1801, the Court heard only 87 cases under its appellate jurisdiction.[18] In

TABLE 9.4 Don't Know Much About the Supreme Court

Supreme Court Justice	Percentage Who Could Name
Sandra Day O'Connor	27
Clarence Thomas	21
John G. Roberts Jr.	16
Antonin Scalia	13
Ruth Bader Ginsburg	12
Anthony Kennedy	7
David Souter	5
Stephen Breyer	3
John Paul Stevens	3

Source: Findlaw.com poll, January 10, 2006, http://company.findlaw.com/pr/2006/011006.supremes.html.

POLITICS NOW

Source: CQ WEEKLY – WEEKLY REPORT, LEGAL AFFAIRS   December 10, 2007   Page 3665

Should Supreme Court Proceedings Be Televised?

Supreme Court TV Bill Snags on Procedure

CAITLIN WEBBER AND KEITH PERINE

The Senate Judiciary Committee endorsed legislation last week that would compel the Supreme Court to televise its public proceedings, but the panel will have to revisit the issue this week because of a procedural snag.

Members voted, 11–7, in favor of the bill (S 344), which would require TV coverage of the Court's open sessions unless a majority of justices vote to block cameras for a particular case. Currently, the Court releases only transcripts and audio recordings.

Technically, however, the panel did not approve the measure. Under committee rules, which allow for proxy voting, a majority of senators must vote in person for a bill in order for it to be approved. The tally of those senators who were present was 5–5. The committee has scheduled another vote for Dec. 13 to ratify last week's vote.

A majority of justices on the bench have spoken out against allowing cameras. Justice Anthony M. Kennedy told the Judiciary Committee in February that televised Court proceedings would "change our collegial dynamic. And we hope that this respect that separation of powers and checks and balances implies would persuade you to accept our judgment in this regard."

Dianne Feinstein of California was the only Democrat to vote against the measure, saying it would "have a negative impact on the way justices relate to each other."

"Congress should not tell the Court how to run its operations, just as the Court should not tell us how to run Congress," she said.

Judiciary's ranking Republican, Arlen Specter of Pennsylvania, who introduced the bipartisan bill in January, disagreed. "We have substantial authority . . . .Congress has also established time limits that the Supreme Court and the other federal courts have to observe," he said.

Chief Justice John G. Roberts Jr. has moved to better publicize the court's proceedings. The Court now publishes same-day transcripts and some audio recordings of oral arguments.

Discussion Questions

1. *Should Congress have the authority to compel the Supreme Court to televise its proceedings? Why or why not?*
2. *How might television cameras change the dynamics of legal proceedings before the Supreme Court?*
3. *What are other possible reasons that would explain why the justices are resistant to having cameras in the courtroom?*

---

the Court's early years, most of the justices' workload involved their circuit-riding duties. From 1862 to 1866, only 240 cases were decided. Creation of the courts of appeals in 1891 resulted in an immediate reduction in Supreme Court filings—from 600 in 1890 to 275 in 1892.[19] As recently as the 1940s, fewer than 1,000 cases were filed annually. Filings increased at a dramatic rate until the mid 1990s, shot up again in the late 1990s, and generally have now leveled off. (To learn more about the Court's caseload, see Figure 9.2.)

The content of the Court's docket is every bit as significant as its size. During the 1930s, cases requiring the interpretation of constitutional law began to take a growing portion of the Court's workload, leading the Court to take a more important role in the policy-making process. At that time, only 5 percent of the Court's cases involved questions concerning the Bill of Rights. By the late 1950s, one-third of filed cases involved such questions; by the 1960s, half did.[20]

As discussed earlier in the chapter, the Court has two types of jurisdiction. The Court has original jurisdiction in "all Cases affecting Ambassadors, other public Ministers and Consuls, and those in which a State shall be a party." It is rare for more than two or three of these cases to come to the Court in a year. The second kind of jurisdiction enjoyed by the Court is its appellate jurisdiction. The Court is not expected to exercise its appellate jurisdiction simply to correct errors of other courts. Instead, appeal to the Supreme Court should be taken only if the case presents important issues of law, or what is termed "a substantial federal question." Since 1988, nearly all appellate cases that have gone to the Supreme Court arrived there on a petition for a **writ of *certiorari*** (from the Latin "to be informed"), which is a request for

You Are a Supreme Court Justice Deciding a Free Speech Case

writ of *certiorari*
A request for the Court to order up the records from a lower court to review the case.

FIGURE 9.2 Supreme Court Caseload, 1950–2008 Terms
Cases the Supreme Court chooses to hear (represented by brown bars) represent a tiny fraction of the total number of cases filed with the Court (represented by green bars).

Source: Administrative Office of the Courts; Supreme Court Public Information Office.

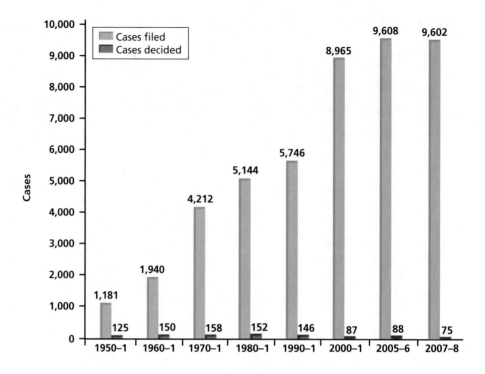

the Supreme Court—at its discretion—to order up the records of the lower courts for purposes of review. (To learn more about this process, see Figure 9.3.)

WRITS OF *CERTIORARI* AND THE RULE OF FOUR   The Supreme Court controls its own caseload through the *certiorari* process, deciding which cases it wants to hear, and rejecting most cases that come to it. All petitions, or writs of *certiorari*, must meet two criteria:

1. The case must come from either a U.S. court of appeals, a special three-judge district court, or a state court of last resort.
2. The case must involve a federal question. Thus, the case must present questions of federal constitutional law or involve a federal statute, action, or treaty.

The clerk of the Court transmits petitions for writs of *certiorari* first to the chief justice's office, where clerks review the petitions, and then to the individual justices' offices. On the Roberts Court, all of the justices except Justice John Paul Stevens (who allows his clerks great individual authority in selecting the cases for him to review) participate in what is called the *cert* pool.[21] Pool participants review their assigned fraction of petitions and share their notes with each other. Those cases that the justices deem noteworthy are then placed on what is called the discuss list prepared by the chief justice's clerks and circulated to the chambers of the other justices. All others are dead listed and go no further. Only about 30 percent of submitted petitions make it to the discuss list. During one of the justices' weekly conference meetings, the cases on the discuss list are reviewed. The chief justice speaks first, then the rest of the justices, according to seniority. The decision process ends when the justices vote, and by custom, *certiorari* is granted according to the **Rule of Four**—when at least four justices vote to hear a case.

Rule of Four
At least four justices of the Supreme Court must vote to consider a case before it can be heard.

THE ROLE OF CLERKS   As early as 1850, the justices of the Supreme Court beseeched Congress to approve the hiring of a clerk to assist each justice. Congress denied the request, so when Justice Horace Gray hired the first law clerk in 1882, he paid the clerk himself. Justice Gray's clerk was a top graduate of Harvard Law School whose duties included cutting Justice Gray's hair and running personal errands. Finally, in 1886, Congress authorized each justice to hire a stenographer clerk for $1,600 a year.

Clerks typically are selected from candidates at the top of the graduating classes of prestigious law schools. They perform a variety of tasks, ranging from searching for arcane facts to playing tennis or taking walks with the justices. Clerks spend most of their time researching material, reading and summarizing cases, and helping justices write opinions. Clerks also make the first pass through the petitions that come to the

You Are a Clerk to Supreme Court Justice Judith Gray

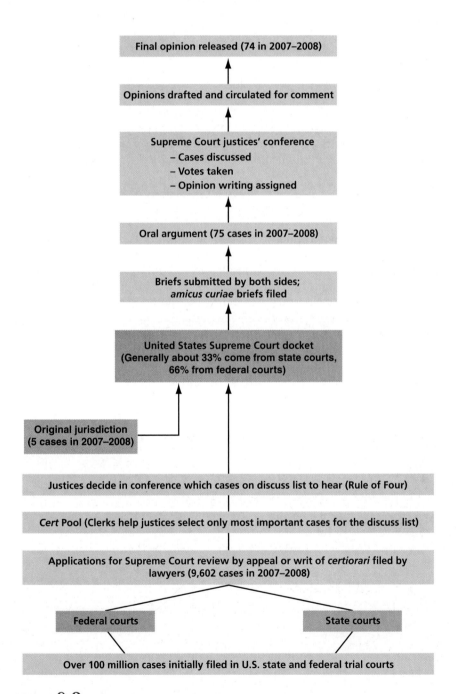

FIGURE 9.3 How a Case Gets to the Supreme Court
This figure illustrates both how cases get on the Court's docket and what happens after a case is accepted for review.

TABLE 9.5   What do Supreme Court Clerks Do?

Supreme Court clerks are among the best and brightest recent law school graduates. Almost all first clerk for a judge on one of the courts of appeals. After their Supreme Court clerkship, former clerks are in high demand. Firms often pay signing bonuses of up to $200,000 to attract clerks, who earn over $180,000 their first year in private practice.

Tasks of a Supreme Court clerk include the following:

- Perform initial screening of the 9,000 or so petitions that come to the Court each term
- Draft memos to summarize the facts and issues in each case, recommending whether the case should be accepted by the Court for full review
- Write "bench memos" summarizing an accepted case and suggesting questions for oral argument
- Write the first draft of an opinion
- Serve as informal conduit for communicating and negotiating with other justices' chambers as to the final wording of an opinion

Court, undoubtedly influencing which cases get a second look. Just how much help they provide in the writing of opinions is unknown.[22] (To learn more about what clerks do, see Table 9.5.)

In 2009, the nine active justices and retired Justice Sandra Day O'Connor employed a total of thirty-eight clerks. This growth in the number of clerks has had many interesting ramifications for the Court. As the number of clerks has grown, so have the number and length of the Court's opinions.[23] And, until recently, the number of cases decided annually increased as more help was available to the justices.

The relationship between clerks and the justices for whom they work is close and confidential, and many aspects of the relationship are kept secret.[24] Clerks may sometimes talk among themselves about the views and personalities of their justices, but rarely has a clerk leaked such information to the press. In 1998, a former clerk to Justice Harry A. Blackmun broke the silence. Edward Lazarus published an insider's account of how the Court really works.[25] He argued that the justices give their young, often ideological, clerks far too much power.

How Does a Case Survive the Process?

It can be difficult to determine why the Court decides to hear a particular case. Sometimes it involves a perceived national emergency, as was the case with appeals concerning the outcome of the 2000 presidential election. The Court does not offer reasons, and "the standards by which the justices decide to grant or deny review are highly personalized and necessarily discretionary," noted former Chief Justice Earl Warren.[26] Political scientists nonetheless have attempted to determine the characteristics of the cases the Court accepts; not surprisingly, they are similar to those that help a case get on the discuss list. Among the cues are the following:

- The federal government is the party asking for review.
- The case involves conflict among the courts of appeals.

Who sits on the Roberts Court? Back row, from left to right: Justices Stephen Breyer, Clarence Thomas, Ruth Bader Ginsburg, and Samuel A. Alito Jr. Front row, from left to right: Justices Anthony Kennedy and John Paul Stevens, Chief Justice John G. Roberts Jr., Justices Antonin Scalia and David Souter.

Photo courtesy: Supreme Court Historical Society

- The case presents a civil rights or civil liberties question.
- The case involves the ideological or policy preferences of the justices.
- The case has significant social or political interest, as evidenced by the presence of interest group *amicus curiae* briefs.

THE FEDERAL GOVERNMENT One of the most important cues for predicting whether the Court will hear a case is the solicitor general's position. The **solicitor general**, appointed by the president, is the fourth-ranking member of the Department of Justice and is responsible for handling most appeals on behalf of the U.S. government to the Supreme Court. The solicitor's staff resembles a small, specialized law firm within the Department of Justice. But, because this office has such a special relationship with the Supreme Court, even having a suite of offices within the Supreme Court building, the solicitor general often is referred to as the Court's "ninth and a half member."[27] Moreover, the solicitor general, on behalf of the U.S. government, appears as a party or as an *amicus curiae* in more than 50 percent of the cases heard by the Court each term. *Amicus curiae* means friend of the court. *Amici* may file briefs or even appear to argue their interests orally before the Court. This special relationship helps to explain the overwhelming success the solicitor general's office enjoys before the Supreme Court. The Court generally accepts 70 to 80 percent of the cases where the U.S. government is the petitioning party, compared with about 5 percent of all others.[28]

CONFLICT AMONG THE COURTS OF APPEALS Conflict among the lower courts is another reason that the justices take cases. When interpretations of constitutional or federal law are involved, the justices seem to want consistency throughout the federal court system. Often these conflicts occur when important civil rights or civil liberties questions arise. Political scientists have noted that the justices' ideological leanings play a role.[29] It is not uncommon to see conservative justices voting to hear cases to overrule liberal lower court decisions, or vice versa. Justices also take cases when several circuit courts are in disagreement over a main issue.

INTEREST GROUP PARTICIPATION A quick way for the justices to gauge the ideological ramifications of a particular civil rights or liberties case is by the nature and amount of interest group participation. Richard C. Cortner has noted that "Cases do not arrive on the doorstep of the Supreme Court like orphans in the night."[30] Instead, most cases heard by the Supreme Court involve either the government or an interest group—either as the sponsoring party or as an *amicus curiae*. Liberal groups, such as the American Civil Liberties Union, People for the American Way, or the NAACP Legal Defense Fund, and conservative groups, including the Washington Legal Foundation, Concerned Women for America, and the American Center for Law and Justice, routinely sponsor cases or file *amicus* briefs either urging the Court to hear a case or asking it to deny *certiorari*.

The positions of both parties in a case are often echoed or expanded in *amicus curiae* briefs filed by interested parties, especially interest groups. Interest groups also provide the Court with information not necessarily contained in the party briefs, help write briefs, and assist in practice oral arguments during moot court sessions. In these moot court sessions, the lawyer who will argue the case before the nine justices goes through several complete rehearsals, with prominent lawyers and law professors role-playing the various justices.

Research by political scientists has found that "not only does [an *amicus*] brief in favor of *certiorari* significantly improve the chances of a case being accepted, but two, three and four briefs improve the chances even more."[31] Clearly, it's the more the merrier, whether the briefs are filed for or against granting review.[32] (To learn how you can participate in Court cases, see Ideas into Action: Be a Friend of the Court.)

solicitor general
The fourth-ranking member of the Department of Justice; responsible for handling all appeals on behalf of the U.S. government to the Supreme Court.

amicus curiae
"Friend of the court"; *amici* may file briefs or even appear to argue their interests orally before the court.

Ideas Into Action

Be a Friend of the Court

Amicus curiae briefs have become an increasingly popular way for interest groups and individuals to express their points of view to state supreme courts as well as the U.S. Supreme Court. This form of judicial lobbying allows citizens to become active participants in what is often viewed as the most insulated branch of government.

State supreme courts and the U.S. Supreme Court adjudicate a number of issues of concern to students. A number of state high courts, for example, have dealt with an ongoing stream of cases dealing with how to finance public education. And, the U.S. Supreme Court has dealt with cases involving mandatory student fees and school vouchers (see chapter 5).

Recently, a number of student groups, including Students for Sensible Drug Policy, participated in the U.S. Supreme Court case of *Morse* v. *Frederick* (2007). This case, also known as the "bong hits for Jesus" case, asked whether the First Amendment allows public schools to restrict the display of signs promoting drug use at school-sponsored events. As a free speech issue, *Morse* was a matter of concern for students and student rights groups across the country. The Court eventually ruled that schools could prohibit such signage.

Explore the docket of the U.S. Supreme Court or your state's high court and identify the cases that may be relevant to students like you. Then, consider:

- What rules govern *amicus* briefs in your state's high court? In the U.S. Supreme Court?
- Are you active in any groups that might file a relevant *amicus* brief? How would you go about preparing this sort of brief? What resources would you need?
- What other ways might you get involved in litigation in your state's high court? The U.S. Supreme Court?

Hearing and Deciding the Case

Once a case is accepted for review, a flurry of activity begins. Lawyers on both sides of the case begin to prepare their written arguments for submission to the Court. In these briefs, lawyers cite prior case law and make arguments as to why the Court should find in favor of their client.

ORAL ARGUMENTS Once a case is accepted by the Court for full review, and after briefs and *amicus* briefs are submitted on each side, oral argument takes place. Oral argument generally is limited to the immediate parties in the case, although it is not uncommon for the U.S. solicitor general to appear to argue orally as an *amicus curiae*. Oral argument at the Court is fraught with time-honored tradition and ceremony. At precisely ten o'clock every morning when the Court is in session, the Court marshal, dressed in a formal morning coat, emerges to intone "Oyez! Oyez! Oyez!" as the nine justices emerge from behind a reddish-purple velvet curtain to take their places on the raised and slightly angled bench. The chief justice sits in the middle. The remaining justices sit to the left and right alternating in seniority.

Almost all attorneys are allotted one half hour to present their cases, and this time includes that required to answer questions from the bench. Although many Court watchers have tried to figure out how a particular justice will vote based on the questioning at oral argument, most researchers find that the nature and number of questions asked do not help much in predicting the outcome of a case.

THE CONFERENCE AND THE VOTE The justices meet in closed conference once a week when the Court is hearing oral arguments. Since the ascendancy of Chief Justice Roger B. Taney to the Court in 1836, the justices have begun each conference session with a round of handshaking. Once the door to the conference room closes, no others are allowed to enter. The justice with the least seniority acts as the doorkeeper for the other eight, communicating with those waiting outside to fill requests for documents, water, and any other necessities.

Conferences highlight the importance and power of the chief justice, who presides over them and makes the initial presentation of each case. Each individual justice then discusses the case in order of his or her seniority on the Court, with the most senior justice speaking next. Most accounts of the decision-making process reveal that at this point some justices try to change the minds of others, but that most enter the conference room with a clear idea of how they will vote on each case.

During the Rehnquist Court, the justices generally voted at the same time they discussed each case, with each justice speaking only once. Initial conference votes were not final, and justices were allowed to change their minds before final votes were taken later. The Roberts Court is much more informal than the Rehnquist Court. The justices' regular Friday conferences now last longer and, unlike the conferences headed by Rehnquist, the new chief justice encourages discussion.[33]

WRITING OPINIONS   After the Court has reached a decision in conference, the justices must formulate a formal opinion of the Court. If the chief justice is in the majority, he selects the justice who will write the opinion. This privilege enables him to wield tremendous power and is a very important strategic decision. If the chief justice is in the minority, the assignment falls to the most senior justice in the majority.

The opinion of the Court can take several different forms. Most decisions are reached by a majority opinion written by one member of the Court to reflect the views of at least five of the justices. This opinion usually sets out the legal reasoning justifying the decision, and this legal reasoning becomes a precedent for deciding future cases. The reasoning behind any decision is often as important as the outcome. Under the system of *stare decisis*, both are likely to be relied on as precedent later by lower courts confronted with cases involving similar issues.

In the process of creating the final opinion of the Court, informal caucusing and negotiation often take place, as justices may hold out for word changes or other modifications as a condition of their continued support of the majority opinion. This negotiation process can lead to divisions in the Court's majority. When this occurs, the Court may be forced to decide cases by plurality opinions, which attract the support of three or four justices. While these decisions do not have the precedential value of majority opinions, they nonetheless have been used by the Court to decide many major cases. Justices who agree with the outcome of the case but not with the legal rationale for the decision may file concurring opinions to express their differing approach. Justices who do not agree with the outcome of a case file dissenting opinions. Although these opinions have little direct legal value, they can be an important indicator of legal thought on the Court and are an excellent platform for justices to note their personal and legal disagreements with other members of the Court.

Judicial Philosophy and Decision Making

Justices do not make decisions in a vacuum. Principles of *stare decisis* dictate that the justices follow the law of previous cases in deciding cases at hand. But, a variety of legal and extra-legal factors have also been found to affect Supreme Court decision making.

Judicial Philosophy, Original Intent, and Ideology

Legal scholars long have argued that judges decide cases based on the Constitution and their reading of various statutes. Determining what the Framers meant—if that is even possible today—often appears to be based on an individual jurist's philosophy.

One of the primary issues concerning judicial decision making focuses on what is called the activism/restraint debate. Advocates of **judicial restraint** argue that courts should allow the decisions of other branches to stand, even when they offend a judge's

judicial restraint
A philosophy of judicial decision making that argues courts should allow the decisions of other branches of government to stand, even when they offend a judge's own sense of principles.

strict constructionist
An approach to constitutional interpretation that emphasizes the Framers' original intentions.

judicial activism
A philosophy of judicial decision making that argues judges should use their power broadly to further justice, especially in the areas of equality and personal liberty.

own principles. Restraintists defend their position by asserting that the federal courts are composed of unelected judges, which makes the judicial branch the least democratic branch of government. Consequently, the courts should defer policy making to other branches of government as much as possible.

Advocates of judicial restraint generally agree that judges should be **strict constructionists**; that is, they should interpret the Constitution as it was written and intended by the Framers. They argue that in determining the constitutionality of a statute or policy, the Court should rely on the explicit meanings of the clauses in the document, which can be clarified by looking at the intent of the Framers.

Advocates of **judicial activism** contend that judges should use their power broadly to further justice, especially in the areas of equality and personal liberty. Activists argue that it is appropriate for the courts to correct injustices committed by the other branches of government. Implicit in this argument is the notion that courts need to protect oppressed minorities.[34]

Although judicial activists are often considered politically liberal and restraintists politically conservative, in recent years a new brand of conservative judicial activism has become prevalent. Liberal activist decisions often expanded the rights of political and legal minorities. But, conservative activist judges view their positions as an opportunity to issue broad rulings that impose their own political beliefs and policies on the country at large.

Some scholars argue that this increased conservative judicial activism has had an effect on the Court's reliance on *stare decisis* and adherence to precedent. Chief Justice William H. Rehnquist noted that while "*stare decisis* is a cornerstone of our legal system . . . it has less power in constitutional cases."[35]

Models of Judicial Decision Making

Most political scientists who study judicial behavior conclude that a variety of forces shape judicial decision making. Many have attempted to explain how judges vote by integrating a variety of models to offer a more complete picture of how judges make decisions.[36] Many of those models attempt to take into account justices' individual behavioral characteristics and attitudes as well as the fact patterns of the case.

BEHAVIORAL CHARACTERISTICS Some political scientists argue that social background differences, including childhood experiences, religious values, education, earlier political and legal careers, and political party loyalties, are likely to influence how a judge evaluates the facts and legal issues presented in any given case.

THE ATTITUDINAL MODEL The attitudinal approach links judicial attitudes with decision making.[37] The attitudinal model holds that Supreme Court justices decide cases according to their personal preferences toward issues of public policy. Among some of the factors used to derive attitudes are a justice's party identification,[38] the party of the appointing president, and the liberal/conservative leanings of a justice.[39]

THE STRATEGIC MODEL   The strategic model argues that justices temper legal doctrine and their own policy beliefs with concerns about how other internal and external variables will affect and be affected by their decision. Scholars have accumulated a body of evidence in support of the strategic model. They have found, for example, that justices are strategic in their votes for *certiorari*.[40] Justices may not vote to hear a case, no matter how interesting, if they suspect they will lose in the final decision. Other internal and external factors may influence strategic decisions. Evidence shows that the chief justice often assigns final opinions to justices based on the organizational needs of the Court.[41] And, at least under some conditions, justices pay attention to their colleagues' preferences in crafting majority opinions.[42] Finally, the Supreme Court appears to be responsive to public opinion,[43] other courts,[44] and other institutions.[45]

Public Opinion

Many political scientists have examined the role of public opinion in Supreme Court decision making. Not only do the justices read legal briefs and hear oral arguments, but they also read newspapers, watch television, and have some knowledge of public opinion—especially on controversial issues.

Whether or not public opinion actually influences justices, its can act as a check on the power of the courts and as an energizing factor. Activist periods on the Supreme Court generally have corresponded to periods of social or economic crisis. For example, the Marshall Court supported a strong national government, much to the chagrin of a series of pro-states' rights Democratic-Republican presidents in the early crisis-ridden years of the republic. Similarly, the Court capitulated to political pressures and public opinion when, after 1936, it reversed many of its earlier decisions that had blocked President Franklin D. Roosevelt's New Deal legislation.

The courts, especially the Supreme Court, also can be the direct target of public opinion. When *Webster* v. *Reproductive Health Services* (1989) was about to come before the Supreme Court, the Court was subjected to unprecedented lobbying as groups and individuals on both sides of the abortion issue marched and sent appeals to the Court. Mail at the Court, which usually average about 1,000 pieces a day, rose to an astronomical 46,000 pieces per day, virtually paralyzing normal lines of communication.

The Supreme Court also appears to affect public opinion. Political scientists have found that the Court's initial rulings on controversial issues such as abortion or capital punishment positively influence public opinion in the direction of the Court's opinion. However, this research also finds that subsequent decisions have little effect.[46]

The Court also is dependent on the public for its prestige as well as for compliance with its decisions. In times of war and other emergencies, for example, the Court frequently has decided cases in ways that commentators have attributed to the sway of public opinion and political exigencies. In *Korematsu* v. *U.S.* (1944), for example, the high Court upheld the obviously unconstitutional internment of Japanese American citizens during World War II.[47] Moreover, Chief Justice William H. Rehnquist himself once suggested that the Court's restriction on presidential authority in *Youngstown Sheet & Tube Co.* v. *Sawyer* (1952), which invalidated President Harry S Truman's seizure of the nation's steel mills, was largely attributable to Truman's unpopularity in light of the Korean War.[48]

Public confidence in the Court, as with other institutions of government, has ebbed and flowed. Public support for the Court was highest after the Court issued *U.S.* v. *Nixon* (1974).[49] At a time when Americans lost faith in the presidency due to the Watergate scandal, they could at least look to the Supreme Court to do the right thing. Although the numbers of Americans with confidence in the courts has fluctuated over time, in 2006, 40 percent of those sampled by Gallup International had a "great deal" or "quite a lot" of confidence in the Supreme Court.[50]

Toward Reform: Power, Policy Making, and the Court

All judges, whether they recognize it or not, make policy. The decisions of the Supreme Court, in particular, have a tremendous impact on American politics and policy. Over the last 250 years, the justices have helped to codify many of the major rights and liberties guaranteed to the citizens of the United States. Although justices need the cooperation of the executive and legislative branches to implement and enforce many of their decisions, it is safe to say that many policies we

Photo Courtesy: Bettman/Corbis

Do unpopular Supreme Court rulings threaten the nation? The Warren Court's broad expansions of civil and political rights led to a great deal of criticism, including a movement to impeach the chief justice. Here, two California billboards present contrasting views of Warren's performance.

judicial implementation
How and whether judicial decisions are translated into actual public policies affecting more than the immediate parties to a lawsuit.

take for granted in the United States would not have come to fruition without the support of the Supreme Court.

Several Courts have played particularly notable roles in the development of the Judiciary's policy making role. As discussed earlier in the chapter, the Marshall Court played an important role in establishing the Supreme Court as a co-equal branch, including establishing the power of judicial review in *Marbury* v. *Madison* (1803). The Warren Court decided a number of civil rights cases that broadly expanded civil and political rights. These decisions drew a great deal of criticism but played a major role in broadening public understanding of the Court as a policy maker. And, the Rehnquist Court made numerous decisions related to federalism (see chapter 3), which caused observers to take note of the Court's ability to adjudicate conflicts between the federal government and the states. Similarly, the Roberts Court reversed the general trend of the Court agreeing with executive actions during times of war by finding in 2008 that the Bush administration's denial of *habeas corpus* rights to prisoners being held at Guantanamo Bay was an unconstitutional exercise of presidential power.[51]

Policy Making

One measure of the power of the courts and their ability to make policy is that more than one hundred federal laws have been declared unconstitutional. Although many of these laws have not been particularly significant, others have.

Another measure of the policy-making power of the Supreme Court is its ability to overrule itself. Although the Court generally abides by the informal rule of *stare decisis*, by one count, it has overruled itself in more than 200 cases.[52] Moreover, in the past few years, the Court repeatedly has reversed earlier decisions in the areas of criminal defendants' rights, women's rights, and the establishment of religion, revealing its powerful role in determining national policy. The modern court also handles a number of issues that had been considered political questions more appropriately left to the other branches of government to decide.

Implementing Court Decisions

President Andrew Jackson, annoyed about a particular decision handed down by the Marshall Court, is alleged to have said, "John Marshall has made his decision; now let him enforce it." Jackson's statement raises a question: how do Supreme Court rulings translate into public policy? In fact, although judicial decisions carry legal and even moral authority, all courts must rely on other units of government to carry out their directives. If the president or members of Congress, for example, don't like a particular Supreme Court ruling, they can underfund programs needed to implement a decision or seek only lax enforcement. **Judicial implementation** refers to how and whether judicial decisions are translated into actual public policies affecting more than the immediate parties to the lawsuit.

How well a decision is implemented often depends on how well crafted or popular it is. Hostile reaction in the South to *Brown* v. *Board of Education* (1954) and the absence of precise guidelines to implement the decision meant that the ruling went largely unenforced for years. The *Brown* experience also highlights how much the Supreme Court needs the support of both federal and state courts as well as other governmental agencies to carry out its judgments. For example, you probably graduated from high school after 1992, when the Supreme Court ruled that public middle school and high school graduations could not include a prayer, yet your own commencement ceremony may have included one.

For effective implementation of a judicial decision, the first requirement is that the members of the implementing population must act to show that they understand the original decision. For example, the Supreme Court ruled in *Reynolds* v. *Sims* (1964) that every person should have an equally weighted vote in electing governmental representatives.[53] This "one person, one vote" rule might seem simple enough at first glance, but in practice it can be very difficult to understand.

The second requirement is that the implementing population actually must follow Court policy. Thus, when the Court ruled that men could not be denied admission to a state-sponsored nursing school, the implementing population—in this case, university administrators and the state board of regents governing the nursing school—had to enroll qualified male students.[54]

Judicial decisions are most likely to be implemented smoothly if responsibility for implementation is concentrated in the hands of a few highly visible public officials, such as the president or a governor. By the same token, these officials also can thwart or impede judicial intentions. Recall from chapter 5, for example, the effect of Governor Orval Faubus's initial refusal to allow black children to attend all-white public schools in Little Rock, Arkansas.

The third requirement for implementation is that the consumer population must be aware of the rights that a decision grants or denies them. Teenagers seeking an abortion, for example, are consumers of the Supreme Court's decisions on abortion. They need to know that most states require them to inform their parents of their intention to have an abortion or to get parental permission to do so.

Thinking Globally

Judicial Independence in Pakistan

In November 2007, President Pervez Musharraf of Pakistan removed several Supreme Court justices and four judges from the provincial high courts immediately following his imposition of emergency rule in the country. A newly reconstituted Supreme Court legalized the dismissal of the judges, but opposition groups in the parliament vowed to reinstate the fired judges, who might be asked to rule on the constitutionality of the president's most recent election. Musharraf was later removed from office.

- How would the role of the Supreme Court change in the United States if the president was able to remove justices who did not support his or her policy agenda?
- How independent should the Supreme Court be? Does today's Court exercise too much influence over the policy-making process, or too little? Explain your reasoning.

★ WHAT SHOULD I HAVE LEARNED?

The judiciary and the legal process—on both the national and state levels—are complex and play a far more important role in the setting of policy than the Framers ever envisioned. To explain the judicial process and its evolution, we have asked the following questions:

- **What are the roots of the federal judiciary?**

  Many of the Framers viewed the judicial branch of government as little more than a minor check on the other two branches, ignoring Anti-Federalist concerns about an unelected judiciary and its potential for tyranny. The Judiciary Act of 1789 established the basic federal court system we have today. It was the Marshall Court (1801–1835), however, that interpreted the Constitution to include the Court's major power, that of judicial review.

- **What is the structure of the American legal system?**

  Ours is a dual judicial system consisting of the federal court system and the separate judicial systems of the fifty states. In each system there are two basic types of courts: trial courts and appellate courts. Each type deals with cases involving criminal and civil law. Original jurisdiction refers to a court's ability to hear a case as a trial court; appellate jurisdiction refers to a court's ability to review cases already decided by a trial court.

■ **How is the federal court system organized?**

The federal court system is made up of constitutional and legislative courts. Federal district courts, courts of appeals, and the Supreme Court are constitutional courts.

■ **How are federal court judges selected?**

District court and court of appeals judges are nominated by the president and subject to Senate confirmation. Supreme Court justices are nominated by the president and must also win Senate confirmation. Important criteria for selection include competence, standards, ideology, rewards, pursuit of political support, religion, race, ethnicity, and gender.

■ **How does the Supreme Court function today?**

Several factors influence the Court's decision to hear a case. Not only must the Court have jurisdiction, but at least four justices must vote to hear the case. Cases with certain characteristics are most likely to be heard. Once a case is set for review, briefs and *amicus curiae* briefs are filed and oral argument scheduled. The justices meet after oral argument to discuss the case, votes are taken, and opinions are written, circulated, and then announced.

■ **What are the key aspects of judicial philosophy and decision making?**

Judges' philosophy and ideology have an extraordinary impact on how they decide cases. Political scientists consider these factors in identifying models of how judges make decisions, including the behavioral, attitudinal, and strategic models.

■ **How does the judiciary affect policy and what efforts have been made to reform its policy-making powers?**

The Supreme Court is an important participant in the policy-making process. The power to interpret the laws gives the Court tremendous policy-making power never envisioned by the Framers.

Key Terms

amicus curiae, p. 267
appellate court, p. 254
appellate jurisdiction, p. 254
brief, p. 257
civil law, p. 255
constitutional court, p. 256
criminal law, p. 254
judicial activism, p. 270

judicial implementation, p. 272
judicial restraint, p. 269
judicial review, p. 248
Judiciary Act of 1789, p. 249
jurisdiction, p. 254
legislative court, p. 256
Marbury v. *Madison* (1803), p. 252
original jurisdiction, p. 254

precedent, p. 257
Rule of Four, p. 264
senatorial courtesy, p. 258
solicitor general, p. 267
stare decisis, p. 257
strict constructionist, p. 270
trial court, p. 254
writ of *certiorari*, p. 263

Researching the Judiciary
In the Library

Baum, Lawrence. *Judges and Their Audiences: A Perspective on Judicial Behavior*. Princeton, NJ: Princeton University Press, 2005.
———. *The Puzzle of Judicial Behavior*. Ann Arbor: University of Michigan Press, 1997.
Epstein, Lee, and Jeffrey A. Segal. *Advice and Consent: The Politics of Judicial Appointments*. New York: Oxford University Press, 2005.

Epstein, Lee, et al. *The Supreme Court Compendium*, 4th ed. Washington, DC: CQ Press, 2007.
Hall, Kermit L., ed. *The Oxford Companion to the Supreme Court of the United States*, 2nd ed. New York: Oxford University Press, 2005.
Hall, Kermit L., and Kevin T. McGuire, eds. *Institutions of American Democracy: The Judicial Branch*. New York: Oxford University Press, 2005.

Lazarus, Edward. *Closed Chambers: The First Eyewitness Account of the Epic Struggles Inside the Supreme Court*. New York: Times Books, 1998.

O'Brien, David M. *Storm Center: The Supreme Court in American Politics*, 8th ed. New York: Norton, 2008.

Perry, H. W. *Deciding to Decide: Agenda Setting in the United States Supreme Court*, reprint ed. Cambridge, MA: Harvard University Press, 2005.

Segal, Jeffrey A., and Harold J. Spaeth. *The Supreme Court and the Attitudinal Model Revisited*. New York: Cambridge University Press, 2002.

Slotnick, Elliot E., and Jennifer A. Segal. *Television News and the Supreme Court: All the News That's Fit to Air*. Boston: Cambridge University Press, 1998.

Sunstein, Cass R., et al. *Are Judges Political? An Empirical Analysis of the Federal Judiciary*. Washington, DC: Brookings Institution, 2006.

Ward, Artemus, and David L. Weiden. *Sorcerer's Apprentices: 100 Years of Law Clerks at the United States Supreme Court*. New York: New York University Press, 2006.

Whittington, Keith E. *Political Foundations of Judicial Supremacy: The Presidency, the Supreme Court, and Constitutional Leadership in U.S. History*. Princeton, NJ: Princeton University Press, 2007.

Woodward, Bob, and Scott Armstrong. *The Brethren: Inside the Supreme Court*, 2nd reprint ed. New York: Avon, 2005.

On the Web

To take a virtual tour of the U.S. Supreme Court and examine current cases on the Court's docket, go to **www.supremecourtus.gov**.

To learn more about the workings of the U.S. justice system, go to the Department of Justice Website at **www.usdoj.gov.**

To learn about the U.S. Senate Judiciary Committee and judicial nominations currently under review, go to the Senate's home page at **www.senate.gov**. You may also find information about pending nominations at the president's Web site at **www.whitehouse.gov**.

To learn about the American Bar Association's legislative and government advocacy, go to **www.abanet.org**.

To examine major Supreme Court decisions from the past to the present, go to Cornell Law School's Supreme Court Collection at **www.law.cornell.edu/supct/**. Streaming audio of oral arguments before the Court may be accessed at Oyez: U.S. Supreme Court Media at **www.oyez.org**.

10

Public Opinion and The News Media

E xit polls have long received attention for their ability to help media outlets predict the outcome of elections before state agencies completely tabulate the results. But, during the 2008 Iowa caucuses, a different, related way to gauge public opinion—the entrance poll—gained prevalence. In an entrance poll, voters are asked about which candidate they are going to vote for and why before they walk into the actual caucus. These polls are favored in caucuses because their results can be released immediately after they are collected. This allows networks to predict what might happen in a caucus while these events are actually occurring.

During the 2008 Iowa caucuses, five major television and cable networks (ABC, CBS, NBC, CNN, and FOX News) and the Associated Press banded together to collect information through an agency known as the National Election Pool. This agency sent pollsters to 40 caucuses for each political party, a total of 80 different meetings.

Entrance polls in Iowa immediately set the tone for the 2008 contest, showing record numbers of first-time caucus goers and young voters. They emphasized the importance of independent voters and correctly predicted strong support for Democratic candidate Barack Obama and Republican candidate Mike Huckabee, both of whom won their party's caucuses. Caucus voters, in addition, seemed to have a widespread interest in political change.

The 2008 entrance polls were notable for a number of other reasons, as well. First, they were the first entrance polls to include a correction to take into account caucus-goers who refused to participate in the survey; evidence shows that younger people are more likely to complete a whole entrance poll than their older counterparts. This correction, which had previously been implemented in exit polls, requires pollsters to collect the demographic information of all of the people who elect not to participate in the poll. This information is used to weight the collected data to accurately represent the population that comes to the polling place or party caucus.

Second, the polling firms charged with conducting the entrance poll made a concerted effort to recruit and train a broader cross-section of interviewers. This, too, was directed at improving the representativeness of the sample; pollsters believe that people

■ **Polling has been used to gauge public opinion on presidential elections since the early 20th century.** At left, George Gallup, the godfather of scientific polling, appears on a television program in 1948. At right, Iowa Caucus-goers register inside Waukee High School in Waukee, Iowa, in 2008.

WHAT SHOULD I KNOW ABOUT...

- the roots of political values: political socialization?
- public opinion and polling?
- the reasons we form and express political opinions?
- the evoluiton of the news media in the United States?
- rules governing the media?
- how the media cover politics?
- media influence, media bias, and public perceptions?

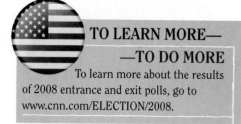

TO LEARN MORE—
—TO DO MORE
To learn more about the results of 2008 entrance and exit polls, go to www.cnn.com/ELECTION/2008.

are more likely to participate in a poll conducted by someone like them. For example, women may be more likely to respond to a poll conducted by a woman, and young people may be more likely to respond to a poll conducted by a young person.

The networks, many major newspapers, and polling organizations routinely report on and often attempt to gauge public opinion about a wide array of events. Still, many citizens question the fairness or bias of the media in all of its forms as well as the accuracy of public opinion polls. Often, as reported by or even commissioned by the media, polls reveal much about what "the public" is thinking. The complex interaction of the media and public opinion are the focus of this chapter

First we will discuss the roots of political values: political socialization. After an examination of the history of public opinion research, we will examine how we form political opinions. Looking next at the news media, we will examine the evolution of the press in the United States and current issues affecting the media. We will also discuss the rules under which the news media operate, how the media cover politics, and how the media influence public opinion.

oots of Political Values: Political Socialization

political socialization
The process through which individuals acquire their political beliefs and values.

Political scientists believe that many of our attitudes about issues are grounded in our political values. We learn these values through **political socialization**. Family, school, peers, and the mass media are often important influences or agents of political socialization. Other factors, too, often influence how political opinions are formed or reinforced. These include religious beliefs, race and ethnicity, gender, age, the region of the country in which you live, and even political events. Your own political knowledge may also shape your ideals.

The Family

The influence of the family on political socialization can be traced to two factors: communication and receptivity. Children, especially during their preschool years, spend tremendous amounts of time with their parents; early on, they learn their parents' political values, even though these concepts may be vague. (To learn more about political socialization, see Ideas into Action: Be a Socialization Agent.) One study found that the most important visible public figures for children under the age of ten were police officers and, to a much lesser extent, the president.[1] Young children almost uniformly view both as "helpful." But, by the age of ten or eleven, children become more selective in their perceptions of the president. By this age, children raised in Democratic households are much more likely to be critical of a Republican president than are those raised in Republican households. In 1988, for example, 58 percent of children in Republican households identified themselves as Republicans, and many had developed strong positive feelings toward Ronald Reagan, the Republican president. (To learn more about the political indentification of young people, see Figure 10.1.)

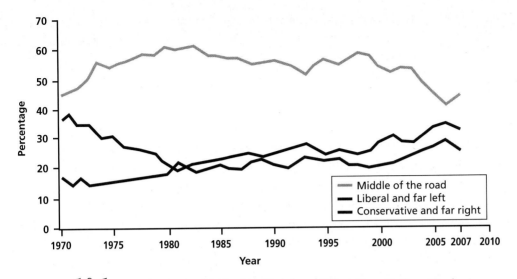

FIGURE 10.1 The Ideological Self-Identification of First-Year College Students

A majority of first-year college students describe themselves as middle of the road; this number has been fairly consistent since the early 1990s although it decreased beginning in the early 2000s. The number of students identifying themselves as liberal and far left declined dramatically during the 1970s and early 1980s but is currently on the rise. The number of students identifying themselves as conservative and far right has also increased, but at a slower rate.

Sources: Reprinted from Harold W. Stanley and Richard G. Niemi, *Vital Statistics on American Politics, 2007–2008* (Washington, DC: CQ Press, 2008), 124.

School and Peers

Researchers report mixed findings concerning the role of schools in the political socialization process. (To learn more about schools and the socialization process, see Join the Debate: Teaching Civics in American High Schools.) There is no question that, in elementary school, children are taught respect for their nation and its symbols. Most school days begin with the Pledge of Allegiance, and patriotism and respect for country are important components of most school curricula. Support for flag and country create a foundation for national allegiance that prevails despite the negative views about politicians and government institutions that many Americans develop later in life. For example, though many Americans debated U.S. action in Iraq in 2003, large numbers of schoolchildren were encouraged to send letters and packages to troops there and elsewhere. In some states, teachers were encouraged to limit anti-war discussion.[2] Measures such as these, however controversial, help to build a sense of patriotism at a young age.

A child's peers—that is, children about the same age—also seem to have an important effect on the socialization process. While parental influences are greatest from birth to age five, a child's peer group becomes increasingly important as the child gets older, especially as he or she gets into middle school or high school.[3]

High schools also can be important agents of political socialization. They continue the elementary school tradition of building good citizens and often reinforce textbook learning with trips to the state or national capital. They also offer courses on current U.S. affairs. Many high schools impose a compulsory service learning requirement, which some studies report positively affects later political participation.[4] Although the formal education of many people in the United States ends with high school, research shows that better-informed citizens vote more often as adults. Therefore, presentation of civic information is especially critical at the high school level, where it reinforces views about participation.

Join the Debate

Teaching Civics in American High Schools

OVERVIEW: Civic education is considered an essential component of political socialization. In many classrooms, for example, children elect the students who will erase chalkboards or serve as class leaders; by participating in classroom elections, students are thus socialized to accept electoral politics as part of legitimate political behavior. Most democratic societies have some form of civic education, if only to teach citizens social norms, virtues, and the "rules of the game" of the democratic process. Historically low voter turnout and close election outcomes have been cited by supporters of civic education as a sign that more needs to be done to teach young people the importance of political participation. Recently, civic education requirements have taken on additional urgency in light of debates about immigration policy and questions regarding the extent to which civic education efforts should focus exclusively on U.S. norms or emphasize commonalities and differences among democratic nations worldwide.

Civic education in secondary education has declined over the last thirty years. The National Assessment of Educational Progress (NAEP) has determined that only 26 percent of all high school seniors may be considered "proficient" in American political knowledge, and a Roper survey discovered that the majority of graduates from America's elite universities were incapable of identifying James Madison (a principal architect of the Constitution and the fourth president) or words from President Abraham Lincoln's Gettysburg Address. As a corrective, the federal government has instituted increased spending and guidelines for secondary American history and government education under the National Endowment for the Humanities' We the People Initiative, a program created to reaffirm and reinstitute civic education in America's classrooms.

French political commentator Alexis de Tocqueville argued that without common values and virtues, there can be no common action and social stability. What is the best way to teach American history, government, and political principles so that all who have contributed to the American experiment are recognized? Is a common civic education necessary, or should political socialization be left to the family? What can be done to increase interest in democratic politics and participation, and how can civic knowledge be restored to the American electorate?

Arguments IN FAVOR of Civic Education in High Schools

■ **There may be a relationship between political participation and civic education.** A Carnegie Corporation study contends that student participation in the management of schools and classrooms, as well as in simulations of democratic institutions and processes, may increase involvement in the American political process.

At the college level, teaching style often changes. Many college courses and texts like this one are designed in part to provide you with the information necessary to think critically about issues of major political consequence. It is common in college for students to be called on to question the appropriateness of certain political actions or to discuss underlying reasons for certain political or policy decisions. Therefore, most researchers believe that college has a liberalizing effect on students. Since the 1920s, studies have shown that students become more liberal each year they are in college. The 1992 and 1996 victories of Bill Clinton and his equally youthful running mate Al Gore, who went out of their way to woo the youth vote, probably contributed to the small bump in the liberal ideological identification of first-year college students in those years.

The Mass Media

The media today are taking on a growing role as socialization agents. Adult Americans spend nearly thirty hours a week in front of their television sets; children spend

- **Civic education teaches citizens how to participate in a democratic society.** Students become politically socialized by taking part in school elections, activities, and extracurricular activities (such as participating in debate teams and publishing school newspapers). Civic education teaches not only cooperation, but also tolerance of dissent and opposing views, as well as political compromise. This prepares students for the realities of pluralistic democratic life.

- **Civic education is a complement to political socialization.** The primary influence on a person's political development comes from family and friends, and mass media and culture also help to shape political values and attitudes. The role of a formal civic education is to teach American history and governmental and political structures and principles, as well as to provide a forum for students to hone their political skills, practice public debate, and learn civic engagement.

Arguments AGAINST Civic Education in High Schools

- **Civic education is innately biased by promoting certain values over** others. In a free, multicultural society, it is inherently wrong to press upon individuals a certain political and social view. Modern democratic governments gather their strength from the many diverse cultures and political views that make up their respective societies. Teaching one sociopolitical view stifles the contributions of different cultures. To this end, the American Historical Society advocates teaching comparative and world history.

- **Parents should be responsible for civic education.** A government-sanctioned education will likely be partial to the government's interests and views. It is proper that parents introduce their children to the nation's political culture. This will help ensure a diversity of views in regard to the nature of government, thereby fostering debate and compromise in the marketplace of political ideas.

- **It is difficult to determine what should constitute a civic education curriculum in a pluralistic society.** Which understanding of American history, politics, and government is to be taught? Different groups have different interpretations and understanding of the historical unfolding of American society. To promote the views of one group over another would be unfair, and to teach all views would overwhelm students with information; the effect may be actually to *discourage* political engagement by subjecting students to information overload.

Continuing the Debate

1. Is there a correlation between civic participation and civic education? Why or why not?
2. Is it the proper place of public schools to engage in civic education, or is this the duty of family and friends?

To Follow the Debate Online, Go To:

www. civiced. org, the Web site of the Center for Civic Education, a group partially funded by the Pew Charitable Trusts to provide resources and programs to promote civic education.

www.carnegie.org/reporter/07/civic/demo_low. html, a page from the Carnegie Foundation web site discussing a number of studies that link civic education and patterns of participation in governance.

even more.[5] Television has a tremendous impact on how people view politics, government, and politicians. Television can serve to enlighten voters and encourage voter turnout.

Over the years, more and more Americans have turned away from traditional sources of news such as nightly news broadcasts on the major networks and daily newspapers in favor of different outlets. In 2008, one study estimated that the same percentage of viewers watched alternative sources such as *The Tonight Show, The Late Show*, or *The Daily Show* as watched more traditional cable news such as CNN or FOX News.[6] TV talk shows, talk radio, online magazines, listservs, and blogs are important sources of information about politics for many, yet the information that people get from these sources often is skewed.

Since the 2004 presidential election, major party candidates have used another form of media to sway and inform voters: the Internet. Candidates running for office in 2008 launched their own Internet sites, and the major networks and newspapers had their own Internet sites reporting on the election. Blogs and social networking sites also played an important role. The Obama campaign relied heavily on Facebook.

Religious Beliefs

Throughout our history, religion has played an extraordinary role in political life. Many colonists came to American shores seeking religious liberty, yet many quickly moved to impose their religious beliefs on others, and some made participation in local politics contingent on religiosity. Since political scientists began to look at the role of religion, numerous scholars have found that organized religion influences the political beliefs and behaviors of its adherents. The effects of organized religion are magnified in American culture, as 82 percent of respondents in a 2007 Gallup poll considered religion an important part of their lives.[7]

Through much of the twentieth century, social scientists found that faith-based political activity occurred largely on the left. From the civil rights movement, to efforts to improve the living standards of farmers and migrant workers, to abolition of the death penalty, religious leaders were evident. The civil rights movement, in particular, was led by numerous religious men, including the Reverend Martin Luther King Jr. and the Reverend Andrew Young (who later became mayor of Atlanta, Georgia, and the U.S. ambassador to the United Nations), as well as more recently the Reverend Jesse Jackson and the Reverend Al Sharpton.

In 1972, for the first time, a religious gap appeared in voting and public opinion. President Richard M. Nixon's re-election campaign was designed to appeal to what he termed "the Silent Majority," who wanted a return to more traditional values after the tumult of the 1960s. By the 1980s, conservative Christians could take credit for the election of Ronald Reagan. Throughout the 1980s, first the Moral Majority and the the Christian Coalition have played increasingly key roles in politics. Today, religion is the second largest predictor of vote choice, after party identification. Regular church-goers have conservative views and vote Republican by a 2 to 1 margin.

In 2006, 55 percent of Americans identified themselves as Protestant, 26 percent as Catholic, and 4 percent as Jewish, while 14 percent claimed to have no religious affiliation. As shown in Figure 10.2, Protestants, especially evangelicals, are the most conservative and Jews the most liberal. And, as liberals, Jews tend to vote Democratic. In 2008, for example, Barack Obama and his running mate, Joe Biden, captured 78 percent of the Jewish vote.[8]

Shared religious attitudes tend to affect voting and stances on particular issues. Catholics as a group, for example, favor aid to parochial schools, while many fundamentalist Protestants support organized prayer in public schools as well as abstinence-only education.

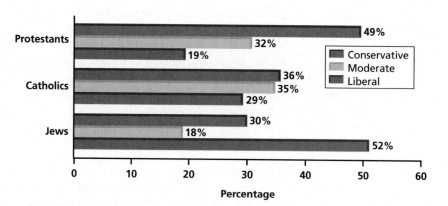

FIGURE **10.2** The Ideological Self-Identification of Protestants, Catholics, and Jews

Source: Data compiled and analyzed by Alixandra B. Yanus from the 2004 American National Election Study.

Analyzing Visuals | Racial and Ethnic Attitudes on Selected Issues

Political opinions held by racial and ethnic groups in the United States differ on many issues. Look at the bar graph comparing the opinions of whites, blacks, and Latino/as on a number of political issues and ask yourself the following questions:

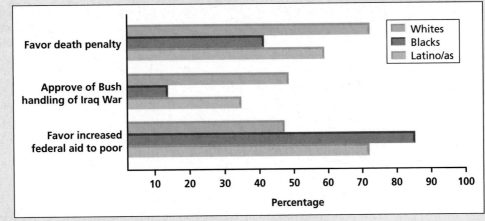

Source: Data compiled and analyzed by Alixandra B. Yanus from the 2004 American National Election Study.

WHAT do you observe about the differences and similarities in opinions among the three different groups?

ON which issues do blacks and whites, Latino/as and blacks, and Latino/as and whites have the most divergent opinions?

ON which issues are these groups likely to have the most similar opinions?

Race and Ethnicity

Differences in political socialization appear at a very early age. Young African American children, for example, generally show very positive feelings about American society and political processes, but this attachment lessens considerably over time. Black children fail to hold the president in the esteem accorded him by white children; indeed, older African American children in the 1960s viewed the government primarily in terms of the U.S. Supreme Court.[9] These differences continue through adulthood.

Race and ethnicity are exceptionally important factors in elections and in the study of public opinion. The direction and intensity of African American opinion on a variety of hot-button issues often are quite different from those of whites. As revealed in Analyzing Visuals: Racial and Ethnic Attitudes on Selected Issues, whites are much more likely to support the war in Iraq than are blacks or Latino/as. Likewise, differences can be seen in other issue areas, including support for preferential treatment to improve the position of the poor.[10] Government-sponsored health insurance for the working poor, for example, is a hot-button issue with Latino/a voters, with 94 percent favoring it. Unlike many non-Latino/a Americans, Hispanics also favor bilingual education and liberalized immigration policies.[11] Asian and Pacific Americans, and American Indians also often respond differently to issues than do whites.

Gender

Poll after poll reveals that women hold very different opinions from men on a variety of issues, as shown in Table 10.1. Women, and particularly unmarried women, are more likely to be Democrats, while white men are increasingly becoming the core of the Republican Party.[12]

"From the time that the earliest public opinion polls were taken, women have held" more liberal attitudes about social welfare issues such as education, juvenile justice, capital punishment, and the environment. Some analysts suggest that women's more nurturing nature and their prominent role as mothers lead women to have more liberal attitudes on issues affecting the family or children. Research by political scientists, however, finds no support for a maternal explanation.[13]

Historically, public opinion polls have also found that women hold more negative views about war and military intervention. However, the gender gap on military issues began to disappear in the late 1990s, when the United States intervened in Kosovo. Many speculated that this occurred because of the increased participation of women in the workforce and the military, the "sanitized nature of much of the war footage" shown on TV, and the humanitarian reasons for involvement.[14]

The gender gap in military affairs also was less visible following the terrorist attacks of September 11, 2001. Right after the attacks, polls showed that 47 percent of women and 53 percent of men voiced their support for the U.S. military intervention in Afghanistan.[15] However, as the memory of 9/11 has receded, the war in Iraq has resulted in a renewed gender gap on foreign affairs. (To learn more about the gender gap, see Table 10.1.)

Age

Age seems to have a decided effect on political socialization. Our view of the proper role of government, for example, often depends on the era in which we were born and our individual experiences with a variety of social, political, and economic forces. Older people continue to be affected by having lived through the Great Depression and World War II. One political scientist predicts that as Baby Boomers age, the age gap in political beliefs about political issues, especially governmental programs, will increase.[16] Young people, for example, resist higher taxes to fund Medicare, while the elderly resist all efforts to limit Medicare or Social Security.

In states such as Florida, to which many northern retirees have flocked seeking relief from cold winters and high taxes, the elderly have voted as a bloc to defeat school tax increases and to pass tax breaks for themselves. As a group, senior citizens are much more likely to favor an increased governmental role in the area of medical insurance.

Region

Regional and sectional differences have been important factors in the development and maintenance of political beliefs since colonial times. As the United States developed into a major industrial nation, waves of immigrants with different religious traditions and customs entered the United States and often settled in areas where other immigrants from their region already lived. For example, thousands of Scandinavians settled in Minnesota, and many Irish settled in the urban centers of the Northeast, as did many Italians and Jews. All brought with them unique views about numerous issues, as well as about the role of government. These political views often have been

TABLE 10.1 Gender Differences on Political Issues

Public opinion polls reveal that men and women tend to hold different views on a number of political issues. Yet, as this table also reveals, on some political issues, little difference is evident.

	Men (%)	Women (%)
Think Iraq War worth the cost	42	35
Favor increased federal spending on war on terrorism	50	36
Favor increased federal spending on Social Security	57	67
Favor ban on late-term (partial birth) abortion	57	60
Think federal government should make it more difficult to buy guns	48	67
Voted for Barack Obama in 2008	49	56

Source: Data compiled and analyzed by Alixandra B. Yanus from the 2004 American National Election Study.

transmitted through generations, and many regional differences continue to affect public opinion today.

One of the most long-standing and dramatic regional differences in the United States is that between the South and the North. Recall that during the Constitutional Convention, most Southerners staunchly advocated a weak national government. Nearly a hundred years later, the Civil War was fought in part because of basic differences in philosophy toward government (states' rights in the South versus national rights in the North). As we know from the results of modern political polling, the South has continued to lag behind the rest of the nation on support for civil rights, while continuing to favor return of power to the states at the expense of the national government.

The South also is much more religious than the rest of the nation, as well as more Protestant. About two-thirds of the South is Protestant (versus about 45 percent for the rest of the nation), and church attendance is highest in the South, where 46 percent report weekly visits. In contrast, only 34 percent of those living in the Northeast go to church or synagogue on a weekly basis.[17] Given the South's higher churchgoing rates, it is not surprising that the Christian Coalition (also discussed in chapter 16) has been very successful at mobilizing voters in that region.

The West, too, now appears different from other sections of the nation. Some people have moved there to avoid city life; other residents have an anti-government bias. Many who have sought refuge there are staunchly against any governmental action, especially on the national level.

The Impact of Events

Key political events play a very important role in a person's political socialization. You probably have teachers or professors who remember what they were doing on the day that President John F. Kennedy was killed—November 22, 1963. This dramatic event is indelibly etched in the minds of virtually all people who were old enough to be aware of it. Similarly, most college students today remember where they were when they heard about the September 11, 2001, attacks on the World Trade Center and the Pentagon. These attacks on American shores evoked a profound sense of patriotism and national unity as American flags were displayed from windows, doors, balconies, and cars. For many Americans, the attacks were life-changing political events.

One problem in discussing the impact of events on political socialization is that many of the major studies on this topic were conducted in the aftermath of Watergate, which, along with the civil rights movement and the Vietnam War, produced a marked increase in Americans' distrust of government. The findings reported in Analyzing Visuals: Faith in Institutions (see page 21) reveal the dramatic drop-off of trust in government that began in the mid-1960s.

War, Peace,
and Public Opinion

Public Opinion and Polling

At first glance, **public opinion** seems to be a very straightforward concept: it is what the public thinks about a particular issue or set of issues at a particular time. Since the 1930s, governmental decision makers have relied heavily on **public opinion polls**—interviews with samples of citizens that are used to estimate what the public is thinking. According to George Gallup (1901–1983), an Iowan who is considered the founder of modern-day polling, polls have played a key role in defining issues of concern to the public, shaping administrative decisions, and helping "speed up the process of democracy" in the United States.[18]

public opinion
What the public thinks about a particular issue or set of issues at any point in time.

public opinion polls
Interviews or surveys with samples of citizens that are used to estimate the feelings and beliefs of the entire population.

Thinking Globally

Public Opinion Regarding Terrorism

Public opinion regarding the degree to which terrorism represents an important national problem differs significantly across countries. In the United States, 44 percent of citizens surveyed in 2007 by the Pew Charitable Trust reported terrorism as a very important problem. Among Canadians, only 24 percent agreed that terrorism is a major concern. In Western Europe, 31 percent of Germans, 54 percent of French, 66 percent of Spanish, and 73 percent of Italians considered terrorism a major problem.

- What factors might account for the different opinions about the danger posed by terrorism across countries?
- Are you surprised that more Americans aren't worried about terrorism? Why are opinions about the importance of terrorism so different across neighboring countries in Western Europe?

The History of Public Opinion Research

As early as 1824, one Pennsylvania newspaper tried to predict the winner of that year's presidential contest. In 1883, the *Boston Globe* sent reporters to selected election precincts to poll voters as they exited voting booths in an effort to predict the results of key contests. But, public opinion polling as we know it today did not begin to develop until the 1930s. Much of this growth was prompted by Walter Lippmann's seminal work, *Public Opinion* (1922). In this piece, Lippmann observed that research on public opinion was far too limited, especially in light of its importance. Researchers in a variety of disciplines, including political science, heeded Lippmann's call to learn more about public opinion. Some tried to use scientific methods to measure political thought through the use of surveys or polls. As methods for gathering and interpreting data improved, survey data began to play an increasingly important role in all walks of life, from politics to retailing.

Literary Digest, a popular magazine that first began presidential polling in 1916, was a pioneer in the use of **straw polls**, unscientific surveys used to gauge public opinion, to predict the popular vote in those four presidential elections. Its polling methods were hailed widely as "amazingly right" and "uncannily accurate."[19] In 1936, however, its luck ran out. *Literary Digest* predicted that Republican Alfred M. Landon would beat incumbent President Franklin D. Roosevelt by a margin of 57 percent to 43 percent of the popular vote. Roosevelt, however, won in a landslide election, receiving 62.5 percent of the popular vote and carrying all but two states.

Literary Digest's 1936 straw poll had three fatal errors. First, its **sample**, a subset of the whole population selected to be questioned for the purposes of prediction or gauging opinion, was drawn from telephone directories and lists of automobile owners. This technique oversampled the upper middle class and the wealthy, groups heavily Republican in political orientation. Moreover, in 1936, voting polarized along class lines. Thus, the oversampling of wealthy Republicans was particularly problematic because it severely underestimated the Democratic vote.

Literary Digest's second problem was timing. Questionnaires were mailed in early September. It did not measure the changes in public sentiment that occurred as the election drew closer.

Its third error occurred because of a problem we now call self-selection. Only highly motivated individuals sent back the cards—a mere 22 percent of those surveyed responded. Those who respond to mail surveys (or today, online surveys) are quite different from the general electorate; they often are wealthier and better educated and care more fervently about issues. *Literary Digest*, then, failed to observe one of the now well-known cardinal rules of survey sampling: "One cannot allow the respondents to select themselves into the sample."[20]

At least one pollster, however, correctly predicted the results of the 1936 election: George Gallup. Gallup had written his dissertation in psychology at the University of Iowa on how to measure the readership of newspapers. He then expanded his research to study public opinion about politics. He was so confident about his methods that he gave all of his newspaper clients a money-back guarantee: if his poll predictions weren't closer to the actual election outcome than those of the highly acclaimed *Literary Digest*, he would refund their money. Although Gallup underpredicted Roosevelt's victory by nearly 7 percent, the fact that he got the winner right was what everyone remembered, especially given *Literary Digest*'s dramatic miscalculation.

straw polls
Unscientific surveys used to gauge public opinion on a variety of issues and policies.

sample
A subset of the whole population selected to be questioned for the purposes of prediction or gauging opinion.

Through the late 1940s, polling techniques became more sophisticated. The number of polling groups also dramatically increased, as businesses and politicians began to rely on polling information to market products and candidates. But, in 1948, the polling industry suffered a severe, although fleeting, setback when Gallup and many other pollsters incorrectly predicted that Thomas E. Dewey would defeat President Harry S Truman.

Nevertheless, as revealed in Figure 10.3, the Gallup Organization continues to predict the winners of the presidential popular vote successfully. Gallup not only predicted the winner, it also accurately predicted Barack Obama's popular vote.

Traditional Public Opinion Polls

Polling has several key phases, including: (1) determining the content and phrasing the questions; (2) selecting the sample; and, (3) contacting respondents.

DETERMINING THE CONTENT AND PHRASING THE QUESTIONS Once a candidate, politician, or news organization decides to use a poll to measure the public's attitudes, special care has to be taken in constructing the questions to be asked. For example, if your professor asked you, "Do you think my grading procedures are fair?" rather than asking, "In general, how fair do you think the grading is in your American Politics course?" you might give a slightly different answer. The wording of the first question tends to put you on the spot and personalize the grading style; the second question is more neutral. Even more obvious differences appear in the real world of polling, especially when interested groups want a poll to yield particular results. Responses to highly emotional issues such as abortion, same-sex marriage, and affirmative action often are skewed depending on the wording of a particular question.

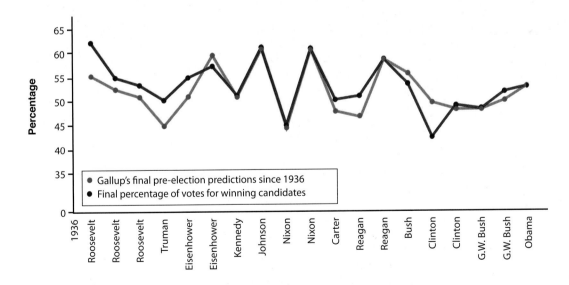

Presidential election winner

FIGURE 10.3 The Success of the Gallup Poll in Presidential Elections, 1936–2008

As seen here, Gallup's final predictions have been remarkably accurate. Furthermore, in each of the years where there is a significant discrepancy between Gallup's prediction and the election's outcome, there was a prominent third candidate. In 1948, Strom Thurmond ran on the Dixiecrat ticket; in 1980, John Anderson ran as the American Independent Party candidate; in 1992, Ross Perot ran as an independent.

Sources: Marty Baumann, "How One Polling Firm Stacks Up," *USA Today* (October 27, 1992): 13A; 1996 data from Mike Mokrzycki, "Pre-election Polls' Accuracy Varied," *Atlanta Journal and Constitution* (November 8, 1996): A12; 2000 data from Gallup Organization, "Poll Releases," November 7, 2000; 2004 and 2008 data from *USA Today* and CNN/Gallup Tracking Poll, USAToday.com.

POLITICS NOW

Source: ST. LOUIS POST DISPATCH   December 9, 2007

Cell Phones Challenge Pollsters

Pollsters Face New Hurdles: Cell Phones

BILL LAMBRECHT

Pollsters taking the pulse of voters this political season are confronting growing obstacles from cell phones—and an electorate that is increasingly walling itself off with caller ID and answering machines. The response rate in phone surveys has plunged from about 40 percent in the 1980s to 20 percent or less now, making it harder and more expensive for pollsters to secure the samples they need. These changes are causing some to wonder about the accuracy of poll results this year, especially when it comes to young adults, who are 50 percent more likely than the rest of the population to use cell phones but who are voting in ever-greater numbers. . . .

According to the most recent government figures, nearly 13 percent of American homes were categorized as cell phone only—meaning that they had no land line. A quarter of young adults are reachable by cell phone only, and that number continues to rise.

Pollsters tend to shun cell phones for several reasons. Among them:

- Cell phone users are able to automatically screen calls and are less likely to answer.

- Area codes of cell phones don't necessarily indicate where the user lives.
- Directories for cell phones are not available, and blocks of numbers available for purchase may not represent the geographical region being polled.
- Mobile phones are typically used by people on the go, perhaps in their cars or in situations where they are distracted and unable to complete long interviews.

Besides narrowing the traditional random sample pool, the switch to cell phones makes it less likely that people reached by pollsters on land lines will be between 18 and 34 years old—a group that is voting more heavily than it used to.

As recently as the 2000 presidential election, pollsters had a nearly 1-in-3 chance of encountering a young adult in a phone call. By the 2006 congressional elections, the percentage of young people in land-line homes had dropped to 20 percent, and by earlier this year, the percentage had dipped into the teens.

For pollsters, this means extrapolating from the responses of young people they do reach—meaning they are talking to fewer young people than their surveys might suggest—or trying to reach people on cell phones.

Del Ali is president of Research 2000, which conducts polls for the [St. Louis] *Post-Dispatch* and other news organizations. He uses cell phone numbers in polls but says he takes extra care to make

sure that young people reached on their cell phones are registered voters in the state or locale targeted. Ali is among pollsters who say a bigger worry is Internet polling.

Pollster John Zogby, a pioneer in Internet surveys, acknowledges that cyberspace polling is still in its infancy. He has been working for years to build a database of 350,000 e-mail addresses of people that he regards as representative of the nation. When conducting a national poll, he'll e-mail 50,000-75,000 people to take part. From the thousands who respond, he'll randomly select people for the poll.

Skeptics say Internet polling is flawed because an e-mail database may not be representative of the population at large. Zogby, who also uses phone surveys, professes confidence in his Internet results and argues that survey research must change with society.

"I know that it is the next wave," he said. "The telephone is becoming ungainly. It's still a useful tool (for polling), but we're anticipating that it won't continue to be a useful tool."

Discussion Questions

1. *How can pollsters surmount the problems that come with a growing population of cell phone users?*
2. *What additional shortcomings might Internet polling have?*
3. *How might you make more people aware of the shortcomings of traditional polling techniques?*

SELECTING THE SAMPLE Once the decision is made to take a poll, pollsters must determine the universe, or the entire group whose attitudes they wish to measure. This universe could be all Americans, all voters, all city residents, all Latino/as, or all Republicans. In a perfect world, each individual would be asked to give an opinion, but such comprehensive polling is not practical. Consequently, pollsters take a sample of the universe in which they are interested. One way to obtain this sample is by **random sampling**. This method of selection gives each potential voter or adult the same chance of being selected. In theory, this sounds good, but it is actually impossible to achieve because no one has lists of every person in a group. Thus, the method of representative poll taking is extremely important in determining the validity and reliability of the results.

random sampling
A method of poll selection that gives each person in a group the same chance of being selected.

Most national surveys and commercial polls use samples of 600 to 1,000 individuals and use a variation of the random sampling method called **stratified sampling**. Simple random, nonstratified samples are not very useful at predicting voting because they may undersample or oversample key populations that are not likely to vote. To avoid these problems, reputable polling organizations use stratified sampling (the most rigorous sampling technique) based on census data that provide the number of residences in an area and their location.

About twenty respondents from each primary sampling unit are picked to be interviewed. Generally four or five city blocks or areas are selected, and then four or five target families from each district are used. Large, sophisticated surveys such as the National Election Study and General Social Survey, which produce the data commonly used by political scientists, attempt to sample from lists of persons living in each household. The key to the success of the stratified sampling method is not to let people volunteer to be interviewed—volunteers as a group often have different opinions from those who do not volunteer.

CONTACTING RESPONDENTS After selecting the methodology to conduct the poll, the next question is how to contact those to be surveyed. Television stations often ask people to call in, and some surveyors hit the streets. Telephone polls, however, are the most frequently used mechanism by which to gauge the temper of the electorate.

The most common form of telephone polls are random-digit dialing surveys, in which a computer randomly selects telephone numbers to be dialed. In spite of some problems (such as the fact that many people do not want to be bothered, especially at dinner time or do not have home phones), most polls done for newspapers and news magazines are conducted in this way. Pollsters are exempt from federal and state do-not-call lists because poll-taking is a form of constitutionally protected speech.

Individual, in-person interviews are conducted by some groups, such as the National Election Study. Some analysts favor such in-person surveys, but others argue that the unintended influence of the questioner or pollster is an important source of errors. How the pollster dresses, relates to the person being interviewed, and even asks the questions can affect responses. (Some of these factors, such as tone of voice or accent, can also affect the results of telephone surveys.)

Political Polls

As polling has become increasingly sophisticated and networks, newspapers, and magazines compete with each other to report the most up-to-the-minute changes in public opinion on issues or politicians, new types of polls have been suggested and put into use. Each type of poll has contributed to our knowledge of public opinion and its role in the political process.

PUSH POLLS All good polls for political candidates contain questions intended to produce information that helps campaigns judge their own strengths and weaknesses as well as those of their opponents.[21] They might, for example, ask if you would be more likely to vote for candidate X if you knew that candidate was a strong environmentalist. These kinds of questions are accepted as an essential part of any poll, but there are concerns as to where to draw the line. Questions that go over the line are called **push polls** and often are a result of ulterior motives. Push polls are designed to give respondents some negative or even untruthful information about a candidate's opponent to push them away from that candidate and toward the one paying for the poll.

TRACKING POLLS During the 1992 presidential elections, **tracking polls**, which were taken on a daily basis by some news organizations, were first introduced to allow presidential candidates to monitor short-term campaign developments and the effects of their campaign strategies. Today, tracking polls involve small samples (usually of

stratified sampling
A variation of random sampling; census data are used to divide the country into four sampling regions. Sets of counties and standard metropolitan statistical areas are then randomly selected in proportion to the total national population.

push polls
Polls taken for the purpose of providing information on an opponent that would lead respondents to vote against that candidate.

tracking polls
Continuous surveys that enable a campaign to chart its daily rise or fall in support.

registered voters contacted at certain times of day) and are conducted every twenty-four hours. The results are then combined into moving three- to five-day averages, as illustrated below in Figure 10.4. Even though these surveys are fraught with reliability problems and are vulnerable to bias, many major news organizations continue their use. (To learn more about tracking polls, see Figure 10.4)

exit polls
Polls conducted at selected polling places on Election Day.

EXIT POLLS In contrast to the entrance polls discussed in the opening vignette, **exit polls** are polls conducted as voters leave selected polling places on Election Day. Generally, large news organizations send pollsters to selected precincts to sample every tenth voter as he or she emerges from the polling site. The results of these polls are used to help the media predict the outcome of key races, often just a few minutes after the polls close in a particular state and generally before voters in other areas—sometimes in a later time zone—have cast their ballots. They also provide an independent assessment of why voters supported particular candidates.

In 1980, President Jimmy Carter's own polling and the results of network exit polls led him to concede defeat three hours before the polls closed on the West Coast. Many Democratic Party officials and candidates criticized Carter and network predictions for harming their chances at victories, arguing that with the presidential election already called, voters were unlikely to go to the polls. In the aftermath of that controversy, all networks agreed not to predict the results of presidential contests until all polling places were closed.

Shortcomings of Polling

The information derived from public opinion polls has become an extremely important part of governance. When the results of a poll are accurate, they express the feelings of the electorate and help guide policymakers. However, when the results of a poll are inaccurate, disastrous consequences often result.

MARGIN OF ERROR All polls contain errors. Typically, the margin of error in a sample of 1,000 will be about 4 percent. If you ask 1,000 people "Do you like ice cream?"

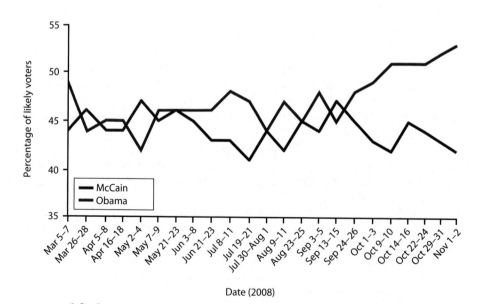

Date (2008)

FIGURE 10.4 A Daily Tracking Poll for the 2008 Presidential Election
The day-to-day fluctuations in presidential and congressional races are often shown through tracking polls. This figure shows the ups and downs of the 2008 presidential election.
Source: USA Today and CNN/Gallup Poll results, http://www.usatoday.com/news/politicselections/nation/polls/usatodaypolls.htm.

and 52 percent say yes and 48 percent say no, the results are too close to tell whether more people like ice cream than not. Why? Because the **margin of error** implies that somewhere between 56 percent (52 + 4) and 48 percent (52 − 4) of the people like ice cream, while between 52 percent (48 + 4) and 44 percent (48 − 4) do not. The margin of error in a close election makes predictions very difficult.

SAMPLING ERROR The accuracy of any poll depends on the quality of the sample that was drawn. Small samples, if properly drawn, can be very accurate if each unit in the universe has an equal opportunity to be sampled. If a pollster, for example, fails to sample certain populations, his or her results may reflect that shortcoming. Often the opinions of the poor and homeless are underrepresented because insufficient attention is given to making certain that these groups are sampled representatively.

By permission of Mike Luckovich and Creators Syndicate, Inc.

How susceptible are polls to short-term forces? This cartoon is a humorous take on the frequent fluctuations many political polls demonstrate as the electorate responds to changing events.

margin of error
A measure of the accuracy of a public opinion poll.

LIMITED RESPONDENT OPTIONS Polls can be inaccurate when they limit responses. If you are asked "How do you like this class?" and are given only like or dislike options, your full sentiments may not be tapped if you like the class very much or feel only so-so about it.

LACK OF INFORMATION Public opinion polls may also be inaccurate when they attempt to gauge attitudes about issues that some or even many individuals do not care about or about which the public has little information. Most academic public opinion research organizations, such as the National Election Study, use some kind of filter question that first asks respondents whether or not they have thought about the question. These screening procedures generally allow surveyors to exclude as many as 20 percent of their respondents, especially on complex issues like the federal budget. Questions on more personal issues such as moral values, drugs, crime, race, and women's role in society get far fewer "no opinion" or "don't know" responses.

DIFFICULTY MEASURING INTENSITY Another shortcoming of polls concerns their inability to measure intensity of feeling about particular issues. Whereas a respondent might answer affirmatively to any question, it is likely that his or her feelings about issues such as abortion, the death penalty, or support for U.S. troops in Afghanistan or Iraq are much more intense than are his or her feelings about the Electoral College or types of voting machines.

Why We Form and Express Political Opinions

Often, the sentiments we express in public opinion polls can be traced to our political socialization. However, most people also are influenced by a number of other factors, including: (1) personal benefits; (2) political knowledge; (3) cues from various leaders or opinion makers; and, (4) their political ideology.

Can public opinion polling measure intensity?
One of the difficulties of public opinion researchers is measuring how strongly people hold their opinons.

Personal Benefits

Most polls reveal that Americans are growing more and more "I" centered. This perspective often leads people to agree with policies that will benefit them personally. You've probably heard the adage "People vote with their pocketbooks." Taxpayers generally favor lower taxes, hence the popularity of candidates pledging "No new taxes." They also begin to question policies such as the war in Iraq as it costs billions and billions of dollars, causing national economic woes.

Some government policies, however, don't really affect us individually. Legalized prostitution and the death penalty, for example, are often perceived as moral issues that directly affect few citizens. Individuals' attitudes on these issues often are based on underlying values they have acquired through the years.

When we are faced with policies that don't affect us personally and don't involve moral issues, we often have difficulty forming an opinion. Foreign policy is an area in which this phenomenon is especially true. Most Americans often know little of the world around them. Unless major issues of national importance are involved, American public opinion on foreign affairs is likely to be volatile in the wake of any new information.

Political Knowledge

Political knowledge and political participation have a reciprocal effect on one another—an increase in one will increase the other.[22] Knowledge about the political system is essential to successful political involvement, which, in turn, teaches citizens about politics and increases their interest in public affairs.[23] And, although few citizens know everything about all of the candidates and issues in a particular election, they can, and often do, know enough to impose their views and values as to the general direction the nation should take.[24]

This is true despite the fact that most Americans' level of knowledge about history and politics is quite low. According to the Department of Education, today's college graduates have less civic knowledge than high school graduates did fifty years ago.[25]

Americans also don't appear to know much about foreign policy; some critics would even argue that many Americans are geographically illiterate. An astounding 49 percent of young Americans could not find New York on a map, and 10 percent of all Americans could not locate the United States.[26]

Cues from Leaders or Opinion Makers

As early as 1966, noted political scientist V. O. Key Jr. argued in *The Responsible Electorate* that voters "are not fools."[27] Still, low levels of knowledge can lead to rapid opinion shifts on issues. The ebb and flow of popular opinion can be affected dramatically (some cynics might say manipulated) by political leaders. Given the visibility of political leaders and their access to the media, it is easy to see the important role they play in influencing public opinion. Political leaders, members of the news media, and a host of other experts have regular opportunities to influence public opinion because of the lack of deep conviction with which most Americans hold many of their political beliefs.[28]

The president, especially, is often in a position to mold public opinion through effective use of the bully pulpit, as discussed in chapter 7.[29] One political scientist concludes that there is a group of citizens—called followers—who are inclined to rally to the support of the president no matter what he does.[30]

DEBATE

Are You a Liberal or a Conservative?

Political Ideology

As discussed in chapter 1, an individual's coherent set of values and beliefs about the purpose and scope of government is called his or her **political ideology**. Americans' attachment to strong ideological positions has varied over time. In sharp contrast to spur-of-the-moment responses, these sets of values, which are often greatly affected by political socialization, can prompt citizens to favor a certain set of policy programs and adopt views about the proper role of government in the policy process.

Conservatives generally are likely to support smaller, less activist governments, limited social welfare programs, and reduced government regulation of business. Increasingly, they also have very strong views on social issues, including abortion and same-sex marriage. In contrast, liberals generally believe that the national government has an important role to play in a wide array of areas, including helping the poor and the disadvantaged. Unlike most conservatives, they generally favor activist governments. Most Americans today, however, identify themselves as moderates.

political ideology
The coherent set of values and beliefs about the purpose and scope of government held by groups and individuals.

VISUAL LITERACY

Who Are Liberals and Conservatives? What's the Difference?

The Evolution of News Media in the United States

The **mass media**—the entire array of organizations through which information is collected and disseminated to the general public—have become a colossal enterprise in the United States. The mass media include print sources, movies, television, radio, and Web-based material. Collectively the mass media make use of broadcast, cable, and satellite technologies to distribute information, which reaches every corner of the United States. The mass media are a powerful tool for both entertaining and informing the public. They reflect American society, but they are also the primary lens through which citizens view American culture and American politics. The **news media,** which are one component of the larger mass media, provide the public with new information about subjects of public interest and play a vital role in the political process.[31]

mass media
The entire array of organizations through which information is collected and disseminated to the general public.

news media
Media providing the public with new information about subjects of public interest.

Print Media

The first example of news media in America came in the form of newspapers, which were published in the colonies as early as 1690. The number of newspapers grew throughout the 1700s, as colonists began to realize the value of a press free from government oversight and censorship. The battle between Federalists and Anti-Federalists over ratification of the Constitution, discussed in chapter 2, played out in various partisan newspapers in the late eighteenth century. Thus, it was not surprising that one of the Anti-Federalists' demands was a constitutional amendment

Timeline: The Development of American News Media

1893 Joseph Pulitzer launches *New York World*—Known for its sensationalism and progressive crusades, Pulitzer's approach is nicknamed "yellow journalism".

1960 Presidential debates—Debates are televised for the first time.

1833 *New York Sun* enters circulation—Single copies sell for one penny (about four dollars in today's currency). The Sun is written to appeal to a mass audience.

1848 Associated Press established—The AP becomes the nation's first wire service.

1920 KDKA in Pittsburgh—First commercial radio station launches and provides detailed campaign coverage.

1789 Rise of the Partisan Press—Alexander Hamilton's *The Gazette of the United States* and Thomas Jefferson's *The National Gazette* are established.

1912 The Columbia School of Journalism admits its first class—Students use the first journalism textbook—*The Practice of Journalism* by Williams and Martin—in their classes.

guaranteeing the freedom of the press. (To learn more about freedom of the press, see The Living Constitution.)

The partisan press eventually gave way to the penny press. In 1833, Benjamin Day founded the *New York Sun*, which cost a penny at the newsstand. Beyond its low price, the *Sun* sought to expand its audience by freeing itself from the grip of a single political party. Inexpensive and politically independent, the *Sun* was the forerunner of modern newspapers, which rely on mass circulation and commercial advertising to produce profit. By 1861, the penny press had so supplanted partisan papers that President Abraham Lincoln announced his administration would have no favored or sponsored newspaper.

Although the print media were becoming less partisan, they were not necessarily becoming more respectable. Mass-circulation dailies sought wide readership, attracting readers with the sensational and the scandalous. The sordid side of politics became the entertainment of the times. One of the best-known examples occurred in the presidential campaign of 1884, when the *Buffalo Evening Telegraph* headlined "A Terrible Tale" about Grover Cleveland, the Democratic nominee.[32] The story alleged that Cleveland, an unmarried man, had fathered a child in 1871, while sheriff of Buffalo, New York. Even though paternity was indeterminate because the child's mother had been seeing other men, Cleveland willingly accepted responsibility, since all the

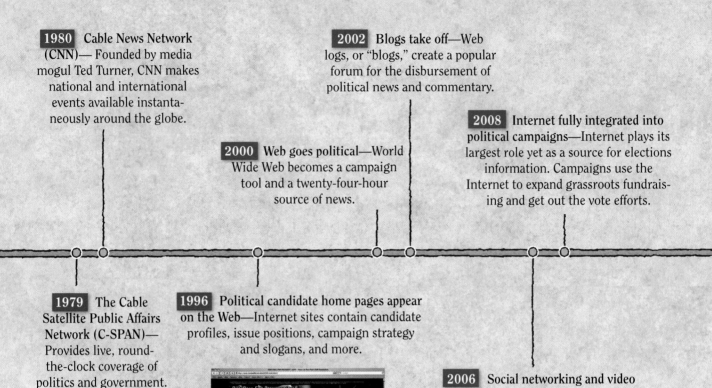

1980 Cable News Network (CNN)— Founded by media mogul Ted Turner, CNN makes national and international events available instantaneously around the globe.

2002 Blogs take off—Web logs, or "blogs," create a popular forum for the disbursement of political news and commentary.

2008 Internet fully integrated into political campaigns—Internet plays its largest role yet as a source for elections information. Campaigns use the Internet to expand grassroots fundraising and get out the vote efforts.

2000 Web goes political—World Wide Web becomes a campaign tool and a twenty-four-hour source of news.

1979 The Cable Satellite Public Affairs Network (C-SPAN)— Provides live, round-the-clock coverage of politics and government.

1996 Political candidate home pages appear on the Web—Internet sites contain candidate profiles, issue positions, campaign strategy and slogans, and more.

2006 Social networking and video sharing explodes—Online social networks and video sharing Web sites transform campaigning by providing for greater transparency of candidates and their campaign practices.

other men were married, and he had dutifully paid child support for years. The strict Victorian moral code that dominated American values at the time made the story even more shocking than it would be today. Fortunately for Cleveland, another newspaper, the *Democratic Sentinel*, broke a story that helped to offset this scandal: Republican presidential nominee James G. Blaine and his wife's first child had been born just three months after their wedding.

Throughout the nineteenth century, payoffs to the press were common. Andrew Jackson, for instance, gave one in ten of his early appointments to loyal reporters.[33] During the 1872 presidential campaign, the Republicans slipped cash to about 300 newsmen.[34] Wealthy industrialists also sometimes purchased investigative cease-fires for tens of thousands of dollars.

In the late 1800s and early 1900s, prominent publishers such as William Randolph Hearst and Joseph Pulitzer expanded the reach of newspapers in their control by practicing what became known as **yellow journalism**—sensationalized reporting that lowered journalistic standards in order to increase readership. Hearst's and Pulitzer's newspapers featured pictures and comics printed in color and sensationalized news stories designed to increase their readership and capture a share of the burgeoning immigrant population market.

yellow journalism
A form of newspaper publishing in vogue in the late nineteenth century that featured pictures, comics, color, and sensationalized, oversimplified news coverage.

The Living Constitution

Congress shall make no law respecting an establishment of religion, or prohibiting the free exercise thereof; or abridging the freedom of speech, or of the press; or the right of the people peaceably to assemble, and to petition the government for a redress of grievances.

FIRST AMENDMENT

The Framers knew that democracy is not easy, that a republic requires a continuous battle for rights and responsibilities. One of those rights is the freedom of the press, preserved in the First Amendment to the Constitution. To protect the press, the Framers were wise enough to keep the constitutional language simple—and a good thing, too. Their view of the press, and its required freedom, was almost certainly less broad than our conception of press freedom today.

It is difficult today to appreciate what a leap of faith it was for the Framers to grant freedom of the press when James Madison brought the Bill of Rights before Congress. Newspapers were largely run by disreputable people, since at the time editors and reporters were judged as purveyors of rumor and scandal. This was the reason Madison, as well as Alexander Hamilton and John Jay, published their newspaper articles advocating the ratification of the Constitution, *The Federalist Papers*, under the pseudonym "Publius."

The printed word was one of the few mediums of political communication in the young nation—it was critical for keeping Americans informed about issues. Therefore, the Framers had to hope that giving the press freedom to print all content, although certain to give rise to sensational stories, would also produce high-quality, objective reporting. Nevertheless, we should note that the Framers were not above using journalism as a way of promoting their political agendas. For example, Thomas Jefferson created a newspaper, the *National Gazette*, to report news favoring his Democratic-Republican Party. Giving the press freedom was also giving opposing politicians an open forum to attack each other.

Not much has changed since the Framers instituted the free press. We still have tabloids and partisan publications in which politicians attack each other, and we still rely on the press to give us important political information that we use to make voting decisions. The First Amendment declares the priority of free expression. The Framers recognized that all kinds of information would have to be protected to maximize opportunities for solid information to be reported. Regulations in response to what offends some people might be the first step on the slippery slope to censorship. The simple, enduring protection the Framers created in the First Amendment continues to make possible the flow of ideas that a democratic society relies upon.

CRITICAL THINKING QUESTIONS

1. While the First Amendment guarantees the rights of a free press, it is silent about their responsibilities to the public. What should the responsibilities of the media and individual journalists be? How would you suggest encouraging them to live up to their responsibilities?

2. The First Amendment was drafted in a time where the press consisted of newspapers, pamphlets, and public speakers. How relevant are the guarantees enshrined in the First Amendment to today's media environment? Are bloggers journalists? Do bloggers deserve the same constitutional protections as traditional journalists?

muckraking
A form of journalism, in vogue in the early twentieth century, concerned with reforming government and business conduct.

The Progressive movement gave rise to a new type of journalism in the early 1920s. **Muckraking** journalists—so named by President Theodore Roosevelt after a special rake designed to collect manure—were devoted to exposing misconduct by government, business, and individual politicians.[35] Muckrakers stimulated demands for anti-trust regulations—laws that prohibit companies, like large steel companies, from controlling an entire industry—and exposed deplorable working conditions in factories, as well as outright exploitation of workers by business owners. An unfortunate side effect of this emphasis on crusades and investigations, however, was the frequent publication of gossip and rumor without sufficient proof.

As the news business grew, so did the focus on increasing its profitability. Newspapers became more careful and less adversarial in their reporting to avoid alienating the advertisers and readers who produced their revenues.

Radio News

The advent of radio in the early part of the twentieth century was a media revolution and a revelation to the average American who rarely, if ever, had heard the voice of a president, governor, or senator. The radio became the center of most homes in the evening, when national networks broadcast the news as well as entertainment shows. Calvin Coolidge was the first president to appear on radio on a regular basis, but President Franklin D. Roosevelt made the radio appearance a must-listen by presenting "fireside chats" to promote his New Deal. The soothing voice of Roosevelt made it difficult for most Americans to believe that what the president wanted could be anything other than what was best for America.

News radio, which had begun to take a back seat to television by the mid-1950s, regained popularity with the development of AM talk radio in the mid-1980s. Controversial radio host Rush Limbaugh began the trend with his unabashed conservative views, opening the door for other conservative commentators such as Laura Ingraham, Sean Hannity, and Michael Reagan (son of the former president). Statistics show that these conservative radio hosts have resurrected the radio as a news medium by giving the information that they broadcast a strong ideological bent.

Television News

Television was first demonstrated in the United States at the 1939 Worlds Fair in New York, but it did not take off as a news source until after World War II. While most homes had televisions by the early 1960s, it would take several years more for television to replace print and radio as the nation's chief news provider. In 1963, most networks provided only fifteen minutes of news per day; only two major networks provided thirty minutes of news coverage. During this period, a substantial majority of Americans still received most of their news from newspapers. But, in 2007, 65 percent of Americans claimed to get their news from television, whereas only 27 percent read newspapers, as shown in Figure 10.5.

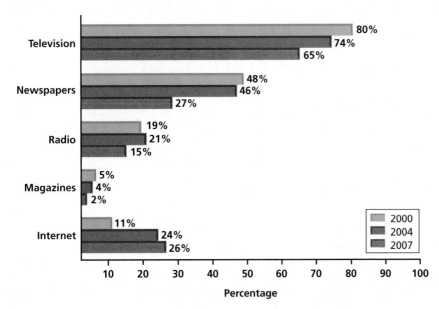

FIGURE 10.5 Where Americans Get Most of Their National and International News: 2000, 2004, and 2007

Source: Pew Research Center for the People and the Press, "Views of Press Values and Performance: 1985–2007," http://people-press.org/reports/.

How do partisan pundits and political satirists affect political coverage? Bill O'Reilly, at right, is one of the country's most visible conservative commentators and the host of the FOX News program *The O'Reilly Factor*. Stephen Colbert, at left, hosts Comedy Central's *The Colbert Report*, which lampoons O'Reilly's conservative views and blustering approach to reporting the news. Both programs have generated loyal audiences and high ratings.

An important distinction exists between network and cable news stations. Network news has lost viewers since 1980, with the loss becoming even steeper after the advent of cable news. Between 2000 and 2004, viewership for all network news programming declined from 45 percent to 35 percent.[36] Cable news has seen an increase in viewership, from 34 percent in 2000 to 38 percent in 2004. This increase is due in large part to the increased availability of services providing twenty-four-hour news channels. By 2006, 58 percent of all U.S. households subscribed to a cable service, and 29 percent of households were using a direct broadcast satellite (such as DirectTV or DISH Network).[37] Thus, the vast majority of Americans receive cable news in addition to their broadcast stations.

Cable and satellite providers give consumers access to a less glitzy and more unfiltered source of news with C-SPAN, a basic cable channel that offers gavel-to-gavel coverage of congressional proceedings, as well as major political events. C-SPAN along iwth C-SPAN2 and C-SPAN3 benefits from having no sponsors distracting from (with commercials or banners) or possibly affecting what it broadcasts. Because the content of C-SPAN can be erudite, technical, and sometimes downright tedious (such as the fixed camera shot of the Senate during a roll-call vote), audiences tend to be very small, but they are very loyal and give C-SPAN its place as a truly content-driven news source.

A recent development in television news is the growth in popularity of comedy news programs. While *Saturday Night Live* and other late-night comedy programs, like those hosted by Jay Leno and David Letterman, have mocked politicians and the news for years, more recent programs like Jon Stewart's *The Daily Show* and Stephen Colbert's *Colbert Report*—a satire of FOX News's *The O'Reilly Factor*—dedicate their entire program to poking fun at world leaders and current issues. One study conducted by the Annenberg Public Policy Center of the University of Pennsylvania revealed comedy programs actually inform viewers as well as entertain them. Regular viewers of *The Daily Show* were found to know more about world events than non-viewers, even when education, party identification, watching cable news, and other factors were taken into consideration.[38]

The New Media

Increasingly, media consumers, especially those under the age of thirty-five, are abandoning traditional media outlets in favor of other sources. While cable news networks

Ideas Into Action

Where Do Young People Get Their Campaign News?

In January 2008, the Pew Research Center for the People and the Press stated in a press release that many young voters (age eighteen to twenty-nine) rely on the Internet for campaign news: 42 percent of young voters, 26 percent of voters age thirty to forty-nine, and 15 percent of voters age fifty or older use the Internet for campaign news. Pew also found that young voters rely on comedy television shows, such as *The Daily Show* and *Saturday Night Live*, for campaign information: 21 percent of young voters use comedy television shows, much higher than the 5 percent of those thirty or older.[a] The fact that young voters might make voting decisions based on a quip from Stephen Colbert or a skit featuring Tina Fey may upset many in academia and in the media. One journalist disparagingly called the age bracket "the Young and the Newsless."[b]

But other data are quite encouraging and point toward a greater level of political awareness and engagement for today's youth. The Pew studies also have revealed that for Americans of all ages, only 4 percent rely exclusively on the Internet to get news about the campaign. Moreover, when online, voters gravitate toward the Web sites with traditional news sources, with MSNBC, CNN, and Yahoo News getting the most traffic.

Pew's most surprising finding, however, was that voters regularly watching *The Daily Show*, *The Colbert Report*, and other late-night comedy shows are more knowledgeable about current affairs than the average voter. What explains this phenomenon is that these shows tend to draw well-educated audiences and those already following politics. Well-informed young voters in particular gravitate to newer media for learning about politics.[c]

So when Jon Stewart reminds the audience, as he often does, that he anchors a fake news show, the audience will listen and, after the "Moment of Zen" segment, check the headlines on the Web site of a major newspaper. After all, when told that *The Daily Show* could be confused with an old form of satire or a new kind of journalism, Stewart said,

"Well, then, that either speaks to the sad state of comedy or the sad state of the news."[d]

- Why are traditional ways of getting the news, such as newspapers, radio, magazines, and television, less appealing to young voters than comedy shows and the Internet? How are traditional media responding to the popularity of the Internet and comedy shows as venues for the news?
- Go to the Web site of *The Daily Show* (www.thedailyshow.com) and watch an archived interview that Jon Stewart conducted with a major 2008 presidential candidate. Next, visit the Web site of ABC News's *This Week* (www.abcnews.go.com/ThisWeek) and watch an interview conducted by George Stephanopoulos with the same candidate. What differences do you notice in the tone and substance of the interviews? What do you see in each format that is either beneficial or harmful to the public interest?
- Go to Comedy Central's Web site for *The Colbert Report* (www.comedycentral.com/colbertreport) and search for archived clips of the "Better Know a District" segment, where the host profiles a congressional district and interviews its member of Congress. Watch three or four of these segments, preferably those closer to where you live. Do these profiles and interviews educate the public in some way? Why or why not?
- In what ways do comedy shows and Internet news sources, including blogs and other user-generated content, enhance the media's role in a democratic society? In what ways do new media undermine the media's role in serving democracy?

[a]Pew Research Center, "Cable and Internet Loom Large in Fragmented Political News Universe" January 11, 2004, and "Social Networking and Online Videos Take Off," January 11, 2008, http://www.pewinternet.org.

[b]Melanie McFarland, "Young People Turning Comedy Shows into Serious News Source," *Seattle Post-Intelligencer*, January 22, 2004, http://seattlepi.nwsource.com.

[c]Pew Research Center, "What Americans Know: 1989–2007," April 15, 2007.

[d] Jon Stewart interview by Bill Moyers, *NOW*, PBS, July 11, 2003.

are still the most regularly viewed, the Internet is gaining ground.[10] The Internet, which began as a Department of Defense project named Advanced Research Projects Agency Network (ARPANET) in the late 1960s, has grown into an unprecedented source of public information for people throughout the world. In 2000, whereas only 9 percent of Americans claimed to receive news from the Internet, 29 percent did in 2007.[39] Of course, few people rely exclusively on the Internet for news, although it is likely in the future that many citizens will use the video components of the World Wide Web to substitute for television news watching.

In an attempt to assert an online presence and make government more accessible, the U.S. government provides its own news to the public over the Internet. Press releases, government forms, statistical data, and other information are available on

Web sites created for all the major departments and agencies. The president and both houses of Congress also have official Web sites that offer basic information regarding the history and function of the respective bodies and current issues before them. Users can also access the complete voting record of individual members of Congress on the Senate and House sites and use the contact information found there to contact any representatives or senators. Individual members of Congress also have their own Web sites that allow them to promote their personalities, activities, and policy views. State governments and an increasing number of local governments have adopted similar online practices.[40]

The Internet also offers access to foreign news media previously unavailable to most Americans. The British Broadcasting Channel (BBC) has a Web site entirely devoted to news and available in over forty languages. International newspapers offer online content, although usually in their native languages. Al-Jazeera, a major Arabic television news source, has an English-language Web site providing news concerning the Middle East. By visiting alternative news sources like these, individuals gain a more nuanced and informed understanding of global issues.

Current Media Trends

The editors of the first partisan newspapers could scarcely have imagined what their profession would become more than two centuries later. The number and diversity of media outlets today are stunning. The print media consist of many thousands of daily and weekly newspapers, magazines, newsletters, and journals. Broadcast media encompass traditional radio and television stations, as well as satellite and cable services. The new media are the latest technologies, such as the Internet, that blur the lines between media sources and create new opportunities for the dissemination of news and other information.

THE INFLUENCE OF MEDIA GIANTS Every newspaper, radio station, television station, and Web site is influential in its own area, but only a handful of media outlets are influential nationally, and an even smaller number of media giants have international influence. The *New York Times*, the *Wall Street Journal*, *USA Today*, and the *Christian Science Monitor* are distributed nationally, and other newspapers, such as the *Washington Post* and the *Los Angeles Times*, have substantial influence from coast to coast. These six newspapers also have a pronounced effect on what the major national broadcast **networks** (ABC, CBS, NBC, and FOX) air on their evening news programs, and what the major cable news networks (CNN, FOX News, MSNBC, and CNBC)

network
An association of broadcast stations (radio or television) that share programming through a financial arrangement.

TABLE 10.2 The News Generation Gap

	18–29 %	30–49 %	50–64 %	65+ %
Regularly watch/listen to:				
Nightly network news	9	24	38	43
Cable TV news	30	31	40	46
Local TV news	42	51	60	65
Morning news show	20	22	26	23
C-SPAN	4	4	6	9
NewsHour with Jim Lehrer	4	4	6	9
National Public Radio	15	21	18	11
Political talk radio shows	21	21	20	14
The Daily Show with Jon Stewart	11	7	4	3
The O'Reilly Factor	4	7	11	14
Did yesterday:				
Read a newspaper	22	33	46	57
Watched TV news	49	53	63	69
Listened to radio news	26	43	39	27

Source: Pew Research Center for the People and the Press, "Maturing Internet New Audience—Broader Than Deep," July 30, 2006, http://people-press.org.

air around the clock. These news shows are carried by hundreds of local stations—called **affiliates**—that are associated with the national networks and may choose to carry their programming. **Wire services,** such as the Associated Press (AP), Reuters, and United Press International (UPI) distribute news around the globe. Most newspapers subscribe to at least one of these services, which not only produce their own news stories but also put on the wire major stories produced by other media outlets.

MEDIA CONSOLIDATION The news media in the United States are multibillion-dollar, for-profit businesses that ultimately are driven by the bottom line. As with all free-market enterprises, the pressure in privately owned media is to increasingly consolidate media ownership, so as to reap the benefits that come from larger market shares and fewer large-scale competitors.

Unlike traditional industries, where the primary concern associated with consolidation is the manipulation of prices made possible by monopolies or near monopolies, the consolidation of the media poses a far greater potential risk. Should the news media become dominated by a few mega-corporations, the fear is that these groups could limit the flow of information and ideas that form the very essence of a free society and that make democracy possible.

INCREASING USE OF EXPERTS Most journalists know a little bit about many subjects but do not specialize in any one area and certainly do not possess enough knowledge to fill the hours of airtime made possible by cable television's twenty-four-hour news cycle. Therefore, especially on cable stations, the news media employ expert consultants from a number of different disciplines ranging from medical ethics to political campaigning. These experts, also referred to as pundits, or the more derogatory term "talking heads," are hired to discuss the dominant issues of the day.

One 1992 study about how experts affect the views of Americans toward foreign policy says that "news from experts or research studies is estimated to have almost as great an impact" as anchorpersons, reporters in the field, or special commentators. Such findings are both good and bad for Americans. On the one hand, the "strong effects by commentators and experts are compatible with a picture of a public that

affiliates
Local television stations that carry the programming of a national network.

wire service
An electronic delivery of news gathered by the news service's correspondents and sent to all member news media organizations.

Photo courtesy: Dana Edelson/NBCU Photo Bank

Do late night comedy shows affect politics? Saturday Night Live cast members portray Senator Barack Obama and Senator Hillary Clinton, the two Democratic contenders for the presidential nomination, in a campaign debate spoof in early 2008. The skit portrayed the moderators of the debate fawning over Obama, while asking particularly harsh questions of Clinton, and mirrored charges of media bias by supporters of Clinton who believed that coverage of Obama was far less critical than coverage of their candidate. Journalists subsequently increased their examinations of Obama's record and statements.

engages in collective deliberation and takes expertise seriously." On the other, "one might argue that the potency of media commentators and of ostensibly nonpartisan TV 'experts' is disturbing. Who elected them to shape our views of the world? Who says they are insightful or even unbiased?"[41]

narrowcasting
Targeting media programming at specific populations within society.

NARROWCASTING In recent years, fierce competition to attract viewers and the availability of additional television channels made possible by cable and satellite television have led media outlets to move toward **narrowcasting**—targeting media programming at specific populations within society. Within the realm of cable news, the two ratings leaders, CNN and FOX News, have begun engaging in this form of niche journalism. The two stations divide audiences by ideology. FOX News emphasizes a conservative viewpoint and CNN increasingly stresses a more liberal perspective, although the FOX view is often more pronounced.[42]

blog
Web-based journal entries that provide an editorial and news outlet for citizens.

TECHNOLOGICAL INNOVATION Ironically, the same technology that has given rise to media giants also has the ability to increase the diversity of available news. **Blogs,** which have rapidly grown in popularity in recent years, are Web-based journal entries that provide an editorial and news outlet for citizens. They have become webs of information, linking together people with common ideological or issue-specific interests. In some instances, information made public on blogs has been picked up by mainstream news outlets, revealing how the new media provide unprecedented opportunities for the flow of information.

While the future of the new media remains as unpredictable as the latest blog entry, it is likely that the new media will continue to blur the lines between print and broadcast, consumer and producer, commentary and fact, and entertainment and news. The distinctions between the Internet and broadcast and cable news are likely to shrink as the technologies merge. Wireless handheld devices that allow users to send e-mail and text messages, make phone calls, browse the Internet, and download music and video clips are increasing in popularity. The emergence of online social networks such as MySpace and Facebook, video- and photo-sharing sites like YouTube and Flickr, and the citizen-encyclopedia, Wikipedia, are also affecting the ways in which Americans share and consume the news and information. The further development of these applications offers the potential for the public to have a greater voice in public affairs and to be more engaged in civic life.

Rules Governing the Media

The First Amendment to the U.S. Constitution, which prohibits Congress from abridging the freedom of the press, does not provide the media with unlimited print and broadcast freedom. A wide array of internal and external checks governs the behavior of the modern media.

Journalistic Standards

The heaviest restrictions placed on reporters do not come from government regulations but from the industry's own professional norms and each journalist's level of integrity, as well as from the oversight provided by editors who are ultimately responsible for the accuracy of the news they produce. To help guide the ethical behavior of journalists, the Society of Professional Journalists publishes a detailed "Code of Ethics" for journalists that includes principles and standards governing issues like avoiding conflicts of interest, dealing ethically with sources, and verifying the information being reported.

Government Regulation of the Electronic Media

The U.S. government regulates the electronic component of the media. Unlike radio or television, the print media are exempt from most forms of government regulation, although even print media must not violate community standards for obscenity, for instance. There are two reasons for this unequal treatment. First, the airwaves used by the electronic media are considered public property and are leased by the federal government to private broadcasters. Second, those airwaves are in limited supply; without some regulation, the nation's many radio and television stations would interfere with one another's frequency signals. It was not, in fact, the federal government but rather private broadcasters, frustrated by the numerous instances in which signal jamming occurred, that initiated the call for government regulation in the early days of the electronic media.

In 1996, Congress passed the sweeping Telecommunications Act, deregulating whole segments of the electronic media. The Telecommunications Act sought to provide an optimal balance of competing corporate interests, technological innovations, and consumer needs. It appeared to offer limitless opportunities for entrepreneurial companies to provide enhanced services to consumers. The result of this deregulation was the sudden merger of previously distinct kinds of media in order to create a more "multimedia" approach to communicating information and entertainment. This paved the way for the creation of multimedia corporations such as Viacom, Time Warner, and Comcast.

In June 2003, the Federal Communications Commission (FCC) attempted to build on these deregulatory changes by proposing to increase the total national audience a corporation could reach from 35 percent to 45 percent. Since total national audience is measured by how many stations a corporation owns, this increase would have allowed corporations to own more television stations.

Both Republicans and Democrats in Congress opposed the FCC changes, arguing that the country needs more and not less media diversification, given increasing media outlet consolidation. Furthermore, many ideologically opposed groups also argued against media consolidation: conservative religious groups believe that large media corporations purvey immoral content, and liberal groups believe that less diversification kills community-based media. Finally, there was a general public outcry, with legislators receiving angry letters and e-mails demanding that Congress stop the FCC.[43] At the end of the year, Congress had passed an amendment to an appropriations bill that raised the 35 percent cap on a national audience to 39 percent, a compromise that allowed the largest corporations to retain their current share—the largest corporation, Viacom, had 38.9 percent of the national audience—but prohibited any further expansion.[44]

The FCC's attempt to enact other controversial deregulatory changes related to media cross-ownership in specific markets was placed on hold. The Third Circuit Court of Appeals issued a stay blocking the FCC's changes and subsequently asked the FCC to revise its proposals. In December 2007, the FCC issued a revised rule lifting the cross-ownership ban for televisions and newspapers in the twenty largest markets, and it established procedures to grant waivers for combinations in smaller markets if they served the public interest.[45]

Content Regulation

The government also subjects the electronic media to substantial **content regulation** that, again, does not apply to the print media. Charged with ensuring that the airwaves "serve the public interest, convenience, and necessity," the FCC has attempted

content regulation
Government attempts to regulate the substance of the mass media.

equal time rule
The rule that requires broadcast stations to sell air time equally to all candidates in a political campaign if they choose to sell it to any.

to promote equity in broadcasting. For example, the **equal time rule** requires that broadcast stations sell air time equally to all candidates in a political campaign if they choose to sell it to any, which they are under no obligation to do. An exception to this rule is a political debate: stations may exclude from this event less well-known and minor-party candidates.

Until 2000, FCC rules required broadcasters to give candidates the opportunity to respond to personal attacks and to political endorsements by the station. In October 2000, however, a federal court of appeals found these rules, long criticized by broadcasters as having a chilling effect on free speech, to be unconstitutional when the FCC was unable to justify these regulations to the court's satisfaction.[46]

Efforts to Control the News Media

In the United States, only government officials can be prosecuted for divulging classified information; no such law applies to journalists. Nor can the government, except under extremely rare and confined circumstances, impose prior restraints on the press—that is, the government cannot censor the press. This principle was clearly established in *New York Times Co.* v. *U.S.* (1971).[47] In this case, the Supreme Court ruled that the government could not prevent publication by the *New York Times* of the Pentagon Papers, classified government documents about the Vietnam War that had been stolen, photocopied, and sent to the *Times* and the *Washington Post* by Daniel Ellsberg, a government employee. "Only a free and unrestrained press can effectively expose deception in the government," Justice Hugo Black wrote in a concurring opinion for the Court. "To find that the President has 'inherent power' to halt the publication of news by resort to the courts would wipe out the First Amendment."

How well do embedded journalists report the news? This image shows Jill Carroll, at right a freelance journalist for *The Christian Science Monitor,* embedded with U.S. troops in Iraq. Carroll was the thirty-first foreign journalist to be kidnapped in Iraq, but was safely released after three months in captivity.

Photo courtesy: Jill Carroll Collection/Getty Images

Similar concerns arose in the United States during the 1991 Persian Gulf War. Reporters were upset that the military was not forthcoming about events on and off the battlefield, while some Pentagon officials and many persons in the general public accused the press of telling the enemy too much in their dispatches. The U.S. government attempted to isolate offending reporters by keeping them away from the battlefield. This maneuver was highly controversial and very unpopular with news correspondents because it directly interfered with their job of reporting the news.

The George W. Bush administration provided an interesting compromise to this dilemma when it gave journalists the opportunity to be embedded with various parts of the military and report about the experiences of each unit when U.S.-led forces invaded Iraq in 2003. Organizations such as the Project for Excellence in Journalism found that embedded journalists typically provided only anecdotal stories, lacked the overall context of the war, and stressed American successes without much coverage of Iraqi civilian casualties. While conceding these limitations, some scholars maintain that an embedded journalist is better than no journalist at all, especially since journalists of foreign news organizations, like al-Jazeera, are able to cover the events from different perspectives.[48]

Whatever one's specific quarrel with the American news media, most Americans would probably prefer that the media tell them too much rather than not enough. Totalitarian and authoritarian societies have a tame journalism, after all. Media excesses may be considered the price of popular sovereignty.

How the Media Cover Politics

The news media focus an extraordinary amount of attention on our politicians and the day-to-day operations of our government. Since 1983, the number of print (newspaper and magazine) reporters accredited at the U.S. Capitol jumped from 2,300 to more than 4,000 today.[49] On the campaign trail, a similar phenomenon has occurred. In the 1960s, a presidential candidate in the primaries would attract a press entourage of at most a few dozen reporters, but today a hundred or more journalists can be seen tagging along with a front-runner. When a victorious candidate reaches the White House, the media are there as well; in 2007, sixty-eight journalists were credentialed as daily White House correspondents.[50] Consequently, a politician's every public utterance is reported and intensively scrutinized and interpreted in the media.

Thinking Globally
Censorship in North Korea

North Koreans live in the most heavily censored country in the world. The North Korean government tightly controls all domestic radio and television stations and newspapers. Radio and television receivers are locked to government-specified frequencies, and the content of all broadcasts is determined by a single government agency.

- Government censorship of the media deprives citizens of information; however, some might argue that the American press has too much freedom. Do you agree? Why or why not?
- What are the consequences of a censored media in repressive nations such as North Korea, Myanmar (Burma), and Cuba? What would you expect to happen if these countries allowed more open access to a variety of news sources?

How the Press and Public Figures Interact

Communication between elected officials or public figures and the media takes different forms. A **press release** is a written document offering an official comment or position on an issue or news event; it is usually printed on paper and faxed or handed directly to reporters, or increasingly, released by e-mail. A **press briefing** is a relatively restricted live engagement with the press, with the range of questions limited to one or two specific topics. In a press briefing, a press secretary or aide represents the elected official or public figure, who does not appear in person. In a full-blown **press conference,** an elected official appears in person to talk with the press at great length about an unrestricted range of topics. Press conferences provide a field on which reporters struggle to get the answers they need and public figures attempt to retain control of their message and spin the news and issues in ways favorable to them.

Politicians and media interact in a variety of other ways as well. Politicians hire campaign consultants who use focus groups and polling in an attempt to gauge how to present the candidate to the media and to the public. Additionally, politicians can attempt to bypass the national news media through paid advertising and by appearing on talk shows and local news programs. (Some of these and other techniques for dealing with the media during a campaign are discussed in greater detail in chapter 12.) Politicians also use the media to attempt to retain a high level of name recognition and to build support for their ideological and policy ideas.

In the past, a reporter would think twice about filing a story critical of a politician's character, and the editors probably would have killed the story had the reporter been foolish enough to do so. The reason? Fear of a libel suit. (Recall from chapter 4 that libel is written defamation of character that unjustly injures a person's reputation.) The first question editors would ask about even an ambiguous or suggestive phrase about a public official was, "If we're sued, can you prove beyond a doubt what you've written?"

Such concerns were significantly reduced in 1964, when the Supreme Court ruled in ***New York Times Co. v. Sullivan*** that simply publishing a defamatory falsehood is not enough to justify a libel judgment.[51] Henceforth, a public official would have to

press release
A document offering an official comment or position.

press briefing
A relatively restricted session between a press secretary or aide and the press.

press conference
An unrestricted session between an elected official and the press.

New York Times Co. v. Sullivan (1964)
The Supreme Court concluded that "actual malice" must be proved to support a finding of libel against a public figure.

prove "actual malice," a requirement extended three years later to all public figures, such as Hollywood stars and prominent athletes.[52] As discussed in chapter 4, the Supreme Court declared that the First Amendment requires elected officials and candidates to prove that the publisher either believed the challenged statement was false or at least entertained serious doubts about its truth and acted recklessly in publishing it in the face of those doubts. The actual malice rule has made it very difficult for public figures to win libel cases.

Covering the Presidency

The three branches of the U.S. government—the executive, the legislative, and the judicial—are roughly equal in power and authority. But, in the world of media coverage, the president is first among equals. All television cables lead to the White House, and a president can address the nation on all networks almost at will.

Since Franklin D. Roosevelt's time, chief executives have used the office and presidential press conference as a bully pulpit to shape public opinion and explain their actions. The presence of the press in the White House enables a president to appear even on very short notice and to televise live, interrupting regular programming. The White House's press briefing room is a familiar sight on the evening news, not just because presidents use it fairly often, but also because the presidential press secretary has almost daily question and answer sessions there.

The post of press secretary to the president has existed only since Herbert Hoover's administration (1929–1933), and the individual holding it is the president's main disseminator of information to the press. For this vital position, some presidents choose close aides with whom they have worked previously and who are familiar with their thinking. Press secretaries must be very adept at dealing with the news media; some worked as journalists prior to becoming a press secretary, and many go on to press jobs after their stint in the White House. For example, Lyndon B. Johnson's press secretary, Bill Moyers, has produced or hosted many PBS documentaries and series.

While the president receives the vast majority of the press's attention, much of this focus is unfavorable. Dwight Eisenhower once opened up a press conference by inviting the press to "nail him to the cross" as they usually did, and this approach suggests the way most presidents approach their formal encounters with the press. A study in the early 1990s found coverage of George Bush's handling of important national problems was almost solely negative.[53] Analysis of the coverage of Bill Clinton's turbulent presidency found a frenzy of negative media coverage immediately following the Lewinsky scandal, followed by a longer period of more even-handed coverage.[54]

The media faced a more difficult challenge in covering the administration of George W. Bush, a president who prided himself on the tight-lipped, no leaks nature of his White House. No member of his staff appeared on television or in print without prior permission, while Bush kept his direct contact with the press to a minimum. President Bush clearly tried to control his image by controlling how much the press directly encountered him and by speaking at highly staged media events, quite often in military settings, where he delivered a scripted message and presented an interesting visual, but answered no questions from the media.[55]

Covering Congress

With 535 voting members representing distinct geographic areas, covering Congress poses a difficult challenge for the media. Nevertheless, the congressional press corps has more than 3,000 members.[56] Most news organizations solve the size and decentralization problems inherent in covering news developments in the legislative branch by concentrating coverage on three groups of individuals. First, the leaders of both parties in both houses receive the lion's share of attention because only they can speak for a majority of their party's members. Usually the majority and minority leaders in each house and the Speaker of the House are the preferred spokespersons, but the whips also receive a substantial share of air time and column inches. Second, key committee chairs command center stage when subjects in their domain are newsworthy. Heads of the most prominent committees (such as Ways and Means or Armed Services) are guaranteed frequent coverage, but even the chairs and members of minor committees or subcommittees can achieve fame when the time and issue are right. For example, a sensational scandal like steroid use in major league baseball may lead to congressional committee hearings that receive extensive media coverage. Third, local newspapers and broadcast stations normally devote some resources to covering their local senators and representatives, even when these legislators are junior and relatively lacking in influence.

As with coverage of the president, media coverage of Congress is disproportionately negative. A significant portion of the media attention given to the House and Senate focuses on conflict among members. Some political scientists believe that such reporting is at least partially responsible for the public's negative perceptions of Congress.[57] Coverage of Congress has been greatly expanded through cable channels C-SPAN and C-SPAN2, which provide coverage of House and Senate sessions as well as many committee hearings. For the first time, Americans can watch their representatives in action without editing or interpretation.

Covering the Supreme Court

While the president and Congress interact with the media on a regular basis, the Supreme Court remains a virtual media vacuum. Despite persistent efforts by C-SPAN and other media outlets to gain access, television cameras have never been permitted to record Supreme Court proceedings. Citing the need to protect the public's perception of the Supreme Court as a nonpolitical and autonomous entity, the justices have given little evidence to suggest that they are eager to reverse their broadcast media ban. Instead, at the end of each term, they release written transcripts and audio recordings of the proceedings, which lack both the visuals and timeliness that could make them fodder for the modern press. Since 2000, however, reporters have been granted on a case-by-case basis the ability to make use of same-day audio recordings. The first instance of this occurred during *Bush* v. *Gore* (2000), which decided the presidential vote in Florida. Since this case, reporters have been granted limited audio access to the Court.

While print and broadcast reporters are granted access to the Court, even if their cameras are not, coverage of the Court remains severely limited when compared with coverage of the executive and legislative branches. There are less than a dozen full-time reporters covering the Supreme Court, and the amount of space dedicated to Court-related stories has continued to shrink. Stories involving complex legal issues are not as easy to sell as well-illustrated stories related to the Congress or president.[58]

Toward Reform: Media Influence, Media Bias, and Public Confidence

There are many important questions concerning the media's relationship with the public. For instance, how much influence do the media actually have on public opinion? Do the media have a discernable ideological bent or bias, as some people suggest? Are people able to resist information that is inconsistent with their preexisting beliefs? And, how much confidence does the public have in the news media?

Media Influence

Some political scientists argue that the content of news coverage accounts for a large portion of the volatility and changes in public opinion and voting preferences of

media effects
The influence of news sources on public opinion.

agenda setting
The constant process of forming the list of issued to be addressed by government.

framing
The process by which a news organization defines a political issue and consequently affects opinion about the issue

Americans, when measured over relatively short periods of time.[59] These changes are called **media effects**. Let's examine how these media-influenced changes might occur. First, reporting can sway people who are uncommitted and have no strong opinion in the first place. So, for example, the media have a greater influence on political independents than on strong partisans.[60] That said, the sort of politically unmotivated individual who is subject to media effects may not vote in a given election, in which case the media influence may be of little particular consequence.

Second, it is likely that the media have a greater impact on topics far removed from the lives and experiences of readers and viewers. News reports can probably shape public opinion about events in foreign countries fairly easily. Yet, what the media say about domestic issues such as rising prices, neighborhood crime, or child rearing may have relatively little effect, because most citizens have personal experience of and well-formed ideas about these subjects.

Third, in a process often referred to as **agenda setting,** news organizations can influence what we think about, even if they cannot determine what we think. Indeed, the press often sets the agenda for a campaign or for government action by focusing on certain issues or concerns.

Fourth, the media influence public opinion through **framing**—the process by which a news organization defines a political issue and consequently affects opinion about the issue. Finally, the media have the power to indirectly influence the way the public views politicians and government.

Media Bias

Whenever the media break an unfavorable story about a politician, the politician usually counters with a cry of "biased reporting"—a claim that the press has told an untruth, has told only part of the truth, or has reported facts out of the complete context of the event. Some research suggests that candidates may charge the media with bias as a strategy for dealing with an assertive press, and that bias claims are part of the dynamic between elected officials and reporters. If a candidate can plausibly and loudly decry bias in the media as the source of his negative coverage, for example, reporters might temper future negative stories or give the candidate favorable coverage to mitigate the calls of bias.[61]

Are journalists biased? The answer is simple and unavoidable. Of course they are. Journalists, like all human beings, have values, preferences, and attitudes galore—some conscious, others subconscious, but all reflected at one time or another in the subjects selected for coverage or the portrayal of events or content communicated. Given that the press is biased, in what ways is it biased and when and how are the biases shown?

For much of the 1980s and 1990s, the argument was that the media had a liberal bias because of the sheer number of journalists who leaned to the left. Studies in the 1980s showed that professional journalists were drawn heavily from the ranks of highly educated social and political liberals.[62] To this day, journalists are substantially Democratic in party affiliation and voting habits, progressive and anti-establishment in political orientation, and to the left of the general public on many economic, foreign policy, and social issues. Indeed, a 2007 survey revealed that, whereas 36 percent of the general public describes themselves as being ideologically conserv-

Thinking Globally
Al-Jazeera and Media Bias

Al-Jazeera is an independent television station that broadcasts from the tiny, oil-rich Islamic country of Qatar—an important U.S. ally. Unlike its regional competitors, when al-Jazeera was founded in 1996, it offered more than state propaganda and limited news content. Over the years, al-Jazeera's broadcasts have caused international controversy. Saudi Arabia, Libya, Algeria, and Kuwait have all expressed outrage over the station's coverage of domestic events, while the United States has criticized al-Jazeera for broadcasting interviews with Osama bin Laden and for referring to Palestinians killed by Israeli forces as martyrs.

- Go to al-Jazeera's English-language Web site, **www.aljazeera.net**. How does its coverage of world news compare with that of American media outlets?
- Why would media coverage in some parts of the world tend to be very critical of the United States? Where would media coverage be most critical of the United States and where would it be most favorable?
- Think about the media outlets you rely on for news. How objective or balanced are they in their coverage? In what ways are they biased?

ative, only 8 percent of those in the national media would do the same. At the same time, the majority of national journalists—53 percent—describe themselves as moderate, while only 39 percent of Americans describe themselves in the same way. Local journalists, moreover, are less liberal than their counterparts in the national media. Whereas 32 percent of the national journalists describe themselves as liberal, only 23 percent of the local journalists describe themselves as liberals, much more in line with most Americans.[63]

Some scholars argue that corporate interests play a significant role in what journalists report, and that they may counter any liberal leanings of reporters. Others argue that the deepest bias among political journalists is the desire to get to the bottom of a good campaign story. Other human biases are also at work in reporting on politics. Whether the press likes or dislikes a candidate is often vital. So, too, is the increasing celebrity status of many people who report the news.

The Public's Perception of the Media

Americans' general assessment of the news media is considerably unfavorable and has been in a downward trend since the 1980s. According to a 2007 survey by the Pew Research Center for the People and the Press, a majority of the public gives the media low ratings on a number of indicators. Pew found that 55 percent of the respondents perceive the news media to be politically biased and 53 percent believe that the press often is inaccurate in their reporting. Moreover, there has been a steady decline in the perceived believability of the major news organizations. In 2004, only 54 percent of the public reported that they can believe most of what they read in their daily newspaper. The ratings for the television networks and local news stations are somewhat better, around 60 percent.

There also is an increasing partisan divide between Democrats and Republicans in their assessments of the media's performance. Whereas large majorities of Republicans see the press as liberal and politically biased, only a little more than one-third of Democrats feel the same way. Democrats and Republicans also get their news from different sources. Recent survey data show that Democrats are more likely to watch CNN than Republicans, and Republicans are nearly twice as likely to watch FOX News as Democrats.

The ideological fragmentation of the media should give pause to those who believe that mass media are essential to providing the facts to educate the public about policies our local, state, and federal governments consider. If those facts are reported with bias (or worse, not reported at all because of bias), then portions of the public learn only the facts they want to learn, making consensus among the public and, thus, their representatives increasingly difficult.

WHAT SHOULD I HAVE LEARNED?

Public opinion and the news media are two factors that have a drastic impact on American politics and public policy. To that end, this chapter has explored the following questions:

- **What is political socialization and how is it the root of political values?**

The first step in forming opinions occurs through a process called political socialization. Our family, school, peers, social groups—including religion, race, ethnicity, gender, and age—as well as where we live and the impact of events all affect how we view political events and issues.

- **How does polling seek to measure and influence public opinion and how are polls conducted?**

Over the years, polling to measure public opinion has become increasingly sophisticated and more accurate because pollsters are better able to sample the public in their effort to determine their attitudes and positions on issues. Polls, however, have several shortcomings, including sampling error, limited respondent options, lack of information, and difficulty measuring intensity.

■ **How do we form and express political opinions?**

Myriad factors enter our minds as we form opinions about political matters. These include a calculation about the personal benefits involved, degree of personal political knowledge, cues from leaders, and political ideology.

■ **How did the news media in the United States evolve?**

News media, a component of the larger mass media, provide the public with key information about subjects of public interest and play a crucial role in the political process. The news media consist of print, broadcast, and new media.

Trends affecting the modern media include the growth of media conglomerates and an attendant consolidation of media outlets, the increasing use of experts, and narrowcasting in order to capture particular segments of the population. Increasingly, the lines between media types are blurred by technological innovations that continue to transform the way information is produced and distributed, as well as the way that the public perceives the media.

■ **What rules govern the media?**

While the media continue to be governed by institutional norms, the government has gradually loosened restrictions on the media. The Federal Communications Commission (FCC) licenses and regulates broadcasting stations but has been quite willing to grant and renew licenses and has reduced its regulation of licensees. Content regulations have loosened, with the courts using a narrow interpretation of libel. The Telecommunications Act of 1996 further deregulated the communications landscape.

■ **How do the media cover politics?**

The media cover every aspect of the political process, including the executive, legislative, and judicial branches of government, though the bulk of media attention focuses on the president. Politicians have developed a symbiotic relationship with the media, both feeding the media a steady supply of news and occasionally being devoured by the latest media feeding frenzy.

■ **How do media influence, media bias, and public confidence shape the issue of media reform?**

By controlling the flow of information, framing issues in a particular manner, and setting the agenda, the media have the potential to exert influence over the public, though generally have far less influence than people believe. While the media do possess biases, a wide variety of news options are available in the United States, providing savvy news consumers an unprecedented amount of information from which to choose. Public opinion regarding the media continues to be largely critical, though Americans continue to give high marks to established news organizations.

Key Terms

affiliates, p. 301

agenda setting, p. 308

blog, p. 302

content regulation, p. 303

equal time rule, p. 304

exit polls, p. 290

framing, p. 308

margin of error, p. 291

mass media, p. 293

media effects, p. 308

muckraking, p. 296

narrowcasting, p. 302

network, p. 300

news media, p. 293

New York Times Co. v. *Sullivan* (1964), p. 305

political ideology, p. 293

political socialization, p. 278

press briefing, p. 305

press conference, p. 305

press release, p. 305

public opinion, p. 285

public opinion polls, p. 285

push polls, p. 289

random sampling, p. 288

sample, p. 286

stratified sampling, p. 289

straw polls, p. 286

tracking polls, p. 289

wire service, p. 301

yellow journalism, p. 295

Researching Public Opinion and The News Media

In the Library

Alvarez, R. Michael, and John Brehm. *Easy Answers, Hard Choices: Values, Information, and American Public Opinion.* Princeton, NJ: Princeton University Press, 2002.

Crouse, Timothy. *The Boys on the Bus*, reprint ed. New York: Random House, 2003.

Erikson, Robert S., and Kent L. Tedin. *American Public Opinion: Its Origins, Contents, and Impact*, 7th ed. New York: Longman, 2007.

Erikson, Robert S., Gerald C. Wright, and John P. McIver. *Statehouse Democracy: Public Opinion and the American States.* New York: Cambridge University Press, 1993.

Graber, Doris A. *Mass Media and American Politics*, 8th ed. Washington, DC: CQ Press, 2007.

Hamilton, James T. *All the News That's Fit to Sell.* Princeton, NJ: Princeton University Press, 2004.

Iyengar, Shanto, and Jenifer A. McGrady. *Media Politics: A Citizen's Guide.* New York: Norton, 2007.

Jamieson, Kathleen Hall, and Paul Waldman. *The Press Effect: Politicians, Journalists, and the Stories That Shape the Political World.* Oxford: Oxford University Press, 2002.

Key, V. O., Jr. *Public Opinion and American Democracy.* New York: Knopf, 1961.

McChesney, Robert W. *The Problem of the Media: U.S. Communication Politics in the Twenty-First Century.* New York: Monthly Review, 2004.

Mutz, Diana Carole. *Impersonal Influence: How Perceptions of Mass Collectives Affect Political Attitudes.* New York: Cambridge University Press, 1998.

Sabato, Larry J. *Feeding Frenzy: Attack Journalism and American Politics*, updated ed. Baltimore, MD: Lanahan, 2000.

Stimson, James A. *The Tides of Consent: How Public Opinion Shapes American Politics.* New York: Cambridge University Press, 2004.

Zaller, John. *The Nature and Origin of Mass Opinions.* New York: Cambridge University Press, 1992.

On the Web

To learn more about the history of the Gallup Organization and poll trends, go to **www.gallup.com.**

To learn more about the American National Election Study (ANES), including the history of this public opinion research project, go to **www.electionstudies.org.**

For the most recent Roper Center polls, go to the Roper Center's public opinion archives page at **www.ropercenter.uconn.edu.**

The Pew Research Center for the People and the Press does national surveys that explore the public's attitudes about the news media and measure the public's use of the Internet and traditional news outlets. Go to **people-press.org.**

The *Columbia Journalism Review* examines the performance of journalists for newspapers, magazines, radio, television, and the Web, and the forces that affect their performance, through a mix of reporting, analysis, and commentary. Go to **www.cjr.org.**

The *American Journalism Review* covers all aspects of print, television, radio, and online media, examining how the media cover specific stories, the broader coverage trends, ethical dilemmas in the field, and the impact of technology. Go to **www.ajr.org.**

11 Political Parties and Interest Groups

In August 2008, the Democrats used the city of Denver to formally launch the nomination of Senator Barack Obama as their candidate for president of the United States. A few weeks later, from Minneapolis, the Republicans followed by formally nominating John McCain as their candidate. The televised convention proceedings and morning papers focused on the nominations of these two people and their personal attributes. Less attention, however, was paid to the importance of the party platforms, the official statements that detail each party's positions on key public policy issues. Party platforms are often taken for granted, certainly by the news media, and even by many political activists. They are rarely noted by American voters, many of whom are more concerned about the personalities of candidates than the details of their policy positions and are also cynical about politicians and political parites, in general.

How wrong the cynics are. Party platforms reflect significant policy differences and worldviews. The 2008 Democratic platform criticized the Republican Bush

administration, claiming that President George W. Bush had overextended the military by rushing into an ill-considered war in Iraq. Democrats also charged that Republican economic policies had put the American Dream at risk by allowing incomes to fall and foreclosures and gas prices to rise. The Democratic platform pledged to renew America's promise and provide leadership on the world stage.

The Republican platform noted that the tragedy of September 11 had not been repeated on American soil and that the Republican Party remained committed to victory in Iraq. The Republican platform also pledged that the men and women on the front lines of the war on terrorism would be given the authority and resources they needed to protect the country and the platform promised to further reduce the tax burden of all Americans.

In addition to seeking to place blame for policy failures (the Democrats) or lay claim to policy successes (the Republicans), detailed policy positions were laid out in each platform. The Democrats advocated cutting taxes for middle class families and most senior citizens, closing corporate loopholes, and restoring fairness to the tax code by raising taxes on the richest Americans. The Republicans vowed to make President Bush's 2001 and 2003 tax cuts permanent; to reduce a variety of taxes on individuals, families, and small businesses; and to eliminate the practice of congressional earmarks and attack wasteful government spending. The Democrats pledged to lead the nation

■ **National party conventions generate excitement and enthusiasm from dedicated delegates.** At left, members of the Democratic Party's Texas delegation celebrate the re-nomination of Franklin Delano Roosevelt for president in 1936. At right, avid supporters of Senator John McCain and Governor Sarah Palin attends the 2008 Republican National Convention in Minneapolis.

WHAT SHOULD I KNOW ABOUT . . .

- the roots of the American party system?
- the functions and organization of the American party system?
- interest group structure and functions?
- regulating interest groups and lobbyists?

TO LEARN MORE—
—TO DO MORE
     To learn more about the Democratic and Republican party platforms, go to www.democrats.org and www.rnc.org. To learn about the platforms of two of the leading third parties, the Libertarians and the Greens, go to www.lp.org and www.gp.org.

towards energy independence by investing in renewable energy technologies and advanced biofuels and increasing the fuel efficiencies of automobiles. They also pledged to lower gasoline prices by cracking down on speculators artificially driving up oil prices. The Republicans advocated accelerating domestic oil exploration and drilling offshore and on federal lands, constructing more oil refineries and nuclear power plants, and offering tax credits to encourage the development of alternative energy sources. The Democrats reiterated their support for *Roe* v. *Wade* and preserving a woman's right to choose a safe and legal abortion. The Republicans continued their strong pro-life stance and advocated for the passage of a Constitutional amendment to outlaw abortion. (To learn more about the party platforms, see Table 11.1.)

When James Madison warned of the dangers of faction in *Federalist No. 10*, he never envisioned the development of political parties, or the role that organized interests would eventually play in politics and policy making. It was not long after the ink was dry on the new Constitution that factions arose concerning the desirability to the new system of government that it created. And, soon after, political parties were formed to reflect those political divisions.

political party
A group of office holders, candidates, activists, and voters who identify with a group label and seek to elect to public office individuals who run under that label.

At the most basic level, a **political party** is a group of office holders, candidates, activists, and voters who identify with a group label and seek to elect to public office individuals who run under that label. Notice that the goal is to *win* office, not just compete for it. This objective is in keeping with the practical nature of Americans and the country's historical aversion to most ideologically driven, purist politics. Nevertheless, the group label—also called party identification—can carry with it clear messages about ideology and issue positions. Although these especially exist for minor, less broad-based parties that have little chance of electoral success, they also apply to the Democrats and the Republicans, the two national, dominant political parties in the United States.

interest group
An organized group that tries to influence public policy.

In contrast to political parties, **interest groups**, which go by a variety of names—special interests, pressure groups, organized interests, political groups, lobby groups, and public interest groups—are organizations that "seek or claim to represent people or organizations which share one or more common interests or ideals."[1] Distinguished political scientist V. O. Key Jr. tried to differentiate political parties from interest groups by arguing that "interest groups promote their interests by attempting to influence government rather than by nominating candidates and seeking responsibility for the management of government."[2]

In this chapter we trace the evolution of the role of political parties and interest groups in America. First, we will examine the roots of the American party system. Then, we will look at the organization and functions of the American party system. After focusing on interest group functions and organization, we will consider efforts to regulate interest groups and lobbyists.

Roots of the American Party System

The broad structure and pragmatic purpose of political parties have been features of the American party system since the founding of the republic. By tracing the history and development of political parties in

TABLE 11.1 Party Platforms: Moderate but Different

As most Americans have moderate political views and the aim of political parties is to attract voters, the platforms of the two dominant parties tend to be moderate in tone and occasionally similar in substance, though the differences below the rhetoric are significant.

	Democratic Platform	Republican Platform
Abortion	The Democratic Party strongly and unequivocally supports *Roe v. Wade* and a woman's right to choose a safe and legal abortion, regardless of ability to pay, and we oppose any and all efforts to weaken or undermine that right. The Democratic Party also strongly supports access to comprehensive affordable family planning services and age-appropriate sex education which empower people to make informed choices and live healthy lives.	We assert the inherent dignity and sanctity of all human life and affirm that the unborn child has a fundamental individual right to life which cannot be infringed. We support a human life amendment to the Constitution, and we endorse legislation to make clear that the Fourteenth Amendment's protections apply to unborn children. We oppose using public revenues to promote or perform abortion and will not fund organizations which advocate it. We support the appointment of judges who respect traditional family values and the sanctity and dignity of innocent human life.
Energy	Democrats are committed to fast-track investment of billions of dollars over the next ten years to establish a green energy sector that will create up to five million jobs. We'll create an energy focused youth job program to give disadvantaged youth job skills for this emerging industry. We must invest in research and development, and deployment of renewable energy technologies as well as technologies to store energy through advanced batteries and clean up our coal plants.	We must draw more American oil from American soil. We will encourage refinery construction and modernization and, with sensitivity to environmental concerns, an expedited permitting process. Republicans will pursue dramatic increases in the use of all forms of safe nuclear power. We must continue to develop alternative fuels, such as biofuels, especially cellulosic ethanol, and hasten their technological advances to next-generation production.
Taxation	We will shut down the corporate loopholes and tax havens and use the money so that we can provide an immediate middle-class tax cut. We'll eliminate federal income taxes for millions of retirees, because all seniors deserve to live out their lives with dignity and respect. For families making more than $250,000, we'll ask them to give back a portion of the Bush tax cuts to invest in health care and other key priorities. We will expand the Earned Income Tax Credit, and dramatically simplify tax filings so that millions of Americans can do their taxes in less than five minutes.	Republicans will lower the tax burden for families by doubling the exemption for dependents. We will continue our fight against the federal death tax. Republicans support tax credits for health care and medical expenses. We support a major reduction in the corporate tax rate so that American companies stay competitive with their foreign counterparts and American jobs can remain in this country. We support a plan to encourage employers to offer automatic enrollment in tax-deferred savings programs.
National Security	We must first bring the Iraq war to a responsible end. We will defeat Al Qaeda in Afghanistan and Pakistan, where those who actually attacked us on 9-11 reside and are resurgent. We will fully fund and implement the recommendations of the bipartisan 9-11 Commission. We must invest still more in human intelligence and deploy additional trained operatives with specialized knowledge of local cultures and languages. We will review the current Administration's warrantless wiretapping program.	We must regularly exercise our ability to quickly respond to acts of bioterrorism and other WMD-related attacks. We must develop and deploy both national and theater missile defenses to protect the American homeland, our people, our Armed Forces abroad, and our allies. We must increase the ranks and resources of our human intelligence capabilities, integrate technical and human sources, and get that information more quickly to the war-fighter and the policy maker.

Note: Excerpts are taken directly from the relevant sections of the 2008 party platforms.
Sources: http://www.democrats.org/a/party/platform.html and http://platform.gop.com/2008Platform.pdf.

the United States, we will see that another prominent feature is a competitive two-party system, even as there have been dramatic shifts in party coalitions and reforms to democratize the system.

The Birth of American Political Parties

It is one of the great ironies of the early republic that George Washington's public farewell, which warned the nation against parties, marked the effective end of the brief era of partyless politics in the United States. (To learn more about American party history, see Figure 11.1.) Washington's unifying influence ebbed as he stepped off the national stage, and his vice president and successor, John Adams, occupied a much less exalted position. To win the presidency in 1796, Adams narrowly defeated his arch-rival Thomas Jefferson, who according to the existing rules of the Constitution became vice president. Over the course of Adams's single term, two competing congressional factions, the Federalists and Democratic-Republicans, gradually organized around these clashing

The Evolution of Political Parties in the United States

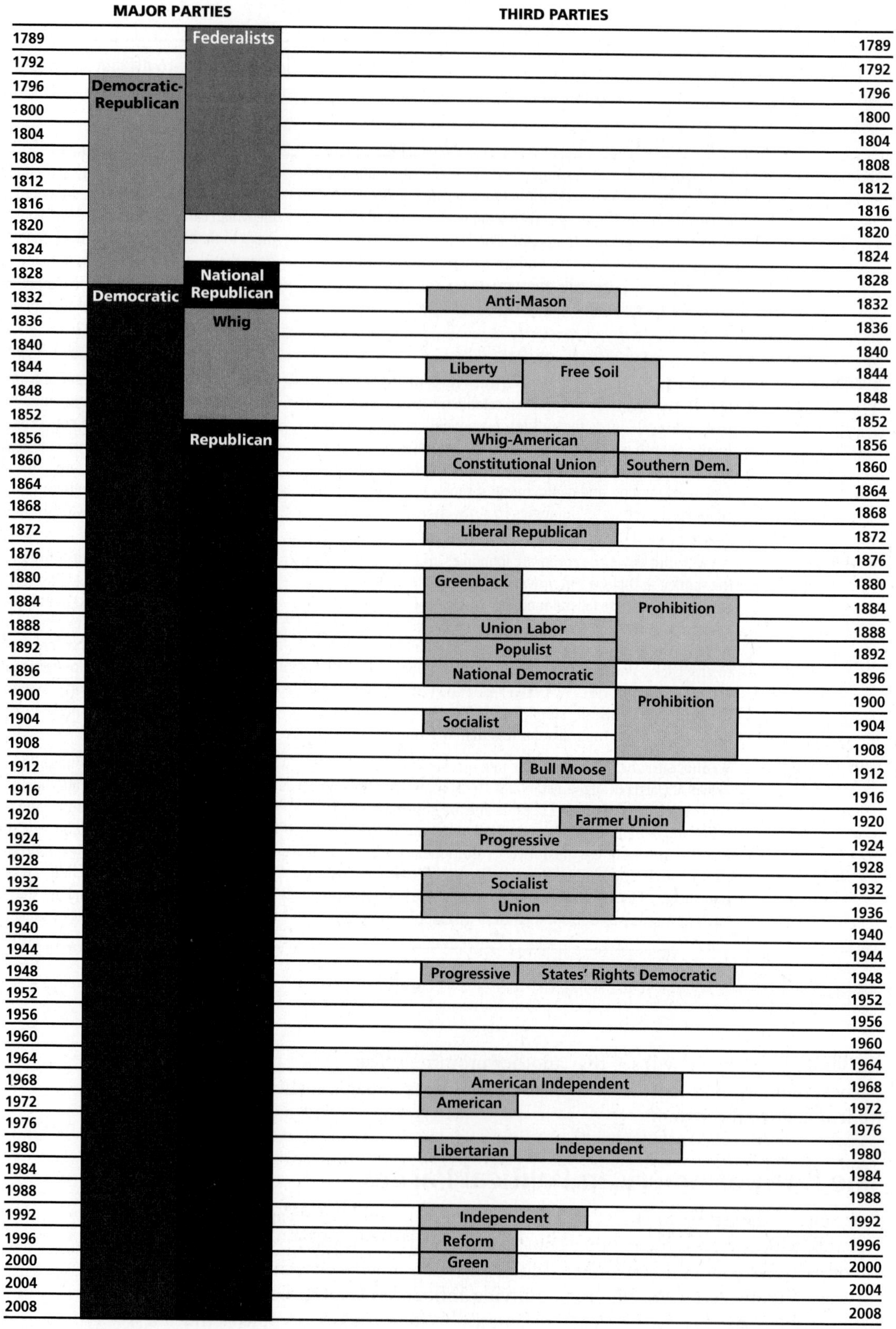

MAJOR PARTIES	THIRD PARTIES

Year	Major Parties	Third Parties	Year
1789	Federalists		1789
1792			1792
1796	Democratic-Republican		1796
1800			1800
1804			1804
1808			1808
1812			1812
1816			1816
1820			1820
1824			1824
1828		National Republican	1828
1832	Democratic	Anti-Mason	1832
1836	Whig		1836
1840			1840
1844		Liberty Free Soil	1844
1848			1848
1852			1852
1856	Republican	Whig-American	1856
1860		Constitutional Union Southern Dem.	1860
1864			1864
1868			1868
1872		Liberal Republican	1872
1876			1876
1880		Greenback	1880
1884		Prohibition	1884
1888		Union Labor	1888
1892		Populist	1892
1896		National Democratic	1896
1900		Prohibition	1900
1904		Socialist	1904
1908			1908
1912		Bull Moose	1912
1916			1916
1920		Farmer Union	1920
1924		Progressive	1924
1928			1928
1932		Socialist	1932
1936		Union	1936
1940			1940
1944			1944
1948		Progressive States' Rights Democratic	1948
1952			1952
1956			1956
1960			1960
1964			1964
1968		American Independent	1968
1972		American	1972
1976			1976
1980		Libertarian Independent	1980
1984			1984
1988			1988
1992		Independent	1992
1996		Reform	1996
2000		Green	2000
2004			2004
2008			2008

FIGURE 11.1 American Party History at a Glance

Note: Chart lists political parties that received at least 1 percent of the presidential vote.

Source: Harold W. Stanley and Richard G. Niemi, *Vital Statistics on American Politics, 2007–2008* (Washington, DC: CQ Press, 2007).

The Living Constitution

It is difficult to imagine modern American politics without the political parties, but where in the text of the Constitution do we find the provision to establish them?

Nowhere in the Constitution do we find a provision establishing political parties. Some might point out that the First Amendment establishes the right to assemble as a constitutional right, and this right certainly helps to preserve and protect parties from governmental oppression during rallies and conventions. However, the right to assembly is not the same as permission for two organizations to mediate elections. Furthermore, James Madison, in *Federalist No. 10*, feared that one of the greatest dangers to the new American republic was a majority tyranny created by the domination of a single faction fighting for one set of interests, so he hoped that extending the sphere of representation among many members of Congress would prevent a majority of representatives from coming together to vote as a bloc.

Of course, parties are *not* like the factions Madison describes. Parties today seem to embody Madison's principle of the extended sphere of representation. Neither of the two major political parties is monolithic in its beliefs; rather, both parties constantly reconsider their platforms in light of the changes of the various constituencies they try to represent. The Republicans have Senator Olympia Snowe (ME), who is pro-choice and pro-environment, and Representative Roy Blunt (MO), who is pro-life and pro-business. Democrats have Representative Dennis Kucinich (OH), who advocates withdrawal from the North American Free Trade Agreement, and Governor Bill Richardson (NM), who balances various racial/ethnic concerns and business interests while trying to protect the border between the U.S. and Mexico. These comparisons illustrate significant differences in interests, an approach Madison supported.

Finally, Madison himself actually belonged to two early American political parties during his public service, first the Federalists and later the Democratic-Republicans. In fact, it is because of the Federalist Party that we have a Constitution today. Federalists compromised with Anti-Federalists to provide a Bill of Rights so long as the Anti-Federalists would stop opposing ratification of the Constitution. So parties are not so much *in* the Constitution as *behind* the Constitution, first behind its ratification and, today, behind its preservation of diverse interests.

CRITICAL THINKING QUESTIONS

1. How could the Constitution be amended in order to officially establish political parties as an institution of government? Would this be a good idea? Why or why not?
2. Why would candidates and office holders with very diverse views join the same political party?

men and their principles: Adams and his Federalist allies supported a strong central government; the Democratic-Republicans of Thomas Jefferson and his allies inherited the mantle of the Anti-Federalists (see chapter 2) and preferred a federal system in which the states retained the balance of power. (Jefferson actually preferred the simpler name "Republicans," a different group from today's party of the same name, but Alexander Hamilton, a leading Federalist, insisted on calling the group "Democratic-Republicans," an attempt to disparage the group by linking them to the radical democrats of the French Revolution.) In the presidential election of 1800, the Federalists supported Adams's bid for a second term, but this time the Democratic-Republicans prevailed with their nominee, Jefferson, who became the first U.S. president elected as the nominee of a political party. (To learn more about factionalism and the Framers, see The Living Constitution.)

Jefferson was deeply committed to the ideas of his party but not nearly as devoted to the idea of a party system. He regarded his party as a temporary measure necessary to defeat Adams, not a long-term political tool or an essential element of democracy. Jefferson's party never achieved widespread loyalty among the citizenry akin to that of today's Democrats and Republicans. Although Southerners were overwhelmingly partial to the

Thinking Globally

Regional Parties in India

India's multi-party parliamentary system consists of several strong regional parties, which have had significant representation in the lower house of India's national parliament. These regional parties have helped national parties form winning coalitions and their members have held numerous cabinet positions.

■ Under what conditions might a regional party emerge in the United States?

■ Which party might be harmed the most by such a regional threat? Why?

Democratic-Republicans and New Englanders favored the Federalists, no broad-based party organizations existed to mobilize popular support. Rather, the congressional factions organized around Adams and Jefferson primarily were designed to settle the dispute over how strong the new federal government would be.[3] Just as the nation was in its infancy, so, too, was the party system.

The Early Parties Fade

What is sometimes called the second party system began around 1824, when Andrew Jackson ran for president. He lost to John Quincy Adams but was successful when he ran again in 1828. Around this time, party membership broadened along with the electorate. After receiving criticism for being elitist and undemocratic, the small caucuses of congressional party leaders that had previously nominated candidates gave way to nominations at large party conventions. In 1832, the Democratic Party, which succeeded the old Jeffersonian Democratic-Republicans, held the first national presidential nomination convention. Formed around President Andrew Jackson's popularity, the Democratic Party attracted most of the newly enfranchised voters, who were drawn to Jackson's charismatic style. His strong personality helped to polarize politics, and opposition to the president coalesced into the Whig Party. Among the Whig Party's early leaders was Henry Clay, the Speaker of the House from 1811 to 1820. The incumbent Jackson, having won a first term as president in 1828, defeated Clay in the 1832 presidential contest. Jackson was the first chief executive who won the White House as the nominee of a truly national, popularly based political party.

The Whigs and the Democrats continued to strengthen after 1832, establishing state and local organizations almost everywhere. Their competition was usually fierce and closely matched, and they brought the United States the first broadly supported two-party system in the Western world.[4] Unfortunately for the Whigs, the issue of slavery sharpened the many divisive tensions within the party, which led to its gradual dissolution and replacement by the new Republican Party. Formed in 1854 by anti-slavery activists, the Republican Party set its sights on the abolition (or at least the containment) of slavery. After a losing presidential effort for John C. Frémont in 1856, the party was able to assemble enough support primarily from former Whigs and anti-slavery northern Democrats to win the presidency for Abraham Lincoln in a fragmented 1860 vote. In that year, the South voted solidly Democratic, beginning a tradition so strong that not a single southern state voted Republican for president again until 1920.

Democrats and Republicans: The Golden Age

From the presidential election of 1860 to this day, the same two major parties, the Republicans and the Democrats, have dominated elections in the United States, and control of an electoral majority has seesawed between them. Party stability, the dominance of party organizations in local and state governments, and the impact of those organizations on the lives of millions of voters were the central traits of the era called the "Golden Age" of political parties.

Emigration from Europe (particularly from Ireland, Italy, and Germany) fueled the development in America of big-city **political machines** that gained control of local and state government during this time. A political machine is a party organization that uses tangible incentives such as jobs and favors to win loyalty among voters. Machines also are characterized by a high degree of leadership control over member activity. Party machines were a central element of life for millions of people in the United States during the Golden Age. For city-dwellers, their party and their government were virtually interchangeable during this time.

political machine
A party organization that recruits voter loyalty with tangible incentives and is characterized by a high degree of control over member activity.

Political parties thus not only served the underlying political needs of the society, but also supplemented the population's desire for important social services. In addition to providing housing, employment, and even food to many voters, parties in most major cities provided entertainment by organizing torchlight parades, weekend picnics, socials, and other community events. Many citizens—even those who weren't particularly "political"—attended, thereby gaining some allegiance to one party or the other. The parties offered immigrants not just services but also the opportunity for upward social mobility as they rose in the organization. As a result, parties generated intense loyalty and devotion among their supporters and office holders that helped to produce startlingly high voter turnouts—75 percent or better in all presidential elections from 1876 to 1900—compared with today's 50–60 percent.[5]

The Modern Era

The modern era seems very different from the Golden Age of parties. Many social, political, technological, and governmental changes have contributed to changes in the nature of the national parties since the 1920s. Historically, the government's gradual assumption of important functions previously performed by the parties, such as printing ballots, conducting elections, and providing social welfare services, had a major impact. Beginning in the 1930s with Franklin Roosevelt's New Deal, social services began to be seen as a right of citizenship rather than as a privilege extended in exchange for a person's support of a party. Also, as the flow of immigrants slowed dramatically in the 1920s, party organizations gradually shrank in many places.

A **direct primary** system, in which party nominees were determined by the ballots of qualified voters rather than at party conventions, gained widespread adoption by the states in the first two decades of the twentieth century. Championed by the Progressive movement, direct primaries removed the power of nomination from party leaders and workers and gave it instead to a much broader and more independent electorate, thus loosening the tie between party nominees and the party organization.

Additional Progressive movement reforms also contributed to reduced party influence in the United States. **Civil service laws,** for example, which require appointment on the basis of merit and competitive examinations, removed opportunities for much of the patronage used by the parties to reward their followers. The development of the civil service is discussed in greater detail in chapter 8.

In the post–World War II era, extensive social changes also contributed to the move away from strong parties. A weakening of the party system gave rise to candidate and **issue-oriented politics.** Rather than a focus on party platforms, contemporary politics focuses on the individuals running for office and specific issues, such as civil rights, tax cutting, or environmentalism. Interest groups and lobbyists have stepped into the void that weaker parties have left behind. Candidates compete for endorsements and contributions from a variety of multi-issue as well as single-issue organizations. Issue politics tends to cut across party lines and encourages voters to **ticket-split**—to vote for candidates of different parties in the same election (a phenomenon we discuss in greater depth in chapter 12). Parties' diminished control over issues and campaigns also have left candidates considerable power in how they conduct themselves during election season and how they seek resources. This new **candidate-centered politics** is an outgrowth of voters focusing directly on the candidates, their particular issues, and character, rather than on their party affiliation.

Another post–World War II social change that has affected the parties is the population shift from urban to suburban locales. Millions of people have moved from the cities to the suburbs, where a sense of privacy and detachment can deter the most energetic party organizers. In addition, population growth in the last half-century has created districts with far more people, making it less feasible to knock on every door or shake every hand.[6]

direct primary
The selection of party candidates through the ballots of qualified voters rather than at party nominating conventions.

civil service laws
These acts removed the staffing of the bureaucracy from political parties and created a professional bureaucracy filled through competition.

issue-oriented politics
Politics that focus on specific issues rather than on party, candidate, or other loyalties.

ticket-split
To vote for candidates of different parties for various offices in the same election.

candidate-centered politics
Politics that focus directly on the candidates, their particular issues, and character, rather than on party affiliation.

Realignment

party realignment
A shifting of party coalition group-ings in the electorate that remains in place for several elections.

critical election
An election that signals a party realignment through voter polariza-tion around new issues.

Periodically in election years, voters make dramatic shifts in partisan preference that drastically alter the political landscape. During these **party realignments,** existing party affiliations are subject to upheaval: many voters may change parties, and the youngest age group of voters may permanently adopt the label of the newly dominant party.[7]

Preceding a major realignment are one or more **critical elections,** which may polarize voters around new issues and personalities in reaction to crucial developments, such as a war or an economic depression. Three tumultuous eras in particular have pro-duced significant critical elections. First, Thomas Jefferson, in reaction against the Federalist Party's agenda of a strong, centralized federal government, formed the Democratic-Republican Party, which took the presidency and Congress in 1800. Sec-ond, in reaction to the growing crisis over slavery, the Whig Party gradually dissolved and the Republican Party gained strength and ultimately won the presidency in 1860. Third, the Great Depression of the 1930s caused large numbers of voters to repudiate Republican Party policies and embrace the Democratic Party. Each of these cases resulted in fundamental and enduring alterations in the party equation.

The last confirmed major realignment, then, happened in the 1928–1936 period, as Republican Herbert Hoover's presidency was held to one term because of voter anger about the Depression. In 1932, Democrat Franklin D. Roosevelt swept to power as the electorate decisively rejected Hoover and the Republicans. This dramatic vote of "no confidence" was followed by substantial changes in policy by the new pres-ident. The majority of voters responded favorably to Roosevelt's New Deal policies, accepted his vision of society, and ratified their choice of the new president's party in subsequent presidential and congressional elections.

The idea that party realignments occurred on a predictable, periodic basis beguiled many political scientists in the 1960s and 1970s, and much attention was focused on awaiting the next sea change in partisan alignment.[8] However, no uniform shift in parti-san alignment has occurred in American politics since the election of Franklin D. Roo-sevelt in 1932. In fact, divided partisan government has been a dominant outcome of elec-tions since World War II. Many scholars today question the value of party realignments in understanding partisanship and policy change. While critical elections share some degree of similarity, each is precipitated by distinctive political changes that are linked to the par-ticular period and issues.[9] Nonetheless, party realignments offer a useful basis for under-standing how pivotal elections may lastingly alter the direction of American politics.

A critical election is not the only occasion when changes in partisan affiliation are accommodated. In truth, every election produces realignment to some degree, since some individuals are undoubtedly pushed to change parties by events and by their reactions to the candidates. Research suggests that partisanship is much more respon-sive to current issues and personalities than had been believed earlier.[10]

Secular Realignment

secular realignment
The gradual rearrangement of party coalitions, based more on demo-graphic shifts than on shocks to the political system.

Although the term *realignment* is usually applied only if momentous events such as war or economic depression produce enduring and substantial alterations in the party coali-tions, political scientists have long recognized that a more gradual rearrangement of party coalitions can occur.[11] Called **secular realignment,** this piecemeal process depends not on convulsive shocks to the political system but on slow, almost barely dis-cernible demographic shifts—the shrinking of one party's base of support and the enlargement of the other's, for example—or simple generational replacement (that is, the dying off of the older generation and the maturing of the younger generation). According to one version of this theory, in an era of weaker party attachments (such as we currently are experiencing), a dramatic, full-scale realignment may not be possible.[12] Still, a critical mass of voters may be attracted for years to one party's banner in waves or streams, if that party's leadership and performance are consistently exemplary.

The prospect of a national realignment is unlikely as long as party ties remain tenuous for so many voters.[13] However, regionally there have been slow but stable partisan realignments that have affected the power bases of the major parties. During the 1990s, the southern states, traditionally Democratic stalwarts since the Civil War, shifted dramatically toward the Republican Party. The Northeast, a longtime reliable voting bloc for Republicans, became increasingly Democratic during the same period. Many factors have contributed to these gradual regional shifts in party allegiance. Southern Democrats were the most conservative of the New Deal coalition, favoring the social status quo and opposing civil rights reform. As the Democratic Party shifted its platform toward more liberal social causes such as civil rights and social spending, many southern voters and politicians shifted their allegiance toward the Republicans. In a region where voting for a Republican was once considered taboo, the South is now one of the most reliable blocs of Republican voters.[14]

DEALIGNMENT AND THE STRENGTH OF POLITICAL PARTIES Over the past two decades, numerous political scientists as well as other observers, journalists, and party activists have become increasingly anxious about **dealignment,** a general decline in partisan identification and loyalty in the electorate.[15] Since parties traditionally provide political information and serve as an engine of political participation, it has been feared that weakening party attachments are undermining political involvement. Many public opinion surveys have shown an increase in independents at the expense of the two major parties. The Center for Political Studies/Survey Research Center (CPS/SRC) of the University of Michigan has charted the rise of self-described independents from a low of 19 percent in 1958 to a peak of 40 percent in 2000, with percentages in recent years consistently hovering just below the high-water mark of 40 percent.

From 1952 to 1964, about three-fourths or more of the electorate volunteered a party choice without prodding, but since 1970 an average of less than two-thirds has been willing to do so. Professed independents (including leaners) have increased from around one-fifth of the electorate in the 1950s to over one-third during the last three decades. In recent years, the number of voters who identify with parties has stabilized, but the number still lags far behind historical norms.

Nevertheless, the parties' decline can easily be exaggerated. Although political parties have evolved considerably and changed form from time to time, they usually have been reliable vehicles for mass participation in a representative democracy. The parties' journeys through U.S. history have been characterized by the same ability to adapt to prevailing conditions that is often cited as the genius of the Constitution. Both major parties exhibit flexibility and pragmatism, which help ensure their survival and the success of the society they serve.

Despite massive changes in political conditions and frequent dramatic shifts in the electorate's mood, the two major parties not only have achieved remarkable longevity but also have almost always provided strong competition for each other and the voters at the national level. Of the thirty presidential elections from 1884 to 2008, for instance, the Republicans won seventeen and the Democrats fifteen.

The sharp rise in party unity scores in Congress discussed earlier in the chapter suggests that the party in government is alive and well. The unprecedented fund-raising of the party organizations suggests, moreover, that political parties are here to stay.

Perhaps most of all, history teaches us that the development of parties in the United States has been inevitable. Human nature alone guarantees conflict in any society; in a free state, the question is simply how to contain and channel conflict productively without infringing on individual liberties. The Framers' utopian hopes for the avoidance of partisan faction, Madison's chief concern, have given way to an appreciation of the parties' constructive contributions to conflict definition and resolution during the years of the American republic. Political parties have become the primary means by which society addresses its irreconcilable differences, and as such they play an essential role in democratic society.

**You Are Redrawing
the Districts in Your State**

dealignment
A general decline in party identification and loyalty in the electorate.

The Functions and Organization of the American Party System

For over 200 years, the two-party system has served as the mechanism American society uses to organize and resolve social and political conflict. Political parties often are the chief agents of change in our political system. They provide vital services to society, and it would be difficult to envision political life without them.

What Do Parties Do?

Political parties in America carry out a wide variety of functions. Among other goals, they mobilize support, provide stability, create unity, run candidates for election, organize the legislature, and formulate policy.

MOBILIZING SUPPORT AND GATHERING POWER Party affiliation is enormously helpful to elected leaders. Therefore the parties aid office holders by giving them room to develop their policies and by mobilizing support for them. When the president addresses the nation and requests support for his policies, for example, his party's members are usually the first to respond to the call, perhaps by flooding Congress with e-mails and phone calls urging action on the president's agenda. Moreover because there are only two major parties in the United States, citizens who are interested in politics or public policy are mainly attracted to one or the other party, creating natural majorities or near majorities for party office holders to command. The party generates a community of interest that bonds disparate groups over time into a **coalition**.

coalition
A group made up of interests or organizations that join forces for the purpose of electing public officials.

A FORCE FOR STABILITY AND MODERATION The parties encourage stability in the type of coalitions they form. There are inherent contradictions in these coalitions that, oddly enough, strengthen the nation even as they strain party unity. Franklin D. Roosevelt's Democratic New Deal coalition, for example, included many African Americans and most southern whites, opposing groups nonetheless joined in common political purpose by economic hardship and, in the case of better-off Southerners, in longtime voting habits.[16]

UNITY, LINKAGE, AND ACCOUNTABILITY Parties are the glue that holds together the disparate elements of the U.S. governmental and political apparatus. The Framers designed a system that divides and subdivides power, making it possible to preserve individual liberty but difficult to coordinate and produce action in a timely fashion. Parties help compensate for this drawback by linking the executive and legislative branches. Although rivalry between these two branches of U.S. government is inevitable, the partisan affiliations of the leaders of each branch constitute a common basis for cooperation, as the president and his fellow party members in Congress usually demonstrate daily.

The party's linkage function does not end there. Party identification and organization foster communication between the voter and the candidate, as well as between the voter and the office holder. The party connection is one means of increasing accountability in election campaigns and in government. Candidates on the campaign trail and elected party leaders in office are required from time to time to account for their performance at party-sponsored forums, nominating primaries, and conventions.

THE ELECTIONEERING FUNCTION The election, proclaimed author H. G. Wells, is "democracy's ceremonial, its feast, its great function," and the political parties assist this ceremony in essential ways. First, the parties help to funnel eager, interested individuals into politics and government. While most candidates are self-recruited, some are also recruited each year by the two parties, as are many of the candidates' staff members—the people who manage the campaigns and go on to serve in key governmental positions once the election has been won.

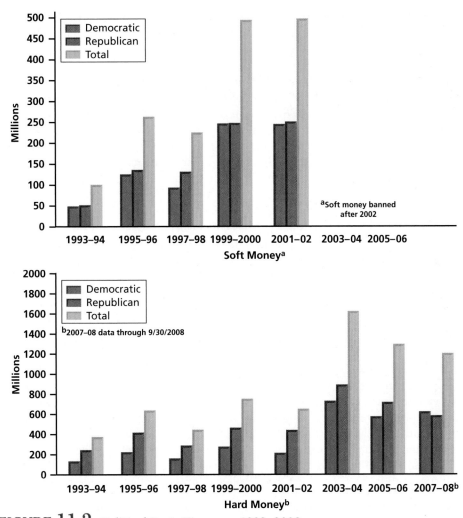

FIGURE 11.2 Political Party Finances, 1993–2008

Note how the Democratic Party had higher receipts than the Republican Party for the first time in the 2007–08 cycle. Also note how the receipts for both parties have substantially increased over time, even following the 2002 Bipartisan Campaign Reform Act (BCRA), which outlawed soft-money contributions (shown in the top graph) to the parties.

Sources: 2003–2008 from Center for Responsive Politics (http://www.opensecrets.org), and earlier years from Harold W. Stanley and Richard Niemi, *Vital Statistics on American Politics, 2003–2004* (Washington, DC: CQ Press, 2004).

Elections can have meaning in a democracy only if they are competitive, and in the United States they probably could not be competitive without the parties. (When we use the term *competitive*, we mean that both parties have sufficient organization, money, and people to run a vigorous election campaign, and to sustain their arguments through the period of governance.)

Currently, both major political parties have supplemented labor-intensive, person-to-person operations with modern technological and communication strategies, and both parites are similar in the objectives they pursue to achieve political power. Nevertheless, each party has its strengths and weaknesses.

The contemporary national Republican Party has considerable organizational prowess, often surpassing the Democrats in fund-raising by large margins. (To learn more, see Figure 11.2.) In recent election cycles, Democrats have worked hard to compete with the Republican Party fund-raising machine, which is fueled by a large number of wealthy donors. In 2006, the Democrats came closer to matching the Republicans in fundraising than in any other modern election season. In 2008, the Democrats' House and Senate campaign committees raised nearly $50 million more than their Republican counterparts. And, while the Republican National Committee maintained an edge by raising over $250 million, which was about $50 million more than the Democratic National Committee, the DNC actually spent more money than the RNC in 2008.

The parties raise so much money because they have developed networks of donors reached by a variety of methods. Both parties have highly successful mail solicitation lists. Republicans also pioneered the use of interactive technologies to attract voters. With these contributions, the parties have spent millions of dollars for national, state, and local opinion surveys. The information provided in such polls is invaluable in the tense concluding days of an election. Both parties operate sophisticated media divisions that specialize in the design and production of television advertisements for party nominees at all levels. And, both parties train the armies of the political volunteers and paid operatives who run the candidates' campaigns. Early in each election cycle, the national parties also help prepare voluminous research reports on opponents, analyzing their public statements, votes, and attendance records.

PARTY AS A VOTING AND ISSUE CUE A voter's party identification can act as an invaluable filter for information, a perceptual screen that affects how he or she digests political news. Parties try to cultivate a popular image and help inform the public about issues through advertising and voter contact. Therefore, party affiliation provides a useful cue for voters, particularly for the least informed and least interested, who can use the party label as a shortcut or substitute for interpreting issues and events they may not fully comprehend. Better-educated and more involved voters also find party identification helpful. After all, no one has the time to study every issue carefully or to become fully knowledgeable about every candidate seeking public office.

national party platform
A statement of the general and specific philosophy and policy goals of a political party, usually promulgated at the national convention.

POLICY FORMULATION AND PROMOTION The **national party platform** is the most visible instrument that parties use to formulate, convey, and promote public policy. Every four years, each party writes for the presidential nominating conventions a lengthy platform explaining its positions on key issues. Typically, about two-thirds of the promises in the victorious party's presidential platform have been completely or mostly implemented. Moreover, about one-half or more of the pledges of the losing party also tend to find their way into public policy, a trend that no doubt reflects the effort of both parties to support broad policy positions that enjoy widespread support in the general public.[17]

LEGISLATIVE ORGANIZATION In no segment of U.S. government is the party more visible or vital than in the Congress. In this century, political parties have dramatically increased the sophistication and impact of their internal congressional organizations. Prior to the beginning of every session, the parties in both houses of Congress gather (or "caucus") separately to select party leaders (House majority and minority leaders, Senate majority and minority leaders, party whips, and so on) and to arrange for the appointment of members of each chamber's committees. In effect, then, the parties organize and operate the Congress.

To promote their policy positions, the leaders of each party in Congress try to advance legislation to further their interests. Party labels, in fact, consistently have been the most powerful predictor of congressional roll-call voting. In the last few years, party-line voting has increased noticeably, as reflected in the upward trend by both Democrats and Republicans shown in Figure 11.3. Although not invariably predictive, a member's party affiliation proved to be the indicator of his or her votes about 88 percent of the time in 2007; that is, the average representative or senator sided with his or her party on about 88 percent of the votes that divided a majority of Democrats from a majority of Republicans that year. In most recent years, unanimous party-line votes have become increasingly common, with Democrats recording a record 272 unanimous roll-call votes in 2007.[18]

There are many reasons for the recent growth of congressional party unity. Both congressional parties, for instance, have gradually become more ideologically homogeneous and internally consistent. Southern Democrats today are typically moderate or liberal like their northern counterparts. Similarly, the vast majority of Republicans in Congress identify themselves as conservative. Partisan gerrymandering, redrawing congressional lines so as to create safe districts, has also increased party cohesion, as

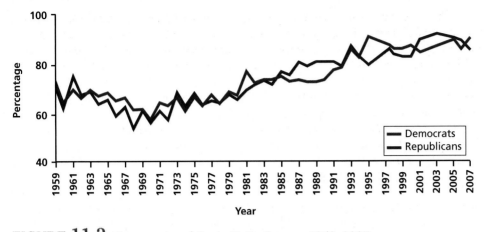

FIGURE 11.3 Congressional Party Unity Scores, 1959–2007

Note how party-based voting has increased conspicuously since the 1970s.

Source: Congressional Quarterly Almanacs (Washington, DC: CQ Press).

members of Congress increasingly represent congressional districts that strongly favor a single party. The political campaign committees have also played a role in this renewed cohesiveness. Each national party committee has been recruiting and training House and Senate candidates as never before, and devising themes and issues aimed at targeted districts. With numbers so close in each chamber of Congress, each party has a singular focus on electing a majority of legislators.

Besides mobilizing Americans on a permanent basis, then, the parties convert the cacophony of hundreds of identifiable social and economic groups into a two-part semi-harmony that is much more comprehensible, if not always on key and pleasing to the ears. The simplicity of two-party politics may be deceptive, given the enormous variety in public policy choices, but a sensible system of representation in the American context might be impossible without it.

CRASHING THE PARTY: MINOR PARTIES IN THE AMERICAN TWO-PARTY SYSTEM

Despite their disadvantages in the United States, minor parties based on causes often neglected by the major parties have significantly affected American politics. Third parties find their roots in sectionalism (as did the South's states' rights Dixiecrats, who broke away from the Democrats in 1948), in economic protest (such as the agrarian revolt that fueled the Populists, an 1892 prairie-states party), in specific issues (such as the Green Party's support of the environment), in ideology (the Socialist, Communist, and Libertarian Parties are examples), and in appealing, charismatic personalities (Theodore Roosevelt's affiliation with the Bull Moose Party in 1912 is perhaps the best case). Many minor parties have drawn strength from a combination of these sources. The American Independent Party enjoyed a measure of success because of a dynamic leader (George Wallace in 1968), a firm geographic base (the South), and an emotional issue (an opposition to federal civil rights legislation). In 1992, Ross Perot, the billionaire with a folksy Texas manner, was a charismatic leader whose campaign was fueled by the deficit issue (as well as by his personal fortune).

Minor-party and independent candidates are not limited to presidential elections. Many also run in congressional elections, and the numbers appear to be growing. In the 2006 congressional elections, for example, nearly 350 minor-party and independent candidates ran for seats in the House and Senate—almost three and half times as many as in 1968 and one and a half times the number that ran in 1980. Only two members of the 111th Congress—Senator Joe Lieberman, who lost the Democratic primary but won reelection as an independent in Connecticut, and freshman Senator Bernie Sanders of Vermont—are independents, and both caucus with the Democrats. Minor-party candidates for the House are most likely to emerge under three conditions: (1) when a House seat becomes open; (2) when a minor-party candidate has previously competed in the district; and, (3) when partisan competition between the two major parties in the district is close.[19]

Above all, third parties make electoral progress in direct proportion to the failure of the two major parties to incorporate new ideas or alienated groups or to nominate attractive candidates as their standard-bearers. Third parties do best when declining trust in the two major political parties plagues the electorate.[20] Usually, though, third parties are eventually co-opted by one of the two major parties, each of them eager to take the politically popular issue that gave rise to the third party and make it theirs in order to secure the allegiance of the third party's supporters.

The Party Organization

Although the distinctions might not be as clear today as they were two or three decades ago, the two major parties remain fairly loosely organized, with national, state, and local branches. (To learn more about Political Party organization, see Figure 11.4.) The different levels of each party represent diverse interests in Washington, D.C., state capitals, and local governments throughout the nation.

NATIONAL COMMITTEES The first national party committees were skeletal and formed some years after the creation of the presidential nominating conventions in the 1830s. First the Democrats in 1848 and then the Republicans in 1856 established national governing bodies—the Democratic National Committee, or DNC, and the Republican National Committee, or RNC—to make arrangements for the national conventions and to coordinate the subsequent presidential campaigns. In addition, to serve their interests, the congressional party caucuses in both houses organized their own national committees, loosely allied with the DNC and RNC.

FIGURE 11.4 Political Party Organization in America: From Base to Pinnacle

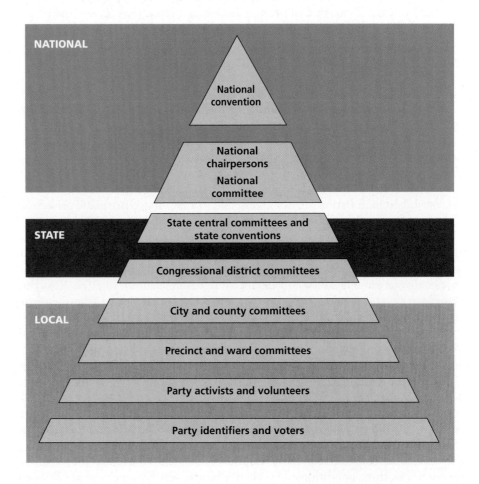

Source: WASHINGTON POST | *April 6, 2008* | *Page B4*

The Impact of a National Committee Chair

The Dems, Now Dancing to His Tune

PERRY BACON JR.

When running for president in 2004, Howard Dean famously screamed at Democrats; in 2008, plenty of Democrats are screaming right back.

But Democrats have some good reasons to stop kicking Dean around. . . . If the Democrats win in 2008, they may come to thank Dr. Dean [chair of the Democratic National Committee] for providing the medicine that cured some of the party's ills.

Sen. Barack Obama's campaign has been groundbreaking on many levels, but its widely hailed use of the Internet to create a large base of small donors largely recycles the breakthrough that powered Dean's 2004 campaign. Despite having had more time to plan for her presidential run, Clinton has often found herself outmaneuvered at creative online fundraising by Obama, and Sen. John McCain may find himself at a sizable fundraising disadvantage to either Democrat. . . .

As the Democrats tried to win back Congress in 2006, Dean found himself back at the center of controversy. The new DNC chairman set out to forge what he called the "50-state strategy," spending millions to start building party organizations in red states such as Alabama. That infuriated congressional Democrats who wanted to spend the money on targeted districts in swing states such as Ohio and Pennsylvania. The Democrats did win some congressional seats in GOP-leaning states such as Indiana, but even Dean might acknowledge that that had less to do with the small number of ground-level organizers he deployed than with weak GOP incumbents forced to defend an unpopular war. Still, Dean got some results: a study by Harvard's Elaine Kamarck found that Democratic turnout in 2006 was higher in places where Dean's new organizers were working.

Dean's basic point was also something Democrats may come to embrace: Far more Democrats live in some very red states than you might guess, and if the Democrats want to build a permanent majority in Congress, they'll need to win at least some seats in those areas.

It's no accident that Obama, not Dean, is benefiting most from some of Dean's insights. The DNC chief's checkered track record makes it hard for some Democrats to laud him. Many Democrats say that he has by and large failed at building strong organizations, with the DNC finding itself with far less cash on hand than the Republican National Committee, despite the paucity of grass-roots enthusiasm for the GOP. Dean is also often described as weak in the two areas party chairs are supposed to excel at: raising money and providing "message discipline." Many Democrats still cringe when the loose-lipped former governor appears on television to push the party's message. Meanwhile, his limited relationships with many party insiders have made it harder for him to referee party disputes, such as stopping Michigan and Florida from moving their primaries up, or persuade the two Democratic brawlers not to bloody each other.

But those shortcomings don't tarnish the underlying point: Howard Dean has been a man ahead of his time. When he leaves Washington for good next year, the improved fortunes he has helped bring to his party may be enough to make him want to scream.

Discussion Questions

1. *What power or influence does the chair of a national party have on the rules of nominating presidential candidates and managing the convention procedures? Did the 2008 disputes over seating in the Florida and Michigan delegations affect the final outcome of the presidential election?*

2. *In retrospect, was Howard Dean's strategy for allocating national party resources a more effective strategy for expanding the Democrats' majorities in Congress and winning the White House than targeting key districts and states?*

There is an informal division of labor among the national committees. Whereas the DNC and RNC focus primarily on aiding presidential campaigns and conducting general party-building activities, the congressional campaign committees work primarily to maximize the number of seats held by their respective parties in Congress. In the past two decades, all six national committees have become major, service-oriented organizations in American politics.[21]

LEADERSHIP The key national party official is the chairperson of the national committee. Although the chair is formally elected by the national committee, he or she is usually selected by the sitting president or newly nominated presidential candidate, who is accorded the right to name the individual for at least the duration of his or her campaign. The chair often becomes the prime spokesperson and arbitrator for the party during the four years between elections. He or she is called on to damp down factionalism, negotiate candidate disputes, and prepare the machinery for the next presidential election. Perhaps most critically, the chair is called upon to raise funds and keep the party financially

How do national parties discipline unruly state parties? Protesters gathered outside a meeting of the DNC Rules and Bylaws Committee in May of 2008 as the committee debated how to treat delegates from Florida and Michigan at the upcoming Democratic National Convention. Both states had violated party rules by holding primaries before February 5, 2008, but both states were also expected to be key battleground states in the presidential election. The Committee's solution was to give each delegate half a vote. Before the convention, however, Senator Barack Obama, assured of winning the nomination, offered a motion to seat all of Michigan and Florida's delegates and grant them full voting rights.

national convention
A party meeting held in the presidential election year for the purposes of nominating a presidential and vice presidential ticket and adopting a platform.

party identification
A citizen's personal affinity for a political party, usually expressed by a tendency to vote for the candidates of that party.

strong. Balancing the interests of all potential White House contenders is a particularly difficult job, and strict neutrality is normally expected from the chair.

NATIONAL CONVENTIONS Every four years, each party holds a **national convention** to nominate its presidential and vice presidential candidates. In addition to nominating the presidential ticket, the convention also fulfills its role as the ultimate governing body for the party. The rules adopted and the party platform that is passed serve as durable guidelines that steer the party until the next convention.

STATES AND LOCALITIES Although national committee activities of all kinds attract most of the media attention, the party is structurally based not in Washington, D.C., but in the states and localities. Except for the campaign finance arena, virtually all government regulation of political parties is left to the states. Most importantly, the vast majority of party leadership positions are filled at subnational levels.

The arrangement of party committees provides for a broad base of support. The smallest voting unit, the precinct, usually takes in a few adjacent neighborhoods and is the fundamental building block of the party. There are more than 100,000 precincts in the United States. The precinct committee members are the foot soldiers of any party, and their efforts are supplemented by party committees above them in the wards, cities, counties, towns, villages, and congressional districts.

The state governing body supervising this collection of local party organizations is usually called the state central (or executive) committee. Its members come from all major geographic units, as determined by and selected under state law. Generally, state parties are free to act within the limits set by their state legislatures without interference from the national party, except in the selection and seating of presidential convention delegates.

Sources of Party Identification

Most American voters identify with a party but do not belong to it. Universal party membership does not exist in the United States: the voter pays no prescribed dues; no formal rules govern an individual's party activities; and voters assume no enforceable obligations to the party even when they consistently vote for its candidates. A party has no real control over its adherents, and the party's voters subscribe to few or none of the commonly accepted tenets of organizational membership, such as regular participation and some measure of responsibility for the group's welfare. Rather, **party identification** or affiliation is an informal and impressionistic exercise whereby a citizen acquires a party label and accepts its standard as a summary of his or her political views and preferences.

For those Americans who do firmly adopt a party label, their party often becomes a central political reference symbol and perceptual screen. For these partisans, party identification is a significant aspect of their political personality and a way of defining and explaining themselves to others. The loyalty generated by the label can be as intense as any enjoyed by sports teams and alma maters.

Individual party identifications are reinforced by the legal institutionalization of the major parties. Because of restrictive ballot laws, campaign finance rules, the powerful inertia of political tradition, and many other factors, voters for all practical purposes are limited to a choice between a Democrat and a Republican in almost all elections—a situation that naturally encourages the pragmatic choosing up of sides. About half of the states require a voter to state a party preference (or independent status) when registering to vote, and they restrict voting in a party primary only to registrants in that particular party, making it an incentive for voters to affiliate themselves with a party.[22]

Photo courtesy: Mannie Garcia/Bloomberg News/Landov

TABLE **11.2** Party Identification by Group Affiliation

		Democratic	Independents	Republican
		Identifiers		Identifiers
Region	Northeast	33	45	23
	Midwest	35	44	21
	South	34	41	26
	West	33	39	29
Gender	Male	30	45	25
	Female	37	39	24
Race	Black	66	31	3
	Hispanic	37	47	17
	White	27	42	30
Age	<30	35	46	19
	30–49	30	42	28
	50+	36	40	24
Income	<30,000	41	15	44
	30,000–74,999	31	30	39
	75,000+	39	32	39
Education	High School or Less	34	24	43
	College	28	32	40
	Advanced Degree	39	22	39
Union Member	Yes	47	22	32
Military Veteran	Yes	29	27	45
Religion Type	Protestant	34	39	37
	Catholic	34	23	43
	Jewish	48	18	34
Evangelical Christian	Yes	31	33	36
Marital Status	Married	28	31	41
	Not Currently Marrried	39	19	42
Ideology	Conservative	21	33	45
	Moderate	35	48	17
	Liberal	53	42	6

Note: In this table, independent leaners are collapsed into the independent column. Partisans and strong partisans are collapsed into the party columns. Due to rounding, not all rows equal 100 percent.
Source: Pew Research Center, *Political Landscape More Favorable to Democrats: Trends in Political Values and Core Attitudes, 1987–2007*, March 22, 2007.

GROUP AFFILIATIONS Just as individuals vary in the strength of their partisan choice, so, too, do groups vary in the degree to which they identify with the Democratic Party or the Republican Party. In modern American politics, the geographic regions are relatively closely contested between the parties. Gender, however, is another matter. In 2008, for example, exit polls showed that women favored Democratic presidential candidate Barack Obama by 13 percentage points over John McCain, his Republican rival. This pro-Democratic trend among women has persisted through many elections cycles.

Race and ethnicity also are extremely significant factors in determining party affiliation. African Americans, for example, almost always are Democrats. Hispanics supplement African Americans as Democratic stalwarts; by more than three to one, Hispanics prefer the Democratic Party. Voting patterns of Puerto Ricans are very similar to those of African Americans, while Mexican Americans favor the Democrats by smaller margins. An exception is the Cuban American population, whose anti–Fidel Castro tilt leads to support for the Republican Party.

Age has long been associated with party identification, as most voters develop their partisan affiliations based on formative political experiences growing up. For example, many voters who were alive during the Great Depression identify strongly with the Democratic Party, whereas many who were young during the Reagan years identify with the Republican Party. Today, generally the very youngest and very oldest voters tend to prefer the Democratic Party, while middle-aged voters disproportionately favor the Republican Party.

Occupation, income, and education also influence party affiliation. The GOP remains predominant among executives, professionals, and white-collar workers, whereas the Democrats lead substantially among trial lawyers, educators, and blue-collar workers. Labor union members are also Democratic by nearly two to one. Women who do not work outside the home are less liberal and Democratic than those who do. Occupation, income, and education are closely related, of course, so many of the same partisan patterns appear in all three classifications. Democratic support drops as one climbs the income scale. Those with a college education tend to support the Republican Party, although those with advanced degrees tend to be Democratic.[23]

Party preferences by religion are also traditional, but with modern twists. White Protestants—especially Methodists, Presbyterians, and Episcopalians—favor the Republicans, whereas Catholics and, even more so, Jewish voters tend to favor the Democratic Party. Decreased polarization is apparent all around, however.[24] Democrats have made inroads among many liberal Protestant denominations over the past three decades, and Republicans can now sometimes claim up to 25 percent of Jewish voters and a nearly equal share of the Catholic vote. Evangelical Christians are somewhat less Republican than commonly believed. The GOP usually has just a 10 percent edge among them, primarily because so many African Americans, who are strongly pro-Democratic, are also members of this group.[25]

Interest Group Structure and Functions

The face of interest group politics in the United States is changing as quickly as laws, political consultants, and technology allow. Big business and trade groups are increasing their activities and engagement in the political system at the same time that there is conflicting evidence concerning whether ordinary citizens join political groups. In an influential 1995 essay and later in a 2000 book, political scientist Robert Putnam argued that fewer Americans are joining groups, a phenomenon he labeled "bowling alone."[26] Others have faulted Putnam, concluding that America is in the midst of an "explosion of voluntary groups, activities and charitable donations [that] is transforming our towns and cities."[27] Although bowling leagues, which were once a very common means of bringing people together, have withered, other groups such as volunteer groups, soccer associations, health clubs, and environmental groups are flourishing. Older groups such as the Elks Club and the League of Women Voters, whose membership was tracked by Putnam, are attracting few new members, but this does not mean that people aren't joining groups; they just aren't joining the ones studied by Putnam.

social capital
The myriad relationships that individuals enjoy that facilitate the resolution of community problems through collective action.

Why is this debate so important? Political scientists believe that involvement in these kinds of community groups and activities enhances the level of **social capital**, "the web of cooperative relationships between citizens that facilitates resolution of collective action problems."[28] The more social capital that exists in a given community, the more citizens are engaged in its governance and well-being, and the more likely they are to work for the collective good.[29] This tendency to form small-scale associations for the public good, or **civic virtue**, as Putnam calls it, creates fertile ground within communities for improved political and economic development.[30] Thus, if Americans truly are joining fewer groups, we might expect the overall quality of government and its provision of services to suffer.

civic virtue
The tendency to form small-scale associations for the public good.

Interest groups are also important because they give the unrepresented or underrepresented an opportunity to have their voices heard, thereby making the government and its policy-making process more representative of diverse populations and perspectives.

Interest Group Formation

David B. Truman, one of the first political scientists to study interest groups, defines an organized interest as "any group that, on the basis of one or more shared attitudes, makes certain claims upon other groups in society for the establishment, maintenance, or enhancement of forms of behavior that are implied by shared attitudes."[31] Interest group theorists use a variety of theories to explain how interest groups form and how they influence public policy. **Pluralist theory** argues that political power is distributed among a wide array of diverse and competing interest groups. Pluralist theorists such as David B. Truman explain the formation of interest groups through **disturbance theory**. According to this approach, anytime there is a disturbance in a political system, a group will arise. Moreover, one wave of groups will give way to another wave of groups representing a contrary perspective (a countermovement). Thus, Truman would argue, all salient issues will be represented in government. The government in turn should provide a forum in which the competing demands of groups and the majority of the U.S. population can be heard and balanced.[32]

Transactions theory arose out of criticisms of the pluralist approach. Transactions theory argues that public policies are the result of narrowly defined exchanges among political actors. Transactions theorists make two main contentions: it is not rational for people to mobilize into groups, and, therefore, the groups that do mobilize will represent elites.

Transactionists also argue that the interest group system will be biased in terms of resources, because the relative cost of mobilization is lower for individuals who have greater amounts of time or money available. According to one political scientist, "The flaw in the pluralist heaven is that the heavenly chorus sings with a strong upper-class bias."[33]

More recently, a new wave of political scientists called the neopluralists have evaluated previous theories and data to find a middle ground. For example one neopluralist perspective, **population ecology theory**, argues that the formation and life of a political organization is conditional on the density and diversity of the interest group population in a given area. This theory builds on the biological idea that the resources of an ecosystem can only support a certain number of any one species. Initial growth of these species usually proceeds in an "s" curve, with a slow period of growth, followed by a rapid increase in population, and an eventual leveling off when the population has reached its maximum capacity. Population ecology theorists believe that interest group growth follows a similar pattern and is constrained by the relative abundance of resources in a particular environment.[34]

pluralist theory
The theory that political power is distributed among a wide array of diverse and competing interest groups.

disturbance theory
The theory that interest groups form in part to counteract the efforts of other groups.

transactions theory
The theory that public policies are the result of narrowly defined exchanges among political actors.

population ecology theory
The theory that the life of a political organization is conditioned on the density and diversity of the interest group population in a given area.

How do special interests develop?
Geography often determines the kinds of special interests that are most common in a given region.

The Ununited Interests of America

Photo courtesy: Tom Toles/Universal Press Syndicate

Interest Group Maintenance

patron
A person who finances a group or individual activity.

All interest groups require adequate funding to build their memberships as well as to advance their policy objectives. Governments, foundations, and wealthy individuals can serve as **patrons**, providing crucial start-up funds for groups, especially public interest groups.[35] Advertising, litigating, and lobbying are expensive. Without financiers, few public interest groups could survive their initial start-up period.

Organizations usually are composed of three kinds of members. At the top are a relatively small number of leaders who devote most of their energies to the single group. The second tier of members is generally involved psychologically as well as organizationally. They are the workers of the group—they attend meetings, pay dues, and chair committees to see that things get done. In the bottom tier are the rank and file, members who don't actively participate. They pay their dues and call themselves group members, but they do little more. Most group members fall into this last category.

collective good
Something of value that cannot be withheld from a nonmember of a group, for example, a tax write-off or a better environment.

free rider problem
Potential members fail to join a group because they can get the benefit, or collective good, sought by the group without contributing the effort.

Groups vary tremendously in their ability to enroll what are called potential members. According to economist Mancur Olson Jr., all groups provide some **collective good**—that is, something of value, such as money, a tax write-off, a good feeling, or a better environment, that can't be withheld from a nonmember.[36] If one union member at a factory gets a raise, for example, all other workers at that factory will, too. Therefore, those who don't join or work for the benefit of the group still reap the rewards of the group's activity. The downside of this phenomenon is called the **free rider problem**. As Olson asserts, potential members may be unlikely to join a group because they realize that they will receive many of the benefits the group acheives, regardless of their participation. Not only is it irrational for free riders to join any group, but the bigger the group, the greater the free rider problem. Thus, groups need to provide a variety of other incentives to convince potential members to join. These can be newsletters, discounts, or simply a good feeling.

The Development of American Interest Groups

Although all kinds of local groups proliferated throughout the colonies and in the new states, it was not until the 1830s, as communications networks improved, that the first national groups emerged. Many of these groups were single-issue groups deeply rooted in the Christian religious revivalism that was sweeping the nation. Concern with humanitarian issues such as temperance (total abstinence from alcoholic beverages), peace, education, slavery, and women's rights led to the founding of numerous associations dedicated to solving these problems. Among the first of these groups was the American Anti-Slavery Society, founded in 1833 by William Lloyd Garrison.

After the Civil War, more groups were founded. For example, the Women's Christian Temperance Union (WCTU) was created in 1874 with the goal of outlawing the sale of liquor. Its members, many of them quite religious, believed that the consumption of alcohol was an evil injurious to family life because many men drank away their paychecks, leaving no money to feed or clothe their families.

Business interests began to play even larger roles in both state and national politics. A popular saying of the day noted that the Standard Oil Company did everything to the Pennsylvania legislature except refine it. Increasingly large trusts, monopolies, business partnerships, and corporate conglomerations in the oil, steel, and sugar industries became sufficiently powerful to control many representatives in the state and national legislatures.

Perhaps the most effective organized interest of the day was the railroad industry. In a move that couldn't take

Thinking Globally

Agricultural Interests in France

In France, less than 5 percent of the population is engaged in agricultural farming, and less than 3 percent of the country's economy is devoted to agriculture. Historically, however, France's National Farmers' Union has been especially powerful and, despite its small size, very adept at resisting limits to agricultural subsidies from the European Union and attempts to open agricultural markets globally.

- What are some of the interest groups in the United States that exercise political influence disproportionate to their size?
- Think of interest groups with which you are familiar in the United States. Would these groups, or similar groups, be active in other parts of the world? Why or why not?

place today because of its clear impropriety, the Central Pacific Railroad sent its own lobbyist to Washington, D.C., in 1861, where he eventually became the clerk (staff administrator) of the committees of both houses of Congress that were charged with overseeing regulation of the railroad industry. Subsequently, Congress awarded the Central Pacific Railroad (later called the Southern Pacific) vast grants of lands along its route and large subsidized loans. The railroad company became so powerful that it later went on to have nearly total political control of the California state legislature.

By the 1890s, a profound change had occurred in the nation's political and social outlook. Rapid industrialization, an influx of immigrants, and monopolistic business practices created a host of problems including crime, poverty, squalid and unsafe working conditions, and widespread political corruption. Many Americans began to believe that new measures would be necessary to impose order on this growing chaos and to curb some of the more glaring problems in society. The political and social movement that grew out of these concerns was called the Progressive movement.

In response to the pressure applied by Progressive-era groups, the national government began to regulate business. Because businesses had a vested interest in keeping wages low and costs down, more business groups organized to consolidate their strength and to counter Progressive moves. Not only did governments have to mediate Progressive and business demands, but they also had to accommodate the role of organized labor, which often allied itself with Progressive groups against big business.

Thinking Globally
The Solidarity Movement in Poland

On occasion, organized labor activities have helped to bring about major political change. A notable example is the Solidarity movement led by Lech Walesa in Poland during the 1980s. The first independent trade union in Soviet-controlled Eastern Europe, the Solidarity movement encouraged political liberalization in Poland and contributed to the fall of communism in Eastern Europe.

- Where else in the world might an organized labor organization, or any interest group, have the ability to significantly alter governments or their policies?
- Do organized interest groups in the United States have too much power or too little? Explain your answer.

The National Association of Manufacturers (NAM) was founded in 1895 by manufacturers who had suffered business losses in the economic panic of 1893 and who believed that they were being affected adversely by the growth of organized labor. The second major business organization came into being in 1912, when the U.S. Chamber of Commerce was created with the assistance of the federal government.

Until the creation of the American Federation of Labor (AFL) in 1886, there was not any real national union activity. The AFL brought skilled workers from several trades together into one stronger national organization for the first time. As the AFL grew in power, many business owners began to press individually or collectively to quash the unions. As business interests pushed states for what are called open shop laws to outlaw unions in their factories, the AFL became increasingly political. It also was forced to react to the success of big businesses' use of legal injunctions to prohibit union organization. In 1914, massive lobbying by the AFL and its members led to passage of the Clayton Act, which labor leader Samuel Gompers hailed as the Magna Carta of the labor movement. This law allowed unions to organize free from prosecution and also guaranteed their right to strike, a powerful weapon against employers.

Membership in labor unions held steady throughout the early and mid-1900s and then skyrocketed toward the end of the Depression. By then, organized labor began to be a potent political force as it was able to turn out its members in support of particular political candidates.

Labor became a stronger force in U.S. politics when the American Federation of Labor (AFL) merged with the Congress of Industrial Organizations (CIO) in 1955. Concentrating its efforts largely on the national level, the new AFL-CIO immediately turned its energies to pressuring the government to protect concessions won from employers at the bargaining table and to other issues of concern to its members, including minimum wage laws, the environment, civil rights, medical insurance, and health care.

More recently, the once fabled political clout of organized labor has been on the wane at the national level. Membership peaked at about 30 percent of the workforce in the late 1940s. Since that time, union membership has plummeted as the nation changed from a land of manufacturing workers and farmers to a nation of white-collar professionals and service workers.

Even worse for the future of the labor movement, at least in the short run, is the split that occurred at the AFL-CIO's 2005 annual meeting, ironically the fiftieth anniversary of the joining of the two unions. Plagued by reduced union membership, and mired in disagreement about how much money to devote to the campaigns of Democrats at a time when Republicans controlled two branches of government, three of the largest member unions plus four additional ones ceded from the AFL-CIO. With the head of the Service Employees International Union (SEIU) noting that the AFL-CIO had grown "pale, male, and stale," the SEIU, the International Brotherhood of Teamsters, and the United Food and Commercial Workers International left to form the Change to Win Coalition.[37]

The Rise of the Interest Group State

public interest group
An organization that seeks a collective good that will not selectively and materially benefit group members.

During the 1960s and 1970s, the Progressive spirit reappeared in the rise of **public interest groups**. Generally, these groups devoted themselves to representing the interests of African Americans, women, the elderly, the poor, and consumers, or to working on behalf of the environment. Many of their leaders and members had been active in the civil rights and anti–Vietnam War movements of the 1960s. Other groups, formed during the Progressive era, such as the American Civil Liberties Union (ACLU) and the NAACP, gained renewed vigor. Many of them had as their patron the liberal Ford Foundation, which helped to bankroll numerous groups, including the Women's Rights Project of the ACLU, the Mexican American Legal Defense and Education Fund, the Puerto Rican Legal Defense and Education Fund, and the Native American Rights Fund (as discussed in chapter 5).[38] The American Association of Retired Persons, now simply called AARP, also came to prominence in this era.

The civil rights and anti-war struggles left many Americans feeling cynical about a government that they believed failed to respond to the will of the majority. They also believed that if citizens banded together, they could make a difference. Thus, two major new public interest groups—Common Cause and Public Citizen—were founded. Common Cause, a good-government group that acts as a watchdog over the federal government, is similar to some of the early Progressive movement's public interest groups. Common Cause effectively has challenged aspects of the congressional seniority system, successfully urged the passage of sweeping campaign financing reforms, and played a major role in the enactment of legislation authorizing federal financing of presidential campaigns. It continues to lobby for accountability in government and for more efficient and responsive governmental structures and practices. Perhaps more well known than Common Cause is Public Citizen, the collection of groups headed by Ralph Nader (who went on to run as a candidate for president in 1996 and subsequent elections).

Conservatives, concerned by the activities of these liberal groups, responded by forming religious and ideological groups that became a potent force in U.S. politics. In 1978, the Reverend Jerry Falwell founded the first major new religious group, the Moral Majority. The Moral Majority was widely credited with assisting in the election of Ronald Reagan as president in 1980 as well as with the defeats of several liberal Democratic senators that same year. Falwell claimed to have sent 3 to 4 million newly registered voters to the polls.[39]

Pat Robertson, a televangelist, formed the Christian Coalition in 1990. Since then, it has grown in power and influence. The Christian Coalition played an important role in the Republicans winning control of the Congress in 1994. In 2008, the group distributed millions of voter guides in churches throughout the United States.

The Christian Coalition also lobbies Congress and the White House. During the Bush administration, the group had the sympathetic ear of the president, who placed a priority on faith-based initiatives. Its role is likely to be significantly diminished in the Obama administration.

TABLE 11.3 Lobbying Techniques

Technique	State-Based Groups		Washington, D.C.-Based Groups (n = 175)
	Lobbyists (n = 595)	Organizations (n = 301)	
Testifying at legislative hearings	98	99	99
Contacting government officials directly to present point of view	98	97	98
Helping to draft legislation	96	88	85
Alerting state legislators to the effects of a bill on their districts	96	94	75
Having influential constituents contact legislator's office	94	92	80
Consulting with government officials to plan legislative strategy	88	84	85
Attempting to shape implementation of policies	88	85	89
Mounting grassroots lobbying efforts	88	86	80
Helping to draft regulations, rules, or guidelines	84	81	78
Raising new issues and calling attention to previously ignored problems	85	83	84
Engaging in informal contacts with officials	83	81	95
Inspiring letter-writing or telegram campaigns	82	83	84
Entering into coalitions with other groups	79	93	90
Talking to media	73	74	86
Serving on advisory commissions and boards	58	76	76
Making monetary contributions to candidates	—	45	58
Attempting to influence appointment to public office	44	42	53
Doing favors for officials who need assistance	41	36	56
Filing suit or otherwise engaging in litigation	36	40	72
Working on election campaigns	—	29	24
Endorsing candidates	—	24	22
Running advertisements in media about position	18	21	31
Engaging in protests or demonstrations	13	21	20

Source: State-Based Groups: Anthony J. Nownes and Patricia Freeman, "Interest Group Activity in the States," *Journal of Politics* 60 (1998): 92. Washington, D.C.-Based Groups: Kay Lehman Schlozman and John Tierney, "More of the Same: Washington Pressure Group Activity in a Decade of Change," *Journal of Politics* 45 (1983): 358.

The Christian Coalition is not the only conservative interest group to play an important role in the policy process as well as in elections at the state and national level. The National Rifle Association (NRA), an active opponent of gun control legislation, saw its membership rise in recent years, as well as its importance in Washington, D.C. The NRA and its political action committee spent more than $11 million to help elect John McCain in 2008. And, conservative groups such as Students for Academic Freedom have made their views known in the area of higher education. More recently, students have formed Students for Concealed Weapons on Campus, as discussed in Ideas into Action: Guns on Campus.

What Do Interest Groups Do?

Interest groups are involved in myriad activites. They lobby all three branches of government, and engage in grassroots lobbying. They also participate in protest activities, and many are actively engaged in the campaign process, among other activities.

LOBBYING Most interest groups put lobbying at the top of their agendas. **Lobbying** is the process by which interest groups attempt to assert their influence on the policy-making process. The term **lobbyist** refers to any representative of a group that attempts to influence a policy maker by one or more of the tactics listed in Table 11.3.

Almost all interest groups lobby by testifying at hearings and contacting legislators. Other groups also provide information that decision makers might not have the time, opportunity, or interest to gather on their own.

Lobbying Congress Efforts to reform lobbying continue to plague members of Congress, who are the targets of a wide variety of lobbying activities: congressional testimony on behalf of a group, individual letters from interested constituents, campaign contributions, or the outright payment of money for votes. Of course, the last item is

lobbying
The activities of a group or organization that seeks to influence legislation and persuade political leaders to support the group's position.

lobbyist
Interest group representative who seeks to influence legislation that will benefit his or her organization or client through political persuasion.

Ideas Into Action

Guns on Campus

Look at the person sitting to the right of you. How would you feel if that person were packing heat? A group of 9,000 students and faculty want to make carrying concealed weapons on campus legal.

Students for Concealed Weapons on Campus works to educate the public about concealed weaponry and to convince state legislatures and school administrations to grant concealment permits to students on campuses across the nation.[a] It gained attention in the wake of the Virginia Tech shootings in 2007 in which thirty-three people were killed by a student gunman on campus. Had students been able to carry weapons legally, the leaders of this new interest group argue, the number of students killed could have been reduced. State legislators in Utah already have passed a law prohibiting gun bans on college campuses.

The Second Amendment of the U.S. Constitution states that "the right of the people to keep and bear Arms, shall not be infringed," yet some Americans argue that the right to bear arms needs some restrictions in today's society, especially in educational settings. The Brady Center to Prevent Gun Violence says that violence on college campuses would increase if concealed weapons were allowed because people between eighteen and twenty-four years of age have the highest rates of drug and alcohol use, mental health problems, and suicide attempts.[b] It argues that even for self-defense purposes, the prevalence of guns on campus would increase fatalities in school shootings because students would be likely to miss their intended targets.

- Would allowing students to carry concealed weapons on campus decrease or increase violence? Why?
- Write a letter to your local state representative and describe why you believe guns should or should not be allowed in your school or university. Be sure to include factual details to support your argument.

NO GUN LEFT BEHIND
The Gun Lobby's Campaign to
Push Guns Into Colleges and Schools

Do guns have a place on college campuses? The Brady Center to Prevent Gun violence does not think so; this advertisement makes a mockery of the idea.

[a]"About Us," Students for Concealed Weapons on Campus, www.concealedcampus.org/about.htm.
[b]"No Gun Left Behind: The Gun Lobb's Campaign to Push Guns into Colleges and Schools," Brady Center to Prevent Gun Violence.

illegal, but there are numerous documented instances of money changing hands for votes. Because, as discussed in chapter 6, lobbying plays such an important role in Congress, many effective lobbyists often are former members of that body, former staff aides, former White House officials or Cabinet officers, or other Washington insiders.

Lobbying the Executive Branch Groups often target one or more levels of the executive branch because there are so many potential access points, including the president, White House staff, and the numerous levels of the executive branch bureaucracy. Groups try to work closely with the administration to influence policy decisions at their formulation and later implementation stages. As with congressional lobbying, the effectiveness of a group often depends on its ability to provide decision makers with important information and a sense of where the public stands on the issue.

An especially strong link exists between interest groups and regulatory agencies (see chapter 8). Because of the highly technical aspects of much regulatory work, many groups employ Washington attorneys and lobbying firms to deal directly with the agencies. So great is interest group influence in the decision-making process of these agencies that many people charge that the agencies have been captured by the interest groups.

Lobbying the Courts The courts, too, have proved a useful target for interest groups.[40] Although you might think that the courts decide cases that affect only the parties involved or that they should be immune from political pressures, interest groups for years have recognized the value of lobbying the courts, especially the Supreme Court, and many political scientists view it as a form of political participation.[41] As shown in Table 11.3, 72 percent of the Washington D.C.-based groups surveyed participated in litigation as a lobbying tool.

Generally, interest group lobbying of the courts can take two forms: direct sponsorship or the filing of *amicus curiae* briefs. Most major U.S. Supreme Court cases noted in this book have been sponsored by an interest group, or one or both of the parties in the case have been supported by an *amicus curiae* brief. Interest groups also file cases in state supreme courts, but in much lower numbers.

Grassroots Lobbying As the term implies, grassroots lobbying is a form of interest group activity that prompts individuals to contact their representatives directly in an effort to affect policy.[42] Although it often involves door-to-door informational or petition drives—a tried and true method of lobbying—the term also encompasses more modern forms of communication such as fax and Internet lobbying of lawmakers.

Interest groups regularly try to inspire their members to engage in grassroots activity, hoping that lawmakers will respond to those pressures and the attendant publicity. In essence, the goal of many organizations is to persuade ordinary voters to serve as their advocates. In the world of lobbying, there are few things more useful than a list of committed supporters. Radio talk-show hosts such as Rush Limbaugh try to stir up their listeners by urging them to contact their representatives in Washington, D.C. Other interest groups now run carefully targeted and costly television advertisements pitching one side of an argument. Some of these undefined masses, as they join together on the Internet or via faxes, may be mobilized into one or more groups.

Protests and Radical Activism An occasional though highly visible tactic used by some groups is protest activity. Although it is much more usual for a group's members to opt for more conventional forms of lobbying or to influence policy through the electoral process, when these forms of pressure-group activities are unsuccessful, some groups (or individuals within groups) resort to more forceful measures to attract attention to their cause. Since the Revolutionary War, violent, illegal protest has been one tactic of organized interests. The Boston Tea Party, for example, involved breaking all sorts of laws, although no one was hurt physically. Other forms of protest, such as Shays's Rebellion, ended in tragedy for some participants. Much more recently, antiwar protestors have been willing to march and risk detention and jail in the United States. And, protesters regularly try to picket or protest meetings of the International Monetary Fund or the World Bank. Political conventions as well as inaugurations also routinely are targeted by protesters.

ELECTION ACTIVITIES In addition to trying to achieve their goals (or at least draw attention to them) through conventional and unconventional forms of lobbying, many interest groups also become involved more directly in the electoral process.

Photo courtesy: Carrie Devorah/WENN

Can Hollywood celebrities effectively lobby Congress? Hayden Panettiere, a star on the television show *Heroes*, protests against inhumane treatment and slaughtering of whales. She has lobbied both Congress and presidential campaigns enthusiastically supporting the cause to "Save the Whales Again."

SIMULATION

You Are the Leader of Concerned Citizens for World Justice

Join the Debate

Should There Be Limits on Interest Group Participation?

OVERVIEW: The First Amendment to the Constitution guarantees the right to freedom of speech, press, association, and the right to "petition the government for a redress of grievances." These are necessary rights in a democracy because they guarantee the right of the people—within the framework of law—to have their voice heard by the government. Grievances can be political or social in nature, and all citizens have the right to petition the government to have their (sometimes narrow) interests or issues addressed. This right includes expressing policy preferences. While political speech and activity as well as the actions of government are regulated by law to prevent the encroachment of undue influence and corruption, the line between appropriate regulation and rights violations may be difficult to discern. Additionally, in order for government to fulfill its functions, it must attempt to balance the claims of diverse competing interests. Because the framework that interest groups and government must operate within is contentious, regulation is necessary. But, when a group lobbies to change government policies, can the government require full disclosure of the group's activities and finances?

Part of the mandate from the Lobbying Disclosure Act of 1995 (LDA) is to facilitate public access to information about lobbying groups as well as about the government's knowledge of their activities. The more recent Honest Leadership and Open Government Act of 2007 has enhanced information about interest group activity by requiring the disclosure of campaign contributions by clients of lobbyists, and by tracking the insertion of earmark provisions in the federal budget by individual members of Congress. The goal is to allow concerned citizens, the media, and watchdog groups to correlate lobbying activities with perceived government response.

The political nature of lobbying activity may mean that interest groups are subject to a higher standard of disclosure and scrutiny. Just as the American people demand transparency in government activity, it seems reasonable that they be provided with information regarding those interest groups monitoring (or supporting) the decisions of government officials. But, what about First Amendment guarantees of free speech and the right to privacy? Could more transparency have the effect of discouraging the expression of concerns and participation in politics? Should interest groups have the same right to privacy as individuals? After all, citizens who contribute less than $200 to campaigns are not required to disclose their influence the political process. why should interest groups be denied this standard of privacy?

Arguments IN FAVOR of Regulating Interest Group Activities

- Interest groups are not given a constitutional role to make or influence policy. Though individuals and groups have the right to lobby the government, they have no unrestricted right to do so. Given literally thousands of interests, the government must have some means to prioritize and determine the legitimacy of various groups. For example, should a local 4-H group have the same voice and access to national policy makers as the National Dairy Association?

- Regulation is necessary to ensure the public knows why and in what

Interest Groups and Campaign Finance

Candidate Recruitment and Endorsements Many interest groups claim to be nonpolitical. But, some interest groups recruit, endorse, and/or provide financial or other forms of support for political candidates. EMILY's List (EMILY stands for "Early money is like yeast—it makes the dough rise") was founded to support pro-choice Democratic women candidates, especially during party primary election contests. It now, however, like its Republican counterpart the WISH List (WISH stands for Women in the House and Senate), recruits and trains candidates in addition to contributing to their campaigns.

Getting Out the Vote Many interest groups believe they can influence public policy by putting like-minded representatives in office. To that end, many groups across the

capacity an interest group is acting. The purpose of federal laws is to ensure accountability in the lobbying process, not to discourage the expression of concerns. The American public needs to know about corruption or misinformation not only coming from the government, but coming from interest groups as well. For instance, the RainbowPUSH Coalition was implicated in lobbying the City of Chicago to keep an after-hours dance club open, even after a fire caused twenty-one deaths. The club owners, RainbowPUSH, and certain Chicago politicians were known to have a business relationship.

- Regulation of interest groups allows the government to level the playing field. Research published by the American Political Science Association (APSA) contends that inequality and unequal access to wealth harms the American democratic process. APSA implies that weathier groups have a larger voice and thus more access to policy makers. Money should not be the only—or even the major—means of influencing public policy. By regulating interest groups, the federal government can help minimize the impact of wealth by letting voters consider the links between interest groups and legislators when they go to the polls.

Arguments AGAINST Regulating Interest Group Activities

- Government regulation of interest groups may stifle political speech. For example, the U.S. Supreme Court upheld the Bipartisan Campaign Reform Act's provision prohibiting groups from issue advertising sixty days prior to a general election. Many scholars and legal experts believe that this is a fundamental violation of political speech rights, as it is now believed that money gives "voice" to the political process—and to deny groups the right to political advertisement is to deny political speech.

- Regulation of groups essentially creates approved speech and politics. By requiring the registration of lobbyists and then regulating their activities, the government is in effect establishing which groups are legitimate and which are not. It is not the government's role to decide the importance of a political group. The government, moreover, should not try to control relationships between politicians and their supporters.

- Government regulation of interest groups is not necessary. In an open, pluralistic society, interest groups are subject to market dynamics. That is, those groups that truly represent broad or

important interests will have their views heard over those that do not. Thus, a natural voice is given to those groups deemed by the American people to represent important interests and issues.

Continuing the Debate

1. Is requiring disclosure of group information a violation of the First Amendment and privacy rights? How can this be reconciled with the public's right to know?
2. Does the political nature of lobbyist activity demand a higher level of governmental scrutiny?

To Follow the Debate Online, Go To:

www.opensecrets.org, the Center for Responsive Politics site devoted to resources and information about making lobbying in the United States transparent and regulated. The center is a nonprofit and nonpartisan policy research organization.

www.aclu.org, the site of the American Civil Liberties Union, which has provided testimony to Congress, courts, and regulatory agencies, opposing the regulation of lobbyists and their activities. Copies of ACLU statements and testimony are available on their site.

ideological spectrum launch massive get out the vote (GOTV) efforts. These include identifying prospective voters and getting them to the polls on Election Day. Well-financed interest groups such as MoveOn.org and Progress for America often produce issue-oriented ads for newspapers, radio, and television designed to educate the public as well as increase voter interest in election outcomes.

Rating the Candidates or Office Holders Many liberal and conservative ideological groups rate candidates to help their members (and the general public) evaluate the voting records of members of Congress. The American Conservative Union (conservative) and the Americans for Democratic Action (liberal)—two groups at ideological polar extremes—routinely rate candidates and members of Congress based on their

Analyzing Visuals	Interest Group Ratings of Selected Members of Congress

Interest groups inform their members, as well as the public generally, of the voting records of office holders, helping voters make an informed voting decision. The table displays the 2007 ratings of selected members of Congress by seven interest groups that vary greatly in their ideologies. After reviewing the table, answer the following critical thinking questions:

Member	ACU	ACLU	ADA	AFL-CIO	CoC	LCV	NARAL
Senate							
Mitch McConnell (R–KY)	92	14	10	11	82	7	0
Dianne Feinstein (D–CA)	0	57	90	89	45	87	100
Mel Martinez (R–FL)	80	14	20	16	100	13	0
Charles Schumer (D-NY)	0	71	90	100	55	93	100
House							
John Boehner (R–OH)	100	0	5	4	79	0	0
Sheila Jackson Lee (D–TX)	0	100	100	100	55	90	100
Ileana Ros-Lehtinen (R–FL)	60	33	25	46	90	30	0
Henry Waxman (D–CA)	0	100	90	100	53	95	100

Key
ACU = American Conservative Union
ACLU = American Civil Liberties Union
ADA = Americans for Democratic Action
AFL-CIO = American Federation of Labor–Congress of Industrial Organizations
CC = Christian Coalition
CoC = Chamber of Commerce
LCV = League of Conservation Voters
NARAL = NARAL Pro-Choice America
Members are rated on a scale from 1 to 100, with 1 being the lowest and 100 being the highest support of a particular group's policies.

WHICH members of the Senate would you consider the most liberal? Which groups' ratings did you use to reach your conclusion?

WHICH members of the House would you consider the most conservative? Which groups' ratings did you use to reach your conclusion?

WOULD it be important to know the votes by each representative that each group used to determine their rating? Explain your answer.

votes on key issues (To learn more, see Analyzing Visuals: Interest Group Ratings of Selected Members of Congress). These scores help voters know more about their representatives' votes on issues that concern them.

Political Action Committees As discussed in chapter 12, corporations, labor unions, and interest groups are allowed to form **political action committees (PACs)**. PACs allow these interests to raise money to contribute to political candidates in national elections. Unlike some contributions to interest groups, contributions to PACs are not tax deductible, and PACs generally don't have members who call legislators; instead, PACs have contributors who write checks specifically for the purpose of campaign donations. PAC money plays a significant role in the campaigns of many congressional incumbents, often averaging over half a House candidate's total campaign spending. PACs generally contribute to those who have helped them before and who serve on committees or subcommittees that routinely consider legislation of concern to that group.

political action committee (PAC)
Federally mandated, officially registered fund-raising committee that represents interest groups in the political process.

Toward Reform: Regulating Interest Groups and Lobbyists

For the first 150 years of our nation's history, federal lobbying practices went unregulated. While the courts remain largely free of lobbying regulations, reforms have altered the state of affairs in Congress and the executive branch. In 1946, in an effort to limit the power of lobbyists, Congress passed the Federal Regulation of Lobbying Act, which required anyone hired to lobby any member of Congress to register and file quarterly financial reports. For years, few lobbyists actually filed these reports and numerous good government groups continued to argue for the strengthening of lobbying laws. Until 1995, however, their efforts were blocked by civil liberties groups such as the ACLU, who argued that registration provisions violate the First Amendment's protections of freedom of speech and of the right of citizens to petition the government.

But, by 1995, public opinion polls began to show that Americans believed the votes of members of Congress were available to the highest bidder. Thus, in late 1995, Congress passed the first effort to regulate lobbying since the 1946 act. The Lobbying Disclosure Act required lobbyists to: (1) register with the clerk of the House and the secretary of the Senate; (2) report their clients and issues and the agency or house they lobbied; and, (3) estimate the amount they were paid by each client. These reporting requirements made it easier for watchdog groups or the media to monitor lobbying activities.

After lobbyist Jack Abramoff pleaded guilty to extensive corruption charges in 2006, Congress pledged to reexamine the role of lobbyists in the legislative process. Nevertheless, while legislators said they wanted higher standards set and Democrats complained about "the GOP culture of corruption," no lobbying reform measures were passed in either house prior to the November 2006 election. After the Democrats took control of both houses of Congress in 2007 in the wake of a variety of lobbying scandals, they were able to pass the **Honest Leadership and Open Government Act of 2007.** Among the act's key provisions were a ban on gifts and honoraria to members of Congress and their staffs, tougher disclosure requirements, and longer time limits on moving from the federal government to the private lobbying sector.

Formal lobbying of the executive branch is not governed by the restrictions in the 1995 Lobbying Disclosure Act or the Honest Leadership and Open Government Act. Executive branch employees are, however, constrained by the 1978 Ethics in Government Act. Enacted in the wake of the Watergate scandal, this act attempts to curtail questionable moves by barring members of the executive branch from representing any clients before their agency for one year after leaving governmental service. Thus, someone who worked in air pollution policy for the Environmental Protection Agency and then went to work for the Environmental Defense Fund would have to wait a year before lobbying his or her old agency.

Honest Leadership and Open Government Act of 2007
Lobbying reform banning gifts to members of Congress and their staffs, toughening disclosure requirements, and increasing time limits on moving from the federal government to the private sector.

WHAT SHOULD I HAVE LEARNED?

■ **What are the roots of the American party system?**

A political party is an organized effort by office holders, candidates, activists, and voters to pursue their common interests by gaining and exercising power through the electoral process. The evolution of U.S. political parties has been remarkably smooth, and the stability of the Democratic and Republican groupings is a wonder. For 150 years, the two-party system has served as the mechanism American society uses to organize and resolve social and political conflict.

■ **What are the functions and organization of the American political parties?**

For 150 years, the two-party system has served as the mechanism American society uses to organize and resolve social and political conflict. The Democratic and Republican Parties, through lengthy nominating processes, provide a screening mechanism for those who aspire to office, helping to weed out unqualified individuals, expose and test candidates' ideas on important policy questions, and ensure a measure of long-term continuity and accountability.

The basic structure of the major parties is complex and amorphous. The state and local parties are generally more important than the national ones, though campaign technologies and fund-raising concentrated in Washington, D.C., have helped to centralize power within national party committees.

Most American voters have a personal affinity for a political party, which summarize his or her political views and preferences and is expressed by a tendency to vote for the candidates of that party.

■ **What are the structure and function of interest groups?**

Interest groups lie at the heart of the American social and political system. Those who study interest groups have offered a variety of definitions to explain what they are. Most definitions revolve around notions of associations or groups of individuals who share some sort of common interest or attitude and who try to influence or engage in activity to affect government policies or the people in government.

National interest groups did not emerge in the United States until the 1830s. Later, from 1890 to 1920, the Progressive movement emerged. The 1960s saw the rise of a variety of liberal interest groups. By the 1970s and through the 1980s, conservatives formed new groups to counteract those efforts.

Interest groups give Americans opportunities to make claims, as a group, on government. The most common activity of interest groups is lobbying. Groups routinely pressure members of Congress and their staffs, the president and the bureaucracy, and the courts; they use a variety of techniques to educate and stimulate the public to pressure key governmental decision makers. Interest groups also attempt to influence the outcome of elections; some run their own candidates for office. Others rate elected officials to inform their members how particular legislators stand on issues of importance to them or establish political action committees (PACs).

■ **What efforts have been made to regulate and reform interest groups and lobbyists?**

It was not until 1946 that Congress passed any laws regulating federal lobbying. Those laws were largely ineffective and were successfully challenged as violations of the First Amendment. In 1995, Congress passed the Lobbying Disclosure Act that required lobbyists to register with both houses of Congress. By 2007, a rash of scandals resulted in the sweeping reforms of the Honest Leadership and Open Government Act, which dramatically limited what lobbyists can do.

Key Terms

candidate-centered politics, p. 319

civic virtue, p. 330

civil service laws, p. 319

coalition, p. 322

collective good, p. 332

critical election, p. 320

dealignment, p. 321

direct primary, p. 319

disturbance theory, p. 331

free rider problem, p. 332

Honest Leadership and Open
Government Act of 2007, p. 341

interest group, p. 314

issue-oriented politics, p. 319

lobbying, p. 335

lobbyist, p. 335

national convention, p. 328

national party platform, p. 324

party identification, p. 328

party realignment, p. 320

patron, p. 332

pluralist theory, p. 331

political action committee (PAC),
p. 340

population ecology theory,
p. 331

political machine, p. 318

political party, p. 314

public interest group, p. 334

secular realignment, p. 320

social capital, p. 330

ticket-split, p. 319

transactions theory, p. 331

Researching Interest Groups

In the Library

Aldrich, John Herbert. *Why Parties? The Origin and Transformation of Political Parties in America*. Chicago: University of Chicago Press, 1995.

Baumgartner, Frank, and Beth Leech. *Basic Interests*. Princeton, NJ: Princeton University Press, 1998.

Berry, Jeffrey M., and Clyde Wilcox. *The Interest Group Society*, 4th ed. New York: Longman, 2007.

Bibby, John F., and Brian Schaffner. *Politics, Parties, and Elections in America*. Boston, MA: Thomson Wadsworth, 2008.

Cigler, Allan J., and Burdett A. Loomis, eds. *Interest Group Politics*, 7th ed. Washington, DC: CQ Press, 2007.

Herrnson, Paul S., Ronald G. Shaiko, and Clyde Wilcox, eds. *The Interest Group Connection*, 2nd ed. Washington, DC: CQ Press, 2005.

Hershey, Marjorie Randon. *Party Politics in America*, 12th ed. New York: Pearson Longman, 2007.

Key, V. O., Jr. *Southern Politics in State and Nation*, new edition. Knoxville: University of Tennessee Press, 1984.

———. *Politics, Parties, and Pressure Groups*, 5th ed. New York: Crowell, 1964.

Kollman, Ken. *Outside Lobbying: Public Opinion and Interest Group Strategies*. Princeton, NJ: Princeton University Press, 1998.

Mayhew, David R. *Electoral Realignments*. New Haven, CT: Yale University Press, 2004.

McGlen, Nancy E., et al. *Women, Politics, and American Society*, 4th ed. New York: Longman, 2004.

Nownes, Anthony J. *Total Lobbying: What Lobbyists Want (and How They Try to Get It)*. New York: Cambridge University Press, 2006.

Olson, Mancur, Jr. *The Logic of Collective Action: Public Goods and the Theory of Groups*. Cambridge, MA: Harvard University Press, 1965.

Rosenstone, Steven J., Roy L. Behr, and Edward H. Lazarus. *Third Parties in America*, 2nd ed. Princeton, NJ: Princeton University Press, 1996.

Sabato, Larry J., and Howard R. Ernst. *Encyclopedia of American Parties and Elections*. New York: Facts on File, 2005.

Schattschneider, E. E. *Party Government*. New York: Holt, Rinehart and Winston, 1942.

Truman, David B. *The Governmental Process: Political Interests and Public Opinion*. New York: Knopf, 1951.

On the Web

The Center for Responsive Politics tracks campaign contributions to political parties, candidates, PACs and other political committees and analyzes the effect on elections and public policy. Visit their Web site at **www.opensecrets.org.**

For a summary of the evolution, current platforms, prominent officeholders, and candidates for both major parties and nearly 50 minor and third parties, go to **www.politics1.com/parties.htm**.

To see how interest groups grade your political representatives, go to Project Vote Smart at **www.votesmart.org** and click on "Interest Group Rating" on the home page.

To learn more about lobbying reform efforts, go to Thomas, the legislative information section of the Library of Congress, at **thomas.loc.gov**. Search for the Lobbying Disclosure Act of 1995 and the Honest Leadership and Open Government Act of 2007 in order to find out more about the lobbying restrictions required by this legislation.

12 Voting, Elections and Campaigns

While it is impossible to mark the exact beginning of the 2008 presidential contest, it is likely that the 2008 race was on the minds of several presidential hopefuls prior to the conclusion of the 2004 contest. Senator John McCain's endorsement in 2004 of George W. Bush, his arch-rival from the 2000 presidential primary, was certainly influenced by McCain's desire to gain support among the party faithful for a 2008 bid. Senator and former First Lady Hillary Rodham Clinton's decision not to run in 2004 was undoubtedly influenced by her upcoming bid for reelection to the Senate in 2006, as well as the fact that the 2008 presidential election, unlike the 2004 race, was likely be highly contested by both parties.

A year before the Democratic and Republican Parties would formally nominate their candidates for president, there seemed to be little doubt that the 2008 quest for the presidency would be the most memorable in recent history. For the first time

■ **Voting rights are a basic corner-stone of American democracy.** At left, a woman stands in a voting booth in 1920, shortly after ratification of the Nineteenth Amendment expanded voting rights to women. At right, an Obama supporter braves a snow bank to support his candidate before the 2008 New Hampshire Primary.

since 1928, none of the candidates would be either the incumbent president or vice president. Among the Democrats, former first lady and current New York Senator Hillary Clinton seemed the inevitable nominee. With her proven ability to raise money, the popularity of the Clinton brand, and a front-loaded nominating contest that seemed likely to reward an early front-runner, Senator Clinton appeared poised to make history as the first woman to lead a major party's presidential ticket. Among the Republicans, Senator John McCain was thought surely to be folding his campaign after he ran out of money in the summer of 2007 and began a free fall in the polls. When no clear front-runner emerged from the rest of the Republican pack, a protracted struggle for the GOP nomination seemed certain.

But, nomination battles often prove difficult to predict. The January 3 Iowa caucuses turned the Democratic nomination race upside down. Senator Barack Obama, who also hoped to make history by becoming the first African American nominee of a major party, was the surprise winner, while Senator Clinton finished a distant third behind John Edwards, a former senator who had been the 2004 vice presidential candidate. With fresh polls coming out of New Hampshire showing Obama surging and building an insurmountable lead, the talk in the media was about Clinton's inevitable demise. But, the voters of the Granite State gave

WHAT SHOULD I KNOW ABOUT . . .
- the roots of voting behavior?
- presidential elections?
- congressional elections?
- the media's role in the campaign process?
- the 2008 presidential election?
- reforming campaign finance?

Clinton a dramatic comeback victory, and she seemed ready to secure the nomination on Super Tuesday, February 5, when twenty-three states and territories would hold their nominating contests. The people voting on Super Tuesday, however, split their votes between Clinton and Obama, ensuring that the battle for the nomination would not end until voters in remaining states had a chance to cast their ballots.

The momentum continued to swing back and forth throughout the spring of 2008. Senator Obama won the next nine consecutive contests, while Senator Clinton won nine of the last sixteen, all the while pledging that she would fight on until all the votes had been counted in the nomination battle. It would not be until the evening of June 3, 2008, after the final contests, that Senator Obama could claim a majority of delegates and declare himself the presumptive Democratic nominee.

Conventional wisdom also suffered at the hands of Republican primary and caucus voters. Former Massachusetts Governor Mitt Romney, who had the best-financed and most well-organized campaign among the Republican front-runners, moved to the top of the opinion polls in Iowa and New Hampshire and was in a strong position to be the beneficiary of the GOP's wide-open field. But, with a shoestring organization and little money, former Arkansas Governor and Baptist minister Mike Huckabee emerged the winner in Iowa. In New Hampshire, John McCain resurrected his campaign and won a dramatic come-from-behind victory. McCain then followed up with victories in South Carolina and Florida, where he ended the nomination hopes of former New York Mayor Rudy Giuliani. On Super Tuesday, McCain won an overwhelming share of Republican delegates, ending Romney's candidacy, and had built up a large enough lead to secure the nomination. On the day that Senator Clinton had hoped to make history, it was Senator McCain who emerged as a big winner, on his way to the Republican nomination.

TO LEARN MORE—
—TO DO MORE

Track the dynamics of the nomination contests by viewing the many polls taken throughout 2007 and 2008 at Real Clear Politics: www.realclearpolitics.com/epolls/2008/president/.

Every four years, on the Tuesday following the first Monday in November, a plurality of voters, simply by casting ballots peacefully across a continent-sized nation, reelects or replaces politicians at all levels of government—from the president of the United States, to members of the U.S. Congress, to state legislators. Americans tend to take this process for granted, but in truth it is a marvel. Many other countries do not enjoy the benefit of competitive elections and the peaceful transition of political power made possible through the electoral process. American political institutions have succeeded in maintaining peaceful elections, even when they are closely contested, as was the case with the 2000 presidential election. Elections take the pulse of average people and gauge their hopes and fears, they provide direction for government action in a process that shapes and reforms all levels of government, and they hold the nation's leaders accountable.

The United States, judging from its frequent elections at all levels of government for more offices than any other nation on earth, is committed to democracy. The nation has steadily increased the size of the electorate (those citizens eligible to vote) by removing restrictions based on property ownership, religion, race, and gender. But, despite the increased access to the ballot box, and various direct democratic devices such as primaries and initiatives opened to the public in the last century, voter turnout remains historically low. After all the blood spilled and energy expended to expand voting rights, some eligible voters still do not bother to go to the polls.

This chapter focuses on the purposes served by elections, the various kinds of elections held in the United States, and patterns of voting over time. After an examination of the roots of voting behavior, we will look at the types of elections held in the United States, specifically presidential and congressional elections. We will explore the media's role in defining campaigns and consider the story of the 2008 presidential election. We will conclude by examining efforts to reform campaign finance.

Roots of Voting Behavior

Research on voting behavior seeks primarily to explain two phenomena: voter turnout (that is, what factors contribute to an individual's decision to vote or not to vote) and vote choice (once the decision to vote has been made, what leads voters to choose one candidate over another).

Patterns in Voter Turnout

Turnout is the proportion of the voting-age public that votes. About 40 percent of the eligible adult population in the United States votes regularly, whereas 25 percent are occasional voters and 35 percent rarely or never vote.

Some of the factors known to influence voter turnout include education, income, age, gender, race and ethnicity, and interest in politics. (To learn about how turnout considerations affected the 2008 presidential election, see Politics Now: Can Turnout Aid One Candidate?)

EDUCATION AND INCOME Highly educated people are more likely to vote than people with less education. A higher income level also increases the likelihood that a person will exercise his or her right to vote.

Other things being equal, college graduates are much more likely to vote than those with less education, and people with advanced degrees are the most likely to vote. People with more education tend to learn more about politics, are less hindered by registration requirements, and are more self-confident about their ability to affect public life.[1] Therefore, one might argue that institutions of higher education provide citizens with opportunities to learn about and become interested in politics.

A considerably higher percentage of citizens with annual incomes over $65,000 vote than do citizens with incomes under $35,000. Income level, to some degree, is connected to education level, as wealthier people tend to have more opportunities for higher education, and more education also may lead to higher income. Wealthy citizens are more likely than poor ones to think that the "system" works for them and that their votes make a difference. People with higher incomes are more likely to recognize their direct financial stake in the decisions of the government, thus spurring them into action.[2]

By contrast, lower-income citizens often feel alienated from politics, possibly believing that conditions will remain the same no matter who holds office. American political parties may contribute to this feeling of alienation. As discussed in chapter 11, unlike parties in many other countries that tend to associate themselves with specific socio-economic classes, U.S. political parties are less directly linked to socio-economic class. One consequence of "classless" parties is that the interests of the poor receive relatively little public attention, feeding feelings of alienation and apathy.

turnout
The proportion of the voting-age public that votes.

POLITICS NOW

Can Turnout Aid One Candidate?

A *Chicago Tribune* analysis looks at battleground states as Democrats push a voter registration drive.

TURNOUT BOOST COULD FAVOR OBAMA

MIKE DORNING

Barack Obama could make major gains in at least nine states the Democratic ticket lost in 2004 if he can achieve a relatively modest increase in turnout among young and African-American voters, a *Tribune* analysis of voting data suggests. That potential helps explain why the Obama campaign chose to forgo federal funding and also why it is engaged in a massive voter registration drive. With its unprecedented resources, the campaign can fund an array of specific targeting operations, and Obama exploited early versions of those to great success during the primary campaign.

If Obama could inspire just 10 percent more Democratic voters under 30 to go to the polls than did four years ago, that alone could be enough to switch Iowa and New Mexico from red to blue, the analysis suggests. Just a 10 percent increase in turnout among blacks would make up more than 40 percent of George W. Bush's 2004 victory margin in Ohio and more than 20 percent of the Republicans' 2004 victory margin in Florida. Turnout increases of 10 percent of both young voters and African-Americans could virtually eliminate the Republicans' 2004 victory margin in Ohio and go

a long way to closing the gap in Colorado, Nevada, Missouri, Virginia and—a bit more of a stretch—possibly North Carolina.

The campaign dispatched an advance guard to the likely battlefields of the November election more than a month before Obama had even locked up the nomination. Its mission: to begin work on an ambitious national voter registration drive that advisers say is a key part of the campaign's strategy.

Campaign volunteers have been registering voters at bars and nightclubs as well as visiting hip-hop parties and even gas stations—where drivers irate over rising fuel prices are a target, said one organizer. More than 250 of the campaign's "organizing fellows" arrived last week in Virginia, a state Democrats did not seriously contest in 2004, and will spend much of the summer there on voter registration.

With the Illinois senator's enthusiastic following that regularly packs arena-sized venues for rallies, and unprecedented organizational resources from his campaign's fundraising successes, his barrier-breaking campaign sees a chance to reshape the electorate this fall to the Democrats' advantage, possibly for several elections into the future....

There's still plenty of time between now and Election Day for the Obama hype to come crashing down. But the Obama campaign sees reason for hope after a primary season in which at least 3.5 million new voters registered and young people of voting age, typically apathetic, turned out as much as older voters in some states. . . .

The Republican Party also is hard at work mobilizing voters it believes will be especially supportive of McCain, including military veterans. The McCain campaign is opening an office even in Democratic-leaning New Jersey....And a Republican official argues that the party's well-developed expertise in "surgical" micro-targeting of narrowly sliced segments of the electorate will give the party an advantage in turnout efforts. . . .

The Obama campaign has structured its voter registration drive as a 50-state effort. But campaign officials said they will concentrate resources on states that are competitive or they hope to make competitive, as well as demographic groups supportive of their candidate that historically have turned out in low numbers. . . .

Still, Republican officials and plenty of others are skeptical. But even if the Obama campaign can force Republicans to spend limited resources to defend previously safe territory, that in itself offers an advantage, political strategists said.

Discussion Questions

1. *Was the Obama campaign's decision to target young people, African Americans, and other groups with historically low turnout rates an effective strategy, given the outcome of the 2008 presidential election? Why or why not?*

2. *What are the possible long-term implications of young voters' support for Barack Obama? Do the results suggest that 2008 was a transformative election year?*

AGE   A strong correlation exists between age and voter participation rates. The Twenty-Sixth Amendment to the Constitution, ratified in 1971, lowered the voting age to eighteen. While this amendment obviously increased the number of *eligible* voters, it did so by enfranchising the group that is least likely to vote. A much higher percentage of citizens age thirty and older vote than do citizens younger than thirty, although voter turnout decreases over the age of seventy, primarily due to difficulties some older voters have getting to their polling locations. Only 58 percent of eligible eighteen- to twenty-four-year-olds registered to vote in the 2004 presidential election.[3] However, record numbers of young people voted in 2008. (To learn more about voters under twenty-five, see Ideas into Action: Motivating Young Voters.)

Ideas Into Action

Motivating Young Voters

In the 2008 presidential election, 53 percent of eligible voters age eighteen to twenty-nine voted—that's 5 percent more than in the 2004 presidential election.[a] While midterm elections typically draw fewer voters than presidential elections, exit polls suggested that the "surge" in the youth vote also was observed in 2006, when 26 percent of young people voted—2 million more than in the 2002 midterms.[b] Still, when compared to the approximately 64 percent of voters thirty and over who voted in the last presidential election, 53 percent can only be described as low.

This lower turnout should disturb young voters, since it directly impacts what issues state and federal governments address. Ongoing military action in Iraq and Afghanistan, the federal deficit, rising health costs, the long-term financial stability of Social Security, high oil prices, and climate change are all issues likely to affect young voters—if not now, then in the future. Rising tuition costs and the extent to which government supports higher education are issues that hit even closer to home, since many students must work to pay their tuition bills and are likely to have loans to repay when they graduate. The stakes are high for young voters, so why aren't they voting?

Surveys consistently have shown that young voters do not vote because they believe their votes do not make a difference, they do not have enough information to make a decision, or they are too busy. Nearly half of students polled claim not to discuss politics with their parents, and over half say that schools do not sufficiently educate them on how to vote![c] Of course, if you do not know how to vote, then you do not vote, and if you never vote, then you never discover that your vote does make a difference.

- Did the parties and candidates in the last election make a real effort to connect with younger voters? Was one party or candidate more effective than others? Explain your answers.
- As the 2010 midterm elections approach, what advice do you have for parties and candidates who want to appeal to young voters?
- Design an educational brochure that can be distributed to high school students in your community explaining how to register to vote and how to locate their polling location. Make sure that the brochure includes information on absentee and early voting. While gathering the information for the brochure, note the procedural difficulties that Americans face in order to vote, and consider possible reforms to make the process more user-friendly.
- Conduct a brief survey of students on your campus to find out how many voted in the 2008 presidential election. Ask those who did not vote, why they did not vote.
- The Harvard Institute of Politics released its 14th Biannual Youth Survey on Politics and Public Service in April 2007. The survey includes responses from 2,500 U.S. citizens eighteen to twenty-four years old, half of whom were enrolled in four-year colleges and universities. You can view the full report at **www.iop.harvard.edu/Research-Publications/Polling/Spring-2008-Survey/Executive-Summary.**

[a]National Election Pool exit polls, www.cnn.com/ELECTION/2008/.
[b]See www.civicyouth.org for information on youth voting drawn from exit poll results in 2002 through 2008.
[c]See www.civicyouth.org/?page_id=154.

GENDER   It is generally accepted that in the period following ratification of the Nineteenth Amendment, women voted at a lower rate than men. Recent polls suggest that today women vote at the same rate as men or at a slightly higher rate. Since women comprise slightly more than 50 percent of the U.S. population, they now account for a majority of the American electorate.

RACE AND ETHNICITY Despite substantial gains in voting rates among minority groups, especially African Americans, race remains an important factor in voter participation. Whites still tend to vote more regularly than do African Americans, Hispanics, and other minority groups.

Several factors help to explain the persistent difference in voting rates between white and black voters. One reason is the relative income and educational levels of the two racial groups. African Americans tend to be poorer and to have less formal education than whites; as mentioned earlier, both of these factors affect voter turnout. Significantly, though, highly educated and wealthier African Americans are more likely to vote than whites of similar background.[4] Another explanation focuses on the

Timeline: The Expansion of Voting Rights

1892 Secret Ballot Introduced—The secret, or Australian ballot, is used for the first time in each state in the vote for president.

1870 Fifteenth Amendment— Prohibits any government from denying a citizen the right to vote on the basis of race, color, or previous condition of servitude.

1920 Nineteenth Amendment— Prohibits any government from denying a citizen the right to vote on the basis of that citizen's sex.

1964 Twenty-Fourth Amendment—Prohibits any government from imposing a poll tax or other tax that would deny a citizen the right to vote in a primary or other election for federal office.

1890 Wyoming Grants Women Voting Rights—Becomes the first state to grant women the right to vote and run for the state legislature.

1960 *Baker v. Carr*— Supreme Court reaffirms the principle of one person, one vote by ruling that U.S. House and state legislative districts for both houses must be equal in population.

1965 Voting Rights Act—Outlaws literacy and other discriminatory tests and devices used to deny citizens the right to vote and strengthens federal enforcement of all voting rights laws.

long-term consequence of the voting barriers that African Americans historically faced in the United States, especially in areas of the Deep South (see chapter 5).

Race also helps explain why the South has long had a lower turnout than the rest of the country. As discussed in chapter 5, in the wake of Reconstruction, the southern states made it extremely difficult for African Americans to register to vote, and only a small percentage of the eligible African American population was registered throughout the South until the 1960s. The Voting Rights Act (VRA) of 1965 helped to change this situation. Often heralded as the most successful piece of civil rights legislation ever passed, the VRA was intended to guarantee voting rights to African Americans nearly a century after passage of the Fifteenth Amendment. The VRA, key provisions of which were extended for another twenty-five years in 2006, targets states that once used literacy or morality tests or poll taxes to exclude minorities from the polls. The act bans any voting device or procedure that interferes with a minority citizen's right to vote, and it requires approval for any changes in voting qualifications or procedures in certain areas where minority registration was not in proportion to the racial composition of the district. It also authorizes the federal government to monitor all elections in areas where discrimination was found to be practiced or where less than 50 percent of the voting-age public was registered to vote in the 1964 election.

The 2000 Census revealed that the Hispanic community in the United States is now slightly larger in size than the African American community; thus, Hispanics have the potential to wield enormous political power. In California, Texas, Florida, Illinois, and New York, five key electoral states, Latino/a voters have emerged as pow-

1993 The National Voter Registration Act—Requires states to offer voter registration services at drivers' license registration centers and social service, military recruiting and other public offices.

2008 Voter turnout reaches its highest level since 1964, with approximately 62% of eligible voters voting in the 2008 presidential election.

1971 Twenty-Sixth Amendment—Prohibits any government from denying a citizen who is eighteen years or older the right to vote on the basis of age.

1995 *Miller v. Johnson*—Supreme Court rules that states cannot design redistricting plans that use race as the overriding and predominant factor.

2008 *Crawford v. Marion County Election Board*—Supreme Court upholds Indiana's law requiring voters to present photo identification at polling places, finding that a state's broad interests in deterring and detecting voter fraud outweighs the burden that may be felt by poor and elderly voters.

2002 Help America Vote Act (HAVA)—Mandates that all states and localities upgrade their election procedures, including their voting machines, registration processes, and poll worker training.

erful allies for candidates seeking office. However, just as voter turnout among African Americans is historically much lower than among whites, the turnout among Hispanic Americans is much lower than turnout among African Americans.[4]

Like any voting group, Hispanics are not easily categorized and voting patterns cannot be neatly generalized. However, several major factors play out as key decision-making variables: country of origin, length of time in the United States, and income levels. Although Hispanic Americans share a common history of Spanish colonialism and similar patterns of nation building, they differ in political processes and agendas. Despite having citizenship, Puerto Ricans can vote in a presidential election only if they live on the mainland and establish residency. Cuban Americans are concentrated in south Florida and tend to be conservative and vote for GOP candidates. Mexican Americans favor Democrats, but their voting patterns are very issue-oriented and vary according to income levels, length of time in the United States, and age.[5]

INTEREST IN POLITICS An interest in politics must also be included as an important factor for voter turnout. Many citizens who vote have grown up in families interested and active in politics. It is believed that interest serves as a gateway that leads people to gather information about candidates and to more fully participate in the political process, including voting.

People who are highly interested in politics constitute only a small minority of the U.S. population. The most politically active Americans—party and issue-group activists—make up less than 5 percent of the country's more than 300 million people.

VISUAL LITERACY

Voting Turnout: Who Votes in the United States

Does voter turnout matter?
Lines like this were common in urban areas during the 2008 elections. In 2008, 62 percent of eligible Americans, over 128 million voters, cast a ballot. Among the more than 14 million voting for the first time, 68 percent voted for Barack Obama.

Those who contribute time or money to a party or a candidate during a campaign make up only about 10 percent of the total adult population. Although these percentages appear low, they translate into millions of Americans who contribute more than just votes to the system.

Why Is Voter Turnout So Low?

The United States has one of the lowest voter participation rates of any nation in the industrialized world. In 1960, 65 percent of the eligible electorate voted in the presidential election, but by 1996, American voter participation had fallen to a record low of 48.8 percent—the lowest general presidential election turnout in modern times. In 2008, participation climbed to 62 percent, the highest it had been since 1964. U.S. nonvoters give a variety of reasons for not voting. A number of these factors are discussed below.

TOO BUSY   According to the U.S. Census Bureau, 20 percent of registered nonvoters reported they did not vote in a recent election because they were too busy or had conflicting work or school schedules. Another 15 percent said they did not vote because they were ill, disabled, or had a family emergency. While these reasons seem to account for a large portion of the people surveyed, they may also reflect the respondents' desire not to seem uneducated about the candidates and issues or apathetic about the political process.

DIFFICULTY OF REGISTRATION   Of those citizens who are registered, the overwhelming majority vote. A major reason for lack of participation in the United States remains the relatively low percentage of the adult population that is registered to vote. (To learn more about the percentage of registered voters by age, race, and gender, see Figure 12.1.) There are several reasons for the low U.S. registration rate. First, while nearly every other democratic country places the burden of registration on the government rather than on the individual, in the United States the registration process still requires individual initiative—a daunting impediment in this age of political apathy. Thus, the cost (in terms of time and effort) of registering to vote is higher in the United States than it is in other industrialized democracies. Second, many nations automatically register all of their citizens to vote. In the United States, however, citizens must jump the extra hurdle of remembering on their own to register.

Indeed, it is no coincidence that voter participation rates dropped markedly after reformers, desiring to combat voter fraud, pushed through strict voter registration laws in the early part of the twentieth century. Correspondingly, several recent studies of the effects of relaxed state voter registration laws show that easier registration leads to higher levels of turnout.[6] When states adopted Election Day registration of new voters, large and significant improvements in turnout occurred among younger voters and the poor.[7]

The National Voter Registration Act of 1993, commonly known as the Motor Voter Act, was a recent attempt to ease the bureaucratic hurdles associated with registering to vote. The law requires states to provide the opportunity to register through drivers' license agencies, public assistance agencies, and the mail. While a large number of Americans have yet to take advantage of the Motor Voter Act, it is likely that the law is at least partially responsible for the increases in voter participation experienced in recent elections.

DIFFICULTY OF ABSENTEE VOTING Stringent absentee ballot laws are another factor in low voter turnout for the United States. Many states, for instance, require citizens to apply in person for absentee ballots, a burdensome requirement given that one's

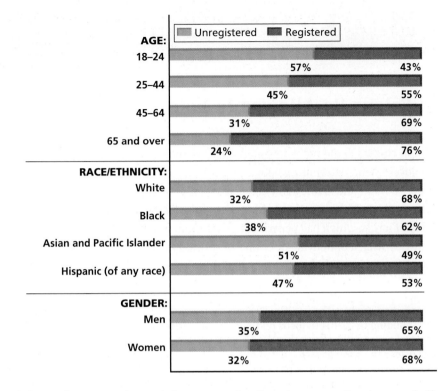

FIGURE 12.1 Percentage of Registered Voters by Age, Race/Ethnicity, and Gender, 2004

Older Americans continue to register at a much higher rate than younger voters. While increasing their representation at the ballot box, minorities still lag behind white voters in registration. Polling in November 2008 suggested that a higher percentage of many of these groups—especially African Americans and young voters—cast ballots in the 2008 presidential election.

Source: U.S. Census Bureau, Current Population Survey, November 2004.

inability to be present in one's home state is often the reason for absentee balloting in the first place.

NUMBER OF ELECTIONS Another explanation for low voter turnout in the United States is the sheer number and frequency of elections. According to a study by the International Institute for Democracy and Electoral Assistance, the United States typically holds twice as many national elections as other Western democracies, a consequence of the relatively short two-year term of office for members of the House of Representatives.[8] American federalism (see chapter 3), with its separate elections at the local, state, and national levels, and its use of primary elections for the selection of candidates, also contributes to the number of elections in which Americans are called on to participate.

Patterns in Vote Choice

Just as there are certain predictable patterns when it comes to American voter turnout, so, too, are there predictable patterns of vote choice. Some of the most prominent correlates of vote choice include partisan identification, race and ethnicity, gender, religion, income, ideology, issues, and campaign-specific developments. Many of these ideas follow the same logic as patterns in voter turnout and are discussed in greater detail there.

PARTY IDENTIFICATION As discussed in chapter 11, party identification is a longterm force in American politics. Party identification, which is dependent on a variety of factors noted in chapter 11, often acts as a lens that shapes how an individual perceives a particular candidate.[9] It also affects how one processes information about candidates and political issues.

ISSUES Individual issues can have important effects in any given election year. In 1992, when Bill Clinton's chief political adviser, James Carville, established "it's the economy stupid" as Clinton's campaign mantra, he was confirming a well-established idea in American politics: perceptions of the economy drive voter decisions.[10] Voters tend to reward the party in government, usually the president's party, during good economic

Join the Debate

Should Felons Be Allowed to Vote?

OVERVIEW: An estimated 5.3 million citizens could not vote in 2008 because they had been convicted of a felony. States, not the federal government, determine whether or not felons can vote, and there is considerable variation in state laws. Vermont and Maine allow convicted felons—even those in prison or on probation or parole—to vote. Convicted felons in Kentucky and Virginia, on the other hand, are barred from voting for life. In 2007, Florida, which had permanently disenfranchised almost 1 million felons, adopted rules allowing those convicted of nonviolent crimes to vote after completing their time in prison. Eighteen other states reconsidered their policies in 2007, and seven adopted changes.

In 2005, one out of every fifteen African American men of voting age and one out of every thirty-six Hispanic men were in prison. In contrast, only one out of 106 white men were incarcerated. The number of women in prisons is considerably less than the number of men, but the patterns are similar: one out every 203 African American women, one out of every 436 Hispanic women, and one out every 859 white women. The racial impact of not allowing felons to vote is even more pronounced when including those on probation and parole. Almost 17 percent of African Americans and 12 percent of Hispanics are disenfranchised because of felonies, but only 2 percent of whites.[a] While the reasons for this pattern are themselves a subject of heated debate, clearly the impact of policies taking away the voting rights of felons affects racial minorities far more heavily than whites.

When an individual commits a felony offense, he or she is demonstrating a basic disregard for the law. One way of responding to that is to focus on the illegal act or acts and another is to consider the felon as so alienated from and hostile to society that he or she should not participate in the governing process. Are we, in other words, dealing with bad behavior or a bad person? The latter perspective provides a justification for banning felons not only from the voting booth but also from serving in top government posts.

Efforts to reform state laws and allow felons the right to vote focus more on behavior than fundamental flaws in character. The assumption is that individuals who commit crimes should be punished but can be rehabilitated. Part of rehabilitation and reintegration into life outside prison walls is participation in the electoral process and in governance generally. Courts have ruled that states may pursue whatever policies they like with regard to felons. The Fourteenth Amendment to the Constitution requires states to provide "equal protection of the laws" to all citizens, which can be interpreted to mean that once someone completes a sentence, they have the same rights as others. However, the Fourteenth Amendment includes a clause that explicitly does not include this protection for persons who participate "in rebellion or other crimes."[b]

Some maintain that a partisan dimension to the debate about the voting rights of felons exists. The public debate focuses on issues of law and order and crime and punishment, but the probable implications for which party gains or loses if felons are not allowed to vote fuels suspicions of partisan strategy. As pointed out in this chapter, African Americans and those with lower levels of income and education tend to vote for Democrats. On the other hand, as also pointed out in this chapter, these same demographic groups tend to have a low rate of voter participation, thus making accusations of partisan bias in this debate somewhat suspect, at least in practice.

retrospective judgment
A voter's evaluation of the performance of the party in power.

prospective judgment
A voter's evaluation of a candidate based on what he or she pledges to do about an issue if elected.

times and punish the party in government during periods of economic downturn. When this occurs, the electorate is exercising **retrospective judgment;** that is, voters are rendering judgment on the performance of the party in power by judging whether the economy has improved under its governance. At other times, voters might use **prospective judgment;** that is, they vote based on what they perceive to be the future direction of the economy. By looking forward, voters can evaluate if a party's positions are likely to serve their interests, while not holding the ruling party accountable for economic conditions that might be beyond the party's control (for example, the economy).

Arguments AGAINST Voting Rights for Felons

- Part of the punishment for committing a serious crime is the revocation of the privilege of voting. The penalties for disregarding the law include a variety of restrictions and lost freedoms. Convicted felons do not enjoy the same rights as the rest of us do to privacy, employment, and movement.

- Prohibiting felons from voting is a race and class neutral policy. If racial minorities or people with lower incomes or lower education are disproportionately represented among felons, that is a social and economic issue that might demonstrate the need for certain policies, but it does not affect the justification for disenfranchising convicted criminals.

- We need to deter crime and one of the ways of doing that is to take the right to vote away from felons. There need to be consequences when someone commits a crime. One of the consequences is to revoke a criminal's right to vote.

Arguments IN FAVOR of Voting Rights for Felons

- Voting is a right of citizenship, not a reward for good behavior. One does not forfeit basic rights of citizenship when making a mistake and committing a crime. Although we incarcerate and place on probation

and parole those who have been convicted of crimes, we do not revoke their basic constitutional rights to humane treatment or to freedom of expression and association. Likewise, we should not allow states to take away the right to vote.

- Felons need to be reintegrated into society, not treated like noncitizens. It is a mixed message to tell felons that they need to get a legitimate job and to act like a law-abiding citizen and then to tell them that they may not vote. Current policies treat felons, even after they have completed their sentences in prison and thus have paid their debt to society, as if they are still criminals rather than functioning members of society.

- Limiting the rights of felons to vote disproportionately affects ethnic minorities and individuals with low levels of income or education. To disenfranchise felons is to double the disadvantages already faced by members of minority groups and lower socio-economic classes. Taking away voting rights of felons works against the objective of integrating our society.

Continuing the Debate

1. When, if at all, should felons be allowed to vote again? If they are no longer incarcerated? If they are no longer on probation or parole?

Photo courtesy: Robert Allfred

Is voting a right or a privilege? Bill Kleiber, far right, provides voter registration information to former inmates in Texas.

For a certain period after they are no longer in the correctional system? Explain your answer.

2. Is the concern about the number of felons who are poor or members of minority groups a legitimate reason for reinstating the voting rights of felons? Why or why not?

To Follow the Debate Online, Go To:

Project Vote, projectvote.org/issues/felon-voting-rights.html
The American Civil Liberties Union, www.aclu.org/votingrights/exoffenders
The Federalist Society, www.fed-soc.org/publications/PubID.185/pub_detail.asp

---

[a]The Pew Center on the States, *One in 100: Behind Bars in America 2008*, www.pewcenteronthestates.org/uploaded-Files/One%20in%20100.pdf; and Bureau of Justice Statistics, *Probation and Parole, 2005*, www.ojp.usdoj.gov/bjs/abstract/ppus05.htm.
[b]Christopher P. Manfredi, "Judicial Review and Criminal Disenfranchisement in the United States and Canada," *Review of Politics* 60:2 (1998): 277–305.

Types of Elections

In the U.S. system, elections happen at various levels and come in numerous types. In **primary elections,** voters decide which of the candidates within a party will represent the party's ticket in the general elections. There are different kinds of primaries. For example, **closed primaries** allow only a party's registered voters to cast a ballot, and **open primaries** allow independents and sometimes members of the other party to participate. Closed primaries are considered healthier for the party system because

primary election
Election in which voters decide which of the candidates within a party will represent the party in the general election.

closed primary
A primary election in which only a party's registered voters are eligible to vote.

open primary
A primary in which party members, independents, and sometimes members of the other party are allowed to vote.

Thinking Globally

How Many Elections?

Between 1945 and 2005, the United States held thirty national elections. In contrast, Iceland held sixteen, Italy held fourteen, and Portugal held a mere nine.

- How frequently should elections be held? Does the United States hold elections too often? Explain your reasoning.
- Is the frequency of elections an important factor in the accountability of elected officials? Why or why not?

crossover voting
Participation in the primary of a party with which the voter is not affiliated.

raiding
An organized attempt by voters of one party to influence the primary results of the other party.

runoff primary
A second primary election between the two candidates receiving the greatest number of votes in the first primary.

general election
Election in which voters decide which candidates will actually fill elective public offices.

initiative
An election that allows citizens to propose legislation and submit it to the state electorate for popular vote.

referendum
An election whereby the state legislature submits proposed legislation to the state's voters for approval.

recall
An election in which voters can remove an incumbent from office by popular vote.

nomination campaign
That part of a political campaign aimed at winning a primary election.

they prevent members of one party from influencing the primaries of the opposition party. Studies of open primaries indicate that **crossover voting**—participation in the primary of a party with which the voter is not affiliated—occurs frequently.[11] Nevertheless, the research shows little evidence of much **raiding**—an *organized* attempt by voters of one party to influence the primary results of the other party.[12]

In ten states, when none of the candidates in the initial primary secures a majority of the votes, there is a **runoff primary,** a contest between the two candidates with the greatest number of votes.[13] Louisiana has a novel twist on the primary system. There, all candidates for office appear on the ballot, and if one candidate receives over 50 percent of the vote, the candidate wins and no general election is necessary. If no candidate wins a majority of the vote, the top two candidates, even if they belong to the same party, face each other in a runoff election.

Once party members vote for their party candidates for various offices, each state holds its general election. In the **general election,** voters decide which candidates will actually fill the nation's elective public offices. These elections are held at many levels, including municipal, county, state, and national. Whereas primaries are contests between the candidates within each party, general elections are contests between the candidates of opposing parties.

Three other types of elections are the initiative, the referendum, and the recall. An **initiative** is a process that allows citizens to propose legislation or state constitutional amendments by submitting them directly to the state electorate for popular vote, provided the initiative supporters receive a certain number of signatures on petitions supporting the placement of the proposal on the ballot. The initiative process is used in twenty-four states and the District of Columbia. A **referendum** is an election whereby the state legislature submits proposed legislation or state constitutional amendments to the state's voters for approval. Although both the referendum and the initiative provide for more direct democracy, they are not free from controversy.

The third type of election (or "deelection") found in many states is the **recall,** in which voters can remove an incumbent from office prior to the next scheduled election. Recall elections are very rare, and sometimes they are thwarted by the official's resignation or impeachment prior to the vote.

Presidential Elections

Variety aside, no U.S. election can compare to the presidential contest. This spectacle, held every four years, brings together all the elements of politics and attracts the most ambitious and energetic politicians to the national stage. Voters in a series of state contests that run through the winter and spring of the election year select delegates who will attend each party's national convention. Following the national convention for each party, held in mid and late summer, there is a final set of fifty separate state elections all held on the Tuesday after the first Monday in November to select the president. This lengthy process exhausts candidates and voters alike, but it allows the diversity of the United States to be displayed in ways a shorter, more homogeneous presidential election process could not.

The Nomination Campaign

The **nomination campaign** begins as soon as the candidate has decided to run—sometimes years prior to an official announcement—and it ends at the party conven-

The Living Constitution

No Person shall be a Representative who shall not have attained to the Age of twenty five Years.

ARTICLE I, SECTION 2

No Person shall be a Senator who shall not have attained to the Age of thirty Years.

ARTICLE I, SECTION 3

...neither shall any person be eligible to that Office [of the Presidency] who shall not have attained to the Age of thirty five Years.

ARTICLE II, SECTION 1

There was little debate among the Framers at the Constitutional Convention that elected officials should have enough experience in life and in politics before being qualified to take on the responsibility of representing the interests of the nation and of their district or state. It is likely that they concurred, as they so often did, with John Locke, who stated in section 118 of his *Second Treatise of Government*, "a Child is born a Subject of no Country or Government. He is under his Father's Tuition and Authority, till he come to Age of Discretion." However, a minor, who is not subject to the authority of the state in the same way as a full citizen, also could not possibly be qualified to vote. The Framers added age requirements higher than the age when one becomes a full citizen as a guarantee that individuals with the necessary experience would be elected. Notice how the age limits scale upward according to the amount of deliberation and decision making that the position involves. House members need to be only twenty-five, but the president must be at least thirty-five, giving whoever would run for that office plenty of time to acquire the political experience necessary for the central role he or she will play.

State governments usually employ similar requirements. For instance, Virginia requires that candidates for the state's House of Delegates and Senate be at least twenty-one years old, while candidates for the state's three most powerful executive positions—governor, lieutenant governor, and attorney general—must be at least thirty years old. South Dakota, however, sets the minimum age limit for its most important executive officers— governor and lieutenant governor—at twenty-one.

Amazingly, the Framers did not impose an age limit on Supreme Court justices, not even the chief justice. Perhaps the Framers thought that the president was not likely to appoint minors to the bench, or at least that they would not be approved by the Senate. Looking at the nine justices today, it is obvious that the Framers were right not to worry.

CRITICAL THINKING QUESTIONS

1. A minimum age requirement is one of the few qualifications for office that the Constitution imposes on candidates running for Congress and the presidency. What additional qualifications would you propose for candidates running for these positions? Why do you think the Framers were reluctant to include additional qualifications for office in the Constitution?

2. Some analysts have suggested imposing a maximum age limit on Supreme Court justices and other federal judges or a limit on how many years a justice or judge can serve. What are some of the advantages and disadvantages of imposing a mandatory retirement age for judges?

tion. During the nomination campaign, the candidate targets the leaders and activists who choose nominees in primaries or conventions. Party leaders are concerned with electability, while party activists are often ideologically and issue oriented, so a candidate must appeal to both bases.

Photo courtesy: Laura J. Gardner/The News and Advance/AP/Wide World Photos

Photo courtesy: Sandy Huffaker/Getty Images

How do candidates campaign for the support of different electoral groups? Senator John McCain (R-AZ), who had publicly feuded with fundamentalist Christian political leaders in the 2000 election, delivered the commencement address at the Reverend Jerry Falwell's Liberty University (left photo) during his losing bid for the presidency in 2008. Senator Barack Obama (D-IL) spoke at the 2008 National Council of La Raza conference during his successful presidential campaign (right photo).

front-loading
The tendency of states to choose an early date on the primary calendar.

Iowa Caucuses

PRIMARIES VERSUS CAUCUSES   The mix of preconvention contests has changed over the years, with the most pronounced trend being the shift from caucuses to primary elections. Only seventeen states held presidential primaries in 1968; the number increased to thirty-eight in 1992, forty-two in 1996, and forty-three in 2000, but declined to forty in 2008. In recent years, the vast majority of delegates to each party's national convention have been selected through the primary system.

The caucus is the oldest, most party-oriented method of choosing delegates to the national conventions. Traditionally, the caucus was a closed meeting of party activists in each state who selected the party's choice for presidential candidate. In the late nineteenth and early twentieth centuries, however, many people viewed these caucuses as elitist and anti-democratic, and reformers succeeded in replacing them with direct primaries in most states. Although there are still presidential nominating caucuses today (in Iowa, for example, as noted above), they are now more open and attract a wider range of the party's membership. Indeed, new participatory caucuses more closely resemble primary elections than they do the old, exclusive party caucuses.[14]

The primary schedule has been altered by a phenomenon often referred to as **front-loading,** the tendency of states to choose an early date on the primary calendar. Seventy percent of all the delegates to both party conventions are now chosen before the end of February. This trend is hardly surprising, given the added press emphasis on the first contests and the voters' desire to cast their ballots before the competition is decided.

Front-loading has important effects on the nomination process. First, a front-loaded primary schedule generally benefits the front-runner, since opponents have little time to turn the contest around once they fall behind. Second, front-loading gives an advantage to the candidate who wins the "invisible primary," that is, the one who can raise the bulk of the money *before* the nomination season begins. Once the primaries begin, there is less opportunity to raise money to finance campaign efforts simultaneously in many states.

However, Internet fund-raising has emerged as a means to soften the advantage of a large campaign fund going into a primary battle, since it allows candidates to raise large sums from many small donors nationwide and to do so virtually overnight. All of the major 2008 presidential candidates relied on online donations to finance their campaigns, but the highly compressed schedule still forced even the best-funded candidates to make difficult decisions on how to allocate their financial resources.

THE PARTY CONVENTIONS   The seemingly endless nomination battle does have a conclusion: the national party convention held in the summer of presidential election years. The out-of-power party traditionally holds its convention first, in late July, followed in mid-August by the party holding the White House. Preempting an hour or more of prime-time network television for four nights and monopolizing the cable networks such as CNN, FOX News, and C-SPAN, these remarkable conclaves give viewers a chance to learn about the candidates.

Today, the convention is fundamentally different from what it was in the past. First, its importance as a party conclave, at which compromises on party leadership and policies can be worked out, has diminished. Second, although the convention still formally selects the presidential ticket, most nominations are settled well in advance. Third, three preconvention factors have lessened the role of the current parties and conventions: delegate selection, national candidates and issues, and the news media.

DELEGATE SELECTION As mentioned in the previous section, the selection of delegates to the conventions is no longer the function of party leaders but of primary elections and grassroots caucuses. Moreover, recent reforms, especially by the Democratic Party, have generally weakened any remaining control by local party leaders over delegates. In fact, most delegates come to their party's convention already committed to supporting a particular candidate.

Who the delegates are, a topic that is less important today than it was when delegates enjoyed more power in the selection process, still reveals interesting differences between the political parties. Both parties draw their delegates from an elite group whose income and educational levels are far above the average American's. Nearly 35 percent of delegates at the 2008 Democratic convention were minorities, and half were women. (To learn more about "firsts" for women at the conventions, see Table 12.1.) Only 7 percent of the delegates to the 2008 Republican convention were racial and ethnic minorities. Despite recent GOP efforts to increase minority representation at its convention, this marks a steep decline from 2004, when 17 percent of the delegates were minorities.

The General Election Campaign

After earning the party's nomination, candidates embark on the **general election campaign**. They must seek the support of interest groups and a majority of voters and decide on the issues they will emphasize. When courting interest groups, a candidate

general election campaign
That part of a political campaign aimed at winning a general election.

Thinking Globally
The Length of Campaigns

While many of the candidates for the 2008 U.S. presidential nominations made their first campaign visits to Iowa and New Hampshire a few days following the 2006 midterm elections, candidates in most parliamentary democracies campaign for only thirty to sixty days. Canadian law requires that the minimum length of a campaign be thirty-six days, although most national campaigns have lasted for an average of two months.

- For the electorate, what might be the advantages and disadvantages of having a much shorter presidential campaign?
- Are certain types of candidates given an advantage (and others left at a disadvantage) by limiting the length of the campaign? In the United States, who might benefit the most if candidates were prohibited from raising money or producing advertisements sixty days prior to an election?

TABLE 12.1 Historic Moments for Women at the Conventions

Since 1980, Democratic Party rules have required that women constitute 50 percent of the delegates to its national convention. The Republican Party has no similar quota. Nevertheless, both parties have tried to increase the role of women at the convention. Some "firsts" and other historic moments for women at the national conventions include:

1876	First woman to address a national convention
1890	First women delegates to conventions of both parties
1940	First woman to nominate a presidential candidate
1951	First woman asked to chair a national party
1972	First woman keynote speaker
1984	First major-party woman nominated for vice president (Democrat Geraldine Ferraro)
1996	Wives of both nominees make major addresses
2000	Daughter of a presidential candidate nominates her father
2004	Both candidates introduced by their daughters
2008	First woman nominated by the Republican Party for vice president (Governor Sarah Palin)

Source: Center for American Women in Politics. Updated by authors.

Photo courtesy: Bettmann/CORBIS

What makes a good campaign slogan? 1964 Republican presidential candidate Barry Goldwater's famous slogan, "In your heart, you know he's right," was quickly lampooned by incumbent Democratic opponent President Lyndon B. Johnson's campaign as "In your guts, you know he's nuts."

seeks both money and endorsements, although the results are mainly predictable: liberal, labor, and minority groups usually back Democrats, while social conservatives and business organizations usually support Republicans. The most active groups often coalesce around emotional issues such as abortion and gun control, and these organizations can produce a bumper crop of money and activists for favored candidates.

Virtually all candidates adopt a brief theme, or slogan, to serve as a rallying cry in their quest for office. In 2008, John McCain adopted the slogan "Country First" in order to remind voters of his experience as a prisoner of war in Vietnam and his ability to work across party lines and defy his own party. Candidates try to avoid controversy in their selection of slogans, and some openly eschew ideology. The clever candidate also attempts to find a slogan that cannot be lampooned easily.

The Key Players: The Candidate and the Campaign Staff

Most observers agree that the most important aspect of any campaign is the quality of the candidate and the attributes of the campaign team. The ability to convey ideas in a persuasive manner, the cornerstone of all political campaigns, ultimately rests in the hands of the candidate. The ability to package and project the candidate's message in the most effective and persuasive manner, the work of the campaign staff, requires expertise in media and public relations. The ability to raise funds, which in turn provide volume to the campaign message, requires the combined effort of a strong candidate and experienced campaign staff.

THE CANDIDATE   Before there can be a campaign, there must be candidates. Candidates run for office for any number of reasons, including personal ambition, the desire to promote ideological objectives or pursue specific public policies, or simply because they think they do a better job than their opponents.[15] In any case, to be successful, candidates must spend a considerable amount of time and energy in pursuit of their desired office, and all candidates must be prepared to expose themselves to public scrutiny and the chance of rejection by the voters.

ticket-splitting
Voting for candidates of different parties for various offices in the same election.

THE CAMPAIGN STAFF   Paid staff, political consultants, and dedicated volunteers work behind the scenes to support the candidate. Collectively, they plan general strategy, conduct polls, write speeches, craft the campaign's message, and design the strategy for communicating that message in the form of television advertisements, radio spots, Web sites, and direct mail pieces. Others are responsible for organizing fundraising events, campaign rallies, and direct voter contacts. The staff, professional and volunteer, keeps the candidate on message and manages the campaign's near-infinite details. The size and nature of the organizational staff varies significantly depending on the type of race. Senate and gubernatorial races, for example, are able to hire for many staff positions and employ a number of different consultants and pollsters, whereas races for state legislatures will likely have a paid campaign manager and rely more heavily on volunteer workers. Presidential campaign organizations, not surprisingly, have the most elaborate structure.

Volunteers are the lifeblood of every national, state, and local campaign. Volunteers answer phone calls, staff candidate booths at festivals and county fairs, copy and distribute campaign literature, and serve as the public face of the campaign. They go door to door to solicit votes, or use computerized telephone banks to call targeted voters with scripted messages, two basic methods of **voter canvass.** Most canvassing, or direct solicitation of support, takes place in the month before the election, when voters are most likely to be paying attention. Closer to Election Day, volunteers begin vital **get out the vote (GOTV)** efforts, calling and e-mailing supporters to remind them to vote and arranging for their transportation to the polls if necessary.

THE CANDIDATE'S PROFESSIONAL STAFF Nearly every campaign at the state and national level is run by a **campaign manager,** who coordinates and directs the campaign. The campaign manager is the person closest to the candidate, the person who delivers the good and bad news about the condition of the campaign and makes the essential day-to-day decisions, such as whom to hire and when to air which television advertisement. The campaign manager helps to determine the campaign's overall strategy, and equally important, works to keep the campaign on message throughout the race.

Key paid positions in addition to the campaign manager, and depending on the race, include the **finance chair,** who is responsible for bringing in the large contributions that fund the campaign, the **pollster,** who takes public opinion surveys to learn what issues voters want candidates to address in speeches, and the **direct mailer,** who supervises direct mail fund-raising. The **communications director** develops the overall media strategy for the candidate, carefully blending press coverage with paid TV, radio, and mail media, not to mention advertisements on Web sites visited by those likely to favor the candidate's positions.

The **press secretary** is charged with interacting and communicating with journalists on a daily basis. It is the press secretary's job to be quoted in the newspapers or on TV explaining the candidate's positions or reacting to the actions of the opposing candidate. Good news is usually announced by the candidate. Bad news, including responding to attacks from the other side, is the preserve of the press secretary (better to have someone not on the ballot doing the dirty work of the campaign).

An indispensable part of modern political campaigns is the campaign's **Internet team,** which manages the campaign's communications, outreach, and fund-raising via the Internet, and increasingly tries to manage the candidate's online visibility. Members of the Internet team monitor and post on blogs popular with the party faithful, and they create candidate profiles intended for a more general audience on social networking sites.

The Electoral College: How Presidents Are Elected

The campaign for the presidency has many facets, but the object of the exercise is clear: winning a majority of the **Electoral College**. This uniquely American institution consists of representatives of each state who cast the final ballots that actually elect a president. The total number of **electors**—the members of the Electoral College—for each state is equivalent to the number of senators and representatives that state has in the U.S. Congress. The District of Columbia is accorded three electoral votes.

The Electoral College was the result of a compromise between those Framers who argued for selection of the president by the Congress and those who favored selection by direct popular election. There are three essentials to understanding the Framers' design of the Electoral College. The system was constructed (1) to work without political parties; (2) to cover both the nominating and electing phases of presidential selection; and, (3) to produce a nonpartisan president.

The Electoral College machinery as originally designed by the Framers was somewhat complex. Each state designated electors (through appointment or popular vote) equal in number to the sum of its representation in the House and Senate. The electors met in their respective states. Each elector had two votes to cast in the Electoral College's selection for the president and vice president, although electors could not vote for more than one candidate from their state. The rules of the college stipulated that each elector was allowed to cast only one vote for any single candidate, and by extension obliged each elector to use his second vote for another candidate. There was no way to designate votes

voter canvass
The process by which a campaign reaches individual voters, either by door-to-door solicitation or by telephone.

get out the vote (GOTV)
A push at the end of a political campaign to encourage supporters to go to the polls.

campaign manager
The individual who travels with the candidate and coordinates the many different aspects of the campaign.

finance chair
A professional who coordinates the fund-raising efforts for the campaign.

pollster
A professional who takes public opinion surveys that guide political campaigns.

direct mailer
A professional who supervises a political campaign's direct mail fund-raising strategies.

communications director
The person who develops the overall media strategy for the candidate, blending free press coverage with paid TV, radio, and mail media.

press secretary
The individual charged with interacting and communicating with journalists on a daily basis.

Internet team
The campaign staff that makes use of Web-based resources to communicate with voters, raise funds, organize volunteers, and plan campaign events.

Electoral College
Representatives of each state who cast the final ballots that actually elect a president.

elector
Member of the Electoral College chosen by methods determined in each state.

for president or vice president; instead, the candidate with the most votes (provided he also received votes from a majority of the electors) won the presidency and the runner-up won the vice presidency. If two candidates received the same number of votes and both had a majority of electors, the election was decided in the House of Representatives, with each state delegation acting as a unit and casting one vote. If no candidate secured a majority, the election would also be decided in the House, with each state delegation casting one vote for any of the top five electoral vote-getters. In both these scenarios, the candidate needed a majority of the total number of states for victory.

THE ELECTORAL COLLEGE IN THE NINETEENTH CENTURY   The Republic's fourth presidential election revealed a flaw in the Framers' Electoral College plan. In 1800, Thomas Jefferson and Aaron Burr were, respectively, the presidential and vice presidential candidates advanced by the Democratic-Republican Party, whose supporters controlled a majority of the Electoral College. Accordingly, each Democratic-Republican elector in the states cast one of his two votes for Jefferson and the other one for Burr. Since there was no way under the constitutional arrangements for electors to earmark their votes separately for president and vice president, the presidential election resulted in a tie between Jefferson and Burr. Even though most understood Jefferson to be the actual choice for president, the Constitution mandated that a tie be decided by the House of Representatives. It was, of course, and in Jefferson's favor, but only after much energy was expended to persuade lame-duck Federalists not to give Burr the presidency.

The Twelfth Amendment, ratified in 1804 and still the constitutional foundation for presidential elections today, was an attempt to remedy the confusion between the selection of vice presidents and presidents that beset the election of 1800. The amendment provided for separate elections for each office, with each elector having only one vote to cast for each. In the event of a tie or when no candidate received a majority of the total number of electors, the election still went to the House of Representatives; now, however, each state delegation would have one vote to cast for one of the three candidates who had received the greatest number of electoral votes.

The Electoral College modified by the Twelfth Amendment has fared better than the college as originally designed, but it has not been problem free. On three occasions during the nineteenth century, the electoral process resulted in the selection of a president who received fewer votes than his opponent. In 1824, neither John Quincy Adams nor Andrew Jackson secured a majority of electoral votes, throwing the election into the House. Although Jackson had more electoral and popular votes than Adams, the House voted for the latter as president. In the 1876 contest between Republican Rutherford B. Hayes and Democrat Samuel J. Tilden, no candidate received a majority of electoral votes; the House decided in Hayes's favor even though he had 250,000 fewer popular votes than Tilden. In the election of 1888, President Grover Cleveland secured about 100,000 more popular votes than did Benjamin Harrison, yet Harrison won a majority of the Electoral College vote, and with it the presidency.

THE ELECTORAL COLLEGE IN THE TWENTIETH AND TWENTY-FIRST CENTURIES
Several near crises pertaining to the Electoral College occurred in the twentieth century. For example, had third-party presidential candidate Ross Perot stayed in the 1992 presidential contest, he could have thrown the election into the House of Representatives. His support had registered from 30 percent to 36 percent in the polls in early 1992, prior to his dropping out of the race. When he reentered the race, some of that backing had evaporated, and he finished with 19 percent of the vote and carried no states. However, Perot drained a substantial number of Republican votes from George Bush, thus splitting the GOP base and enabling Bill Clinton to win many normally GOP-leaning states.[16]

Throughout the 2000 presidential campaign, many analysts foresaw that the election would likely be the closest since the 1960 race between John F. Kennedy and Richard M. Nixon. Few realized, however, that the election would be so close that the winner would not be officially declared for more than five weeks after Election Day.

**Close Calls
in Presidential Elections**

And, no one could have predicted that the Electoral College winner, George W. Bush, would lose the popular vote and become president after the Supreme Court's controversial decision in *Bush* v. *Gore* (2000) stopped the recount in Florida. With the margin of the Electoral College results so small (271 for Bush, 267 for Gore), a Gore victory in any number of closely contested states could have given him a majority in the Electoral College. As it turned out, Al Gore became only the fourth person to win the popular vote and lose the presidency.

Keep in mind that through **reapportionment,** representation in the House of Representatives and consequently in the Electoral College is altered every ten years to reflect population shifts. Reapportionment is simply the reallocation of the number of seats allocated to each state in the House of Representatives that takes place after each national census. The number of House seats has been fixed at 435 since 1910 Since that time, the average size of congressional districts has tripled in population, from 211,000 following the 1910 Census to 647,000 in the 2000 Census.[17]

Projections for the upcoming 2010 census show a sizable population shift from the Midwest and the Democratic-dominated Northeast to the South and West, where Republicans are much stronger. If these projections hold, Texas will gain four congressional districts, and therefore four additional seats in the House of Representatives and four additional votes in the Electoral College. Arizona and Florida will gain two seats and two votes, while four other states will gain one. New York and Ohio stand to lose

reapportionment
The reallocation of the number of seats in the House of Representatives allocated to each state after each decennial census.

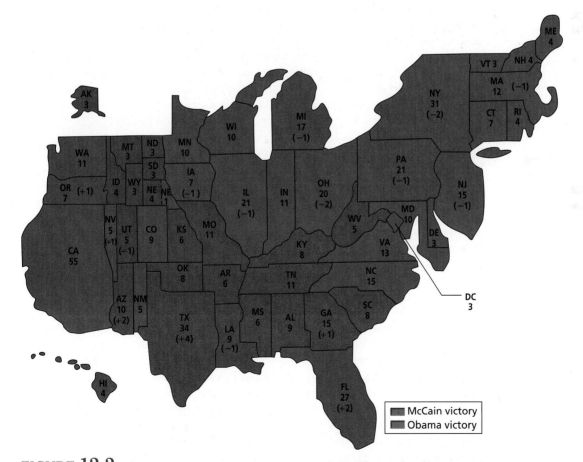

FIGURE 12.2 The States Drawn in Proportion to Their Electoral College Votes
This map visually represents the respective electoral weights of the fifty states in the 2008 presidential election. For each state, the projected gain or loss of Electoral College votes based on the upcoming 2010 Census is indicated in parentheses.

Note: States drawn in proportion to number of electoral votes. Total electoral votes: 538.

Source: http://synapse.princeton.edu/~sam/ev_projection_current_map.jpg and http://www.edssurvey.com/images/File/NR_Appor07wTables.pdf.

two seats and two votes, while eight states stand to lose a single seat and electoral vote. If Barack Obama runs for reelection and wins the same states in 2012 that he won in 2008, he will win 5 fewer votes. (To learn more about the 2008 Electoral College map, see Figure 12.2.)

Congressional Elections

Compared with presidential elections, congressional elections receive scant national attention. Unlike major-party presidential contenders, most candidates for Congress labor in relative obscurity. There are some celebrity nominees for Congress—television stars, sports heroes, even local TV news anchors. In 2000, First Lady Hillary Rodham Clinton made history with her Senate campaign and gained the nation's attention by becoming the only first lady to win elective office. The vast majority of party nominees for Congress, however, are little-known state legislators and local office holders who receive remarkably limited coverage in many states and communities. For them, just establishing name identification in the electorate is the biggest battle.

The Incumbency Advantage

incumbency
The holding of an office.

The current system enhances the advantages of **incumbency** (that is, already being in office). Those people in office tend to remain in office. Of the 396 incumbents running for the House in 2008, only 18 lost on election day. In a "bad" year for House incumbents, such as the Democratic wave of 2006, "only" 94 percent of incumbents will win, but the senatorial reelection rate can drop much lower on occasion (79 percent in 2006). To the political novice, these reelection rates might seem surprising, as public trust in government and satisfaction with Congress has remained remarkably low during the very period that reelection rates have been on the rise.

redistricting
Redrawing congressional districts to reflect increases or decreases in seats allotted to the states as well as population shifts within a state.

gerrymandering
The legislative process through which the majority party in each statehouse tries to assure that the maximum number of representatives from its political party can be elected to Congress through the redrawing of legislative districts.

REDISTRICTING   Because the Constitution requires that representation in the House be based on state population, and that each state have at least one representative, congressional districts must be redrawn by state legislatures to reflect population shifts, so that each member in Congress will represent approximately the same number of residents. Exceptions to this rule are states such as Wyoming and Vermont, whose statewide populations are less than average congressional districts. This process of redrawing congressional districts to reflect increases or decreases in seats allotted to the states, as well as population shifts within a state, is called **redistricting**. Redistricting is a largely political process that the majority party in a state uses to ensure formation of voting districts that protect their majority.

This redistricting process often involves **gerrymandering**—the drawing of boundaries in a way to produce a particular electoral outcome without regard to the shape of the district. Because of enormous population growth, the partisan implications of redistricting, and the requirement under the Voting Rights Act for minorities to get an equal chance to elect candidates of their choice, legislators end up drawing oddly shaped districts to achieve their goals.[18] Redistricting plans routinely meet with court challenges across the country. Following the 2000 Census and the subsequent redistricting in 2002, the courts threw out legislative maps in a half-dozen states, primarily because of state constitutional concerns about compactness.[19]

Over the years, the Supreme Court has ruled that:

- Congressional as well as state legislative districts must be apportioned on the basis of population.[20]
- District lines must be contiguous; you must be able to draw the boundaries of the district with one unbroken line.

- Purposeful gerrymandering of a congressional district to dilute minority strength is illegal under the Voting Rights Act of 1965.[21]
- Redrawing of districts for obvious racial purposes to enhance minority representation is constitutional if race is not the "predominate" factor over all other factors that are part of traditional redistricting, including compactness.[22]

THE IMPACT OF SCANDALS   Scandals come in many varieties in this age of investigative journalism. The old standby of financial impropriety has been supplemented by other forms of career-ending incidents, such as sexual improprieties. Incumbents implicated in scandals typically do not lose reelections—because they simply choose to retire rather than face defeat.[23] Representative Mark Foley (R–FL) resigned shortly before the 2006 elections after newspaper reports that he had sent sexually explicit instant messages and emails to underage male congressional pages. The House Majority Leader, Tom DeLay (R–TX), also resigned before the election after being indicted for violating campaign finance laws, and Representative Bob Ney (R–OH) resigned after being convicted on corruption charges. Although their districts had been normally safe for Republicans, these scandals helped Democrats claim all three seats. In 2008, the man who defeated Foley in 2006, Tim Mahoney (D-FL), was himself defeated after he was accused of sexual harassment and two extra-marital relationships with staff members were revealed.

Presidential Coattails

The defeat of a congressional incumbent can also occur as a result of the presidential coattail effect. Successful presidential candidates usually carry into office congressional candidates of the same party in the year of their election.

Midterm Elections

Elections in the middle of presidential terms, called **midterm elections,** present a threat to incumbents of the president's party. Just as the presidential party usually gains seats in presidential election years, it usually loses seats in off years as shown in Table 12.2. The problems and tribulations of governing normally cost a president some popularity, alienate key groups, or cause the public to want to send the president a message of one sort or another. An economic downturn or presidential scandal can underline and expand this circumstance, as the Watergate scandal of 1974 and the recession of 1982 demonstrated. The 2002 midterm elections, however, bucked that trend, marking the first time since 1934 and Franklin D. Roosevelt that a first-term president gained seats for his party in a midterm election. The 2002 election was likely an anomaly, as it was the first election following the September 11 terrorist attacks, and voters most likely sought political stability by supporting the president's party.

Most apparent is the tendency of voters to punish the president's party much more severely in the sixth year of an eight-year presidency, a phenomenon associated with retrospective voting. After only two years, voters are still willing to "give the guy a chance," but after six years, voters are often restless for change.

Senate elections are less inclined to follow these off-year patterns than are House elections. The idiosyncratic nature of Senate contests is due to their intermittent scheduling (only one-third of the seats come up for election every two years) and the existence of well-funded, well-known candidates who can sometimes swim against whatever political tide is rising.

midterm election
An election that takes place in the middle of a presidential term.

Critical Congressional
(Mid-Term) Elections

The 2008 Congressional Elections

Democrats began the 2008 congressional election cycle with momentum at their backs and a favorable electoral landscape. Just two years earlier, they had gained thirty

TABLE 12.2 Congressional Election Results, 1948–2008

The party of the president in power almost always loses seats in midterm elections, especially in the midterm election of the second term. In a phenomenon sometimes called the "sixth-year itch," voters are tired of the incumbent president and reward the opposition party with big gains in Congress. The recent exceptions showed the American people's unhappiness with impeachment efforts against Bill Clinton and their support for George W. Bush due to concerns related to the war on terrorism.

| | Gain (+) or Loss (−) for President's Party | | | | |
| | Presidential Election Years | | | Midterm Election Years | |
President/Year	House	Senate	Year	House	Senate
Truman (D): 1948	+76[a]	+9	1950	−29	−6
Eisenhower (R): 1952	+24	+2	1954	−18	−1
Eisenhower (R): 1956	−2	0	1958	−48	−13
Kennedy (D): 1960	−20	−2	1962	−4	+3
Johnson (D): 1964	+38	+2	1966	−47	−4
Nixon (R): 1968	+7	+5	1970	−12	+2
Nixon (R): 1972	+13	−2	Ford (R): 1974	−48	−5
Carter (D): 1976	+2	0	1978	−15	−3
Reagan (R): 1980	+33	+12	1982	−26	+1
Reagan (R): 1984	+15	−2	1986	−5	−8
G. Bush (R): 1988	−3	−1	1990	−9	−1
Clinton (D): 1992	−10	0	1994	−52	−9[b]
Clinton (D): 1996	+10	−2	1998	+5	0
G. W. Bush (R): 2000	−2	−4	2002	+6	+2
G. W. Bush (R): 2004	+3	+4	2006	−30	−6
Obama (D): 2008	+19[c]	+6[c]	2010	—	—

[a] Gains and losses are the difference between the number of seats won by the president's party and the number of seats won by that party in the previous election.

[b] Includes the switch from Democrat to Republican of Alabama U.S. Senator Richard Shelby one day after the election.

[c] Does not include the results of races called after Noember 10, 2008.

seats in the House and six in the Senate, giving the Democratic Party control of both Houses of Congress for the first time since 1994. Moreover, Democratic candidates pulled off stunning upsets in three special elections to fill seats vacated by Republicans from conservative districts in early 2008. With twenty-nine Republicans from the House and five from the Senate not seeking re-election, but only six Democrats from the House retiring, Democrats had fewer seats to defend and could go on the offensive in more competitive races than embattled Republicans.

Democrats also benefited from a slight fundraising advantage, which reached record levels in 2008. Whereas Democratic candidates raised a combined total of approximately $500 million, Republican candidates raised a combined total of approximately $425 million. Together, the nearly $1 billion represented the most ever raised for congressional elections. The biggest fundraisers of all the congressional candidates were Senator Norm Coleman (R-MN) and his Democratic challenger, comedian Al Franken. The incumbent Coleman raised over $15 million, while Franken raised even more, over $17 million and was the top fundraiser in 2008. The biggest fundraiser in the House was Jared Polis, running for a Democratic open seat in Colorado, who amassed almost $7.5 million to keep the seat Democratic. In addition, the Democratic Party committees in the House and Senate out-raised their Republican counterparts by over $75 million.

The national political climate also favored the Democrats, given widespread disapproval of President Bush and Republicans in Congress and an increase in Democratic partisan identification. Barack Obama also inspired great confidence among Democrats. With Obama at the top of the ticket, all Democratic candidates would benefit from increased turnout among Democratic-leaning constituencies.

Thus, it was expected that the Democrats would build on their gains from 2006, but it was not certain whether they would be able to win enough Senate races to reach sixty seats, the number of votes needed to break a filibuster. Of the 35 seats up for election in 2008, Democrats needed not only to win all the open seats, but also to defeat several vulnerable Republican incumbents in traditionally blue states. And, to reach the magic number of sixty, they would have to pull off some upsets against incumbents in several red states such as Georgia, Alaska, Kentucky, Mississippi, and North Carolina. A favorable political environment helped Democrats win at least six more seats in the Senate. Pending the outcome of a recount in Minnesota, a run-off in Georgia, and late arriving absentee ballots in Alaska, the Democratic gains could be as high as nine seats (for the most up-to-date status of the races not called on Election Day, see http://cnn.com/ELECTION/2008/results/president/). As expected, Democrats won open seats in Colorado, New Mexico and Virginia. In New Hampshire, former Governor Jeanne Shaheen defeated one-term incumbent Senator John Sununu in a re-match of their 2002 contest by a decisive 52 percent to 45 percent margin. In Oregon, Jeff Merkley defeated two-term incumbent Gordon Smith by a margin of three percent. Both Sununu and Smith had two of the more moderate voting records in their party and had stressed their opposition to President Bush in their advertising. This strategy failed both incumbents in two states that have become more Democratic in recent years. Democrat Kay Hagan successfully ousted first-term incumbent Elizabeth Dole in North Carolina, a state that still tends to vote Republican. With Hagan and Shaheen elections, there are 17 women serving in the 111th Congress, an all-time high.

In the House races, Democrats captured eleven open seats vacated by Republicans and defeated 14 incumbents. Democratic gains were nationwide. The GOP minimized their losses slightly by defeating four one-term Democratic incumbents who previously had scored upset wins in heavily Republican districts. Overall, the Democrats came away with a net gain of at least 21 seats and maybe even as many as 25, depending on the outcome of pending ballots, runoffs, and recounts in five districts (see http://clerk.house.gov/ for the most up-to-date information on partisan divisions in the 111th Congress). Over the course of two election cycles, Democrats had gained over 50 seats. As a result, the Democrats begin the 111th Congress with a commanding 80-seat advantage in the House to go with at least a 14-seat majority in the Senate. Barack Obama's victory means the Democrats will control both chambers of Congress and the presidency for the first time since the 103rd Congress.

You Are a Media Consultant
to a Political Candidate

The Media's Role in the Campaign Process

What voters actually see and hear of the candidate is primarily determined by the paid media, free media, and the new media. The **paid media,** are political advertisements or other pieces that the campaign creates and pays to have disseminated. The campaign staff and consultants determine the amount, form, and content of paid media. The **free media** are the stories about a campaign that news programs choose to broadcast, or newspapers and magazines choose to print, and which cost the campaign nothing. The **new media** are new technologies, such as the Internet, which blur the lines between paid and free media sources. The new media, made possible by a wide array of technological innovations, are generated in part by the campaign but are also driven by individuals from outside the campaign. These individuals may contribute to the candidate's existing online effort, maintain Web sites and groups on social networking sites, and write blogs about the candidate and his or her policies.

Paid Media

Positive ads stress the candidate's qualifications, family and personal ties, and issue positions with no direct reference to the opponent. Positive ads are usually favored by the incumbent candidate. **Negative ads** attack the opponent's character and platform. And, with the exception of the candidate's brief, legally required statement that he or she approved the ad, a negative ad may not even mention the candidate who is paying for the airing. **Contrast ads** compare the records and proposals of the candidates, with

paid media
Political advertisements purchased for a candidate's campaign.

free media
Coverage of a candidate's campaign by the news media.

new media
New technologies, such as the Internet, that blur the line between paid and free media sources.

positive ad
Advertising on behalf of a candidate that stresses the candidate's qualifications, family, and issue positions, without reference to the opponent.

negative ad
Advertising on behalf of a candidate that attacks the opponent's platform or character.

contrast ad
Ad that compares the records and proposals of the candidates, with a bias toward the sponsor.

spot ad
Television advertising on behalf of a candidate that is broadcast in sixty-, thirty-, or ten-second duration.

Television and Presidential Campaigns

inoculation ad
Advertising that attempts to counteract an anticipated attack from the opposition before the attack is launched.

a bias toward the candidate sponsoring the ad. Most paid advertisements are short **spot ads** that range from ten to sixty seconds long. In his successful 2008 bid for the White House, however, President Barack Obama purchased airtime on seven networks the week before the election to broadcast a 30-minute advertisement intended to sway undecided voters.

Before the 1980s, well-known incumbents usually ignored negative attacks from their challengers, believing that the proper stance was to be above the fray. But, after some well-publicized defeats of incumbents in the early 1980s in which negative television advertising played a prominent role,[24] incumbents began attacking their challengers in earnest. The new rule of politics became "An attack unanswered is an attack agreed to." In a further attempt to stave off brickbats from challengers, incumbents began anticipating the substance of their opponents' attacks and airing **inoculation ads** early in the campaign to protect themselves in advance from the other side's spots.

Free Media

While candidates have control over what advertisements are run (paid media), they have little control over how journalists will cover their campaign and convey it to voters. During campaign season, the news media constantly report political news. What they report is largely based on news editors' decisions of what is newsworthy or "fit to print." The press often reports what candidates are doing, such as giving speeches, holding fundraisers, or meeting with party leaders. Even better from the candidate's perspective, the news media may report on a candidate's success, perhaps giving that candidate the brand of a "winner," making him or her that much more difficult to beat. Reporters may also investigate rumors of a candidate's misdeeds or unflattering personal history, such as run-ins with the law, alleged use of drugs, or a failed marriage.

The media's expectations can have an effect on how the public views the candidates. Using poll data, journalists often predict the margins by which they expect contenders to win or lose. A clear victory of 5 percentage points can be judged a setback if the candidate had been projected to win by 12 or 15 points. The tone of the media coverage—that a candidate is either gaining or losing support in polls—can affect whether people decide to give money and other types of support to a candidate.[25]

The New Media

Contemporary campaigns have an impressive new array of weapons at their disposal: faster printing technologies, reliable databases, instantaneous Internet publishing and mass e-mail, autodialed pre-recorded messages, video technology, and enhanced telecommunications and teleconferencing. As a result, candidates can gather and disseminate information more quickly and effectively than ever.

One outcome of these changes is the ability of candidates to employ "rapid-response" techniques: the formulation of prompt and informed responses to changing events on the campaign battlefield. In response to breaking news of a scandal or issue, for example, candidates can conduct background research, implement an opinion poll and tabulate the results, devise a containment strategy and appropriate "spin," and deliver a reply. This makes a strong contrast with the campaigns of the 1970s and early 1980s, dominated primarily by radio and TV advertisements, which took much longer to prepare and had little of the flexibility enjoyed by the contemporary e-campaign.[29]

The first use of the Internet in national campaigning came in 1992 when the Democratic presidential ticket of Bill Clinton and Al Gore maintained a Web site that stored electronic versions of their biographical summaries, speeches, press releases, and position papers. The Internet remained something of a virtual brochure until the 2000 elections, when candidates began using e-mail and their Web sites as vehicles for fund-raising, recruiting volunteers, and communicating

Photo courtesy: Bettmann/CORBIS; Rich Wilking/Reuters/CORBIS

Photo courtesy: Frederick Breedon IV/UPI/Landov

How have the rules and format for presidential debates changed since the first televised debates? Presidential debates have come a long way since an ill-at-ease Richard M. Nixon was visually bested by John F. Kennedy in the first set of televised debates. John McCain and Barack Obama's second debate in 2008 was in a town meeting format, where the candidates were able to respond to questions directly posed by audience members.

with supporters. By 2006, most campaign Web sites featured downloadable and streaming video and were integrated into the candidate's overall communication and mobilization strategy. In 2008, all of the major candidates running for president and nearly 90 percent of the Democratic and Republican congressional candidates maintained a campaign Web site.

With the advent of blogs, a candidate's Web site can take on a life of its own. Blogs enable supporters and the occasional stealthy opponent to post messages on the candidate's Web site and to engage in a nearly contemporaneous exchange of ideas with other supporters and with the candidate's Internet team. While it is possible that this form of dialogue can be empowering for supporters and encourage civic involvement, the way that candidates have used blogs calls this possibility into question.

The newest Internet tools to have emerged in campaigns are social networking sites such as Facebook and MySpace, which allow candidates to cultivate a sense of community and build a personal network of supporters. Since the 2006 midterm elections, social networking sites have created a space for candidates to develop personal profiles that allow them to list their professional qualifications and personal interests, share photographs, post campaign updates, and host free-flowing discussion forums.

The Main Event: The 2008 Presidential Campaign

The 2008 election may go down in history for being one of the nation's longest and most contentious electoral marathons. The outcome was a source of anxiety not only for millions of Americans, but also for people around the globe, many of whom viewed America's presidential choice as a referendum on George W. Bush's policies abroad. Senator Barack Obama, the 47-year-old Democratic nominee for president, initially was unable to capitalize fully on the fundamental advantages that favored the Democratic Party. Many Americans were unsure whether Obama had the experience to serve in the nation's highest office at a time of global economic instability and threats to national security. Despite his years of experience in Congress and military service, Americans also expressed doubts about 72-year-old Senator John McCain, the Republican Party's nominee. Many were unsure that McCain could understand the plight of ordinary Americans and resolve the major problems of the day; others worried about McCain's age—he would be the oldest man ever to be elected president if he won the election. Polls taken throughout the summer and fall of 2008 showed nearly 10 percent of Americans undecided between Senators Obama and McCain. Another 15 percent claimed that they could switch their support before Election Day.

The Party Nomination Battles

With no incumbent president or vice president running for reelection, the nomination contests in both parties drew a crowded field of candidates. The Democrats had former Iowa Governor Tom Vilsack; Representative Dennis Kucinich (OH); former senator and the party's 2004 vice presidential nominee, John Edwards (NC); Senator Joe Biden (DE); Senator Chris Dodd (CT); New Mexico Governor Bill Richardson; and former Senator Mike Gravel (AK). The most anticipated announcements came in February when first-term Senator Barack Obama (IL) and former First Lady and two-term Senator Hillary Clinton (NY) announced their candidacies.

The initial field of candidates for the Republicans was even larger. Senator Sam Brownback (KS) led the way with an announcement in January 2007. He would soon be joined by Senator John McCain (AZ); Representatives Duncan Hunter (CA), Ron Paul (TX), and Tom Tancredo (CO); former New York City Mayor Rudolph Giuliani; former Governors James Gilmore (VA), Mike Huckabee (AR), Mitt Romney (MA), and Tommy Thompson (WI); former Ambassador Alan Keyes; and businessman John Cox. Former Senator Fred Thompson (TN) became the thirteenth candidate when he announced his candidacy on the *Tonight Show with Jay Leno*.

The Democratic candidates spent the spring and summer of 2007 in the typical primary season fashion: fund-raising, debating, giving speeches and meeting personally with voters, particularly in the states with early nomination contests. Senator Clinton began the race as the clear front-runner and emerged the winner of the "invisible primary." By autumn, she had raised the most money, secured the most endorsements from major party leaders and Democratic constituencies, and was the leader in the national polls. Clinton seemed to be the focus of many of the other candidates' attacks during the 17 debates before the Iowa caucuses and any stumbles she experienced garnered intense scrutiny and attention from the media. Senator Obama, whose electrifying address to the Democratic National Convention in 2004 had catapulted him into the national spotlight, was the main beneficiary of that hostility. Obama combined a firm anti-war stance with rhetoric that tapped into Democrats' frustration with the Washington establishment and a desire for real change in terms of both policy and tone. His star power within the party and growing grassroots confidence in his electability helped Obama match Clinton's fundraising totals and climb in opinion polls.

Obama was the clear winner of the Iowa caucuses, with John Edwards finishing second, and Clinton finishing a close third. Not only did a win in Iowa generate momentum for Obama's campaign, but it also demonstrated that an African American candidate could win significant support from white voters. Also telling was the effectiveness of Obama's intricate field organization and the great enthusiasm he was generating among young voters. With the field of frontrunners narrowed to Clinton, Edwards, and Obama, the focus shifted to New Hampshire, where Senator Obama was surging ahead in the polls with the primary less than a week away. Rather than deliver the expected knockout blow to Senator Clinton's candidacy, Obama finished second to Clinton, an outcome that surprised every pollster and pundit in the field. Clinton's victory was attributed to a strong debate performance and strong turnout and support among women.

How do debates affect the party nomination battle? Individual campaigns negotiate with other campaigns and the major news organizations to schedule debates during the party nomination races. Here, Democratic and Republican primary presidential candidates shake hands at the request of moderator Charles Gibson of ABC News when the two parties held back-to-back debates at St. Anselm College on January 5, 2008. The debates were co-sponsored by Facebook and the local ABC affiliate. The 2008 campaign marked the first time that new media organizations such as Facebook and YouTube participated in the debate process.

Photo courtesy: Neil Hamburg/Bloomberg News/Landov

Senator Clinton next won a close popular-vote victory in Nevada but suffered a resounding defeat in South Carolina, possibly due to negative attacks on Obama by Clinton supporters, including the candidate's husband, that some perceived to be racially-tinged. Most observers assumed that the nomination would be decided on February 5, Super Tuesday, when 25 states and territories would hold primaries and caucuses. Yet, the strength of Clinton's and Obama's candidacies resulted in a close race pitting two well-funded candidates with significant numbers of avid supporters against one another. Super Tuesday resulted in a draw. After a bruising nomination battle that threatened to split the Democratic Party, the nomination contest at last came to a close on June 5, when Senator Clinton officially conceded to Senator Obama.

The Republican contest was the one that was supposed to be long and dramatic, given the absence of a front-runner among a crowded field of top-tier candidates. Through 15 debates in 2007, each candidate sought to portray himself as the conservative best able to win an election in a climate that was unfavorable to Republicans. Mitt Romney established an early lead in the polls in Iowa and New Hampshire. There did not seem to be a widespread movement towards Romney among social conservatives, however, as many had concerns about his Mormon faith and the moderate image he had presented to the public during his political career in Massachusetts. Fred Thompson seemed to be the most reliably conservative option, but his lackluster performance on the campaign trail disappointed many frustrated conservatives unable to throw their overwhelming support to any of the candidates.

Mike Huckabee, the former Arkansas governor and an ordained Baptist minister was the big winner in Iowa, with Romney finishing second. Playing the role of underdog, McCain won a convincing victory in New Hampshire and effectively won the nomination on Super Tuesday by winning nine of 21 contests and 61 percent of Republican delegates. Romney won seven states but only 21 percent of the delegates with his best performances coming in caucuses and smaller states. Huckabee had a respectable showing, but could not seem to expand his coalition beyond his evangelical base. The Republican race officially continued for another month, until McCain had enough delegates to clinch the nomination.

The Democratic and Republican Conventions

An almost two month gap would separate the end of the primary season and the first day of the Democratic National Convention. Speculation had centered on whether Obama would ask his Democratic rival, Senator Hillary Clinton, to be his running mate. Some in the party base argued that a "dream ticket" of Obama and Clinton was needed to unify the party and win in November. In the end, Obama chose Senator Joe Biden of Delaware, whose working class upbringing and foreign policy credentials were seen as broadening the ticket's appeal.

The Democratic National Convention was held August 25-28 in Denver, Colorado. One of the most highly anticipated speeches came on the second night of the convention when Senator Clinton, who had come closer than any woman before her to winning the U.S. presidency, gave her full support to Obama in front of an enthusiastic crowd in the convention hall and 26 million viewers at home and asked her supporters to back her former opponent. Former president Bill Clinton was followed by vice presidential nominee Joe Biden on Wednesday night. On the final night of the convention, Senator Obama accepted his party's nomination in front of 86,000 supporters at Invesco Field, with another 39 million watching on television. This speech by the first African American to win the nomination of a major party for president marked the 45th Anniversary of the Reverend Martin Luther King's "I Have a Dream" speech. Observers judged it a significant achievement and an important milestone in American history.

Less than 12 hours after the Democratic convention had ended, in what most agreed was a tactic to reduce Obama's post-convention bounce, Senator McCain announced the selection of Alaska Governor Sarah Palin as his running mate. Palin was only the second woman to run for the vice presidency on a major party ticket and the first Republican woman to be selected.

McCain's announcement generated great excitement among the Republican base. Governor Palin was presented to the public as a rising star in Alaskan politics with a strong record of government reform. The mother of five children, including a special needs infant, Palin's strong pro-life views connected on a very personal level with social conservatives and Evangelicals. In a brief speech after McCain introduced her as his running mate, Palin referenced Hillary Clinton's campaign for the White House, in what was seen as a clear bid to win the support of disaffected supporters of Senator Clinton. Intense media scrutiny of Palin began immediately after McCain's announcement. Over the next few days, journalists, pundits, and bloggers took part in a frenzied examination of her family, personal life, political record, and policy positions.

The 2008 Republican National Convention was held September 1-4 in the Xcel Center in St. Paul, Minnesota. Because New Orleans was again under threat of a massive hurricane, the first night of the convention was scaled back considerably. The night was to feature President Bush and Vice President Cheney as speakers, but both of their appearances were cancelled. Their absence may have benefited the McCain campaign, given that both men were widely unpopular. Moreover, the latest tracking polls showed that the Democrats were getting their post-convention bounce. By Tuesday, the Obama-Biden ticket had jumped out to a six-point advantage. Republicans hoped to turn things around on Wednesday night, when Sarah Palin addressed the convention and 38 million television viewers. In an accomplished speech, Palin introduced herself to America and delivered biting criticisms of the Democratic nominee, the mainstream media, and Washington, D.C., while touting her running mate as a fellow maverick and American hero. Palin's speech was rapturously received in the convention center and received high marks from media commentators and political analysts.

In a somewhat anti-climactic appearance the following night, John McCain accepted his party's nomination with a speech that revealed in very personal terms his motivation for service. McCain explained his dedication to "Country First"—the slogan for his campaign—as stemming from the lessons he had learned as a prisoner of war in Vietnam and discussed his record of doing what was right for the nation, regardless of his party's support. While McCain's speech did not have the flair or generate the enthusiasm that Obama and Palin's speeches did, it was watched by a record-breaking 40 million television viewers.

The Debates and the General Election Campaign

The first presidential debate was scheduled to take place on Friday, September 26, on the campus of the University of Mississippi. By this point, the Republicans' optimism was beginning to fade. A growing economic crisis had made the economy, not foreign policy, the primary concern for a majority of the country. Since most Americans trusted Democrats more on economic policy, this policy focus harmed McCain's standing in the polls. In addition, President Bush's proposal to address nearly frozen credit markets was met with great skepticism among the electorate and on Capitol Hill. Sensing an opportunity to demonstrate his problem-solving abilities, Senator McCain "suspended" his campaign and suggested postponing the first debate in order to work on the financial crisis until a compromise had been reached. When the initial bill failed to pass the House due to opposition mostly from conservative Republicans, McCain appeared to be an obstacle to a solution. On Friday morning, McCain announced that he would participate in the debate as planned. The format featured questions posed by the moderator, PBS host Jim Lehrer, with responses and rebuttals by the candidates. While neither candidate broke new ground on the issues, Obama consistently came across as calm, confident, and having a firm grasp of policy. McCain's performance was somewhat uneven, although he demonstrated his experience and expertise in national security matters quite convincingly. For a Friday evening, the audience for the first debate was exceptionally high, with 52.4 million

Americans watching on television. Opinion polls found that a majority of viewers believed that Obama was the winner.

Another concern for the McCain campaign was the increasingly negative impression that voters were forming about Sarah Palin. After having been sheltered from major news organizations during the first weeks of the campaign, interviews were arranged with ABC World News anchor Charlie Gibson and CBS Evening News anchor Katie Couric. Neither of these interviews went well. The Couric interview was especially problematic, as Palin frequently appeared flustered by rather innocuous questions and provided confusing answers on more serious ones. Palin was able to regain her footing and reassure nervous supporters during the only Vice Presidential debate with Joe Biden, who was nevertheless considered the strongest performer of the two candidates. Over 70 million people watched the debate, the most ever for a Vice Presidential debate. Palin would continue to be a big draw in public and on television. On October 18, 14 million Americans watched her impressive appearance on Saturday Night Live, a record audience for the late night comedy show.

A town-hall format was used for the second presidential debate, which was held on October 7 at Belmont University in Nashville. Moderator Tom Brokaw of NBC News asked questions prepared by about 125 undecided registered voters selected by the Gallup polling organization. The expectations and stakes were high for Senator McCain, who was very experienced with the town-hall format and needed a strong performance in order to alter the dynamics of the race. As with the first debate, no major gaffes or new substantive information was revealed. Again, however, Senator Obama received higher marks from viewers.

A television viewing audience of 56.5 million watched the final debate on October 15 at Hofstra University on Long Island. With CBS veteran correspondent Bob Schieffer serving as moderator, this debate focused on domestic policy with the two candidates seated close together at a table. This was clearly McCain's strongest performance, as he had his opponent on the defensive for most of the early part of the debate. He also introduced the country to "Joe the Plumber," an Ohio voter who was videotaped having a friendly argument with Senator Obama over Obama's tax proposals. Most of the public saw Obama as the winner, giving the Democratic ticket a clean sweep of the four debates and strong momentum going into the final weeks of the campaign.

Opinion polls taken after the last debate indicated that Senator Obama had maintained a lead over Senator McCain that had begun to build during the week of the financial crisis. On the day of the first debate, the Rasmussen Reports daily presidential tracking poll showed that Obama was the choice of 50 percent of likely voters, while McCain was the choice of 45 percent. Support for both tickets fluctuated only slightly from that point forward, with Obama-Biden peaking at 52 percent several times and never dropping below 50 percent. Support for McCain-Palin, on the other hand, never reached above 47 percent. The picture for the Republicans was even more disappointing at the state level, where Obama led in all the battleground states except Missouri throughout October. But even more troubling was the numbers coming out of states that were thought to be reliably Republican. Polls showed leads averaging six percent for Obama in Virginia and only one percent leads for McCain in Indiana and North Carolina. Indiana and Virginia had not voted for a Democrat for president since 1964, while North Carolina last voted Democratic in 1976. Additional signs of trouble were apparent from the numbers coming out of Georgia, Montana, and North Dakota.

McCain's hope to change the dynamics of the race had rested on a strong showing in the debates or a major misstep by Obama. The Democrats stayed on message, however, criticizing President George W. Bush's handling of the economy and tying Senator McCain to the unpopular president and his policies. In addition to offering a general promise of "change we can believe in," Obama put forth a plan to cut taxes for 95 percent of all Americans, invest in alternative sources of energy, and make health care more accessible and affordable. He also promised to withdraw American troops from Iraq within a specified period of time and place more emphasis on capturing Osama bin Laden and funding the war against a resurgent Taliban in Afghanistan.

With nearly $300 million spent on over 535,000 airings of campaign ads, including a 30-minute long advertisement aired on seven networks the week before the election, the Obama campaign not only stayed on message, but it made sure that the message was made clear to millions of swing voters across the country.

Senator McCain spent most of the campaign attempting to distance himself from President Bush and prove that he was a maverick—a more authentic agent of change than his opponent. In both cases, McCain was largely unsuccessful. In the summer, the McCain campaign had made some headway by arguing for a withdrawal from Iraq without arbitrary timetables and pushing a proposal to lift the federal ban on off-shore drilling for oil. Growing stability in Iraq and falling energy prices in anticipation of a looming global recession, however, made it difficult to keep these two issues at the top of the policy agenda.

McCain also had made some progress sowing seeds of doubt in voters' minds about Obama's readiness to be president. While McCain had tax cuts and a health insurance reform plan of his own, the campaign focused on Obama's policy positions and his association with a 1960s radical in a series of highly negative attack ads throughout the fall. To the bewilderment of many observers, McCain's campaign made no mention of Obama's relationship with his former pastor, the Reverend Jeremiah Wright, whose fiery sermons had been excerpted to great effect by conservative broadcasters and pundits. Nor was there much mention of Senator McCain's numerous bipartisan legislative achievements and initiatives. In the final two weeks of the campaign, with Samuel "Joe the Plumber" Wurzelbacher frequently by his side, McCain zeroed in on Obama's tax and spending proposals, claiming that Obama's brief conversation with Wurzelbacher provided evidence of a Democratic plan to pursue redistributive economic policies once Obama was in office.

Election Results and Analysis

As the first returns and exit polls were announced from states in the Eastern and Central time zones, it was clear that Obama's lead in the polls was accurate. The outcomes in reliably red states with early poll closings—Indiana, Georgia, North Carolina, and Virginia—were deemed by the network and cable news bureaus as "too close to call" for most of the evening. The same was true for Florida and Ohio, two battleground states that George W. Bush had won and that McCain needed to keep in order to have any chance of winning. But soon after the polls closed in New Hampshire and Pennsylvania, two states that Kerry had won in 2004 and that McCain needed to win to compensate for likely losses in Colorado and New Mexico, the news media called both states for Obama. Around 9:30 pm EST, the networks called Ohio for Obama and the only question remaining was his margin of victory. As soon as California was called for Obama at 11:00 pm EST, the networks declared Barack Obama the forty-fourth president of the United States.

Senator McCain immediately called Obama to congratulate him on his historic win and then gave a gracious concession speech in front of supporters in Phoenix. President-elect Obama gave his victory speech at Chicago's Grant Park in front of over 100,000 supporters. To chants of "Yes we did!" Obama gave a highly conciliatory speech, noting the historic significance of his victory and praising the power of American democracy.

When polls in the remaining states closed and the final tallies were completed, Obama had won a landslide in the Electoral College, 365 to 173. Obama won all of the states that Kerry had won in 2004 and the major battleground states of Ohio and Florida by narrow, but clear margins. He also won convincingly in Colorado, Iowa, Nevada, and New Mexico, four states that Bush had won in 2004. The big surprises were in Virginia, where Obama won by five percent, and in Indiana and North Carolina, both of which he won by less than one percentage point. Obama also won one electoral vote from the 2nd Congressional District in Nebraska, which is one of just two states to allocate votes by congressional district.

In the popular vote, Obama won 53 percent to McCain's 46 percent—the highest percentage of the vote won by a Democratic nominee since 1964. (Go to http://www.cnn.com/ELECTION/2008/results/president/ to see the final counts and percentages in each state). The 2008 election also had the highest voter turnout since 1964, with over 62 percent of eligible citizens casting more than 128 million votes.

Most analysts expected the 2008 election to be similar to the 2000 election, with most "red states" remaining red and most "blue states" remaining blue. The Obama campaign was convinced, however, that they had the opportunity to expand the blue portion of the electoral map by investing in an extensive field organization that covered all 50 states, much of it built on organizations already put in place during the primaries and caucuses. The Obama campaign's decision to opt out of the public financing system allowed them to raise an unprecedented sum of money to fund their ground operation and to buy extensive airtime for campaign advertisements. In contrast, the McCain campaign pursued a more traditional strategy, assuming that much of their base was secure and focused their attention on the states that had been decided by narrow margins in the past two elections. McCain's decision to agree to limits on his spending in return for federal financing also contributed to his defeat, since it resulted in an inadequate amount of resources devoted to voter mobilization. In October, for example, the McCain campaign had to abandon battleground states that Kerry had won in 2004, which allowed the Obama campaign to redirect even more resources to the states still considered in play.

Obama's impressive seven percent win was fueled by strong performances among key voting groups. Although McCain won the support of 55 percent of white voters, Obama won the support of women of all races by 13 percentage points and the support of men of all races by one percent. This was the first time that a Democrat had won a majority of men since 1976. Ninety-five percent of African Americans supported Obama. Strategically important given their status as America's fastest-growing ethnic group and concentration in key electoral states was the preference of Latino/a voters: 67 percent voted for Obama and only 31 percent for McCain. In 2004, Kerry won Latino/as by a margin of only 53 percent to 44 percent. Young voters, those between the ages of 18 and 29, also strongly supported Obama over McCain, by a margin of 66 percent to 32 percent.

Barack Obama ran a disciplined, innovative campaign in a year that strongly favored a Democratic victory. Obama was able to inspire a majority of the electorate, including numerous young people and racial and ethnic minorities, with a message of change and hope during the worse economic crisis to face the nation since the Great Depression. His election as the first African American president of the United States was seen by many as the culmination of the American dream. And, as is the tradition in American politics, Americans of all ideological stripes began uniting behind their new president in the days following the election.

oward Reform: Campaign Finance

In the early 1970s Congress enacted its most ambitious round of campaign laws to date. The Federal Election Campaign Act (FECA) and its later amendments established disclosure requirements, established the Presidential Public Funding Program, which provides partial public funding for presidential candidates who meet certain criteria, and created the Federal Election Commission (FEC), an independent federal agency tasked with enforcing the nation's election laws.

The most recent round of reforms was set in motion by Senators John McCain (R–AZ) and Russell Feingold (D–WI) who co-sponsored the Bipartisan Campaign Reform Act (BCRA) of 2002 in the Senate, while Representatives Chris Shays (R–CT)

Thinking Globally

Campaign Finance in Japan

In contrast to multimillion-dollar U.S. political campaigns, direct expenses for the comparatively short campaigns before Japanese elections are relatively modest. The use of campaign posters and pamphlets is strictly regulated, candidates appear on Japan's noncommercial public television station to give short campaign speeches, and neither candidates nor political parties may advertise in the mass media until twelve days before an election. Unlike in the United States, most of this campaign activity is publicly funded.

■ What are the advantages and disadvantages of a more regulated campaign system such as the one in place in Japan?
■ Does public funding for an election make the process more fair? Why or why not?

and Martin Meehan (D–MA) sponsored the House version. BCRA included a "fast track" provision that any suits challenging the constitutionality of the reforms would be immediately placed before a U.S. district court, and giving appellate powers to the U.S. Supreme Court. The reason for this provision was simple: to thwart the numerous lobbying groups and several high-profile elected officials who threatened to tie up BCRA in the courts for as long as they could. No sooner did President Bush sign BCRA than U.S. Senator Mitch McConnell (R–KY) and the National Rifle Association separately filed lawsuits claiming that the BCRA violated free speech rights.

In a 5–4 decision in *McConnell* v. *Federal Election Commission* (2003), the U.S. Supreme Court held that the government's interest in preventing corruption overrides the free speech rights to which the parties would otherwise be entitled and, thus, found that BCRA's restrictions on soft-money donations and political advertising did not violate free speech rights.[26] In *Federal Election Commission* v. *Wisconsin Right to Life* (2007), however, the Supreme Court invalidated BCRA's strict ban on genuine issue ads during the "blackout" period on the grounds that the timing of the ad does not automatically designate it as electioneering.[31] These two cases indicate that the Supreme Court has very narrowly upheld the BCRA measures restricting speech both in the form of political contributions (soft money) and in political advertising, but also has opened the door to challenges to how the Federal Election Commission will enforce BCRA.

Current Rules

The Supreme Court's *McConnell* decision in 2003 means that political money is now regulated by the federal government under the terms of the BCRA, which supplanted most of the provisions of the Federal Election Campaign Act. The BCRA outlaws unlimited and unregulated contributions to parties, known as soft money, and limits the amounts that individuals, interest groups, and political parties can give to candidates for president, U.S. senator, and U.S. representative. (To learn more about contribution limits, see Table 12.3). The goal of all limits is the same: to prevent any single group or individual from gaining too much influence over elected officials, who naturally feel indebted to campaign contributors.

INDIVIDUAL CONTRIBUTIONS Individual contributions are donations from individual citizens. The maximum allowable contribution under federal law for congressional and presidential elections was $2,300 per election to each candidate in 2007–2008, with primary and general elections considered separately. Individuals in 2007–2008 were also limited to a total of $108,200 in gifts to all candidates, political action committees, and parties combined per two-year election cycle. These limits will rise at the rate of inflation in subsequent cycles. Most candidates receive a majority of all funds directly from

TABLE 12.3 Individual Contribution Limits per Election Cycle Before and After Bipartisan Campaign Reform Act (2002)

	Before	After[a]
Contributions per candidate	$1,000	$2,300
Contributions per national party committee	$20,000	$38,500
Total contributions per 2-year cycle	$50,000	$108,200
Soft money	Unlimited	Banned

[a]These limits are for 2007–2008. BCRA limits are adjusted in odd-numbered years to account for inflation.
Source: Campaign Finance Institute, http://www.cfinst.org/studies/ElectionAfterReform/pdf/EAR_Appendix1.pdf.

individuals, and most individual gifts are well below the maximum level. Finally, individuals who spend over $10,000 to air "electioneering communication," that is, "any broadcast, cable, or satellite communication which refers to a clearly identified candidate for Federal office" within sixty days of a general election or thirty days of a primary election, are now subject to a strict disclosure law. The rationale behind this regulation is that spending on an ad favoring a candidate is effectively the same as a contribution to the candidate's campaign and requires the same scrutiny as other large donations.[27]

POLITICAL ACTION COMMITTEE (PAC) CONTRIBUTIONS When interest groups such as labor unions, corporations, trade unions, and ideological issue groups seek to make donations to campaigns, they must do so by establishing **political action committees (PACs)**. PACs are officially recognized fund-raising organizations that are allowed by federal law to participate in federal elections. (Some states have similar requirements for state elections.) Under current rules, a PAC can give no more than $5,000 per candidate per election (primary, general, and special election), and $15,000 each year to each of the units of the national parties.

Approximately 4,000 PACs are registered with the FEC. In 2006, PACs contributed $359 million to Senate and House candidates, while individuals donated $785 million. On average, PAC contributions accounted for 37 percent of the war chests (campaign funds) of House candidates and 14 percent of the treasuries of Senate candidates. Incumbents benefit the most from PAC money; incumbents received $289 million, much more than the $70 million given to challengers during the 2006 election cycle.[28] By making these contributions, PACs hope to secure entrée to candidates after they have been elected in order to influence them on issues important to the PAC, since they might reciprocate campaign donations with loyalty to the cause. Corporate PACs give primarily to incumbents because incumbents tend to win, and lobbyists want to guarantee access for their clients. Single-issue and more ideologically based PACs are often willing to support challengers and more untried candidates who pledge to support their positions if elected.[29]

In an attempt to control PACs, the BCRA has a limit on the way PACs attempt to influence campaigns. The law strictly forbids PACs from using corporate or union funds for the electioneering communications discussed earlier. PACs can use corporate or labor contributions only for administrative costs. The purpose of this rule is to prevent corporations or unions from having an undue influence on the outcome of elections by heavily advertising toward specific audiences in the weeks leading up to elections. (To learn about PAC expenditures in 2008, see Figure 12.3.)

political action committee (PAC)
Federally mandated, officially registered fund-raising committee that represents interest groups in the political process.

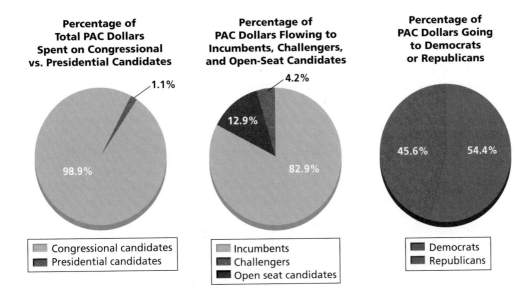

FIGURE 12.3
Expenditures by PACs in the 2008 Election Cycle
PACs contributed a total of $29 million to candidates competing in the 2008 election.
Source: Federal Election Commission, http://www.fec.gov; http://www.opensecrets.org.

Percentage of Total PAC Dollars Spent on Congressional vs. Presidential Candidates
1.1%
98.9%
Congressional candidates
Presidential candidates

Percentage of PAC Dollars Flowing to Incumbents, Challengers, and Open-Seat Candidates
4.2%
12.9%
82.9%
Incumbents
Challengers
Open seat candidates

Percentage of PAC Dollars Going to Democrats or Republicans
45.6%   54.4%
Democrats
Republicans

POLITICAL PARTY CONTRIBUTIONS Candidates also receive donations from the national and state committees of the Democratic and Republican Parties. As mentioned in chapter 11, political parties can give substantial contributions to their congressional nominees. Under the current rules, national parties can give up to $5,000 to a House candidate in the general election and $39,900 to a Senate candidate. In 2006, the Republican and Democratic parties funneled over $768 million to their standard-bearers, via direct contributions and coordinated expenditures. In competitive races, the parties may provide 15–17 percent of their candidates' total war chests.

MEMBER-TO-CANDIDATE CONTRIBUTIONS In Congress and in state legislatures, well-funded, electorally secure incumbents often contribute campaign money to their party's needy incumbent and non-incumbent legislative candidates.[30] This activity began in some state legislatures (notably California), but it is now well-established at the congressional level.[31] Generally, members contribute to other candidates by establishing their own PACs—informally dubbed "leadership" PACs—through which they distribute campaign support to candidates.

In general, members give their contributions to the same candidates who receive the bulk of congressional campaign committee resources. Thus, member contributions at the congressional level have emerged as a major supplement to the campaign resources contributed by the party campaign committees.[32]

CANDIDATES' PERSONAL CONTRIBUTIONS Candidates and their families may donate to the campaign. The U.S. Supreme Court ruled in *Buckley* v. *Valeo* (1976) that no limit could be placed on the amount of money candidates can spend from their own families' resources, since such spending is considered a First Amendment right of free speech.[33] For wealthy politicians, this allowance may mean personal spending in the millions. For example, Mitt Romney spent a record $42 million of his own money in his failed quest for the 2008 Republican presidential nomination. While self-financed candidates often garner a great deal of attention, most candidates commit much less than $100,000 in family resources to their election bids.[34]

public funds
Donations from the general tax revenues to the campaigns of qualifying presidential candidates.

matching funds
Donations to presidential campaigns from the federal government that are determined by the amount of private funds a qualifying candidate raises.

PUBLIC FUNDS **Public funds** are donations from general tax revenues to the campaigns of qualifying candidates. Only presidential candidates (and a handful of state and local contenders) receive public funds. Under the terms of the FECA (which first established public funding of presidential campaigns), a candidate for president can become eligible to receive public funds during the nominating contest by raising at least $5,000 in individual contributions of $250 or less in each of twenty states. The candidate can apply for federal **matching funds,** whereby every dollar raised from individuals in amounts less than $251 is matched by the federal treasury on a dollar-for-dollar basis. Of course, this assumes there is enough money in the Presidential Election Campaign Fund to do so. The fund is accumulated by taxpayers who designate $3 of their taxes for this purpose each year when they send in their federal tax returns. During the 2008 primaries, all of the major candidates except John Edwards opted out of the federal matching funds, allowing them to raise considerably more money than the government would have provided.

For the general election, the two major-party presidential nominees can accept an $85 million lump-sum payment from the federal government after the candidate accepts his or her nomination. If the candidate accepts the money, it becomes the sole source for financing the campaign. A candidate may refuse the money and be free from the spending cap the government attaches to it, as Barack Obama did in 2008, subsequently setting a record for the most spent by a candidate for a presidential campaign.

A third-party candidate receives a smaller amount proportionate to his or her November vote total if that candidate gains a minimum of 5 percent of the vote. Note that in such a case, the money goes to third-party campaigns only *after* the election is over; no money is given in advance of the general election.

Analyzing Visuals | The Ten Most Active 527 Groups in 2008

Examine the table showing the most financially active 527 groups participating in the 2008 elections and answer the following questions:

Committee	Expenditures	Pro-Democratic	Pro-Republican
Service Employees International Union	$25,058,103	✔	
America Votes	$19,672,551	✔	
American Solutions Winning the Future	$17,470,711		✔
The Fund for America	$11,514,130	✔	
EMILY's List	$10,349,746	✔	
GOPAC	$8,100,840		✔
College Republican National Committee	$6,458,084		✔
Citizens United	$5,238,329		✔
Alliance for New America	$4,890,620	✔	
Working for Working Americans	$2,049,833	✔	
Gay & Lesbian Victory Fund	$5,145,721	✔	
Club for Growth	$4,246,547		✔

LOOKING at the information in the table, what conclusions can you draw about the relative success of Democratic and Republican fund-raising efforts with regard to 527 groups in 2008?

GIVEN what you know about some of the individual 527s listed in the table, what conclusions can you draw about the effectiveness of various 527 strategies with regard to the 2008 presidential election?

Source: http://www.opensecrets.org.

Soft Money and the 527 Loophole

Soft money, as discussed above, is campaign money raised and spent by political parties for expenses such as overhead and administrative costs and for grassroots activities such as political education and GOTV efforts. Soft-money donations are now prohibited under the 2002 Bipartisan Campaign Finance Reform Act (BCRA), and third-party issue ads, if coordinated with a federal candidate's campaign, can now be considered campaign contributions and are thus regulated by the FEC. The last election cycle for the parties to use soft money was 2001–2002, and the amount raised, nearly $430 million for Republican and Democrats combined,[35] highlights why the reform seemed necessary. Republicans raised $219 million in soft money from pharmaceutical, insurance, and energy companies. Democrats raised just under $211 million in soft money from unions and law firms. With soft money banned, the hope was that wealthy donors and interest groups would be deprived of their privileged and potentially corrupting influence on parties and candidates. The hope was that, like every other citizen, they would have to donate within the placed on individuals and PACs. Unfortunately, these reforms have not worked, and the 2004 election revealed the latest campaign finance loophole.

The most significant unintended result of the BCRA in 2004 was the emergence of political entities known as **527 political committees**—the numbers come from the provisions of the Internal Revenue tax code that establish their legal status. These committees are essentially unregulated interest groups that focus on specific causes or policy positions and attempt to influence voters. (To learn more about 527 activity in 2008, see Analyzing Visuals: The Ten Most Active 527 Groups in 2008.)

According to the tax code, 527s may not directly engage in advocacy for or against a candidate, but they can advocate on behalf of political issues. This allowed them to circumvent the direct advocacy prohibition by creating what detractors called "sham issue ads" naming a particular candidate and stating how the candidate supported or harmed a particular interest, but without directly stating the 527 group's opinion on how to vote in the election. Thus, money that would have entered the system as unregulated soft money in previous election cycles ended up in the hands of 527 organizations in 2004, funding several television advertisements and direct mailings.[36] To limit

soft money
The virtually unregulated money funneled by individuals and political committees through state and local parties.

527 political committees
Nonprofit and unregulated interest groups that focus on specific causes or policy positions and attempt to influence voters.

You Are a Campaign Manager: Lead Obama to Battleground State Victory

McCain and the Swingers: Help McCain Win Swing States and Swing Voters

501(c)(3) committees
Nonprofit and tax-exempt groups that can educate voters about issues and are not required to release the names of their contributors.

Campaign Finance Regulations

the influence of such ads on voters, the BCRA now forbids their airing in the thirty days before a primary and sixty days before a general election.

The 527s exist in both political camps, though the Democrats, the party out of power in 2004, were first to aggressively pursue them. Two of the largest pro-Democratic committees in the 2004 election were the Media Fund and Americans Coming Together (ACT), both raising millions of dollars from people eager to see a Democrat in the White House. These committees bought TV, radio, and print advertising to sell their message, focusing on the battleground or "swing" states that were not firmly in the Bush or Kerry camps. Even though most political observers predicted that President Bush would easily outspend Senator Kerry in the presidential contest, the Democratic 527s considerably aided the Democratic campaign. Through the end of the 2004 election, pro-Democratic 527 groups spent more than $200 million, more than double that of their Republican counterparts. In 2008 527's contributed approximately $425 million.

Another loophole that groups and individuals have used to circumvent the BCRA is to direct soft money donations to tax-exempt, non-profit **501(c)(3) committees**. These committees, also known by their designation in the federal tax code, are prohibited from conducting political campaign activities to influence elections to public office. But like 527s, 501(c)(3)s are permitted to educate voters on political issues as long as they do not overtly advocate a specific position. These committees are beginning to rival 527s in popularity as conduits for soft money, however, because they do not have to release the names of donors, who therefore can remain anonymous until their tax returns are filed in the following year.

Reformers will once again attempt to reform their reforms, but the abolition of 527 committees or restrictions on 501(c)(3)s are highly unlikely—and the money supporting them would most likely reappear in some other way. Overall, however, one lesson of the Bipartisan Campaign Reform Act is obvious: no amount of clever legislating will rid the American system of campaign money. Interested individuals and groups will always find ways to have their voices heard. The challenge is to find a way to force contributors to disclose their contributions in a timely fashion, so that the public may take this information into account when deciding how to vote.

WHAT SHOULD I HAVE LEARNED?

Voting, elections, and campaigns are essential parts of American government and the democratic principles we hold dear.

■ What are the roots of voting behavior in the United States?

Whether they are casting ballots in congressional or presidential elections, voters behave in certain distinct ways and exhibit unmistakable patterns to political scientists who study them. Elections in the United States include primary elections, general elections, initiatives, referenda, and recall elections.

■ What are the key elements of presidential elections?

No U.S. election can compare to the presidential contest. This spectacle, held every four years, brings together all the elements of politics and attracts the most ambitious and energetic politicians to the national stage. No longer closed affairs dominated by deals cut in "smoke filled rooms," today's conventions are more open made-for-television events in which the party platform is drafted and adopted, and the presidential ticket is formally nominated.

■ What are the key elements of congressional elections?

Compared with presidential elections, which are played out on the national stage, congressional elections are a different animal. Most candidates for Congress labor in relative obscurity. The 2008 midterm elections resulted in an expanded Democratic majority in both houses of Congress.

■ What is the media's role in campaigns?

Candidates for public office seek to gain favorable coverage in the media. They gain access with paid media, and with free media. The Internet increasingly makes this possible, since candidates can use it as a cheap medium to relate directly to voters and activists.

■ What does the 2008 presidential campaign teach us about voting, campaigns, and elections?

The events of the 2008 election demonstrate how all of the components of voting, campaigns and elections come together in modern politics.

■ What does the future hold for campaign finance reform?

As a result of the rise of soft money, Congress passed the Bipartisan Campaign Finance Reform

Act, in 2002. BCRA was promptly challenged but was upheld with very few exceptions by the Supreme Court. Though BCRA was successful in banning the unregulated soft money that flowed through the political parties, it exposed another loophole in the existing campaign finance laws, the unregulated money that now flows through 527 and 501(c)(3) groups.

Key Terms

campaign manager, p. 361
closed primary, p. 355
communications director, p. 361
contrast ad, p. 367
crossover voting, p. 356
direct mailer, p. 361
elector, p. 361
Electoral College, p. 361
finance chair, p. 361
501(c)(3) committees, p. 380
527 political committees, p. 379
free media, p. 367
front-loading, p. 358
general election, p. 356
general election campaign, p. 359
gerrymandering p. 364

get out the vote (GOTV), p. 361
incumbency, p. 364
initiative, p. 356
inoculation ad, p. 368
Internet team, p. 361
matching funds, p. 378
midterm election, p. 365
negative ad, p. 367
new media, p. 367
nomination campaign, p. 356
open primary, p. 355
paid media, p. 367
political action committee (PAC), p. 377
pollster, p. 361
positive ad, p. 367

press secretary, p. 361
primary election, p. 355
prospective judgment, p. 354
public funds, p. 378
raiding, p. 356
reapportionment, p. 363
recall, p. 356
redistricting, p. 364
referendum, p. 356
retrospective judgment, p. 354
runoff primary, p. 356
soft money, p. 379
spot ad, p. 368
ticket-splitting, p. 360
turnout, p. 347
voter canvass, p. 361

Researching Voting, Elections, and Campaigns

In the Library

Ansolabehere, Stephen, and Shanto Iyengar. *Going Negative: How Political Ads Shrink and Polarize the Electorate.* New York: Free Press, 1997.

Campbell, Angus, Philip E. Converse, Warren E. Miller, and Donald E. Stokes. *The American Voter*, reprint ed. Chicago: University of Chicago, 1980.

Carroll, Susan J., and Richard L. Fox, eds. *Gender and Elections: Shaping the Future of American Politics.* New York: Cambridge University Press, 2006.

Green, Donald P., and Alan S. Gerber. *Get Out the Vote: How to Increase Voter Turnout,* 2nd ed. Washington, DC: Brookings Institution, 2008.

Halperin, Mark, and John F. Harris. *The Way to Win: Taking the White House in 2008.* New York: Random House, 2006.

Herrnson, Paul S. *Congressional Elections: Campaigning at Home and in Washington,* 5th ed. Washington, DC: CQ Press, 2007.

Jacobson, Gary C. *The Politics of Congressional Elections,* 7th ed. New York: Longman, 2008.

Key, V. O., Jr., with Milton C. Cummings. *The Responsible Electorate.* Cambridge, MA: Harvard University Press, 1966.

Lewis-Beck, Michael S., Helmut Norpoth, William G. Jacoby, and Herbert F. Weisberg. *The American Voter Revisited.* Ann Arbor: University of Michigan Press, 2008.

Nivola, Pietro, and David W Brady. *Red and Blue Nation? Consequences and Correction of America's Polarized Politics.* Washington, DC: Brookings Institution, 2008.

Sabato, Larry J. *Marathon: The 2008 Election.* New York: Longman, 2008.

Sabato, Larry J. *The Sixth Year Itch: The Rise and Fall of George W. Bush's Presidency.* New York: Longman, 2007.

Skewes, Elizabeth A. *Message Control: How News Is Made on the Presidential Campaign Trail.* Lanham, MD: Rowman and Littlefield, 2007.

Trent, Judith S., and Robert V. Friedenberg. *Political Campaign Communication: Principles and Practices,* 6th ed. Westport, CT: Praeger, 2008.

Wattenberg, Martin P. *Is Voting for Young People? With a Postscript on Citizen Engagement.* New York: Longman, 2007.

On the Web

To learn more about the Federal Election Commission (FEC), which monitors and enforces campaign finance and election laws, go to **www.fec.gov.**

Project Vote Smart, **www.vote-smart.org,** is a nonpartisan resource for researching the voting records, issue positions, public statements, and campaign finances for current office holders and candidates. The site also includes a search engine to identify your member of Congress, voter registration information, and key issues being debated in your state.

For comprehensive election information that includes the political biographies and issue positions of the major candidates, county-by-county election results, exit poll data, primary and caucus rules and delegate allocation, and an explanation of the Electoral College, go to **www.cnn.com/ELECTION/2008/.**

To learn more about Facebook's profiles of elected officials and candidates, debates on contemporary issues, and the latest political news and commentary, go to **www.facebook.com/politics/?us.**

13

Social and Economic Policy

Picture the following scenario: the president is George Bush, the economy is in a downturn, there is turmoil in Iraq, and the issue of health care reform is one of the central issues in an upcoming presidential campaign. While this certainly could be a description of 2008, the scenario is drawn from the events of 1992. Back then, George Bush (the father of George W. Bush) was in the White House, the nation was in an economic recession, and Iraq was recovering from the 1991 Persian Gulf War. In addition, Americans were increasingly worried about the skyrocketing costs of medical care, a growing number of uninsured citizens, and escalating prices for pharmaceuticals. According to public opinion polls, voters placed reform of the health care system at the top of the list of issues the next president should address. How did the country wind up in nearly the same place sixteen years later?

During the 1992 presidential election, Bill Clinton made the issue of health care reform one of the main themes of his campaign to win the White House. Throughout the autumn months of 1992, Clinton regularly condemned President Bush for failing

The government's role in providing a social safety net has changed markedly over the last century. Sociologist and progressive reformer Jane Addams, shown at left, provided education and support to Chicago's poor at a time when social services were considered the responsibility of private citizens. While running for the 2008 Democratic presidential nomination, Senator Hillary Clinton, shown at right, unveiled an ambitious health care plan intended to provide all Americans with adequate health coverage.

to take action on an emerging national crisis. He promised that under a Clinton administration, there would be major reform of the nation's health care system. After he prevailed in the election, Clinton quickly sought to fulfill his campaign promise by creating a task force led by his wife, Hillary Rodham Clinton, to provide health care to all Americans. After about a year of preparation, Clinton's health care task force released its proposal to much fanfare, but the plan stalled in Congress under fierce opposition from Republican leaders.[1]

Among the main causes of its demise was a rise in public concern over the impact of the plan on the ability of individuals to choose their own physicians. In order to reach its goal of universal health care coverage, the Clinton reform called for restrictions on individual choices to help control the spiraling costs of health services. Declining public support for the Clinton plan was undoubtedly aided by a series of television ads funded by the health insurance industry that warned Americans they would lose control of their health care under the Clinton proposal. Arguments against the Clinton plan were summed up in a statement by then Republican Senator Bob Dole, who told the *Washington Post*, "More cost. Less choice. More taxes. Less quality. More government control. Less control for you and your family. That's what the president's government-run plan is likely to give you."[2]

WHAT SHOULD I KNOW ABOUT . . .

- the roots of public policy and the policy-making process?
- social welfare policy?
- reforming economic policy?

383

Without serious reform efforts throughout the late 1990s and first half of this decade, the health care situation in the nation continued to deteriorate. By the time the presidential election of 2008 rolled around, the problems with health care in America had once again emerged as a central issue. However, all the leading candidates had learned from the failures of the Clinton administration and proposed reforms that recognized the political liabilities of limiting individual choice.

Ironically, one of the two Democratic front-runners for the presidential nomination was none other than Hillary Clinton, now a second-term senator from New York. Not surprisingly, it was Senator Clinton who created the most aggressive plan for reforming America's health care system. As a Democratic presidential candidate, Clinton proposed a major reform that promised health insurance for all Americans and control of the skyrocketing costs of medical care. Unlike her plan in the 1990s, the new proposal would provide universal coverage through a more "choice driven" mechanism. Her "American Health Choices Plan" would give families tax credits to help pay for health insurance and require large businesses to help pay for their employees' insurance costs. Clinton's plan would not require small businesses to take part, but it would offer tax credits to encourage them to participate. In unveiling her proposal, Clinton warned that her Republican opponents would "try to equate this plan with government-run health care. Don't let them fool you again." She stressed that her plan would let individuals "keep the doctors you know and trust," and expand "personal choice" while keeping costs down.[3]

Clinton's key Democratic rival, Senator Barack Obama, and the eventual Republican nominee, Senator John McCain, also released health care reform proposals. Like Clinton, Obama and McCain shied away from any measure that would give the appearance of limiting individual choice. Instead, they called for various policies that would use tax incentives and subsidies to allow individuals to gain access to health insurance. They also called for allowing consumers the option of reimporting drugs from other countries to help reduce costs of prescriptions.[4]

While it's clear that health care played a prominent role in the 2008 presidential campaign, it is unclear if the heavy attention will lead to the types of fundamental change proposed by the candidates. After all, in 1992 the nation seemed primed to send a president to Washington who would fix the nation's ailing health care system. A decade and a half later, the nation is still waiting for that reform. The failure to address the nation's health care system has raised questions regarding the policy-making process and efforts to tackle such a mammoth social issue. Has the failure to achieve health care reform been caused by the partisan conflict that so often dominates in Washington, D.C., or is the lack of progress more reflective of the broader difficulties associated with making public policies in a democracy?

TO LEARN MORE—
—TO DO MORE
To learn more about health care reform efforts in the United States, go to the Kaiser Family Foundation's Web site at www.kaiseredu.org.

public policy
An intentional course of action followed by government in dealing with some problem or matter of concern.

Public policy is a purposive course of action followed by government in dealing with some problem or matter of concern.[5] Public policies are governmental policies based on law; they are authoritative and binding on people. Individuals, groups, and government agencies that do not comply with policies can be penalized through fines, loss of benefits, or even jail terms. As the phrase "course of action" implies, policies develop or unfold over time. They involve more than a legislative decision to enact a law or executive order is carried out.

Whether a policy is vigorously enforced, enforced in only some instances, or not enforced at all helps determine its meaning and impact.

In this chapter, we will discuss social and economic policy. Policies in both areas follow similar patterns, in what is called the policy-making process. After considering the roots of the policy-making process, we will examine social welfare policy and the government's involvement in the economy. Finally, we will examine the government's role in stabilizing the economy.

 **oots of Public Policy: The Policy-Making Process**

Political scientists and other social scientists have developed many theories and models to explain the formation of public policies. Here, we present a popular model used to describe the policy-making process that views it as a sequence of stages or functional activities. (This model, depicted in Figure 17.1, can be used to analyze any of the issues discussed in this book.) Public policies do not just happen; rather, they are typically the products of a predictable pattern of events. Models for analyzing the policy-making process do not always explain *why* public policies take the specific forms that they do, however. That depends on the political struggles over particular policies. Nor do models necessarily tell us *who* dominates or controls the formation of public policy.

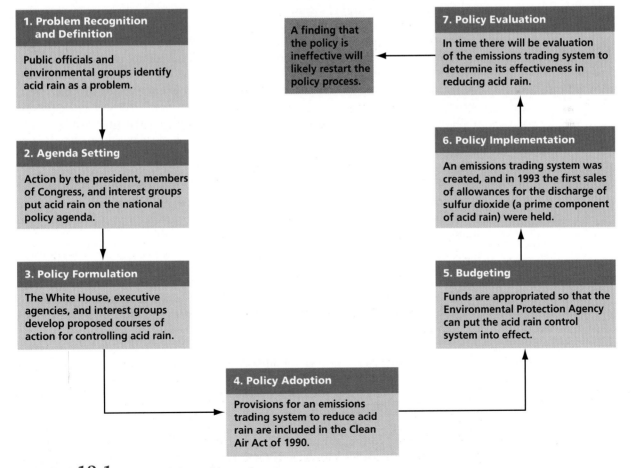

1. Problem Recognition and Definition

Public officials and environmental groups identify acid rain as a problem.

2. Agenda Setting

Action by the president, members of Congress, and interest groups put acid rain on the national policy agenda.

3. Policy Formulation

The White House, executive agencies, and interest groups develop proposed courses of action for controlling acid rain.

4. Policy Adoption

Provisions for an emissions trading system to reduce acid rain are included in the Clean Air Act of 1990.

5. Budgeting

Funds are appropriated so that the Environmental Protection Agency can put the acid rain control system into effect.

6. Policy Implementation

An emissions trading system was created, and in 1993 the first sales of allowances for the discharge of sulfur dioxide (a prime component of acid rain) were held.

7. Policy Evaluation

In time there will be evaluation of the emissions trading system to determine its effectiveness in reducing acid rain.

A finding that the policy is ineffective will likely restart the policy process.

FIGURE **13.1** Stages of the Public Policy Process

Policy making typically can be thought of as a process of sequential steps, although in practice these steps may merge together in a less distinct manner:

1. **Problem recognition**—identification of an issue that disturbs the people and leads them to call for governmental intervention.
2. **Agenda setting**—government recognition that a problem is worthy of consideration for governmental intervention.
3. **Policy formulation**—identification of alternative approaches to addressing the problems placed on government's agenda.
4. **Policy adoption**—the formal selection of public policies through legislative, executive, judicial, and bureaucratic means.
5. **Budgeting**—the allocation of resources to provide for the proper implementation of public policies.
6. **Policy implementation**—the actual administration or application of public policies to their targets.
7. **Policy evaluation**—the determination of a policy's accomplishments, consequences, or shortcomings.

With this overview in mind, let's now look in more detail at the various stages of the policy process or cycle.

Problem Recognition and Definition

At any given time, there are many conditions that disturb or distress people, such as polluted air and water, the outsourcing of jobs overseas, natural disasters, the rising cost of college tuition, and possible terrorist attacks. All disturbing conditions do not automatically become problems in need of public policy solutions, however. Some of them may be accepted as trivial, inevitable, or beyond the control of government.

For a condition to become a problem, there must be some criterion—a standard or value—that leads people to believe that the condition does not have to be accepted and, further, that it is something with which government can deal effectively and appropriately. For example, natural disasters such as hurricanes are unlikely to be identified as a policy problem because there is little that government can do about them directly. The consequences of hurricanes—the human distress and property destruction that they bring—are another matter. Relief from the devastation of natural disasters can be a focus of government action, and agencies such as the Federal Emergency Management Agency (FEMA) have been set up to reduce these hardships. When these agencies fail to fulfill their roles, as FEMA did in the wake of Hurricane Katrina in 2005, the public requires answers for why government has not done its job.

Usually there is not a single, agreed-on definition of a problem. Indeed, political struggle often occurs at this stage because how the problem is defined helps determine what sort of action is appropriate. For example, if we define access to transportation for people with disabilities as a transportation problem, then an acceptable solution is to adapt the regular transportation system or establish other means of transport, such as a special van service. If we define access to transportation as a civil rights problem, however, then people with disabilities are entitled to equal access to the regular transportation system. The civil rights view triumphed with congressional passage of the Americans with Disabilities Act in 1990, which mandated that local and state governments must make transportation accessible to the elderly and to all people with disabilities.

Note that public policies themselves are frequently viewed as problems or the causes of other problems. Thus, for some people, gun control legislation is a solution to gun violence. To the National Rifle Association (NRA), however, any law that restricts gun ownership is a problem because the NRA views such laws as inappropriately infringing on an individual's constitutional right to keep and bear arms. To social conservatives, legal access to abortion is a problem; for social liberals, laws restricting abortion access fall into the problem category.

Agenda Setting

Once a problem is recognized and defined as such by a significant segment of society, it must be brought to the attention of public officials and it must secure a place on an **agenda**, a set of issues to be discussed or given attention. Every political community—national, state, and local—has a **systemic agenda**. The systemic agenda is essentially a discussion agenda; it comprises "all issues that are commonly perceived by the members of the political community as meriting public attention and as involving matters within the legitimate jurisdiction" of governments.[6] A **governmental** or **institutional agenda** includes only problems to which legislators or other public officials feel obliged to devote active and serious attention. Not all problems that attract the attention of officials are likely to have been widely discussed by the general public, and not all issues on the systemic agenda end up on the institutional agenda. Problems or issues (an issue emerges when disagreement exists over what should be done about a problem) may move onto an institutional agenda, whether from the systemic agenda or elsewhere, in several ways. These include crisis situations, political campaigns, and interest group lobbying, among many others.

Policy Formulation

Policy formulation is the crafting of appropriate and acceptable proposed courses of action to ameliorate or resolve public problems. It has both political and technical components. The political aspect of policy formulation involves determining generally what should be done to reduce acid rain, for example—whether standard setting and enforcement or emissions testing should be used. The technical facet involves correctly stating in specific language what one wants to authorize or accomplish, so as to adequately guide those who must implement policy and to prevent distortion of legislative intent. Political scientist Charles O. Jones suggests that formulation may take different forms.[7]

Routine formulation is "a repetitive and essentially changeless process of reformulating similar proposals within an issue area that is well established on the government agenda." For instance, the formulation of policy for veterans' benefits represents a standard process of drafting proposals similar to those established in the past.

Analogous formulation handles new problems by drawing on experience with similar problems in the past. What has been done in the past to cope with the activities of terrorists? What has been done in other states to deal with child abuse or divorce law reform?

Creative formulation involves attempts to develop new or unprecedented proposals that represent a departure from existing practices and that will better resolve a problem. For example, plans to develop an anti-missile defense system to shoot down incoming missiles represents a departure from previous defense strategies of mutual destruction.

Policy formulation may be undertaken by various players in the policy process: the president, presidential aides, agency officials, specially appointed task forces and commissions, interest groups, private research organizations (or "think tanks"), and legislators and their staffs. The people engaged in formulation are usually looking ahead toward policy adoption. Particular provisions may be included or excluded from a proposal in an attempt to enhance its likelihood of adoption.

Policy Adoption

Policy adoption is the approval of a policy proposal by the people with requisite authority, such as a legislature or chief executive. This approval gives the policy legal force. Because most public policies in the United States result from legislation, policy

agenda
A set of issues to be discussed or given attention.

systemic agenda
All public issues that are viewed as requiring governmental attention; a discussion agenda.

governmental (institutional) agenda
The changing list of issues to which governments believe they should address themselves.

policy formulation
The crafting of appropriate and acceptable proposed courses of action to ameliorate or resolve public problems.

policy adoption
The approval of a policy proposal by the people with the requisite authority, such as a legislature.

adoption frequently requires the building of majority coalitions necessary to secure the enactment of legislation.

In chapter 6, we discuss how power is diffused in Congress and how the legislative process comprises a number of roadblocks or obstacles that a bill must successfully navigate before it becomes law. A majority is needed to clear a bill through each of these obstacles; hence, not one majority but a series of majorities is needed for congressional policy adoption. To secure the needed votes, a bill may be watered down or modified at each of these decision points. Or, the bill may fail to win a majority at one of them and die, at least for the time being.

The adoption of major legislation requires much negotiation, bargaining, and compromise. In some instances, years or even decades may be needed to secure the enactment of legislation on a controversial matter. Congress considered federal aid to public education off and on over several decades before it finally won approval in 1965, for example. At other times, the approval process may move quickly.

Not all policy adoption necessitates formation of majority coalitions. Although a president has many aides and advisers and is bombarded with information and advice, the final decision to veto a bill passed by Congress rests with him.

Budgeting

Where the Money Goes

Most policies require money in order to be carried out; some policies, such as those providing income security, essentially involve the transfer of money from taxpayers to the government and back to individual beneficiaries. Funding for most policies and agencies is provided through the budgetary process. Whether a policy is well funded or poorly funded has a significant effect on its scope, impact, and effectiveness.

A policy can be nullified by a refusal to fund, which was the fate of the Homeownership and Opportunity for People Everywhere (Hope VI) program. In 2006, the Bush administration decided not to seek funds for HOPE VI, a program within the Department of Housing and Urban Development (HUD) that demolished obsolete and severely distressed public housing while introducing community service and self-sufficiency initiatives. President Bush had tried to eliminate HOPE VI twice before by not funding it, but each time Congress directed financial resources to HUD to keep the program alive. However, in 2006, Congress followed the president's lead, and HOPE VI was terminated.[8]

Other policies or programs often suffer from inadequate funding. Thus, the Occupational Safety and Health Administration (OSHA) can afford to inspect annually only a small fraction of the workplaces within its jurisdiction. Similarly, the Department of Housing and Urban Development has funds sufficient to provide rent subsidies only to approximately 20 percent of the eligible low-income families.

The budgetary process also gives the president and the Congress an opportunity to review the government's many policies and programs, to inquire into their administration, to appraise their value and effectiveness, and to exercise some influence on their conduct. Not all of the government's hundreds of programs are fully examined every year. But, over a period of several years, most programs come under scrutiny.

Policy Implementation

policy implementation
The process of carrying out public policy through governmental agencies and the courts.

Policy implementation is the process of carrying out public policies, most of which are implemented by administrative agencies. Some, however, are enforced in other ways. Product liability and product dating are two examples. Product liability laws such as the Food and Drug Act of 1906, the National Traffic and Motor Vehicle Safety Act of 1966, and the Consumer Product Safety Act of 1972 are typically enforced by lawsuits initiated in the courts by injured consumers or their survivors. In contrast, state product-dating laws are implemented more by voluntary compliance when grocers take out-of-date products off their shelves or when consumers choose

POLITICS NOW

Source: WASHINGTON POST   April 3, 2007   Page A1

Supreme Court Action on Clean Air

High Court Faults EPA Inaction on Emissions

ROBERT BARNES AND JULIET EILPERIN

The Supreme Court rebuked the Bush administration yesterday for refusing to regulate greenhouse gas emissions, siding with environmentalists in the Court's first examination of the phenomenon of global warming. The Court ruled 5 to 4 that the Environmental Protection Agency violated the Clean Air Act by improperly declining to regulate new-vehicle emissions standards to control the pollutants that scientists say contribute to global warming.

"EPA has offered no reasoned explanation for its refusal to decide whether greenhouse gases cause or contribute to climate change," Justice John Paul Stevens wrote for the majority. The agency "identifies nothing suggesting that Congress meant to curtail EPA's power to treat greenhouse gases as air pollutants," the opinion continued.

The issue at stake in the case, one of two yesterday that the Court decided in favor of environmentalists, is somewhat narrow. But environmentalists and some lawmakers said it could serve as a turning point, placing new pressure on the Bush administration to address global warming. The Natural Resources Defense Council said in a statement that the ruling "repudiates the Bush administration's do-nothing policy on global warming," undermining the government's refusal to view carbon dioxide as an air pollutant subject to EPA regulation.

The ruling could also lend important authority to efforts by the states either to force the federal government to reduce greenhouse gas emissions or to be allowed to do it themselves. New York is leading an effort to strengthen regulations on power-plant emissions. California has passed a law seeking to cut carbon dioxide emissions from automobiles starting in 2009; its regulations have been adopted by 10 other states and may soon be adopted by Maryland.

The decision in *Commonwealth of Massachusetts et al. v. Environmental Protection Agency* et al. also reinforced the division on the Supreme Court, with its four liberal members in the majority and its four most conservative members dissenting. Justice Anthony M. Kennedy's role as the key justice in this term's 5 to 4 decisions was again on display, as he sided with Stevens, Stephen G. Breyer, Ruth Bader Ginsburg and David H. Souter.

The case dates from 1999, when the International Center for Technology Assessment and other groups petitioned the EPA to set standards for greenhouse gas emissions for new vehicles. Four years later, the EPA declined, saying that it lacked authority to regulate greenhouse gases and that even if it did, it might not choose to because of "numerous areas of scientific uncertainty" about the causes and effects of global warming. Massachusetts, along with other states and cities, took the agency to court.

The Court majority said that the EPA clearly had the authority to regulate the emissions and that its "laundry list" of reasons for not doing so were not based in the law. "We need not and do not reach the question whether on remand EPA must make an endangerment finding.... We hold only that EPA must ground its reasons for actions or inaction in the statute," Stevens wrote.

Chief Justice John G. Roberts Jr. wrote one dissent, which was joined by Justices Samuel A. Alito Jr., Antonin Scalia and Clarence Thomas. He said that global warming may be a "crisis," even "the most pressing environmental problem of our time," but that it is an issue for Congress and the executive branch. He said the Court's majority used "sleight-of-hand" to even grant Massachusetts the standing to sue.

Scalia wrote another dissent, which Roberts and others also joined, saying the EPA had done its duty when it considered the petition and decided not to act. He said the Court "has no business substituting its own desired outcome for the reasoned judgment of the responsible agency."

Discussion Questions

1. *In the* Massachusetts v. EPA *(2007) decision, there was significant disagreement among the Supreme Court justices about the role of the courts in requiring the EPA to regulate greenhouse gases. Do you agree with the Court's decision in this case? What is the primary reason you support or oppose this decision?*

2. *The Clean Air Act and its primary amendments were passed before global warming and climate change had become widely accepted scientific views. Should the courts order an agency to interpret older laws to apply to current concerns, or is it the responsibility of Congress to update the laws? Explain your reasoning.*

3. *Should state governments have the ability to use the federal courts to require federal agencies to change the way they interpret acts of Congress? Why or why not?*

not to buy food products after the use dates stamped on them expire. The courts also get involved in implementation when they are called on to interpret the meaning of legislation, review the legality of agency rules and actions, and determine whether institutions such as prisons and mental hospitals conform to legal and constitutional standards. (To learn more, see Politics Now: Supreme Court Action on Clean Air.)

Administrative agencies may be authorized to use a number of techniques to implement the public policies within their jurisdictions. These techniques can be categorized as authoritative, incentive, capacity, or hortatory, depending on the behavioral assumptions on which they are based.[9]

Authoritative techniques for policy implementation rest on the notion that people's actions must be directed or restrained by government in order to prevent or eliminate activities or products that are unsafe, unfair, evil, or immoral. Consumer products must meet certain safety regulations, and radio stations can be fined heavily or have their broadcasting licenses revoked if they broadcast obscenities. Many government agencies have authority to issue rules and set standards to regulate such matters as meat and food processing, the discharge of pollutants into the environment, the healthfulness and safety of workplaces, and the safe operation of commercial airplanes. Compliance with these standards is determined by inspection and monitoring, and penalties may be imposed on people or companies that violate the rules and standards set forth in a particular policy. For example, under Title IX, the federal government can terminate funds to colleges or universities that discriminate against female students. Its detractors sometimes stigmatize this pattern of action as "command and control regulation," although in practice it often involves much education, bargaining, and persuasion in addition to the exercise of authority. In the case of Title IX, for instance, the Department of Education will try to negotiate with a school to bring it into compliance before funding is terminated.

Incentive techniques for policy implementation encourage people to act in their own best interest by offering payoffs or financial inducements to get them to comply with public policies. Such policies may provide tax deductions to encourage charitable giving or the purchase of alternative fuel vehicles such as hybrid automobiles. Farmers receive subsidies to make their production (or nonproduction) of wheat, cotton, and other goods more profitable. Conversely, sanctions such as high taxes may discourage the purchase and use of such products as tobacco or liquor, and pollution fees may reduce the discharge of pollutants by making this action more costly to businesses.

Capacity techniques provide people with information, education, training, or resources that will enable them to participate in desired activities. The assumption underlying the provision of these techniques is that people have the incentive or desire to do what is right but lack the capacity to act accordingly. Job training may enable able-bodied people to find work, and accurate information on interest rates will enable people to protect themselves against interest-rate gouging. Financial assistance can help the needy acquire better housing and warmer winter coats and perhaps allow them to lead more comfortable lives.

Hortatory techniques encourage people to comply with policy by appealing to people's "better instincts" in an effort to get them to act in desired ways. In this instance, the policy implementers assume that people decide how to act according to their personal values and beliefs. During the Reagan administration, First Lady Nancy Reagan implored young people to "Just say no" to drugs. Hortatory techniques also include the use of highway signs displaying slogans like "Don't Be a Litterbug" and "Don't Mess with Texas" to discourage littering. Campaigns like "Smokey the Bear's 'Only You Can Prevent Forest Fires'" are meant to encourage compliance with fire and safety regulations in national parks and forests.

Effective administration of public policies depends partly on whether an agency is authorized to use appropriate implementation techniques. Many other factors also come into play, including the clarity and consistency of policies' statutory mandates, adequacy of funding, political support, and the will and skill of agency personnel. Often government will turn to a combination of authoritative, incentive, capacity, and hortatory approaches to reach their goals. For example, public health officials employ all of these tools in their efforts to reduce tobacco use. These techniques include laws prohibiting smoking in public places, taxes on the sales of tobacco products, warning labels on packs of cigarettes, and anti-smoking commercials on television. There is no easy formula that will guarantee successful policy implementation; in practice, many policies only partially achieve their goals.

Policy Evaluation

Practitioners of **policy evaluation** seek to determine what a policy is actually accomplishing. They may also try to determine whether a policy is being fairly or efficiently administered. Policy evaluation may be conducted by a variety of players: congressional committees, through investigations and other oversight activities; presidential commissions; administrative agencies themselves; university researchers; private research organizations, such as the Brookings Institution; and the Government Accountability Office (GAO), formerly named the General Accounting Office.

The GAO, created in 1921, is an important evaluator of public policies. Every year, the GAO conducts hundreds of studies of government agencies and programs, either at the request of members of Congress or on its own initiative. The titles of two of its 2008 evaluations convey a notion of the breadth of its work: "Biosurveillance: Preliminary Observations on Department of Homeland Security's Biosurveillance Initiatives" and "Influenza Pandemic: Federal Agencies Should Continue to Assist States to Address Gaps in Pandemic Planning."

Social scientists and qualified investigators design studies to measure the societal impact of programs and to determine whether these programs are achieving their specified goals or objectives. The national executive departments and agencies often have officials and units responsible for policy evaluation; so do state governments. Evaluation research and studies can stimulate attempts to modify or terminate policies and thus restart the policy process. Legislators and administrators may formulate and advocate amendments designed to correct problems or shortcomings in a policy. In 1988, for example, legislation was adopted to correct weaknesses in the enforcement of the Fair Housing Act of 1968, which banned discrimination in the sale or rental of most housing. Policies are also terminated as a result of the evaluation process; for example, through the Airline Deregulation Act of 1978, Congress eliminated the Civil Aeronautics Board and its program of economic regulation of commercial airlines. This action was taken on the assumption that competition in the marketplace would better protect the interests of airline users. Competition indeed reduced the cost of flying on many popular routes.

The demise of programs is relatively rare, however; more often, a troubled program is modified or allowed to limp along because it provides a popular service. For example, the nation's passenger rail system, Amtrak, remains dependent on government funds. While its northeastern lines are financially self-sufficient, many of Amtrak's longer distance routes are not able to operate without significant government subsidies. Nevertheless, the more rural routes remain popular with legislators in western states, and thus Amtrak continues to receive federal support.[10]

While policy evaluation has become more rigorous, systematic, and objective over the past few decades, judgments by policy makers still are often based on anecdotal and fragmentary evidence rather than on solid facts and thorough analyses. Sometimes a program is judged to be a good program simply because it is politically popular or fits the ideological beliefs of an elected official. Having described the policy-making process on a general level, we now turn our attention to the evolution of domestic policies related to income security and health care.

policy evaluation
The process of determining whether a course of action is achieving its intended goals.

Social Welfare Policy

Social welfare policy is a term that designates a broad and varied range of government programs designed to protect people from want and deprivation, to improve

social welfare policy
Government programs designed to improve quality of life.

their health and physical well-being, provide educational and employment training opportunities, and otherwise enable them to lead more satisfactory, meaningful, and productive lives. The issue of who is deserving and what they deserve is at the heart of the debate over social welfare programs. Over time, the focus of social welfare programs has expanded from providing minimal assistance to the destitute to helping the working poor attain a degree of security and provide for their health, nutrition, income security, employment, and education needs. Most social welfare programs in the United States are largely a product of the twentieth century.

The Origins of Social Welfare

As U.S. society became more urban and industrial, self-sufficiency declined and people became more interdependent and reliant on a vast system of production, distribution, and exchange. The ostentation of the very wealthy and the suffering of the many on the bottom rung of the social ladder created fears of an economic revolution if the gap between rich and poor was not reduced. Some industrialized European countries, where class-consciousness ran stronger, established new social welfare programs around this time, with those governments assuming more of a direct responsibility for the well-being of their people. The Great Depression of the 1930s reinforced the notion that hard work alone would not provide economic security for everyone, and it showed that state governments and private charities lacked adequate resources to alleviate economic want and distress. Beginning with the Social Security Act of 1935, which we will describe below, a variety of national programs aimed at providing economic security have emerged.

Social Security Act
A 1935 law that established old-age insurance (Social Security) and assistance for the needy, children, and others, and unemployment insurance.

INCOME SECURITY   Passage of the **Social Security Act** in 1935 represented the beginning of a permanent welfare state in America and a dedication to the ideal of greater equity.[11] The act consisted of three major components: (1) old-age insurance (what we now call Social Security); (2) public assistance for the needy, aged, blind, and families with dependent children (later, people with disabilities were added); and, (3) unemployment insurance and compensation.

The core of the Social Security Act was the creation of a compulsory old-age insurance program funded equally by employer and employee contributions. The act imposed a payroll tax, collected from the employer, equal to 1 percent from both employee and employer starting in 1937. The Social Security Act also addressed the issue of unemployment, requiring employers to pay 3 percent of a worker's salary into an insurance fund. If workers became unemployed, they could draw from this fund for a given period of time. During the time laid-off workers drew from the insurance fund, they were required to seek other jobs. This

Photo courtesy: Bettmann/CORBIS

What policy initiatives came about during the Great Depression? The Great Depression, beginning in late 1929 and continuing throughout the 1930s, dramatically pointed out to average Americans the need for a broad social safety net and gave rise to a host of income, health, and finance legislation.

component of the Social Security Act served two basic purposes: on the individual level, it provided income to laid-off workers, expanding the social safety net; on the broader economic level, it acted as an automatic stabilizer, increasing the amount of money in the nation's economy when financial resources were scarce.

Social Security is credited with replacing a piecemeal collection of local programs with a national system. This national system was widely praised but also was perceived to contain two basic flaws: the payroll tax was regressive (the tax fell disproportionately on lower-income contributors), and some workers were excluded from the program. Over the next decades, Social Security was expanded to include a much greater percentage of American workers. The program also became one of the most successful and popular government programs. In the 1930s, poverty rates were highest among the elderly. Today, seniors have the lowest rate of poverty among any age group in the United States.

HEALTH CARE   Governments in the United States have long been active in the health care field. Local governments began to establish public health departments in the first half of the nineteenth century, and state health departments followed in the second half. Discoveries related to the causes of diseases and human ailments in the late nineteenth and early twentieth centuries led to significant advances in improving public health. Public sanitation and clean-water programs, pasteurization of milk, immunization programs, and other activities greatly reduced the incidence of infectious and communicable diseases. Public health policies have also been highly effective in reducing the incidence of infectious diseases such as measles, infantile paralysis (poliomyelitis), and smallpox. The increase in American life expectancy from forty-seven in 1900 to over seventy-eight in 2008 is tightly linked to public health programs.

Beginning in 1798 with the establishment of the National Marine Service (NMS) for "the relief of sick and disabled seamen," which was the forerunner of the Public Health Service, the national government has provided health care for some segments of the population. Repeated efforts have been made to expand health care coverage to all Americans, as discussed in the opening vignette. The current Medicare and Medicaid programs that sharply increased access to health care for both the elderly (in the case of Medicare) and the poor (in the case of Medicaid) were first passed by Congress in 1965. The share of health care expenditures financed by public spending rose from under 25 percent in 1960 to almost 40 percent in 1970. During this time, public expenditures on health care as a percent of total gross domestic product (GDP) rose by more than 100 percent, from 1.3 percent to 2.7 percent. Total expenditures rose from 5.3 percent of GDP in 1960 to 7.4 percent in 1970.[12]

Social Welfare

Income security and health care remain two key domestic policy areas that involve citizens, interest groups, and government. Both areas encompass many complex policies and programs. Although all levels of government (national, state, and local) are involved with the development and implementation of income security and health care policy, we emphasize the national government's role.

Income security programs protect people against loss of income because of retirement, disability, unemployment, or death or absence of the family breadwinner. Although cases of total deprivation are now rare, many people are unable to provide a minimally decent standard of living for themselves and their families. They are poor in a relative if not an absolute sense. In 2008, the poverty threshold for a four-person family unit was $21,200.[13]

Income security programs fall into two general categories. Social insurance programs are **non-means-based programs** that provide cash assistance to qualified beneficiaries. **Means-tested programs** require that people must have incomes below

Welfare Reform

non-means-based program
Program such as Social Security where benefits are provided irrespective of the income or means of recipients.

means-tested program
Income security program intended to assist those whose incomes fall below a designated level.

specified levels to be eligible for benefits. Benefits of means-tested programs may come either as cash or in-kind benefits, such as food stamps.

NON-MEANS-BASED PROGRAMS   Social insurance programs operate in a manner somewhat similar to private automobile or life insurance. Contributions are made by or on behalf of the prospective beneficiaries, their employers, or both. When a person becomes eligible for benefits, the monies are paid as a matter of right, regardless of the person's wealth or unearned income (for example, from dividends and interest payments).

Old Age, Survivors, and Disability Insurance   As mentioned earlier, this program began as old-age insurance, providing benefits only to retired workers. Its coverage was extended to survivors of covered workers in 1939 and to the permanently disabled in 1956. Customarily called Social Security, it is not, as many people believe, a pension program that collects contributions from workers, invests them, and then returns them with interest to beneficiaries. Instead, the current workers pay taxes that directly go toward providing benefits for retirees. In 2008, an employee tax of 7.65 percent was levied on the first $102,000 of wages or salaries and placed into the Social Security Trust Fund. An equal tax was levied on employers. Nearly all employees and most of the self-employed (who pay a 15.3 percent tax) are now covered by Social Security. People earning less than $102,000 pay a greater share of their income into the Social Security Fund, since wages or salaries above that amount are not subject to the Social Security tax. The Social Security tax therefore is considered a regressive tax because it captures larger proportions of incomes from lower-and middle-income individuals than from high-wage earners.

People born before 1938 are eligible to receive full retirement benefits at age sixty-five. The full retirement age gradually rises until it reaches sixty-seven for persons born in 1960 or later. Individuals can opt to receive reduced benefits as early as age sixty-two. In November 2007, the average monthly Social Security benefit for retired workers was $1,053.70, with the maximum monthly benefit set at $2,116. Social Security is the primary source of income for many retirees and keeps them from living in poverty. However, eligible people are entitled to Social Security benefits regardless of how much *unearned* income (for example, dividends and interest payments) they also receive. Beginning with a change in 2004, Social Security recipients between the age of sixty-two and sixty-four had one dollar withheld from their earnings for every two dollars earned after a specific amount of earnings was reached. For recipients age sixty-five, one dollar was withheld for every three dollars earned after the threshold was reached. Social Security recipients older than sixty-five were allowed to earn an unlimited amount of money without any reduction of Social Security benefits.[14]

The trustees of the Social Security Trust Fund predicted in 2006 that, starting in about 2010, Social Security Fund expenditures would begin to increase rapidly as the Baby Boom generation (roughly speaking, those born in the two decades immediately following World War II) reached retirement age. It was estimated that by 2017, payments would exceed revenues collected. Viewing costs and revenues as a proportion of taxable payrolls (to correct for the value of the dollar over time), one can see that projected revenues remain relatively constant over time, while costs are projected to rise substantially. (To learn more about social security costs and revenues, see Figure 17.2.) Aside from the retirement of Baby Boomers, other factors pressuring the fund include increased life expectancies and low fertility rates. In other words, Americans are living longer and having fewer children who as workers will contribute to the Social Security Fund.

After George W. Bush was elected in 2000, he promoted his vision of privatizing Social Security through investments in stocks and bonds, and he created a President's Commission to Strengthen Social Security. This panel consisted of sixteen members, with Daniel Patrick Moynihan, the former Democratic senator from New York, and Richard Parsons, co-chief operating officer of AOL Time Warner, serving as co-chairs. By the end of 2001, the panel disappointed proponents of privatization with their set

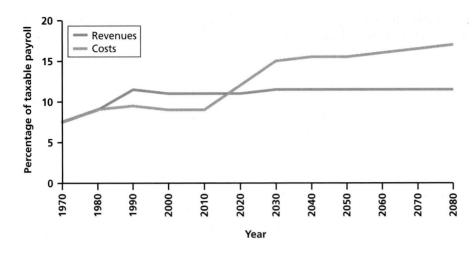

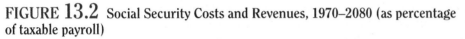

FIGURE 13.2 Social Security Costs and Revenues, 1970–2080 (as percentage of taxable payroll)

Source: Social Security Administration, Status of the Social Security and Medicare Programs, Summary of the 2004 Annual Reports, www.ssa.gov.

of recommendations. The panel provided three options: (1) allowing workers to invest up to 2 percentage points of their payroll tax in personal accounts; (2) allowing workers to invest up to 4 percentage points of their payroll tax in personal accounts, to a maximum of $1,000 per year; and, (3) allowing workers to invest an additional 1 percent of their earnings in a personal account. Proponents of privatization had hoped for a single recommendation. Congress ignored the recommendations, no doubt influenced by the slump in the stock market and unpopular panel observations. The panel noted they believed that ultimately benefits would have to be cut or more money would have to be assigned to the program. Following his reelection in 2004, Bush reaffirmed his support for Social Security privatization.

Despite controlling both houses of Congress and the presidency after the 2004 elections, Republicans were unable to achieve any substantial reform of Social Security. This may be explained by continued public skepticism regarding President Bush's plan. According to a 2005 poll by the Pew Research Center for the People and the Press, only about four in ten Americans supported the concept of individualized accounts as part of the Social Security system.[15] Given the central role that these accounts played in Bush's reform efforts, it was not a surprise that his plan was unable to gather the necessary support in Congress. Simply put, many Republican legislators could not risk aligning themselves with the president because of the possibility of a backlash at the polls. In fact, Democratic candidates used President Bush's support for Social Security privatization against their Republican opponents with some success in the 2006 midterm elections. Their takeover of both houses of Congress in 2007 and the 2008 financial meltdown meant an end—for the time-being, at least—to Republican efforts to significantly reform or privatize the program.

Unemployment Insurance As mentioned earlier, unemployment insurance is financed by a payroll tax paid by employers. The program pays benefits to workers who are covered by the government plan and are unemployed through no fault of their own. The Social Security Act provided that if a state set up a comparable program and levied a payroll tax for its support, most of the federal tax would be forgiven (that is, not collected). The states were thus accorded a choice: either set up and administer an acceptable unemployment program, or let the national government handle the matter. Within a short time, all states had their own programs.

Analyzing Visuals | Unemployment Rates by State

This map shows the rates of unemployment across the United States in the summer of 2008. Based on your analysis of this map and your understanding of the chapter discussion, answer the following critical thinking questions:

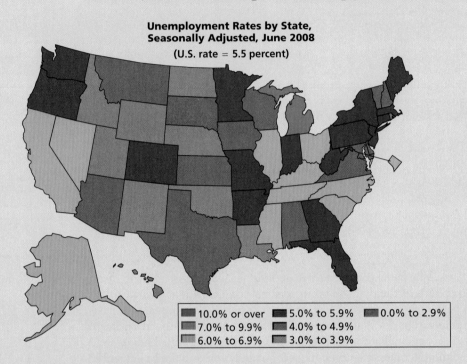

**Unemployment Rates by State,
Seasonally Adjusted, June 2008**
(U.S. rate = 5.5 percent)

- 10.0% or over
- 7.0% to 9.9%
- 6.0% to 6.9%
- 5.0% to 5.9%
- 4.0% to 4.9%
- 3.0% to 3.9%
- 0.0% to 2.9%

WHICH states are suffering from the highest levels of unemployment, and why do you think that is so?

WHY do unemployment rates vary substantially from state to state?

DO you detect any similarities among states with the lowest rates of unemployment?

DO you think the unemployment rate played a role in the 2008 presidential elections?

Source: Bureau of Labor Statistics, Local Area Unemployment Statistics, www.bls.gov/web/laumstrk.htm.

Unemployment insurance covers employers of four or more people, but not part-time or occasional workers. Benefits are paid to unemployed workers who have neither been fired for personal faults nor quit their jobs, and who are willing and able to accept suitable employment. State unemployment programs differ considerably in levels of benefits, length of benefit payment, and eligibility for benefits. For example, in 2008, average weekly benefit payments ranged from $404 in Hawaii and $388 in Massachusetts to $179 in Mississippi.[16] In general, less generous programs exist in southern states, where labor unions are less powerful. Nationwide, only about half of the people who are counted as unemployed at any given time are receiving benefits.

In June 2008, the unemployment rate stood at 5.5 percent. (To learn more, see Analyzing Visuals: Unemployment Rates by State.) But, there are considerable differences across the nation. In Utah and Wyoming, unemployment rates were slightly above 3 percent, while levels of unemployment in Michigan and Rhode Island were over 7 percent. Unemployment rates also vary considerably across races and by age. For example, levels of unemployment for African American males are approximately twice that of whites, with unemployment rates of 15 percent or greater common among young African American males.[17]

MEANS-TESTED PROGRAMS Means-tested income security programs are intended to help the needy; that is, individuals or families whose incomes fall below specified levels, such as a percentage of the official poverty line. Included in the means-tested categories are the Supplemental Security Income (SSI), Temporary Assistance for Needy Families (TANF), and food stamp programs.

Supplemental Security Income This program began under the Social Security Act as a grant-in-aid program to help the needy aged or blind. Grants were financed jointly by the national and state governments, but the states played a major role in determining standards of eligibility and benefit levels. In 1950, Congress extended coverage to needy people who were permanently and totally disabled.

With the support of the Nixon administration, Congress reconfigured the grant programs into the Supplemental Security Income (SSI) program in 1974. Primary funding for SSI is provided by the national government, which prescribes uniform benefit levels throughout the nation. To be eligible, beneficiaries can own only a limited amount of possessions. In 2008, monthly payments were about $477 for an individual and $720 for a married couple.[18] The states may choose to supplement the federal benefits, and forty-eight states do.

For years, this program generated little controversy, as modest benefits go to people who obviously cannot provide for themselves. However, there was a growing perception among conservatives as well as Democratic President Bill Clinton that many social welfare programs were flawed. In 1996, access to SSI and other programs was limited by legislation. Under George W. Bush's administration, funding for SSI has remained fairly stable, with about $38 billion directed to the program in fiscal year 2008.[19]

Family and Child Support In 1950, Aid to Families with Dependent Children (AFDC), the predecessor to the Temporary Assistance for Needy Families (TANF) program, was broadened to include not only dependent children without fathers but also mothers or other adults with whom dependent children were living. The AFDC rolls expanded greatly since 1960 because of the increasing numbers of children born to unwed mothers, the growing divorce rate, and the migration of poor people to cities, where they are more likely to apply for and be provided with benefits.

Photo courtesy: James Nubile/The Image Works

What is workfare? Workfare is a welfare strategy that gives adults the opportunity to learn skills that can lead to employment. Here, one workfare recipient tends to children at a day-care-center job.

Because of its clientele, the AFDC program was the focus of much controversy. Critics who pointed to the rising number of recipients claimed that it encouraged promiscuity, out-of-wedlock births, and dependency that resulted in a permanent class of welfare families. In what was hailed as the biggest shift in social policy since the Great Depression, a new welfare bill, the Personal Responsibility and Work Opportunity Reconciliation Act (PRWORA) of 1996, created the Temporary Assistance for Needy Families (TANF) program to replace AFDC. The shift from AFDC to TANF was meant to foster a new philosophy of work rather than welfare dependency. The most fundamental change enacted in the new law was the switch in funding for welfare from an open-ended matching program to a block grant to the states. PRWORA also gave states more flexibility in reforming their welfare programs toward work-oriented goals.

Significant features of the welfare plan included: (1) a requirement for single mothers with a child over five years of age to work within two years of receiving benefits; (2) a provision that unmarried mothers under the age of eighteen were required to live with an adult and attend school in order to receive welfare benefits; (3) a five-year lifetime limit for aid from block grants; (4) a requirement that mothers must provide information about a child's father in order to receive full welfare payments; (5) cutting off food stamps and Supplemental Security Income for legal immigrants; (6) cutting off cash welfare benefits and food stamps for convicted drug felons; and, (7) limiting food stamps to three months in a three-year period for persons eighteen to fifty years old who are not raising children and not working.[20]

In 2002, the Bush administration released a detailed plan for TANF reauthorization. The plan proposed to strengthen work rules to ensure that all welfare families were engaged in meaningful activities that would lead to self-sufficiency. These meaningful activities included not only work but also allowed "individuals participating in substance abuse treatment, rehabilitative services, and work-related training" to qualify for TANF benefits.[21] The administration proposed increasing the proportion of TANF families that would have to participate in work activities and increasing the number of hours of required work.[22] Between 2002 and 2006, Congress passed a number of extensions to keep the TANF program in operation, with President Bush signing a reauthorization in February 2006. This reauthorization did not address the issue of increased work hours but did strengthen enforcement of child support provisions.[23]

Food Stamp Program The initial food stamp program (1939–1943) was primarily an effort to expand domestic markets for farm commodities. Food stamps provided the poor with the ability to purchase more food, thus increasing the demand for American agricultural produce. Attempts to reestablish the program during the Eisenhower administration failed, but in 1961, a $381,000 pilot program began under the Kennedy administration. It was made permanent in 1964 and extended nationwide in 1974. Although strongly opposed by Republicans in Congress, Democrats put together a majority coalition when urban members agreed to support a wheat and cotton price support program wanted by rural and southern Democrats in return for their support of food stamps.

In the beginning, recipients had to pay cash for food stamps, but this practice ceased in 1977. Benefiting low-income families, the program has helped to combat hunger and reduce malnutrition. Food stamps went to more than 26 million beneficiaries in 2007 at a cost of $33 billion. The average participant received $95 worth of stamps per month.[24] The national government operates several other food programs for the needy. These programs include a special nutritional program for women, infants, and children (WIC); a school breakfast and lunch program; and an emergency food assistance program.

entitlement program
Income security program to which all those meeting eligibility criteria are entitled.

THE EFFECTIVENESS OF INCOME SECURITY PROGRAMS Many of the income security programs, including Social Security, Supplemental Security Income, and food stamps, are **entitlement programs**. That is, Congress sets eligibility criteria—such as age, income level, or unemployment—and those who meet the criteria are legally "entitled" to receive benefits. Unlike such programs as public housing, military construction, and space exploration, spending for entitlement programs is mandatory. Year after year, funds *must* be provided for them unless the laws creating the programs are changed. This feature of entitlement programs has made it difficult to control spending for them.

Income security programs have not eliminated poverty and economic dependency, but they have improved the lives of large numbers of people. Millions of elderly people in the United States would be living below the poverty line were it not for Social Security. The economic crisis of 2008 is likely to lead to renewed debates about the best way for national, state, and local governments to help struggling Americans.

Health Care

Currently, many millions of people receive medical care through the medical branches of the armed forces, the hospitals and medical programs of the Department of Veterans Affairs, and the Indian Health Service. The government spent $69 billion in 2007 for health and human services and estimated that it would spend $71 billion in the 2009 fiscal year for health and human services, the construction and operation of facilities, and the salaries of doctors and other medical personnel.[25]

Comparing Health Systems

The national government finances most medical research, primarily through the National Institutes of Health (NIH). The National Cancer Institute; the National Heart, Lung, and Blood Institute; the National Institute of Allergy and Infectious Diseases; and the other NIH institutes and centers spend more than $10 billion annually on biomedical research. NIH scientists and scientists at universities, medical schools, and other research facilities receiving NIH research grants conduct the research. Most Americans accept and support extensive government spending on medical research. Congress, in fact, often appropriates more money for medical research than the president recommends.

Comparing Welfare Systems

The United States spends significant sums of money on public health, a larger proportion of its gross domestic product than most other industrialized democracies. Much of the increase in funding for health care has gone to the Medicare and Medicaid programs. Reasons for growth in medical spending include the public's increased expectations, increased demand for services, advances in health care technology, the perception of health care as a right, and the third-party payment system.[26] In many ways the issue of soaring health care costs underlies most of the current problems affecting the American health care system and limits the range of alternatives available to government officials.

A quick review of the increase in health care costs over the past fifteen years helps to demonstrate the magnitude of the problem. Per capita spending on health care in the United States increased by 123 percent in the fourteen-year period between 1990 and 2004. But, per capita income in America increased by only 59 percent during the same time frame, meaning that individual financial resources grew at less than half the rate of the cost of health care. Behind this dramatic increase in health care costs are a number of important factors. First, more people are living longer and are requiring costly and extensive care in their declining years. Second, the range and sophistication of diagnostic practices and therapeutic treatments, which are often quite expensive, have increased. Third, the expansion of private health insurance, along with Medicare and Medicaid, has reduced the direct costs of health care to most people and increased the demand for services. More people, in short, can afford care. They may also be less aware of the costs of care. Fourth, the costs of health care have also increased because of its higher quality and because labor costs have outpaced productivity in the provision of hospital care.[27] Fifth, U.S. health care focuses less on preventing illnesses and more on curing them, a more costly approach.

While all areas of health care experienced significant increases in cost since 1990, there were areas within the broader health field that underwent the sharpest spike in prices. Prescription drug costs increased at rates even greater than those for physicians and hospital stays through 2005, thus increasing the pressure for the federal government to provide some prescription drug benefits as part of Medicare. Because government health care programs such as Medicare and Medicaid are directly affected by soaring prices, policy makers have been challenged to keep these programs fully funded. In 2008, national expenditures for both the Medicare and Medicaid programs were $661 billion. Projected increases for Medicare and Medicaid are expected to grow between 2008 and 2013 at a faster pace than other key areas of the federal budget.

Medicare
The federal program established in the Lyndon B. Johnson administration that provides medical care to elderly Social Security recipients.

MEDICARE **Medicare**, which covers persons receiving Social Security benefits, is administered by the Center for Medicare and Medicaid Services in the Department of Health and Human Services. Medicare coverage has two components, Parts A and B. Benefits under Part A come to all Americans automatically at age sixty-five, when they qualify for Social Security. It covers hospitalization, some skilled nursing care, and home health services. Individuals have to pay about $700 in medical bills before they are eligible for Part A benefits. Medicare is financed by a payroll tax of 1.45 percent paid by both employees and employers on the total amount of one's wages or salary.

Part B, which is optional, covers payment for physicians' services, outpatient and diagnostic services, X-rays, and some other items not covered by Part A. Excluded from coverage are eyeglasses, hearing aids, and dentures. This portion of the Medicare program is financed partly by monthly payments from beneficiaries and partly by general tax revenues.

In 2003, President Bush signed into law the Medicare Prescription Drug Improvement and Modernization Act, which since January 2006 provides some prescription drug coverage for seniors who opt to participate. Participants pay a monthly premium of approximately $35; after a $250 annual deductible, they have 75 percent of their prescription costs paid for. For those whose annual prescription drug costs exceed $5,100, the new program pays 95 percent of prescription costs over that amount. There are some odd gaps in the prescription drug coverage, however. Many congressional Democrats found the bill too weak in helping the average senior and claimed its primary beneficiaries would be the pharmaceutical and insurance industries. But, even some Democrats voted for its final passage, as they agreed with the leaders of the American Association of Retired Persons (AARP) that it was time to do something, and this seemed the only plan with a chance to pass.[28]

The addition of the prescription drug benefit troubled many conservatives because of the added costs it is projected to impose on a system that, whatever its merits, is extraordinarily expensive. The actual costs of this new program were understated during the congressional debate, and that leads many to wonder how the federal budget can withstand the additional pressure. Attempts to limit or cap expenditures for the program have had only marginal effects. With millions of Baby Boomers set to retire in the next fifteen years, the system will be under even greater strain.

Medicaid
An expansion of Medicare, this program subsidizes medical care for the poor.

MEDICAID   Enacted into law at the same time as Medicare, the **Medicaid** program provides comprehensive health care, including hospitalization, physician services, prescription drugs, and long-term nursing-home care (unlike Medicare) to all who qualify as needy under TANF and SSI. In 1986, Congress extended Medicaid coverage to pregnant women and children in low-income families whose total earnings were less than 133 percent of the official poverty level. The states were also accorded the option of extending coverage to all pregnant women and to all children under one year of age in families with incomes below 185 percent of the poverty level. By 1993, twenty-nine states had chosen to provide this coverage. In 2008, Medicaid served over 58 million people at a cost of $204 billion.[29] Nursing facility services, in-patient general hospital services, home health services, and prescription drugs represented major categories of spending within the Medicaid program. The national government pays 50 to 79 percent of Medicaid costs, based on average per capita income, which awards more financial support to poor than to wealthy states. Each state is responsible for the administration of its own program and sets specific standards of eligibility and benefit levels for Medicaid recipients within the boundaries set by national guidelines. In some states, nearly all needy people are covered by Medicaid, while in others, only about one-third of the needy are protected. Some states also award coverage to the "medically indigent," that is, to people who do not qualify for welfare but for whom large medical expenses would constitute a severe financial burden.

While the average amount paid for by the states varies, the portion of state budgets going to Medicaid is similar—ever upward. If Medicaid expenditures continue to grow at their present rate, the proportion of funding that is available for other programs will be reduced.

Thinking Globally
Health Care Policy

All industrialized nations provide some kind of publicly funded health care. In Canada, universal health care is provided by private practitioners with partial or total government funding. In Finland, Spain, Israel, and Cuba, the government operates health care facilities and employs health care professionals. In the United States, the Veterans Health Administration and the medical departments of the U.S. Army, Navy, and Air Force are examples of health care systems funded and operated by the federal government.

- The United States does not offer publicly funded universal health care. Should it adopt such a program? Why or why not?
- What are the pros and cons of a health care system where the government operates the facilities and hires the health care providers?
- What countries are most likely to adopt publicly funded universal health care coverage? What characteristics do these countries have in common?

Toward Reform: Economic Policy

During the nation's first century, the states were responsible for managing economic affairs. The national government defined its economic role narrowly, although it did collect tariffs (taxes on imported goods), fund public improvements, and encourage private development. (To learn more, see The Living Constitution: The Sixteenth Amendment.) Congress became active in setting economic policy and enacting economic regulation only after people realized that the states alone could not solve the problems affecting the economy.

The Nineteenth Century

Although the U.S. economic system is a mixed free-enterprise system characterized by the private ownership of property, private enterprise, and marketplace competition, the national government has long played an important role in fostering economic development through its policies on taxes, tariffs, the use of public lands, and the creation of a national bank (see chapter 3). For much of the nineteenth century, however, national regulatory programs were few and were restricted to such tasks as steamboat inspection and the regulation of trade with American Indian tribes.

Following the Civil War, the United States entered a period of rapid economic growth. Small business owners, reformers, and farmers in the Midwest pressured the government to control these new forces. After nearly two decades of pressure from farmers, owners of small businesses, and reformers in the cities, Congress adopted the Interstate Commerce Act in 1887 to regulate the railroad industry. Enforced by the new Interstate Commerce Commission (ICC), the act required that railroad rates should be "just and reasonable."[30]

Three years later, Congress dealt with the problem of "trusts," the name given to large-scale, monopolistic businesses that dominated many industries, including oil, sugar, whiskey, salt, and meatpacking. The Sherman Anti-Trust Act of 1890 prohibits

The Living Constitution

The Congress shall have power to lay and collect taxes on incomes, from whatever source derived, without apportionment among the several States, and without regard to any census or enumeration.

SIXTEENTH AMENDMENT

Ratified on February 3, 1913, the Sixteenth Amendment modified the Article I prohibition against levying a "direct tax" on individual property, unless the tax in question addresses the rule of apportionment as set forth in Article I, sections 2 and 9. This amendment was yet another revision made to the Constitution in response to a U.S. Supreme Court decision, namely the 1895 *Pollock* v. *Farmers' Loan & Trust Co.*—a judgment in which a divided Court held that Congress could not tax incomes uniformly throughout the United States.

The authority to tax is one of the fundamental rights inherent in legitimate government, and it is the hallmark of good and just governance to tax citizens fairly and equitably. The Constitution gives the House of Representatives sole authority to originate revenue bills, since the Framers believed the House, as the institution that directly represents the people, should determine how taxes should be raised and apportioned. Indeed, during the ratification debates, concern was expressed in regard to the Senate's ability to amend revenue bills as being a potential means for unjust taxation, since the Senate would not directly represent the people in its political capacity.

As the nineteenth century drew to a close, the Supreme Court became aware that in the new industrial age, the *Pollock* decision could threaten national solvency. As a result, the Court began to redefine "direct taxation" so as to help the federal government adapt to the new era. For example, the Court held in 1911 that corporate income could be taxed as an "excise measured by income." And, in its first appraisal of the newly ratified Sixteenth Amendment, the Court began to view income taxes as a form of indirect taxation. The Sixteenth Amendment has thus guaranteed the federal government a consistent and continuous revenue stream, and it is up to the Congress and the president to ensure fair taxation for all Americans.

CRITICAL THINKING QUESTIONS

1. While the Sixteenth Amendment's authorization of the federal income tax has helped to increase the national government's powers, the federal tax system is often criticized in terms of its fairness. Are there alternatives to the current federal income tax system that would be fairer for the American people?

2. There have been calls to amend the Constitution in order to establish a fairer and simpler federal tax system. Should the Constitution be used to create the specific rules of the tax system, or should Congress be responsible for constructing the taxes employed by the federal government?

all restraints of trade, including price-fixing, bid-rigging, and market allocation agreements. It also prohibits all monopolization or attempts to monopolize, including domination of a market by one company or a few companies. The Interstate Commerce Act and the Sherman Anti-Trust Act were the key legislative responses of the national government to the new industrialization.

The Progressive Era

The Progressive movement drew much of its support from the middle class and sought to reform America's political, economic, and social systems. There was a desire

What was public sentiment toward big business in the late 1800s? Here, a political cartoonist depicts the perception that the U.S. government was dominated by various trusts in the nineteenth century.

to bring corporate power under the control of government and make it more responsive to democratic ends. Progressive administrations under presidents Theodore Roosevelt and Woodrow Wilson established or strengthened regulatory programs to protect consumers and to control railroads, business, and banking.

The Pure Food and Drug Act and the Meat Inspection Act, both enacted in 1906, marked the beginning of consumer protection as a major responsibility of the national government. These laws prohibited adulteration and mislabeling of food and drugs and set sanitary standards for the food industry.

The Depression and the New Deal marked a major turning point in U.S. history in general and in U.S. economic history in particular. During the 1930s, the **laissez-faire** state was replaced with an **interventionist state**, in which the government began to play an active and extensive role in guiding and regulating the private economy. Until the 1930s, the national government's role in the economy was consistent with a broad interpretation of laissez-faire doctrine in that the government mostly provided a framework of rules within which the economy was left alone to operate. The New Deal, however, established the national government as a major regulator of private businesses, as a provider of Social Security, and as ultimately responsible for maintaining a stable economy.

While the New Deal was not (and is not) without critics, most people today accept the notion that the government should play a role in the economy. The New Deal brought about a number of reforms in almost every area, including finance, agriculture, labor, and industry.

laissez-faire
A French term literally meaning "to allow to do, to leave alone." It is a hands-off governmental policy that is based on the belief that governmental involvement in the economy is wrong.

interventionist state
Alternative to the laissez-faire state; the government takes an active role in guiding and managing the private economy.

FINANCIAL REFORMS   Major New Deal banking laws included the Glass-Steagall Act (1933). The Glass-Steagall Act required the separation of commercial and investment banking and set up the Federal Deposit Insurance Corporation (FDIC) to insure bank deposits, originally for $5,000 per account. Legislation was also passed to control abuses in the stock markets. The Securities Act (1933) required that prospective investors be given full and accurate information about the stocks or securities being offered to them. The Securities Exchange Act (1934) created the Securities and Exchange Commission (SEC), an independent regulatory commission. The SEC was authorized to regulate the stock exchanges, enforce the Securities Act, and reduce the number of stocks bought on margin (that is, with borrowed money).

AGRICULTURE AND LABOR   During the New Deal, Congress passed several laws designed to boost farm income by restricting agriculture production in order to bring it into better balance with demand. At the same time, Congress passed the National Labor Relations Act. Better known as the Wagner Act after its sponsor, Senator Robert Wagner (D–NY), this statute guaranteed workers' rights to organize and bargain collectively through unions of their own choosing. The act prohibited a series of "unfair labor practices," such as discriminating against employees because of their union activities. The National Labor Relations Board (NLRB) was created to carry out the act and to conduct elections to determine which union, if any, employees wanted to represent them. Unions prospered under the protection provided by the Wagner Act.

The last major piece of New Deal economic legislation passed by Congress was the Fair Labor Standards Act (FLSA) of 1938. Intended to protect the interests of low-paid workers, the law set twenty-five cents per hour and forty-four hours per week as initial minimum standards. Within a few years, wages rose to forty cents per hour, and hours declined to forty per week. The act also banned child labor.

INDUSTRY REGULATIONS   During the New Deal, Congress established new or expanded regulatory programs for several industries. The Federal Communications Commission (FCC), created in 1934 to replace the old Federal Radio Commission, was given extensive jurisdiction over the radio, telephone, and telegraph industries. The Civil Aeronautics Board (CAB) was put in place in 1938 to regulate the commercial aviation industry. The Motor Carrier Act of 1935 put the trucking industry under the jurisdiction of the Interstate Commerce Commission (ICC). Like railroad regulation, the regulation of industries such as trucking and commercial aviation extended to such matters as entry into the business, routes of service, and rates.

Economic and Social Regulations

economic regulation
Government regulation of business practices, industry rates, routes, or areas serviced by particular industries.

Economists and political scientists frequently distinguish between economic regulation and social regulation. **Economic regulation** focuses on such matters as control of entry into a business, prices or rates businesses charge, and service routes or areas. Economic regulation is usually tailored to the conditions of particular industries, such as railroads or stock exchanges. In contrast, **social regulation** sets standards for the quality and safety of products and the conditions under which goods are produced and services rendered. Social regulation strives to protect and enhance the quality of life.

social regulation
Government regulation of the quality and safety of products as well as the conditions under which goods and services are produced.

Most of the regulatory programs established through the 1950s fell into the category of economic regulation. From the mid-1960s to the mid-1970s, however, the national government passed social regulatory legislation affecting consumer protection, health and safety, and environmental protection. Congress based this legislation on its commerce clause authority.

As a consequence of this flood of social regulation, many industries that previously had limited dealings with government found they now had to comply with government regulation in the conduct of their operations. For example, the automobile industry, which previously had been lightly touched by anti-trust, labor relations, and other general statutes, found that its products were now affected by motor vehicle emissions standards and federally mandated safety standards.

Deregulation

deregulation
A reduction in market controls (such as price fixing, subsidies, or controls on who can enter the field) in favor of market-based competition.

Deregulation is the reduction in market controls (such as price fixing, subsidies, or controls on who can enter the field) in favor of market-based competition. Advocates of deregulation contended that regulation often encouraged lack of competition and monopolistic exploitation, discrimination in services, and inefficiency in operation of regulated industries. For instance, regulatory standards meant that no new major commercial airline was permitted to enter the industry after the Civil Aeronautics Board (CAB) began to regulate the industry in 1938. Consequently, consumers paid higher prices for airfares and had fewer choices than they would in a more competitive market. Critics contended that regulatory commissions like the CAB and the Interstate Commerce Commission were more responsive to the interests of the regulated firms than to the public interest.

For some time, there were no changes in economic regulation despite these criticisms. In the mid-1970s, however, President Gerald R. Ford, seeing regulation as one cause of the high inflation that existed at the time, decided to make deregulation a major objective of his administration. Deregulation was also a high priority for Ford's successor, President Jimmy Carter, and legislation that deregulated commercial airlines, railroads, motor carriers, and financial institutions was enacted during Carter's term as president. All successive presidents have maintained an active deregulatory agenda, though the effects of deregulation have been mixed, as illustrated by the airline, communication, and agricultural sectors.

The Airline Deregulation Act of 1978 completely eliminated economic regulation of commercial airlines over several years. Although many new passenger carriers flocked into the industry when barriers to entry were first removed, they were unable to compete successfully with the existing major airlines. Consequently, there are now fewer major carriers than under the regulatory regime, although new airlines continue to emerge. Competition has lowered some passenger rates, but there is disagreement as to the extent to which passengers have benefited. For example, since enactment of the Airline Deregulation Act, small communities across the United States have been losing service as airlines make major cuts in their routes, despite government subsidies to help maintain service.[31]

As the government removed or modified long-standing regulations in other industries, there was public disagreement over who benefited the most. The landmark Telecommunications Act of 1996 deregulated the radio industry, allowing companies to own an unlimited number of stations nationwide. Deregulation strengthened the

Photo courtesy: Mark Wilson/Getty Images

How important is the chair of the Federal Reserve to the nation's economic well-being? Ben Bernanke, center, after President George W. Bush announced his nomination to replace Federal Reserve Board Chair Alan Greenspan, at left. In the midst of the 2008 economic crisis, Bernanke moved aggresively to stabilize the markets and reassure jittery investors.

Thinking Globally

Economic Freedom

We can learn how hospitable a country is to business by looking at the rankings of countries on the Economic Freedom of the World index prepared by the Economic Freedom network (www.freetheworld.com). Hong Kong has the highest rating for economic freedom, followed by Singapore. Nations with the least economic freedom include Zimbabwe, Myanmar (Burma), and Venezuela.

- According to the authors of the index, economic freedom is defined by personal choice, voluntary exchange, freedom to compete, and security of privately owned property. What other factors might help to define economic freedom around the world?
- Canada, Great Britain, and the United States all scored an 8.1 (out of 10) on the 2007 economic freedom index. Estonia, a former Soviet republic, scored an 8.0. Is it surprising that a formerly communist-controlled country ranks so closely to long-standing democracies in terms of its business climate? Why or why not?

position of efficient companies and drove the less efficient into bankruptcy. However, the resulting industry consolidation also resulted in fewer individual owners, less minority ownership, and less diversity of content.

Politicians and citizens alike have expressed concern about concentrated corporate ownership of the media. As Representative Maurice Hinchey (D–NY) wrote in February 2006, "Over the past three decades the number of major U.S. media companies fell by more than half; most of the survivors are controlled by fewer than ten huge media conglomerates."[32] Corporate corruption has also raised concerns about such powerful conglomerates.

In spite of the mixed record, economic deregulation has remained a top policy priority among American politicians. The same cannot be said of deregulation efforts in the social sphere. Strong support continues for social regulation to protect consumers, workers, and the environment. Moreover, in some areas in which economic deregulation occurred, there have been calls to "reregulate." This has occurred in the airline industry because of concern about safety and industry domination by a small number of companies. The subprime mortgage crisis that developed in 2007 and the severe economic downturn of 2008 brought new calls for reregulation in the financial sector.

Stabilizing the Economy

economic stability
A situation in which there is economic growth, rising national income, high employment, and steadiness in the general level of prices.

inflation
A rise in the general price levels of an economy.

recession
A short-term decline in the economy that occurs as investment sags, production falls off, and unemployment increases.

Economic stability is a condition in which there is economic growth, a rising national income, high employment, and a steadiness in the general level of prices. Conversely, economic instability involves either inflation or recession. **Inflation** occurs when there is too much demand for the available supply of goods and services, with the consequence that general price levels rise as buyers compete for the available supply. Prices may also rise if large corporations and unions have sufficient economic power to push prices and wages above competitive levels. A **recession** is marked by a decline in the economy. Investment sags, production falls off, and unemployment increases.

The government manages the economy through monetary and fiscal policies. Monetary policies influence the economy through changes in the money supply, while fiscal policies influence the behavior of consumers and businesses through government spending and taxing decisions.

monetary policy
A form of government regulation in which the nation's money supply and interest rates are controlled.

money
A system of exchange for goods and services that includes currency, coins, and bank deposits.

Board of Governors
In the Federal Reserve System, a seven-member board that sets member banks' reserve requirements, controls the discount rate, and makes other economic decisions.

MONETARY POLICY: CONTROLLING THE MONEY SUPPLY   The government conducts **monetary policy** by managing the nation's money supply and influencing interest rates. In an industrialized economy, all those making exchanges—consumers, businesses, and government—use money. That is, prices of goods and services are set in **money** units (dollars), and the amount of money in circulation influences the quantity of goods and services demanded, the number of workers hired, the decisions to build factories, and so on. Money is more than just the currency and coin in our pockets: it includes balances in our checkbooks, deposits in bank accounts, and the value of other assets.

The Federal Reserve System is responsible for changing the money supply. As it makes these changes, it attempts to promote economic stability. The **Board of Governors** has responsibility for the formation and implementation of monetary policy because of its ability to control the credit-creating and lending activities of the nation's banks. When individuals and corporations deposit their money in financial institutions such as commercial banks (which accept deposits and make loans) and savings and loan

Discovering Your Tax Burden

It's no secret that Americans complain about paying taxes. But, while few Americans relish filing a tax return, fewer still actually track the total tax burden placed on them by federal, state, and local governments. Income taxes, sales taxes, property taxes, municipal taxes, and wage taxes all contribute revenue that governments use to provide services for their citizens. The number and type of taxes that affect Americans vary dramatically, depending on where they live.

If you live in New Hampshire, for example, you don't pay any sales taxes, but you do pay some of the highest property taxes in the country. Drivers in San Francisco pay the highest taxes in the nation to fill up their gas tanks. In Chicago, smokers pay more taxes than any other Americans for engaging in that particular vice.

Identify the types of taxes that are levied in your state and municipality. Then, consider the following questions:

- At the Tax Foundation site www.taxfoundation.org, examine the data on taxes in your state and municipality. What taxes are placed on individuals in your municipality? How many of those taxes did you pay last year? What is the total amount of taxes that you paid last year, including income taxes, property taxes, excise taxes, and sales taxes?

- What benefits and services do you receive for the taxes that you pay? Consider local and state services (e.g., garbage collection, police and fire protection, education) and federal services (e.g., health care and income security). Do you believe that the benefits of government are worth the financial impact of the taxes you pay? Why or why not?

- To learn more about debates related to tax policy, go to the following Web sites: www.taxpolicycenter.org, a joint effort sponsored by the Urban Institute and Brookings Institution; www.taxfoundation.org, the site of a tax research organization based in Washington, D.C.; www.atr.org, site of Americans for Tax Reform, a conservative, anti-tax lobbying organization; www.americanprogress.org, where the Center for American Progress, a liberal think tank, offers tax policy information in the issues section.

---

associations, these deposits serve as the basis for loans to borrowers. In effect, the loaning of money creates new deposits or financial liabilities—new money that did not previously exist. Created in 1913 to adjust the money supply to the needs of agriculture, commerce, and industry, the Federal Reserve System comprises the Federal Reserve Board (FRB—formally, the Board of Governors of the Federal Reserve System; informally, "the Fed"), the Federal Open Market Committee (FOMC), the twelve Federal Reserve Banks in regions throughout the country, and other member banks.[33]

Monetary authority is allocated to the FRB, the Federal Reserve Bank boards of directors, and the FOMC. In actuality, however, all three are dominated by the FRB and its chair. Public officials and the financial community pay great attention to the utterances of the Fed's chair for clues to the future course of monetary policy. The primary monetary policy tools are the setting of reserve requirements for member banks, control of the discount rate, and open market operations.

Reserve requirements set by the Federal Reserve designate the portion of the banks' deposits that most banks must retain as backing for their loans. The reserves determine how much or how little banks can lend to businesses and consumers. For example, if the FRB changed the reserve requirements and allowed banks to keep $10 on hand rather than $15 for every $100 in deposits that it held, it would free up some additional money for loans. The **discount rate** is the rate of interest at which the Federal Reserve Board lends money to member banks. In **open market operations,** the FRB buys and sells government securities in the open market. The FRB can also use "moral suasion" to influence the actions of banks and other members of the financial community by suggestion, exhortation, and informal agreement. Because of its commanding position as a monetary policy maker, the media, economists, and market observers pay attention to verbal signals about economic trends and conditions emitted by the FRB and its chair.

reserve requirements
Government requirements that a portion of member banks' deposits must be retained to back loans made.

discount rate
The rate of interest at which member banks can borrow money from their regional Federal Reserve Bank.

open market operations
The buying and selling of government securities by the Federal Reserve Bank in the securities market.

Join the Debate

Economic Stimulus Payments

OVERVIEW: In April and May 2008, the U.S. government sent checks to individual taxpayers in an attempt to stimulate the economy and keep it from going into a long and harsh recession. The economy was steadily declining. Workers were losing their jobs. Spending—except on food and gasoline—was going down. Families were not able to make mortgage payments and were losing their homes. These factors lowered demand for more goods, which meant businesses cut back production, leading to more workers laid off, which meant less consumer spending and more foreclosures. In an attempt to stop the cycle, Congress and President George W. Bush agreed to fund a $168 billion package that included the checks to taxpayers, some tax incentives for business investments, and increased guarantees to lenders of home mortgages.

The purpose of the 2008 stimulus payments was to encourage lower- and middle-income people to spend money. The checks went to those who filed a tax return for 2007 and earned at least $3,000 if single and $6,000 if filing jointly as a married couple. Most who received a check got $600, or $1,200 if filing jointly. If someone earned more than $75,000 ($150,000 if married) in 2007, the check was for increasingly reduced amounts ($30 less for each $1,000 above $75,000), and the wealthy got nothing. Each dependent child generated an additional $300 payment.

The political calculus for sending money back to taxpayers seemed clear. Symbolically, policy makers were signaling that they were concerned and doing something to improve the economy generally and the fate of individuals specifically. This stimulus package, in contrast to some previous tax cuts, targeted benefits for the majority of wage earners instead of the rich.

What was less clear was the economic calculus. How far would a $600 check go in stimulating growth in jobs and businesses? Especially given higher food and fuel prices, would consumers be able to buy a new car or kitchen appliance? Was $600 going to be enough to keep someone from defaulting on a home mortgage? Would people use their check to pay off some of their credit card debt instead of buying something new?

The Congressional Budget Office reviewed the history of previous programs similar to the 2008 payment approach. They found that consumers spent only 12 to 24 percent of the money they received in 1975 and 20 to 40 percent in 2001. The intended impact on the economy, in other words, was modest, but there was some effect. The CBO testimony prompted some legislators to propose even more targeted relief through extending eligibility for unemployment compensation for those laid off from their jobs and through expanding the food stamp program. The majority of representatives and senators rejected these proposals though the global financial crisis that began in late 2008 put all options back on the table.

Arguments IN FAVOR of Economic Stimulus Payments

- The government can and should act to keep an economic downturn from turning into a long and harsh recession. By making it possible

---

How the FRB uses these tools depends in part on its views of the state of the economy. If inflation appears to be the problem, then the Fed would likely restrict or tighten the money supply. If a recession with rising unemployment appears to threaten the economy, then the FRB would probably act to loosen or expand the money supply in order to stimulate the economy.

fiscal policy
Federal government policies on taxes, spending, and debt management, intended to promote the nation's macroeconomic goals, particularly with respect to employment, price stability, and growth.

FISCAL POLICY: TAXING AND SPENDING   **Fiscal policy** is the deliberate use of the national government's taxing and spending policies to influence the overall operation of the economy and maintain economic stability. The president and Congress formulate fiscal policy and conduct it through the federal budget process. The powerful instruments of fiscal policy are budget surpluses and deficits. These are achieved by manipulating the overall or "aggregate" levels of revenue and expenditures.

According to standard fiscal policy, there is a level of total or aggregate spending at which the economy will operate at full employment. Total spending is the sum of

for people to spend more money, the demand for goods will increase and thus spark growth in jobs and the economy. When a cycle of layoffs and lower spending has begun, government action can halt that dynamic. Stimulus payments not only help workers, businesses, and investors but also yield increased tax revenues that may more than offset the costs of the stimulus package.

■ **Economic stimulus efforts directed to low- and middle-income families are effective.** Stimulus payments sent to low- and middle-income taxpayers are likely to be spent immediately. An uptick in consumer spending is exactly what is needed to avoid further economic downturn.

■ **The stimulus payments send an important message to consumers, businesses, and investors.** Adopting a stimulus program allows Congress and the president to reassure citizens that the health of the economy is a concern and that it is being addressed. To do nothing erodes confidence and contributes to a continued decline in the economy.

Arguments AGAINST Economic Stimulus Payments

■ **It is a mistake for government to interfere with market forces.**

Economic woes require economic adjustments, not government intervention. A downturn in the economy is due to a variety of factors, like foreign competition, unsound lending practices, and labor and production inefficiencies. The artificial injection of spending money by the government diverts attention from the real problems.

■ **An indebted government is in no position to indebt itself further with stimulus spending.** Deficit spending—spending more money than is available—is irresponsible and passes on to future generations the burdens and challenges posed by a large and growing debt. With the national debt over $9.3 trillion in 2008, the economic stimulus package may have made political sense but could not be justified economically.

■ **Stimulus payments are more likely to be spent on rising food and fuel costs and on credit card debt than on purchases that stimulate the economy.** Low- and middle-income families will use their $600 stimulus check to pay for food or gasoline or some other basic necessity rather than for a new purchase. The government can help distressed individuals more directly by extending unemployment compensation or providing food stamp supplements. If the objective

is to help businesses, significant measures to adjust to foreign competition or solve other problems would be the better course.

Continuing the Debate

1. Should the government try to stimulate economic activity by sending people a check? Does this approach divert attention from the real reasons for an economic downturn? Explain your answers.

2. Is it likely that $600 or $1,200 checks will be spent on new purchases that will spark economic growth, or is it more likely that the money will be used for other purposes? Are there more effective approaches to halting a downturn? Explain.

To Follow the Debate Online, Go To:

www.cbo.gov, where the Congressional Budget Office has a series of studies and reports on economic stimulus proposals.

www.brookings.edu for Brookings Institution reports and testimony supporting the 2008 economic stimulus legislation of the federal government.

www.epi.org, the Web site of the Economic Policy Institute, a nonpartisan, nonprofit organization that raised concerns about the 2008 stimulus package.

consumer spending, private investment spending, and government spending. If consumer and business spending does not create demand sufficient to cause the economy to operate at full employment, then the government should make up the shortfall by increasing spending in excess of revenues. This was essentially what the economist John Maynard Keynes recommended for the national government during the Great Depression. If inflation is the problem confronting policy makers, then government can reduce demand for goods and services by reducing its expenditures and running a budget surplus.[34]

One type of fiscal policy is discretionary fiscal policy, which involves deliberate decisions by the president and Congress to run budget surpluses or deficits. This can be done by increasing or decreasing spending while holding taxes constant, by increasing or cutting taxes while holding spending stable, or by some combination of changes in taxing and spending. (To learn more about how taxes affect you individually, see Ideas into Action: Discovering Your Tax Burden.)

★ WHAT SHOULD I HAVE LEARNED?

This chapter examined the policy-making process, social welfare policies, and economic policies.

■ **What are the roots of public policy and the policy-making process?**

The policy-making process can be viewed as a sequence of functional activities beginning with the identification and definition of public problems. Once identified, problems must get on the governmental agenda. Other stages of the process include policy formulation, policy adoption, budgeting for policies, policy implementation, and the evaluation of policy.

■ **How did social welfare policy evolve?**

The origins of social welfare policy can be traced back to early initiatives in the nation's history. Only after the Great Depression, however, was a public-sector role in the delivery of social services broadly accepted. Most income security programs generally take two forms: non-means-based programs and means-based programs, which indicate that all people who meet eligibility criteria are automatically entitled to receive benefits. Governments in the United States have a long history of involvement in the health of Americans. Most state and local governments have health departments, and the U.S. government has several public health and medical research divisions. Medicare and Medicaid are the two most prominent national programs. As the cost of health care has risen, however, new demands have been made to restrain the rate of growth in costs.

■ **How did economic policy evolve?**

Efforts by the national government to regulate the economy began with anti-monopoly legislation during the Progressive era. Then, during the New Deal, a host of new programs were created by Congress and the president to correct the lingering effects of the Great Depression. Full employment, employee-employer relations, and social regulation became new concerns of government even before social regulation which involves the reduction in market controls, emerged as an attractive political issue.

The national government continues to shape monetary policy by regulating the nation's money supply and interest rates. Monetary policy is controlled by the Federal Reserve Board. Fiscal policy, which involves the deliberate use of the national government's taxing and spending policies, is another tool of the national government and involves the president and Congress setting the national budget.

Key Terms

agenda, p. 387
Board of Governors, p. 406
deregulation, p. 404
discount rate, p. 407
economic regulation, p. 404
economic stability, p. 406
entitlement program, p. 398
fiscal policy, p. 408
governmental (institutional) agenda, p. 387
inflation, p. 406

interventionist state, p. 403
laissez-faire, p. 403
means-tested program, p. 393
Medicaid, p. 400
Medicare, p. 400
monetary policy, p. 406
money, p. 406
non-means-based program, p. 393
open market operations, p. 407
policy adoption, p. 387
policy evaluation, p. 391

policy formulation, p. 387
policy implementation, p. 388
public policy, p. 384
recession, p. 406
reserve requirements, p. 407
social regulation, p. 404
Social Security Act, p. 392
social welfare policy. p. 391
systemic agenda, p. 387

Researching Social and Economic Policy

In the Library

Bitner, Richard. *Greed, Fraud, and Ignorance: A Subprime Insider's Look at the Mortgage Collapse.* Colleyville, TX: LTV Media, 2008.

Chernow, Ron. *Alexander Hamilton.* New York: Penguin, 2004.

Fleckenstein, William, and Fred Sheehan. *Greenspan's Bubbles: The Age of Ignorance at the Federal Reserve.* New York: McGraw Hill, 2008.

Iley, Richard A., and Mervyn K. Lewis. *Untangling the U.S. Deficit: Evaluating Causes, Cures and Global Imbalances.* Northampton, MA: Edward Elgar, 2007.

Isaacs, Stephen, and James Knickman, eds. *To Improve Health and Health Care.* Vol. 8. San Francisco: Jossey-Bass, 2005.

Lindbloom, Charles E., and Edward J. Woodhouse. *The Policy-Making Process,* 3rd ed. Englewood Cliffs, NJ: Prentice Hall, 1993.

Oberlander, Jonathan. *The Political Life of Medicare.* Chicago: University of Chicago Press, 2003.

Rich, Robert, and William White. *Health Policy, Federalism, and the American States.* Washington, DC: Urban Institute, 1996.

Rubin, Robert E., with Jacob Weisberg. *In an Uncertain World: Tough Choices from Wall Street to Washington.* New York: Random House, 2003.

Sherraden, Michael. *Inclusion in the American Dream: Assets Poverty and Public Policy.* Oxford: Oxford University Press, 2005.

Skocpol, Theda. *The Missing Middle: Working Families and the Future of American Social Policy.* New York: Norton, 2000.

Weil, Alan, and Kenneth Finegold, eds. *Welfare Reform: The Next Act.* Washington, DC: Urban Institute, 2002.

On the Web

To understand how public policies are prioritized and analyzed, go to **www.ncpa.org.**

To learn more about how public policies are budgeted, go to **www.cbpp.org.**

To learn more about the most current Social Security benefits and statistics, go to **www.ssa.gov.**

To learn more about current welfare provisions, go to **www.progress.org.**

For other health care policy initiatives and consumer health information, go to **www.nih.gov.**

To learn about the government bureau for economic analysis, go to **www.bea.doc.gov.**

To compare various business cycle indicators, go to **www.tcb-indicators.org.**

To learn more about regulation of financial markets via the Federal Reserve Board, go to **www.federalreserve.gov.**

To learn about current fiscal policy, go to **www.gpoaccess.gov/usbudget/index.html.**

Someone Talked!

Foreign and Defense Policy

The war on terrorism declared by President George W. Bush after the September 11, 2001, attacks on the United States has been a multifaceted, global undertaking that includes military action overseas, increased security measures at home, cooperation among domestic and international intelligence agencies, diplomacy, and the prevention of terrorists' access to weapons of mass destruction. It involves domestic strategies, such as efforts to improve homeland security, as well as international activities, such as the promotion of democracy abroad, military strikes against terrorist organizations and the states that sponsor them, and diplomatic initiatives designed to thwart the spread of religious extremism and nuclear proliferation. In the context of the war on terrorism, the division of U.S. policies into "foreign affairs" and "domestic affairs" is somewhat artificial.

After the events of 9/11, striking the appropriate balance between foreign and domestic affairs so that American interests and objectives are achieved and the American public is protected remains a continuing challenge for the president and others involved in the foreign and defense policy process. For example, three days after the 9/11 attacks,

Hon. Alberto Gonzales

President Bush authorized the National Security Administration (NSA) to eavesdrop on telephone calls and e-mails between American citizens and foreigners suspected of terrorist ties without first seeking a court warrant. The NSA's Terrorist Surveillance Program continued until January 2007, when the White House resumed seeking surveillance warrants from the Federal Intelligence Surveillance Court. When it was disclosed, the NSA's spying program created a great deal of controversy because the 1978 Foreign Intelligence Surveillance Act (FISA) requires the special intelligence court to approve any interception of communications involving U.S. citizens. The program generated debate in Congress over the legality of President Bush's decision to order the NSA to conduct warrantless surveillance of Americans' communications. The Department of Justice, however, argued that the president's constitutional role as commander in chief provides adequate justification for his authorization of such a program. Critics argue that the program violates U.S. law, that the president is unnecessarily extending the reach of the federal government, and that the NSA's limited resources should be targeted at more precise threats to national security.

The debate intensified in the wake of revelations of a much larger data-mining project designed to track the domestic phone records of millions of ordinary U.S. citizens and analyze them for signs that Americans are communicating with suspected terrorists. In a White House press briefing on May 11, 2006, President Bush strongly defended his administration's surveillance and monitoring efforts: "We're not mining or trolling through the personal lives of

■ What is the appropriate scope of the government's power to combat threats to national security? At left, a World War II-era poster warns Americans of the potentially deadly consequences of talking about military deployments or troop movement publicly. At right, former Attorney General Alberto Gonzales testifies before Congress about the Bush Administration's controversial domestic eavesdropping program.

WHAT SHOULD I KNOW ABOUT . . .

■ the roots of U.S. foreign and defense policy?
■ foreign and defense policy decision making?
■ twenty-first-century challenges in foreign and defense policy?

413

millions of innocent Americans," he stated. "Our efforts are focused on links to al-Qaeda and their known affiliates."[1]

In August 2007, Congress passed a temporary law that expanded the president's power to monitor communications passing through the United States that involve suspected terrorists. This law expired in February 2008 and efforts to revise the FISA law hinged on a variety of hotly debated issues, including the level of oversight over domestic surveillance that should be exercised and whether to grant retroactive immunity to private telecommunications companies that participated in the NSA's earlier warrantless spying programs.

In the summer of 2008, Congress reached an agreement on the issue and passed the FISA Amendments Act. On July 10, 2008, President Bush signed the bill into law. Important provisions of the law include protections for telecommunications companies from lawsuits for past or future cooperation with the intelligence community and language that allows federal law enforcement agencies to conduct surveillance of any person for up to one week (an increase from the previous forty-eight hours) without a warrant as long as the FISA court is notified. The American Civil Liberties Union (ACLU) has filed a lawsuit challenging the law (*Amnesty et al v. McConnell*) as a violation of free speech and privacy under the First and Fourth Amendments to the Constitution.

Current domestic surveillance programs blur the distinction between domestic and foreign policies and raise complicated constitutional questions about the reach of the federal government in the context of combating terrorism. Domestic issues, such as the privacy rights of ordinary Americans, have become part of the discussion of how best to pursue a defense policy that will thwart terrorism here and abroad. The Bush administration's war on terrorism dramatically changed how the United States conducts foreign and defense policy, ushering in a period of unprecedented unilateral military action abroad, aggressive detention practices for those suspected of terrorist activities, and controversial spying programs at home.

Following the end of the Cold War (1947–1991), U.S. foreign policy began a period of transition. Many wondered what role the United States would play in a world with only one remaining superpower. Most hoped that the world would be a safer place in the new millennium. After September 11, 2001, however, Americans recognized a new and deadly threat: terrorism. Many citizens wondered how the United States, with its superior military resources, could have fallen prey to a devastating series of terrorist attacks on a single fateful day.

Like social and economic policy, U.S. foreign and defense policy has evolved. Today, the United States is a powerful and influential presence on the world stage. It was not always this way. When the United States was founded, it was a weak country on the margins of world affairs, with an uncertain future.

Even so, the United States was fortunate. Separated from Europe and Asia by vast oceans, it had abundant resources and industrious people. The United States often stood apart from world engagements, following a policy of **isolationism**, that is, avoiding participation in foreign affairs. However, isolationism was rarely absolute. Even in its early years, the United States engaged in foreign affairs, and it was always a trading nation. Another consistent hallmark of U.S. policy was **unilateralism**, that is, acting

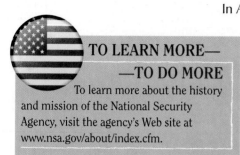

TO LEARN MORE—
—TO DO MORE
To learn more about the history and mission of the National Security Agency, visit the agency's Web site at www.nsa.gov/about/index.cfm.

isolationism
A national policy of avoiding participation in foreign affairs.

unilateralism
A national policy of acting without consulting others.

without consulting others. **Moralism** was also central to U.S. self-image in foreign policy, with most Americans believing their country had higher moral standards than European and other countries. Many Americans were also proud of their **pragmatism**—their ability to find ways to take advantage of a situation. Thus, when European nations went to war, Americans sold goods to both sides and profited handsomely. When opportunities to acquire more land arose, Americans aggressively pursued them.

In this chapter, we first will trace the origins of current U.S. foreign and defense policy in the years since the United States became a world power. After studying foreign and defense policy decision making, we wil discuss twenty-first-century foreign policy challenges.

moralism
The policy of emphasizing morality in foreign affairs.

pragmatism
The policy of taking advantage of a situation for national gain.

Roots of U.S. Foreign and Defense Policy

Throughout the 1950s and into the 1960s, the world seemed divided into two camps, one led by the United States and the other by the communist Soviet Union. John F. Kennedy became president in 1961 during this Cold War period. Kennedy brought a sense of optimism and activism to the United States that captivated many Americans. "Ask not what your country can do for you," Kennedy urged Americans in his inaugural address, "but what you can do for your country."[2]

Containing the Soviet Union while at the same time establishing cordial relations with it to lessen the peril of nuclear war was high on President Kennedy's foreign and military policy agenda. Thus, in 1961, Kennedy met Khrushchev in Vienna, Austria. The meeting did not go well. Both leaders returned to their respective countries and increased military spending. In 1962, the Soviet Union began to deploy intermediate-range ballistic missiles in Cuba, only ninety miles from Florida, leading to the **Cuban Missile Crisis**.[3] The United States reacted strongly, placing a naval blockade around Cuba and warning the Soviet Union to withdraw the missiles or suffer the consequences. After several days during which the world was closer to nuclear war than it had ever been, Khrushchev backed down and withdrew the missiles. The world breathed a sigh of relief.

The Cuban Missile Crisis led to a period of improved U.S.-Soviet relations. During the crisis, the United States and the Soviet Union had marched to the edge of nuclear war, and neither liked what they had seen. Thus, in 1963, the two nations concluded a partial nuclear test ban treaty and installed a "hot line" between Washington and Moscow to allow the leaders of the two countries to talk directly during crises.

The Cuban Missile Crisis confirmed the majority of Americans' belief that the Soviet Union was an expansionist power. Most Americans believed that containment was the correct strategy, and that the United States remained the moral defender of liberty and justice, acting pragmatically but always with restraint to prevent communist expansion. Few questioned the morality of containment, the necessity for pragmatism, or the need for internationalism and American-led multilateralism.

Then came the **Vietnam War**.[4] The United States sought to contain communism from spreading from North Vietnam into South Vietnam starting in the 1950s, but it was in the mid-1960s that U.S. bombing and ground operations began, and they escalated quickly. While many in South Vietnam were grateful for U.S. assistance, others were actively supporting the communists. The United States became embroiled in a civil war in which it was difficult to determine friend from foe. Eventually, the U.S. presence in Vietnam grew to more than 500,000 troops, 58,000 of whom were killed. As deaths mounted and costs grew, many Americans asked questions they had rarely asked before.

Cuban Missile Crisis
The 1962 confrontation that nearly escalated into war between the United States and the Soviet Union over Soviet deployment of medium-range ballistic missiles in Cuba.

SIMULATION

**You Are President
John F. Kennedy**

Vietnam War
Between 1965 and 1973, the United States deployed up to 500,000 troops to Vietnam to try to prevent North Vietnam from taking over South Vietnam; the effort failed and was extremely divisive within the United States.

The Living Constitution

To provide for calling forth the Militia to execute the Laws of the Union, suppress Insurrections and repel Invasions;

To provide for organizing, arming, and disciplining, the Militia, and for governing such Part of them as may be employed in the Service of the United States, reserving to the States respectively, the Appointment of the Officers, and the Authority of training the Militia according to the discipline proscribed by Congress;

ARTICLE I, SECTION 8

With the Constitution's Article I militia clauses, a significant defect of the Articles of Confederation was corrected. A fundamental weakness of the earlier document was that it did not grant the central U.S. government adequate means for national defense, and this defect was understood to hamper the Revolutionary War effort. In the view of the Framers, a government without the force to administer its laws or to defend its citizens was either a weak government or no government at all, and these clauses consequently give the federal government authority to call up the state militias in times of national emergency or distress. The clauses address the understanding that military training, proficiency, and organization should be uniform across state and national forces so as to ensure effectiveness and efficiency in military operations.

Despite the fact that the militia clauses passed the convention, many Anti-Federalists were concerned that the federal government could call together the state militias for unjust ends. They held the position that state governments should control their militias in order to prevent any perfidy on the part of the federal government. To this end, the states were given authority to name militia officers and train their forces. During the War of 1812—to the consternation of President James Madison—two state governments withheld their militias, because they believed it was the purview of the state to set the terms for the use of its guards. The Supreme Court has since held that, except for constitutional prohibitions, the Congress has "unlimited" authority over the state militias. The National Defense Act of 1916 mandated the use of the term "National Guard" and gave the president the authority to mobilize the National Guard during times of national emergency or war.

Throughout U.S. history, the National Guard has proved effective and essential in defending the United States. With the extensive use of the National Guard to assist American efforts in Iraq and in the struggle against terrorism, its role has expanded. The militia clauses ensure the unity, effectiveness, and strength of the United States military not only during wartime, but also during other national emergencies.

CRITICAL THINKING QUESTIONS

1. According to the Constitution, the president is the commander in chief of the armed forces. But, Congress has the power to organize the military, fund it, and call it to duty. How does this division of authority work in practice?
2. Should individual states retain the right to withhold National Guard troops if the state government does not approve of the way in which the president intends to use them?

Was the United States on the side of justice in Vietnam, or had it only replaced France there as a colonial power? How much killing and how great a cost would the United States bear to prevent the expansion of communism? Was communism still the enemy it had been? Increasingly, U.S. citizens became less persuaded that their mission in Vietnam was moral or that communism was universally dangerous. By the end of the 1960s, Ameri-

What are the lessons of the Vietnam War? Many Americans visit the Vietnam War Memorial in Washington, D.C., to grieve for and honor those in the U.S. military who gave their lives during the conflict in Southeast Asia.

cans were not as sure of their moral superiority as they had been, nor were they sure that containment was the proper strategy on which to base their foreign and military policy. President Lyndon B. Johnson, who had presided over the massive U.S. military escalation in Vietnam, became so unpopular by 1968 that he chose not to run for reelection.

Détente and Human Rights: 1969–1981

When Richard M. Nixon was inaugurated as president in 1969, he declared it was time to move from "an era of confrontation" to "an era of negotiation" in relations with the Soviet Union.[5] Recognizing that nuclear war would destroy life as it existed, searching for a way to exit Vietnam, and trying to improve East–West relations without conceding international leadership or renouncing containment, Nixon undertook policies that began this transformation. The improvement in U.S.-Soviet relations was called **détente**.[6]

The changed nature of U.S.-Soviet relations brought about by détente was best illustrated by the frequency of summit meetings. From 1972 to 1979, American and Soviet leaders met six times, but détente was more than summitry. It also included increased trade, arms control agreements, and cultural exchanges. Détente improved East–West relations in Europe as well. For example, the heads of government of almost every nation in Europe and North America attended a meeting in Helsinki, Finland, in 1975.

When Jimmy Carter became president in 1977, he intended to pursue détente. However, he rejected Nixon's foreign policy cynicism that had emphasized pragmatism to the virtual exclusion of moralism. Carter instead emphasized **human rights**, that is, the protection of people's basic freedoms and needs. This found a sympathetic ear among many Americans. Once again, they believed, the United States would emphasize morality in foreign policy. Some Americans wondered, however, if Carter's emphasis on human rights was misdirected and was weakening the United States.[7]

Concern about American weakness grew in 1979 when radical Iranians, with the support of Iran's fundamentalist Islamic government, overran the U.S. embassy in Tehran and held the embassy staff captive. The Iranian hostage crisis eroded Carter's support in the United States. For over a year, the country was powerless to win the hostages' release. A failed rescue attempt added to American humiliation. (The hostages were not released until the day that Carter left office in 1981.)

Détente finally died in 1979 when the Soviet Union invaded Afghanistan. Described by Carter in his 1980 State of the Union Address as "the most serious

détente
The relaxation of tensions between the United States and the Soviet Union that occurred during the 1970s.

human rights
The belief that human beings have inalienable rights such as freedom of speech and freedom of religion.

threat to peace since the Second World War,"[8] the Soviet invasion led to an immediate increase in U.S. defense spending.

Containment Revisited and Renewed: 1981–1989

The tense U.S.-Soviet relations during Jimmy Carter's last year as president became confrontational during President Ronald Reagan's first term in office. Reagan accelerated the U.S. arms buildup and, in response to Soviet influence in developing countries, initiated an activist foreign policy that included the invasion of Grenada, a pro-Soviet island nation in the Caribbean, and support for the Contras, an insurgency attempting to overthrow the pro-Soviet Sandinista government in Nicaragua in Central America. In addition, Reagan emphasized morality in American foreign policy and pushed to create an open international economic system.[9]

By 1984, however, relations between the United States and the Soviet Union were beginning to improve. The two countries upgraded their hotlines and agreed to expand arms-control talks. Most importantly, the rhetoric from both capitals deescalated. What happened? First, the 1984 U.S. presidential election constrained U.S. rhetoric. Although most Americans supported the arms buildup, they were concerned about confrontation with the Soviets. In response, Reagan moderated his statements. Second, U.S. foreign and military policy initiatives had an impact on Moscow as, in addition to its arms buildup, the United States implemented the **Reagan Doctrine**, under which the United States provided arms to anti-Soviet movements fighting pro-Soviet governments in Afghanistan, Angola, Mozambique, and Nicaragua. These programs increased the cost of Soviet involvement there and led Soviet leaders to rethink their foreign policy. Finally, the Soviet Union had serious internal problems. Its economy was performing poorly and it had a leadership crisis, with three Soviet leaders dying between 1982 and 1985. These problems had to be addressed. To do this, the Soviet Union needed a less confrontational relationship with the United States.

Recognizing this, Soviet President Mikhail Gorbachev worked with Reagan to improve relations after Gorbachev became the Soviet leader in 1985. Even before Gorbachev's reforms took hold, Gorbachev and Reagan laid the groundwork for a transformation in relations.[10] At the third of five summit meetings, the two leaders signed an agreement to destroy all intermediate-range nuclear weapons. Gorbachev introduced "perestroika"—reforms in domestic, foreign, and military policies that transformed the Soviet Union and U.S.-Soviet relations. Although the reforms were intended to address the serious problems that the Soviet Union faced, they eventually led to the end of the Cold War and the demise of the Soviet Union.[11]

Reagan Doctrine
Policy that the United States would provide military assistance to anti-communist groups fighting against pro-Soviet governments.

Searching for a New International Order: 1989–2001

George Bush, vice president during President Reagan's two terms, assumed the presidency in 1989 pledging to continue Reagan's foreign policy directions. However, the pace and scope of change in

Photo courtesy: Tannen Murray/Image Works

How important is the role of diplomacy to successful U.S. foreign policy? After several tense years in U.S.-Soviet relations, the emergence of Mikhail Gorbachev as Soviet premier in 1985 led to the adoption of stunning reforms in the Soviet Union and a series of increasingly friendly summit meetings between Gorbachev and U.S. President Ronald Reagan.

Eastern Europe and the Soviet Union raised questions about the entire direction of U.S. foreign policy. The first question came from Eastern Europe. In 1989, the people of many Eastern European states revolted against their governments. During previous rebellions, Soviet troops stationed in Eastern Europe subdued the rebellions. This time, Gorbachev ordered Soviet troops to remain in their barracks. The rebellions continued, and in every communist country in Eastern Europe, the government fell.

The United States was not quite sure how to respond. At first, Bush proceeded cautiously. As it became clear that the revolutions were irreversible, the United States and other democratic states helped the new noncommunist Eastern European states try to establish democratic political and free market economic systems. Remarkably, in a matter of months, the so-called "Iron Curtain" in Europe had collapsed, with almost no serious bloodshed.

The 1990 Iraqi invasion of Kuwait produced a new challenge. The Bush administration believed that the invasion threatened vital U.S. interests, and the United Nations passed a resolution authorizing the use of force to expel Iraq from Kuwait. Shortly after Congress voted to support the use of military force against Iraq, the Persian Gulf War began in January 1991. In an attack called Operation Desert Storm, U.S. and allied forces defeated Iraq in a matter of weeks. The objective—expelling Iraq from Kuwait—had been achieved with few U.S. casualties.[12] The conduct of Operation Desert Storm reflected the principles of the **Powell Doctrine** articulated by Colin Powell, President Bush's chair of the Joint Chiefs of Staff.

Powell Doctrine
The Powell Doctrine advocates an all-or-nothing approach to military intervention. Among other criteria, it emphasizes the use of overwhelming force to ensure a quick and decisive victory, and the adoption of an exit strategy prior to any intervention.

Meanwhile, startling events were unfolding in the Soviet Union. Under Gorbachev, the Soviet Union posed less and less of a threat as the United States and Soviet Union forged an increasingly close relationship. Weakened by a failed coup attempt against Gorbachev in the summer of 1991, its economy in shambles, and torn by internal dissent and the desires of nationalities for independence, the Soviet Union collapsed.[13] The Cold War was over, as was the need for containment. Once again Americans asked questions: What would U.S. strategy now be? With the Cold War over, should the United States cut defense spending, and if so, how much? How much aid should the United States send to its former enemy to help it survive its collapse? What criteria would guide decisions about where and when to employ U.S. forces abroad in a world with only one remaining superpower?

These were the complex questions Bill Clinton faced when he assumed the presidency in 1993. Defining the American role in this world presented a challenge. Clinton's agenda centered on implementing engagement and enlargement, shaping new international economic relationships, deciding when U.S. armed forces should be used overseas, and puzzling over what role the United States should play in the post–Cold War world. **Engagement** meant that the United States would not retreat into isolationism as it did after World War I and for a short time after World War II. Engagement implied that the United States relied on negotiations and cooperation rather than confrontation and conflict, although it would use force when necessary. **Enlargement** meant that the United States would promote democracy, open markets, and other Western political, economic, and social values. In practice, engagement and enlargement led to the implementation of the Partnership for Peace program with former communist states in Eastern Europe and the former Soviet Union and the expansion of NATO, a defense alliance established during the Cold War.

engagement
Policy implemented during the Clinton administration that the United States would remain actively involved in foreign affairs.

enlargement
Policy implemented during the Clinton administration that the United States would actively promote the expansion of democracy and free markets throughout the world.

Deciding when to use U.S. armed forces overseas is a vexing problem. As we have seen, from the end of World War II to the collapse of the Soviet Union, U.S. military intervention was usually tied to containing communism. With the Soviet Union gone, this easy benchmark for deciding when to intervene no longer existed. The administration faced different types of crises in countries in Africa, Eastern Europe, Asia, the Middle East, and the Caribbean and intervened militarily in a number of those countries, but no pattern related to the use of U.S. military force overseas became evident. In some cases the U.S. response was largely humanitarian, other situations dictated peacekeeping or peace enforcement efforts, and still others involved combat activities.

Timeline: Major Acts of Terrorism Affecting the United States, 1990 - Present

January 15, 1990 U.S. embassy bombing—Attack in Lima, Peru, by local revolutionaries.

June 26, 1996 Khobar Towers bombing—Truck bomb explodes outside of the U.S. military's Khobar Towers housing facility in Khobar, Saudi Arabia. Twenty killed and over 300 injured.

September 11, 2001 9/11 terrorist attacks—Planes hijacked by members of al-Qaeda destroy the World Trade Center in New York City and damage the Pentagon in Washington, D.C. A fourth hijacked airplane crashes in Pennsylvania. Nearly 3,000 dead and thousands more injured. The deadliest terrorist attack on U.S. soil in the nation's history.

April 14, 1993 Assassination attempt— Attempted assassination of former President George Bush by Iraqi intelligence during a visit to Kuwait.

October 12, 2000 U.S.S. Cole attack—Attack on the destroyer U.S.S. Cole in Aden, Yemen. A small boat loaded with explosives rams the destroyer.

February 26, 1993 World Trade Center bombing in New York City—Car bomb explodes in an underground garage; six killed and over a thousand injured. Khaled Shaikh Mohammed and more than six others are charged with planning and financing the attack.

August 7, 1998 U.S. embassy bombings—Attacks on embassies in East Africa including Nairobi, Kenya and Dar es Salaam, Tanzania.

April 19, 1995 Oklahoma City bombing—Bombing of the Alfred P. Murrah Federal Building in Oklahoma City, Oklahoma, by anti-government extremists Timothy McVeigh and Terry Nichols. 168 people killed; over 800 injured. The deadliest terrorist attack on U.S. soil until the 9/11 attacks.

North American Free Trade Agreement (NAFTA)
Agreement that promotes free movement of goods and services among Canada, Mexico, and the United States.

World Trade Organization (WTO)
International governmental organization created in 1995 that manages multilateral negotiations to reduce barriers to trade and settle trade disputes.

al-Qaeda
Worldwide terrorist organization led by Osama bin Laden; responsible for numerous terrorist attacks against U.S. interests, including 9/11 attacks against the World Trade Center and the Pentagon.

International economic issues were another focus of Clinton's activities. He guided the **North American Free Trade Agreement (NAFTA)** into law, establishing the free flow of goods among Canada, Mexico, and the United States. The United States under Clinton also played an important role in initiating two other major free trade areas: the Free Trade Area of the Americas and the Asia-Pacific Economic Cooperation agreement, as well as creating the **World Trade Organization (WTO)**, charged with overseeing world trade, judging trade disputes, and lowering tariffs.[14]

The War on Terrorism: 2001 to the Present

During his first months as president, George W. Bush (a son of former President George Bush) conducted an active foreign policy. Relations with Latin America, Europe, Russia, and China all loomed large on the new president's agenda, as did security, international economics, immigration, drugs, and the environment. However, suddenly and unexpectedly, the Bush administration's foreign and defense priorities became clearly focused.

On September 11, 2001, members of **al-Qaeda**, a terrorist network founded and funded by Muslim fundamentalist Osama bin Laden, hijacked four jetliners, flying two

December 6, 2004 U.S. consulate bombing—Attack on U.S. Consulate in Jeddah, Saudi Arabia.

March 20, 2002
U.S. embassy bombing—Car bombing at a shopping center near the U.S. Embassy in Lima, Peru, three days before an official visit by President George W. Bush.

July 7, 2005
London bombings—Bombs explode on a double-decker bus and three London Underground trains, killing 56 people and injuring over 700, on the first day of the 31st G-8 Conference. Attacks are the first suicide bombings in Western Europe.

October-November 2001 Anthrax attacks—Anthrax spores mailed to several television networks in New York and to the offices of two Democratic senators in Washington, D.C. Five people die and 17 are sickened. FBI implicates American biodefense scientist, but questions linger after the scientist commits suicide in 2008.

September 13, 2006 U.S. embassy attack—Gunmen attack security guards outside the U.S. Embassy in Damascus, Syria.

2005- 2009
Attacks in Iraq, Afghanistan, Pakistan— Numerous attacks on U.S. contractors and armed forces in Iraq, Pakistan, and Afghanistan; kidnapping and executions of journalists, military personnel, and private contractors.

July 30, 2004
U.S. embassy bombing— Attack on U.S. Embassy in Uzbekistan.

into the twin towers of New York's World Trade Center. The impact destroyed the towers and killed almost 3,000 people. Another hijacked plane slammed into the Pentagon, killing 189 individuals. The fourth plane headed toward Washington, D.C., but crashed into a field in Pennsylvania after passengers charged the hijackers and forced them to lose control of the plane.[15]

After the 9/11 attacks, President Bush, declaring a **war on terrorism**, organized a coalition of nations to combat the threat posed by terrorist groups such as al-Qaeda. He also demanded that Afghanistan's **Taliban** government, which had provided safe haven for bin Laden and al-Qaeda's terrorist training camps, turn bin Laden over to the United States. When the Taliban refused, the Bush administration launched Operation Enduring Freedom against al-Qaeda and the Taliban regime in October 2001. The military operation included air strikes against Taliban and al-Qaeda targets and support for the Northern Alliance, an Afghani opposition force battling Taliban control. By the end of 2001, the Taliban were overthrown and the United States was committed to peace enforcement in Afghanistan and assistance with the transition to a democratic government.

The terrorist attacks of September 11, 2001, had a profound impact on U.S. foreign policy. (To learn more about acts of terrorism affecting the United States, see the Timeline.) Despite its superpower status and nuclear superiority, the United States

war on terrorism
Initiated by George W. Bush after the September 11, 2001, attacks to weed out terrorist operatives throughout the world, using diplomacy, military means, improved homeland security, stricter banking laws, and other means.

Taliban
Fundamentalist Islamic government of Afghanistan that provided terrorist training bases for al-Qaeda.

Join the Debate

Should the United States Pull Out of the United Nations?

OVERVIEW: The United Nations came into existence in 1945 in the wake of two world wars and the desire of most nations for an international organization dedicated to pursuing global justice, peace, and human rights. To back up its mandate, the United States and the United Nations have usually worked together to help maintain relative global security. For example, UN member nations helped defend South Korea from invasion by North Korea, provided a blueprint to help mediate peace in the Middle East, and voted for sanctions against South Africa to help end racial apartheid. The UN has also helped millions living in famine and aided countless refugees fleeing war and natural disasters by providing food, shelter, clothing, and medical relief.

Since the end of the Cold War, the United States and the United Nations have developed competing and sometimes antagonistic views with regard to the UN's mandate and global role. In 1992, for example, the UN released a bold initiative—the Agenda for Peace—to recast the UN's peacekeeping role. The move was viewed by some U.S. policy makers as giving the UN control over U.S. military and foreign policy resources and it received a great deal of criticism in Congress.

Furthermore, due to disagreements with the United States over a variety of issues, including its military and foreign policy role in the Middle East, its refusal to ratify the Kyoto climate change treaty, and its opposition to a treaty to abolish land mines, the UN voted the United States off the UN Human Rights Commission in 2001. This action infuriated the Bush administration, because countries that engage in human rights violations, such as Sudan, Libya,

and Cuba, retained their seats on the commission. The United States walked out of the UN conference on racism in 2001 because it objected to criticisms of Israel in a draft of the conference's final declaration. The strain between the Bush administration and the United Nations increased even more in 2003 when the UN Security Council refused to sanction military action against Iraq.

On the other hand, the UN also faced criticism for a major financial scandal involving its Oil for Food program, which had been created during Saddam Hussein's regime in order to give the Iraqi people humanitarian aid while sanctions against Hussein's government were in place. A son of the U.N. Secretary General at the time was implicated in this scandal. Nearly $1 billion disappeared into hidden bank accounts and fake corporations, and the U.S. Congress launched an investigation into where the money went.

Arguments IN FAVOR of the United States Pulling Out of the United Nations

■ It is difficult for the United Nations to act, and even when it does, it is incapable of enforcing its own resolutions. In 2006, Iran made public its intention to develop nuclear weapons, but the UN could not forge a consensus regarding how to respond. China and Russia balked at imposing sanctions on Iran, creating an impasse within the Security Council. When the UN has passed resolutions on Israel, Palestine, Iraq, and Darfur, there has been no significant implementation. When the United States attacked and occupied Iraq in 2003, it claimed that it was in part enforcing UN resolutions that the UN itself was incapable or unwilling to enforce. Getting the global community to act with one voice can be extremely

appeared vulnerable in a way it had not previously. President Bush responded by inaugurating a global campaign against terrorists and their supporters. Like other presidents before him, George W. Bush was putting his distinctive stamp on how the country should address threats to national security. Bush and his foreign policy team concluded that a more ambitious, "muscular" posture was needed to fight threats to U.S. interests. Instead of relying on the reactive strategies of deterrence and containment or the strategies of enlargement and engagement that had characterized the Clinton administration's approach to foreign policy, the Bush administration advocated a proactive doctrine of preemptive military action, commonly referred to as the **Bush Doctrine**.

Bush Doctrine
Policy advocated by President George W. Bush of using preemptive military action against a perceived threat to U.S. interests.

difficult, given the diverse interests of the countries that are represented on the Security Council and within the larger UN body.

- **The United States is not accountable to international organizations when pursuing its own interests.** The United States and the United Nations have divergent interests and understandings of international law and diplomacy. Placing members of the American armed forces under UN command cedes control to an organization that may not always act in the best interests of the United States. The United States must maintain its ability to act in whatever way it sees fit to defend its interests at home and abroad.

- **Adhering to UN resolutions results in giving up American sovereignty.** Some supporters of U.S. withdrawal from the United Nations believe the UN is attempting to create a "world government" and that to accede to UN mandates and resolutions is to relinquish U.S. sovereignty and U.S. control over its own citizens. Many see the UN as one more instance of the international community trying to institute international government.

Arguments AGAINST the United States Pulling Out of the United Nations

- **The UN engages in peacekeeping and nation building when the United States will not.** The UN is currently engaged in about fifteen peacekeeping operations, with more than 72,000 uniformed personnel from member nations in places such as Lebanon, Haiti, and Sudan. The UN can provide peacekeeping support when the United States is either unable or unwilling, thus preventing humanitarian disaster and conflict. This is an essential function if global security and stability are to be maintained.

- **The United States must lead by example.** Because the United States has a unique world military and economic position, it can use its various strengths and principles to promote global peace and justice. Why should other nations respond to UN resolutions and decrees when the United States does not? By acceding to UN requests, the United States can set an example for other nations to follow, and this may help facilitate other nations' compliance with UN wishes to ensure global security. Instead of attempting to form and maintain coalitions to support various actions, the United States can provide leadership and work within the United Nations.

- **International institutions provide global stability and promote peaceful conflict resolution.** Since the establishment of the United Nations, there have been no worldwide wars. The UN was able to provide security for South Korea and it acts as an international forum for conflict mediation. Though imperfect, the UN affords a medium in which human rights policy is debated and developed and international security and stability discussed. For example, the UN has taken on the cause of disarmament and elimination of weapons of mass destruction and thereby provides legitimacy in this policy domain, whereas the United States cannot. Because the United States is a world power, its membership in the UN gives the organization credibility and validity.

Continuing the Debate

1. Does adhering to UN mandates mean giving up national sovereignty? Explain.
2. What can be done to reconcile U.S. and UN interests? Do the United States and the United Nations have similar interests?
3. Is the United States better off acting unilaterally rather than trying to achieve agreement within the United Nations?

To Follow the Debate Online, Go To:

www.unausa.org, the Web site for the United Nations Association of the United States of America, a nonprofit, nonpartisan organization that seeks to provide effective leadership by the United States in the United Nations.

www.eagleforum.org, the Web site of the Eagle Forum, a conservative advocacy group that opposes continued membership and participation of the United States in the United Nations.

When the United States launched its war against Saddam Hussein's regime in Iraq in March 2003, it signaled the implementation of the Bush Doctrine. In past conflicts of this magnitude, the United States had intervened militarily in response to a direct attack (such as Pearl Harbor), or to defend other countries that had been invaded (such as South Korea or Kuwait). The 2003 U.S.-led invasion of Iraq was part of a new strategy that sought to promote American security through preemptive military strikes against potentially dangerous nations. Based on faulty intelligence information that suggested the Hussein regime was developing **weapons of mass destruction (WMDs)**—nuclear, chemical, or biological weapons—and believing that Iraq was a safe harbor and potential breeding ground for terrorists, the U.S. govern-

weapons of mass destruction (WMDs)
Biological, chemical, and nuclear weapons, which present a sizeable threat to U.S. security.

United Nations (UN)
An international governmental organization created shortly before the end of World War II to guarantee the security of nations and to promote global economic, physical, and social well-being.

ment chose to act. U.S. action, however, did not have the support of the **United Nations (UN)**, the international governmental organization created near the end of World War II to guarantee the security of nations and promote global economic, physical, and social well-being. The UN Security Council refused to endorse the recourse to war. The failure of the United States to win approval from the Security Council for the 2003 invasion of Iraq led to vigorous debate at home and abroad, and U.S. actions created hard feelings among many of America's traditional allies. (To learn more about the relations between the United States and its allies, see Join the Debate: Should the United States Pull Out of the United Nations?)

The overthrow of Saddam Hussein's government in the spring of 2003 was relatively quick. The U.S.-led bombing campaign destroyed much of the military and governmental infrastructure in Iraq within days. The Iraqi armed forces seemed helpless and disorganized. Within weeks, U.S. and other allied forces entered Hussein's palaces, tore down statues of the dictator around the country, and began to create a post-Saddam government in Iraq. American forces ultimately captured Saddam Hussein himself on December 13, 2003.

Over time, coalition forces failed to find evidence of an active nuclear weapons program in Iraq—the original justification provided by the Bush administration for a preemptive military strike. As evidence of WMDs failed to materialize, the Bush administration changed its justification for war, arguing that Saddam Hussein posed a severe danger to the world because of his long history of brutality, and emphasizing the goal of promoting democracy in the Middle East through his removal from power.

In the months after President Bush declared an end to major combat, soldiers from the United States and its allies found themselves under attack from mortar fire, roadside bombings, and suicide missions by various insurgents. As the American military presence in Iraq continued, war deaths and injuries mounted. By the end of 2006, more than 2,900 U.S. service men and women had lost their lives in Iraq and more than 22,000 had been injured.[16]

A positive development, however, was the January 2005 election in which the Iraqi people chose representatives for a 275-member national assembly. The election marked an important step in the process of turning over control of the country from the U.S.-led coalition to the Iraqis themselves. But throughout 2006, Iraqi insurgents and foreign terrorists continued their attacks against the U.S.-led coalition forces, and increasing sectarian violence led many observers to characterize the chaos in Iraq as a civil war among Sunni, Shi'ite, and Kurdish factions.

In early 2007, President Bush announced an American troop surge designed to reduce sectarian violence in Iraq and enable the Iraqi government to make political progress. Escalating violence in Baghdad, however, along with other tensions, made it almost impossible for the Iraqi government to achieve results. By the end of 2007, General David H. Petraeus, the top military official in Iraq, reported a significant decline in suicide attacks and civilian casualties; yet 2007 remained the deadliest year for U.S. troops. By mid-2008, more than 4,000 U.S. military personnel and Department of Defense civilians had died in Iraq, and 30,000 had been reported wounded.

The September 11 terrorist attacks gave the United States two overarching foreign and defense policy priorities: defense of the homeland and pursuing the global war on terrorism. Few Americans disagree with these priorities, but disagreements and controversies continue regarding the means to these ends and the effectiveness of government policies. (To learn morea about terrorism responses on campus, see Ideas into Action: The Impact of the War on Terrorism on American Campuses.) Moreover, other foreign and defense policy issues, such as the threat of a nuclear-armed Iran, increased extremist violence in Afghanistan, the security of Pakistan's nuclear arsenal, and the humanitarian crisis in Sudan, have also captured the public's attention.

The Impact of the War on Terrorism on American Campuses

American campuses have become part of a national strategy to improve homeland security. Even though most of the 9/11 hijackers were on tourist or work visas, two were in the United States on student visas. Concern over terrorists on student visas increased more when, several months after the attacks, the Immigration and Naturalization Service (INS) admitted it had processed a pre-9/11 visa application from one of the hijackers and granted a student visa to him even after he had conducted one of the attacks and died. In March 2003, the INS came under the Department of Homeland Security (DHS) as the U.S. Citizenship and Immigration Services (USCIS).

The most notable impact on campuses of the efforts to improve security was the implementation of the Student and Exchange Visitor Information System (SEVIS) required by the USA Patriot Act of 2001. SEVIS is a Web-based registration and tracking system operated by the DHS to monitor nearly 1 million international students and their dependents. Last year Immigration and Customs Enforcement officers investigated 3,129 students not complying with visa rules and made 1,108 arrests.

Experts say the computer-based system has improved national security by giving the DHS faster and more reliable information on the whereabouts and activities of foreign students. But, the system has also significantly increased the burden of accountability on universities and international students. Universities and colleges must report the comings and goings of every international student and visiting foreign professor. In April 2008, the DHS announced that it would double the fees paid by international students—from $100 to $200—to help cover the costs of SEVIS.

- Is it fair to require colleges and universities to track their international students and visitors? Should the federal government pay college administrators for such a task, or is such a process the financial responsibility of the colleges and universities that accept foreign students into their programs?
- Do you agree with the decision by the Department of Homeland Security to double the fees associated with studying in the United States to support the costs of maintaining the SEVIS system?
- Is the SEVIS system a violation of privacy for international students and their dependents?
- What kind of impact is SEVIS having at your college or university? Do you know how many international students are currently enrolled at your institution?
- If you were to study abroad, would your host country track your academic progress and whereabouts?

Sources: U.S. House of Representatives, Committee on Science, "Dealing with Students and Scholars in an Age of Terrorism: Visa Backlogs and Tracking Systems," March 26, 2003; Homeland Security Presidential Directive 2, October 2001; Lynn Franey and Samuel Siringi, "Post-Sept 11 Requirements Put Squeeze on Colleges," *Kansas City Star* (April 27, 2008).

Having discussed the history of U.S. foreign policy during the twentieth century and the new direction of foreign policy during the presidency of George W. Bush, we turn to how foreign policy is made and the major players involved.

Foreign and Defense Policy Decision Making

The executive branch is the most powerful branch of government in the formulation and implementation of U.S. foreign and defense policy. Congress also influences and shapes policy, as do the military-industrial complex, the news media, and the public.

The Executive Branch

The executive branch is the locus for creating and implementing U.S. foreign and defense policy; within the executive branch, the president is the most important individual. Among executive departments, the Department of State is primarily responsible for diplomatic activity and the Department of Defense for military policy. Other executive agencies, such as the National Security Council, the Joint Chiefs of Staff, and the Central Intelligence Agency provide additional resources for the president. The relatively new Department of Homeland Security has a role to play in foreign and defense policy making as well.

THE PRESIDENT The president is preeminent in foreign and defense policy for several reasons. The president alone is in charge of all executive-branch resources. The president has greater access to and control over information, and the president alone can act with little fear that his actions will be countermanded.

American presidents have often used their authority to order U.S. armed forces to engage in actions without seeking approval from others. Ronald Reagan ordered air strikes against Libya and the invasion of Grenada; George Bush ordered the invasion of Panama; and Bill Clinton ordered cruise missile attacks against Afghanistan, Iraq, and Sudan. Although these presidents informed congressional leaders of their intended actions, they made the decisions and undertook the actions on their own authority. For far more extensive and serious military commitments—such as the 1991 Persian Gulf War and the 2003 U.S.-led invasion of Iraq—the president sought and received congressional approval in advance.

THE DEPARTMENTS OF STATE AND DEFENSE The Departments of State and Defense have responsibility for implementing U.S. diplomatic and military policy respectively. The **Department of State** employs more than 30,000 people who gather information on foreign political, economic, social, and military situations; represent the United States in negotiations and international organizations; staff U.S. embassies and consulates in more than 180 countries, and manage numerous international assistance programs.

The **Department of Defense** contributes to policy formulation and provides the forces to undertake military operations. Under the secretary of defense and other appointed civilian officials, the Department of Defense directs U.S. forces from the Pentagon, a complex across the Potomac River from Washington, D.C. With thousands of civilian employees and millions of active-duty, National Guard, and reserve military personnel, the Department of Defense is among the most influential executive departments.

Within the Department of Defense, the **Joint Chiefs of Staff** is an important advisory body to the president, the secretary of defense, and the National Security Council. The Joint Chiefs of Staff provides a link between senior civilian leadership in the Department of Defense and the professional military, and the office often assists with the coordination of the various branches of the armed forces.

The Department of Defense is also home to some of the nation's most sophisticated intelligence organizations, including the **National Security Agency (NSA)**, which gathers intelligence from electronic and other sources and undertakes code breaking; the **Central Intelligence Agency (CIA)**, which collects and analyzes information necessary to meet national security requirements; and the **National Security Council (NSC)**, which advises the president on foreign and military affairs. The CIA is the best-known intelligence agency, but it is only one of many government organizations engaged in intelligence work within the Department of Defense. The Departments of State, Homeland Security, Treasury, and Energy also maintain intelligence units. The CIA is an independent agency and its head, the director of central intelligence, reports directly to the president. The Intelligence Reform and Terrorism Prevention Act of 2004 established a director of national intelligence who oversees the entire intelligence community. After the 9/11 terrorist attacks, the CIA and the rest of the intelligence community were criticized for failing to identify clues that could

---

You Are the President of the United States

Department of State
Chief executive-branch department responsible for formulation and implementation of U.S. foreign policy.

Department of Defense
Chief executive-branch department responsible for formulation and implementation of U.S. military policy.

Joint Chiefs of Staff
Advisory body to the president that includes the army chief of staff, the air force chief of staff, the chief of naval operations, and the marine commandant.

National Security Agency (NSA)
Intelligence agency primarily responsible for gathering intelligence from electronic and nonelectronic sources and for breaking foreign information transmission codes.

Central Intelligence Agency (CIA)
Executive agency responsible for collection and analysis of information and intelligence about foreign countries and events.

National Security Council (NSC)
Executive agency responsible for advising the president about foreign and defense policy and events.

have prevented the attacks and for relying too heavily on electronic means of gathering intelligence and not heavily enough on human sources. Controversy over faulty intelligence about Iraq, the agency's serious lack of human intelligence sources in a number of trouble spots, and its connection to secret prisons and controversial interrogation techniques generated a great deal of criticism on Capitol Hill and among the public.[17] (To learn more about controversial private security firms in Iraq, see Politics Now: Blackwater.)

The National Security Council was set up to institutionalize the system by which the U.S. government integrates foreign and military policy and to coordinate U.S. activities on a range of foreign policy and defense issues. Former NSC advisers include Henry Kissinger, Colin Powell, and Condoleezza Rice. The NSC includes the president, the vice president, the secretaries of state and defense, the chair of the Joint Chiefs of Staff, and the director of the CIA.

THE DEPARTMENT OF HOMELAND SECURITY Following the 9/11 terrorist attacks on the United States, the Office of Homeland Security was created by executive order and tasked to coordinate the executive branch's efforts to "detect, prepare for, prevent, protect against, respond to, and recover from terrorist attacks against the United States." Legislation in late 2002 converted this office into the Cabinet-level **Department of Homeland Security (DHS)**. This was the largest reorganization of the federal government since the creation of the Department of Defense in 1947. The homeland security reorganization brought the functions of twenty-two existing agencies, approximately thirty newly created agencies or offices, and 180,000 employees under a single department. The mission of the department is to protect the American public from future acts of terror by engaging in activities designed to thwart terrorist activities and respond to any future crises.

> **Department of Homeland Security**
> Cabinet department created after the 9/11 attacks to coordinate domestic U.S. security efforts against terrorism.

The department is the locus for federal, state, and local homeland security coordination. Staff members work with state, local, and private-sector partners to identify threats, determine vulnerabilities, and target resources. The department includes the Transportation Security Administration (TSA), the organization responsible for aviation security; the Federal Emergency Management Agency (FEMA), the primary federal disaster relief organization; Customs and Border Protection; the Coast Guard; the Secret Service; and immigration services and enforcement.

Immigration

Congress

The U.S. Constitution gave Congress fewer responsibilities in foreign and defense policy than the president; nevertheless, the legislative branch plays an important role in the policy process. Most would agree that Congress is the second most important actor in shaping American foreign and defense policy.[18] Congress influences foreign and defense policy through its congressional leadership, oversight, approval of treaties and appointments, appropriations, and the War Powers Act.

From World War II until the late 1960s, Congress deferred to the president and the military on foreign and defense issues and rarely exercised its oversight responsibilities outside appropriations. The Vietnam War changed this. As questions emerged about U.S. policy toward Vietnam, Congress questioned executive leadership in other areas of foreign and military policy as well. This expanded oversight is now the norm. For example, in 2005 and 2006, the Senate Foreign Relations Committee questioned Bush administration officials and military leaders about growing sectarian violence in Iraq and the NSA's domestic spying program.

POLITICS NOW

Source: WASHINGTON POST   December 24, 2007

Private Security Firms in Iraq

Warnings Unheeded on Guards in Iraq

STEVE FAINARU

The U.S. government disregarded numerous warnings over the past two years about the risks of using Blackwater Worldwide and other private security firms in Iraq, expanding their presence even after a series of shooting incidents showed that the firms were operating with little regulation or oversight, according to government officials, private security firms and documents.

The warnings were conveyed in letters and memorandums from defense and legal experts and in high-level discussions between U.S. and Iraqi officials. They reflected growing concern about the lack of control over the tens of thousands of private guards in Iraq, the largest private security force ever employed by the United States in wartime.

Neither the Pentagon nor the State Department took substantive action to regulate private security companies until Blackwater guards opened fire Sept. 16, 2007, at a Baghdad traffic circle, killing 17 Iraqi civilians and provoking protests over the role of security contractors in Iraq.

"Why is it they couldn't see this coming?" said Christopher Beese, chief administrative officer for ArmorGroup International, a British security firm with extensive operations in Iraq. "That amazes me. Somebody—it could have been military officers, it could have been State—anybody could have waved a flag and said, 'Stop, this is not good news for us.'"

Private security firms rushed into Iraq after the March 2003 invasion. The U.S. military, which entered the country with 130,000 troops, needed additional manpower to protect supply convoys, military installations and diplomats. Last year, the Pentagon estimated that 20,000 hired guns worked in Iraq; the Government Accountability Office estimated 48,000.

On Feb. 7, 2006, Blackwater guards allegedly killed three Kurdish civilians outside the northern city of Kirkuk. The incident was one of several shootings that caused friction between the U.S. and Iraqi governments. On Christmas Eve 2006, a Blackwater employee killed the bodyguard of an Iraqi vice president in the Green Zone. Six weeks later, a Blackwater sniper killed three security guards for the state-run media network. On May 24, a Blackwater team shot and killed a civilian driver outside the Interior Ministry gates, sparking an armed standoff between the Blackwater guards and Iraqi security forces in downtown Baghdad.

By June 6, concerns about Blackwater had reached Iraq's National Intelligence Committee, which included senior Iraqi and U.S. intelligence officials. Maj. Gen. Hussein Kamal, who heads the Interior Ministry's intelligence directorate, called on U.S. authorities to crack down on private security companies.

U.S. military officials told Kamal that Blackwater was under State Department authority and outside their control, according to notes of the meeting. The matter was dropped.

"We set this thing up for failure from the beginning," said T.X. Hammes, a retired Marine colonel who advised the new Iraqi army from January to March 2004. "We're just sorting it out now," Hammes said. "I still think, from a pure counterinsurgency standpoint, armed contractors are an inherently bad idea, because you cannot control the quality, you cannot control the action on the ground, but you're held responsible for everything they do."

U.S. officials argue that security contractors save money and free up troops for more urgent tasks, such as fighting insurgents. "Certainly there have been moments of frustration where people here have said, 'Maybe we should just take over the whole operation, even if it stretches our forces more,'" Pentagon spokesman Geoff Morell said. "But the reality is that we think our resources are better utilized taking it to the bad guys than guarding warehouses and escorting convoys."

The State Department investigated previous Blackwater shootings and found no indication of wrongdoing, according to a senior official involved in security matters. He said the U.S. Embassy discussed any concerns the Iraqi government had about the company's conduct. "I'm not aware of the significant warnings," said the official, who spoke on condition of anonymity because of ongoing investigations related to the Sept. 16 shooting.

But the laws governing security contractors still have not been clarified. On Sept. 30, 2006, Congress passed a provision aimed at giving the military authority over all contractors in Iraq, including Blackwater. But the provision has not been implemented by the Pentagon. The 15-month delay "has led to much confusion over who will be covered . . . and has called into question whether the Department plans to utilize this provision," Sen. Lindsey O. Graham (R-S.C.) and Sen. John F. Kerry (D-Mass.), who sponsored the provision, wrote in a letter to Defense Secretary Robert M. Gates shortly after the Sept. 16 incident.

The Pentagon is studying whether the provision can withstand legal scrutiny, Pentagon spokesman Bryan Whitman said.

Discussion Questions

1. *In previous wars, the Department of Defense prohibited private security contractors from participating in combat. This policy was revised in 2005. Should private security forces be involved in combat situations? Why or why not? What role, if any, should private security firms play in military operations?*

2. *What degree of oversight should the Pentagon exercise over private security forces hired by the Department of Defense? How can the Pentagon effectively regulate the actions of private security personnel?*

3. *Should private security personnel be held legally accountable to the country in which they operate? Or, should they operate with legal immunity? Explain your reasoning.*

The Constitution gives the Senate explicit power to approve treaties, but the Senate has rejected treaties only twenty times in U.S. history.[19] The Senate's power to approve treaties is important, however. Presidents want to avoid the embarrassment of Senate rejection of a treaty, the delay of a filibuster, or senatorial refusal to consider a treaty. Presidents can avoid the treaty process by using executive agreements, which unlike treaties do not require Senate approval.

Although the Constitution gives the president the power to appoint ambassadors and others involved in foreign and defense policy, it gives the Senate the responsibility to provide advice and consent on these appointments. For example, in 2005, President Bush nominated John R. Bolton to serve as the U.S. ambassador to the United Nations. Bolton, a former State Department official, has close ties to the Bush family and pursued aggressive tactics against the 2000 presidential vote recount in Florida. His nomination as ambassador to the UN caused a prolonged filibuster by Senate Democrats, who opposed Bolton for a number of reasons, including his skepticism of the United Nations, his opposition to the International Criminal Court, and his harsh management tactics. Ultimately President Bush installed Bolton as ambassador via a congressional recess appointment that lasted until a new Congress convened in January 2007.

Congress has a key role in shaping foreign and defense policy through its power to appropriate funds, and it influences when and where the United States fights through its control of the budget. While the power to go to war is shared by the executive and legislative branches of government, the power to appropriate funds belongs to the legislature alone. (To learn more about U.S. defense spending since 1940, see Figure 14.1.)

You Are the Newly Appointed Ambassador to the Country of Dalmatia

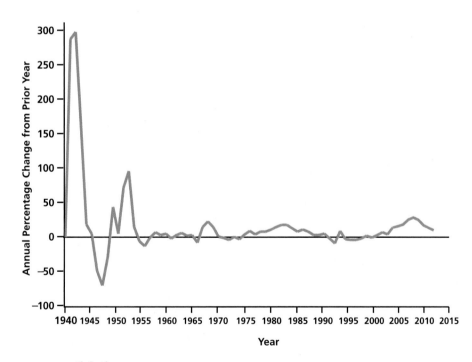

FIGURE 14.1 U.S. Defense Spending, 1940–2012

The figure shows the percentage change from the prior year in the amount of current dollars spent on U.S. defense (data for 2007–2012 are estimated). As the figure illustrates, nothing in modern American history compares to the increase in spending after the United States entered World War II in 1941. Other significant increases in defense spending were related to the Cold War in the early 1950s and the Vietnam War in the 1960s. President George W. Bush's defense increases to fight the war on terrorism after 2001 are the highest since the end of the Cold War in the 1980s.

Source: Harold W. Stanley and Richard G. Niemi, eds., *Vital Statistics on American Politics, 2007–2008* (Washington, DC: CQ Press, 2008). Reprinted by permission.

War Powers Act
Passed by Congress in 1973; the president is limited in the deployment of troops overseas to a sixty-day period in peacetime (which can be extended for an extra thirty days to permit withdrawal) unless Congress explicitly gives its approval for a longer period.

Throughout American history, there have been cases where Congress and the executive branch disagreed on U.S. military actions overseas. During the Vietnam War, however, Congress tried to define and limit the president's and the executive branch's ability to engage in military action overseas by passing the **War Powers Act**. The act requires the president to consult with Congress before deploying American troops into hostile situations. Under certain conditions, the president is required to report to Congress within forty-eight hours of the deployment. A presidential report can trigger a sixty-day clock that requires congressional approval for any continued military involvement past the sixty-day window. If Congress does not give explicit approval within sixty days, the president then has thirty days to withdraw the troops. Under the act, the president could respond to an emergency such as rescuing endangered Americans but could not engage in a prolonged struggle without congressional approval. The War Powers Act is controversial and has not been an effective restraint on presidential military adventurism.

The Military-Industrial Complex

military-industrial complex
The grouping of the U.S. armed forces and defense industries.

President Dwight D. Eisenhower, a former general who commanded Allied forces during World War II, warned in his 1961 farewell address that the United States had developed a **military-industrial complex** that included the military and defense industries. This complex, Eisenhower feared, could become an increasingly dominant factor in U.S. politics with "potential for the disastrous rise of misplaced power."[20]

The military-industrial complex has the potential to acquire power for several reasons. First, it has economic clout. During the Cold War, as much as 7 percent of the U.S. gross national product was spent on defense. Second, it has access to technical expertise and political information. Third, the military and defense industries share many interests. For example, both benefited economically when tensions between the United States and the Soviet Union increased. Fourth, personal and professional relationships between the military and defense industries are close, with many newly retired military officers going to work for defense industries. Finally, the military and defense industry officials work closely with legislators and their staffs. Planned or unplanned, undue influence can accompany close working relations.

The News Media

News media reports provide the public with valuable information on government actions and policy initiatives related to foreign and defense policy. From World War II to the Vietnam War, the press tended to support the president in foreign and defense policy. As a rule, editors assumed that government statements were true and printed them as fact. In the mid-1960s, this changed as U.S. involvement in Vietnam grew and reporters based in Vietnam realized that the daily military briefings at times were untrue. This led many journalists to investigate government statements rather than merely repeating them as fact. Some observers complain that since Vietnam and the Watergate scandal during Richard M. Nixon's presidency, the news media have become too intent on investigating and challenging the government, but others argue that freedom of the press is a crucial, constitutionally protected right in the United States and that investigative reporting is critical for a full accounting of government activities. In 2004, the media broke the news about abuse of prisoners at Iraq's Abu Ghraib prison by U.S. military personnel, launching a public outcry and government investigations. (To learn more, see Analyzing Visuals: Abu Ghraib Prisoner Abuse.)

Analyzing Visuals | Abu Ghraib Prisoner Abuse

Photos of American soldiers demeaning, taunting, and torturing Iraqi detainees in Abu Ghraib prison in Iraq shocked the world when they were published in 2004. Acts of torture violate the Geneva conventions of warfare, to which the United States is a signatory. The resulting scandal led to investigations by both Congress and the Pentagon and a series of trials against the alleged abusers, most of whom were young, lower-level soldiers. Nine army reservists were convicted of abusing detainees; eight received prison sentences. Pentagon officials maintain that the abuse at Abu Ghraib was the product of rogue soldiers who chose to break the rules. Those involved argue they were ordered to use aggressive interrogation techniques by CIA interrogators and personnel higher up in the chain of command. Reports about the use of waterboarding, an interrogation technique widely viewed as torture, generated renewed debate about what is and isn't torture and the treatment of suspected terrorists in U.S. custody. Examine the photograph and answer the following questions:

Photo courtesy: New Yorker magazine

WHAT has been the impact—nationally and internationally—of the use of torture on suspected terrorists by the United States?

ARE there instances in which you would condone torture of an enemy? Why or why not?

DOES the use of torture by the United States jeopardize the safety of American troops? Why or why not?

The Public

The American public affects foreign and defense policy through expressions of public opinion, elections, and public action. However, as a rule, the American public is more interested in domestic affairs than foreign and defense policy. (To learn more about historical trends in public opinion, see Figure 14.2.)

In the United States and other democracies, foreign policy or defense crises generally increase presidential popularity, but sometimes the increase is temporary. President

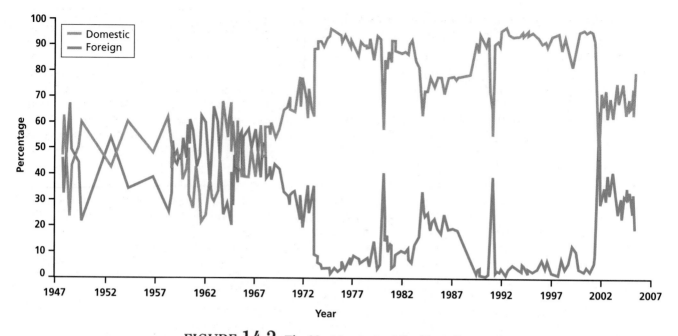

FIGURE 14.2 **The Most Important Problem: Domestic or Foreign, 1947–2007**

Note: Typical question: "What do you think is the most important problem facing this country today?"

Source: Harold W. Stanley and Richard G. Niemi, eds., *Vital Statistics on American Politics, 2007–2008* (Washington, DC: CQ Press, 2008). Reprinted by permission.

George W. Bush's approval ratings skyrocketed from 51 percent to 86 percent shortly after September 11, 2001—the largest "rally effect" ever reported by the Gallup polling organization. Bush's popularity remained high during the war in Afghanistan, fell somewhat at the beginning of the war in Iraq in 2003, and then declined significantly as the war dragged on despite the president's "Mission Accomplished" event on an aircraft carrier in May 2003. By 2008, Bush's job approval rating had slipped to 30 percent or lower in some polls, due in large part to the conflict in Iraq and the economic downturn.

nongovernmental organization (NGO)
An organization that is not tied to a government.

In addition to expressions of public opinion, U.S. citizens exercise electoral control on foreign and defense policy during elections. Citizens may also influence U.S. policy through activism, especially when they join or work with **nongovernmental organizations (NGOs)**, international organizations that seek a set of objectives but are not formally connected to a government. Amnesty International, for example, monitors human rights violations worldwide and seeks to galvanize world opinion to influence the behaviors of offending governments.

Comparing Foreign and Security Policy

Toward Reform: Twenty-First-Century Challenges

As the international community has grown more interconnected over time, forging U.S. foreign and defense policies that both protect American interests and benefit those outside our borders has become more consequential and increasingly challenging. How can the United States best support democracy abroad? What can the United States do to promote peace between Israelis and Palestinians? What is the best way to deter states like Iran from developing nuclear capabilities? What policies are appropriate for relations with increasingly powerful states such as China?

Promoting Democracy in the Middle East

Promoting democracy in the Middle East is a difficult task that can have unexpected consequences. Though Saddam Hussein's government in Iraq was easily toppled in 2003, the situation there is far less secure than initially predicted by the Bush administration. Many Iraqis, even those glad to be free of Hussein's tyrannical rule, are troubled by the lawlessness unleashed by Hussein's overthrow. Many resent the U.S. occupation but remain skeptical of the democratically elected government's effectiveness should the United States withdraw its troops. While some parts of Iraq are successfully rebuilding and remain relatively calm, the overall situation remains enormously volatile. Oil pipelines are routinely sabotaged, Iraqi police forces often come under attack, and Iraqis face great uncertainty about the future. The United States has begun turning over control of security to Iraqi forces, but whether the Iraqi government has the capacity to control sectarian violence in the absence of a U.S. presence is an open question.

Iraq remains an unfinished piece of business, as does Afghanistan, which is under assault from reorganized Taliban militias. Additionally, since the U.S. overthrow of the Taliban regime in Afghanistan in 2001, opium production has surged.[21] Today, Afghanistan is the world's largest producer of opium. According to the IMF, drug revenue accounts for roughly 75 percent of the country's economy and opium trafficking has contributed to government corruption at all levels.

Transnational Threats to Peace

Terrorist organizations are an ever evolving threat that is not easily contained or defeated with traditional military activities. Operating as nonstate actors, terrorists "blur the line between civilians and the military" and "confound war plans and diplomatic practices based upon enemies with fixed territory and political sovereignty."[22] Some groups, such as al-Qaeda, possess sophisticated economic, political, and military resources and are actively seeking to obtain weapons of mass destruction—nuclear, chemical, or biological weapons. Meeting these threats is a key element of the war on terrorism, which the Bush administration repeatedly cautioned will be both long and costly.

Because of its reliance on computers, the United States is vulnerable to information warfare: attacks on information systems. How serious is the threat of information warfare? Government studies have highlighted the vulnerabilities of U.S. infrastructures, including communications and telephones, banking, power grids, water systems, fuel supply networks, and other systems that rely on computers.[23] Indeed, in a 1997 war game, government hackers penetrated computers on military bases, gained access to computers on a navy cruiser, could have closed down the U.S. electric power grid, and positioned themselves to disable the emergency 911 network.[24]

Thinking Globally

The International Criminal Court

The United States, India, and China have declined membership in the International Criminal Court (ICC)—a UN-established institution with jurisdiction over crimes against humanity, war crimes, and genocide. More than one hundred nations have joined the ICC, including the European Union nations, Canada, and most of Latin America.

- Can a multilateral institution such as the ICC function effectively without the support of powerful nations such as the United States and China? Why or why not?
- Should the United States join the ICC? What arguments can you make in favor of membership and what arguments support continued nonparticipation?

What role should former U.S. presidents play in crafting American foreign policy? During a controversial April 2008 visit to the Middle East, former president and Nobel Peace Prize winner Jimmy Carter attends a wreath-laying ceremony at Palestinian leader Yasser Arafat's grave. Carter's diplomatic efforts were criticized by the Bush administration and the Israeli government.

Photo courtesy: Thaer Ganaim/Office of the Palestinian President/Getty Images

WHAT SHOULD I HAVE LEARNED?

Foreign and defense policy are important functions of the U.S. government. This chapter stressed the evolution of foreign and defense policy over time, the role of public and private agencies, and the challenges that American policy makers face in the twenty-first century. In examining these issues, this chapter answered the following questions:

■ **What are the roots of U.S. foreign and defense policy?**

After World War II, foreign and defense policy became major concerns, especially issues such as U.S.-Soviet relations, nuclear weapons, and the Vietnam War. Despite debate, an underlying consensus existed that American policy should focus on containing the Soviet Union. After the Soviet Union collapsed, no immediate consensus emerged on the direction of U.S. foreign policy. The terrorist attacks that took place on September 11, 2001, caused the United States to focus much of its energy on a war against terrorism.

■ **What is the process of foreign and defense policy decision making?**

Balances found in other parts of the U.S. political system are generally absent in foreign and defense policy. The executive branch of government dominates foreign and defense policy, with the Departments of State and Defense being particularly important. Within the executive branch, the president is preeminent. Until the War Powers Act, few constraints were placed on presidential prerogatives in foreign and defense policy. Presidential power experienced a post-9/11 resurgence as concerns about national security often eclipsed executive accountability and the protection of civil liberties. Institutions outside the executive also play a role in U.S. foreign and defense policy. These include Congress, the military-industrial complex, the news media, and the public.

■ **What challenges confront the United States in the twenty-first century?**

The United States faces major challenges in foreign and defense policy during the twenty-first century, especially homeland defense and the global war on terrorism. Other challenges include promoting democratic values globally and addressing transnational threats to peace.

Key Terms

al-Qaeda, p. 420
Bush Doctrine, p. 422
Central Intelligence Agency (CIA), p. 426
Cuban Missile Crisis, p. 415
Department of Defense, p. 426
Department of Homeland Security, p. 427
Department of State, p. 426
détente, p. 417
engagement, p. 419
enlargement, p. 419
human rights, p. 417
isolationism, p. 414

Joint Chiefs of Staff, p. 426
military-industrial complex, p. 430
moralism, p. 415
National Security Agency (NSA), p. 426
National Security Council (NSC), p. 426
nongovernmental organization (NGO), p. 432
North American Free Trade Agreement (NAFTA), p. 420
Powell Doctrine, p. 419
pragmatism, p. 415

Reagan Doctrine, p. 418
Taliban, p. 421
unilateralism, p. 414
United Nations, p. 424
Vietnam War, p. 415
war on terrorism, p. 421
War Powers Act, p. 430
weapons of mass destruction (WMDs), p. 423
World Trade Organization (WTO), p. 420

Researching Foreign and Defense Policy

In the Library

Allison, Graham F., and Philip Zelikow. *Essence of Decision: Explaining the Cuban Missile Crisis*, 2nd ed. New York: Pearson, 1999.

Ambrose, Stephen, and Douglas Brinkley (contributor). *Rise to Globalism: American Foreign Policy Since 1938*, 8th ed. New York: Penguin, 1997.

Axelrod, Alan. *American Treaties and Alliances*. Washington, DC: CQ Press, 2000.

Bacevich, Andrew J. *American Empire: The Realities and Consequences of U.S. Diplomacy*. Cambridge, MA: Harvard University Press, 2002.

Boot, Max. *The Savage Wars of Peace: Small Wars and the Rise of American Power*. New York: Basic Books, 2002.

Byman, Daniel, and Matthew C. Waxman. *The Dynamics of Coercion: American Foreign Policy and the Limits of Military Might*. Cambridge: Cambridge University Press, 2002.

Clarke, Richard A. *Against All Enemies: Inside America's War on Terror*. New York: Free Press, 2004.

Ervin, Clark Kent. *Open Target: Where America Is Vulnerable to Attack*. New York: Palgrave Macmillan, 2006.

Forsythe, David P., Patrice C. McMahon, and Andrew Wedeman. *American Foreign Policy in a Globalized World*. New York: Routledge, 2006.

Goldstein, Joshua S. *International Relations*, 6th ed. New York: Longman, 2008.

Halberstam, David. *War in a Time of Peace: Bush, Clinton, and the Generals*. New York: Scribner's, 2001.

Hook, Steven W. *U.S. Foreign Policy: The Paradox of World Power*. Washington, DC: CQ Press, 2005.

Howard, Russell D., James J. F. Forest, and Joanne C. Moore. *Homeland Security and Terrorism: Readings and Interpretations*. New York: McGraw-Hill, 2006.

Johnson, Loch K. *Seven Sins of American Foreign Policy*. New York: Longman, 2007.

Kennan, George F. *American Diplomacy, 1900–1950*. Chicago: University of Chicago Press, 1951.

Lowenthal, Mark M. *Intelligence: From Secrets to Policy*, 2nd ed. Washington, DC: CQ Press, 2003.

Nye, Joseph S., Jr. *The Paradox of American Power: Why the World's Only Superpower Can't Go It Alone*. New York: Oxford University Press, 2002.

Papp, Daniel S. *The Impact of September 11 on Contemporary International Relations*. New York: Longman, 2003.

Talbott, Strobe, and Nayan Chanda, eds. *The Age of Terror: America and the World After September 11*. New York: Basic Books, 2002.

On the Web

To see the reach and worldwide involvement of the United Nations, go to **www.unsystem.org.**

To learn more about the Department of Defense and U.S. military operations around the globe, go to **www.defenselink.mil.**

To learn more about the State Department, go to **www.state.gov.**

To learn more about the CIA and the larger intelligence community, go to **www.cia.gov.**

To learn about the specific workings of the IMF and World Bank, go to **www.imf.org, www.worldbank.org.**

To learn more about strategic security, nuclear nonproliferation, and weapons of mass destruction, among other national security issues, visit the Federation of American Scientists at **www.fas.org.**

The Declaration of Independence

In Congress, July 4, 1776

The Unanimous Declaration of the Thirteen United States of America

When in the Course of human events it becomes necessary for one people to dissolve the political bands which have connected them with another, and to assume, among the powers of the earth, the separate and equal station to which the Laws of Nature and of Nature's God entitle them, a decent respect to the opinions of mankind requires that they should declare the causes which impel them to the separation.

We hold these truths to be self-evident, that all men are created equal, that they are endowed by their Creator with certain unalienable Rights, that among these are Life, Liberty and the pursuit of Happiness. That to secure these rights, Governments are instituted among Men, deriving their just powers from the consent of the governed. That whenever any Form of Government becomes destructive of these ends, it is the Right of the People to alter or to abolish it, and to institute new Government, laying its foundation on such principles and organizing its powers in such form, as to them shall seem most likely to effect their Safety and Happiness. Prudence, indeed, will dictate that Governments long established should not be changed for light and transient causes; and accordingly all experience hath shewn that mankind are more disposed to suffer, while evils are sufferable, than to right themselves by abolishing the forms to which they are accustomed. But when a long train of abuses and usurpations, pursuing invariably the same Object evinces a design to reduce them under absolute Despotism, it is their right, it is their duty, to throw off such Government, and to provide new Guards for their future security. —Such has been the patient sufferance of these Colonies; and such is now the necessity which constrains them to alter their former Systems of Government. The history of the present King of Great Britain is a history of repeated injuries and usurpations, all having in direct object the establishment of an absolute Tyranny over these States. To prove this, let Facts be submitted to a candid world.

He has refused his Assent to Laws, the most wholesome and necessary for the public good.

He has forbidden his Governors to pass Laws of immediate and pressing importance, unless suspended in their operation till his Assent should be obtained; and when so suspended, he has utterly neglected to attend to them.

He has refused to pass other Laws for the accommodation of large districts of people, unless those people would relinquish the right of Representation in the Legislature, a right inestimable to them and formidable to tyrants only.

He has called together legislative bodies at places unusual, uncomfortable, and distant from the depository of their Public Records, for the sole purpose of fatiguing them into compliance with his measures.

He has dissolved Representative Houses repeatedly, for opposing with manly firmness his invasions on the rights of the people.

He has refused for a long time, after such dissolutions, to cause others to be elected; whereby the Legislative Powers, incapable of Annihilation, have returned to the People at large for their exercise, the State remaining in the mean time exposed to all the dangers of invasion from without, and convulsions within.

He has endeavored to prevent the population of these States; for that purpose obstructing the Laws of Naturalization of Foreigners; refusing to pass others to encourage their migration hither, and raising the conditions of new Appropriations of Lands.

He has obstructed the Administration of Justice, by refusing his Assent to Laws for establishing Judiciary powers.

He has made Judges dependent on his Will alone, for the tenure of their offices, and the amount and payment of their salaries.

He has erected a multitude of New Offices, and sent hither swarms of Officers to harass our people, and eat out their substance.

He has kept among us, in times of peace, Standing Armies without the Consent of our legislatures.

He has affected to render the Military independent of and superior to the Civil power.

He has combined with others to subject us to a jurisdiction foreign to our constitution, and unacknowledged by our laws, giving his Assent to their Acts of pretended Legislation:

For quartering large bodies of armed troops among us:

For protecting them, by a mock Trial, from punishment for any Murders which they should commit on the Inhabitants of these States:

For cutting off our Trade with all parts of the world:

For imposing Taxes on us without our Consent:

For depriving us in many cases, of the benefits of Trial by Jury:

For transporting us beyond Seas to be tried for pretended offences:

For abolishing the free System of English Laws in a neighboring Province, establishing therein an Arbitrary government, and enlarging its Boundaries so as to render it at once an example and fit instrument for introducing the same absolute rule into these Colonies:

For taking away our Charters, abolishing our most valuable Laws, and altering fundamentally the Forms of our Governments:

For suspending our own Legislatures, and declaring themselves invested with power to legislate for us in all cases whatsoever.

He has abdicated Government here, by declaring us out of his Protection and waging War against us.

He has plundered our seas, ravaged our Coasts, burnt out towns, and destroyed the lives of our people.

He is at this time transporting large Armies of foreign Mercenaries to compleat the works of death, desolation and tyranny, already begun with circumstances of Cruelty and perfidy scarcely paralleled in the most barbarous ages, and totally unworthy the Head of a civilized nation.

He has constrained our fellow Citizens taken Captive on the high Seas to bear Arms against their Country, to become the executioners of their friends and Brethren, or to fall themselves by their Hands.

He has excited domestic insurrections amongst us, and has endeavored to bring on the inhabitants of our frontiers, the merciless Indian Savages, whose known rule of warfare, is an undistinguished destruction of all ages, sexes and conditions.

In every stage of these Oppressions We have Petitioned for Redress in the most humble terms: Our repeated Petitions have been answered only by repeated injury: A Prince, whose character is thus marked by every act which may define a Tyrant, is unfit to be the ruler of a free people.

Nor have We been wanting in attention to our British brethren. We have warned them from time to time of attempts by their legislature to extend an unwarrantable jurisdiction over us. We have reminded them of the circumstances of our emigration and settlement here. We have appealed to their native justice and magnanimity; and we have conjured them by the ties of our common kindred to disavow these usurpations, which would inevitably interrupt our connections and correspondence. They too have been deaf to the voice of justice and consanguinity. We must, therefore, acquiesce in the necessity, which denounces our Separation, and hold them, as we hold the rest of mankind, Enemies in War, in Peace Friends.

We, therefore, the Representatives of the United States of America, in General Congress, Assembled, appealing to the Supreme Judge of the world for the rectitude of our intentions, do, in the Name, and by Authority of the good People of these Colonies, solemnly publish and declare, That these United Colonies are, and of Right ought to be Free and Independent States; that they are Absolved from all Allegiance to the British Crown, and that all political connection between them and the State of Great Britain, is and ought to be totally dissolved: and that as Free and Independent States, they have full power to levy War, conclude Peace, contract Alliances, establish Commerce, and to do all other Acts and Things which Independent States may of right do. And for the support of this Declaration, with a firm reliance on the protection of Divine Providence, we mutually pledge to each other our Lives, our Fortunes and our sacred Honor.

JOHN HANCOCK

NEW HAMPSHIRE
Josiah Bartlett
William Whipple
Matthew Thornton

MASSACHUSETTS BAY
Samuel Adams
John Adams
Robert Treat Paine
Elbridge Gerry

RHODE ISLAND
Stephen Hopkins
William Ellery

CONNECTICUT
Roger Sherman
Samuel Huntington
William Williams
Oliver Wolcott

NEW YORK
William Floyd
Philip Livingston
Francis Lewis
Lewis Morris

NEW JERSEY
Richard Stockton

John Witherspoon
Francis Hopkinson
John Hart
Abraham Clark

PENNSYLVANIA
Robert Morris
Benjamin Rush
Benjamin Franklin
John Morton
George Clymer
James Smith
George Taylor
James Wilson
George Ross

DELAWARE
Caesar Rodney
George Read
Thomas McKean

MARYLAND
Samuel Chase
William Paca
Thomas Stone
Charles Carroll

VIRGINIA
George Wythe

Richard Henry Lee
Thomas Jefferson
Benjamin Harrison
Thomas Nelson, Jr.
Francis Lightfoot Lee
Carter Braxton

NORTH CAROLINA
William Hooper
Joseph Hewes
John Penn

SOUTH CAROLINA
Edward Rutledge
Thomas Heyward, Jr.
Thomas Lynch, Jr.
Arthur Middleton

GEORGIA
Button Gwinnett
Lyman Hall
George Walton

Federalist No. 10

November 22, 1787

James Madison

To the People of the State of New York.

Among the numerous advantages promised by a well constructed Union, none deserves to be more accurately developed than its tendency to break and control the violence of faction. The friend of popular governments, never finds himself so much alarmed for their character and fate, as when he contemplates their propensity to this dangerous vice. He will not fail therefore to set a due value on any plan which, without violating the principles to which he is attached, provides a proper cure for it. The instability, injustice and confusion introduced into the public councils, have in truth been the mortal diseases under which popular governments have every where perished; as they continue to be the favorite and fruitful topics from which the adversaries to liberty derive their most specious declamations. The valuable improvements made by the American Constitutions on the popular models, both ancient and modern, cannot certainly be too much admired; but it would be an unwarrantable partiality, to contend that they have as effectually obviated the danger on this side as was wished and expected. Complaints are every where heard from our most considerate and virtuous citizens, equally the friends of public and private faith, and of public and personal liberty; that our governments are too unstable; that the public good is disregarded in the conflicts of rival parties; and that measures are too often decided, not according to the rules of justice, and the rights of the minor party; but by the superior force of an interested and over-bearing majority. However anxiously we may wish that these complaints had no foundation, the evidence of known facts will not permit us to deny that they are in some degree true. It will be found indeed, on a candid review of our situation, that some of the distresses under which we labor, have been erroneously charged on the operation of our governments; but it will be found, at the same time, that other causes will not alone account for many of our heaviest misfortunes; and particularly, for that prevailing and increasing distrust of public engagements, and alarm for private rights, which are echoed from one end of the continent to the other. These must be chiefly, if not wholly, effects of the unsteadiness and injustice, with which a factious spirit has tainted our public administrations.

By a faction I understand a number of citizens, whether amounting to a majority or minority of the whole, who are united and actuated by some common impulse of passion, or of interest, adverse to the rights of other citizens, or to the permanent and aggregate interests of the community.

There are two methods of curing the mischiefs of faction: the one, by removing its causes; the other, by controlling its effects.

There are again two methods of removing the causes of faction: the one by destroying the liberty which is essential to its existence; the other, by giving to every citizen the same opinions, the same passions, and the same interests.

It could never be more truly said than of the first remedy, that it is worse than the diease. Liberty is to faction, what air is to fire, an aliment without which it instantly expires. But it could not be a less folly to abolish liberty, which is essential to political life, because it nourishes faction, than it would be to wish the annihilation of air, which is essential to animal life, because it imparts to fire its destructive agency.

The second expedient is as impracticable, as the first would be unwise. As long as the reason of man continues fallible, and he is at liberty to exercise it, different opinions will be formed. As long as the connection subsists between his reason and his self-love, his opinions and his passions will have a reciprocal influence on each other; and the former will be objects to which the latter will attach themselves. The diversity in the faculties of men from which the rights of property originate, is not less an insuperable obstacle to a uniformity of interests. The protection of these faculties is the first object of Government. From the protection of different and unequal faculties of acquiring property, the possession of different degrees and kinds of property immediately results: and from the influence of these on the sentiments and views of the respective proprietors, ensues a division of the society into different interests and parties.

The latent causes of faction are thus sown in the nature of man; and we see them everywhere brought into different degrees of activity, according to the different circumstances of civil society. A zeal for different opinions concerning religion, concerning Government and many other points, as well of speculation as of practice; an attachment to different leaders ambitiously contending for pre-eminence and power; or to persons of other descriptions whose fortunes have been interesting to the human passions, have in turn divided mankind into parties, inflamed them with mutual animosity, and rendered them much more disposed to vex and oppress each other, than to cooperate for their common good. So strong is this propensity of mankind to fall into mutual animosities, that where no substantial occasion presents itself, the most frivolous and fanciful distinctions have been sufficient to kindle their unfriendly passions, and excite their most violent conflicts. But the most common and durable source of factions, has been the various and unequal distribution of property. Those who hold, and those who are without property, have ever formed distinct interests in society. Those who are creditors, and those who are debtors, fall under a like discrimination. A landed interest, a manufacturing interest, a mercantile interest, a monied interest, with many lesser interests, grow up of necessity in civilized nations, and divide them into different classes, actuated by different sentiments and views. The regulation of these various and interfering interests forms the principal task of modern Legislation, and involves the spirit of party and faction in the necessary and ordinary operations of Government.

No man is allowed to be a judge in his own cause; because his interest would certainly bias his judgment, and, not improbably, corrupt his integrity. With equal, nay with greater reason, a body of men, are unfit to be both judges and parties, at the same time; yet, what are many of the most important acts of legislation, but so many judicial determinations, not indeed concerning the rights of single persons, but concerning the rights of large bodies of citizens, and what are the different classes of legislators, but advocates and parties to the causes which they determine? Is a law proposed concerning private debts? It is a question to which the creditors are parties on one side, and the debtors on the other. Justice ought to hold the balance between them. Yet the parties are and must be themselves the judges; and the most numerous party, or, in other words, the most powerful faction must be expected to prevail. Shall domestic manufactures be encouraged, and in what degree, by restrictions on foreign manufactures? are questions which would be differently decided by the landed and the manufacturing classes; and probably by neither, with a sole regard to justice and the public good. The apportionment of taxes on the various descriptions of property, is an act which seems to require the most exact impartiality; yet, there is perhaps no legislative act in which greater opportunity and temptation are given to a predominant party, to trample on the rules of justice. Every shilling with which they over-burden the inferior number, is a shilling saved to their own pockets.

It is in vain to say, that enlightened statesmen will be able to adjust these clashing interests, and render them all subservient to the public good. Enlightened statesmen will not always be at the helm: Nor, in many cases, can such an adjustment be made at all, without taking into view indirect and remote considerations, which will rarely prevail over the immediate interest which one party may find in disregarding the rights of another, or the good of the whole.

The inference to which we are brought, is, that the *causes* of faction cannot be removed; and that relief is only to be sought in the means of controlling its *effects*.

If a faction consists of less than a majority, relief is supplied by the republican principle, which enables the majority to defeat its sinister views by regular vote: It may clog the administration, it may convulse the society; but it will be unable to execute and mask its violence under the forms of the Constitution. When a majority is included in a faction, the form of popular government on the other hand enables it to sacrifice to its ruling passion or interest, both the public good and the rights of other citizens. To secure the public good, and private rights, against the danger of such a faction, and at the same time to preserve the spirit and the form of popular government, is then the great object to which our enquiries are directed: Let me add that it is the great desideratum, by which alone this form of government can be rescued from the opprobrium under which it has so long labored, and be recommended to the esteem and adoption of mankind.

By what means is this object attainable? Evidently by one of two only. Either the existence of the same passion or interest in a majority at the same time, must be prevented; or the majority, having such co-existent passion or interest, must be rendered, by their number and local situation, unable to concert and carry into effect schemes of oppression. If the impulse and the opportunity be suffered to coincide, we well know that neither moral nor religious motives can be relied on as an adequate control. They are not found to be such on the injustice and violence of individuals, and lose their efficacy in proportion to the number combined together; that is, in proportion as their efficacy becomes needful.

From this view of the subject, it may be concluded, that a pure Democracy, by which I mean, a Society, consisting of a small number of citizens, who assemble and administer the Government in person, can admit of no cure for the mischiefs of faction. A common passion or interest will, in almost every case, be felt by a majority of the whole; a communication and concert results from the form of Government itself; and there is nothing to check the inducements to sacrifice the weaker party, or an obnoxious individual. Hence it is, that such Democracies have ever been spectacles of turbulence and contention; have ever been found incompatible with personal security, or the rights of property; and have in general been as short in their lives, as they have been violent in their deaths. Theoretic politicians, who have patronized this species of Government, have erroneously supposed, that by reducing mankind to a perfect equality in their political rights, they would, at the same time, be perfectly equalized and assimilated in their possessions, their opinions, and their passions.

A republic, by which I mean a government in which the scheme of representation takes place, opens a different prospect, and promises the cure for which we are seeking. Let us examine the points in which it varies from pure democracy, and we shall comprehend both the nature of the cure and the efficacy which it must derive from the union.

The two great points of difference, between a democracy and a republic, are, first, the delegation of the government, in the latter, to a small number of citizens, elected by the rest; secondly, the greater number of citizens, and greater sphere of country, over which the latter may be extended.

The effect of the first difference is, on the one hand, to refine and enlarge the public views, by passing them through the medium of a chosen body of citizens, whose wisdom may best discern the true interest of their country, and whose patriotism and love of justice, will be least likely to sacrifice it to temporary or partial considerations. Under such a regulation, it may well happen, that the public voice, pronounced by the representatives of the people, will be more consonant to the public good, than if pronounced by the people themselves, convened for the purpose. On the other hand the effect may be inverted. Men of factious tempers, of local prejudices, or of sinister designs, may by intrigue, by corruption, or by other means, first obtain the suffrages, and then betray the interest of the people. The question resulting is, whether small or extensive republics are most favorable to the election of proper guardians of the public weal, and it is clearly decided in favor of the latter by two obvious considerations.

In the first place, it is to be remarked that, however small the republic may be, the representatives must be raised to a certain number, in order to guard against the cabals of a few; and that however large it may be, they must be limited to a certain number, in order to guard against the confusion of a multitude. Hence, the number of representatives in the two cases not being in proportion to that of the constituents, and being proportionally greatest in the small republic, it follows, that if the proportion of fit characters be not less in the large than in the small republic, the former will present a greater option, and consequently a greater probability of a fit choice.

In the next place, as each Representative will be chosen by a greater number of citizens in the large than in the small Republic, it will be more difficult for unworthy candidates to practise with success the vicious arts, by which elections are too often carried; and the suffrages of the people being more free, will be more likely to center on men who possess the most attractive merit, and the most diffusive and established characters.

It must be confessed, that in this, as in most other cases, there is a mean, on both sides of which inconveniences will be found to lie. By enlarging too much the number of electors, you render the representatives too little acquainted with all their local circumstances and lesser interests; as by reducing it too much, you render him unduly attached to these, and too little fit to comprehend and pursue great and national objects. The Federal Constitution forms a happy combination in this respect; the great and aggregate interests being referred to the national, the local and particular, to the state legislatures.

The other point of difference is, the greater number of citizens and extent of territory which may be brought within the compass of Republican, than of Democratic Government; and it is this circumstance principally which renders factious combinations less to be dreaded in the former, than in the latter. The smaller the society, the fewer probably will be the distinct parties and interests composing it; the fewer the distinct parties and interests, the more frequently will a majority be found of the same party; and the smaller the number of individuals composing a majority, and the smaller the compass within which they are placed, the more easily will they concert and execute their plans of oppression. Extend the sphere, and you take in a greater variety of parties and interests; you make it less probable that a majority of the whole will have a common motive to invade the rights of other citizens; or if such a common motive exists, it will be more difficult for all who feel it to discover their own strength, and to act in unison with each other. Besides other impediments, it may be remarked, that where there is a consciousness of unjust or dishonorable purposes, communication is always checked by distrust, in proportion to the number whose concurrence is necessary.

Hence it clearly appears, that the same advantage, which a Republic has over a Democracy, in controlling the effects of faction, is enjoyed by a large over a small Republic—is enjoyed by the Union over the States composing it. Does this advantage consist in the substitution of Representatives, whose enlightened views and virtuous sentiments render them superior to local prejudices, and to schemes of injustice? It will not be denied, that the Representation of the Union will be most likely to possess these requisite endowments. Does it consist in the greater security afforded by a greater variety of parties, against the event of any one party being able to outnumber and oppress the rest? In an equal degree does the increased variety of parties, comprised within the Union, increase this security? Does it, in fine, consist in the greater obstacles opposed to the concert and accomplishment of the secret wishes of an unjust and interested majority? Here, again, the extent of the Union gives it the most palpable advantage.

The influence of factious leaders may kindle a flame within their particular States, but will be unable to spread a general conflagration through the other States: a religious sect, may degenerate into a political faction in a part of the Confederacy but the variety of sects dispersed over the entire face of it, must secure the national Councils against any danger from that source: a rage for paper money, for an abolition of debts, for an equal division of property, or for any other improper or wicked project, will be less apt to pervade the whole body of the Union, than a particular member of it; in the same proportion as such a malady is more likely to taint a particular county or district, than an entire State.

In the extent and proper structure of the Union, therefore, we behold a Republican remedy for the diseases most incident to Republican Government. And according to the degree of pleasure and pride, we feel in being Republicans, ought to be our zeal in cherishing the spirit, and supporting the character of Federalists.

PUBLIUS

Federalist No. 51

To the People of the State of New York.
February 6, 1788
James Madison

To what expedient then shall we finally resort for maintaining in practice the necessary partition of power among the several departments, as laid down in the constitution? The only answer that can be given is, that as all these exterior provisions are found to be inadequate, the defect must be supplied, by so contriving the interior structure of the government, as that its several constituent parts may, by their mutual relations, be the means of keeping each other in their proper places. Without presuming to undertake a full development of this important idea, I will hazard a few general observations, which may perhaps place it in a clearer light, and enable us to form a more correct judgment of the principles and structure of the government planned by the convention.

In order to lay a due foundation for that separate and distinct exercise of the different powers of government, which to a certain extent, is admitted on all hands to be essential to the preservation of liberty, it is evident that each department should have a will of its own; and consequently should be so constituted, that the members of each should have as little agency as possible in the appointment of the members of the others. Were this principle rigorously adhered to, it would require that all the appointments for the supreme executive, legislative, and judiciary magistracies, should be drawn from the same fountain of authority, the people, through channels, having no communication whatever with one another. Perhaps such a plan of constructing the several departments would be less difficult in practice than it may in contemplation appear. Some difficulties however, and some additional expense, would attend the execution of it. Some deviations therefore from the principle must be admitted. In the constitution of the judiciary department in particular, it might be inexpedient to insist rigorously on the principle; first, because peculiar qualifications being essential in the members, the primary consideration ought to be to select that mode of choice, which best secures these qualifications; secondly, because the permanent tenure by which the appointments are held in that department, must soon destroy all sense of dependence on the authority conferring them.

It is equally evident that the members of each department should be as little dependent as possible on those of the others, for the emoluments annexed to their offices. Were the executive magistrate, or the judges, not independent of the legislature in this particular, their independence in every other would be merely nominal.

But the great security against a gradual concentration of the several powers in the same department, consists in giving to those who administer each department, the necessary constitutional means, and personal motives, to resist encroachments of the others. The provision for defense must in this, as in all other cases, be made commensurate to the danger of attack. Ambition must be made to counteract ambition. The interest of the man must be connected with the constitutional right of the place. It may be a reflection on human nature, that such devices should be necessary to control the abuses of government. But what is government itself but the greatest of all reflections on human nature? If men were angels, no government would be necessary. If angels were to govern men, neither external nor internal controls on government would be necessary. In framing a government which is to be administered by men over men, the great difficulty lies in this: You must first enable the government to control the governed; and in the next place, oblige it to control itself. A dependence on the people is no doubt the primary control on the government; but experience has taught mankind the necessity of auxiliary precautions.

This policy of supplying by opposite and rival interests, the defect of better motives, might be traced through the whole system of human affairs, private as well as public. We see it particularly displayed in all the subordinate distributions of power; where the constant aim is to divide and arrange the several offices in such a manner as that each may be a check on the other; that the private interest of every individual, may be a sentinel over the public rights. These inventions of prudence cannot be less requisite in the distribution of the supreme powers of the state.

But it is not possible to give to each department an equal power of self defense. In republican government the legislative authority, necessarily, predominates. The remedy for this inconveniency is, to divide the legislature into different branches; and to render them by different modes of election, and different principles of action, as little connected with each other, as the nature of their common functions, and their common dependence on the society, will admit. It may even be necessary to guard against dangerous encroachments by still further precautions. As the weight of the legislative authority requires that it should be thus divided, the weakness of the executive may require, on the other hand, that it should be fortified. An absolute negative, on the legislature, appears at first view to be the natural defense with which the executive magistrate should be armed. But perhaps it would be neither altogether safe, nor alone sufficient. On ordinary occasions, it might not be exerted with the requisite firmness; and on extraordinary occasions, it might be prefidiously abused. May not this defect of an absolute negative be supplied, by some qualified connection between this weaker department, and the weaker branch of the stronger department, by which the latter may be led to support the constitutional rights of the former, without being too much detached from the rights of its own department? If the principles on which these observations are founded be just, as I persuade myself they are, and they be applied as a criterion, to the several state constitutions, and to the federal constitution, it will be found, that if the latter does not perfectly correspond with them, the former are infinitely less able to bear such a test.

There are moreover two considerations particularly applicable to the federal system of America, which place that system in a very interesting point of view.

First. In a single republic, all the power surrendered by the people, is submitted to the administration of a single government; and usurpations are guarded against by a division of the government into distinct and separate departments. In the compound republic of America, the power surrendered by the people, is first divided between two distinct governments, and then the portion allotted to each, subdivided among distinct and separate departments. Hence a double security arises to the rights of the people. The different governments will control each other; at the same time that each will be controlled by itself.

Second. It is of great importance in a republic, not only to guard the society against the oppression of its rulers; but to guard one part of the society against the injustice of the other part. Different interests necessarily exist in different classes of citizens. If a majority be united by a common interest, the rights of the minority will be insecure. There are but two methods of providing against this evil: The one by creating a will in the community independent of the majority, that is, of the society itself, the other by comprehending in the society so many separate descriptions of citizens, as will render an unjust combination of a majority of the whole, very improbable, if not impracticable. The first method prevails in all governments possessing an hereditary or self appointed authority. This at best is but a precarious security; because a power independent of the society may as well espouse the unjust views of the major, as the rightful interests, of the minor party, and may possibly be turned against both parties. The second method will be exemplified in the federal republic of the United States. While all authority in it will be derived from and dependent on the society, the society itself will be broken into so many parts, interests and classes of citizens, that the rights of individuals or of the minority, will be in little danger from interested combinations of the majority. In a free government, the security for civil rights must be the same as for religious rights. It consists in the one case in the multiplicity of interests, and in the other, in the multiplicity of sects. The degree of security in both cases will depend on the number of interests and sects; and this may be presumed to depend on the extent of country and number of people comprehended under the same government. This view of the subject must particularly recommend a proper federal system to all the sincere and considerate friends of republican government: Since it shows that in exact proportion as the territory of the union may be formed into more circumscribed confederacies or states, oppressive combinations of a majority will be facilitated, the best security under the republican form, for the rights of every class of citizens, will be diminished; and consequently, the stability and independence of some member of the government, the only other security, must be proportionally increased. Justice is the end of government. It is the end of civil society. It ever has been, and ever will be pursued, until it be obtained, or until liberty be lost in the pursuit. In a society under the forms of which the stronger faction can readily unite and oppress the weaker, anarchy may as truly be said to reign, as in a state of nature where the weaker individual is not secured against the violence of the stronger: And as in the latter state even the stronger individuals are prompted by the uncertainty of their condition, to submit to a government which may protect the weak as well as themselves: So in the former state, will the more powerful factions or parties be gradually induced by a like motive, to wish for a government which will protect all parties, the weaker as well as the more powerful. It can be little doubted, that if the state of Rhode Island was separated from the confederacy, and left to itself, the insecurity of rights under the popular form of government within such narrow limits, would be displayed by such reiterated oppressions of factious majorities, that some power altogether independent of the people would soon be called for by the voice of the very factions whose misrule had proved the necessity of it. In the extended republic of the United States, and among the great variety of interests, parties and sects which it embraces, a coalition of a majority of the whole society could seldom take place on any other principles than those of justice and the general good; and there being thus less danger to a minor from the will of the major party, there must be less pretext also, to provide for the security of the former, by introducing into the government a will not dependent on the latter; or in other words, a will independent of the society itself. It is no less certain than it is important, notwithstanding the contrary opinions which have been entertained, that the larger the society, provided it lie within a practicable sphere, the more duly capable it will be of self government. And happily for the *republican cause*, the practicable sphere may be carried to a very great extent, by a judicious modification and mixture of the *federal principle*.

PUBLIUS

Presidents, Congresses, and Chief Justices: 1789–2009

Term	President and Vice President	Party of President	Congress	Majority Party		Chief Justice of the United States
				House	Senate	
1789–1797	**George Washington** John Adams	None	1st 2nd 3rd 4th	(N/A) (N/A) (N/A) (N/A)	(N/A) (N/A) (N/A) (N/A)	John Jay (1789–1795) John Rutledge (1795) Oliver Ellsworth (1796–1800)
1797–1801	**John Adams** Thomas Jefferson	Federalist	5th 6th	(N/A) Fed	(N/A) Fed	Oliver Ellsworth (1796–1800) John Marshall (1801–1835)
1801–1809	**Thomas Jefferson** Aaron Burr (1801–1805) George Clinton (1805–1809)	Democratic-Republican	7th 8th 9th 10th	Dem-Rep Dem-Rep Dem-Rep Dem-Rep	Dem-Rep Dem-Rep Dem-Rep Dem-Rep	John Marshall (1801–1835)
1809–1817	**James Madison** George Clinton (1809–1812)[a] Elbridge Gerry (1813–1814)[a]	Democratic-Republican	11th 12th 13th 14th	Dem-Rep Dem-Rep Dem-Rep Dem-Rep	Dem-Rep Dem-Rep Dem-Rep Dem-Rep	John Marshall (1801–1835)
1817–1825	**James Monroe** Daniel D. Tompkins	Democratic-Republican	15th 16th 17th 18th	Dem-Rep Dem-Rep Dem-Rep Dem-Rep	Dem-Rep Dem-Rep Dem-Rep Dem-Rep	John Marshall (1801–1835)
1825–1829	**John Quincy Adams** John C. Calhoun	National-Republican	19th 20th	Nat'l Rep Dem	Nat'l Rep Dem	John Marshall (1801–1835)
1829–1837	**Andrew Jackson** John C. Calhoun (1829–1832)[c] Martin Van Buren (1833–1837)	Democratic	21st 22nd 23rd 24th	Dem Dem Dem Dem	Dem Dem Dem Dem	John Marshall (1801–1835) Roger B. Taney (1836–1864)
1837–1841	**Martin Van Buren** Richard M. Johnson	Democratic	25th 26th	Dem Dem	Dem Dem	Roger B. Taney (1836–1864)
1841	**William H. Harrison**[a] John Tyler (1841)	Whig				Roger B. Taney (1836–1864)
1841–1845	**John Tyler** (VP vacant)	Whig	27th 28th	Whig Dem	Whig Whig	Roger B. Taney (1836–1864)
1845–1849	**James K. Polk** George M. Dallas	Democratic	29th 30th	Dem Whig	Dem Dem	Roger B. Taney (1836–1864)
1849–1850	**Zachary Taylor**[a] Millard Fillmore	Whig	31st	Dem	Dem	Roger B. Taney (1836–1864)
1850–1853	**Millard Fillmore** (VP vacant)	Whig	32nd	Dem	Dem	Roger B. Taney (1836–1864)

Term	President and Vice President	Party of President	Congress	Majority Party		Chief Justice of the United States
				House	Senate	
1853–1857	**Franklin Pierce** William R. D. King (1853)[a]	Democratic	33rd 34th	Dem Rep	Dem Dem	Roger B. Taney (1836–1864)
1857–1861	**James Buchanan** John C. Breckinridge	Democratic	35th 36th	Dem Rep	Dem Dem	Roger B. Taney (1836–1864)
1861–1865	**Abraham Lincoln**[a] Hannibal Hamlin (1861–1865) Andrew Johnson (1865)	Republican	37th 38th	Rep Rep	Rep Rep	Roger B. Taney (1836–1864) Salmon P. Chase (1864–1873)
1865–1869	**Andrew Johnson** (VP vacant)	Republican	39th 40th	Union Rep	Union Rep	Salmon P. Chase (1864–1873)
1869–1877	**Ulysses S. Grant** Schuyler Colfax (1869–1873) Henry Wilson (1873–1875)[a]	Republican	41st 42nd 43rd 44th	Rep Rep Rep Dem	Rep Rep Rep Rep	Salmon P. Chase (1864–1873) Morrison R. Waite (1874–1888)
1877–1881	**Rutherford B. Hayes** William A. Wheeler	Republican	45th 46th	Dem Dem	Rep Dem	Morrison R. Waite (1874–1888)
1881	**James A. Garfield**[a] Chester A. Arthur	Republican	47th	Rep	Rep	Morrison R. Waite (1874–1888)
1881–1885	**Chester A. Arthur** (VP vacant)	Republican	48th	Dem	Rep	Morrison R. Waite (1874–1888)
1885–1889	**Grover Cleveland** Thomas A. Hendricks (1885)[a]	Democratic	49th 50th	Dem Dem	Rep Rep	Morrison R. Waite (1874–1888) Melville W. Fuller (1888–1910)
1889–1893	**Benjamin Harrison** Levi P. Morton	Republican	51st 52nd	Rep Dem	Rep Rep	Melville W. Fuller (1888–1910)
1893–1897	**Grover Cleveland** Adlai E. Stevenson	Democratic	53rd 54th	Dem Rep	Dem Rep	Melville W. Fuller (1888–1910)
1897–1901	**William McKinley**[a] Garret A. Hobart (1897–1899)[a] Theodore Roosevelt (1901)	Republican	55th 56th	Rep Rep	Rep Rep	Melville W. Fuller (1888–1910)
1901–1909	**Theodore Roosevelt** (VP vacant, 1901–1905) Charles W. Fairbanks (1905–1909)	Republican	57th 58th 59th 60th	Rep Rep Rep Rep	Rep Rep Rep Rep	Melville W. Fuller (1888–1910)
1909–1913	**William Howard Taft** James S. Sherman (1909–1912)[a]	Republican	61st 62nd	Rep Dem	Rep Rep	Melville W. Fuller (1888–1910) Edward D. White (1910–1921)
1913–1921	**Woodrow Wilson** Thomas R. Marshall	Democratic	63rd 64th 65th 66th	Dem Dem Dem Rep	Dem Dem Dem Rep	Edward D. White (1910–1921)
1921–1923	**Warren G. Harding**[a] Calvin Coolidge	Republican	67th	Rep	Rep	William Howard Taft (1921–1930)
1923–1929	**Calvin Coolidge** (VP vacant, 1923–1925) Charles G. Dawes (1925–1929)	Republican	68th 69th 70th	Rep Rep Rep	Rep Rep Rep	William Howard Taft (1921–1930)
1929–1933	**Herbert Hoover** Charles Curtis	Republican	71st 72nd	Rep Dem	Rep Rep	William Howard Taft (1921–1930) Charles Evans Hughes (1930–1941)

| Term | President and Vice President | Party of President | Congress | Majority Party | | Chief Justice of the United States |
				House	Senate	
1933–1945	**Franklin D. Roosevelt**[a] John Nance Garner (1933–1941) Henry A. Wallace (1941–1945) Harry S Truman (1945)	Democratic	73rd 74th 75th 76th 77th 78th	Dem Dem Dem Dem Dem Dem	Dem Dem Dem Dem Dem Dem	Charles Evans Hughes (1930–1941) Harlan F. Stone (1941–1946)
1945–1953	**Harry S Truman** (VP vacant, 1945–1949) Alben W. Barkley (1949–1953)	Democratic	79th 80th 81st 82nd	Dem Rep Dem Dem	Dem Rep Dem Dem	Harlan F. Stone (1941–1946) Frederick M. Vinson (1946–1953)
1953–1961	**Dwight D. Eisenhower** Richard M. Nixon	Republican	83rd 84th 85th 86th	Rep Dem Dem Dem	Rep Dem Dem Dem	Frederick M. Vinson (1946–1953) Earl Warren (1953–1969)
1961–1963	**John F. Kennedy**[a] Lyndon B. Johnson (1961–1963)	Democratic	87th	Dem	Dem	Earl Warren (1953–1969)
1963–1969	**Lyndon B. Johnson** (VP vacant, 1963–1965) Hubert H. Humphrey (1965–1969)	Democratic	88th 89th 90th	Dem Dem Dem	Dem Dem Dem	Earl Warren (1953–1969)
1969–1974	**Richard M. Nixon**[b] Spiro Agnew (1969–1973)[c] Gerald R. Ford (1973–1974)[d]	Republican	91st 92nd	Dem Dem	Dem Dem	Earl Warren (1953–1969) Warren E. Burger (1969–1986)
1974–1977	**Gerald R. Ford** Nelson A. Rockefeller[d]	Republican	93rd 94th	Dem Dem	Dem Dem	Warren E. Burger (1969–1986)
1977–1981	**Jimmy Carter** Walter Mondale	Democratic	95th 96th	Dem Dem	Dem Dem	Warren E. Burger (1969–1986)
1981–1989	**Ronald Reagan** George Bush	Republican	97th 98th 99th 100th	Dem Dem Dem Dem	Rep Rep Rep Dem	Warren E. Burger (1969–1986) William H. Rehnquist (1986–2005)
1989–1993	**George Bush** Dan Quayle	Republican	101st 102nd	Dem Dem	Dem Dem	William H. Rehnquist (1986–2005)
1993–2001	**Bill Clinton** Al Gore	Democratic	103rd 104th 105th 106th	Dem Rep Rep Rep	Dem Rep Rep Rep	William H. Rehnquist (1986–2005)
2001–2009	**George W. Bush** Dick Cheney	Republican	107th 108th 109th 110th	Rep Rep Rep Dem	Dem Rep Rep Dem	William H. Rehnquist (1986–2005) John G. Roberts Jr. (2005–)
2009–2013	**Barack Obama** Joe Biden	Democratic	111th	Dem	Dem	John G. Roberts Jr.

[a]Died in office.
[b]Resigned from the presidency.
[c]Resigned from the vice presidency.
[d]Appointed vice president.

Selected Supreme Court Cases

- *Agostini v. Felton (1997):* The Court agreed to permit public school teachers to go into parochial schools during school hours to provide remedial education to disadvantaged students because it was not an excessive entanglement of church and state.

- *Ashcroft v. Free Speech Coalition (2002):* The Court ruled that the Child Online Protection Act of 1998 was unconstitutional because it was too vague in its reliance on "community standards" to define what is harmful to minors.

- *Atkins v. Virginia (2002):* Execution of the mentally retarded is prohibited by the Eighth Amendment's cruel and unusual punishment clause.

- *Avery v. Midland (1968):* The Court declared that the one-person, one-vote standard applied to counties as well as congressional and state legislative districts.

- *Ayotte v. Planned Parenthood of Northern New England (2006):* A New Hampshire abortion law that did not provide an exception for the woman's health was unconstitutional.

- *Baker v. Carr (1962):* Watershed case establishing the principle of one person, one vote, which requires that each legislative district within a state have the same number of eligible voters so that representation is equitably based on population.

- *Barron v. Baltimore (1833):* Decision that limited the application of the Bill of Rights to the actions of Congress alone.

- *Batson v. Kentucky (1986):* Peremptory challenges cannot be used to exclude all people of a given race (in this case, African Americans) from a jury pool.

- *Benton v. Maryland (1969):* Incorporated the Fifth Amendment's double jeopardy clause.

- *Board of Regents v. Southworth (2000):* Unanimous ruling from the Supreme Court which stated that public universities could charge students a mandatory activities fee that could be used to facilitate extracurricular student political speech so long as the programs are neutral in their application.

- *Boerne v. Flores (1997):* The Court ruled that Congress could not force the Religious Freedom Restoration act upon the state governments.

- *Bowers v. Hardwick (1986):* Unsuccessful attempt to challenge Georgia's sodomy law. The case was overturned by *Lawrence* v. *Texas* in 2003.

- *Bradwell v. Illinois (1873):* In this case, a woman argued that Illinois's refusal to allow her to practice law despite the fact that she had passed the bar violated her citizenship rights under the privileges and immunities clause of the Fourteenth Amendment; the justices denied her claim.

- *Bragdon v. Abbott (1998):* The Court ruled that individuals infected with HIV but not sick enough to qualify as having AIDS were protected from discrimination by the 1990 Americans with Disabilities Act (ADA).

- *Brandenburg v. Ohio (1969):* The Court fashioned the direct incitement test for deciding whether certain kinds of speech could be regulated by the government. This test holds that advocacy of illegal action is protected by the First Amendment unless imminent action is intended and likely to occur.

- *Brown v. Board of Education (1954):* Supreme Court decision holding that school segregation is inherently unconstitutional because it violates the Fourteenth Amendment's guarantee of equal protection; marked the end of legal segregation in the United States.

- *Brown v. Board of Education II (1955):* Follow-up to *Brown* v. *Board of Education*, this case laid out the process for school desegregation and established the concept of dismantling segregationist systems "with all deliberate speed."

- *Brown University v. Cohen (1997):* Landmark Title IX case that put all colleges and universities on notice that discrimination against women would not be tolerated, even when, as in the case of Brown University, the university had tremendously expanded sports opportunities for women.

- *Buckley v. Valeo (1976):* The Court ruled that money spent by an individual or political committee in support or opposition of a candidate (but independent of the candidate's campaign) was a form of symbolic speech, and therefore could not be limited under the First Amendment.

- *Bush v. Gore (2000):* Controversial 2000 election case that made the final decision on the Florida recounts, and thus determined the result of the 2000 election.

- *Cantwell v. Connecticut (1940):* The case in which the Supreme Court incorporated the freedom of religion, ruling that the freedom to believe is absolute, but the freedom to act is subject to the regulation of society.

- *Chandler v. Miller (1997):* The Supreme Court refused to allow Georgia to require all candidates for state office to pass a urinalysis thirty days before qualifying for nomination or election, concluding that this law violated the search and seizure clause.

- *Chaplinsky v. New Hampshire (1942):* Established the Supreme Court's rationale for distinguishing between protected and unprotected speech.

- *Chicago, B&Q R.R. Co. v. Chicago (1897):* Incorporated the Fifth Amendment's just compensation clause.

- *Chisholm v. Georgia (1793):* The Court interpreted its jurisdiction under Article III, section 2, of the Constitution to include the right to hear suits brought by a citizen of one state against another state.

- *City of Cleburne v. Cleburne Living Center (1985):* Established that zoning restrictions against group homes for the retarded have a rational basis.

- *Civil Rights Cases (1883):* Name attached to five cases brought under the Civil Rights Act of 1875. In 1883, the Supreme Court decided that discrimination in a variety of public accommodations, including theaters, hotels, and railroads, could not be prohibited by the act because it was private and not state discrimination.

- *Clinton v. City of New York (1998):* The Court ruled that the line-item veto was unconstitutional because it gave powers to the president denied him by the U.S. Constitution.

- *Clinton v. Jones (1997):* The Court refused to reverse a lower court's decision that allowed Paula Jones's civil case against President Bill Clinton to proceed.

- *Cohens v. Virginia (1821):* The Court defined its jurisdiction to include the right to review all state criminal cases; additionally, this case built on *Martin* v. *Hunter's Lessee*, clarifying the Court's power to declare state laws unconstitutional.

- *Colorado Republican Federal Campaign Committee v. Federal Election Commission (1996):* The Supreme Court extended its ruling in *Buckley* v. *Valeo* to also include political parties.

- *Cooper v. Aaron (1958):* Case wherein the Court broke with tradition and issued a unanimous decision against the Little Rock School Board, ruling that the district's evasive schemes to avoid the *Brown II* decision were illegal.

- *Craig v. Boren (1976):* The Court ruled that keeping drunk drivers off the roads may be an important governmental objective, but allowing women aged eighteen to twenty-one to drink alcoholic beverages while prohibiting men of the same age from drinking is not substantially related to that goal.

- *Cruzan by Cruzan v. Director, Missouri Department of Health (1990):* The Court rejected any attempt to extend the right to privacy into the area of assisted suicide. However, the Court did note that individuals could terminate medical treatment if they were able to express, or had done so in writing, their desire to have medical treatment terminated in the event they became incompetent.

- *DeJonge v. Oregon (1937):* Incorporated the First Amendment's right to freedom of assembly.

- *Doe v. Bolton (1973):* In combination with *Roe* v. *Wade*, established a woman's right to an abortion.

- *Dred Scott v. Sandford (1857):* Concluded that the U.S. Congress lacked the constitutional authority to bar slavery in the territories; this decision narrowed the scope of national power while it enhanced that of the states. This case marks the first time since *Marbury* v. *Madison* that the Supreme Court found an act of Congress unconstitutional.

- *Duncan v. Louisiana (1968):* Incorporated the Sixth Amendment's trial by jury clause.

- *Engel v. Vitale (1962):* The Court ruled that the recitation in public classrooms of a non-denominational prayer was unconstitutional and a violation of the establishment clause.

- *Fletcher v. Peck (1810):* The Court ruled that state legislatures could not make laws that voided contracts or grants made by earlier legislative action.

- *Furman v. Georgia (1972):* The Supreme Court used this case to end capital punishment, at least in the short run. (The case was overturned by *Gregg* v. *Georgia* in 1976.)

- *Garcia v. San Antonio Metropolitan Transport Authority (1985):* In this case, the court ruled that Congress has the broad power to impose its will on state and local governments, even in areas that have traditionally been left to state and local discretion.

- *Georgia v. Randolph (2006):* The Court ruled that both residents of a home must consent to a search before that search is regarded as constitutional.

- *Gibbons v. Ogden (1824):* The Court upheld broad congressional power over interstate commerce.

- *Gideon v. Wainwright (1963):* Granted indigents the right to counsel.

- *Gitlow v. New York (1925):* Incorporated the free speech clause of the First Amendment, ruling that the states were not completely free to limit forms of political expression.

- *Gonzales v. O Centro Espirita Beneficente União do Vegetal (2006):* Under the Religious Freedom Restoration Act, the government has to make an exception to the Controlled Substances Act for a substance used in religious services.

- *Gonzales v. Oregon (2006):* Held that the Justice Department does not have the authority to block physician assisted suicides.

- *Gonzales v. Raich (2005):* Upheld power of Congress to ban and prosecute the possession and use of marijuana for medical purposes, even in states that permitted it.

- *Gratz v. Bollinger (2003):* The Court struck down the University of Michigan's undergraduate point system, which gave minority applicants twenty automatic points simply because they were minorities.

- *Gray v. Sanders (1963):* The Court held that voting by unit systems is unconstitutional.

- *Gregg v. Georgia (1976):* Overturning *Furman* v. *Georgia*, the case ruled that Georgia's rewritten death penalty statute is constitutional.

- *Griswold v. Connecticut (1965):* Supreme Court case that established the Constitution's implied right to privacy.

- *Grutter v. Bollinger (2003):* The Court voted to uphold the constitutionality of the University of Michigan law school's affirmative action policy, which gave preference to minority students.

- *Hamdan v. Rumsfeld (2006):* The Court ruled that detainees in the war on terrorism were entitled to the protections of the Geneva Convention and the procedural rights of the Uniform Code of Military Justice, since Congress had not approved of President George W. Bush's system of military tribunals. Congress passed the Military Commissions Act in 2006 to address the Court's ruling in *Hamdan*.

- *Hamdi et al v. Rumsfeld (2004):* The government does not have the authority to detain a U.S. citizen charged as an enemy combatant in the war on terrorism without providing basic due process protections under the Fifth Amendment.

- *Harris v. Forklift Systems (1993):* The Court ruled that a federal civil rights law created a "broad rule of workplace equality."

- *Hill v. McDonough (2006):* Challenging the form of execution prescribed in a defendant's sentence is not a proper use of a *habeas corpus* petition.

- *House v. Bell (2006):* A Tennessee death-row inmate who had otherwise exhausted his federal appeals was provided an exception due to the availability of DNA evidence suggesting his innocence; the case recognized the potential exculpatory power of DNA evidence.

- *Hoyt v. Florida (1961):* The Court ruled that an all-male jury did not violate a woman's rights under the Fourteenth Amendment.

- *Hudson v. Michigan (2006):* Evidence obtained in violation of the "knock and announce" rule is not subject to the restrictions of the exclusionary rule.

- *Hunt v. Cromartie (1999, 2001):* Continuation of redistricting litigation begun with *Shaw* v. *Reno* (1993). The Court reversed district court conclusions that the North Carolina legislature had used race-driven criteria in violation of the equal protection clause to redraw district lines.

- *Immigration and Naturalization Service v. Chadha (1983):* The Court ruled that the legislative veto as it was used in many circumstances was unconstitutional because it violated the separation of powers principle.

- *J.E.B. v. Alabama (1994):* The use of peremptory challenges to exclude jurors of a particular gender is unconstitutional.

- *Kelo v. New London (2004):* The Court ruled that government could take private property and then sell it to private developers so long as that property was slated for economic development that would benefit the surrounding community.

- *Klopfer v. North Carolina (1967):* Incorporated the Sixth Amendment's right to a speedy trial.

- *Korematsu v. U.S. (1944):* In this case, the Court ruled that the internment of Japanese Americans during World War II was not unconstitutional.

- *Lawrence v. Texas (2003):* The Court reversed its 1986 ruling in *Bowers* v. *Hardwick* by finding a Texas statute that banned sodomy to be unconstitutional.

- *League of United Latin American Citizens et al. v. Perry (2006):* Part of the 2004 Texas redistricting plan violated the Voting Rights Act because it deprived Hispanic citizens of the right to elect a representative of their choosing.

- *Lemon v. Kurtzman (1971):* The Court determined that direct government assistance to religious schools is unconstitutional. In the majority opinion, the Court created what has become known as the "Lemon Test" for deciding if a law is in violation of the establishment clause.

- *Lynch v. Donnelly (1984):* In a defeat for the ACLU, the Court held that a city's inclusion of a crèche in its annual Christmas display in a private park did not violate the establishment clause.

- *Malloy v. Hogan (1964):* Incorporated the Fifth Amendment's self-incrimination clause.

- *Mapp v. Ohio (1961):* Incorporated a portion of the Fourth Amendment by establishing that illegally obtained evidence cannot be used at trial.

- *Marbury v. Madison (1803):* Case in which the Court first asserted the power of judicial review in finding that a congressional statute extending the Court's original jurisdiction was unconstitutional.

- *Martin v. Hunter's Lessee (1816):* The Court's power of judicial review in regard to state law was clarified in this case.

- *Maryland v. Craig (1990):* The confrontation clause of the Sixth Amendment does not guarantee defendants an absolute right to come face to face with their accusers.

- *Ex parte McCardle (1869):* Post–Civil War case that reinforced Congress's power to determine the jurisdiction of the Supreme Court.
- *McCleskey v. Kemp (1987):* The Court ruled that the imposition of the death penalty did not violate the equal protection clause.
- *McCleskey v. Zant (1991):* On this appeal of the 1987 *McCleskey* case, the Court produced new standards designed to make it much more difficult for death-row inmates to file repeated appeals.
- *McConnell v. FEC (2003):* Generally speaking, the Bipartisan Campaign Finance Reform Act of 2002 does not violate the First Amendment.
- *McCreary County v. ACLU of Kentucky (2005):* The Court ruled that the display of the Ten Commandments in public schools and courthouses violated the establishment clause.
- *McCulloch v. Maryland (1819):* The Court upheld the power of the national government and denied the right of a state to tax the bank. The Court's broad interpretation of the necessary and proper clause paved the way for later rulings upholding expansive federal powers.
- *Miller v. California (1973):* Case wherein the Supreme Court began to formulate rules designed to make it easier for states to regulate obscene materials and to return to communities a greater role in determining what is obscene.
- *Minor v. Happersett (1875):* The Supreme Court once again examined the privileges and immunities clause of the Fourteenth Amendment, ruling that voting was not a privilege of citizenship.
- *Miranda v. Arizona (1966):* The Fifth Amendment requires that individuals arrested for a crime must be advised of their right to remain silent and to have counsel present.
- *Morrison v. U.S. (2000):* The Court ruled that Congress has no authority under the commerce clause to enact a provision of the Violence Against Women Act providing a federal remedy to victims of gender-motivated violence.
- *Muller v. Oregon (1908):* Case that ruled Oregon's law barring women from working more than ten hours a day was constitutional; also an attempt to define women's unique status as mothers to justify their differential treatment.
- *Near v. Minnesota (1931):* By ruling that a state law violated the freedom of the press, the Supreme Court incorporated the free press provision of the First Amendment.
- *Nebraska Press Association v. Stuart (1976):* Prior restraint case; the Court ruled that a trial judge could not prohibit the publication or broadcast of information about a murder trial.
- *Nevada Department of Human Resources v. Hibbs (2003):* The court upheld the ability of state employees to sue under the Family and Medical Leave Act.
- *New York Times Co. v. Sullivan (1964):* Supreme Court ruling that simply publishing a defamatory falsehood is not enough to justify a libel judgment. "Actual malice" must be proved to support a finding of libel against a public figure.
- *New York Times Co. v. U.S. (1971):* Also called the Pentagon Papers case; the Supreme Court ruled that any attempt by the government to prevent expression carried "a heavy presumption" against its constitutionality.
- *NLRB v. Jones and Laughlin Steel Co. (1937):* Case that upheld the National Labor Relations Act of 1935, marking a turning point in the Court's ideology toward the programs of President Franklin D. Roosevelt's New Deal.
- *In re Oliver (1948):* Incorporated the Sixth Amendment's right to a public trial.
- *Palko v. Connecticut (1937):* Set the Court's rationale of selective incorporation, a judicial doctrine whereby most but not all of the protections found in the Bill of Rights are made applicable to the states via the Fourteenth Amendment.
- *Parker v. Gladden (1966):* Incorporated the Sixth Amendment's right to an impartial trial.
- *Planned Parenthood v. Casey (1992):* This case was an unsuccessful attempt to challenge Pennsylvania's restrictive abortion regulations.

- *Plessy v. Ferguson (1896): Plessy* challenged a Louisiana statute requiring that railroads provide separate accommodations for blacks and whites. The Court found that separate but equal accommodations did not violate the equal protection clause of the Fourteenth Amendment.

- *Pointer v. Texas (1965):* Incorporated the Sixth Amendment's right to confrontation of witnesses.

- *Printz v. U.S. (1997):* The Court found that Congress lacks the authority to compel state officers to execute federal laws, specifically relating to background checks on handgun purchasers.

- *Quilici v. Village of Morton Grove (1983):* The Supreme Court refused to review a lower court's ruling upholding the constitutionality of a local ordinance banning handguns against a Second Amendment challenge.

- *R.A.V. v. City of St. Paul (1992):* The Court concluded that St. Paul, Minnesota's Bias-Motivated Crime Ordinance violated the First Amendment because it regulated speech based on the content of the speech.

- *Reed v. Reed (1971):* Turned the tide in terms of constitutional litigation, ruling that the equal protection clause of the Fourteenth Amendment prohibited unreasonable classifications based on sex.

- *Regents of the University of California v. Bakke (1978):* A sharply divided Court concluded that the university's rejection of Bakke as a student had been illegal because the use of strict affirmative action quotas was inappropriate.

- *Reno v. American Civil Liberties Union (1997):* The Court ruled that the 1996 Communications Decency Act prohibiting transfer of obscene or indecent materials over the Internet to minors violated the First Amendment because it was too vague and overbroad.

- *Reynolds v. Sims (1964):* The Court decided that every person should have an equally weighted vote in electing governmental representatives.

- *Robinson v. California (1962):* Incorporated the Eighth Amendment's right to freedom from cruel and unusual punishment.

- *Roe v. Wade (1973):* The Supreme Court found that a woman's right to an abortion was protected by the right to privacy that could be implied from specific guarantees found in the Bill of Rights and the Fourteenth Amendment.

- *Romer v. Evans (1996):* A Colorado constitutional amendment precluding any legislative, executive, or judicial action at any state or local level designed to bar discrimination based on sexual preference was ruled not rational or reasonable.

- *Rompilla v. Beard (2005):* Counsel must make a reasonable effort to examine information pertaining to the case they are trying.

- *Roper v. Simmons (2005):* Execution of minors violates the Eighth Amendment's prohibition on cruel and unusual punishment.

- *Roth v. U.S. (1957):* The Court held that in order to be obscene, material must be "utterly without redeeming social value."

- *Santa Fe Independent School District v. Doe (2000):* The Court ruled that student-led, student-initiated prayer at high school football games violated the establishment clause.

- *Schenck v. U.S. (1919):* Case in which the Supreme Court interpreted the First Amendment to allow Congress to restrict speech that is "of such a nature as to create a clear and present danger that will bring about the substantive evils that Congress has a right to prevent."

- *Seminole Tribe v. Florida (1996):* Congress cannot impose a duty on states forcing them to negotiate with Indian tribes; the state's sovereign immunity protects it from a congressional directive about how to do business.

- *Shaw v. Reno (1993):* First in a series of redistricting cases in which the North Carolina legislature's reapportionment of congressional districts based on the 1990 Census was contested because the plan included an irregularly shaped district in which race seemed to be a dominant consideration. The Court ruled that districts created with race as the dominant consideration violated the equal protection clause of the Fourteenth Amendment.

- *In re Sindram (1991):* The Court chastised Michael Sindram for filing his petition *in forma pauperis* to require the Maryland courts to expedite his request to expunge a $35 speeding ticket from his record.

- *The Slaughterhouse Cases (1873):* The Court upheld Louisiana's right to create a monopoly on the operation of slaughterhouses, despite the Butcher's Benevolent Association's claim that this action deprived its members of their livelihood and the privileges and immunities granted by the Fourteenth Amendment.

- *Smith v. Massachusetts (2005):* Double jeopardy clause prohibits judges from reconsidering verdicts reached earlier in a trial, even in light of new evidence.

- *South Dakota v. Dole (1987):* The Court ruled that it was permissible for the federal government to require states that wanted transportation funds to pass laws setting twenty-one as the legal drinking age.

- *Stenberg v. Carhart (2000):* The Court ruled that a Nebraska "partial birth" abortion statute was unconstitutionally vague and unenforceable, calling into question the laws of twenty-nine other states.

- *Stromberg v. California (1931):* The Court overturned the conviction of a director of a Communist youth camp under a state statute prohibiting the display of a red flag.

- *Swann v. Charlotte-Mecklenberg School District (1971):* The Supreme Court ruled that all vestiges of *de jure* discrimination must be eliminated at once.

- *Tennessee v. Lane (2004):* Upheld application of the Americans with Disabilities Act to state courthouses.

- *Texas v. Johnson (1989):* The Court overturned the conviction of a Texas man found guilty of setting fire to an American flag.

- *Thornburg v. Gingles (1986):* At-large election of state legislators violates the Voting Rights Act because it dilutes the voting strength of African Americans.

- *Tinker v. Des Moines Independent School District (1969):* Upheld student's rights to express themselves by wearing black armbands symbolizing protest of the Vietnam War.

- *Tory v. Cochran (2005):* Prohibiting defamation of an individual after that person's death is an overly broad exercise of prior restraint.

- *U.S. v. Curtiss-Wright Export Corporation (1936):* The Court upheld the rights of Congress to grant the president authority to act in foreign affairs and to allow the president to prohibit arms shipments to participants in foreign wars.

- *U.S. v. Grubbs (2006):* A warrant does not need to describe the reason for its existence, only the person and things to be seized.

- *U.S. v. Lopez (1995):* The Court invalidated a section of the Gun Free School Zones Act, ruling that regulating guns did not fall within the scope of the commerce clause, and therefore was not within the powers of the federal government. Only states have the authority to ban guns in school zones.

- *U.S. v. Miller (1939):* The last time the Supreme Court addressed the constitutionality of the Second Amendment; ruled that the amendment was only intended to protect a citizen's right to own ordinary militia weapons.

- *U.S. v. Nixon (1974):* In a case involving President Richard M. Nixon's refusal to turn over tape recordings of his conversations, the Court ruled that executive privilege does not grant the president an absolute right to secure all presidential documents.

- *U.S. v. Patane (2004):* Physical evidence obtained in un-Mirandized voluntary statements is admissible in court.

- *U.S. Term Limits v. Thornton (1995):* The Supreme Court ruled that states do not have the authority to enact term limits for federal elected officials.

- *Washington v. Glucksberg (1997):* A state ban on physician assisted suicide does not violate the Fourteenth Amendment's due process clause.

- *Washington v. Texas (1967):* Incorporated the Sixth Amendment's right to a compulsory trial.
- *Webster v. Reproductive Health Services (1989):* In upholding several restrictive abortion regulations, the Court opened the door for state governments to enact new restrictions on abortion.
- *Weeks v. U.S. (1914):* Case wherein the Supreme Court adopted the exclusionary rule, which bars the use of illegally obtained evidence at trial.
- *Westberry v. Sanders (1964):* Established the principal of one person, one vote for congressional districts.
- *Wolf v. Colorado (1949):* The Court ruled that illegally obtained evidence did not necessarily have to be eliminated from use during trial.
- *Youngstown Sheet & Tube Co. v. Sawyer (1952):* The Court invalidated President Harry S Truman's seizure of the nation's steel mills.
- *Zelman v. Simmons-Harris (2002):* The Court concluded that governments can give money to parents to allow them to send their children to private or religious schools.

Glossary

A

administrative adjudication: A quasi-judicial process in which a bureaucratic agency settles disputes between two parties in a manner similar to the way courts resolve disputes.

administrative discretion: The ability of bureaucrats to make choices concerning the best way to implement congressional intentions.

Administrative Procedures Act: A statute containing Texas's rule-making process.

advisory referendum: A process in which voters cast nonbinding ballots on an issue or proposal.

affiliates: Local television stations that carry the programming of a national network.

affirmative action: Policies designed to give special attention or compensatory treatment to members of a previously disadvantaged group.

agenda: A set of issues to be discussed or given attention.

agenda setting: The constant process of forming the list of issues to be addressed by government.

agriculture commissioner: The elected state official in charge of regulating and promoting agriculture.

the Alamo: A San Antonio mission that was defended by Texans during their war for independence.

al-Qaeda: Worldwide terrorist organization led by Osama bin Laden, responsible for numerous attacks against U.S. interests, including 9/11 attacks against the World Trade Center and the Pentagon.

American Creed: A set of ideas that provide a national identity, limit government, and structure politics in America.

American dream: An American ideal of a happy, sucessful life, which often includes wealth, a house, a better life for one's children, and, for some, the ability to grow up to be president.

amicus curiae: "Friend of the court"; a third party to a lawsuit who files a legal brief for the purpose of raising additional points of view in an attempt to influence a court's decision.

Anglos: Non-Hispanic whites.

annexation: Enlargement of a city's corporate limits by incorporating surrounding territory into the city.

Anti-Federalists: Those who favored strong state governments and a weak national government; opposed the ratification of the U.S. Constitution.

appellate courts: Courts that generally review only findings of law made by lower courts.

appellate jurisdiction: The power vested in an appellate court to review and/or revise the decision of a lower court.

application for discretionary review: Request for Texas Court of Criminal Appeals review, which is granted if four judges agree.

apportionment: The process of allotting congressional seats to each state following the decennial census according to the state's proportion of the population.

Articles of Confederation: The compact among the thirteen original states that was the basis of their government. Written in 1776, the Articles were not ratified by all the states until 1781.

at-large-by-place: An election system in which all positions on the council or governing body are filled by city-wide elections, with each position designated as a seat, and candidates must choose which place to run for.

attorney general: The elected official who is the chief counsel for the state of Texas.

authoritarian system: A system of government that bases its rule on force rather than consent of the governed.

B

balanced budget: A budget in which the legislature balances expenditures with expected revenues, with no deficit.

ballot measure: An election option such as the initiative or referendum that enables voters to enact public policy.

bicameral legislature: A legislature divided into two houses; the U.S. Congress and the state legislatures are bicameral except Nebraska, which is unicameral.

bicameral Texas legislature: The legislature has two bodies, a House of Representatives and a Senate.

biennial legislature: A legislative body that meets in regular session only once in a two-year period.

bill: A proposed law.

bill of attainder: A law declaring an act illegal without a judicial trial.

Bill of Rights: The first ten amendments to the U.S. Constitution, which largely guarantee specific rights and liberties.

Black Codes: Laws denying most legal rights to newly freed slaves; passed by southern states following the Civil War.

block grant: Broad grant with few strings attached; given to states by the federal government for specified activities, such as secondary education or health services.

blog: A Web log; Web-based journal entries that provide an editorial and news outlet for citizens.

Bretton Woods Agreement: International financial agreement signed shortly before the end of World War II that created the World Bank and the International Monetary Fund.

brief: A document containing the legal written arguments in a case filed with a court by a party prior to a hearing or trial.

broadcast media: Television, radio, cable, and satellite services.

Brown v. Board of Education (1954): U.S. Supreme Court decision holding that school segregation is inherently unconstitutional because it violates the Fourteenth Amendment's guarantee of equal protection; marked the end of legal segregation in the United States.

budget execution authority: The authority to move money from one program to another program or from one agency to another agency.

bureaucracy: A set of complex hierarchical departments, agencies, commissions, and their staffs that exist to help a chief executive officer carry out his or her duties. Bureaucracies may be private organizations or governmental units.

Bush Doctrine: Policy advocated by President George W. Bush of using preemptive military action against a perceived threat to U.S. interests.

business cycles: Fluctuations between expansion and recession that are a part of modern capitalist economies.

C

Cabinet: The formal body of presidential advisers who head the fifteen executive departments. Presidents often add others to this body of formal advisers.

campaign consultant: The private-sector professionals and firms who sell to a candidate the technologies, services, and strategies required to get that candidate elected.

campaign manager: The individual who travels with the candidate and coordinates the many different aspects of the campaign.

candidate-centered politics: Politics that focuses directly on the candidates, their issues, and character rather than party affiliation.

candidate debate: Forum in which political candidates face each other to discuss their platforms, records, and character.

captured agency: A government regulatory agency that consistently makes decisions favorable to the private interests that it regulates.

Carter Doctrine: Policy announced after the 1979 Soviet invasion of Afghanistan that the Persian Gulf area was a vital U.S. interest and the United States would fight to maintain access to it.

categorical grant: Grant for which Congress appropriates funds for a specific purpose.

Central Intelligence Agency: Executive agency responsible for collection and analysis of information and intelligence about foreign countries and events.

charter school: Public school sanctioned by a specific agreement that allows the program to operate outside the usual rules and regulations.

checks and balances: A governmental structure that gives each of the three branches of government some degree of oversight and control over the actions of the others.

chief budget officer: The governor, who is charged with preparing the state budget proposal for the legislature.

chief executive officer: The governor, as the top official of the executive branch of Texas state government.

chief of state: The governor in his or her role as the official head representing the state of Texas in its relationships with the national government, other states, and foreign dignitaries.

citizen: Member of the political community to whom certain rights and obligations are attached.

city commission: A form of city government in which elected members serve on the legislative body and also serve as head administrators of city programs.

civic virtue: The tendency to form small-scale associations for the public good.

civil law: Codes of behavior related to business and contractual relationships between groups and individuals.

civil liberties: The personal guarantees and freedoms that the federal government cannot abridge by law, constitution, or judicial interpretation.

civil rights: The government-protected rights of individuals against arbitrary or discriminatory treatment by governments or individuals based on categories such as race, sex, national origin, age, religion, or sexual orientation.

Civil Rights Act of 1964: Legislation passed by Congress to outlaw segregation in public facilities and racial discrimination in employment, education, and voting; created the Equal Employment Opportunity Commission.

Civil Rights Cases (1883): Name attached to five cases brought under the Civil Rights Act of 1875. In 1883, the Supreme Court decided that discrimination in a variety of public accommodations, including theaters, hotels, and railroads, could not be prohibited by the act because it was private, not state, discrimination.

civil service laws: These acts removed the staffing of the bureaucracy from political parties and created a professional bureaucracy filled through competition.

civil service system: The system created by civil service laws by which many appointments to the federal bureaucracy are made.

civil society: Society created when citizens are allowed to organize and express their views publicly as they engage in an open debate about public policy.

clear and present danger test: Test articulated by the Supreme Court in *Schenck v. U.S.* (1919) to draw the line between protected and unprotected speech; the Court looks to see "whether the words used . . ." could "create a clear and present danger that they will bring about substantive evils" that Congress seeks "to prevent."

clemency: The governor's authority to reduce the length of a person's prison sentence.

closed primary: A primary election in which only a party's registered voters are eligible to vote.

cloture: Mechanism requiring sixty senators to vote to cut off debate.

coalition: A group made up of interests or organizations that join forces for the purpose of electing public officials.

cockroach: A member of a constitutional convention who opposes any changes in the current constitution.

collective good: Something of value that cannot be withheld from a nonmember of a group, for example, a tax write-off or a better environment.

collective security: The concept that peace would be secured if all countries collectively opposed any country that invaded another.

commander in chief: The governor in his or her role as head of the state militia.

commissioners court: The legislative body of a county in Texas.

committee: A subunit of the legislature, appointed to work on designated subjects.

Committees of Correspondence: Organizations in each of the American colonies created to keep colonists abreast of developments with the British; served as powerful molders of public opinion against the British.

communications director: The person who develops the overall media strategy for the candidate, blending the free press coverage with the paid TV, radio, and mail media.

comprehensive revision: Constitutional revision through the adoption of a new constitution.

comptroller of public accounts: The elected official who is the state's tax collector.

concurrent powers: Authority possessed by both the state and national governments that may be exercised concurrently as long as that power is not exclusively within the scope of national power or in conflict with national law.

concurrent resolution: A legislative document intended to express the will of both chambers of the legislature, even though it does not possess the authority of law.

confederation: Type of government where the national government derives its powers from the states; a league of independent states.

conference committee: Joint committee created to iron out differences between Senate and House versions of a specific piece of legislation.

congressional review: A process whereby Congress can nullify agency regulations by a joint resolution of legislative disapproval.

conservative: One thought to believe that a government is best that governs least and that big government can only infringe on individual, personal, and economic rights.

constitution: A document establishing the structure, functions, and limitations of a government.

constitutional amendment: A change, addition, or deletion to a constitution.

constitutional county court: Constitutionally mandated court for criminal and civil matters.

constitutional courts: Federal courts specifically created by the U.S. Constitution or by Congress pursuant to its authority in Article III.

Constitutional Revision Commission: Group established to research and draft a constitution for a constitutional convention.

constitutionalism: Limits placed on government through a written document.

containment: Strategy to oppose expansion of Soviet power, particularly in Western Europe and East Asia, with military power, economic assistance, and political influence.

content regulation: Governmental attempts to regulate the electronic media.

contrast ad: Ad that compares the records and proposals of the candidates, with a bias toward the sponsor.

conventional political participation: Political participation that attempts to influence the political process through well-accepted, often moderate forms of persuasion, such as writing letters to government officials, making political contributions, and voting.

cooperative federalism: The relationship between the national and state governments that began with the New Deal.

council–manager: A form of city government in which the city council and mayor hire a professional manager to run the city.

county attorney: Elected official serving as the legal officer for county government and also as a criminal prosecutor.

county auditor: Official appointed by a district judge to audit county finances.

county chairperson: Party leader in a county.

county clerk: Elected official who serves as the clerk for the commissioners court and for county records.

county commissioner: Elected official who serves on the county legislative body, the commissioners court.

county convention: County party meeting to select delegates and adopt resolutions.

county court at law: Statutory county court to relieve county judge of judicial duties.

county executive committee: Precinct chairpersons in a county that assist the county chairpersons.

county judge: Elected official who is the chief administrative officer of county government, serves on the commissioners court, and may also have some judicial functions.

county tax assessor-collector: Elected official who collects taxes for the county (and perhaps for other local governments).

county treasurer: Elected official who serves as the money manager for county government.

court of appeals: Intermediate appellate court for criminal and civil appeals.

criminal district attorney: Elected official who prosecutes criminal cases.

criminal law: Codes of behavior related to the protection of property and individual safety.

critical election: An election that signals a party realignment through voter polarization around new issues.

crossover voting: Participation in the primary of a party with which the voter is not affiliated.

Cuban Missile Crisis: The 1962 confrontation that nearly escalated into war between the United States and Soviet Union over Soviet deployment of medium-range ballistic missiles in Cuba.

cumulative voting: A method of voting in which voters have a number of votes equal to the number of seats being filled, and voters may cast their votes all for one candidate or split them among candidates in various combinations.

D

de facto discrimination: Racial discrimination that results from practice (such as housing patterns or other social factors) rather than the law.

de jure discrimination: Racial segregation that is a direct result of law or official policy.

dealignment: A general decline in partisan identification and loyalty in the electorate.

debt: The total outstanding amount the government owes as a result of borrowing in the past.

Declaration of Independence: Document drafted by Thomas Jefferson in 1776 that proclaimed the right of the American colonies to separate from Great Britain.

deep background: Information provided to a journalist that will not be attributed to any source.

deficit spending: Government spending in the current budget cycle that exceeds government revenue.

delegate: Role played by elected representatives who vote the way their constituents would want them to, regardless of their own opinions.

democracy: A system of government that gives power to the people, whether directly or through elected representatives.

Department of Defense: Chief executive-branch department responsible for formulation and implementation of U.S. military policy.

Department of Homeland Security: Cabinet department created after the 9/11 attacks to coordinate domestic U.S. security efforts against terrorism.

Department of State: Chief executive-branch department responsible for formulation and implementation of U.S. foreign policy.

departments: Major administrative units with responsibility for a broad area of government operations. Departmental status usually indicates a permanent national interest in a particular governmental function, such as defense, commerce, or agriculture.

deregulation: A reduction in market controls (such as price fixing, subsidies, or controls on who can enter a field) in favor of market-based competition.

détente: The relaxation of tensions between the United States and the Soviet Union that occurred during the 1970s.

direct democracy: A system of government in which members of the polity meet to discuss all policy decisions and then agree to abide by majority rule.

direct incitement test: A test articulated by the Supreme Court in *Brandenberg* v. *Ohio* (1969) that holds that advocacy of illegal action is protected by the First Amendment unless imminent lawless action is intended and likely to occur.

direct mailer: A professional who supervises a political campaign's direct-mail fund-raising strategies.

direct primary: The selection of party candidates through the ballots of qualified voters rather than at party nomination conventions.

discharge petition: Petition that gives a majority of the House of Representatives the authority to bring an issue to the floor in the face of committee inaction.

discount rate: The rate of interest at which member banks can borrow money from their regional Federal Reserve Bank.

district attorney (DA): Elected official who prosecutes criminal cases.

district clerk: Elected official who is responsible for keeping the records for the district court.

district court: Court of general jurisdiction for serious crimes and high-dollar civil cases.

disturbance theory: Political scientist David B. Truman's theory that interest groups form in part to counteract the efforts of other groups.

divided government: The political condition in which different political parties control the White House and Congress.

domestic dependent nation: A type of sovereignty that makes an Indian tribe in the United States outside the authority of state governments but reliant on the federal government for the definition of tribal authority.

double jeopardy clause: Part of the Fifth Amendment that protects individuals from being tried twice for the same offense.

dual federalism: The belief that having separate and equally powerful levels of government is the best arrangement.

due process clause: Clause contained in the Fifth and Fourteenth Amendments. Over the years, it has been construed to guarantee to individuals a variety of rights ranging from economic liberty to criminal procedural rights to protection from arbitrary governmental action.

due process rights: Procedural guarantees provided by the Fourth, Fifth, Sixth, and Eighth Amendments for those accused of crimes.

E

earmark: Funds that an appropriations bill designates for a particular purpose within a state or congressional district.

economic interest group: A group with the primary purpose of promoting the financial interests of its members.

economic regulation: Government regulation of business practices, industry rates, routes, or areas serviced by particular industries.

economic stability: A situation in which there is economic growth, rising national income, high employment, and steadiness in the general level of prices.

Eighth Amendment: Part of the Bill of Rights that states: "Excessive bail shall not be required, nor excessive fines imposed, nor cruel and unusual punishments inflicted."

elector: Member of the Electoral College chosen by methods determined in each state.

Electoral College: Representatives of each state who cast the final ballots that actually elect a president.

electorate: Citizens eligible to vote.

Embargo Act: Passed by Congress in 1807 to prevent U.S. ships from leaving U.S. ports for foreign ports without the approval of the federal government.

engagement: Policy implemented during the Clinton administration that the United States would remain actively involved in foreign affairs.

engrossed bill: A bill that has been given final approval on third reading in one chamber of the legislature.

enlargement: Policy implemented during the Clinton administration that the United States would actively promote the expansion of democracy and free markets throughout the world.

enrolled bill: A bill that has been given final approval in both chambers of the legislature and is sent to the governor.

entitlement program: Income security program to which all those meeting eligibility criteria are entitled.

enumerated powers: Seventeen specific powers granted to Congress under Article I, section 8, of the U.S. Constitution; these powers include taxation, coinage of money, regulation of commerce, and the authority to provide for a national defense.

Equal Employment Opportunity Commission: Federal agency created to enforce the Civil Rights Act of 1964, which forbids discrimination on the basis of race, creed, national origin, religion, or sex in hiring, promotion, or firing.

equal protection clause: Section of the Fourteenth Amendment that guarantees that all citizens receive "equal protection of the laws."

Equal Rights Amendment: Proposed amendment that would bar discrimination against women by federal or state governments.

equal time rule: The rule that requires broadcast stations to sell air time equally to all candidates in a political campaign if they choose to sell it to any.

equality: The belief that all individuals should be treated similarly, regardless of socio-economic status.

establishment clause: The first clause in the First Amendment; it prohibits the national government from establishing a national religion.

ex post facto **law:** Law passed after the fact, thereby making previously legal activity illegal and subject to current penalty; prohibited by the U.S. Constitution.

exclusionary rule: Judicially created rule that prohibits police from using illegally seized evidence at trial.

executive agreement: Formal government agreement entered into by the president that does not require the advice and consent of the U.S. Senate.

executive commissioner of health and human services commission: The official appointed by the governor to oversee the state's multi-agency health and human service programs.

Executive Office of the President (EOP): Establishment created in 1939 to help the president oversee the executive branch bureaucracy.

executive order: Rule or regulation issued by the president that has the effect of law. All executive orders must be published in the *Federal Register*.

executive privilege: An implied presidential power that allows the president to refuse to disclose information regarding confidential conversations or national security to Congress or the judiciary.

exit polls: Polls conducted at selected polling places on Election Day.

extradition clause: Part of Article IV that requires states to extradite, or return, criminals to states where they have been convicted or are to stand trial.

extraterritorial jurisdiction (ETJ): The area outside a city's boundaries over which the city may exercise limited control.

F

fairness doctrine: Rule in effect from 1949 to 1985 requiring broadcasters to cover events adequately and to present contrasting views on important public issues.

federal budget deficit: The amount by which federal expenditure exceeds federal revenue.

Federal Employees Political Activities Act: 1993 liberalization of the Hatch Act. Federal employees are now allowed to run for office in nonpartisan elections and to contribute money to campaigns in partisan elections.

Federal Reserve Board: A seven-member board that sets member banks' reserve requirements, controls the discount rate, and makes other economic decisions.

federal system: System of government where the national government and state governments share some powers, derive all authority from the people, and the powers of the national government are specified in a constitution.

The Federalist Papers: A series of eighty-five political papers written by John Jay, Alexander Hamilton, and James Madison in support of ratification of the U.S. Constitution.

Federalists: Those who favored a stronger national government and supported the proposed U.S. Constitution; later became the first U.S. political party.

Fifteenth Amendment: One of the three Civil War amendments; specifically enfranchised newly freed male slaves.

Fifth Amendment: Part of the Bill of Rights that imposes a number of restrictions on the federal government with respect to the rights of persons suspected of committing a crime. It provides for indictment by a grand jury, protection against self-incrimination, and prevents the national government from denying a person life, liberty, or property without the due process of law. It also prevents the national government from taking property without fair compensation.

fighting words: Words that, "by their very utterance inflict injury or tend to incite an immediate breach of peace." Fighting words are not subject to the restrictions of the First Amendment.

filibuster: A formal way of halting action on a bill by means of long speeches or unlimited debate in the Senate.

finance chair: A professional who coordinates the fund-raising efforts for the campaign.

First Amendment: Part of the Bill of Rights that imposes a number of restrictions on the federal government with respect to the civil liberties of the people, including freedom of religion, speech, press, assembly, and petition.

First Continental Congress: Meeting held in Philadelphia from September 5 to October 26, 1774, in which fifty-six delegates (from every colony except Georgia) adopted a resolution in opposition to the Coercive Acts.

first reading: The Texas Constitution requires three readings of a bill by the legislature; first reading is when the bill is introduced, its caption is read aloud, and it is referred to committee.

fiscal policy: Federal government policies on taxes, spending, and debt management, intended to promote the nation's macro-economic goals, particularly with respect to employment, price stability, and growth.

527 political committees: Nonprofit and unregulated interest groups that focus on specific causes or policy positions and attempt to influence voters.

Fourteenth Amendment: One of the three Civil War amendments; guarantees equal protection and due process of the laws to all U.S. citizens.

Fourth Amendment: Part of the Bill of Rights that reads: "The right of the people to be secure in their persons, houses, papers, and effects, against unreasonable searches and seizures, shall not be violated, and no Warrants shall issue, but upon probable cause, supported by Oath or affirmation, and particularly describing the place to be searched, and the persons or things to be seized."

framing: The process by which a news organization defines a political issue and consequently affects opinion about the issues.

free exercise clause: The second clause of the First Amendment. It prohibits the U.S. government from interfering with a citizen's right to practice his or her religion.

free media: Coverage of a candidate's campaign by the news media.

free rider problem: Potential members fail to join a group because they can get the benefit, or collective good, sought by the group without contributing to the effort.

frontier era: The period when Texas constituted a border between American civilization and an area inhabited by a hostile, indigenous population.

front-loading: The tendency of states to choose an early date on the primary calendar.

full faith and credit clause: Section of Article IV of the Constitution that ensures judicial decrees and contracts made in one state will be binding and enforceable in any other state.

full-time equivalent (FTE): A unit of measurement for number of employees.

fundamental freedoms: Those rights defined by the Court to be essential to order, liberty, and justice.

G

General Agreement on Tariffs and Trade: Devised shortly after World War II as an interim agreement until a World Trade Organization could be created to help lower tariffs and increase trade.

general election: Election in which voters decide which candidates will actually fill elective public offices.

general election campaign: That part of a political campaign aimed at winning a general election.

general-law cities: Cities with fewer than 5,000 residents, governed by a general state law rather than by a locally adopted charter.

general ordinance-making authority: The legal right to adopt ordinances covering a wide array of subject areas, authority that cities have but counties do not.

germane: Related to the topic.

gerrymandering: The legislative process through which the majority party in each statehouse tries to assure that the maximum number of representatives from its political party can be elected to Congress through the redrawing of legislative districts.

get out the vote (GOTV): A push at the end of a political campaign to encourage supporters to go to the polls.

Gibbons v. Ogden (1824): The Court upheld broad congressional power over interstate commerce. The Court's broad interpretation of the Constitution's commerce clause paved the way for later rulings upholding expansive federal powers.

global warming: The increase in global temperatures that results from carbon emissions from burning fossil fuels such as oil and coal.

good government: A term used for policies that open up agencies to public participation and scrutiny and that minimize conflicts of interest.

government: The formal vehicles through which policies are made and affairs of state are conducted.

government corporation: Business established by Congress to perform functions that can be provided by private businesses (such as the U.S. Postal Service).

governmental (institutional) agenda: The changing list of issues to which governments believe they should address themselves.

governmental party: The office holders and candidates who run under a political party's banner.

governor: Chief elected executive in state government.

governor's message: Message that the governor delivers to the legislature, pronouncing policy goals, budget priorities, and authorizations for the legislature to act.

grandfather clause: Voting qualification provision in many Southern states that allowed only those whose grandfathers had voted before Reconstruction to vote unless they passed a wealth or literacy test.

Great Compromise: A decision made during the Constitutional Convention to give each state the same number of representatives in the Senate regardless of size; representation in the House was determined by population.

gross domestic product (GDP): The total market value of all goods and services produced in a country during a year.

H

hard money: Legally specified and limited contributions that are clearly regulated by the Federal Election Campaign Act and by the Federal Election Commission.

Hatch Act: Law enacted in 1939 to prohibit civil servants from taking activist roles in partisan campaigns. This act prohibited federal employees from making political contributions, working for a particular party, or campaigning for a particular candidate.

hold: A tactic by which a senator asks to be informed before a particular bill is brought to the floor. This stops the bill from coming to the floor until the hold is removed.

home rule: The right and authority of a local government to govern itself, rather than have the state govern it.

human rights: The belief that human beings have inalienable rights such as freedom of speech and freedom of religion.

I

ideology: A set or system of beliefs that shapes the thinking of individual and how they view the world.

impeach: A vote by the House to formally accuse a government official of official wrongdoing.

impeachment: The power delegated to the House of Representatives in the Constitution to charge the president, vice president, or other "civil officers," including federal judges, with "Treason, Bribery, or other High Crimes and Misdemeanors." This is the first step in the constitutional process of removing such government officials from office.

implementation: The process by which a law or policy is put into operation by the bureaucracy.

implied powers: Powers derived from the enumerated powers and the necessary and proper clause. These powers are not stated specifically but are considered to be reasonably implied through the exercise of delegated powers.

impressment: The British practice in the early eighteenth century of stopping ships at sea to seize sailors suspected of having deserted the Royal Navy.

incorporation doctrine: An interpretation of the Constitution that holds that the due process clause of the Fourteenth Amendment requires that state and local governments also guarantee those rights.

incumbency: The holding of an office.

independent executive agency: Governmental unit that closely resembles a Cabinet department but has a narrower area of responsibility (such as the Central Intelligence Agency) and is not part of any Cabinet department.

independent regulatory commission: An agency created by Congress that is generally concerned with a specific aspect of the economy.

indirect (representative) democracy: A system of government that gives citizens the opportunity to vote for representatives who will work on their behalf.

individualism: The belief that each person should act in accordance with his or her own conscience.

inflation: A rise in the general price levels of an economy.

inherent powers: Powers that belong to the national government simply because it is a sovereign state.

initiative: A process that allows citizens to propose legislation and submit it to the state electorate for popular vote.

inoculation ad: Advertising that attempts to counteract an anticipated attack from the opposition before the attack is launched.

insurance commissioner: The official appointed by the governor to direct the Department of Insurance and regulate the insurance industry.

intent calendar: The Senate calendar listing bills on which the author or sponsor has given notice of intent to move to suspend the regular order of business in order that the Senate may consider them.

interagency councils: Working groups created to facilitate coordination of policy making and implementation across a host of governmental agencies.

interest group: An organized group that tries to influence public policy.

international governmental organization (IGO): An organization created by the governments of at least two and often many countries that operates internationally with the objectives of achieving the purposes that the member countries agree on.

International Monetary Fund: International governmental organization created shortly before the end of World War II to stabilize international financial relations through fixed monetary exchange rates.

Internet team: Campaign staff that uses Web-based resources to communicate with voters, raise funds, organize volunteers, and plan events.

interstate compacts: Contracts between states that carry the force of law; generally now used as a tool to address multistate policy concerns.

interventionist state: Alternative to the laissez-faire state; the government takes an active role in guiding and managing the private economy.

iron triangles: The relatively stable relationships and patterns of interaction that occur among an agency, interest groups, and congressional committees or subcommittees.

isolationism: A national policy of avoiding participation in foreign affairs.

issue networks: The loose and informal relationships that exist among a large number of actors who work in broad policy areas.

issue-oriented politics: Politics that focuses on specific issues rather than on party, candidate, or other loyalties.

J

Jim Crow laws: Laws enacted by southern states that discriminated against blacks by creating "whites only" schools, theaters, hotels, and other public accommodations.

Joint Chiefs of Staff: Advisory body to the president that includes chief of staff of the army, chief of staff of the air force, chief of naval operations, and marine commandant.

joint committee: Includes members from both houses of Congress, conducts investigations or special studies.

joint resolution: A legislative document that either proposes an amendment to the Texas Constitution or ratifies an amendment to the U.S. Constitution.

judicial activism: A philosophy of judicial decision making that argues judges should use their power broadly to further justice, especially in the areas of equality and personal liberty.

judicial implementation: Refers to how and whether judicial decisions are translated into actual public policies affecting more than the immediate parties to a lawsuit.

judicial restraint: A philosophy of judicial decision making that argues courts should allow the decisions of other branches of government to stand, even when they offend a judge's own sense of principles.

judicial review: Power of the courts to review acts of other branches of government and the states.

Judiciary Act of 1789: Established the basic three-tiered structure of the federal court system.

jurisdiction: Authority vested in a particular court to hear and decide the issues in any particular case.

justice of the peace court: Local county court for minor crimes and civil suits.

L

laissez-faire: A French term literally meaning "to allow to do, to leave alone." It is a hands-off governmental policy that is based on the belief that government involvement in the economy is wrong.

land commissioner: The elected official responsible for managing and leasing the state's property, including oil, gas, and mineral interests.

League of Nations: Created in the peace treaty that ended World War I, it was an international governmental organization dedicated to preserving peace.

Legislative Budget Board (LBB): A joint legislative committee (with a large staff) that prepares the state budget and conducts evaluations of agencies' programs.

Legislative Council: A joint legislative committee (with a large staff) that provides legal advice, bill drafting, copyediting and printing, policy research, and program evaluation services for members of the legislature.

legislative courts: Courts established by Congress for specialized purposes, such as the Court of Military Appeals.

legislative party caucus: An organization of legislators who are all of the same party, and which is formally allied with a political party.

legislative process: The process the legislature follows in considering and enacting legislation.

libel: False written statements or written statements tending to call someone's reputation into disrepute.

liberal: One considered to favor extensive governmental involvement in the economy and the provision of social services and to take an activist role in protecting the rights of women, the elderly, minorities, and the environment.

liberal constitution: Constitution that incorporates the basic structure of government and allows the legislature to provide the details through statutes.

libertarian: One who favors a free market economy and no governmental interference in personal liberties.

liberty: The belief that government should not infringe upon a person's individual rights.

line-item veto: The authority of a chief executive to delete part of a bill passed by the legislature that involves taxing or spending. The legislature may override a veto, usually with a two-thirds majority of each chamber.

lobbying: The activities of a group or organization that seeks to influence legislation and persuade political leaders to support the group's position.

lobbyist: Interest group representative who seeks to influence legislation that will benefit his or her organization through political persuasion.

local election: Election conducted by local governments to elect officials.

Local Government Code: The Texas statutory code containing state laws about local governments.

logrolling: Vote trading; voting yea to support a colleague's bill in return for a promise of future support.

M

machine: A party organization that recruits its members with tangible incentives and is characterized by a high degree of control over member activity.

majority leader: The elected leader of the party controlling the most seats in the House of Representatives or the Senate; is second in authority to the Speaker of the House and in the Senate is regarded as its most powerful member.

majority party: The political party in each house of Congress with the most members.

majority rule: The central premise of direct democracy in which only policies that collectively garner the support of a majority of voters will be made into law.

manager: A professional executive hired by a city council or county board to manage daily operations and to recommend policy changes.

mandate: A command, indicated by an electorate's votes, for the elected officials to carry out their platforms.

manifest destiny: Theory that the United States was divinely mandated to expand across North America to the Pacific Ocean.

***Marbury* v. *Madison* (1803):** Supreme Court first asserted the power of judicial review in finding that the congressional statute extending the Court's original jurisdiction was unconstitutional.

margin of error: A measure of the accuracy of a public opinion poll.

markup: A process in which legislative committee members offer changes to a bill before it goes to the floor in either house for a vote.

Marshall Plan: European Recovery Program, named after Secretary of State George C. Marshall, of extensive U.S. aid to Western Europe after World War II.

mass media: The entire array of organizations through which information is collected and disseminated to the general public.

matching funds: Donations to presidential campaigns from the federal government that are determined by the amount of private funds a qualifying candidate raises.

***McCulloch* v. *Maryland* (1819):** The Supreme Court upheld the power of the national government and denied the right of a state to tax the bank. The Court's broad interpretation of the necessary and proper clause paved the way for later rulings upholding expansive federal powers.

means-tested program: Income security program intended to assist those whose incomes fall below a designated level.

media consultant: A professional who produces political candidates' television, radio, and print advertisements.

media effects: The influence of news sources on public opinion.

Medicaid: An expansion of Medicare, this program subsidizes medical care for the poor.

Medicare: The federal program established in the Lyndon B. Johnson administration that provides medical care to elderly Social Security recipients.

mercantilism: An economic theory designed to increase a nation's wealth through the development of commercial industry and a favorable balance of trade.

merit system: The system by which federal civil service jobs are classified into grades or levels, to which appointments are made on the basis of performance on competitive examinations.

midterm election: Election that takes place in the middle of a presidential term.

military-industrial complex: The grouping of the U.S. armed forces and defense industries.

minority leader: The elected leader of the party with the second highest number of elected representatives in the House of Representatives or the Senate.

minority party: The political party in each house of Congress with the second most members.

Miranda rights: Statements that must be made by the police informing a suspect of his or her constitutional rights protected by the Fifth Amendment, including the right to an attorney provided by the court if the suspect cannot afford one.

Miranda v. Arizona (1966): A landmark Supreme Court ruling that held the Fifth Amendment requires that individuals arrested for a crime must be advised of their right to remain silent and to have counsel present.

monarchy: A form of government in which power is vested in hereditary kings and queens who govern in the interests of all.

monetary policy: A form of government regulation in which the nation's money supply and interest rates are controlled.

money: A system of exchange for goods and services that includes currency, coins, and bank deposits.

Monroe Doctrine: President James Monroe's 1823 pledge that the United States would oppose attempts by European states to extend their political control into the Western Hemisphere.

moralism: The policy of emphasizing morality in foreign affairs.

muckraking: A form of journalism, in vogue in the early twentieth century, concerned with reforming government and business conduct.

multilateralism: The U.S. foreign policy that actions should be taken in cooperation with other states after consultation.

municipal corporation: A city.

municipal court: City court with limited criminal jurisdiction.

N

narrowcasting: Targeting media programming at specific populations within society.

national convention: A party conclave (meeting) held in the presidential election year for the purposes of nominating a presidential and vice presidential ticket and adopting a platform.

national party platform: A statement of the general and specific philosophy and policy goals of a political party, usually promulgated at the national convention.

National Security Agency (NSA): Intelligence agency responsible for gathering intelligence from electronic and other sources and for code breaking.

National Security Council (NSC): Executive agency responsible for advising the president about foreign and defense policy and events.

natural law: A doctrine that society should be governed by certain ethical principles that are part of nature and, as such, can be understood by reason.

necessary and proper clause: The final paragraph of Article I, section 8, of the U.S. Constitution, which gives Congress the authority to pass all laws "necessary and proper" to carry out the enumerated powers specified in the Constitution; also called the elastic clause.

negative ad: Advertising on behalf of a candidate that attacks the opponent's platform or character.

network: An association of broadcast stations (radio or television) that share programming through a financial arrangement.

New Deal: The name given to the program of "Relief, Recovery, Reform" begun by President Franklin D. Roosevelt in 1933 to bring the United States out of the Great Depression.

New Federalism: Federal/state relationship proposed by Reagan administration during the 1980s; hallmark is returning administrative powers to the state governments.

New Jersey Plan: A framework for the Constitution proposed by a group of small states; its key points were a one-house legislature with one vote for each state, the establishment of the acts of Congress as the "supreme law" of the land, and a supreme judiciary with limited power.

new media: Technologies such as the Internet that blur the line between media sources and create new opportunities for the dissemination of news and other information.

New York Times Co. v. Sullivan (1964): The Supreme Court concluded that "actual malice" must be proved to support a finding of libel against a public figure.

news media: Media providing the public with new information about subjects of public interest.

9/11 Commission: The National Commission on Terrorist Attacks upon the United States; a bipartisan, independent group authorized by Congress and President Bush in 2002 to study the circumstances surrounding the September 11, 2001, terrorist attacks, including preparedness and response. Its 2004 report includes recommendations for guarding against future attacks.

Nineteenth Amendment: Amendment to the Constitution that guaranteed women the right to vote.

Ninth Amendment: Part of the Bill of Rights that reads "The enumeration in the Constitution, of certain rights, shall not be construed to deny or disparage others retained by the people."

Nixon Doctrine: The policy implemented at the end of the Vietnam War that the United States would provide arms and military equipment to countries but not do the fighting for them.

nomination campaign: That part of a political campaign aimed at winning a primary election.

nongovernmental organization (NGO): An organization that is not tied to a government.

non-means-based program: Program such as Social Security where benefits are provided irrespective of the income or means of recipients.

nonparty legislative caucus: An organization of legislators that is based on some attribute other than party affiliation.

North American Free Trade Agreement (NAFTA): Agreement that promotes free movement of goods and services among Canada, Mexico, and the United States.

North Atlantic Treaty Organization (NATO): The first peacetime military treaty the United States joined, NATO is a regional political and military organization created in 1950.

O

off the record: Information provided to a journalist that will not be released to the public.

Office of Management and Budget (OMB): The office that prepares the president's annual budget proposal, reviews the budget and programs of the executive departments, supplies economic forecasts, and conducts detailed analyses of proposed bills and agency rules.

oligarchy: A form of government in which the right to participate is conditioned on the possession of wealth, social status, military position, or achievement.

on background: Information provided to a journalist that will not be attributed to a named source.

on the record: Information provided to a journalist that can be released and attributed by name to the source.

open market operations: The buying and selling of government securities by the Federal Reserve Bank in the securities market.

open primary: A primary in which party members, independents, and sometimes members of the other party are allowed to vote.

organizational party: The workers and activists who staff the party's formal organization.

original jurisdiction: The jurisdiction of courts that hear a case first, usually in a trial. Courts determine the facts of a case under their original jurisdiction.

overrepresentation and underrepresentation: Higher and lower numbers, respectively, than would be expected from a group in comparison with that group's numbers in the general population.

oversight: Congressional review of the activities of an agency, department, or office.

P

paid media: Political advertisements purchased for a candidate's campaign.

pardon: The authority of a government to cancel someone's conviction of a crime by a court and to eliminate all sanctions and punishments resulting from conviction.

party caucus or conference: A formal gathering of all party members.

party identification: A citizen's personal affinity for a political party, usually expressed by his or her tendency to vote for the candidates of that party.

party in the electorate: The voters who consider themselves allied or associated with the party.

party realignment: A shifting of party coalition groupings in the electorate that remains in place for several elections.

patron: Person who finances a group or individual activity.

patronage: Jobs, grants, or other special favors that are given as rewards to friends and political allies for their support.

Pearl Harbor: Naval base in Hawaii attacked by Japan on December 7, 1941, initiating U.S. entry into World War II.

Pendleton Act: Reform measure that created the Civil Service Commission to administer a partial merit system. The act classified the federal service by grades, to which appointments were made based on the results of a competitive examination. It made it illegal for federal political appointees to be required to contribute to a particular political party.

per diem: Legislators' per day allowance covering room and board expenses while on state business.

permanent party organization: Party organization that operates throughout the year, performing the party's functions.

personal liberty: A key characteristic of U.S. democracy. Initially meaning freedom from governmental interference, today it includes demands for freedom to engage in a variety of practices free from governmental discrimination.

petition for review: Request for Texas Supreme Court review, which is granted if four justices agree.

piecemeal revision: Constitutional revision through constitutional amendments that add or delete items.

Plessy v. *Ferguson* (1896): Plessy challenged a Louisiana statute requiring that railroads provide separate accommodations for blacks and whites. The Court found that separate but equal accommodations did not violate the equal protection clause of the Fourteenth Amendment.

plural executive: An executive branch in which power and policy implementation are divided among several executive agencies rather than centralized under one person; the governor does not get to appoint most agency heads.

pocket veto: If Congress adjourns during the ten days the president has to consider a bill passed by both houses of Congress, without the president's signature, the bill is considered vetoed.

policy adoption: The approval of a policy proposal by the people with the requisite authority, such as a legislature.

policy evaluation: The process of determining whether a course of action is achieving its intended goals.

policy formulation: The crafting of appropriate and acceptable proposed courses of action to ameliorate or resolve public problems.

policy implementation: The process of carrying out public policy through governmental agencies and the courts.

political action committee (PAC): Federally mandated, officially registered fund-raising committee that represents interest groups in the political process.

political culture: Commonly shared attitudes, beliefs, and core values about how government should operate.

political equality: The principle that all citizens should participate equally in government; implied by the phrase "one person, one vote."

political ideology: The coherent set of values and beliefs about the purpose and scope of government held by groups and individuals.

political party: A group of office holders, candidates, activists, and voters who identify with a group label and seek to elect to public office individuals who run under that label.

political socialization: The process through which individuals acquire their political beliefs and values.

politico: Role played by elected representatives who act as trustees or as delegates, depending on the issue.

politics: The study of who gets what, when, and how—or how policy decisions are made.

poll tax: Tax levied in many southern states and localities that had to be paid before an eligible voter could cast a ballot.

pollster: A professional who takes public opinion surveys that guide political campaigns.

popular consent: The idea that governments must draw their powers from the consent of the governed.

popular sovereignty: The notion that the ultimate authority in society rests with the people.

populists: People who support the promotion of equality and of traditional values and behaviors.

pork: Legislation that allows representatives to bring home the bacon to their districts in the form of public works programs, military bases, or other programs designed to benefit their districts directly.

positive ad: Advertising on behalf of a candidate that stresses the candidate's qualifications, family, and issue positions, without reference to the opponent.

Powell Doctrine: An all-or-nothing approach to military intervention advocated by Colin Powell: use overwhelming force for quick, decisive victory, and have an exit strategy before any intervention.

pragmatism: The policy of taking advantage of a situation for national gain.

precedent: Prior judicial decision that serves as a rule for settling subsequent cases of a similar nature.

precinct chairperson: Party leader in a voting precinct.

precinct convention: Precinct party meeting to select delegates and adopt resolutions.

preemption: A concept derived from the Constitution's supremacy clause that allows the national government to override or preempt state or local actions in certain areas.

president of the Texas Senate: The lieutenant governor of Texas, serving in his constitutional role as presiding officer of the Senate.

president pro tempore: The official chair of the Senate; usually the most senior member of the majority party.

press briefing: A relatively restricted session between a press secretary or aide and the press.

press conference: An unrestricted session between an elected official and the press.

press release: A document offering an official comment or position.

press secretary: The individual charged with interacting and communicating with journalists on a daily basis.

primary election: Election in which voters decide which of the candidates within a party will represent the party in the general election.

print media: The traditional form of mass media, comprising newspapers, magazines, newsletters, and journals.

prior restraint: Constitutional doctrine that prevents the government from prohibiting speech or publication before the fact; generally held to be in violation of the First Amendment.

privileges and immunities clause: Part of Article IV of the Constitution guaranteeing that the citizens of each state are afforded the same rights as citizens of all other states.

proportional representation: A voting system that apportions legislative seats according to the percentage of the vote won by a particular political party.

prospective judgment: A voter's evaluation of a candidate based on what he or she pledges to do about an issue if elected.

pro-tempore (pro-tem): A legislator who serves temporarily as legislative leader in the absence of the Senate president or House Speaker.

public counsels: Officials appointed by the governor to represent the public before regulatory agencies.

public funds: Donations from the general tax revenues to the campaigns of qualifying presidential candidates.

public interest group: An organization that seeks a collective good that will not selectively and materially benefit the members of the group.

public opinion: What the public thinks about a particular issue or set of issues at any point in time.

public opinion polls: Interviews or surveys with samples of citizens that are used to estimate the feelings and beliefs of the entire population.

public policy: An intentional course of action followed by government in dealing with some problem or matter of concern.

Public Utility Commission: A full-time, three-member paid commission appointed by the governor to regulate public utilities in Texas.

push polls: "Polls" taken for the purpose of providing information on an opponent that would lead respondents to vote against that candidate.

Q

quasi-judicial: Partly judicial; authorized to conduct hearings and issue rulings.

quorum: The minimum number required to conduct business (as in a legislative body).

R

raiding: An organized attempt by voters of one party to influence the primary results of the other party.

Railroad Commission: A full-time, three-member paid commission elected by the people to regulate oil and gas and some transportation entities.

random sampling: A method of poll selection that gives each person in a group the same chance of being selected.

Reagan Doctrine: Policy that the United States would provide military assistance to anti-communist groups fighting against pro-Soviet governments.

reapportionment: The reallocation of the number of seats in the House of Representatives after each decennial census.

recall: A process in which voters can petition for a vote to remove office holders between elections.

recession: A short-term decline in the economy that occurs as investment sags, production falls off, and unemployment increases.

redistrict: Redraw election-district boundaries.

redistricting: The redrawing of congressional districts to reflect population changes or for political advantage.

referendum: An election whereby the state legislature submits proposed legislation to the state's voters for approval.

regional primary: A proposed system in which the country would be divided into five or six geographic areas and all states in each region would hold their presidential primary elections on the same day.

regular session: The biennial 140-day session of the Texas legislature, beginning in January of odd-numbered years.

regulations: Rules that govern the operation of a particular government program that have the force of law.

republic: A government rooted in the consent of the governed; a representative or indirect democracy.

reservation land: Land designated in a treaty that is under the authority of an Indian nation and is exempt from most state laws and taxes.

reserve (or police) powers: Powers reserved to the states by the Tenth Amendment that lie at the foundation of a state's right to legislate for the public health and welfare of its citizens.

reserve requirements: Government requirements that a portion of member banks' deposits must be retained to back loans made.

retrospective judgment: A voter's evaluation of the performance of the party in power.

revisionist: A member of a constitutional convention who will not accept less than a total revision of the current constitution.

revolving door: An exchange of personnel between private interests and public regulators.

right to privacy: The right to be let alone; a judicially created doctrine encompassing an individual's decision to use birth control or secure an abortion.

***Roe v. Wade* (1973):** The Supreme Court found that a woman's right to an abortion was protected by the right to privacy that could be implied from specific guarantees found in the Bill of Rights applied to the states through the Fourteenth Amendment.

Roosevelt Corollary: Concept developed by President Theodore Roosevelt early in the twentieth century that it was the U.S. responsibility to assure stability in Latin America and the Caribbean.

rule making: A quasi-legislative administrative process that has the characteristics of a legislative act.

Rule of Four: At least four justices of the Supreme Court must vote to consider a case before it can be heard.

runoff primary: A second primary election between the two candidates receiving the greatest number of votes in the first primary.

S

sampling error or margin of error: A measure of the accuracy of a public opinion poll.

Second Continental Congress: Meeting that convened in Philadelphia on May 10, 1775, at which it was decided that an army should be raised and George Washington of Virginia was named commander in chief.

second reading: The Texas Constitution requires three readings of a bill by the legislature; the second reading is when debate and consideration of amendments occur before the whole chamber.

secular realignment: The gradual rearrangement of party coalitions, based more on demographic shifts than on shocks to the political system.

select (or special) committee: Temporary committee appointed for specific purpose, such as conducting a special investigation or study.

selective incorporation: A judicial doctrine whereby most but not all of the protections found in the Bill of Rights are made applicable to the states via the Fourteenth Amendment.

Senate two-thirds rule: The rule in the Texas Senate requiring that every bill win a vote of two-thirds of the senators present to suspend the Senate's regular order of business, so that the bill may be considered.

senatorial courtesy: Process by which presidents, when selecting district court judges, defer to senators of their own party who represent the state where the vacancy occurs; also the process by which a governor, when selecting an appointee, defers to the state senator in whose district the nominee resides.

seniority: Time of continuous service on a committee.

separation of powers: A way of dividing power among three branches of government in which members of the House of Representatives, members of the Senate, the president, and the federal courts are selected by and responsible to different constituencies.

Seventeenth Amendment: Made senators directly elected by the people; removed their selection from state legislatures.

Sharpstown scandal: The legislative scandal of 1969–1972, which resulted in a bribery conviction of the House Speaker and others and set the stage for the 1973 reform session.

Shays's Rebellion: A 1786 rebellion in which an army of 1,500 disgruntled and angry farmers led by Daniel Shays marched to Springfield, Massachusetts, and forcibly restrained the state court from foreclosing mortgages on their farms.

sheriff: Elected official who serves as the chief law enforcement officer in a county.

simple resolution: A legislative document proposing an action that affects only the one chamber in which it is being considered, such as a resolution to adopt House rules or to commend a citizen.

single-member district: An election system for legislative bodies in which each legislator runs from and represents a single district, rather than the entire geographic area encompassed by the government.

Sixteenth Amendment: Authorized Congress to enact a national income tax.

Sixth Amendment: Part of the Bill of Rights that sets out the basic requirements of procedural due process for federal courts to follow in criminal trials. These include speedy and public trials, impartial juries, trials in the state where crime was committed, notice of the charges, the right to confront and obtain favorable witnesses, and the right to counsel.

slander: Untrue spoken statements that defame the character of a person.

social capital: The myriad relationships that individuals enjoy that facilitate the resolution of community problems through collective action.

social conservative: One who believes that traditional moral teachings should be supported and furthered by the government.

social contract: An agreement between the people and their government signifying their consent to be governed.

social contract theory: The belief that people are free and equal by God-given right and that this in turn requires that all people give their consent to be governed; espoused by John Locke and influential in the writing of the Declaration of Independence.

social regulation: Government regulation of the quality and safety of products as well as the conditions under which goods and services are produced.

Social Security Act: A 1935 law that established old-age insurance (Social Security) and assistance for the needy, children, and others, and unemployment insurance.

social welfare policy: Government programs designed to improve quality of life.

soft money: The virtually unregulated money funneled by individuals and political committees through state and local parties.

solicitor general: The fourth-ranking member of the Department of Justice; responsible for handling all appeals on behalf of the U.S. government to the Supreme Court.

sovereign immunity: The right of a state to be free from lawsuit unless it gives permission to the suit. Under the Eleventh Amendment, all states are considered sovereign.

Spanish-American War: Brief 1898 war against Spain because of Spanish policies and presence in Cuba and U.S. desire to attain overseas territory.

Speaker of the House: The only officer of the House of Representatives specifically mentioned in the Constitution; elected at the beginning of each new Congress by the entire House; traditionally a member of the majority party.

Speaker of the Texas House: The state representative who is elected by his or her fellow representatives to be the official leader of the House.

Speaker's lieutenants: House members who make up the Speaker's team, assisting the Speaker in leading the House, either informally, or in a role as a committee chair or other institutional leader.

Speaker's race: The campaign to determine who shall be the Speaker of the Texas House for a given biennium.

Speaker's team: The leadership team in the House, consisting of the Speaker and his or her most trusted allies among the members, most of whom the Speaker appoints to chair House committees.

special election: Election held at a time other than general or primary elections.

special (called) session: A Texas legislative session of up to thirty days, called by the governor, during an interim between regular sessions.

spoils system: The firing of public-office holders of a defeated political party and their replacement with loyalists of the newly elected party.

spot ad: Television advertising on behalf of a candidate that is broadcast in sixty-, thirty-, or ten-second duration.

staggered terms: Terms of office for members of boards and commissions that begin and end at different times, so that a governor is not usually able to gain control of a majority of the body for a long time.

Stamp Act Congress: Meeting of representatives of nine of the thirteen colonies held in New York City in 1765, during which representatives drafted a document to send to the king listing how their rights had been violated.

standing committee: Committee to which proposed bills are referred.

stare decisis: In court rulings, a reliance on past decisions or precedents to formulate decisions in new cases.

State Board of Education: The fifteen-member elected body that sets some education policy for the state and has limited authority to oversee the Texas Education Agency and local school districts.

state convention: Party meeting held to adopt the party's platform, elect the party's executive committee and state chairperson, and in a presidential election year, elect delegates to the national convention and choose presidential electors.

state executive committee: Sixty-two-member party committee that makes decisions for the party between state conventions.

state party chairperson: Party leader for the state.

state senatorial district convention: Party meeting held when a county is a part of more than one senatorial district.

statutory constitution: Constitution that incorporates detailed provisions in order to limit the powers of government.

stratified sampling: A variation of random sampling; Census data are used to divide a country into four sampling regions. Sets of counties and standard metropolitan statistical areas are then randomly selected in proportion to the total national population.

straw polls: Unscientific surveys used to gauge public opinion on a variety of issues and policies.

strict constructionist: An approach to constitutional interpretation that emphasizes the Framers' original intentions.

strict scrutiny: A heightened standard of review used by the Supreme Court to determine the constitutional validity of a challenged practice.

strong mayor–council: A form of city government in which the mayor has strong powers to run the city by hiring, managing, and firing staff and controlling executive departments; the mayor also serves on the council.

substantive due process: Judicial interpretation of the Fifth and Fourteenth Amendments' due process clause that protects citizens from arbitrary or unjust laws.

succession: The constitutional declaration that the lieutenant governor succeeds to the governorship if there is a vacancy.

suffrage movement: The drive for voting rights for women that took place in the United States from 1890 to 1920.

sunset law: A law that sets a date for a program or regulation to expire unless reauthorized by the legislature.

superdelegate: Delegate slot to the Democratic Party's national convention that is reserved for an elected party official.

supremacy clause: Portion of Article VI of the U.S. Constitution mandating that national law is supreme to (that is, supercedes) all other laws passed by the states or by any other subdivision of government.

suspect classification: Category or class, such as race, that triggers the highest standard of scrutiny from the Supreme Court.

symbolic speech: Symbols, signs, and other methods of expression generally also considered to be protected by the First Amendment.

systemic agenda: All public issues that are viewed as requiring governmental attention; a discussion agenda.

T

Taliban: Fundamentalist Islamic government of Afghanistan that provided terrorist training bases for al-Qaeda.

tariffs: Taxes on imports used to raise government revenue and to protect infant industries.

Tejanos: Native Texans of Mexican descent.

temporary party organization: Party organization that exists for a limited time and includes several levels of conventions.

Tenth Amendment: Part of the Bill of Rights that reiterates powers not delegated to the national government are reserved to the states or to the people.

term limits: Restrictions that exist in some states about how long an individual may serve in state or local elected offices.

Texan Creed: A set of ideas—primarily individualism and liberty—that shape Texas politics and government.

Texas Association of Counties: Professional association and lobbying arm for county governments.

Texas Commission on Environmental Quality: As of 2002, the new name for the Texas Natural Resource Conservation Commission.

Texas Court of Criminal Appeals: Court of last resort in criminal cases.

Texas Education Agency: The state agency that oversees local school districts and disburses state funds to districts.

Texas Municipal League: Professional association and lobbying arm for city governments.

Texas Rangers: A mounted militia formed to provide order on the frontier.

Texas secretary of state: The state official appointed by the governor to be the keeper of the state's records, such as state laws, election data and filings, public notifications, and corporate charters.

Texas Supreme Court: Court of last resort in civil and juvenile cases.

think tank: Institutional collection of policy-oriented researchers and academics who are sources of policy ideas.

third reading: The Texas Constitution requires three readings of a bill by the legislature; third reading is the final reading in a chamber, unless the bill returns from the other chamber with amendments.

Thirteenth Amendment: One of the three Civil War amendments; specifically bans slavery in the United States.

Three-Fifths Compromise: Agreement reached at the Constitutional Convention stipulating that each slave was to be counted as three-fifths of a person for purposes of determining population for representation in the U.S. House of Representatives.

ticket-split: To vote for candidates of different parties for various offices in the same election.

Title IX: Provision of the Educational Amendments of 1972 that bars educational institutions receiving federal funds from discriminating against female students.

totalitarianism: A form of government in which power resides in a leader who rules according to self-interest and without regard for individual rights and liberties.

tracking polls: Continuous surveys that enable a campaign to chart its daily rise or fall in support.

trade association: A group that represents a specific industry.

trial courts: Courts of original jurisdiction where a case begins.

trial de novo: New trial, necessary for an appeal from a court that is not a court of record.

Truman Doctrine: U.S. policy initiated in 1947 of providing economic assistance and military aid to countries fighting against communist revolutions or political pressure.

trustee: Role played by elected representatives who listen to constituents' opinions and then use their best judgment to make final decisions.

turnout: The proportion of the voting-age public that votes.

Twenty-Fifth Amendment: Adopted in 1967 to establish procedures for filling vacancies in the office of president and vice president as well as providing for procedures to deal with the disability of a president.

Twenty-Second Amendment: Adopted in 1951, prevents a president from serving more than two terms or more than ten years if he came to office via the death or impeachment of his predecessor.

U

unconventional political participation: Political participation that attempts to influence the political process through unusual or extreme measures, such as protests, boycotts, and picketing.

unfunded mandates: National laws that direct states or local governments to comply with the federal rules or regulations (such as clean air or water standards) but contain no federal funding to defray the cost of meeting these requirements.

unilateralism: A national policy of acting without consulting others.

unitary system: System of government where the local and regional governments derive all authority from a strong national government.

unit rule: A traditional party practice under which the majority of a state delegation can force the minority to vote for its candidate.

United Nations (UN): An international governmental organization created shortly before the end of World War II to guarantee the security of nations and to promote global economic, physical, and social well-being.

U.S. v. Nixon (1974): Key Supreme Court ruling on power of the president, finding that there is no absolute constitutional executive privilege to allow a president to refuse to comply with a court order to produce information needed in a criminal trial.

V

veto: The formal, constitutional authority of the chief executive to reject bills passed by both houses of the legislative body, thus preventing their becoming law without further legislative action.

veto power: The formal, constitutional authority of the president to reject bills passed by both houses of Congress, thus preventing their becoming law without further congressional action.

Vietnam War: Between 1965 and 1973, the United States deployed up to 500,000 troops to Vietnam to try to prevent North Vietnam from taking over South Vietnam; the effort failed and was extremely divisive within the United States.

Virginia Plan: The first general plan for the Constitution, proposed by James Madison and Edmund Randolph. Its key points were a bicameral legislature, an executive chosen by the legislature, and a judiciary also named by the legislature.

voter canvass: The process by which a campaign gets in touch with individual voters, either by door-to-door solicitation or by telephone.

W

war on terrorism: Initiated by President George W. Bush after the 9/11 attacks to weed out terrorist operatives throughout the world, using diplomacy, military means, improved homeland security, stricter banking laws, and other means.

War Powers Act: Passed by Congress in 1973; the president is limited in the deployment of troops overseas to a sixty-day period in peacetime (which can be extended for an extra thirty days to permit withdrawal) unless Congress explicitly gives its approval for a longer period.

weak mayor–council: A form of city government in which the mayor has no more power than any other member of the council.

weapons of mass destruction: Biological, chemical, and nuclear weapons, which present a sizeable threat to U.S. security.

whip: One of several representatives who keep close contact with all members and take nose counts on key votes, prepare summaries of bills, and in general act as communications links within the party.

winner-take-all system: An electoral system in which the party that receives at least one more vote than any other party wins the election.

wire service: An electronic delivery of news gathered by the news service's correspondents and sent to all member news media organizations.

World Bank: International governmental organization created shortly before the end of World War II to provide loans for large economic development projects.

World Trade Organization: International governmental organization created in 1995 that manages multilateral negotiations to reduce barriers to trade and settle trade disputes.

writ of certiorari: A request for the Court to order up the records from a lower court to review the case.

writ of habeas corpus: A court order in which a judge requires authorities to prove that a prisoner is being held lawfully and that allows the prisoner to be freed if the judge is not persuaded by the government's case. Habeas corpus rights imply that prisoners have a right to know what charges are being made against them.

Y

yellow journalism: A form of newspaper publishing in vogue in the late nineteenth century that featured pictures, comics, color, and sensationalized, oversimplified news coverage.

Chapter 1

1. Thomas Byrne Edsall, "The Era of Bad Feelings," *Civilization* (March/April 1996): 37.

2. Jack C. Plano and Milton Greenberg, *The American Political Dictionary*, 6th ed. (New York: Holt, Rinehart and Winston, 1982).

3. U.S. Agency for International Development, "Agency Objectives: Civil Society," November 16, 2001.

4. Terrence Ball and Richard Dagger, *Political Ideologies and the Democratic Ideal* (New York: Longman, 2004), 2.

5. Isaiah Berlin, *The Crooked Timber of Humanity: Chapters in the History of Ideas* (New York: Vintage, 1992), 1.

6. Jack C. Plano and Milton Greenberg, *The American Political Dictionary*, 9th ed. (Fort Worth, TX: Harcourt Brace, 1993), 16.

7. Susan A. MacManus, *Young v. Old: Generational Combat in the 21st Century* (Boulder, CO: Westview, 1995), 3.

8. Dennis Cauchon, "Who Will Take Care of an Older Population?" *USA Today* (October 25, 2005): 1–2B.

9. Democracy Corps Poll, November 29–December 3, 2007.

10. CBS News Poll, February 27, 2006, www.cbsnews.com/ntdocs/pdf/poll_katrina_022706.pdf.

11. Jon Cohen and Dan Balz, "U.S. Outlook is Worse Since '92, Poll Finds," *Washington Post* (May 13, 2008).

Chapter 2

1. See Richard B. Bernstein with Jerome Agel, *Amending America* (New York: New York Times Books, 1993), 138–40.

2. *Oregon* v. *Mitchell*, 400 U.S. 112 (1970).

3. Bernstein with Agel, *Amending America*, 139.

4. For an account of the early development of the colonies, see D. W. Meining, *The Shaping of America*, vol. 1: *Atlantic America, 1492–1800* (New Haven, CT: Yale University Press, 1986).

5. For an excellent chronology of the events leading up to the writing of the Declaration of Independence and the colonists' break with Great Britain, see Calvin D. Lonton, ed., *The Bicentennial Almanac* (Nashville, TN: Thomas Nelson, 1975).

6. See Garry Wills, *Inventing America: Jefferson's Declaration of Independence* (New York: Random House, 1978). Wills argues that the Declaration was signed solely to secure foreign aid for the ongoing war effort.

7. For more about the Articles of Confederation, see Merrill Jensen, *The Articles of Confederation* (Madison: University of Wisconsin Press, 1940).

8. Charles A. Beard, *An Economic Interpretation of the Constitution of the United States*, reissue ed. (Mineola, NY: Dover, 2004).

9. John Patrick Diggins, "Power and Authority in American History: The Case of Charles A. Beard and His Critics," *American Historical Review* 86 (October 1981): 701–30; Robert Brown, *Charles Beard and the Constitution: A Critical Analysis of "An Economic Interpretation of the Constitution"* (Princeton, NJ: Princeton University Press, 1956).

10. Jackson Turner Main, *The Anti-Federalists: Critics of the Constitution, 1781–1788* (Chapel Hill: University of North Carolina, 2004).

11. See Gordon S. Wood, *The Creation of the American Republic, 1776–1787*, reissue ed. (New York: Norton, 1993).

12. For more on the political nature of compromise at the convention, see Calvin C. Jillson, *Constitution Making: Conflict and Consensus in the Federal Constitution of 1787* (New York: Agathon, 1988).

13. Bernard Bailyn, *The Ideological Origins of the American Revolution* (Cambridge, MA: Belknap Press, 1967).

14. Richard E. Neustadt, *Presidential Power: The Politics of Leadership from FDR to Carter* (New York: Macmillan, 1980), 26.

15. Federal Republicans favored a republican or representative form of government (do not confuse this term with the modern Republican Party, which came into being in 1854; see chapter 12). Ultimately, the word *federal* referred to the form of government embodied in the new Constitution, and *confederation* referred to a "league of states," as under the Articles, and later was applied in the "Confederacy" of 1861–1865.

16. See Ralph Ketcham, ed., *The Anti-Federalist Papers and the Constitutional Debates* (New York: New American Library, 1986).

17. See Herbert J. Storing, *What the Anti-Federalists Were For* (Chicago: University of Chicago Press, 1981), for a fuller discussion of Anti-Federalist views.

18. See Alan P. Grimes, *Democracy and the Amendments to the Constitution* (Lexington, MA: Lexington, 1978).

19. David E. Kyvig, *Repealing National Prohibition* (Chicago: University of Chicago Press, 1978).

20. See Jane J. Mansbridge, *Why We Lost the ERA* (Chicago: University of Chicago Press, 1986).

21. *Marbury* v. *Madison*, 5 U.S. 137 (1803).

22. Speech by Attorney General Edwin Meese III before the American Bar Association, July 9, 1985, Washington, DC. See also Antonin Scalia and Amy Gutman, eds. *A Matter of Interpretation: Federal Courts and the Law* (Princeton, NJ: Princeton University Press, 1998).

23. Speech by Associate Justice William J. Brennan Jr., at Georgetown University, Text and Teaching Symposium, October 10, 1985, Washington, DC.

24. Bruce Ackerman, *We the People: Foundations* (Cambridge, MA: Belknap Press, 1991).

Chapter 3

1. Evan Thomas, "How Bush Blew It," *Newsweek* (September 19, 2005), available online at www.msnbc.msn.com/id/9287434/site/newsweek/page/3.

2. See Spencer S. Hsu, "Katrina Report Spreads Blame: Homeland Security, Chertoff Singled Out," *Washington Post* (January 12, 2006): A1.

3. John Mountjoy, "Interstate Cooperation: Interstate Compacts Make a Comeback," *Council of State Governments*, available online at www.csg.org.

4. *McCulloch* v. *Maryland*, 17 U.S. 316 (1819).

5. *Gibbons* v. *Ogden*, 22 U.S. 1 (1824).

6. *Dred Scott* v. *Sandford*, 60 U.S. 393 (1857).

7. *Plessy* v. *Ferguson*, 163 U.S. 537 (1896).

8. *Panhandle Oil Co.* v. *Knox*, 277 U.S. 218, 223 (1928).

9. *Indian Motorcycle Co.* v. *U.S.*, 238 U.S. 570 (1931).

10. *Pensacola Telegraph* v. *Western Union*, 96 U.S. 1 (1877).

11. *Pollock* v. *Farmers Loan and Trust*, 157 U.S. 429 (1895); and *Springer* v. *U.S.*, 102 U.S. 586 (1881).

12. John O. McGinnis, "The State of Federalism," testimony before the Senate Government Affairs Committee, May 5, 1999.

13. *NLRB* v. *Jones and Laughlin Steel Co.*, 301 U.S. 1 (1937).

14. *U.S.* v. *Darby Lumber Co.*, 312 U.S. 100 (1941).

15. *Wickard* v. *Filburn*, 317 U.S. 111 (1942).

16. Morton Grodzins, "Centralization and Decentralization in the American Federal System," in Robert A. Goldwin, ed., *A Nation of States* (Chicago: Rand McNally, 1963), 3–4.

17. Alice M. Rivlin, *Reviving the American Dream* (Washington, DC: Brookings Institution, 1992), 92.

18. Rivlin, *Reviving the American Dream*, 98.

19. Richard P. Nathan et al., *Reagan and the States* (Princeton, NJ: Princeton University Press, 1987), 4.

20. T. R. Reid, "States Feel Less Pinch in Budgets, Services," *Washington Post* (May 9, 2004): A3.

21. Michael Powell, "Art of Politickin'; As the Republican Rivals Get Out in South Carolina, It's Survival of the Folksiest," *Washington Post* (February 19, 2000): C1.

22. Ken Dilanian, "War Costs May Total $2.4 Trillion," *USA Today* (October 24, 2007): 1A.

23. Gene Healy and Timothy Lynch, "Power Surge: The Constitutional Record of George W. Bush," *Cato Institute* (2006) 20.

24. Marianne Arneberg, "Cuomo Assails Judicial Hodgepodge," *Newsday* (August 15, 1990); 15.

25. *Webster* v. *Reproductive Health Services,* 492 U.S. 490 (1989).

26. *Stenberg* v. *Carhart,* 530 U.S. 914 (2000).

27. *Ayotte* v. *Planned Parenthood of Northern New England,* 546 U.S. 320 (2006).

28. *Gonzales* v. *Carhart,* 550 U.S. _____ (2007).

29. *U.S.* v. *Lopez,* 514 U.S. 549 (1995).

30. *Seminole Tribe* v. *Florida,* 517 U.S. 44 (1996).

31. *Boerne* v. *Flores,* 521 U.S. 507 (1997).

32. *Printz* v. *U.S.,* 521 U.S. 898 (1997).

33. *Florida Prepaid* v. *College Savings Bank,* 527 U.S. 627 (1999).

34. *U.S.* v. *Morrison,* 529 U.S. 598 (2000). *Raich* 545 U.S. 1 (2005).

35. Linda Greenhouse, "The Rehnquist Court and Its Imperiled States' Rights Legacy," *New York Times* (June 12, 2005): A3.

36. Linda Greenhouse, "In a Momentous Term, Justices Remake the Law and the Court," *New York Times* (July 1, 2003): A18.

37. *Nevada Department of Human Resources* v. *Hibbs,* 538 U.S. 72 (2003).

38. *Gonzales* v. *Oregon,* 546 U.S. 243 (2006).

39. *U.S.* v. *Georgia,* 546 U.S. 151 (2006).

Chapter 4

1. Paul Duggan, "Lawyer Who Wiped Out D.C. Ban Says It's About Liberties, Not Guns," *Washington Post* (March 18, 2007): A1.

2. D.C. v. Heller, 554 U.S. _____ (2008).

3. The absence of a bill of rights led Mason to refuse to sign the proposed Constitution, noting that he "would sooner chop off his right hand than put it to the Constitution as it now stands." Quoted in Eric Black, *Our Constitution: The Myth That Binds Us* (Boulder, CO: Westview, 1988), 75.

4. *Barron* v. *Baltimore,* 32 U.S. 243 (1833).

5. *Allgeyer* v. *Louisiana,* 165 U.S. 578 (1897).

6. *Gitlow* v. *New York,* 268 U.S. 652 (1925).

7. *Near* v. *Minnesota,* 283 U.S. 697 (1931). For more about Near, see Fred W. Friendly, *Minnesota Rag: The Dramatic Story of the Landmark Case That Gave New Meaning to Freedom of the Press* (New York: Random House, 1981).

8. *Palko* v. *Connecticut,* 302 U.S. 319 (1937).

9. *Zobrest* v. *Catalina Foothills School District,* 506 U.S. 813 (1992).

10. *Engel* v. *Vitale,* 370 U.S. 421 (1962).

11. *Lemon* v. *Kurtzman,* 403 U.S. 602 (1971).

12. *Widmar* v. *Vincent,* 454 U.S. 263 (1981).

13. *Rosenberger* v. *University of Virginia,* 515 U.S. 819 (1995).

14. *Mitchell* v. *Helms,* 530 U.S. 793 (2000).

15. *Zelman* v. *Simmons-Harris,* 536 U.S. 639 (2002).

16. *Lee* v. *Weisman,* 505 U.S. 577 (1992).

17. *McCreary County* v. *ACLU of Kentucky,* 545 U.S. 844 (2005).

18. *Employment Division, Dept. of Human Resources of Oregon* v. *Smith,* 494 U.S. 872 (1990).

19. *Boerne* v. *Flores,* 521 U.S. 507 (1997).

20. *Gonzales* v. *O Centro Espírita Beneficente União Vegetal,* 546 U.S. 418 (2006).

21. Tony Mauro, "Stern's Raunch Is Better than Silence," USA Today (May 12, 2004): 13A.

22. David M. O'Brien, *Constitutional Law and Politics,* vol. 2: *Civil Rights and Civil Liberties* (New York: Norton, 1991), 345.

23. See Frederick Siebert, *The Rights and Privileges of the Press* (New York: Appleton-Century, 1934), 886, 931–40.

24. *Schenck* v. *U.S.,* 249 U.S. 47 (1919).

25. *Brandenburg* v. *Ohio,* 395 U.S. 444 (1969).

26. *New York Times Co.* v. *U.S.,* 403 U.S. 713 (1971).

27. *Nebraska Press Association* v. *Stuart,* 427 U.S. 539 (1976).

28. *Abrams* v. *U.S.,* 250 U.S. 616 (1919).

29. *Stromberg* v. *California,* 283 U.S. 359 (1931).

30. *Tinker* v. *Des Moines Independent Community School District,* 393 U.S. 503 (1969).

31. *R.A.V.* v. *City of St. Paul,* 505 U.S. 377 (1992).

32. *Virginia* v. *Black,* 538 U.S. 343 (2003).

33. *Chaplinsky* v. *New Hampshire,* 315 U.S. 568 (1942).

34. *New York Times Co.* v. *Sullivan,* 376 U.S. 254 (1964).

35. *Chaplinsky* v. *New Hampshire,* 315 U.S. 568 (1942).

36. *Miller* v. *California,* 413 U.S. 15 (1973).

37. *Barnes* v. *Glen Theater,* 501 U.S. 560 (1991).

38. *Reno* v. *American Civil Liberties Union,* 521 U.S. 844 (1997); David G. Savage, "Ban on 'Virtual' Child Porn Is Upset by Court," *Los Angeles Times* (April 17, 2002): A1; *Ashcroft* v. *American Civil Liberties Union,* 542 U.S. 656 (2004).

39. *U.S.* v. *Williams,* 553 U.S. _____ (2008).

40. *DeJonge* v. *Oregon,* 229 U.S. 353 (1937).

41. *Barron* v. *Baltimore,* 32 U.S. 243 (1833).

42. *Dred Scott* v. *Sandford,* 60 U.S. 393 (1857).

43. *U.S.* v. *Miller,* 307 U.S. 174 (1939).

44. *D.C.* v. *Heller,* 554 U.S. 554 _____ (2008).

45. *U.S.* v. *Sokolov,* 490 U.S. 1 (1989).

46. *U.S.* v. *Matlock,* 415 U.S. 164 (1974).

47. *Georgia* v. *Randolph,* 547 U.S. 103 (2006).

48. *Johnson* v. *U.S.,* 333 U.S. 10 (1948).

49. *Winston* v. *Lee,* 470 U.S. 753 (1985).

50. *South Dakota* v. *Neville,* 459 U.S. 553 (1983).

51. *Michigan* v. *Tyler,* 436 U.S. 499 (1978).

52. *Hester* v. *U.S.,* 265 U.S. 57 (1924).

53. *Carroll* v. *U.S.,* 267 U.S. 132 (1925).

54. *U.S.* v. *Arvizu,* 534 U.S. 266 (2002).

55. *Skinner* v. *Railway Labor Executives' Association,* 489 U.S. 602 (1989).

56. *Vernonia School District* v. *Acton,* 515 U.S. 646 (1995).

57. *Board of Education of Independent School District No. 92 of Pottawatomie County* v. *Earls,* 536 U.S. 822 (2002).

58. *Counselman* v. *Hitchcock,* 142 U.S. 547 (1892).

59. *Brown* v. *Mississippi,* 297 U.S. 278 (1936).

60. *U.S.* v. *Patane,* 542 U.S. 630 (2004).

61. *Weeks* v. *U.S.,* 232 U.S. 383 (1914).

62. *Mapp* v. *Ohio,* 367 U.S. 643 (1961).

63. *Johnson* v. *Zerbst,* 304 U.S. 458 (1938).

64. *Gideon* v. *Wainwright,* 372 U.S. 335 (1963).

65. *Argersinger* v. *Hamlin,* 407 U.S. 25 (1972).

66. *Rothgery* v. *Gillespie County,* 554 _____ (2008).

67. *Rompilla* v. *Beard,* 545 U.S. 347 (2005).

68. *Strauder* v. *West Virginia,* 100 U.S. 303 (1880).

69. *Taylor* v. *Louisiana,* 419 U.S. 522 (1975).

70. *Batson* v. *Kentucky,* 476 U.S. 79 (1986).

71. *J.E.B.* v. *Alabama,* 511 U.S. 127 (1994).

72. *Maryland* v. *Craig,* 497 U.S. 836 (1990).

73. See Michael Meltsnet, *Cruel and Unusual: The Supreme Court and Capital Punishment* (New York: Random House, 1973).

74. *Furman* v. *Georgia,* 408 U.S. 238 (1972).

75. *Gregg* v. *Georgia,* 428 U.S. 153 (1976).

76. *House* v. *Bell,* 547 U.S. 518 (2006).

77. *Hill* v. *McDonough,* 547 U.S. 573 (2006).

78. *Baze* v. *Rees,* 553 U.S. _____ (2008).

79. *Olmstead v. U.S.*, 277 U.S. 438 (1928).

80. *Griswold v. Connecticut*, 381 U.S. 481 (1965).

81. *Eisenstadt v. Baird*, 410 U.S. 113 (1972).

82. *Roe v. Wade*, 410 U.S. 113 (1973).

83. *Webster v. Reproductive Health Services*, 492 U.S. 490 (1989).

84. *Planned Parenthood of Southeastern Pennsylvania v. Casey*, 502 U.S. 1056 (1992).

85. *Bowers v. Hardwick*, 478 U.S. 186 (1986).

86. *Lawrence v. Texas*, 539 U.S. 558 (2003).

87. *Cruzan v. Director, Missouri Dept. of Health*, 497 U.S. 261 (1990).

88. *Vacco v. Quill*, 521 U.S. 793 (1997).

89. Office of the Attorney General, Memorandum for Asa Hutchinson, Administrator, the Drug Enforcement Administration, November 6, 2001.

90. *Gonzales v. Oregon*, 546 U.S. 243 (2006).

91. Jennifer Levin, "Alternative Reality About Public, War," *Associated Press* (May 29, 2007).

92. "Surveillance Under the USA Patriot Act," American Civil Liberties Union, April 3, 2003.

93. *Rasul v. Bush*, 542 U.S. 466 (2004).

94. *Boumediene v. Bush* 553 U.S. _____ (2008).

95. *Hamdan v. Rumsfeld*, 548 U.S. 557 (2006).

96. Shane Scott, David Johnston, and James Risen, "Secret U.S. Endorsement of Severe Interrogations," *New York Times* (October 7, 2007): A1.

97. Scott, Johnston, and Risen, "Secret U.S. Endorsement of Severe Interrogations."

Chapter 5

1. Dan Eggen, "Civil Rights Focus Shift Roils Staff at Justice," *Washington Post* (December 13, 2005): A1.

2. Adam Zagorin, "Why Were These U.S. Attorneys Fired?" *Time* (March 7, 2007).

3. Eggen, "Civil Rights Focus Shift Roils Staff at Justice."

4. Dan Eggen, "Politics Alleged in Voting Cases," *Washington Post* (January 23, 2006): A1.

5. David E. Rosenbaum et al., "New Twist in Texas Districting Dispute," *New York Times* (December 3, 2005).

6. *League of United Latin American Citizens v. Perry*, 547 U.S. 399 (2006).

7. *Civil Rights Cases*, 109 U.S. 3 (1883).

8. *Plessy v. Ferguson*, 163 U.S. 537 (1896).

9. *Williams v. Mississippi*, 170 U.S. 213 (1898); *Cummins v. Richmond County Board of Education*, 175 U.S. 528 (1899).

10. *Missouri* ex rel. *Gaines v. Canada*, 305 U.S. 337 (1938).

11. *Sweatt v. Painter*, 339 U.S. 629 (1950); and *McLaurin v. Oklahoma*, 339 U.S. 637 (1950).

12. *Brown v. Board of Education*, 347 U.S. 483 (1954).

13. But see Gerald Rosenberg, *The Hollow Hope: Can Courts Bring About Social Change?* (Chicago: University of Chicago Press, 1991).

14. Quoted in Williams, *Eyes on the Prize*, 10.

15. *Brown v. Board of Education II*, 349 U.S. 294 (1955).

16. Quoted in Williams, *Eyes on the Prize*, 37.

17. *Cooper v. Aaron*, 358 U.S. 1 (1958).

18. Jo Freeman, *The Politics of Women's Liberation* (New York: Longman, 1975), 57.

19. *Hoyt v. Florida*, 368 U.S. 57 (1961).

20. *Reed v. Reed*, 404 U.S. 71 (1971).

21. *Craig v. Boren*, 429 U.S. 190 (1976).

22. *Mississippi University for Women v. Hogan*, 458 U.S. 718 (1982).

23. *Craig v. Boren*, 429 U.S. 190 (1976).

24. *Orr v. Orr*, 440 U.S. 268 (1979).

25. *J.E.B. v. Alabama* ex rel. *TB*, 440 U.S. 268 (1979).

26. *U.S. v. Virginia*, 518 U.S. 515 (1996).

27. *Nguyen v. INS*, 533 U.S. 53 (2001).

28. *Rostker v. Goldberg*, 453 U.S. 57 (1981).

29. *Michael M. v. Superior Court of Sonoma County*, 450 U.S. 464 (1981).

30. *Rostker v. Goldberg*, 453 U.S. 57 (1981).

31. *U.S. v. Virginia*, 518 U.S. 515 (1996).

32. *Meritor Savings Bank v. Vinson*, 477 U.S. 57 (1986).

33. *Oncale v. Sundowner Offshore Services, Inc.*, 523 U.S. 75 (1998).

34. *Hishon v. King & Spalding*, 467 U.S. 69 (1984).

35. *Johnson v. Transportation Agency*, 480 U.S. 616 (1987).

36. *Hernandez v. Texas*, 347 U.S. 475 (1954).

37. *White v. Register*, 412 U.S. 755 (1973).

38. *San Antonio Independent School District v. Rodriguez*, 411 U.S. 1 (1973).

39. *Edgewood Independent School District v. Kirby*, 777 SW 2d 391 (1989).

40. "MALDEF Pleased with Settlement of California Public Schls Inequity Case, *Williams v. California*," August 13, 2004.

41. Michael McNutt, "Group Supports Indians in Office," *Daily Oklahoman* (May 15, 2006).

42. Roger Daniels, *Asian America: Chinese and Japanese in the United States Since 1850* (Seattle: University of Washington Press, 1988).

43. *Yick Wo v. Hopkins*, 118 U.S. 356 (1886).

44. *Ozawa v. U.S.*, 260 U.S. 178 (1922).

45. Andrew L. Aoki, and Don T. Nakanishi, "Asian Pacific Americans and the New Minority Politics," *PS: Political Science and Politics* 34 (2001): 606.

46. *Korematsu v. U.S.*, 323 U.S. 214 (1944).

47. Diane Helene Miller, *Freedom to Differ: The Shaping of the Gay and Lesbian Struggle for Civil Rights* (New York: New York University Press, 1998).

48. Sarah Brewer, David Kaib, and Karen O'Connor, "Sex and the Supreme Court: Gays, Lesbians, and Justice," in Craig A. Rimmerman, Kenneth D. Wald, and Clyde Wilcox, eds., *The Politics of Gay Rights* (Chicago: University of Chicago Press, 2000).

49. Evan Gerstmann, *The Constitutional Underclass: Gays, Lesbians, and the Failure of Class-Based Equal Protection* (Chicago: University of Chicago Press, 1999).

50. Deborah Ensor, "Gay Veterans Working for Change," *San Diego Union* (April 13, 2002): B1.

51. John White, " 'Don't Ask' Costs More than Expected," *Washington Post* (February 14, 2006): A4.

52. *Romer v. Evans*, 517 U.S. 620 (1996).

53. *Lawrence v. Texas*, 539 U.S. 558 (2003).

54. David Pfeiffer, "Overview of the Disability Movement: History, Legislative Record and Political Implications," *Policy Studies Journal* (Winter 1993): 724–42; and "Understanding Disability Policy," *Policy Studies Journal* (Spring 1996): 157–74.

55. Joan Biskupic, "Supreme Court Limits Meaning of Disability," *Washington Post* (June 23, 1999): A1.

56. *Sutton v. United Air Lines, Inc.*, 527 U.S. 471 (1999).

57. *Tennessee v. Lane*, 541 U.S. 509 (2004).

58. *Regents of the University of California v. Bakke*, 438 U.S. 265 (1978).

59. *Grutter v. Bollinger*, 539 U.S. 306 (2003).

60. *Gratz v. Bollinger*, 539 U.S. 306 (2003).

61. Victoria Colliver, "Class Action Considered in Wal-Mart Suit," *San Francisco Chronicle* (September 25, 2003): B1.

62. *Ledbetter v. Goodyear Tire and Rubber Co.*, 550 U.S. _ (2007).

63. "Wal-Mart's Immigrant Labor Problem," *Tampa Tribune* (November 14, 2003): 10.

Chapter 6

1. For an outstanding account of Pelosi's campaign for the whip post, see Juliet Eilperin, "The Making of 'Madam Whip': Fear and Loathing—

and Horse Trading—The Race for the House's No. 2 Democrat," *Washington Post* (January 6, 2002): W27.

2. "Mother of All Whips," *Pittsburgh Post-Gazette* (February 9, 2002): A11.

3. "What Is the Democratic Caucus?" http://dcaucusweb.house.gov/about/what_is.asp.

4. Barbara Sinclair, "The Struggle over Representation and Law-making in Congress: Leadership Reforms in the 1990s," in James A. Thurber and Roger H. Davidson, eds., *Remaking Congress: Change and Stability in the 1990s* (Washington, DC: CQ Press, 1995), 105.

5. Woodrow Wilson, *Congressional Government: A Study in American Government* (New York: Meridian Books, 1956; originally published in 1885), 79.

6. Roger H. Davidson, "Congressional Committees in the New Reform Era: From Combat to the Contract," in Thurber and Davidson, *Remaking Congress*, 28.

7. Christopher Deering and Steven S. Smith, *Committees in Congress*, 3rd ed. (Washington, DC: CQ Press, 1997).

8. Woodrow Wilson, *Congressional Government* (New York: Houghton Mifflin, 1885).

9. Kenneth A. Shepsle, *The Giant Jigsaw Puzzle: Democratic Committee Assignments in the Modern House* (Chicago: University of Chicago Press, 1978).

10. Tim Groseclose and Charles Stewart III, "The Value of Committee Seats in the House, 1947–91," *American Journal of Political Science* 42 (April 1998): 453–74.

11. Gary W. Cox and Jonathan N. Katz, "Why Did the Incumbency Advantage in U.S. House Elections Grow?" *American Journal of Political Science* 40 (May 1996): 478–97; Kenneth N. Bickers and Robert M. Stein, "The Electoral Dynamics of the Federal Pork Barrel," *American Journal of Political Science* 40 (November 1996): 1300–26; and Diana Evans, *Greasing the Wheels: Using Pork Barrel Projects to Build Majority Coalitions in Congress* (New York: Cambridge University Press, 2004).

12. Marjorie Randon Hershey, "Congressional Elections," in Gerald M. Pomper et al., *The Election of 1992: Reports and Interpretations* (Chatham, NJ: Chatham House, 1993), 159.

13. Alan I. Abramowitz, "Incumbency, Congressional Spending, and the Decline of Competition in House Elections," *Journal of Politics* 53 (February 1991): 34–56.

14. Mildred L. Amer, "Membership of the 110th Congress: A Profile." *Congressional Research Service* (December 15, 2006).

15. "Congress Has Wealth to Weather Economic Downturn." (March 13, 2008), www.opensecrets.org/2006/03/congress-has-wealth-toweather.html.

16. *Congressional Quarterly Weekly Report* (January 6, 2001).

17. Norman Ornstein, "GOP Moderates Can Impact Policy—If They Dare," *Roll Call* (February 12, 2003).

18. Byron York, "Bored by Estrada? Owen May Be a Reprise," *The Hill* (March 19, 2003): 43.

19. John W. Kingdon, *Congressmen's Voting Decisions*, 3rd ed. (Ann Arbor: University of Michigan Press. 1989).

20. Ken Kollman, "Inviting Friends to Lobby: Interest Groups, Ideological Bias, and Congressional Committees," *American Journal of Political Science* 41 (April 1997): 519–44. See also Marie Hojnacki and David C. Kimball, "Organized Interests and the Decision of Whom to Lobby in Congress," *American Political Science Review* 92 (December 1998): 775–90.

21. Barbara S. Romzek and Jennifer A. Utter, "Congressional Legislative Staff: Political Professionals or Clerks?" *American Journal of Political Science* 41 (October 1997): 1251–79; Susan Webb Hammond, "Recent Research on Legislative Staffs," *Legislative Studies Quarterly* (November 1996): 543–76; and Michael T. Heaney, "Brokering Health Policy: Coalitions, Parties, and Interest Group Influence," *Journal of Health Politics, Policy, and Law* 31 (October 2006): 887–944.

22. Keith Krehbiel, "Cosponsors and Wafflers from A to Z," *American Journal of Political Science* 39 (November 1995): 906–23.

23. William F. West, "Oversight Subcommittees in the House of Representatives," *Congress and the Presidency* 25 (Autumn 1998): 147–60.

24. This discussion draws heavily on Steven J. Balla, "Legislative Organization and Congressional Review," Paper delivered at the 1999 meeting of the Midwest Political Science Association.

25. Cindy Skrzycki, "Reforms' Knockout Act, Kept Out of the Ring," *Washington Post* (April 18, 2006). D1.

26. *Wall Street Journal* (April 13, 1973): 10.

27. Quoted in Stewart M. Powell, "Lee Fight Signals Tougher Battles Ahead on Nomination," *Commercial Appeal* (December 21, 1997): A15.

Chapter 7

1. "Two Hundred Years of Presidential Funerals," *Washington Post* (June 10, 2004): C14.

2. "The Fold: Presidential Funerals; Farewell to the Chiefs," *Newsday* (June 9, 2004): A38.

3. Gail Russell Chaddock, "The Rise of Mourning in America," *Christian Science Monitor* (June 11, 2004): 1.

4. Richard E. Neustadt, *Presidential Power and the Modern Presidency* (New York: Free Press, 1991).

5. Quoted in Edward S. Corwin, *The President: Office and Powers, 1787–1957*, 4th ed. (New York: New York University Press, 1957), 11.

6. Benjamin I. Page and Mark P. Petracca, *The American Presidency* (New York: McGraw-Hill, 1983), 262.

7. Jim Lobe, "Bush 'Unsigns' War Crimes Treaty," AlterNet.com, May 6, 2002. See also Lincoln P. Bloomfield Jr., "The U.S. Government and the International Criminal Court," Remarks to the Parliamentarians for Global Action, Consultative Assembly of Parliamentarians for the International Criminal Court and the Rule of Laws, Address delivered at the United Nations, New York, September 12, 2003.

8. "War Powers: Resolution Grants Bush Power He Needs," *Rocky Mountain News* (September 15, 2001): B6.

9. *Public Papers of the Presidents* (1963), 889.

10. Quoted in Neustadt, *Presidential Power*, 9.

11. Quoted in Page and Petracca, *The American Presidency*, 57.

12. Samuel Kernell, *Going Public: New Strategies of Presidential Leadership*, 4th ed. (Washington, DC: CQ Press, 2006), 3.

13. Jeffrey Cohen, "Presidential Rhetoric and the Public Agenda," *American Journal of Political Science* 39 (February 1995): 87–107.

14. Neustadt, *Presidential Power*, 1–10.

15. George Reedy, *The Twilight of the Presidency* (New York: New American Library 1971), 38–39.

16. Kernell, *Going Public*.

17. See Louis Fisher, *Constitutional Conflicts Between Congress and the President*, 7th ed. (Lawrence: University Press of Kansas, 2007).

18. Franklin D. Roosevelt, Press Conference, July 23, 1937.

19. See Lance LeLoup and Steven Shull, *The President and Congress: Collaboration and Conflict in National Policymaking* (Boston: Allyn and Bacon, 1999).

20. See Cary Covington, J. Mark Wrighton, and Rhonda Kinney, "A 'Presidency-Augmented' Model of Presidential Success on House Roll Call Votes," *American Journal of Political Science* 39 (November 1995): 1001–24; and Wayne P. Steger, "Presidential Policy Initiation and the Politics of Agenda Control," *Congress and the Presidency* 24 (Spring 1997): 102–14.

21. Quoted in Thomas E. Cronin, *The State of the Presidency*, 2nd ed. (Boston: Little, Brown, 1980), 169.

22. Robert A. Caro, *Master of the Senate: The Years of Lyndon Johnson* (New York: Knopf, 2002).

23. Paul C. Light, *The President's Agenda: Domestic Policy Choice from Kennedy to Carter* (Baltimore, MD: Johns Hopkins University Press, 1983).

24. Mary Leonard, "Bush Begins Talks on Human Cloning," *Boston Globe* (January 17, 2002): A6.

Chapter 8

1. Gardiner Harris, "Bush Plan Shows U.S. Is Not Ready for Deadly Flu," *New York Times* (October 8, 2005).

2. Anita Manning and David Jackson, "Bird Flu Plan Lacks a Key Detail," *USA Today* (May 4, 2006): 2A.

3. Harris, "Bush Plan Shows U.S. Is Not Ready for Deadly Flu."

4. Harris, "Bush Plan Shows U.S. Is Not Ready for Deadly Flu."

5. Stephen Barr, "Users Mostly Rate Agencies Favorably," *Washington Post* (April 13, 2000): A29.

6. Harold D. Lasswell, *Politics: Who Gets What, When and How* (New York: McGraw-Hill, 1938).

7. David Osborne and Ted Gaebler, *Reinventing Government* (Reading, MA: Addison-Wesley, 1992), 20–21.

8. Office of Personnel Management, *The Fact Book*, http://www.opm.gov/feddata/factbook/2005/factbook2005.pdf.

9. "Blackwater Boss Grilled over Iraq," *BBC News* (October 2, 2007).

10. "A Century of Government Growth," *Washington Post* (January 3, 2000): A17. On the difficulty of counting the exact number of government agencies, see David Nachmias and David H. Rosenbloom, *Bureaucratic Government: U.S.A.* (New York: St. Martin's Press, 1980).

11. The classic work on regulatory commissions is Marver Bernstein, *Regulating Business by Independent Commission* (Princeton, NJ: Princeton University Press, 1955).

12. H. H. Gerth and C. Wright Mills, *From Max Weber* (New York: Oxford University Press, 1958).

13. Karen DeYoung, "Saudis Detail Steps on Charities; Kingdom Seeks to Quell Record on Terrorist Financing," *Washington Post* (December 3, 2002): A1.

14. Michael Lipsky, *Street-Level Bureaucracy: Dilemmas of the Individual in Public Services* (New York: Russell Sage Foundation, 1980).

15. Cornelius M. Kerwin, *Rulemaking: How Government Agencies Write Law and Make Policy*, 2nd ed. (Washington, DC: CQ Press, 1999), xv.

16. George A. Krause, "Presidential Use of Executive Orders, 1953–1994," *American Politics Quarterly* 25 (October 1997): 458–81.

17. Irene Murphy, *Public Policy on the Status of Women* (Lexington, MA: Lexington Books, 1974).

18. Rosemary O'Leary, *Environmental Change: Federal Courts and the EPA* (Philadelphia: Temple University Press, 1993).

19. Wendy Hansen, Renee Johnson, and Isaac Unah, "Specialized Courts, Bureaucratic Agencies, and the Politics of U.S. Trade Policy," *American Journal of Political Science* 39 (August 1995): 529–57.

Chapter 9

1. Linda Greenhouse, "In Steps Big and Small. Supreme Court Moved Right," *New York Times* (July 1 2007): A1.

2. Linda Greenhouse. "On Court That Defied Labeling, Kennedy Made Boldest Mark," *New York Times* (June 29, 2008): A1.

3. Administrative Office of the Courts; Supreme Court Public Information Office.

4. *Marbury v. Madison*, 5 U.S. 137 (1803).

5. *Martin v. Hunter's Lessee*, 14 U.S. 304 (1816).

6. *Fletcher v. Peck*, 10 U.S. 87 (1810); *Martin v. Hunter's Lessee*, 14 U.S. 304 (1816); *Cohens v. Virginia*, 19 U.S. 264 (1821).

7. *McCulloch v. Maryland*, 17 U.S. 316 (1819).

8. *Marbury v. Madison*, 5 U.S. 137 (1803).

9. *Marbury v. Madison*, 5 U.S. 137 (1803).

10. This discussion draws heavily on Jack C. Plano and Milton Greenberg, *The American Political Dictionary*, 10th ed. (Fort Worth, TX: Harcourt Brace, 1996), 247.

11. David W. Neubauer, *Judicial Process: Law, Courts, and Politics* (Pacific Grove, CA: Brooks/Cole, 1991), 57.

12. Cases involving citizens from different states can be filed in state or federal court.

13. Sheldon Goldman and Elliot E. Slotnick, "Clinton's First Term Judiciary: Many Bridges to Cross," *Judicature* (May/June 1997): 254–55.

14. Quoted in Lawrence Baum, *The Supreme Court*, 3rd ed. (Washington, DC: CQ Press, 1989), 108.

15. See Barbara A. Perry, *A Representative Supreme Court? The Impact of Race, Religion, and Gender on Appointments* (New York: Greenwood, 1991).

16. Clarence Thomas was raised a Catholic but attended an Episcopalian church at the time of his appointment, having been barred from Catholic sacraments because of his remarriage. He again, however, is attending Roman Catholic services.

17. John Brigham, *The Cult of the Court* (Philadelphia: Temple University Press, 1987).

18. Stephen L. Wasby, *The Supreme Court in the Federal Judicial System*, 4th ed. (Chicago: Nelson-Hall, 1988), 194.

19. Wasby, *The Supreme Court in the Federal Judicial System*, 194.

20. Wasby, *The Supreme Court in the Federal Judicial System*, 199. Much of this change occurred as the result of an increase in state criminal cases, of which nearly 100 percent concerned constitutional questions.

21. Justice Stevens chooses not to join this pool. According to one former clerk, "He wanted an independent review," but Stevens examines only about 20 percent of the petitions, leaving the rest to his clerks. Tony Mauro, "Ginsburg Plunges into the Cert Pool," *Legal Times* (September 6, 1993): 8.

22. Paul Wahlbeck, James F. Spriggs II, and Lee Sigelman, "Ghostwriters on the Court? A Stylistic Analysis of U.S. Supreme Court Opinion Drafts," *American Politics Research 30* (March 2002): 166–92. Wahlbeck, Spriggs, and Sigelman note that "between 1969 and 1972—the period during which the justices each became entitled to a third law clerk . . . the number of opinions increased by about 50 percent and the number of words tripled."

23. Richard A. Posner, *The Federal Courts: Crisis and Reform* (Cambridge, MA: Harvard University Press, 1985), 114.

24. Todd C. Peppers, *Courtiers of the Marble Palace: The Rise and Influence of the Supreme Court Law Clerk* (Palo Alto, CA: Stanford University Press, 2006).

25. Edward Lazarus, *Closed Chambers: The First Eyewitness Account of the Epic Struggles Inside the Supreme Court* (New York: Random House, 1998).

26. "Retired Chief Justice Warren Attacks . . . Freund Study Group's Composition and Proposal," *American Bar Association Journal* 59 (July 1973): 728.

27. Kathleen Werdegar, "The Solicitor General and Administrative Due Process," *George Washington Law Review* (1967–1968): 482.

28. Rebecca Mae Salokar, *The Solicitor General: The Politics of Law* (Philadelphia: Temple University Press, 1992), 3.

29. See, for example, Lawrence Baum, *The Supreme Court*, 4th ed. (Washington, DC: CQ Press, 1992), 106.

30. Richard C. Cortner, *The Supreme Court and Civil Liberties* (Palo Alto, CA: Mayfield, 1975), vi.

31. Gregory A. Caldeira and John R. Wright, "Amicus Curiae Before the Supreme Court: Who Participates, When and How Much?" *Journal of Politics* 52 (August 1990): 803.

32. See also John R. Hermann, "American Indians in Court: The Burger and Rehnquist Years," Ph.D. dissertation, Emory University, 1996.

33. Linda Greenhouse, "With O'Connor Retirement and a New Chief Justice Comes an Awareness of Change," *New York Times* (January 28, 2006): A10.

34. Donald L. Horowitz, *The Courts and Social Policy* (Washington, DC: Brookings Institution, 1977), 538.

35. *Webster v. Reproductive Health Services*, 492 U.S. 490 (1989).

36. See, for example, Tracey E. George and Lee Epstein, "On the Nature of Supreme Court Decision Making," *American Political Science Review* 86 (1992): 323–37; Melinda Gann Hall and Paul Brace, "Justices' Responses to Case Facts: An Interactive Model," *American Politics Quarterly* (April 1996): 237–61; Lawrence Baum, *The Puzzle of Judicial Behavior* (Ann Arbor: University of Michigan Press, 1997); and Gregory N. Flemming, David B. Holmes, and Susan Gluck Mezey, "An Integrated Model of Privacy Decision Making in State Supreme Courts," *American Politics Quarterly* 26 (January 1998): 35–58.

37. Jeffrey A. Segal and Harold J. Spaeth, *The Supreme Court and the Attitudinal Model Revisited* (New York: Cambridge University Press, 2002).

38. Gerard Gryski, Eleanor C. Main, and William Dixon, "Models of State High Court Decision Making in Sex Discrimination Cases," *Journal of Politics* 48 (1986): 143–55; and C. Neal Tate and Roger Handberg, "Time Binding and Theory Building in Personal Attribute Models of

Supreme Court Voting Behavior, 1916–1988," *American Political Science Review* 35 (1991): 460–80.

39. Donald R. Songer and Sue Davis, "The Impact of Party and Region on Voting Decisions in the U.S. Courts of Appeals, 1955–86," *Western Political Quarterly* 43 (1990): 830–44.

40. H.W. Perry, *Deciding to Decide: Agenda Setting in the United States Supreme Court* (Cambridge, MA: Harvard University Press, 1991); and Gregory A. Caldeira, John R. Wright, and Christopher Zorn, "Strategic Voting and Gatekeeping in the Supreme Court," *Journal of Law, Economics, and Organization* 15 (1999): 549–72.

41. Forrest Maltzman and Paul J. Walhbeck, "May It Please the Chief? Opinion Assignments in the Rehnquist Court," *American Journal of Political Science* 40 (1996): 421–43.

42. James F. Spriggs, Forrest Maltzman, and Paul J. Wahlbeck, "Bargaining on the U.S. Supreme Court: Justices' Responses to Majority Opinion Drafts," *Journal of Politics* 61 (1999): 485–506.

43. Kevin T. McGuire and James A. Stimson, "The Least Dangerous Branch Revisited: New Evidence on Supreme Court Responsiveness to Public Preferences," *Journal of Politics* 66 (2004): 1018–35.

44. Charles M. Cameron, Donald R. Songer, and Jeffrey A. Segal, "Strategic Auditing in a Political Hierarchy: An Informational Model of the Supreme Court's Certiorari Decisions," *American Political Science Review* 94 (2000): 101–16.

45. Pablo T. Spiller and Rafael Gely, "Congressional Control or Judicial Independence: The Determinants of U.S. Supreme Court Labor-Relations Decisions, 1949–1988," *RAND Journal of Economics* 23 (1992): 463–92.

46. Timothy R. Johnson and Andrew D. Martin, "The Public's Conditional Response to Supreme Court Decisions," *American Political Science Review* 92 (June 1998): 299–309.

47. *Korematsu v. U.S.*, 323 U.S. 214 (1944).

48. *Youngstown Sheet & Tube Co. v. Sawyer*, 343 U.S. 579 (1952). The Supreme Court ruled that President Truman's seizure and operation of U.S. steel mills in the face of a strike threat were unconstitutional, because the Constitution implied no such broad executive power. See Alan Westin, *Anatomy of a Constitutional Law Case* (New York: Macmillan, 1958); and Maeva Marcus, *Truman and the Steel Seizure Case* (New York: Columbia University Press, 1977).

49. *U.S. v. Nixon*, 418 U.S. 683 (1974).

50. Gallup Poll, June 1–4, 2006, Lexis-Nexis RPOLL.

51. *Boumediene v. Bush*, 553 U.S._____ (2008).

52. "Supreme Court Cases Overruled by Subsequent Decision," U.S. Government Printing Office. Accessed online at http://www.gpoaccess.gov/constitution/pdf/con041.pdf.

53. *Reynolds v. Sims*, 377 U.S. 533 (1964).

54. *Mississippi University for Women v. Hogan*, 458 U.S. 718 (1982).

Chapter 10

1. Robert D. Hess and David Easton, "The Child's Changing Image of the President," *Public Opinion Quarterly* 14 (Winter 1960): 632–42; and Fred I. Greenstein, *Children and Politics* (New Haven, CT: Yale University Press, 1965).

2. Laura Pappano, "Potential War Poses Threat to Teachers," *Boston Globe* (March 9, 2003): B9.

3. James Simon and Bruce D. Merrill, "Political Socialization in the Classroom Revisited: The Kids Voting Program," *Social Science Journal* 35 (1998): 29–42.

4. Simon and Merrill, "Political Socialization in the Classroom Revisited."

5. *Statistical Abstract of the United States, 1997* (Washington, DC: Government Printing Office, 1997), 1011.

6. Pew Project for Excellence in Journalism, 2008.

7. Gallup Poll, December 6–9, 2007.

8. USA Today and CNN/Gallup Tracking Poll, USAToday.com.

9. Edward S. Greenberg, "The Political Socialization of Black Children," in Edward S. Greenberg, ed., *Political Socialization* (New York: Atherton Press, 1970), 131.

10. Jon Hurwitz and Mark Peffley, "Public Perceptions of Race and Crime: The Role of Racial Stereotypes," *American Journal of Political Science* 41 (April 1997): 375–401.

11. Elaine S. Povich, "Courting Hispanies: Group's Votes Could Shift House Control," *Newsday* (April 21, 2002): A4.

12. Karen M. Kaufmann and John Petrocik, "The Changing Politics of American Men: Understanding Sources of the Gender Gap," *American Journal of Political Science* 43 (July 1999): 864–87.

13. Margaret Trevor, "Political Socialization, Party Identification, and the Gender Gap," *Public Opinion Quarterly* 63 (Spring 1999): 62–89.

14. Alexandra Marks, "Gender Gap Narrows over Kosovo," *Christian Science Monitor* (April 30, 1999): 1.

15. Pew Research Center for People and the Press, 2002.

16. Susan A. MacManus, *Young v. Old: Generational Combat in the 21st Century* (Boulder, CO: Westview, 1995).

17. Pew Forum on Religion and Public Life, "U.S. Religions Landscape Survey," http://Religious.Pewforuming.

18. Alan M. Winkler, "Public Opinion," in Jack Greene, ed., *The Encyclopedia of American Political History* (New York: Charles Scribner's Sons, 1988), 1038.

19. *Literary Digest* 125 (November 14, 1936): 1.

20. Robert S. Erikson, Norman Luttbeg, and Kent Tedin, *American Public Opinion: Its Origin, Contents, and Impact* (New York: Wiley, 1980), 28.

21. Francis J. Connolly and Charley Manning, "What 'Push Polling' Is and What It Isn't," *Boston Globe* (August 16, 2001): A21.

22. Suzanne Soule, "Will They Engage? Political Knowledge, Participation and Attitudes of Generations X and Y," paper prepared for the 2001 German and American Conference, 6.

23. Soule, "Will They Engage?" quoting Richard G. Niemi and Jane Junn, *Civic Education* (New Haven, CT: Yale University Press, 1998).

24. Quoted in Everett Carll Ladd, "Fiskin's 'Deliberative Poll' Is Flawed Science and Dubious Democracy," *Public Perspective* (December/January 1996): 41.

25. "Don't Know Much About..." *Christian Science Monitor* (May 16, 2002): 8.

26. "Don't Know Much About History, Geography..." *Pittsburgh Post-Gazette* (January 22, 2003): E2; Laurence D. Cohen, "Geography for Dummies," *Hartford Courant* (December 8, 2002): C3.

27. V. O. Key Jr., *The Responsible Electorate: Rationality in Presidential Voting, 1936–1960* (Cambridge, MA: Belknap Press of Harvard University, 1966).

28. Richard Nodeau et al., "Elite Economic Forecasts, Economic News, Mass Economic Judgements and Presidential Approval," *Journal of Politics* 61 (February 1999): 109–35.

29. Michael Towle, Review of *Presidential Responsiveness and Public Policymaking: The Public and the Policies* by Jeffrey E. Cohen, *Journal of Politics* 61 (February 1999): 230–2.

30. John E. Mueller, *War, Presidents, and Public Opinion* (New York: Wiley, 1973), 69.

31. See Mitchell Stephens, *A History of News: From the Drum to the Satellite* (New York: Viking, 1989).

32. For a delightful rendition of this episode, see Shelley Ross, *Fall from Grace* (New York: Ballantine, 1988), chapter 12.

33. Richard L. Rubin, *Press, Party, and Presidency* (New York: Norton, 1981), 38–39.

34. Stephen Bates, *If No News, Send Rumors* (New York: St. Martin's, 1989), 185.

35. See Doris A. Graber, *Mass Media and American Politics*, 3rd ed. (Washington, DC: CQ Press, 1989), 12; and Thomas C. Leonard, *The Power of the Press: The Birth of American Political Reporting* (New York: Oxford University Press, 1986), chapter 7.

36. Pew Research Center, "Cable and Internet Loom Large."

37. J. D. Power and Associates report, "Although Cable Continues to Lose Market Share to Satellite Providers, Cable Subscribers Are Switching to Digital Service at a Rapid Pace," http://www.jdpower.com.

38. Annenberg National Election Study, 2004, http://www.annenberg publicpolicycenter.org.

39. Pew Research Center for the People and the Press, "Internet News Audience Highly Critical of News Organizations—Views of Press Values and Performance: 1985–2007," August 9, 2007.

40. Darrell West, *Digital Government: Technology and Public Sector Performance* (Princeton, NJ: Princeton University Press, 2005).

41. Donald L. Jorand and Benjamin I. Page, "Shaping Foreign Policy Opinions: The Role of TV News," *Journal of Conflict Resolution* 36 (June 1992): 227–41.

42. Pew Research Center, "Maturing Internet News Audience."

43. Christopher Stern, "FCC Chairman's Star a Little Dimmer," *Washington Post* (July 25, 2003): E01, http://www.washington post.com.

44. Mark K. Miller. "On Hold: Rankings Change Little as Regulatory Uncertainty Keeps Station Trading in Neutral," *Broadcasting and Cable* (April, 19, 2004): 50.

45. Frank Ahrens, "Divided FCC Enacts Rules on Media Ownership," *Washington Post,* December 19, 2007, D01; Stephen Labaton, "FCC Reshapes Rules Limiting Media Industry," *The New York Times,* December 19, 2007, A1

46. *RTNDA* v. *FCC,* 229 F3d 269 (DC Cir. 2000).

47. *New York Times Co.* v. *U.S.,* 403 U.S. 713 (1971).

48. Jillian Harrison, "Embedded Journalism Limited in Perspective, Tufts U. Professors Say," *University Wire,* April 15, 2003.

49. U.S. Senate press gallery and U.S. House of Representatives radio-television correspondents' gallery.

50. List of White House correspondents, http://www.washington post.com/wp-srv/politics/administration/whbriefing/correspondents.html.

51. *New York Times Co.* v. *Sullivan,* 376 U.S. 254 (1964). See also Steven Pressman, "Libel Law: Finding the Right Balance," *Editorial Research Reports* 2 (August 18, 1989): 462–71.

52. *Curtis Publishing Co.* v. *Butts,* 388 U.S. 130 (1967); *Associated Press* v. *Walker,* 388 U.S. 130 (1967).

53. Thomas Patterson, *Out of Order* (New York: Vintage, 1994).

54. John R. Zaller, "Monica Lewinsky's Contribution to Political Science," *PS: Political Science and Politics* 31 (June 1998): 182–9.

55. Lori Robertson, "In Control," *American Journalism Review* (February/March 2005).

56. Harold W. Stanley and Richard G. Niemi, *Vital Statistics on American Politics,* 4th ed. (Washington, DC: CQ Press, 1994), 28.

57. John R. Hibbing and Elizabeth Theiss-Morse, *Congress as Public Enemy: Political Attitudes Toward American Political Institutions* (New York: Cambridge University Press, 1995).

58. Karen Aho, "Broadcasters Want Access, but Will They Deliver Serious Coverage?" *Columbia Journalism Review* 5 (September/October 2003), http://www.cjr.org.

59. Benjamin I. Page, Robert Y. Shapiro, and Glenn R. Dempsey, "What Moves Public Opinion?" *American Political Science Review* 81 (March 1987): 23–44.

60. Shanto Iyengar and Donald R. Kinder, *News That Matters,* reprint ed. (Chicago: University of Chicago Press, 1989).

61. David Domke, David P. Fan, Dhavan V. Shah, and Mark D. Watts, "The Politics of Conservative Elites and the 'Liberal Media' Argument," *Journal of Communication* 49 (Fall 1999): 35–58.

62. American Society of Newspaper Editors, *The Changing Face of the Newsroom* (Washington, DC: ASNE, 1989), 33; William Schneider and I. A. Lewis, "Views on the News," *Public Opinion* 8 (August/September 1985): 6–11, 58–59; and S. Robert Lichter, Stanley Rothman, and Linda S. Lichter, *The Media Elite* (Bethesda, MD: Adler and Adler, 1986).

63. Pew Research Center for the People and the Press, "The Web: Alarming, Appealing and a Challenge to Journalistic Values," March 17, 2008.

Chapter 11

1. Graham Wilson, *Interest Groups in the United States* (New York: Oxford University Press, 1981), 4.

2. V. O. Key, *Politics, Parties, and Pressure Groups* (New York, Crowell, 1942), 23.

3. John H. Aldrich, *Why Parties? The Origin and Transformation of Party Politics in America* (Chicago: University of Chicago Press, 1995).

4. By contrast, Great Britain did not develop truly national, broad-based parties until the 1870s.

5. See *Historical Statistics of the United States: Colonial Times to 1970,* part 2, series Y-27-28 (Washington, DC: Government Printing Office, 1975), based on unpublished data prepared by Walter Dean Burnham. See also Harold W. Stanley and Richard G. Niemi, *Vital Statistics on American Politics 2005–2006* (Washington, DC: CQ Press, 2006), for contemporary turnout figures.

6. U.S. Census Bureau, Population Profile of the United States: 2000 (Internet release), available from http://www.census.gov/population/popprofile/2000/profile2000.pdf.

7. On the subject of party realignment, see Walter Dean Burnham, *Critical Elections and the Mainsprings of American Politics* (New York: Norton, 1970); Kristi Andersen, *The Creation of a Democratic Majority* (Chicago: University of Chicago Press, 1979); and John R. Petrocik, "Realignment: New Party Coalitions and the Nationalization of the South," *Journal of Politics* 49 (May 1987): 347–75.

8. See Burnham, *Critical Elections and the Mainsprings of American Politics,* for a defense of realignment theory.

9. For a perspective on reconsidering the relevance and validity of critical realignments, see David Mayhew, *Electoral Realignments* (New Haven, CT: Yale University Press, 2004).

10. Morris P. Fiorina, *Retrospective Voting in American National Elections* (New Haven, CT: Yale University Press, 1981); and Charles H. Franklin and John E. Jackson, "The Dynamics of Party Identification," *American Political Science Review* 77 (1983): 957–73.

11. See, for example, V. O. Key Jr., "A Theory of Critical Elections," *Journal of Politics* 17 (February 1955): 3–18.

12. See Everett Carll Ladd, "The Brittle Mandate: Electoral Dealignment and the 1980 Presidential Election," *Political Science Quarterly* 96 (1981): 1–25.

13. Everett Carll Ladd, "Like Waiting for Godot: The Uselessness of 'Realignment' for Understanding Change in Contemporary American Politics," in Byron Shafer, ed., *The End of Realignment? Interpreting American Electoral Eras* (Madison: University of Wisconsin Press, 1991).

14. For a discussion of secular realignment in the South, see Jeffrey M. Stonecash, "Class and Party: Secular Realignment and the Survival of Democrats Outside the South," *Political Research Quarterly* 53:4 (2000): 731–52.

15. For a discussion of recent trends in party strength, see Morris P. Fiorina, "Parties and Partisanship: A 40-Year Retrospective," *Political Behavior* 24 (2002): 93–115.

16. Earl Black and Merle Black, *The Rise of Southern Republicans* (Cambridge, MA: Harvard University Press, 2002).

17. See David E. Price, *Bringing Back the Parties* (Washington, DC: CQ Press, 1984), 284–8.

18. Catharine Richert, "Party Unity: United We Stand Opposed," *CQ Weekly* (January 14, 2008): 143.

19. Christian Collet and Martin P. Wattenberg, "Strategically Unambitious: Minor Party and Independent Candidates in the 1996 Congressional Elections," in John C. Green and Daniel M. Shea, eds., *The State of the Parties: The Changing Role of Contemporary American Parties,* 3rd ed. (Lanham, MD: Rowman and Littlefield, 1999).

20. Marc J. Hetherington, "The Effect of Political Trust on the Presidential Vote, 1968–1992," *American Political Science Review* 93 (1999): 311–26.

21. John Clifford Green, Paul S. Herrnson, and John C. Green, eds., *Responsible Partisanship: The Evolution of American Political Parties Since the 1950s* (Lawrence: University Press of Kansas, 2003).

22. See Steven E. Finkel and Howard A. Scarrow, "Party Identification and Party Enrollment: The Difference and the Consequence," *Journal of Politics* 47 (May 1985): 620–42.

23. Flanigan and Zingale, *Political Behavior of the American Electorate,* 2006.

24. The presidential election of 1960 may be an extreme case, but John F. Kennedy's massive support among Catholics and Richard M. Nixon's less substantial but still impressive backing by Protestants demonstrates the polarization that religion could once produce. See Philip E. Converse,

"Religion and Politics: The 1960 Election," in Angus Campbell et al., *Elections and the Political Order* (New York: Wiley, 1966), 96–124.

25. The Pew Forum on Religion and Public Life, U.S. Religious Landscape Survey, February 2008.

26. Robert D. Putnam, "Bowling Alone: America's Declining Social Capital," *Journal of Democracy* 6 (1995): 650–65; and Putnam, *Bowling Alone: The Collapse and Revival of American Community* (New York: Simon and Schuster, 2000).

27. Everett Carll Ladd, quoted in Richard Morin, "Who Says We're Not Joiners," *Washington Post* (May 2, 1999): B5.

28. John Brehm and Wendy Rahn, "Individual-Level Evidence for the Causes and Consequences of Social Capital," *American Journal of Political Science* 41 (July 1997): 999.

29. Mark Schneider et al., "Institutional Arrangements and the Creation of Social Capital: The Effects of Public School Choice," *American Political Science Review* 91 (March 1997): 82–93.

30. Nicholas Lemann, "Kicking in Groups," *Atlantic Monthly* (April 1996), NEXIS.

31. David B. Truman, *The Governmental Process: Political Interests and Public Opinion* (New York: Knopf, 1951), 33.

32. Truman, *The Governmental Process*, ch. 16.

33. E. E. Schattschneider, *The Semisovereign People* (New York: Holt Rinehart, and Winston, 1960), 35.

34. David Lowery and Virginia Gray, "The Population Ecology of Gucci Gulch or the Natural Regulation of Interest Group Numbers in the American States," *American Journal of Political Science* 39 (February 1995): 1–29.

35. Walker, *Mobilizing Interest Groups in America*.

36. Mancur Olson Jr., *The Logic of Collective Action: Public Goods and the Theory of Groups* (Cambridge, MA: Harvard University Press, 1965).

37. Chris Kutalik, "What Does the AFL-CIO Split Mean?" *Labor Notes*, (September 2005): http://www.labornotes.org.

38. Jack L. Walker, "The Origins and Maintenance of Interest Groups in America," *American Political Science Review* 77 (June 1983): 390–406.

39. Peter Steinfels, "Moral Majority to Dissolve: Says Mission Accomplished," *New York Times* (June 12, 1989): A14.

40. Some political scientists speak of "iron rectangles," reflecting the growing importance of a fourth party, the courts, in the lobbying process.

41. Clement E. Vose, "Litigation as a Form of Pressure Group Activity," *Annals* 319 (September 1958): 20–31.

42. Robert A. Goldberg, *Grassroots Resistance: Social Movements in Twentieth Century America* (Belmont, CA: Wadsworth, 1991).

Chapter 12

1. William A. Galston, "Civic Education and Political Participation," *Political Science and Politics* 37 (2004): 263–6.

2. Steven J. Rosenstone and John Mark Hanson, *Mobilization, Participation, and Democracy in America* (New York: Macmillan, 1993).

3. U.S. Census Bureau, "Voting and Registration in the Election of November 2004," http://www.census.gov/prod/2006pubs/p20-556.pdf.

4. Thomas M. Guterbock and Bruce London, "Race, Political Orientation, and Participation: An Empirical Test of Four Competing Theories," *American Sociological Review* 48 (1983): 439–53.

5. Carol A. Cassel, "Hispanic Turnout: Estimates from Validated Voting Data," *Political Science Quarterly* 55 (June 2002): 391–408.

6. Benjamin Highton, "Easy Registration and Voter Turnout," *Journal of Politics* 59 (1997): 565–75.

7. Stephen Knack and J. White, "Election-Day Registration and Turnout Inequality," *Political Behavior* 22 (March 2000): 29–44.

8. International Institute for Democracy and Electoral Assistance, "Global Database," http://www.idea.int/vt/survey/voter_turnout_pop2.cfm.

9. Martin P. Wattenberg, *The Decline of American Political Parties, 1952–1996* (Cambridge, MA: Harvard University Press, 1998).

10. Michael S. Lewis-Beck and Mary Stegmaier, "Economic Determinants of Electoral Outcomes," *Annual Review of Political Science* 3 (2000): 183–219.

11. Paul Allen Beck, *Party Politics in America*, 8th ed. (New York: Longman, 1998); David Adamany, "Cross-over Voting and the Democratic Party's Reform Rules," *American Political Science Review* 70 (1976): 536–41; Ronald Hedlund and Meredith W. Watts, "The Wisconsin Open Primary: 1968 to 1984," *American Politics Quarterly* 14 (1986): 55–74; and Gary D. Wekkin, "The Conceptualization and Measurement of Crossover Voting," *Western Political Quarterly* 41 (1988): 105–14.

12. Gary D. Wekken, "Why Crossover Voters Are Not 'Mischievous' Voters," *American Politics Quarterly* 19 (1991): 229–47; and Todd L. Cherry and Stephan Kroll, "Crashing the Party: An Experimental Investigation of Strategic Voting in Primary Elections," *Public Choice* 114 (2003): 387–420.

13. Of these ten states, South Dakota is the only state outside the South to hold a runoff primary. A runoff is held only if no candidate receives at least 35 percent of the vote, however. See "Statutory Election Information of the Several States," *The Green Papers*, http://www.thegreenpapers.com/slg/sei.phtml?format=sta.

14. Elaine Ciulla Kamarck and Kenneth M. Goldstein, "The Rules Matter: Post-Reform Presidential Nominating Politics," in L. Sandy Maisel, *The Parties Respond: Changes in American Parties and Campaigns* (Boulder, CO: Westview, 1994), 174.

15. See "Candidates and Nominations," in Paul S. Herrnson, *Congressional Elections: Campaigning at Home and in Washington*, 4th ed. (Washington, DC: CQ Press, 2004), 35–68.

16. R. Michael Alvarez and Jonathan Nagler, "Economics, Issues, and the Perot Candidacy: Voter Choice in the 1992 Presidential Election," *American Journal of Political Science* 39 (1995): 714–44.

17. U.S. Census Bureau, Census 2000 and earlier censuses.

18. "How to Rig an Election," *Economist* (April 25, 2002).

19. Matthew Mosk and Lori Montgomery, "Md. Court Spurns Assembly Map: Glendening Plan Ruled Unconstitutional; Judges to Redraw Lines," *Washington Post* (June 12, 2002).

20. *Wesberry v. Sanders*, 376 U.S. 1 (1964).

21. *Thornburg v. Gingles*, 478 U.S. 30 (1986).

22. *Shaw v. Reno*, 113 S.Ct. 2816 (1993).

23. Gary C. Jacobson and Michael A. Dimock, "Checking Out: The Effects of Bank Overdrafts on the 1992 House Elections," *American Journal of Political Science* 38 (1994): 601–24; and Herrnson, *Congressional Elections*.

24. Five liberal Democratic U.S. senators, including George McGovern of South Dakota, were defeated in this way in 1980, for example.

25. Diana C. Mutz, "Effects of Horse-Race Coverage on Campaign Coffers: Strategic Contributing in Presidential Primaries," *Journal of Politics* 57 (November 1995): 1015–42.

26. *McConnell v. Federal Election Committee*, 540 U.S. 93 (2003).

27. Joseph E. Cantor, *Campaign Finance: An Overview* (Washington, DC: Congressional Research Service, March 29, 2007).

28. See http://www.opensecrets.org.

29. See "The Internet Campaign," in Herrnson, *Congressional Elections*.

30. Amy Keller, "Helping Each Other Out: Members Dip into Campaign Funds for Fellow Candidates," *Roll Call* (June 15, 1998): 1.

31. For member contribution activity at the state level, see Jay K. Dow, "Campaign Contributions and Intercandidate Transfers in the California Assembly," *Social Science Quarterly* 75 (1994): 867–80. For member contribution activity at the congressional level, see Bruce A. Larson, "Ambition and Money in the U.S. House of Representatives: Analyzing Campaign Contributions from Incumbents' Leadership PACs and Reelection Committees" (Ph.D. dissertation, University of Virginia, 1998). For a briefer account, see Paul S. Herrnson, "Money and Motives: Spending in House Elections," in Lawrence C. Dodd and Bruce I. Oppenheimer, eds., *Congress Reconsidered*, 6th ed. (Washington, DC: CQ Press, 1997).

32. Larson, "Ambition and Money in the U.S. House of Representatives."

33. *Buckley v. Valeo*, 424 U.S. 1 (1976).

34. Jeffrey Milyo and Thomas Groseclose, "The Electoral Effects of Incumbent Wealth," *Journal of Law and Economics* 42 (1999): 699–722.

35. See http://www.commoncause.org.

36. Federal Election Commission Release, "Party Financial Activity Summarized," December 14, 2004, http://www.fec.gov.

Chapter 13

1. Robert Pear, "Health Care Plan Isn't Cast in Stone," *New York Times* (January 22, 1994).
2. Ann Devroy, "President Insists Congress Enact Reforms in Welfare, Health Care," *Washinton Post* (January 26, 1994): A1.
3. Perry Bacon Jr. and Ann Kornblut, "Clinton Presents Plan for Universal Coverage," *Washinton Post* (September 18, 2007): A1.
4. Kaiser Family Foundation, "2008 Presidential Candidate Health Care Proposals: Side by Side Summary," www.health08.org/sidebyside.cfm.
5. James E. Anderson, *Public Policymaking: An Introduction*, 2nd ed. (Boston: Houghton Mifflin, 1994), 5. This discussion draws on Anderson's study.
6. Roger W. Cobb and Charles D. Elder, *Participation in American Politics: The Dynamics of Agenda-Building*, 2nd ed. (Baltimore, MD: Johns Hopkins University Press, 1983), 85.
7. Charles O. Jones, *An Introduction to the Study of Public Policy*, 3rd ed. (Monterey, CA: Brooks/Cole, 1984), 87–89.
8. Judy Sarasohn, "Bush's '06 Budget Would Scrap or Reduce 154 Programs," *Washington Post* (February 22, 2005): A13.
9. This discussion draws on Anne Schneider and Helen Ingram, "Behavioral Assumptions of Policy Tools," *Journal of Politics* 52 (May 1990): 510–29.
10. Government Accountability Office, "Amtrak Management: Systematic Problems Require Actions to Improve Efficiency, Effectiveness, and Accountability," GAO-06-145, April 2005, www.gao.gov.
11. Ronald Edsforth, *The New Deal: America's Response to the Great Depression* (Oxford: Blackwell, 2000), 231.
12. Robert Rich and William White, "Health Care Policy and the American States: Issues of Federalism," in Rich and White, eds., *Health Policy, Federalism, and the American States* (Washington, DC: Urban Institute Press, 1996), 20.
13. Department of Health and Human Services, aspe.hhs.gov.
14. Fact Sheet, Social Security, www.ssa.gov.
15. Pew Research Center for the People and the Press, "Survey Finds Bush Failing in Social Security Reform," March 3, 2005.
16. Economic Policy Institute, "State Unemployment Insurance Policies as of June 2004," www.epinet.org.
17. Bureau of Labor Statistics, "Employment Situation Summary," www.bls.gov.
18. Social Security Administration, ssa-custhelp.ssa.gov.
19. Budget of the United States Government, Fiscal Year 2007, Historical Tables, Section 11, Outlays for Payments, www.whitehouse.gov/omb/budget/fy2007/pdf/hist.pdf.
20. Steven G. Koven, Mack C. Shelley II, and Bert E. Swanson, *American Public Policy: The Contemporary Agenda* (Boston: Houghton Mifflin, 1998), 271.
21. The White House, "Working Toward Independence," news release, February 2002, www.whitehouse.gov.
22. Nanette Relave, "TANF Reauthorization and Work Requirements," *Reauthorization Resource*, February 2002, www.welfareinfo.org.
23. Department of Health and Human Services, "Welfare Reform Reauthorized," February 8, 2006, www.hhs.gov.
24. Department of Agriculture, "Food Stamp Program Annual Summary," March 24, 2006, www.fns.usda.gov.
25. "Fiscal Year 2006: Mid-Session Review Budget of the U.S. Government," July 13, 2005, www.whitehouse.gov/omb/budget/fy2006/pdf/06msr.pdf.
26. Mark Rushefsky and Kant Patel, *Politics, Power, and Policy Making: The Case of Health Care Reform in the 1990s* (Armonk, NY: M. E. Sharpe, 1998), 27.
27. Henry J. Aaron, *Serious and Unstable Condition: Financing America's Health Care* (Washington, DC: Brookings Institution, 1991), ch. 2.
28. John F. Dickerson, "Can We Afford All This?" *Time* (December 8, 2004), 48–51; Edward Walsh and Bill Brubaker, "Drug Benefits Impact Detailed," *Washington Post* (December 8, 2003): A10.
29. Congressional Budget Office, "Medicaid: Federal Outlays in Billions of Dollars," 2005, www.house.gov; Kaiser Family Foundation, "HIV/AIDS Policy Fact Sheet," September 2005, www.kff.org.
30. After 108 years of operation, the ICC expired at the end of 1995 as part of the effort by congressional Republicans to reduce federal regulations and allow market forces more freedom in which to operate.
31. Micheline Maynard, "Airlines' Cuts Making Cities No-Fly Zones," *New York Times* (May 21, 2008), www.nytimes.com.
32. Maurice Hinchey, "More Media Owners," *Nation* (February 6, 2006), www.thenation.com.
33. About 38 percent of the nation's commercial banks are members of the Federal Reserve System. See www.richmondfed.org.
34. James E. Anderson, David W. Brady, Charles S. Bullock III, and Joseph Stewart Jr., *Public Policy and Politics in America*, 2nd ed. (Monterey: Brooks/Cole, 1984), 38–40.

Chapter 14

1. "President Bush Discusses NSA Surveillance Program," White House press briefing, May 11, 2006, http://www.whitehouse.gov.
2. John F. Kennedy, inaugural address, January 20, 1961, Public Papers of the Presidents of the United States (Washington, DC: Government Printing Office).
3. See Graham Allison, *Essence of Decision: Explaining the Cuban Missile Crisis* (Boston: Little, Brown, 1971).
4. For a discussion of U.S., Soviet, and Chinese views of the Vietnam War, see Daniel S. Papp, *Vietnam: The View from Moscow, Beijing, Washington* (Jefferson, NC: McFarland, 1981).
5. Richard M. Nixon, inaugural address, January 20, 1969, Public Papers of the Presidents of the United States (Washington, DC: Government Printing Office).
6. Michael Froman, *The Development of the Idea of Détente* (New York: St. Martin's, 1982).
7. R. C. Schroeder, "Human Rights Policy," *CQ Research Reports* 1 (1979), CQ Researcher Online, http://library.cqpress.com.
8. Jimmy Carter, State of the Union Address, January 21, 1980, Public Papers of the Presidents of the United States (Washington, DC: Government Printing Office).
9. See Colin S. Gray, "Strategic Forces," in Joseph Kruzel, ed., *1986–1987 American Defense Annual* (Lexington, MA: Lexington Books, 1986). For a discussion of Reagan's early international economic policies, see Jeffrey E. Garten, "Gunboat Economics," *Foreign Affairs* 63 (1985): 538–99.
10. See Stephen E. Ambrose, *Rise to Globalism: American Foreign Policy Since 1938*, 8th revised ed. (New York: Penguin, 1998); Steven W. Hook and John Spanier, *American Foreign Policy Since World War II*, 15th ed. (Washington, DC: CQ Press, 2000); Richard Mandelbaum and Strobe Talbott, *Reagan and Gorbachev* (New York: Vintage, 1987); and Richard A. Melanson, *American Foreign Policy Since the Vietnam War*, 3rd ed. (Armonk, NY: M. E. Sharpe, 2000).
11. Karen Brutents and Larisa Galperin, "Origins of the New Thinking," *Russian Social Science Review* 47:1 (2006): 73–102; David Laibman, "The Soviet Demise: Revisionist Betrayal, Structural Defect, or Authoritarian Distortion?" *Science and Society* 69:4 (2005): 594–606; and John Muelle, "What Was the Cold War About? Evidence from Its Ending," *Political Science Quarterly* 119:4 (2004/2005): 609–31.
12. For good discussions of the events that led to the decline and fall of the Soviet Union, see William Head and Earl H. Tilford Jr., *The Eagle in the Desert: Looking Back on U.S. Involvement in the Persian Gulf War* (Westport, CT: Praeger, 1996).
13. See Geoffrey Hosking, *The Awakening of the Soviet Union* (Cambridge, MA: Harvard University Press, 1990); David Remnick, *Lenin's Tomb: The Last Days of the Soviet Empire* (New York: Random House, 1993); and Jeffrey T. Checkel, *Ideas and International Political Change: Soviet/Russian Behavior and the End of the Cold War* (New Haven, CT: Yale University Press, 1997).
14. Jeffrey J. Schott, *The WTO After Seattle* (Washington, DC: Institute for International Economics, 2000); and Bhagirath L. Das, *World Trade Organization: A Guide to New Frameworks for International Trade* (New York: St. Martin's, 2000).
15. See Daniel S. Papp, *The Impact of September 11 on Contemporary International Relations* (New York: Pearson, 2003).
16. The U.S. Department of Defense provides figures for confirmed U.S. military deaths and other casualties but does not maintain records of Iraqi

military or civilian casualties. Information concerning Iraqi deaths is compiled largely from various news reports. During 2006 alone, it is estimated that 5,000–10,000 Iraqi police and military and 15,000–20,000 civilians lost their lives.

17. U.S. Senate, Select Committee on Intelligence, Report of the Select Committee on Intelligence on the U.S. Intelligence Community's Prewar Intelligence Assessments on Iraq (Washington, DC: Government Printing Office, 2004); Josh Meyer and Greg Miller, "The Prisoner Problem," *Los Angeles Times* (September 7, 2006): A1; and David Stout, "Senate Panel Defies Bush on Detainee Bill," *New York Times* (September 14, 2006): A10.

18. James M. Lindsay, "Congress, Foreign Policy, and the New Institutionalism," *International Studies Quarterly* 38 (June 1994): 281–304.

19. *Congress A to Z*, 4th ed. (Washington, DC: CQ Press, 2003).

20. For Eisenhower's thoughts on the subject, see Dwight D. Eisenhower, *The White House Years* (Garden City, NY: Doubleday, 1963–1965).

21. Testimony of U.S. Ambassador Maureen Quinn, Afghanistan coordinator at the Department of State; Mary Beth Long, deputy assistant secretary of defense for counter-narcotics; and Michael A. Braun, chief of operations for the Drug Enforcement Administration before the U.S. House of Representatives Committee on International Relations, March 17, 2005.

22. Steven W. Hook, *U.S. Foreign Policy: The Paradox of World Power* (Washington, DC: CQ Press, 2005), 319.

23. President's Commission on Critical Infrastructure Protection, *Critical Foundations: Protecting America's Infrastructures* (Washington, DC: Government Printing Office, 1997).

24. John Christensen, "Bracing for Guerrilla Warfare in Cyberspace," CNN Interactive, April 6, 1999; and Kenneth H. Bacon, Department of Defense news briefing, April 16, 1998.

AARP (American Association of Retired Persons), 334, 338, 400
ABC, 19, 300
Abolitionists, 117, 144
Abortion
    and Bush, 131
    and George W. Bush, 217
    "partial-birth," 101–102, 254
    and privacy rights, 129–130
    and Reagan, 131, 217
    state restrictions on, 101–102, 103f
    Supreme Court on, 101–102, 104f, 130–131, 273
Absentee voting, 352
Abu Ghraib prison (Iraq), 431f
Accountability
    in federal bureaucracy, 236–241
    in political parties, 322
Ackerman, Bruce, 48
Adams, John
    and Alien and Sedition Acts, 116
    and Declaration of Independence, 30
    election of 1796, 315
    and State of the Union address, 62
    and Supreme Court, 252, 253
Adams, John Quincy, 60, 315, 362
Adams, Samuel, 27, 28f
Administrative adjudication, 235
Administrative agencies, 390
Administrative discretion, 235
Administrative Procedures Act (1946), 235
Advanced Research Projects Agency Network, 299
Advertisements
    campaign, 367–368
    contrast, 367–368
    and 527 political committees, 379
    inoculation, 368
    negative, 367
    positive, 367
    spot, 368
Affiliates, television, 300–301
Affirmative action, 166
Afghanistan, 238–239, 417, 418, 421, 426, 433
AFL-CIO, 333–334, 340f
African Americans. See also Civil rights movement; Slavery
    and Black Codes, 144
    civil rights for, 80, 142, 144–145
    and Civil War Amendments, 92, 142, 144–145
    in Congress, 183, 184f
    and Democratic Party, 329
    interest groups serving, 334
    in jury pools, 126
    and New Deal coalition, 322
    political ideology of, 282f, 283
    population trends of, 15f
    in prisons, 354
    and segregation, 144, 146–150
    as Supreme Court justices, 261

unemployment rates for, 396
voter registration among, 353f
voter turnout of, 349–350
voting rights for, 144
Age
    and party identification, 329, 329t
    as political socialization agent, 284
    and population, 15, 19f
    and use of news sources, 300t
    and voter registration, 353f
    and voter turnout, 26, 348
    and voting rights, 24–26
Agenda for Peace (UN), 422
Agendas
    explanation of, 387
    governmental, 387
    systemic, 387
Agenda setting, 308, 387
Agnew, Spiro T., 201
Agricultural Adjustment Act (1938), 95
Agricultural Adjustment Administration (AAA), 94
Aid to Families with Dependent Children (AFDC), 99, 397–398
Airline Deregulation Act (1978), 391, 404
Airline industry, 404, 405
Akaka, Daniel, 183f
Alabama, 150
Alaska, 14, 99
Albright, Madeleine, 40
Alcohol, temperance movement, 48f, 76, 332
Ali, Del, 288
Alien and Sedition Acts (1798), 116–117
Alito, Samuel A., Jr., 261f, 266f
    confirmation process for, 262
    effect on Court, 244–246
    on EPA regulatory responsibility, 389
    profile of, 259t, 261
al-Jazeera, 300, 304, 308
al-Qaeda
    domestic surveillance on, 414
    explanation of, 420–421
    media coverage by al-Jazeera, 308
    pursuit of weapons of mass destruction by, 433
    and terrorist attacks of September 11, 2001, 177, 420–421
Amendments. See also specific amendments
    and Article V of Constitution, 42, 46–47, 46f
    Civil War, 92, 142, 144–145
    informal methods for, 48–49
American Anti-Slavery Society, 144, 332
American Association of People with Disabilities, 164
American Association of Retired Persons (AARP). See AARP (American Association of Retired Persons)
American Association of University Women (AAHW), 102
American Center for Law and Justice, 267

American Civil Liberties Union (ACLU)
    FISA lawsuit by, 414
    formation of, 334
    and free exercise issues, 115
    and free speech issues, 115, 119
    ratings of congressional members, 340f
    and Supreme Court, 267
    on USA Patriot Act, 134
American colonies. See Colonial America
American Conservative Union, 339–340, 340f
American dream, 19
American Federation of Labor (AFL), 333
American Independent Party, 325
American Indian Law Center (University of New Mexico), 159–160
American Indian Nations. See Native Americans
American Indians. See Native Americans
American Legion, 234
American Political Science Association (APSA), 339
American Revolution. See Revolutionary War
Americans Coming Together (ACT), 379
American's Creed, 6
Americans for Democratic Action, 339–340, 340f
Americans with Disabilities Act (ADA) (1990), 163–164, 386
American Woman Suffrage Association, 76, 145, 147
American Women (President's Commission on the Status of Women), 153
Amicus curiae
    explanation, 267, 268
    function of, 267, 336
    and segregation, 149
Amnesty Act (1872), 74
Amnesty et al. v. McConnell, 414
Amtrak, 230, 391
Anderson, John B., 287f
Angola, 418
Annan, Kofi, 203
Annenberg Public Policy Center, 298
Anthony, Susan B., 75, 145
Anti-Federalists
    and Bill of Rights, 111, 315, 317
    explanation of, 42
    political views of, 43t, 315
    and right to bear arms, 121, 416
The Anti-Federalists (Main), 34
Anti-trust policy, 401–402
Appellate courts, 254, 257
Appellate jurisdiction, 254, 255, 255f
Apportionment, 173
Appropriations Committee, House, 181
Aristotle, 7, 7t
Arizona, 96, 363
Arkansas, 150
Army Corps of Engineers, 82, 84
Arroyo, Gloria Macapagal, 201

Articles of Confederation
  and Anti-Federalists, 42–43
  and executive branch, 223
  explanation of, 31–32, 38, 39t
  and judiciary, 32
  limitations of, 32, 198, 416
Ashcroft, John, 132
Asian and Pacific Americans, 15f,
    .160–161, 183, 353f
Asia-Pacific Economic Cooperation
    agreement, 420
Assault weapons ban, 122
Assisted suicide, 132
Associated Press (AP), 276, 301
Association of Community Organizations
    for Reform Now (ACORN), 164
Attitudinal model, of judicial decision
    making, 270
Attorney General, 132, 136, 140–142, 223
Australia, 173, 256
Authoritative techniques, 390
Avery, Bill, 162
Avian influenza, 220–222

Baby Boomers, 15, 284, 394
Baghdad, Iraq, 424, 431f
Bahamonde, Marty, 82–84
Banking industry, 406
Barber, James David, 212t
Barbour, Haley, 82
Barron v. Baltimore (1833), 73, 111, 121
Bassal, Sarah, 186f
Baston v. Kentucky (1986), 126
Baze v. Rees (2007), 128
BCRA. See Bipartisan Campaign Reform
    Act (2002) (BCRA)
Beard, Charles A., 34
Beese, Christopher, 428
Berlin, Isaiah, 12
Bernanke, Ben, 405f
Bias. See Media bias
Bicameral legislatures, 172
Biden, Joe, 209f
Bilingualism, 17
Bill of Rights. See also specific amendments
  background of, 111–112
  civil liberty guarantees, 110
  due process, 111–112
  explanation of, 6, 42, 45, 67, 111
  and incorporation doctrine, 112–113,
    112t
  protections in, 11, 44t
Bills
  in committees, 180–181, 187–190, 188f
  explanation of, 173
  pathways for, 187–190, 188f
  voting decisions for, 184–187
Bills of attainder, 88, 122
bin Laden, Osama, 308, 420–421
Bipartisan Campaign Reform Act (2002)
    (BCRA), 375–376, 376t, 378–380
Birmingham, Alabama, 151, 152f
Birth control, 18, 129–130
Black, Hugo, 125, 304
Black Codes, 144
Black Monday, 149

Blackmun, Harry A., 130–131, 266
Blackwater Worldwide, 428
Blaine, James G., 295
Blanco, Kathleen, 82–84, 83f
Block grants, 99
Blogs, 19, 281, 302, 339
Blow, Henry, 92
Blunt, Roy, 317
Board of Governors, Federal Reserve, 406
Board of Regents v. Southworth (2000), 119
Boehner, John, 340f
Boerne, City of v. Flores (1997), 74
Bolton, John R., 429
Bork, Robert H., 250, 262
Boston Globe, 286
Boston Massacre, 29
Boston Tea Party, 29, 337
Bowers v. Hardwick (1986), 131
Brady, James, 122
Brady, Sarah, 122
Brady Bill, 122
Brady Campaign to Prevent Gun Violence,
    71
Brady Center to Prevent Gun Violence, 67,
    337
Brandeis, Louis, 128
Brandenburg v. Ohio (1969), 117
Brazil, 87
Brennan, William J., Jr., 130
Breyer, Stephen, 266f
  Court voting record of, 104f
  on EPA regulatory responsibility, 389
  profile of, 245, 259t
Briefs, 257
British Broadcasting Corporation (BBC),
    300
Broadcast media, 300–302
Brown, Michael, 82–84
Brown v. Board of Education (1954)
  and amicus briefs, 148–149
  challenges to, 66
  description of, 149
  impact of, 64, 149–150
  and Plessy decision, 148–149, 272–273
Brown v. Board of Education II (1955), 150
Budget. See Federal budget; Federal
    budgetary process
Buffalo Evening Telegraph, 294
Bull Moose Party, 325
Bully pulpit, 212, 306
Bureaucracy, 220, 223–226. See also Federal
    bureaucracy
Bureau of the Budget, 215–216
Burger, Warren, 120, 124
Burke, Edmund, 183
Burr, Aaron, 60, 362
Bush, George, 200f
  on abortion, 131
  cabinet appointments of, 202t
  and election of 1992, 362
  foreign policy of, 418–419, 426
  judicial appointments of, 258t,
    260f, 261
  and Operation Desert Storm, 205, 419
  and press conferences, 306
  signing statements of, 216

Bush, George W., 83f, 251f, 405f
  and abortion, 217
  appointments of, 194, 201, 429
  approval ratings for, 213, 283f, 432
  and budget issues, 100–101, 238–239
  cabinet appointments of, 202, 202t
  and Cheney, 209
  and Christian Coalition, 334
  and civil liberties, 110
  and discrimination cases, 141
  and economic stimulus payments,
    408–409
  and election of 2000 (See Presidential
    election of 2000)
  and election of 2004 (See Presidential
    election of 2004)
  emergency responsiveness of, 82–84 (See
    also Hurricane Katrina)
  and environmental issues, 96, 389
  and Executive Office of the President,
    211
  executive orders of, 217
  and federalism, 100–101
  and gun control issues, 122
  and International Criminal Court, 429
  and Iraq War, 204f, 205, 206, 213, 215,
    238–239, 283f, 422–425, 427, 432
  judicial appointments of, 194, 258t, 260f
  and Medicare Prescription Drug,
    Improvement, and Modernization
    Act, 400
  NRA campaign contribution to, 335
  opposition to Title IX, 236
  and Patriot Act, 213, 216
  and preemption statutes, 100–101
  presidential visits by, 213
  and press conferences, 306
  religious faith of, 211
  role in legislative process, 215
  signing statements of, 216
  and Social Security, 394–395
  and Supplemental Security Income, 397
  and United Nations, 203, 422
  use of disability provision, 80
  use of military tribunals, 62, 135, 217
  use of private contractors, 227
  and use of torture, 134–136, 135f
  and war on terrorism, 62, 412–414, 432
  and War Powers Act, 430
  and welfare reform, 398
  withdraws from International Criminal
    Court, 203
Bush, Laura, 210
Bush Doctrine, 237, 422–425
Bush v. Gore (2000), 307, 362. See also
    Presidential election of 2000
Byrd, Robert, 45, 193f, 233f

Cabinet
  appointments to, 202, 202t
  Constitution on, 231
  departments of, 230f, 239–240
  function of, 209, 210t
  size and structure of, 209–210
Cable television, 19, 298
Calder v. Bull (1798), 58

Calhoun, John C., 53
California, 97, 160–162, 255f, 256
Campaign contributions
  from candidate personal funds, 378
  from individuals, 376
  and Internet, 327, 358
  member-to-candidate, 377
  from political action committees, 186,
    376–377
  from political parties, 377
  from public funds, 378
Campaign finance. *See also* 527 political
    committees; Political action
    committees (PACs)
  and hard money, 323f
  public financing, 378
  and soft money, 323f, 375–376, 378–380
  Supreme Court on, 339, 375–376
Campaign finance reform. *See* Bipartisan
    Campaign Reform Act (2002)
    (BCRA)
Campaign managers, 360–361
Campaigns. *See also* Primaries
  general election, 356, 359
  length of, 358
  media coverage of, 367–369 (*See also*
    Media campaigns)
  nominating, 357–359
  slogans for, 359
  staffing for, 360–361
  technology use in, 368–369
Campaign staff, 360–361
Campaign web sites, 338–339
Canada
  bicameral legislative model, 173
  campaign length limits in, 358
  economic freedom rating of, 406
  on extradition for U.S. death penalty, 127
  federal system in, 87
  and North American Free Trade
    Agreement, 420
  universal health care in, 401
Candidate-centered politics, 319
Candidate debates, 359f
Candidates, 360–361
Canvassing, 360
Capacity techniques, 390
Capital punishment. *See* Death penalty
Capitol Building, U.S., 249f
Carlson, Tom, 162
Carnegie Corporation, 280
Carter, Jimmy, 200f
  cabinet appointments of, 202t
  and deregulation, 404
  and election of 1980, 290
  foreign policy of, 417–418
  and Iranian hostage crisis, 417–418
  judicial appointments of, 258t, 260f
  Middle East peace efforts of, 433f
  and Mondale, 209
  and Panama Canal Treaty, 203
  pardons granted by, 207
  and War Powers Act, 193
Carter Doctrine, 417–418
Categorical grants, 97–99
Catholics

and immigrants, 157
and party identification, 329t, 330
political ideology of, 282, 282f
on Supreme Court, 259t, 261
Cato Institute, 108–109
Caucuses. *See* Party caucuses
CBS, 19, 276, 300
Celebrity journalists, 309
Center for Medicare and Medicaid
    Services, 400
Center for Political Studies/Survey
    Research Center (CPS/SRC), 321
Central High School (Little Rock
    Arkansas), 150
Central Intelligence Agency, 426–427
Central Intelligence Agency (CIA)
  Abu Ghraib prisoner abuse by, 431
  and foreign policy, 426–427
  function of, 211
  use of interrogation techniques, 135f, 136
Central Pacific Railroad, 333
Chambers, Ernie, 162
Chaplinsky v. *New Hampshire* (1942), 120
Chavez, Cesar, 157
Chavez, Hugo, 232
Checks and balances
  explanation of, 36–37, 37f, 38
  and veto power, 203
Cheney, Dick, 80, 209
Children, political socialization, 278
China, 87, 226
Chinese Americans. *See* Asian and Pacific
    Americans
Chinese Exclusion Act (1886), 160
Chisholm v. *Georgia* (1793), 72, 279
Christian Coalition, 282, 285, 334
Christianity, 12
Christian Science Monitor, 300
Church of England, 8
Citizens, 5. *See also* Naturalization
Civics education, 280–281
Civic virtue, 330
Civil Aeronautics Board (CAB), 391, 403,
    404
Civilian Conservation Corps (CCC), 94
Civil law, 255–256
Civil liberties. *See also* Bill of Rights
  explanation of, 110
  limits on during war on terrorism,
    133–135
  during wars, 117
Civil Liberties Act (1988), 161
Civil rights
  and affirmative action, 166
  for African Americans, 92, 142,
    144–145
  and Civil War Amendments, 144–145
  for disabled individuals, 163–164
  and employment issues, 166–167
  explanation of, 110, 142
  for gays and lesbians, 161–162
  for Hispanic Americans, 157–159
  Johnson's contribution to, 151–152
  for Native Americans, 159–160
  and Progressive era, 146–149
  Supreme Court on, 145–146, 148–150

for women, 147, 153–154, 166–167
Civil Rights Act (1866), 73, 144
Civil Rights Act (1875), 145–146
Civil Rights Act (1964)
  background of, 140, 151–153
  challenges to, 57
  and employment discrimination, 153
  impact of, 79, 163
  and persons with disabilities,
    163–164
  provisions of, 152–153
  and sex discrimination, 153–154
  Title VII, 156
Civil Rights Act (1991), 166
Civil Rights Cases (1883), 146
Civil rights movement. *See also* Women's
    rights movement
  and desegregation, 148–150
  and federal bureaucracy, 226
  groups involved in, 147, 147f, 150–151
  and March on Washington, 151
  origins of, 10
  protest activities during, 150–151, 152f
  rise of public interest groups during, 334
Civil servants. *See* Federal bureaucrats
Civil Service Commission, 224
Civil service laws, 319
Civil Service Reform Act (1883), 224
Civil service system, 224, 319. *See also*
    Federal bureaucracy
Civil society, 11
Civil unions. *See* Same-sex marriage
Civil War
  and *Dred Scott* decision, 92
  federal bureaucracy during and after, 223
  and federal grant program, 95–98
  and federalism, 92
  and free speech, 117
  and Lincoln, 207–208, 223
Civil War Amendments, 92, 142, 144–147.
    See also Fifteenth Amendment;
    Fourteenth Amendment; Thirteenth
    Amendment
Clay, Henry, 317
Clayton Act (1914), 333
Clean Air Act (1990), 388–391
Clear and present danger test, 117
Cleveland, Grover, 294–295, 362
Clientele agencies, 229–230
Clinton, Bill, 204f
  cabinet appointments of, 202, 202t
  and devolution revolution, 99
  and election of 1992, 280, 362
  and election of 1996, 280
  executive orders of, 217
  foreign policy of, 419–420, 426
  and gays and lesbians in military,
    161–162
  and gun control legislation, 122
  impeachment of, 54, 63, 192, 193, 200
  judicial appointments of, 194, 258,
    258t, 260f
  and marriage legislation, 89
  and media, 198
  and North American Free Trade
    Agreement, 420

presidential visits by, 213
and press conferences, 306
role in legislative process, 215
signing statements of, 216
signs International Criminal Court treaty, 203
staff reductions of, 211
and Sudan, 206
use of campaign web sites, 368
and welfare reform, 397
Clinton, Hillary Rodham, 370f
and election of 2008, 327, 344–346, 384
(*See also* Presidential election of 2008)
and health care reform, 383, 384
as senator, 344, 364
Clinton v. *New York* (1998), 56
Closed primaries, 353–354
Cloture, 189
CNBC, 19, 300
CNN (Cable News Network), 262, 276, 299, 300, 302, 358
Coalitions, 320, 322
Coast Guard, U.S., 427
Coattails effect, congressional elections, 365
Coercive Acts (1774), 29
Colbert, Stephen, 298, 298f
Cold War, 418
Cole, Tom, 183
Coleman, Norm, 366
Coleman v. *Miller* (1939), 81
Collective good, 332
Colleges. *See* Universities/colleges
Colonial America
and Declaration of Independence, 30–31
and First Continental Congress, 30
independence of, 28–29, 198
overview of, 26–27
religion in, 113, 282
and Second Continental Congress, 30
timeline of, 28–29
timelines of, 294
trade and taxation in, 27
Comcast, 301
Comedy news programming, 298, 298f, 299, 301f
Commander in chief, 7, 40, 43, 61, 193, 203, 205
Commentaries on the Constitution (1833), 55
Commerce clause, 101
Committee on Unfinished Portions, 36
Committee on Veterans Affairs, House, 234
Committees, Congressional. *See* Congressional committees
Committees of Correspondence, 29–30
Common Cause, 334
Common defense, 7
Common Sense, 30
Commonwealth of Massachusetts et al. v. *Environmental Protection Agency*, 389
Communications directors, 361
Communism, 415–417
Communist Party, 325
Concerned Women for America, 267
Concurrent powers, 87, 87f
Confederation, 86f

Conference committees, 179
Congress, U.S. *See also* House of Representatives, U.S.; Senate, U.S.
accomplishments of, 188f
and affirmative action, 166
caucuses of, 185–186
and civil rights, 145–146, 151–153
committee system in, 179–182
considerations for decision making in, 184–187
and constituents, 184–185
and Constitution, 38–39, 170–171, 174t
defense appropriations, 427, 429f
and disabled individuals, 163–164
and Equal Rights Amendment, 154
foreign policy influence of, 427–430
and immigration, 177
interest group ratings of, 339–340, 340f
investigatory powers of, 240
and judiciary, 193–194
law-making function of, 187–190
lobbying to, 186, 335–336
media coverage of, 306–307
and media regulation, 301–302
naturalization power of, 173, 177
and obscenity, 120
111th parties by state, 176f
organization of, 174–182, 174t
oversight responsibilities of, 231–232, 240, 427–430
party unity voting in, 324–325, 325f
and political parties, 175f, 176f, 178, 184
powers of, 388
and president, 191–192
presidential power to convene, 202
regulation of commerce by, 91
and slavery, 143
and Social Security privatization, 394–395
staff and support agencies for, 186–187
and theories of representation, 183–184
and veto power, 203
and Vietnam War, 205, 427
Congress Education Project, 161
Congressional Budget Office (CBO), 408
Congressional Caucus for Women's Issues, 186
Congressional committees
bills in, 180–181, 187–190, 188f
chairs of, 181–182
media coverage of hearings in, 307
membership in, 181
role of, 179
types of, 179–181
Congressional districts, 363
Congressional elections. *See also* Elections
of 1994, 99
of 2002, 170
of 2006, 364
of 2008, 364, 366–367
coattails in, 365
and incumbency, 364–365
midterm, 365–366, 365t
and redistricting, 364
and scandals, 365
Congressional Muslim Staffers

Association, 186f
Congressional Record, 55
Congressional Research Service (CRS), 187
Congressional review, 192
Congressional Review Act (1996), 192
Congress members
African Americans as, 183, 184f
approval ratings of, 182, 185f
Asian Americans as, 183
day in the life of, 182t
education levels of, 183
elections of, 93, 172–173, 182–183
function of, 181
Hispanic Americans as, 183, 184f
and incumbency, 182–183
interest group ratings of, 340f
profile of, 183
staff and support agencies for, 186–187
veterans as, 183
women as, 170–171, 183, 186f
Congress of Industrial Organizations (CIO), 333
Conservatives, 12, 293, 297, 298f, 302, 337. *See also* Political ideology
Constituents, legislative decision making and, 184–185
Constitution, U.S. *See also* Amendments; Bill of Rights; Framers (U.S. Constitution); *specific amendments*
amendment procedure (Article V), 42, 46–47, 46f, 65
and checks and balances, 36–37, 37f, 38
and civil rights, 110, 142
concurrent powers under, 87, 88f
on Congress, 38–39, 170–171, 174t
denied powers under, 87–88
executive branch (Article II), 39–40, 60–63, 198, 201–208, 229, 231
explanation of, 34
and federalism, 37, 79
and *Federalist Papers*, 43–44
and foreign policy, 414
full faith and credit clause (Article IV), 42, 64–65, 88, 89
function of, 5–6, 39t
and impeachment, 36, 173, 193
influences on, 9–10
and interstate compacts, 88–90, 90t
judicial branch (Article III), 40–42, 63–64, 126, 247–254, 256
legislative branch (Article I), 38–39, 52–59, 87, 89–87, 173, 174t, 416
and national defense, 414
national powers under, 86–87, 86f
and Native Americans, 159–160
Preamble to, 2–4, 36
principles addressed in, 5–6
privileges and immunities clause (Article IV), 88
ratification procedures (Article VII), 44–45, 66
and separation of church and state, 42
and separation of powers, 36–38, 37f
signing of, 36
and social change, 48–49
state powers under, 87, 88f

supremacy clause (Article VI), 42, 65–66, 87, 91
Constitutional Convention. *See also* Framers (U.S. Constitution)
    characteristics and motives of delegates to, 33–34, 172, 173
    and executive branch, 36, 198
    Great Compromise at, 35, 172
    and New Jersey Plan, 33, 34
    role of Congress at, 172
    and Virginia Plan, 34
Constitutional courts, 256
Constitution Day, 45
Constitutions, 34. *See also* Constitution, U.S.
Consumer Product Safety Act (1972), 388
Containment, 415–417
Content regulation, media, 301–302
Contraceptives, 129–130
Contract with America, 99, 215
Contras, 418
Contrast ads, 367–368
Conventions. *See* National conventions
Coolidge, Calvin, 93, 297
Cooper v. *Aaron* (1958), 66, 150
Cooperative federalism, 95
Cortner, Richard C., 267
Council of Economic Advisors, 211
Court of Appeals, 257
Court of International Trade, 241
Courts. *See* Judiciary; Supreme Court, U.S.
Court TV, 263
Craig v. *Boren* (1976), 155
The Creation of the American Republic (Wood), 34
Criminal defendants' rights
    and cruel and unusual punishment, 126–127
    and exclusionary rule, 125
    and jury trials, 126
    and right to counsel, 125
    and searches and seizures, 122–123
    and self-incrimination, 123–124
Criminal law, 254–255
Critical elections, 319
Crossover voting, 354
Cruel and unusual punishment, 126–127. *See also* Death penalty
C-SPAN, 19, 262, 298, 307, 358
Cuba, 401, 422
Cuban Americans, 157, 329, 351. *See also* Hispanic Americans
Cuban Missile Crisis, 415
Cultural diversity, 15, 18, 183, 184*f. See also* Ethnicity; Minorities; Race
Cuomo, Mario M., 101
Customary courts, 256
Customs and Border Protection, 427
Cyprus, 6

Daniel Shays, 32*f
Daughters of Liberty, 27, 28
Day, Benjamin, 294
D.C. Court of Appeals, 257
Dealignment, 320–321
Dean, Howard, 327

Death. *See* Right to die
Death penalty
    arguments for and against, 128–129
    and DNA tests, 127
    and extradition, 127
    by lethal injection, 127
    and mentally retarded convicts, 127
    methods of execution, 127
    public opinion on, 283*f
    and states' rights, 87
    Supreme Court on, 126–127
    in Texas, 129*f
Debates, presidential, 359*f
Declaration of Independence, 9–10, 30–31, 142
Declaration of Rights and Resolves, 30
Defense of Marriage Act (1996), 89, 191, 194
Defense spending, 238–239, 418, 427, 429*f. See also* Military policy
DeJonge v. *Oregon* (1937), 121
DeLay, Tom, 365
Delegates, 183, 359
Democracy, 8, 10–12
Democratic National Committee (DNC), 326
Democratic National Convention. *See also* National conventions
    in 2008, 328*f
Democratic Party
    and African Americans, 329
    fundraising operations of, 322–323, 323*f
    and gender, 329, 329*t
    historical background of, 315–318, 316*f
    ideological makeup of, 318, 320
    and judicial nominations, 258
    and labor unions, 329*t, 330
    and Northeast, 318
    and organization in Congress, 175*f, 178
    origins of, 318
    platform of, 312–314, 314*t
    and presidential elections (*See specific elections*)
    and religious affiliation, 329*t, 330
    and Social Security privatization, 394–395
    and youth voters, 26
Democratic-Republicans, 116, 315–318, 316*f, 319, 362
Democratic Sentinel, 295
Demographics. *See* Population
Denmark, 173
Department of Agriculture, 223
Department of Defense, 238–239, 299, 426–427, 430. *See also specific wars*
Department of Health and Human Services, 400
Department of Homeland Security, 229, 240, 425, 427
Department of Housing and Urban Development (HUD), 226, 388
Department of Justice, 133, 140–142, 413
Department of Labor, 240
Department of State, 223, 426, 428
Department of Transportation, 226
Department of Veteran Affairs, 234, 399

Departments, cabinet, 230*f, 239–240
Deregulation, 404–405. *See also* Regulation
Desegregation, 146–149, 149*f, 204*f
Détente, 417–418
Deterrence, 422
Devolution revolution, 99, 103, 104*f
Dewey, Thomas E., 287
Dingell, John, 178
Direct democracy, 10
Direct incitement test, 117
Direct mailers, 361
Direct primaries, 319
Disabled individuals, 163–164
Discharge petitions, 180
Discount rate, 406
Discrimination. *See also* African Americans
    against disabled individuals, 163–164
    employment, 162, 166–167
    against gays and lesbians, 161–162
    against Hispanics, 218–219
    against Native Americans, 159–160
    racial, 157–159, 349–350
    sex, 154–156
    against women, 146
District courts, 255*f, 256–257, 259
District of Columbia. *See* Washington, D.C.
District of Columbia v. *Heller* (2008), 109, 121
Disturbance theory, 331
Diversity. *See* Cultural diversity; Race
Divided government, 184
Dixiecrat Party, 325
DNA tests, 127, 128
Dole, Bob, 383
Dole, Elizabeth, 340*f
Domestic policy. *See* Public policy
Domestic tranquility, 6–7
"Don't Ask, Don't Tell" policy, 161–162
Doolittle, John, 365
Dred Scott v. *Sandford* (1857), 73, 92, 121, 145
Drivers License Compact, 90
Drug testing, 123
Dual federalism, 92–93
DuBois, W. E. B., 147*f
Due process rights
    explanation of, 111–112, 122
    and incorporation doctrine, 112–113, 112*t
    substantive, 112
    Supreme Court on, 111–112
    and terrorism detainees, 134–136, 135*f

Earmarks, 181
Eastern Europe, 419
East India Company, 29
Ebbert, Terry, 84
Economic freedom rankings, 406
Economic Interpretation of the Constitution of the United States (Beard), 34
Economic policy
    and deregulation, 404–405
    fiscal, 407
    interventionist state, 402
    Keynesian, 407

laissez-faire, 402
  in nineteenth century, 401–402
  stimulus payments, 408–409
Economic regulation, 224. *See also*
      Regulation
Economic stability, 405
Economic stimulus payments, arguments
      for and against, 408–409
Economy
  and fiscal policy, 407
  and monetary policy, 406
  stability in, 405–409
Education, 96, 100, 152, 280–281, 347. *See
      also* Public schools;
      Universities/colleges
Education Amendment Act (1972), 156,
      236, 390
Education and the Workforce Committee,
      House, 181
Edwards, John, 282, 345, 370f, 378
Eighteenth Amendment, 46, 76
Eighth Amendment, 70, 104, 126–127,
      135–136
Eisenhower, Dwight D.
  and civil rights, 150, 204f
  foreign policy of, 430
  leadership of, 205, 207
  and press conferences, 306
  tenure in office of, 78
  and voting age, 24
Elderly individuals, 15. *See also* Age
Electioneering, 322–323
Elections. *See also* Congressional elections;
      Presidential election of 2000;
      Presidential election of 2004;
      Presidential election of 2008;
      Presidential elections
  function of, 322–323
  general, 356, 359
  initiatives, 356
  number of, 352
  primary (*See* Primaries)
  recall, 356
  referenda, 356
  types of, 353–356
Electoral College
  and Constitution, 36, 39, 60–63, 199
  and election of 2000, 307, 362
  explanation of, 361–363
  historical background of, 362
  state proportional votes in, 363f
  and Twelfth Amendment, 362
  in twenty-first century, 362–363
Electronic media, 301–302. *See also*
      Internet; Radio; Television
Eleventh Amendment, 71–72
Elks Club, 330
Ellsberg, Daniel, 304
Emancipation Proclamation
      (1863), 144
Embedded journalists, 304, 305f
Emerling, Sarah, 100
Emerson, Ralph Waldo, 30
EMILY's List, 338
Employment, Civil Rights Act (1964)
      and, 153

Employment discrimination, 153, 162,
      166–167
Engagement, 419
Engel v. *Vitale* (162), 113
England. *See* Great Britain
English Bill of Rights (1687), 55
Enlargement, 419
Enlightenment, 8
Entitlement programs, 398–399
Entrance polls, 276–278
Enumerated powers, 38, 52, 86, 88f
Environmental policy, 96–97, 389
Environmental Protection Act, 96
Environmental Protection Agency (EPA),
      96, 230, 389
Environmental regulation, 96–97, 389
Equal Employment Opportunity
      Commission (EEOC), 153, 154, 226
Equality, 10–11
"Equal Opportunity to Govern"
      amendment, 40
Equal Pay Act (1963), 153–154, 156
Equal protection clause
  and gays and lesbians, 162
  and Hispanics, 158
  and juror selection, 126
  and separate-but-equal doctrine, 149
  Supreme Court on, 154–156, 158
  and women's rights, 154
Equal Rights Amendment (ERA), 47, 154
Equal time rule, 302
Espionage Act (1917), 117
Essay Concerning Human Understanding
      (Locke), 9
Establishment clause, 113–115
Estonia, 406
Ethics Reform Act (1989), 55
Ethnicity. *See also* Cultural diversity;
      Minorities; Race
  and immigration trends, 15
  and party identification, 329, 329t
  as political socialization agent, 283
  and population, 15f
  and voter turnout, 348–351
Europe, 20, 121, 417. *See also specific
      countries*
European Union (EU), 6, 119
Evangelical Christians, 13, 282, 329t, 330
Exclusionary rule, 125
Executive agreements, 203, 203t, 429
Executive branch. *See also* Federal
      bureaucracy; Presidents
  congressional oversight of, 191–193
  and Constitution, 39–40, 60–63, 198,
      201–208
  and Executive Office of the President,
      211, 216
  and foreign policy, 425–427
  growth of, 205–208, 224, 225f
  lobbying to, 336
  organization of, 210t, 229–232, 230f
  and roots of federal bureaucracy, 223–226
Executive Office of the President (EOP),
      211, 216
Executive orders, 217, 240
Executive privilege, 200

Exit polls, 290
Ex post facto laws, 58, 88, 122
Extradite, governors' power to, 64, 88
Extradition clause, 88

Facebook, 281, 302
Fair Housing Act (1968), 391
Fair Labor Standards Act (FLSA) (1938),
      95, 403
Falwell, Jerry, 334
Families, 15, 18, 278
Family and Medical Leave Act (FMLA)
      (1993), 72, 103
Faubus, Orville, 150
Federal agency regions, 228f
Federal budget, 7f, 100–101, 238–239
Federal budgetary process, 215–217, 388
Federal bureaucracy
  accountability of, 236–241
  and administrative adjudication, 235
  attitudes toward, 220–222
  and business, 224, 226
  and Civil War period, 223
  congressional oversight of, 240
  emergency responsiveness of, 220–222
  executive branch and roots of, 223–226
  executive oversight of, 237, 240
  formal organization of, 229–232, 230f
  judicial control of, 240–241
  and merit system, 223–224
  policy making by, 235
  and political activities, 232–233, 233t
  rule making by, 235
  and spoils system, 223–224
  in twentieth century, 224–227
Federal bureaucrats, 226–229, 227f, 228f
Federal Bureau of Investigation (FBI), 261
Federal Communications Commission
      (FCC), 231, 301–302, 403
Federal court system, 249–252, 255f, 257.
      See also Judiciary; Supreme Court, U.S.
Federal Deposit Insurance Corporation
      (FDIC), 230, 403
Federal Election Campaign Act (FECA),
      375, 378
Federal Election Commission (FEC), 375
Federal Election Commission v. *Wisconsin
      Right to Life* (2007), 375
Federal Emergency Management Agency
      (FEMA), 82–84, 386
Federal employees. *See* Federal bureaucrats
Federal Employees Political Activities Act
      (1993), 233, 233t
Federal Housing Administration (FHA), 94
Federal Intelligence Surveillance Act
      (FISA) (1978), 413–414
Federal Intelligence Surveillance Court, 413
Federalism
  cooperative, 95
  dual, 92–93
  and George W. Bush, 100–101
  and Marshall Court, 90–91
  and New Deal, 93–98
  and Reagan Revolution, 98–99
  and Supreme Court, 38, 90–91, 101–104,
      101f, 104f

Federalist Papers, 43f
  background of, 43–44, 48, 296
  No. 8, 207
  No. 10, 43–44, 190, 314
  No. 51, 43–44
  No. 58, 56
  No. 70, 60
  No. 76, 250–251
  No. 77, 202, 250–251
  No. 78, 247, 252
  No. 84, 70–71
Federalists
  and Alien and Sedition Acts, 116–117
  and Bill of Rights, 111, 315, 317
  explanation of, 42, 43t
  historical background of, 316f, 317
  political views of, 315
Federal Open Market Committee, 406
Federal Radio Commission, 403
Federal Register, 216, 235
Federal Reserve Board (FRB), 231, 406
Federal Reserve System, 406
Federal system
  and concurrent powers under
    Constitution, 87, 88f
  and denied powers under Constitution,
    87–88
  explanation of, 37, 85, 86f
  and national powers under Constitution,
    86–87, 86f
  and relations among states, 88–90
  and relations within states, 89
  and state powers under Constitution, 86f,
    87, 88f
Feingold, Russ, 375
Feinstein, Dianne, 263, 340f
Felons, voting rights, 354–355
The Feminine Mystique (Friedan), 153
Fifteenth Amendment, 74–75, 92, 144–145
Fifth Amendment, 68–69, 113, 123–124
Fighting words, 120
Filibusters, 152, 178, 189, 250–251
Filipinos. *See* Asian and Pacific Americans
Finance chairs, 361
Finland, 401
Firearms. *See* Gun control
Fireside chats (Roosevelt), 297
First Amendment
  and freedom of assembly, 121
  and freedom of religion, 113, 133 (*See
    also* Religious freedom)
  and freedom of speech and press, 112,
    116–117, 133, 296 (*See also* Free
    press; Free speech)
  and freedom of speech and right to
    privacy, 338
  text of, 67, 296
First Bank of the United States, 90
First Continental Congress, 30
First Lady, 210. *See also specific first ladies*
Fiscal policy, 407
501(c) committees, 379–380
527 political committees, 378–380, 379f
Flag, U.S., 3f, 6, 49, 118
Flickr, 302
Florida, 102, 284, 362, 363

Foley, Mark, 365
Food and Drug Act (1906), 388
Food and Drug Administration, 222
Food Stamp program, 398
Ford, Gerald, 200f
  and deregulation, 404
  funeral of, 198
  judicial appointments of, 258t
  pardon of Nixon by, 62, 205
  succession to presidency by, 80, 201
  and War Powers Act, 193
Ford, Harold, 171
Ford Foundation, 157
Foreign policy. *See also* Iraq War; Military
  policy; *specific presidents*
  and Congress, 192–193, 427–430
  and containment, 415
  and Cuban Missile Crisis, 415
  and defense policy decisions, 425–432
  and engagement and enlargement, 419
  historical background of, 416
  and military-industrial complex, 430
  and news media, 430
  between 1989 and 2001, 418–420
  in 1980s, 418
  promoting democracy in Middle East,
    433
  and public opinion, 431–432
  roots of, 415–425
  and Supreme Court, 207
  and terrorism, 433
  and transnational threats, 433
  twenty-first century challenges, 432–433
  and weapons of mass destruction, 206,
    423–424
Foreign policy making, 211, 425–427
Foreign Relations Committee, Senate, 427
Foudy, Julie, 236f
Founders. *See* Framers (U.S. Constitution)
Founding Fathers. *See* Framers (U.S.
  Constitution)
Fourteenth Amendment
  background of, 10, 92, 111, 142
  and citizenship, 177
  and due process, 111–112
  equal protection clause of, 142, 149,
    154–156, 158, 160–162
  and repeal of Three-Fifths Compromise,
    53
  and selective incorporation, 111–112,
    112t
  text of, 73–74
Fourth Amendment, 68, 122–123, 133–134
FOX, 19, 276, 300, 302, 358
Framers (U.S. Constitution). *See also*
  Constitution, U.S.; Constitutional
  Convention
  characteristics and motives of, 5–6, 10,
    33–34, 113, 172, 173
  and civil rights, 142
  and Congress, 215
  on divided government, 84–85
  and Electoral College, 362
  and executive branch, 36, 198
  and freedom of press, 296
  and Great Compromise, 35

  and judiciary, 48, 246
  and ratification, 44
  slaveowners among, 33
Framing, media messages, 308
France, 87, 127, 332
Franken, Al, 366
Franklin, Benjamin, 17, 30, 33, 199
Freedom of assembly, 121
Freedom of religion. *See* Religious freedom
Freedom rides, 151
Free exercise clause, 113, 115–116
Free media, 367, 368
Free press, 112, 116–117, 296. *See also* Free
  speech
Free rider problem, 332
Free Soil Party, 92
Free speech. *See also* Free press
  and Alien and Sedition Acts, 116–117
  and Civil War, 117
  and Congress and obscenity, 120
  and fighting words, 120
  and First Amendment, 116–117
  and hate speech, unpopular speech, and
    speech zones, 118–119
  and libel and slander, 120
  and lobbying, 338–339
  and obscenity, 120
  post-Civil War, 117
  and prior restraint, 118
  and symbolic speech, 118
  and World War I, 117
Free speech zones, 119
Free Trade Area of the Americas, 420
Frémont, John C., 318
French and Indian War, 27
Friedan, Betty, 153
Friends of the Filipino People, 161
Front-loading, 358
Fugitive Act (1793), 64
Full faith and credit clause, 42, 88, 89
Fulton, Robert, 91
Fulton, Tony, 162
Fundamental freedoms, 112–113, 112t
Furman v. *Georgia* (1972), 127

Gaines, Lloyd, 148
Gallup, George, 276f, 285
Gallup Organization, 287
Gallup Polls, 271, 282, 282f, 286,
  287, 287f
Garfield, James A., 80, 224
Garner, John Nance, 209
Garner, Tyron, 131f
Garrison, William Lloyd, 144, 332
Gay and Lesbian Advocates and
  Defenders, 161
Gay marriage. *See* Same-sex marriage
Gays and lesbians, 131–132, 161–162
Gender. *See also* Women
  and juror selection, 126
  and party identification, 329, 329t
  as political socialization agent, 283–284,
    284t
  and vote choice, 329, 329t
  and voter registration, 353f
General Accounting Office. *See*

Government Accountability Office (GAO)

General elections, 356, 359. *See also specific elections*

General Social Survey, 289

General welfare, 7

Geneva Convention, 62, 136, 431

Geographic region
  and party identification, 329, 329t
  as political socialization agent, 284–285

George III, king of England, 29, 30

Georgia, 30, 142

Gephardt, Richard, 171

Germany, 20, 87

Gerrymandering, 364. *See also* Redistricting

Get out the vote (GOTV) efforts, 338–339, 360

Ghana, 256

Gibbons v. *Ogden* (1824), 91

GI Bill, 225

Gideon, Clarence Earl, 125

Gideon v. *Wainwright* (1963), 69, 125

Gingrich, Newt, 99, 99f, 170, 178

Ginsburg, Ruth Bader, 266f
  Court voting record of, 104f
  on EPA regulatory responsibility, 389
  and full faith and credit clause, 89
  profile of, 245, 259t

Gitlow, Benjamin, 112

Gitlow v. *New York* (1925), 67, 112, 117

Glasmeier, Amy, 164

Glass ceiling, 170

Glass-Steagall Act (1933), 403

Going public, 212

Golden Age, 318

Gold Rush, 15, 145

Goldwater, Barry, 40, 215, 360f

Gompers, Samuel, 333

Gonzales, Alberto, 136, 141–142

Gonzales v. *Carhart* (2007), 104f

Gonzales v. *Oregon* (2006), 104f

Gonzales v. *Raich* (2005), 104f

Gorbachev, Mikhail, 418, 418f

Gore, Al, 60, 280, 362. *See also* Presidential election of 2000

Government. *See also* Federal bureaucracy; Local governments; National government; State governments
  current attitudes toward, 18–21, 21f
  distrust of, 4, 285
  divided, 85f, 184
  explanation of, 5
  functions of, 5–6
  impact of diversity on, 21
  as news source, 299–300
  origins of term, 5
  public expectations of, 18–21, 21f
  reform of, 4, 18–21
  role in economy, 402–403
  roots of American, 8–10
  social contract theory of, 9
  types of, 7–8, 8t

Government Accountability Office (GAO), 187

Governmental agenda, 387

Government corporations, 230

Graham, Lindsey O., 428

Grandfather clauses, 146

Granholm, Jennifer, 40, 61

Grant, Ulysses S., 74, 78

Grants, block, 99

Grants-in-aid, categorical, 97–99

Grassroots activities, 336

Gravel v. *U.S.* (1972), 55

Gray, Horace, 264–265

Great Britain
  bicameral legislative model, 173
  economic freedom rating of, 406
  events leading to Revolutionary War with, 26–27
  and French and Indian War, 27
  judicial review in, 279
  Parliament, 26, 44
  public opinion on United States, 20
  religious persecution in, 8
  taxation of colonies by, 27
  unitary system in, 85

Great Compromise, 35, 172

Great Depression
  effects of, 392f
  events leading to, 93
  financial reforms, 402–403
  and New Deal programs, 20, 208, 224, 402–403
  party realignment during, 319–320

Great Society, 98, 226

Greenhouse, Linda, 103

Green Party, 325

Greenpeace, 97f

Greenspan, Alan, 405f

Gregg v. *Georgia* (1976), 127

Grenada, 418, 426

Griner, Tom, 115

Griswold, Estelle, 130f

Griswold v. *Connecticut* (1965), 67, 71, 129–130

Grutter v. *Bollinger* (2003), 166

Gubernatorial elections. *See* Elections

Gulf of Tonkin Resolution, 205

Gun control
  interest groups opposing, 337
  legislation addressing, 121–122
  Supreme Court on, 103, 108–110, 121

Gun rights. *See* Second Amendment

Habeas corpus, 62–63, 122, 134, 246, 272

Hamdan v. *Rumsfeld* (2006), 62

Hamilton, Alexander
  background of, 40
  and *Federalist Papers*, 43, 60, 70–71, 202, 247, 250–252, 296
  on judiciary, 246, 247, 250–252
  and ratification of Constitution, 44
  on role of national government, 32
  on war powers, 207

Hammes, T. X., 428

Hands on Network, 84

Hannity, Sean, 297

Hard money, 323f

Harlan, John Marshall, 118, 146–147

Harper v. *Board of Elections* (1966), 79

Harrison, Benjamin, 60, 362

Harrison, William H., 80, 200

Hastings, Alcee, 54

Hatch, Carl, 232

Hatch, Orrin, 40

Hatch Act (1939), 232–233

Hate speech, 118–119

Hawaii, 14, 160, 396

Hayes, Rutherford B., 362

Health care programs
  background of, 393, 399–401
  and Clinton task force on, 382–384
  expenditures for, 399–400
  Medicaid, 399–401
  medical intervention costs, 18t
  Medicare, 15, 18t, 284, 393, 399–400
  and Medicare Prescription Drug, Improvement, and Modernization Act, 400
  public expenditures for, 393

Hearst, William Randolph, 295

Heller v. *District of Columbia* (2008), 67

Henry, Patrick, 27

Henry VIII, king of England, 8

Hernandez v. *Texas* (1954), 157, 157f

Higher education. *See* Universities/colleges

Hinchey, Maurice, 404

Hinckley, John, Jr., 122

Hispanic Americans. *See also* Cuban Americans
  civil rights issues for, 157–159
  in Congress, 183, 184f
  and Democratic Party, 329, 329t
  discrimination against, 157–159
  and immigration, 157
  political ideology of, 283, 283f, 283f
  population trends of, 15, 15f, 16–17
  in prisons, 354
  and Supreme Court, 157–159
  voter registration among, 353f
  voting trends of, 350–351

Hispanization, Huntington thesis of, 16–17

Hoasca tea, 116

Hobbes, Thomas, 9–10

Hold, 188

Holland, 27

Home Building and Loan Assn. v. *Blaisdell* (1934), 59

Homeland security. *See* Department of Homeland Security; War on terrorism

Home-ownership and Opportunity for People Everywhere (Hope VI), 388

Homosexuals. *See* Gays and lesbians

Honest Leadership and Open Government Act (2007), 338

Hong Kong, 406

Hoover, Herbert, 93, 319–320

Hortatory techniques, 390

House v. *Bell* (2006), 127

House of Representatives, U.S. *See also* Congress, U.S.
  and apportionment and redistricting, 173, 363
  committees in, 179
  and Contract with America, 99, 215

impeachment power of, 173, 193, 200
incumbency advantage and elections to, 364–365
leadership positions in, 176–177
organization of, 174t, 175–178
oversight of executive branch by, 191–192, 427–430
oversight of judiciary by, 193–194
and representation, 14, 36, 173
requirements for election to, 172
Senate vs., 174t
term length of, 173
Huckabee, Mike, 277, 370f
Huerta, Dolores, 157
Hughes, Charles Evans, 121
Human rights, 417
Human Rights Commission (United Nations), 422
Huntington, Samuel, 16
Huntington Theory of Hispanization, 16–17
Hurricane Gustav, 84
Hurricane Katrina, 19, 82–84, 100, 386, 432
Hurricane Rita, 100
Hussein, Saddam, 7, 423–424. See also Iraq War
Hutchison, Kay Bailey, 180–181

Ibrahim, Saad Eddin, 237
Iceland, 356
Idaho, 155
Ideology. See Political ideology
Illegal immigrants, 158
Illinois, 96, 127
Immigration
    Catholics on, 157
    and Congress, 177
    Department of Homeland Security regulations on, 425
    to escape religious persecution, 8, 15, 26
    and ethnic and racial diversity, 15, 18
    Hispanic, 1–159??, 157
    Huntington's thesis on, 16–17
    and political machines, 318
    protest against proposals for, 159
    public opinion on, 18
Impeachment
    of Andrew Johnson, 63
    of Clinton, 54, 63
    Constitutional basis for, 36, 173, 193, 248
    explanation of, 173, 199–200
Implementation, 234
Implied powers, 39, 86
Incentive techniques, 390
Income, voter turnout and, 347
Income security programs
    effectiveness of, 398–399
    means-based, 393–394
    means-tested, 397–399
    as social welfare policy, 392–393
Income Tax Act (1894), 75
Incorporation doctrine, 112–113, 112t
Incumbency, 182–183, 364–365
Independent executive agencies, 230–232

Independent regulatory commissions, 224, 231–232
Independents. See Third parties
India, 31, 226, 318
Indian Health Service, 399
Indigenous Democratic Network (INDN), 160
Indirect democracy, 10
Individualism, 11
Industrialization, 18
Inflation, 405
Ingraham, Laura, 297
Inherent powers, 61, 208
Initiatives, 356
Inoculation ads, 368
I.N.S. v. Chadha (1983), 56
Institutional agenda, 387
Interagency councils, 234
Interest groups. See also Lobbying; Lobbyists; Political action committees (PACs)
    arguments for and against limits on, 338–339
    explanation of, 314
    formation of, 331
    function of, 335–340
    historical background of, 332–335
    and judicial nominees, 262
    lobbying function of, 335
    lobbying of Supreme Court, 262
    overview of, 330
    patron funding of, 332
    in Progressive era, 333
    ratings of congress members by, 339–340, 340f
    rise of public, 334–335
    serving African Americans, 334
    and Supreme Court cases, 267, 336
Interest group theories, 331
Internal Revenue Service (IRS), 235
International Center for Technology Assessment, 388–391
International Criminal Court (ICC), 203, 429
International Institute for Democracy and Electoral Assistance, 352
International Monetary Fund (IMF), 337
International Socialist Organization, 119
Internet. See also Web sites
    blogs, 19, 302, 339
    campaign fundraising on, 327, 358, 361
    campaign news on, 19, 281, 299, 368–369
    and campaign strategy, 368–369
    and free speech issues, 120
    government press releases on, 299–300
    and mobilization of interest groups, 336
    as news source, 297f, 299–300
    and public opinion measurement, 288
Internet campaign teams, 361
Interns, 187
Interstate commerce, 91
Interstate Commerce Act (1887), 93, 401–402, 404
Interstate Commerce Commission (ICC), 224, 401, 403

Interstate compacts, 89–90, 90t
Interventionist state, 402
Intolerable Acts (1774), 29
Iowa caucus, 26, 276–278, 277f
Iran, 87, 417, 422
Iranian hostage crisis, 417
Iraq, 422, 424, 426. See also Persian Gulf War
Iraq War
    arguments for and against funding of, 238–239
    and Baghdad violence, 424
    casualties of, 424
    and Congress, 205, 240, 427
    embedded journalists in, 304, 305f
    funding of, 238–239
    and George W. Bush, 204f, 205, 206, 217, 238–239, 422–425, 427, 432
    media coverage of, 304, 305f
    and Mission Accomplished controversy, 432
    and prisoner abuse, 133, 431f
    private security firms in, 428
    public opinion on, 20, 432
    and weapons of mass destruction claim, 206, 423–424
Ireland, 15
Iron triangles, 234, 234f
Islam, 12
Isolationism, 414, 419
Israel, 173, 179, 401
Issue networks, 234
Issue-oriented politics, 319
Italy, 356

Jackson, Andrew
    and Democratic Party, 315–316
    election of 1824, 362
    election of 1832, 315
    political cartoon on spoils system of, 223f
    spoils system of, 223–224, 295
    on Supreme Court, 272
Jackson, Jesse, 282
Jahncke, Cornelia, 130f
James I, king of England, 26–27
Japan, 20, 87, 376
Japanese Americans, 160–161, 161f, 271. See also Asian and Pacific Americans
Jay, John, 40, 249, 260, 296
Jeanne Clery Disclosure of Campus Security Policy and Campus Crime Statistics Act (1990), 102
Jefferson, Thomas
    and Alien and Sedition Acts, 116–117
    and Anti-Federalists, 315
    and Declaration of Independence, 9, 11, 30–31
    and Democratic-Republican party, 319
    and election of 1796, 315
    and election of 1800, 60, 362
    influence of Locke on, 9
    on majority rule, 191
    and Marbury decision, 254
    and National Gazette, 296
    on separation of church and state, 113
    and State of the Union address, 62

on term limits, 78
on United States, 4
Jews, 18, 259t, 261, 282f
Jim Crow laws, 144, 146
Johnson, Andrew, 63, 74, 144, 193
Johnson, Lyndon B.
    and civil rights, 151–152
    executive orders of, 217, 240
    and federal bureaucracy, 226
    and Great Society program, 98
    judicial appointments of, 258t, 261
    on presidential legislative role, 215
    and presidential power, 192
    succession to presidency of, 201
    and Vietnam War, 192, 205, 417
    and voting age, 24
Joint Chiefs of Staff, 426, 427
Joint committees, 179
Journalism, 294–297, 302. See also Media;
    Media coverage
Journalists. See also Media; Media coverage
    bribery of, 295
    as celebrities, 309
    covering politics, 305–307
    embedded, 304, 305f
    and interaction between public figures,
        305–306
    interest in character, 305
    political ideology of, 308–309
    standards for, 302–303
Judges. See also Judicial appointments;
    Supreme Court appointments
    models of decision making by, 270
    philosophy and ideology of, 269–270
    as policy makers, 244–248, 247t,
        271–273
    profile of federal, 259
    salaries of, 248
    tenure of, 247
Judicial activism, 270
Judicial appointments. See also Presidential
    appointments; specific presidents
    background of, 259, 260f
    previous experience of, 259
    by recent presidents, 258t
    Senate confirmation of, 193–194
    to Supreme Court, 258t, 259, 259t, 260f
        (See also Supreme Court
        appointments)
Judicial implementation, 272–273
Judicial restraint, 269–270
Judicial review
    background of, 248, 252–254
    doctrine of, 251
    explanation of, 38, 193, 248
    impact of Marbury v. Madison on,
        252–254
    power of, 247, 247t
Judiciary. See also Federal court system;
    Supreme Court, U.S.
    and Articles of Confederation, 32
    and civil liberty issues, 108–110
    and Congress, 193–194
    and Constitution, 40–42, 63–64, 126,
        246, 256
    and criminal and civil law, 254–256

and decision making, 269–271
    establishment of, 6
    jurisdiction of, 254, 255f
    lobbying to, 336
    oversight of federal bureaucracy by,
        240–241
    overview of, 254
    and policy making, 244–248, 247t,
        271–273
    role of, 246
Judiciary Act (1789), 63, 249, 256
Judiciary Committee, Senate, 181, 261–263
Jurisdiction
    appellate, 254, 255f, 262
    of courts of appeals, 257
    of district courts, 254–255, 255f, 255f,
        256–257
    explanation of, 254, 255f
    original, 252, 255, 255f, 263
    of Supreme Court, 40–42, 254
Jury pools, 146, 157, 256
Jury trials, 126, 146, 157, 249, 256
Justice, 6

Kamal, Hussein, 428
Kamarck, Elaine, 327
Katzenbach v. McClung (1964), 57, 74
Kelo v. New London (2004), 69
Kennedy, Anthony, 261, 266f
    on abortion, 131
    Court voting record of, 104f
    on EPA regulatory responsibility, 389
    profile of, 245, 259t
    on televised proceedings, 263
Kennedy, John F.
    assassination of, 151, 201, 285
    and civil rights, 151
    and Cuban Missile Crisis, 415
    and debates with Nixon, 359f
    on presidency, 205
    trip to France, 204f
    and women's rights, 153
Kentucky, 354
Kerry, John, 282, 379, 428. See also
    Presidential election of 2004
Key, V. O., Jr., 292, 314
Khrushchev, Nikita, 415
King, Martin Luther, Jr., 150–151, 153, 282
Kingston, Jack, 178
Kissinger, Henry, 40, 427
Know Nothing Party, 18
Korean War, 271
Korematsu v. U.S. (1944), 161, 271
Kosovo, 284
Kucinich, Dennis, 317
Ku Klux Klan, 18
Kuwait, 419. See also Persian Gulf War

Labor unions, 329t, 330, 333, 403
Laissez-faire, 402
Lambda Legal Defense and Education
    Fund, 161
Land-grant colleges, 95–98
Landon, Alfred M., 286
Lasswell, Harold D., 222–223
Latin America, 418

Latinos. See Hispanic Americans
Lawrence, John Geddes, 131f
Lawrence v. Texas (2003), 131–132, 162
Lazarus, Edward, 266
League of Conservation Voters (LCV),
    340f
League of United Latin American Citizens
    (LULAC), 127, 157, 159
League of Women Voters, 330
Ledbetter, Lilly, 167
Lee, Richard Henry, 30
Lee, Sheila Jackson, 340f
Legislation
    pathways for, 187–190, 188f
    presidential proposals for, 214–217
Legislative branch. See Congress, U.S.;
    House of Representatives, U.S.;
    Senate, U.S.
Legislative courts, 256
Legislative decision making
    and colleagues and caucuses, 185–186
    and constituents, 184–185
    and interest groups, lobbyists, and
        political action committees, 186
    and political parties, 184
    and staff and support agencies, 186–187
Legislatures. See also Congress, U.S.; House
    of Representatives, U.S.; Senate, U.S.
    bicameral, 172–173
Lemon v. Kurtzman (1971), 113–114
Leo XIII, (pope), 165
Lesbian, Gay, Bisexual, and Transgender
    Center, 118–119
Lesbian Rights Project, 161
Lesbians. See Gays and lesbians
Lethal injection, 127
Leviathan (Hobbes), 9, 9f
Levin, Carl, 193f
Levy, Robert A., 108–109
Libel, 120
Liberals, 13, 293. See also Political ideology
Libertarian Party, 325
Libertarians, 12
Liberty, 7, 10
Libya, 422, 426
Lichtenstein, Allen, 115
Lieberman, Joe, 325
Life expectancy, 15, 393
Limbaugh, Rush, 297, 336
Lincoln, Abraham
    assassination of, 197, 200
    and Civil War, 207–208, 223
    and election of 1860, 318
    establishes Department of Agriculture,
        223
    and free speech issues, 117
    and habeas corpus, 62–63
    on Harriet Beecher Stowe, 145
    on press, 294
    on United States, 4
Lincoln University, 148
Lippmann, Walter, 286
Literary Digest, 286
Little Rock, Arkansas, 150, 204f
Livingston, Robert (colonial era), 30
Living wage, 164–165

Lobbying. *See also* Interest groups
    for Central Pacific Railroad, 332–333
    to Congress, 335–336
    to executive branch, 336
    explanation of, 353
    grassroots, 336
    to judiciary, 336
    to military-industrial complex, 430
    protest activities as, 336–337
    regulation of, 338–339
    and Supreme Court nominees, 262
Lobbying Disclosure Act (LDA)
        (1995), 338
Lobbyists
    explanation of, 335
    and legislative decision making, 186
    techniques used by, 335t
Local governments, 89
Locke, John, 9, 11, 31, 38, 357
Logrolling, 185
Los Angeles Times, 300
Louisiana, 146–147, 355

Machines. *See* Political machines
Madison, James
    background of, 43
    and Bill of Rights, 71, 104, 296
    on Constitution, 44, 46, 47, 247
    and *Federalist Papers,* 43–44, 56, 84,
        190, 314
    political parties of, 317
    as secretary of state, 253, 256
    and Virginia Plan, 33, 34
    and War of 1812, 206, 416
Magazines. *See* News magazines
Main, Jackson Turner, 34
Maine, 354
Majority leaders, House and Senate, 177
Majority party, 174
Majority rule, 11
Malcolm X, 153
Mapp v. *Ohio* (1961), 68, 125
Marbury, William, 253, 256
Marbury v. *Madison* (1803), 38, 46, 63–64,
        248, 252–254, 256, 272
March on Washington for Jobs and
        Freedom (1963), 151
Marcos, Ferdinand, 161
Margin of error, 291
Marijuana, medical use of, 104f
Markup, bills, 189
Marshall, John, 52, 58, 90–91, 251,
        252–254, 253f, 271, 272
Marshall, Thurgood, 148, 149, 261
Martin v. *Hunter's Lessee* (1816), 248
Maryland, 90–91, 127
Maryland v. *Craig* (1990), 126
Mason, George, 111
Massachusetts, 89, 162, 164, 389
Massachusetts Bay Colony, 26
Mass media, 293. *See also* Media
Matching funds, 378
Mathis, David, 100
Mayflower Compact, 8
McCain, John, 193f, 356f, 370*f*

and campaign finance reform, 375
    campaign slogan, 359
    and election of 2008, 312, 327, 345
    health care reform plan, 384
    and "natural-born" presidency
        requirement, 40
    and role in election of 2004, 344
McCain-Feingold Act. *See* Bipartisan
        Campaign Reform Act (2002)
        (BCRA)
McCardle, Ex parte (1867), 62–63
McConnell, Mitch, 179f, 340*f,* 375
McConnell v. *Federal Election Committee*
        (2003), 375
McCorvey, Norma, 130–131
McCulloch, James, 90–91
McCulloch v. *Maryland* (1819), 58, 71,
        90–91, 252
McLaurin, George, 149f
Means-tested programs, 397–399
Meat Inspection Act (1906), 402
Media. *See also* Free press; Journalism;
        Journalists; *specific media*
    agenda setting by, 308
    alternative news sources, 281
    consolidation of, 301–302
    and foreign policy, 430
    framing of political issues by, 308
    influence of, 307–308
    and interaction between public figures,
        305–306
    mass, 293
    narrowcasting, 302, 308
    national influence of, 300–302
    new, 298–300, 367, 368–369
    news, 293
    overview of, 19
    as political socialization agent, 280–281
    and presidents, 198
    print, 293–294
    public perception of, 21f, 309
    use of experts by, 301–302
Media bias, 307, 308–309
Media campaigns
    explanation of, 367
    and free media, 367, 368
    and new media, 368–369
    use of technology, 368–369
Media coverage
    of campaigns, 367–369
    of character issues, 305
    of Congress, 306–307
    of Iraq War, 304, 305f
    of national conventions, 358
    of presidents, 306
    of wars, 430
Media effects, 308
Media Fund, 379
Media regulation, 302–304
Medicaid, 15, 18t, 393, 399–401
Medicare, 15, 18t, 284, 393, 399–400
Medicare Prescription Drug, Improvement,
        and Modernization Act (2003), 400
Meehan, Martin, 375
Mentally retarded convicts, 127
Mercantilism, 27

Merit system, 223–224, 226–229
Mexican American Legal Defense and
        Education Fund (MALDEF),
        157–159, 334
Mexican Americans, 329, 351. *See also*
        Hispanic Americans
Mexico, 87, 90, 127, 157, 159, 420
Michigan, 40
Michigan State University, 95
Middle East, 433
Midterm elections. *See also* Congressional
        elections
    explanation of, 365–366, 365t
    and president's party, 365t, 366–367
    of 2006, 325, 364
Military. *See also specific wars*
    embedded journalists with, 304, 305f
    gays and lesbians in, 161–162
    media coverage of, 430
    president as commander in chief of, 7,
        43, 61, 193, 203, 205
    and prisoner abuse, 133, 431f
    use of federal contractors, 229
    views of women on, 284, 284t
Military Commissions Act (2006), 62, 133,
        134–135
Military draft, 156
Military-industrial complex, 430
Military policy, 415–417, 419, 422–425,
        432. *See also* Defense spending;
        Foreign policy
Military Reconstruction Act (1867), 74
Military tribunals, 62, 135, 217
Militias, 416
Miller v. *California* (1973), 120
Millionaires Club, 183
Mine Safety and Health Administration,
        233f
Minimum rationality test, 154
Minnesota, 59, 96, 284
Minor v. *Happersett* (1875), 75
Minorities. *See also* Cultural diversity;
        Ethnicity; Race; *specific groups*
    and civil rights issues, 142
    in Congress, 183, 184f
    as federal bureaucrats, 227f
    as judicial appointees, 260f
    preservation of rights for, 10
    presidential appointment of, 202
    in prisons, 354–355
    and redistricting, 142, 364
Minority leaders, 177, 178–179
Minority party, 174, 190–191
Minutemen, 30, 30f
Miranda, Ernesto, 124, 124f
Miranda v. *Arizona* (1966), 68, 69, 124
Miranda rights, 68, 124
Mississippi, 99, 142
Missouri, 114
Missouri Compromise of 1820, 92, 143
Model bureaucracies, 234–234
Monarchy, 7, 26
Mondale, Walter, 209
Monetary policy, 406
Money, 406
Monopolies, 93, 401–402

Montesquieu, Baron de, 36–38
Montgomery, Alabama, 150
Moralism, 415
Moral Majority, 282, 334
Morell, Geoff, 428
Morrill Land Grant Act (1862), 95–98
Morse v. *Frederick* (2007), 268
Motor Carrier Act (1935), 403
Motor-voter laws, 352
Mott, Lucretia, 144
Movement for a Free Philippines, 161
Movie industry, 116
Moyers, Bill, 306
Moynihan, Daniel Patrick, 394
Mozambique, 418
MSNBC, 19, 299, 300
Mubarak, Hosni, 237
Muckraking, 296–297
Mukasey, Michael, 136
Murtha, John P., 178
Muslims, 12, 133
Myanmar, 406
MySpace, 302, 339

NAACP Legal Defense Fund (LDF). *See*
    National Association for the
    Advancement of Colored People
    (NAACP)
Nader, Ralph, 334
NAFTA. *See* North American Free Trade
    Agreement (NAFTA)
Nagin, Ray, 82–84, 83f
NARAL Pro-Choice America, 103f, 340f
Narrowcasting, 302
National Aeronautics and Space
    Administration (NASA), 230
National American Woman Suffrage
    Association (NAWSA), 147
National Assessment of Education Progress
    (NAEP), 280
National Association for the Advancement
    of Colored People (NAACP)
    and bus system segregation, 150
    establishment of, 147
    function of, 334
    Legal Defense and Education Fund,
        126–127, 148–149, 267
    membership of, 147
    and school desegregation, 148–149
    and suffrage movement, 147
National Association of Manufacturers
    (NAM), 333+
National Cancer Institute, 399
National committees, 326–327, 326f
National Conference of State Legislatures,
    99
National conventions
    and delegate selection, 359
    explanation of, 328
    media coverage of, 358
    minorities as delegates at, 359
    and party platforms, 312–314
National Council of La Raza, 157
National Defense Act (1916), 416
National Election Pool, 276–278
National Election Study (NES), 289, 291

National Endowment for the Humanities,
    280
National Firearms Act (1934), 121
National Gazette, 296
National government. *See also* Government
    New Deal and growth of, 93–98
    and overlap of state, 87
    powers under Constitution, 86–87, 86f
    press releases from, 299–300
    role in economy, 402–403
    strengthening of, 93
National Guard, 82, 416
National Health, Lung, and Blood
    Institute, 399
National Institute of Allergy and Infectious
    Diseases, 399
National Institutes of Health (NIH), 399
National Labor Relations Act (1935), 95,
    403
National Labor Relations Board (NLRB),
    231, 257, 403
National Marine Service (NMS), 393
National Organization for Women
    (NOW), 153, 154, 240
National party platforms, 312–314, 314t,
    324
National Recovery Administration (NRA),
    94
National Republican Party, 316f
National Rifle Association (NRA), 67,
    334–335, 375, 386
National Security Agency, 413–414, 426
National Security Council (NSC), 211
National Traffic and Motor Vehicle Safety
    Act (1966), 388
National Voter Registration Act (1993), 352
National Woman's Party, 77, 147, 148f
National Woman Suffrage Association
    (NWSA), 76–77, 145, 147
National Women's Political Caucus, 154
Native American Rights Fund (NARF),
    160
Native Americans, 116, 159–160
Naturalization, 173, 177
Natural law, 11
Natural Resources Defense Council, 389
NBC, 19, 276, 300
Near v. *Minnesota* (1931), 112
Nebraska, 162
Nebraska Press Association v. *Stuart* (1976),
    118
Necessary and proper clause, 38–39, 86, 173
Negative ads, 367
Networks, television, 298, 300–302
Neustadt, Richard E., 198, 212
Nevada v. *Hibbs* (2003), 72, 104f
New Deal
    and economy, 208, 402–403
    explanation of, 208
    and federalism, 93–98
    government programs during, 20, 93–98,
        208, 318–319
    and Great Depression, 208, 224
    growth of federal bureaucracy during,
        224
    impact of, 48, 93–98

    impact on African Americans, 322
    and industry regulation, 403
    and labor unions, 403
    Supreme Court on, 48, 94–95, 101, 271
New England town meetings, 10
New Federalism, 98–101
New Hampshire, 44, 345
New Jersey, 44, 91, 127
New Jersey Plan, 33, 34–35
New media, 298–300, 367, 368–369. *See
    also* Internet
News magazines, 297f
News media, 293, 294–295, 430. *See also*
    Media; News sources
Newspapers, 293–297, 297f
News sources. *See also* Media
    age and use of, 300t
    alternative, 281
    comedy news programming, 298, 298f,
        299, 301f
    and conservatives, 302
    Internet as, 19, 281, 297f, 299–300,
        368–369
    print media as, 293–294, 300–302
    radio as, 297, 297f
    television as, 19, 297–298, 297f
New York State, 91, 256, 363
New York Sun, 294
New York Times, 300
New York Times Co. v.*Sullivan* (1964), 120,
    305–306
New York Times Co. v. *U.S.* (1964), 118,
    118f
New York Times Co. v. *U.S.* (1971), 63, 304
New York v. *U.S.* (1992), 71
New Zealand, 173
Ney, Bob, 365
Niagara Movement, 147f
Nicaragua, 418
Niche journalism, 302
Nigeria, 87
9/11. *See* Terrorist attacks of September 11,
    2001
Nineteenth Amendment, 76–77, 147, 348
Ninth Amendment, 44t, 70–71, 104, 111
Nixon, Richard M., 200f, 204f
    abuse of power by, 193
    debates with Kennedy, 359f
    and election of 1972, 282
    Ford's pardon by, 62, 205
    judicial appointments of, 120, 258t, 261
    and news media, 430
    and pornography, 120
    presidential visits by, 213
    resignation of, 80, 200
    and vice presidents, 201
    and Vietnam War, 205
    and voting age, 24
    and War Powers Act, 192, 205, 206
    and Watergate scandal, 262, 430
Nixon Doctrine, 417
Nixon v. *U.S.* (1993), 53
No Child Left Behind Act (2001), 96, 100
Nominating campaigns, 357–359
Nongovernmental organizations (NGOs),
    432

Non-means based programs, 394–396
Nonviolent protest, 150–151
North, as political socialization agent, 285
North American Free Trade Agreement
    (NAFTA), 420
North Atlantic Treaty Organization
    (NATO), 419, 420
Northeast, and Democratic Party, 318
North Korea, 209, 304
Not Dead Yet group, 164
Nuclear weapons, 422. *See also* Weapons of
    mass destruction (WMD)

Obama, Barack, 19*f*, 213*f*, 356*f*, 370*f*
    and election of 2008, 277, 281, 292*f*, 312,
        327, 345–346, 378 (*See also*
        Presidential election of 2008)
    health care reform plan, 384
    as senator, 183
    use of Internet, 327
Obscenity, 120
Occupational Safety and Health
    Administration (OSHA), 229, 232,
    388
O Centro Espirita Beneficente União do
    Vegetal church, 116
O'Connor, Sandra Day
    on abortion, 131
    Court voting record of, 104*f*
    on homosexuality and privacy rights, 131
    law clerks of, 266
    profile of, 261, 262
    on Supreme Court nominations, 259
Office of Faith-Based and Community
    Initiatives, 211
Office of Homeland Security. *See*
    Department of Homeland Security
Office of Management and Budget (OMB),
    211, 216–217
Office of the Vice President, 211
Ohio, 65, 363
Oil for Food program (United Nations),
    422
Oklahoma, 123
Old Age, Survivors, and Disability
    Insurance, 394–395
Oligarchy, 8
Olive Branch Petition, 30*f*
Olson, Mancur, Jr., 332
Onassis, Jacqueline Kennedy, 204*f*
O'Neill, Tip, 170
Open fields doctrine, 123
Open market operations, 406. *See also*
    Federal Reserve System
Open primaries, 353–354
Operation Desert Storm. *See* Persian Gulf
    War
Operation Enduring Freedom, 420–421
Oregon, 25, 116, 132
Oregon v. *Mitchell* (1970), 81
O'Reilly, Bill, 298*f*
Organized labor. *See* Labor unions
Original jurisdiction, 252, 254, 255*f*
Oversight, of executive branch, 191–193,
    427–430
Owen, Priscilla, 251*f*

PACs. *See* Political action committees
    (PACs)
Page, William Tyler, 6
Paid media, 367–368
Paige, Roderick, 235
Paine, Thomas, 30
Pakistan, 203
Palin, Sarah, 209*f*
Palko, Frank, 113
Palko v. *Connecticut* (1937), 113
Panama, 426
Panama Canal, 203
Panama Canal Treaty, 203
Pandemic Influenza Strategic Plan,
    220–222
Panettiere, Hayden, 336*f*
Pardons, 62, 74, 205
Parks, Rosa, 150
Parsons, Richard, 394
"Partial-birth" abortion, 101–102, 254
Partial Birth Abortion Ban Act (2003), 102
Partisanship, 184
Partnership for Peace, 419
Party caucuses
    delegate selection in, 359
    explanation of, 174–175, 177
    primaries vs., 358
Party conferences, 177
Party identification
    and age, 329, 329t
    and campaign news sources, 302
    and education, 329t, 330
    of Evangelical Christians, 329, 329t
    explanation of, 328, 329f
    family influences on, 278
    and gender, 329, 329t
    and geographic region, 329, 329t
    and ideology, 324
    and loyalty, 328
    of Protestants, 329t, 330
    race and ethnicity in, 329, 329t
    and religion, 329t, 330
    and social and economic factors, 330
    sources of, 328–330
    in third parties, 329t
    of women, 329, 329t
Party platforms, 312–314, 314t, 324
Party realignments, 319–320
Patane, Samuel, 124
Paterson, William, 33
Patraeus, David H., 424
Patriot Act. *See* USA Patriot Act (2001)
Patronage, 224
Patrons, interest group, 332
Paul, Alice, 148*f*
Pay equity, 166–167
PCC on Terrorist Financing, 234
Peacekeeping operations, United Nations,
    422–423
Peers, as agents of political socialization,
    279–280
Pelosi, Nancy, 170, 178
Pendleton, George H., 224
Pendleton Act (1883), 224, 226–227
Pennsylvania, 32, 44, 332
Penny press, 294

Pension Office, 223
Pentagon Papers case. *See New York Times
    Co.* v. *Sullivan* (1964)
The Pentagon Papers, 118, 118*f*, 304
People for the American Way, 267
Perot, Ross, 287*f*, 325, 362
Persian Gulf War, 304, 419, 426
Personal liberty, 10
Personal Responsibility and Work
    Opportunity Reconciliation Act
    (PRWORA) (1996), 99, 398
Pew Research Center for the People and the
    Press, 299, 309
Philippines, 161, 201
Pilgrims, background of, 8
Pinckney, Charles, 40
*Planned Parenthood of Southeastern
    Pennsylvania* v. *Casey* (1992), 131
Plato, 7
Pledge of Allegiance, 3, 4, 194, 279
Plessy v. *Ferguson* (1896), 92, 146–149,
    272–273
Pluralist theory, 331
Pocket vetoes, 189–190
Poland, 334
Police powers, 87
Policy adoption, 387–388
Policy coordinating committees (PCCs),
    234
Policy formulation, 387
Policy implementation, 388–391
Polis, Jared, 366
Political action committees (PACs). *See also*
    Interest groups
    and campaign contributions, 186,
        376–377, 377*f*
    election activities of, 186, 340
    explanation of, 376
    and legislative decision making, 186
Political campaigns. *See* Campaigns
Political candidates
    campaign contributions from personal
        funds of, 378
    interest groups ratings of, 339–340, 340*f*
    media interest in character of, 305
    recruitment of, 338
Political cartoons
    on Bush's domestic surveillance, 33*f*
    on death penalty in Texas, 129*f*
    on federalism and Supreme Court, 101*f*
    on immigration, 17*f*
    on interest groups, 331*f*
    on monopolies, 402*f*
    on polling, 287*f*
    on separation of church and state, 114*f*
    on spoils system, 223*f*
Political culture, 10
Political equality, 10–11
Political events, 285
Political ideology
    of college students, 279*f*, 280
    of conservatives, 13, 13*f*, 293
    explanation of, 12–13, 293
    functions of, 12
    of Hispanics, 283, 283*f*
    labels for, 13

of liberals, 13, 13f, 293
of libertarians, 12
and media, 302
of moderates, 13, 13f
and party identification, 324
and political socialization, 293
of religious groups, 282, 282f
and vote choice, 353
Political knowledge, 292
Political machines, 318
Political participation, 232–233, 233t, 336.
    See also Voter turnout
Political parties. *See also specific parties*
    accountability within, 322
    campaign contributions from, 377
    coalitions, 320, 322
    and Congress, 174–175, 175f, 176f, 178
    and critical elections, 319
    dealignment of, 320–321
    explanation of, 312–314
    finances of (1993-2008), 323f
    functions of, 321–326
    get out the vote efforts, 338–339
    during Golden Age, 318
    group affiliations, 328–330, 329f
    historical background of, 314–318, 316f
    and legislative agendas of presidents, 215
    and legislative decision making, 184
    legislative organization of, 324–325
    in modern era, 318–319
    national committee chairpersons, 327
    platforms of, 312–314, 314t, 324
    realignments in, 319–320
    and redistricting, 142, 364
    secular realignments, 320–321
    in states and localities, 328
    structure of, 326–328, 326f
    and third partyism, 325–326, 329t
Political party identification. *See* Party
    identification
Political socialization
    age in, 284
    explanation of, 278
    family in, 278
    gender in, 283–284, 284t
    mass media in, 280–281
    political events in, 285
    race and ethnicity in, 283
    regional differences in, 284–285
    religious beliefs in, 282, 282f
    school and peers in, 279–280
Politicians, effect on public opinion,
    292–293
Politicos, 184
Politics, 5, 18–19, 291–293, 319
Pollock v. *Farmers' Loan & Trust Co.* (1895),
    75
Polls. *See* Public opinion polls
Pollsters, 361
Poll taxes, 79, 146
Pollution. *See* Environmental regulation
Popular consent, 11
Popular sovereignty, 11
Popular vote, election of 2000, 307, 362
Population
    age of, 14, 14f, 15, 15f, 18

Population ecology theory, 331
Pork, defined, 181
Pornography, 120
Portugal, 356
Positive ads, 367
Potato famine, 15
Powell, Colin, 419, 427
Powell Doctrine, 419
Powell v. *McCormack* (1969), 55
Pragmatism, 415
Prayer, 113–114, 273
Precedents, 257
Preemption, 100–101, 422–425
Presidential appointments. *See also* Judicial
    appointments
    confirmation of, 193
    power to make, 202
    Senate procedure for, 173, 193
    of women, 202t
Presidential Election Campaign Fund, 378
Presidential election of 2000
    Bush platform in, 100
    and Electoral College, 362
    and Florida, 362
    and McCain, 344
    popular vote in, 362
    and Supreme Court, 60, 266, 362
    and vice presidency, 209
Presidential election of 2004
    fundraising in, 335
    and same-sex marriage, 162
    voter turnout in, 352f
Presidential election of 2008
    health care reform issues, 384
    media coverage of, 281
    minority voting trends, 349–351
    overview, 369–375
    primaries in, 344–346
    role of Internet in, 327, 358, 361
    slogans for, 359
    tracking polls for, 290f
    voter turnout, 349–351
    youth vote, 25–26, 348, 350
Presidential elections. *See also* Elections
    of 1796, 315
    of 1800, 60, 362
    of 1832, 315
    of 1860, 318
    of 1884, 294–295
    of 1904, 78
    of 1912, 78
    of 1932, 320
    of 1936, 286
    of 1948, 287
    of 1972, 282
    of 1980, 290
    of 1992, 280, 353, 362
    of 1996, 280
    and accuracy of polls, 287f
    coattails from, 365
    nomination campaigns, 357–359
    party realignments in, 319–320
    polls of, 290
    primaries vs. caucuses, 358
    secular realignments in, 320–321
Presidential Funding Program, 375

Presidential power
    as commander in chief, 7, 40, 43, 61,
        193, 203, 205
    to convene Congress, 202
    development and expansion of, 205–208
    to give pardons, 62, 74, 205
    to make appointments, 202 (*See also*
        Judicial appointments; Presidential
        appointments)
    to make treaties, 202–203
    to order engagement of armed forces, 419
    to veto, 203
Presidential Succession Act (1947), 200
President pro tempore, 54, 178
Presidents. *See also* Executive branch; *specific
    presidents*
    approval ratings for, 212, 214f
    citizenship requirements for, 40–41
    and Congress, 191–192
    control of bureaucracy by, 237, 240
    election of, 198, 199
    and federal budgetary process, 215–217
    funeral plans for, 196–198
    and importance of public opinion,
        211–214
    judicial appointments of, 258t
    leadership abilities of, 212
    legislative role of, 214–217
    media coverage of, 306
    mobilization of public opinion, 212
    overview of, 198
    personalities of, 212t
    persuasive powers of, 212
    as policy makers, 214–217
    press conferences of, 305
    press secretary of, 306
    qualifications for, 199–200
    rankings for, 208t
    roles of, 204f
    roots of, 199–201
    rules of succession to, 200
    terms of office, 36, 199–200
President's Commission on the Status
    of Women (1963), 153
President's Commission to Strengthen
    Social Security, 394–395
Press briefings, 305
Press conferences, 305
Press corps. *See also* Journalism; Journalists;
    Media coverage
    coverage of Congress by, 306–307
    coverage of presidency by, 306
    and interaction between public figures,
        305–306
Press releases, 305
Press secretaries, 306, 361
Primaries
    caucuses vs., 358
    closed, 353–354
    direct, 319
    explanation of, 353–354
    media coverage of, 305
    runoff, 355
    of 2008, 344–346
    types of, 353–355
Print media, 293–294, 300–302. *See also*

Newspapers; *specific media*
Printz v. *U.S.* (1997), 104f
Prior restraint, 116, 118
Prisoner abuse (Iraq War), 133, 431f
 and news media, 431f
Privacy rights
 and abortion, 130–131
 and birth control, 129–130
 and homosexuality, 131–132
 and right to die, 132
 scope of, 127–129
 Supreme Court on, 127–129
 timeline of, 132–133
Privileges and immunities clause, 88
Progressive era issues, 146–149, 333, 402–403
Progressive movement, 146–149, 333, 402–403
Project for Excellence in Journalism, 304
Property rights, constitutional, 9
Proportional representation, 179
Prospective judgment, 353
PROTECT Act (2003), 120
Protest, 115, 150–151, 159, 336–337
Protestants
 early settlements in America by, 8
 and party identification, 329t, 330
 political ideology of, 282, 282f
 in South, 285
 split from Church of England by, 8
 on Supreme Court, 259t, 261
Public Citizen, 334
Public funds, 378
Public Health Service, 393
Public interest groups, 334–335. *See also* Interest groups
Public opinion
 on domestic vs. foreign problems, 432f
 on equal rights amendment, 154
 and ethnicity differences, 283f
 explanation of, 285
 on foreign policy, 431–432
 on gays and lesbians, 162
 on government, 20, 285
 on immigration, 18
 on Iraq War, 20, 432
 on Kosovo involvement, 284
 on media, 309
 media and polarization of, 302
 on military policy, 432
 and political ideology, 293
 politicians' effect on, 292–293
 on presidential performance, 212, 214f
 presidents' mobilization of, 212
 on Supreme Court, 271
 on term limits, 78
 on terrorism, 285, 286
 on United States, 20
 on Warren, 272f
Public opinion influences
 age, 284
 cues from leaders, 292–293
 family, 278
 gender, 283–284, 284t
 geographic region, 284–285
 mass media, 280–281, 307–308

 personal benefits, 292
 political events, 285
 political ideology, 293
 political knowledge, 292
 race and ethnicity, 283, 283f
 religion, 282, 282f
 school and peers, 279–280
Public Opinion (Lippmann), 286
Public opinion polls
 of cell phone users, 288
 entrance, 276–278
 exit, 290
 explanation of, 285
 Gallup, 282, 282f, 287f
 historical background of, 286–287
 and Internet, 288
 margin of error, 291
 measures used for, 291
 political, 289–290
 push polls as, 289–290
 questions in, 287–288
 respondents in, 289
 samples, 288–289
 sampling error on, 291
 shortcomings of, 291
 straw polls, 286
 by telephone, 288, 289
 tracking, 290, 290f
 traditional, 287–289
Public policy
 adoption of, 387–388
 and agenda setting, 387
 and budgeting, 388
 and executive orders, 217
 explanation of, 384–385
 and federal bureaucracy, 235
 formulation of, 387
 implementation of, 388–391
 and judiciary, 244–246, 271–273
 and political parties, 324
 and problem recognition and definition, 386–387
 process for creating, 385–391
 stages of, 385f
Public schools
 civics education in, 280–281
 desegregation of, 148–149, 152, 204f
 drug testing in, 123
 inequalities in, 158
 separation between church and state issues in, 113–114
Publius, 43
Puerto Rican Legal Defense and Education Fund, 157, 334
Puerto Ricans, 157, 351. *See also* Hispanic Americans
Puerto Rico, 157
Pulitzer, Joseph, 295
Pure Food and Drug Act (1906), 402
Puritans, 8
Push polls, 289–290
Putnam, Robert, 330

Quartering Act (1774), 29

Race. *See also* Cultural diversity; Ethnicity;

 Minorities
 of Congress members, 183, 184f
 and death penalty, 128
 and immigration, 15
 and party identification, 329, 329t
 as political socialization agent, 283
 and voter turnout, 348–351
Racial discrimination, 157–159
Racism, 144–145
Radio
 conservative talk, 297, 336
 FDR's fireside chats on, 208, 297
 historical background of, 297
 as news source, 297, 297f
 regulation of, 403
Raiding, 354
Rainbow Push Coalition, 339
Randolph, Edmund, 33, 34
Randolph, Jennings, 25
Random sampling, 289
R.A.V. v. *City of St. Paul* (1992), 118
Reagan, Michael, 297
Reagan, Nancy, 390
Reagan, Ronald, 200f, 204f, 418f
 on abortion, 131, 217
 and affirmative action, 166
 assassination attempt on, 122
 cabinet appointments of, 202t
 and conservative Christians, 282, 334
 and Contras, 418
 foreign policy of, 418, 426
 funeral of, 196–198
 judicial appointments of, 258t, 260f, 261
 and New Federalism, 98
 popularity of, 278
 signing statements of, 216
 and taxation, 99
 tenure in office of, 78
 use of disability provision, 80
 and War Powers Act, 193
Reagan Doctrine, 418
Reagan Revolution, 98–99
Realignments, 319–320
Reapportionment, 363
Recall elections, 356
Recession, 405
Redistricting
 effects of, 363
 explanation of, 173, 364
 impact on minorities, 142, 364
 Supreme Court on, 142, 273
 in Texas, 142
Reed v. *Reed* (1971), 155
Referendum, 356
Reformation, 8
Regents of the University of California v. *Bakke* (1978), 166
Regulation. *See also* Deregulation; Environmental regulation
 of airline industry, 391, 404, 405
 of commerce, 91
 economic, 224, 403–404
 of electronic media, 301–302
 explanation of, 235
 of lobbying, 338–339
 social, 403–404

of transportation industry, 403
of trusts, 401–402
Rehnquist, William H.
    on abortion rights, 101
    and Bill Clinton's impeachment trial, 54
    as chief justice, 269
    Court voting record of, 104f
    and Family and Medical Leave Act,
        103–104
    and *Gideon* v. *Wainright*, 125
    on judicial decision making, 271
    on right to die, 132
    on salaries for judges, 248
    on search and seizure, 123
    on *stare decisis*, 270
Reid, Harry, 179f
Religion. *See also* Separation between
        church and state
    in Colonial America, 8, 113, 282
    Native American, 116
    and party identification, 329t, 330
    and political agendas, 11–12
    as political socialization agent, 282, 282f
    in South, 285
    of Supreme Court appointees, 259t, 261
Religious freedom
    and establishment clause, 113–115
    and First Amendment, 113, 114f
    and free exercise clause, 115–116
    historical background of, 113
Religious Freedom Restoration Act (1993),
        102, 116
Religious interest groups, 334
Religious persecution, 8, 15, 26, 113
Religious Right, 13
Representation
    in House of Representatives, 14, 36, 173
    theories of, 183–184
Representative democracy, 10
Republic, 10
Republican National Committee
        (RNC), 326
Republican Party
    and Contract with America, 99
    fundraising operations of, 322–323, 323f
    historical background of, 316f
    ideological makeup of, 11, 318, 320
    and judicial nominations, 258
    and organization in Congress, 175f, 178
    origin of, 318
    platform of, 312–314, 314t
    and presidential elections (*See specific
        elections*)
    and religious affiliation, 329t, 330
    and Social Security privatization,
        394–395
    and South, 318
Research 2000, 288
Reserve powers, 87
Reserve requirements, 406. *See also* Federal
        Reserve System
The Responsible Electorate (Key),
        292–293
Retrospective judgment, 353
Revolutionary War, 27, 95
Reynolds v. *Sims* (1964), 273

Rice, Condoleezza, 133, 427
Richardson, Bill, 317
Richmond Newspapers v. *Virginia*
        (1980), 71
Right to counsel, 125
Right to die, 132
Right to privacy. *See* Privacy rights
Roberts, John G., Jr., 266f
    and audio recordings and transcripts, 263
    as chief justice, 101–102, 104, 244–246,
        269, 272
    Court voting record of, 104f, 272
    on EPA regulatory responsibility, 389
    profile of, 259t, 261
    on salaries for judges, 248
Robertson, Pat, 334
Rockefeller, Nelson A., 80, 183, 201
Roe v. *Wade* (1973), 130–131
Roman Catholic Church, 8, 18
Romer v. *Evans* (1996), 162
Romney, George, 40
Roosevelt, Eleanor, 120, 153
Roosevelt, Franklin D.
    and election of 1932, 320
    and election of 1936, 286
    funeral of, 197
    and Garner, 209
    internment of Japanese Americans
        by, 161
    and media, 198
    and New Deal, 20, 93–98, 215, 224, 320,
        402–403 (*See also* New Deal)
    and presidential power, 208
    radio fireside chats by, 208, 296
    and Supreme Court, 94–95, 261
    tenure in office, 78, 199
Roosevelt, Theodore
    on bully pulpit, 212
    and election of 1904, 78
    and election of 1912, 78, 325
    on muckraking, 296
    and Progressive movement, 402
Ros-Lehtinen, Ileana, 340f
Roth v. *U.S.* (1957), 120
Rubin, Amina, 186f
Rule making, 235
Rule of Four, 264
Rules Committee, House, 179
Runoff primaries, 355
Russia, 87. *See also* Soviet Union
Ryan, George, 127

Same-sex marriage, 64, 89, 162
Samples, public opinion polls, 286
Sampling error, 291
San Antonio Independent School District
        v. *Rodriguez* (1973), 158
Sanders, Bernie, 325
Sandinistas, 418
Saudia Arabia, 114, 153
Scalia, Antonin, 266f
    and abortion, 131
    Court voting record of, 104f
    on EPA regulatory responsibility, 389
    on homosexuality, 132
    profile of, 259t, 261

Schenck v. *U.S.* (1919), 117
School prayer, Supreme Court and,
        113–114
Schools. *See also* Education; Public schools;
        Universities/colleges
    civics education in, 280–281
    desegregation of, 148–149, 149f, 152,
        204f
    as political socialization agents, 279–280
    sexual discrimination in, 156
Schwarzenegger, Arnold, 40, 61
Scott, Dred, 92, 92f
Search and seizure, 122–123
Second Amendment, 67, 109–110, 121,
        337
Second Bank of the United States, 90
Second Continental Congress, 30
Second Treatise on Civil Government
        (Locke), 9, 357
Secretary of State, 40
Secret Service, 427
Sectionalism, 325
Secular realignments, 320–321
Securities Act (1933), 403
Securities and Exchange Commission
        (SEC), 231, 257, 403
Securities Exchange Act (1934), 403
Segregation, 144–149, 149f
Select committees, 179, 180t
Selective incorporation, 112–113, 112t
Self-incrimination, 123–124
Senate, U.S. *See also* Congress, U.S.
    committees in, 179
    confirmation of presidential
        appointments by, 173, 193, 250–251,
        429
    election to, 93, 172–173
    and foreign policy, 427–430
    House of Representatives vs., 174t
    impeachment trials in, 173, 200
    incumbency advantage in, 364–365
    judicial recommendations of, 193–194,
        250–251
    organization of, 174t, 178–179
    oversight of executive branch by,
        191–193, 427–430
    oversight of judiciary by, 193–194
    and representation, 36
    requirements for election to, 172–173
    term length of, 172–173
    treaty approval by, 173, 203, 429
Senatorial courtesy, 193–194, 258
Seneca Falls Convention, 144
Seniority, committee chairs and, 181–182
Separate-but-equal doctrine, 147, 148–149,
        149f
Separation between church and state, 42,
        113–115
Separation of powers, 36–38, 37f
September 11, 2001 terrorist attacks. *See*
        Terrorist attacks of September 11,
        2001
Seriatim opinions, 252
Seventeenth Amendment, 62, 75–76, 93,
        173
Seventh Amendment, 69–82

Sex discrimination, 155
Sexual harassment, 156
Sexual orientation. *See* Gays and Lesbians
Sharpton, Al, 282
Shays, Chris, 375
Shays's Rebellion, 32f, 36, 337
Sherman, Roger, 30
Sherman Antitrust Act (1890), 93, 402
Singapore, 173, 406
Single-issue groups, 332
Sit-ins, 151
Sixteenth Amendment, 57, 75, 93, 224
Sixth Amendment, 69, 125–126, 135
Slander, 120
Slavery. *See also* African Americans
    background of, 143
    and Constitutional Convention, 33, 35
    European policies on, 144
    and free speech issues, 117
    and political parties, 318
    in South, 143
    Supreme Court on, 73, 91–93, 144–145
Slogans, election, 359
Snowe, Olympia, 317
Social capital, 330
Social change, 48–49
Social conservatives, 13
Social contract theory, 9, 11
Social democracy, 94
Social groups, party identification, 330
Social insurance programs. *See* Social
    welfare policy
Social issues, 330
Socialist Party, 325
Socialization agents, 278
Social networking web sites, 281, 302, 361
Social regulation, 403–404. *See also*
    Regulation
Social Security
    and aging population, 15, 18t
    attempt to privatize, 395–396
    background of, 20, 392–393
    function of, 392–393
    and George W. Bush, 395–396
    percentage of taxable payroll, 395f
    and political ideology, 284
    Supplemental Security Income, 397
Social Security Act (1935), 392
Social Security Trust Fund, 394
Social welfare policy
    explanation of, 391–392
    family and child support, 397–398, 397f
    food stamps, 398
    health care, 393, 399–401
    income security, 392–399
    means-tested, 397–399
    and Medicare Prescription Drug,
        Improvement, and Modernization
        Act, 400
    non-means-based, 394–396
    origins of, 392–393
    unemployment insurance, 395–396, 396f
    welfare reform, 397–398
Society of Professional Journalists, 302
Sodomy laws, 131–132
Soft money, 323f, 375–376, 378–380

Solem v. *Helm* (1983), 70
Solicitor general, 267
Sons of Liberty, 27, 28
Souter, David H., 266f
    on abortion, 131
    Court voting record of, 104f
    on EPA regulatory responsibility, 389
    profile of, 245, 259t
    on school prayer, 114
South, 143, 285, 318, 349
South Carolina v. *Dole* (1984), 78
South Dakota, 357
Southern Christian Leadership Conference
    (SCLC), 150–151
Southern Pacific Railroad, 333
South Korea, 173
Southworth, Scott, 119
Sovereign immunity, 102
Soviet Union. *See also* Russia
    and Cold War, 415
    collapse of communism in, 418
    and Cuban Missile Crisis, 415
    domestic, foreign, and military reforms
        in, 418
    invasion of Afghanistan by, 418
    and Reagan, 418
Spain, 401
Speaker of the House, 176
Spears, Britney, 254
Special committees. *See* Select committees
Specter, Arlen, 263
Speech. *See also* Free speech
    hate, 118–119
    protected, 118–119
    symbolic, 118
    unprotected, 119–121
Spoils system, 223–224
Spot ads, 368
Stamp Act (1765), 27–28
Stamp Act Congress, 28
Standard Oil Company, 332
Standing committees, 179, 180–181, 180t,
    187, 189
Stanislaus II, 40
Stanton, Elizabeth Cady, 75, 144, 145
Stare decisis, 257, 269, 270, 272
State constitutions, 416
State governments
    budget issues in, 99
    and concurrent powers, 87, 88f
    powers under Constitution, 87, 88f
    and relationship between federal, 87, 88f
State of the Union Address, 39, 62, 212
States. *See also specific states*
    political party structure in, 328
    procedure for admitting to union, 42
    relations among, 88–90
    relations within, 89
    sovereign immunity of, 102
    and Supreme Court, 104f
Stem cell research, 87
Stenberg v. *Carhart* (2000), 101–102
Stevens, John Paul, 266f
    Court voting record of, 104f
    on EPA regulatory responsibility, 389
    profile of, 245, 259t

Stewart, Jon, 298, 299
Stewart, Potter, 261
Stimulus payments, 408–409
Stock market, 403
Stone, Lucy, 75
Story, Joseph, 55
Stowe, Harriet Beecher, 145
Strategic model, 270
Stratified sampling, 289
Straw polls, 286
Strict constructionists, 270
Strict scrutiny, 155
Stromberg v. *California* (1931), 118
Student and Exchange Visitor Information
    System (SEVIS), 425
Student Nonviolent Coordinating
    Committee (SNCC), 151
Students for Concealed Weapons on
    Campus, 337
Students for Sensible Drug Policy, 268
Student visas, 425
Substantive due process, 112
Sudan, 206, 422, 426
Suffrage movement, 147, 148f, 194–144.
    See also Voting rights
Sugar Act (1764), 27–28
Supplemental Security Income, 397
Supplemental Security Income (SSI), 397,
    400
Supremacy clause, 42, 87, 91
Supreme Court, U.S. *See also* Federal court
    system; Judiciary; *specific cases; specific
    justices*
    on abortion, 101–102, 104f, 130–131,
        273
    and ACLU, 267
    on actual malice, 306
    on affirmative action, 166
    and African Americans, 261
    on Bill of Rights, 112–113, 112t
    on birth control, 129–130
    on campaign finance, 339, 375
    caseload of, 262–264, 264f
    and Catholics, 259t, 261
    chambers of, 279f
    on civil liberties, 110
    on civil rights, 145–146, 149–153
    closed conferences of, 268–269
    criteria for cases heard by, 266–267
    on death penalty, 127
    on disabled individuals, 163
    on drug testing, 123
    on due process, 111–112
    on environmental regulation, 389
    on equal protection clause, 154–156
    on exclusionary rule, 125
    on executive privilege, 200, 272
    and federalism, 38, 90–91, 101–104,
        101f, 104f
    on flag burning, 49
    on foreign policy, 207
    and Fourth Amendment, 122–123
    on freedom of assembly, 121
    on free exercise clause, 113, 115–116

on free speech and press issues, 112, 116–117

on full faith on credit clause, 89

function of, 38, 257–258

on gun control, 103, 108–110, 121

on *habeas corpus*, 272

on Hispanic rights, 157–159

historical background of, 247–254

on homosexual rights, 131–132, 162

interest group lobbying of, 336

and interest groups, 267

interpretation of Constitution by, 48

and Jackson, 272

on Japanese American internment, 271

and Jay, 249

jurisdiction of, 40–42, 254, 255*f*, 262–264

and jury trials, 126

and justices' ideological leanings, 267

law clerks for members of, 248, 264–266, 266*t*

on liberties of criminal defendants, 122–127

lobbying by interest groups to, 262

media coverage of, 307

on military issues, 416

name of, defined, 247

on New Deal, 48, 94–95, 101, 271

oral arguments in, 267, 268

paths for cases to be heard by, 265*f*

power of, 244–246, 247*t*

on presidential election of 2000, 60, 266

on privacy rights, 127–129

public knowledge about, 262, 262*t*

public opinion on, 271

on redistricting, 142, 273, 364

on religious establishment issues, 113–115

on right to counsel, 125

and Roosevelt, 94–95, 261

on school prayer, 113–114

on searches on seizures, 122–123

on segregation, 146–149

on self-incrimination, 123–124

on sex discrimination, 156

on slavery, 73, 91–93, 143

staffing of, 258

standards of review for, 155, 155t

and states, 104f

structure of, 249–252

televised proceedings of, 263

on terrorism detainees, 134–136, 135f

timeline of, 252–253

transcripts of proceedings, 262

on voting laws, 25

Warren on, 266

Wilson on, 48

written opinions of, 269

Supreme Court appointments. *See also specific justices*

by Adams, 252, 253

confirmation process for, 261–262

explanation of, 259

justices' profiles, 259*t*

and Nixon, 120

nomination criteria for, 259–261

public awareness level of, 262t

by Washington, 249

of women justices, 261

Supreme Court clerks, 248, 264–266, 266*t*

Surveillance. *See* Warrantless surveillance

Suspect classifications, 155

Swann v. *Charlotte-Mecklenburg Board of Education* (1971), 64

Sweatt, H. M., 148

Sweden, 94, 173

Symbolic speech, 118

Systemic agenda, 387

Taft, William H., 123

Taliban, 421

Taney, Roger B., 71, 91–93, 121, 268

Taxation

of Colonial America, 27

in Great Britain, 27

income taxes, 75

poll taxes, 79, 146

and Reagan, 99

and Sixteenth Amendment, 93

Tax rebate checks, 408–409

Tea Act (1773), 28

Technological advances. *See also* Internet

and cell phones, 102, 288

in news coverage, 294–295, 302

and political campaigns, 368–369

in war on terrorism, 425

Tecumseh, Oklahoma, 123

Telecommunications Act (1996), 301, 404

Telephone polls, 288, 289

Television

cable, 19, 298

comedy news programming, 298, 298f, 299, 301f

and election results, 290

and free speech issues, 116

government regulation of, 301–302

national convention coverage on, 358

national influence of, 297–298

networks, 298, 300–302

as news source, 19, 297–298, 297f

as political socialization agent, 281

and presidential debates, 359f

satellite, 298

Supreme Court coverage proposals, 262, 263

White House coverage by, 306

Temperance movement, 48f, 76, 332

Temporary Assistance for Needy Families (TANF), 99, 397–398, 400

Tennessee v. *Lane* (2004), 104f, 163

Tennessee Valley Authority (TVA), 232f

Tenth Amendment, 71, 87, 111

Terminally ill patients, 132

Term limits, 78

Terrorism, 420–421, 433. *See also* Department of Homeland Security; War on terrorism

Terrorist attacks of September 11, 2001

and al-Qaeda-linked operatives, 177, 420–421

effects of, 285, 421–422

public opinion following, 28/4

role of government following, 6–7

Texas, 129f, 130, 142, 256, 363

Texas A&M University, 95

Texas State University for Negroes, 148

Third Amendment, 67–68

Third parties

effects of, 325–326

growth of, 321

historical background of, 316*f*

in midterm elections, 325

and party identification, 329t

public funds for presidential candidates from, 378

Thirteenth Amendment, 73, 92, 144

Thomas, Clarence, 266*f*

confirmation hearings for, 262

Court voting record of, 104f

on EPA regulatory responsibility, 389

profile of, 245, 259*t*, 261

Three-Fifths Compromise, 35, 48, 53

Thurmond, Strom, 152, 287*f*

Ticket-splitting, 319

Tilden, Samuel L., 362

Till, Emmett, 151f

Time Warner, 301

Tinker v. *Des Moines Independent Community School District* (1969), 118

Title IX, Education Amendments (1972), 156, 236, 390

Title VII. *See* Civil Rights Act (1964)

Tocqueville, Alexis de, 280

Torcaso v. *Watkins* (1961), 66

Totalitarianism, 7–8

Townsend, Frances, 221, 221*f*

Townshend Acts (1767), 28

Tracking polls, 290, 290f

Trade, 27, 420

Transactions theory, 331

Transportation Security Administration, 427

Treaties

list of, 203t

presidential power to make, 202–203

Senate approval of, 173, 429

Treaty of Paris (1763), 27

Treaty of Paris (1783), 32

Trial courts, 254

Trials, jury. *See* Jury trials

Truman, David B., 331

Truman, Harry S

and civil rights, 149, 154

and election of 1948, 287

inherent power and, 61–62

pardons granted by, 207

on presidency, 205

and Supreme Court, 271

Trustees, representatives as, 183

Trusts, regulation of, 401–402

Turnout. *See* Voter turnout

Twelfth Amendment, 72, 362

Twentieth Amendment, 77

Twenty-First Amendment, 46–47, 77–78

Twenty-Second Amendment, 78, 199

Twenty-Third Amendment, 78–79

Twenty-Fourth Amendment, 79

Twenty-Fifth Amendment, 79–80

Twenty-Sixth Amendment, 25, 80–81, 348
Twenty-Seventh Amendment, 81
Tyler, John, 80, 193, 200

"Ugly American" perception, 20
Uncle Tom's Cabin (Stowe), 145
Unemployment insurance, 395–396
Unemployment rates, 396f
Unfunded mandates, 99
Unfunded Mandates Reform Act (1995), 99
Unicameral legislatures, 173
Uniform Code of Military Justice, 62
Unilateralism, 414–415
Unitary system, 85, 86f
United Farm Workers Union, 157, 161
United Kingdom. *See* Great Britain
United Nations (UN)
    Agenda for Peace, 422
    arguments for and against membership
        in, 422–423
    and George W. Bush, 203, 422, 424
    Human Rights Commission of, 422
    and International Criminal Court, 203,
        429
    and Iraq, 422
    Oil for Food program, 422
    peacekeeping operations of, 422–423
    Security Council, 422–424
United Press International (UPI), 301
United States. *See also* Colonial America;
        Population
    changing demographics of, 13–18, 15f
    development of journalism in, 294–295
    distrust of, 20
    economic freedom rating of, 406
    and North American Free Trade
        Agreement, 420
    number of governments in, 85f
    party realignments in, 319–320
    size and population of, 14, 14f
United Students Against Sweatshops
        (USAS), 164
Universities/colleges. *See also specific schools*
    as agents of political socialization, 280
    female athletes in, 236
    gender equity in athletics, 236
    and ideological interests, 337
    impact of terrorist attacks of 9/11 on, 425
    land-grant, 95–98
    mandatory fees in, 119
    segregation in, 148–149, 149f
    and students with disabilities, 163
    violence against women on, 102
University of Alabama v. Garrett
        (2001), 104f
University of Georgia, 95
University of Iowa, 286
University of Michigan, 162, 321
University of Missouri Law School, 148
University of New Mexico, 160
University of Oklahoma, 148
University of Pennsylvania, 298
University of Texas Law School, 148
University of Virginia, 114
University of Wisconsin, 119

U.S. Census, 173, 350, 364
U.S. Chamber of Commerce, 333, 340f
U.S. Interagency Council on the Homeless,
    234
U.S. Citizenship and Immigration Service,
    177, 425
U.S. Civil Service, 226–229
U.S. Postal Service, 226
U.S. Trade Representative, 211
U.S. v. Curtiss-Wright (1936), 207
U.S. v. Darby Lumber Co. (1941), 71
U.S. v. Georgia (2006), 104, 104f
U.S. v. Lopez (1995), 71, 102, 104f
U.S. v. Miller (1939), 121
U.S. v. Morrison (2000), 74, 104f
U.S. v. Nixon (1974), 63, 200, 271
U.S. v. Printz (1997), 71
U.S. v. Salerno (1982), 70
U.S. Term Limits v. Thornton (1995), 52
U.S. v. Williams (2008), 120
USA Patriot Act (2001)
    ACLU concerns on, 134
    and First Amendment infringements,
        133–135
    and Fourth Amendment infringements,
        133–134
    George W. Bush support for, 213, 216
    and search and seizure, 123
    and Student and Exchange Visitor
        Information System, 425
USA Today, 300

Venezuela, 232, 406
Vermont, 162, 354, 364
Veterans Housing Authority loans, 225–226
Veterans of Foreign Wars, 234
Vetoes, 56, 189–190, 203
Viacom, 301
Vice presidents, 199, 209, 362
Vietnam War
    amnesty for draft evaders, 207
    Asian American opposition to, 161
    and Congress, 205, 427
    explanation of, 415–417
    and Gulf of Tonkin Resolution, 205
    and Johnson, 192, 205, 417
    and Nixon, 205
    and *Pentagon Papers*, 118, 304
Vietnam War Memorial, 417f
Villard, Oswald Garrison, 147
Violence Against Women Act (1994), 103
Violence on campuses, 102
Virginia, 32, 354, 357
Virginia House of Burgesses, 10, 26
Virginia Plan, 34–35
Virginia Tech, 102, 337
Volstead Act (1919), 76, 78
Vote choice, 352–353
Voter canvass, 360
Voter registration, 351–352, 353f
Voter turnout. *See also* Political participation
    and absentee voting, 352
    and age, 26, 348
    among Hispanic Americans, 350–351
    and education, 347

and ethnicity, 348–351
and gender, 348
and income, 347
and interest in politics, 351
and number of elections, 352
patterns in, 347–351
reasons for low, 351–352, 352f
Voting restrictions, 144–145
Voting rights
    for African Americans, 144, 147
    and age, 24–26
    constitutional provision for, 2–3
    exercise of, 11
    for felons, 354–355
    timeline of, 348–349
    for women, 147, 348
Voting Rights Act (1965)
    background of, 77, 140
    effects of, 79, 157–158, 349–350
    Justice Department violation of, 142
    and redistricting, 142, 364

Wagner, Robert, 403
Wagner Act (1935), 403
Walesa, Lech, 334
Wallace, George, 325
Wall Street Journal, 300
Wal-Mart, 137, 166–167
Warner, John, 193f
War of 1812, 416
War on Poverty. *See* Great Society
War on terrorism. *See also* Terrorism
    black sites, 135
    and due process rights for detainees,
        134–136, 135f
    explanation of, 420–425
    and George W. Bush, 62, 412–414,
        420–425, 432
    impact on college students, 425
    limits on civil liberties during, 133–135
    and National Guard, 416
    public opinion on, 284, 286
    technological advances in, 425
    timeline of, 420–421
    and use of military tribunals, 62,
        135, 217
War Powers Act (1973)
    arguments for and against, 206–207
    explanation of, 192–193, 205, 427
    function of, 206, 430
    and Nixon, 192
Warrantless searches, 122
Warrantless surveillance, 413–414
Warren, Earl
    and *Gideon v. Wainright*, 125
    on *Miranda* rights, 124
    on operation of Supreme Court, 266
    opinions of, 272, 272f
    public opinion on, 272f
    on segregation, 149
Wars, 117, 163. *See also specific wars*
Washington, D.C., 79, 257
Washington, George
    and Constitutional Convention, 33
    and Continental Army, 30

election of, 199
funeral of, 197
on political parties, 315
on role of national government, 32
and State of the Union address, 62
Supreme Court appointments of, 249
Washington, Martha, 210
Washington Legal Foundation, 267
Washington Post, 300, 304
Water-boarding, 135f, 136
Watergate scandal, 200, 262, 271, 285, 430
Waxman, Henry, 340f
Weapons of mass destruction (WMD), 206, 423–424. *See also* Nuclear weapons
Webber, Jim, 115
Weber, Max, 234–234
Web sites. *See also* Internet
campaign, 338–339
for newspapers, 300
social networking, 281, 302, 339, 361
Webster v. *Reproductive Health Services* (1989), 101, 131, 271
Weeks v. *U.S.* (1914), 125
Weems v. *U.S.* (1910), 70
Weicker, Lowell Jr., 40
Welfare reform, 99
Wells, H. G., 322
West region, as political socialization agent, 285
Whig Party, 316f, 317–319
Whips, House, 170, 176, 177
White House
cable television coverage of, 306
journalists assigned to, 305
staff, 211, 336
Wikipedia, 302
Wilson, Edith Bollling Galt, 210
Wilson, Woodrow
on balance of power, 180
on Committees, 179
on Congress, 179
and freedom of speech and press, 117
and health issues, 80, 210
and Progressive movement, 402
on Supreme Court, 46
Wire services, 301
WISH List, 338
Wolf v. *Colorado* (1949), 68
Women. *See also* Gender
campus violence against, 102
and civil rights issues, 142, 147, 153–154, 166–167
in college sports, 236
in Congress, 170–171, 183, 184f, 186f
and Democratic Party, 329, 329t
discrimination against, 146, 153
as federal bureaucrats, 227f
as judicial appointees, 260f
in jury pools, 126
and military draft, 156
as national convention delegates, 359, 359t
and party identification, 329, 329t
presidential appointments of, 202t
on Supreme Court, 261
and vote choice, 329
voter registration among, 353f
voting rights for, 147, 348
Women's Christian Temperance Union (WCTU), 48f, 332
Women's Equality Amendment proposal (2007), 154, 156
Women's Equality Amendment (proposed), 154
Women's rights, 153–154, 156. *See also* Abortion
Women's rights movement, 144–145, 147, 153–154
Wood, George S., 34
World Anti-Slavery Society, 144
World Bank, 337
World Trade Organization (WTO), 420
World War I, 117
World War II, 225–226, 271
World Wide Web. *See* Internet
Writ of *certiorari*, 263–264, 267, 270
Writ of *mandamus*, 253
Wyoming, 364

Yahoo News, 299
Yellow journalism, 295
Yick Wo v. Hopkins (1886), 160
Young, Andrew, 282
Youngstown Sheet & Tube Co. v. Sawyer (1952), 61–62, 271
YouTube, 302

Zimbabwe, 406
Zogby, John, 288